# PAST IMPERFECT

alternative essays in American history

EDITED BY

# BLANCHE WIESEN COOK
John Jay College, C.U.N.Y.

# ALICE KESSLER HARRIS
Hofstra University

# RONALD RADOSH
Queensborough Community College, C.U.N.Y.

ALFRED A. KNOPF 🐕 NEW YORK

# PAST IMPERFECT

## alternative essays in American history

### from reconstruction to the present

volume II

Library of Congress Cataloging in Publication Data

Cook, Blanche Wiesen, comp.
    Past imperfect: alternative essays in American history

    Includes bibliographies.
    CONTENTS: v. 1. From colonial times to the Civil War.-v. 2. From Reconstruction to the present.
    1. United States—History—Essays. 2. United States—Social conditions—Essays.
I. Harris, Alice Kessler, joint comp. II. Radosh, Ronald, joint comp. III. Title.
E178.6.C68    973    72-5167
ISBN 0-394-31694-0 (v. 2)

Designed by James M. Wall

Cover designed by Batten, Friedman, and Kveloff

Manufactured in the United States of America

First Edition
987654321

TO THE MEMORY OF

RADICAL SCHOLARS AND ACTIVISTS

William L. Neumann and Robert Starobin

# acknowledgments

The preparation of this book has been a cooperative venture. We want particularly to thank the following people: Charles B. Forcey read the outline in an early stage; Gerald E. Markowitz, Allen Davis, Milton Mankoff, and Herbert G. Gutman read the entire manuscript and made valuable contributions throughout; Eli Faber, Jesse Lemisch, and Jacques Marchand provided fruitful suggestions for the colonial section. We are especially grateful to Clare Coss whose insights extended our vision at critical points.

We would like to thank Ilona Harris and Katherine Welch who cut and pasted, and Laura and Daniel Radosh.

This cooperative effort would not have worked without the critiques and ideas as well as the unfailing good humor provided by our editors Arthur Strimling and Elaine Rosenberg.

# contents

# PAST
# IMPERFECT
## alternative essays in American history

# introduction

Today, more than ever before, we hear students ask, "Why study history?" For some historians the answer has always been clear: history helps us to understand the living. Marc Bloch, an eminent medievalist who studied the daily lives of people under feudalism, wrote that "Common sense dictates that we no longer avoid" the issues raised by the present. For Bloch, "understanding the living was the master quality of the historian." When, for example, he went with Henri Pirenne, another medievalist, to visit Stockholm, of all the sights in the ancient capital Pirenne wanted to see the new city hall first. Pirenne explained to Bloch that if he "were an antiquarian he would have eyes only for the old stuff." But, he said, "I am an historian, and therefore I love life."

For those who love life our world presents many challenges. Human history is the history of man's failure to achieve a decent society. While it has involved scientific discoveries, creative achievements, and humanistic pursuits, it has also consisted of oppression, war, and the poverty of most of humanity.

As we approach the end of the twentieth century, scientists and humanists who survey our planet have concluded that human life may disappear with us. Many scientists who have traveled around the earth searching for answers about the future have returned with dire predictions of imminent disaster. We have, they insist, depleted our natural resources and polluted our water and air to such a degree that we may have destroyed the wellsprings of our own lives. The violence we traffic in with each other is reflected in the violence that has been done to our planet.

A study of history will not provide the blueprints by which to build a truly humane society. But we cannot prepare for the future without perceiving accurately the world we have made—as well as the means we have used to make it and the reasons for selecting those particular means. In order not to be imprisoned by the patterns of the past we must attempt to understand them.

A knowledge of American history makes it possible to understand the present conditions of our nation and enables us to think about appropriate and possible alternatives. But the traditional study of history has worked to blind us to the realities of the present and to the dynamics by which we have gotten there. Ours has been presented as a history of heroes and leaders who, it would appear, have had a basically agreeable constituency, and no worthy opposition. The role of the ordinary citizen, the history of oppressed minorities, and the nature of the power structure have been omitted from our textbooks, which have been written to serve an established system and inflate its myths. And, in the classroom, history is still largely dulled and obscured by people who remain unwilling not only to answer important questions but even to ask them.

The people who have recorded our past have ranged from those who have idealized American democracy to those who have doubted its very existence. In the early twentieth century some progressive historians explored areas of the past that revealed conflict at all levels of society. The questions they raised were quickly submerged during World War II when the calls for unity demanded a glorification of our past. The "consensus" school of traditional or mainstream American historiography that emerged then dominated the discipline between World War II and the war in Indochina. It held that the United States was a melting pot of harmony and happiness where the privileged classes and institutions of feudal Europe never existed and where, as a result, conflict and violence were always and would forever be avoided by democratic consensus.

Historians such as Louis Hartz, Daniel Boorstin, and Oscar Handlin begin with the assumption that America is basically a good, liberal, and benevolent nation, in which resources are widely shared, decisions are made pragmatically, and access to power is available to all who strive for it. They tend to see America as a society in which social mobility minimizes class distinctions. They believe that all Americans participate in this liberal vision and that the ideology and actions of the nation's leaders represent the thinking of all classes and groups. These historians have concluded that not only does democracy work but that its institutions must be protected. As a result, they see dissent as merely disruptive and rival ideologies as temporary aberrations in an otherwise united nation. Divisive elements such as racism, sexism, and nativism rarely appear in their books. On the contrary, they celebrate a faith in the postulated freedoms of our founding fathers. For many, recent history has not only toppled that faith, it has also revealed that traditional or mainstream interpretations of history have served to obscure the very real tensions that have existed from the beginning.

Unlike their mainstream colleagues who see our history as the unfolding of the American dream, radical historians argue that our society was never based on the belief that democracy and equality were synonymous. That assumption was made possible by historians who systematically ignored both the divisive aspects of our past and the victims of its ideological assumptions. If they had focused on America's divided and violent reality instead of on its mythical harmonies, it is not impossible that our recent past might have been different. Radical historians see the origins of events not only in the social, economic, and political situation but also in the motives of that class which owns the nation's corporations and governs the state. These motives are generally not to be found in its public statements but are camouflaged behind the rhetoric of equal opportunity. The ability of this class to prevail, frequently despite inimical conditions and public opposition, must be examined. Moreover, radical historians do not limit their attention to the operations of political and economic leaders but look to people at all levels and conditions of life for the impact and origins of events.

Traditionally, in periods of crisis, some historians have emerged to reassess and to rewrite history. And, for a time, they are called radical historians. When, for example, Marc Bloch wrote about history from a Nazi concentration camp, his writing was influenced by his politics, his religion, and the invasion of his country.* In the United States, progressive historians such as Carl Becker, James Harvey Robinson, and Charles Beard responded to the political activities and "muckraking" of social reformers that revealed poverty, racism, and the rampant power of corporations. Unable to explain present conditions in terms of what had been previously written about life in the United States, these progressive historians began to explore the discrepancy between the rhetoric of the past and the realities of their present. The most recent stimulus to reassess

---

*Born of Jewish parents in Lyon, Marc Bloch was active in the French Resistance. In 1944 he was captured by the Germans, tortured, and executed. His last book, The Historian's Craft, was written during the war and published posthumously by Alfred A. Knopf in 1953.

American history grew out of the civil rights movement in the late 1950s and early 1960s. Nothing that we had learned about our past could explain the bitter racism that was then exposed. A new interpretation was needed—one that would make sense of what was happening. In the early 1960s the search received impetus at the University of Wisconsin. There, in a journal called *Studies on the Left* and in the research of young faculty members and graduate students, a new past began to emerge. The quest for a new history was spearheaded by such scholars as William Appleman Williams, Eugene Genovese, Staughton Lynd, and Howard Zinn. The movement gathered momentum when the war in Indochina stimulated many to investigate the sources of perpetual conflict abroad, and historians all over the country began seeking explanations for our distorted national priorities.

Some used a Marxian framework in their analysis of America's past. Beginning with the assumption, in the words of Eugene Genovese, "that the root of the great qualitative leaps in social development are to be sought in the rise, development, and confrontation of social classes," these historians taught us much about the sources of conflict inherent in the structure of American society. Conflict both at home and abroad did not appear for the first time in the 1960s; it was built into the nature of a class structure that treated workers as commodities in the name of national growth. Economic motivation in the guise of Manifest Destiny, efficient technology, and progress blocked the achievement of our ideals of equality and individualism.

The Marxian analysis stimulated many historians to seek answers to a multitude of related questions. The abuse of national resources, social injustice, the intensity of war and violence, the impact of racism, and the nature of the class structure all became subjects of investigation. These inquiries have led to further exploration of the psychological and sociological dimensions of our political and economic condition. Consequently, radical historians, motivated by concern with contemporary crisis, have directed their energies to the investigation of potential sources for social change.

Radicals begin with the fundamental precepts which rule their lives and guide their consciences. They regard certain values as basic to human life and do not believe that they are merely matters of opinion. The most important of these values places the survival, well-being, and creativity of the whole of the human community above all other concerns. The inability to achieve these values in a society whose ideology has proclaimed them to be fundamental requires explanation. Esther Kingston Mann has pointed out that "a radical historian writes with the assumption that those values have been repressed, ignored or distorted . . . by specific kinds of economic exploitation, specific instances of failure of governments to protect the interests of the majority of the community, and specific mechanisms which have discouraged the general expansion of individual and social creativity."

Despite fundamental changes in American historiography the debate that has engaged many historians since the beginning of the nineteenth century still continues. Can a scholar primarily concerned with the conditions of his own society, pejoratively called a presentist, also be a historian? Further, can one concerned with those conditions that relate to more than his own limited area of specialization really view the past with the objectivity required of a scholar? Because the contributions made by radical historians have grown out of contemporary issues, some mainstream historians have criticized their work. These traditional historians assert that the only real history is that which explores "objective" facts for their own sake. All the rest, they insist, is propaganda.

The notion that the historian is merely an instrument through which objective or "real" facts are supposed to pass untouched remains popular—and many scholars continue to grind their humanity into footnotes. Fifty years ago Carl Becker addressed himself to that syndrome in an essay entitled "What Are Historical Facts?" Becker wrote that facts, untouched, "do not say anything, do not impose any meaning." All meaning and significance, he maintained, is imposed by the historian: "The historian cannot eliminate the personal equation . . . no one can. . . . The universe speaks to us only in response to our purposes. The present influences our idea of the past, and our idea of the past influences the present."

The business of a historian is to reconstruct the lives and works of people in time—to join, as Marc Bloch wrote, "the study of the dead and of the living." Why bother to study the past at all if not for the light which it may shed on the crisis of the present? If all historians had listened to the admonitions of Johns Hopkins' philosopher Arthur O. Lovejoy when he wrote that the role of historians should not be confused with that of the social reformer and that the more a historian based his interests on problems of his own time "the worse historian he is likely to be," all historians would be engaged in the art of mental masturbation. Advising historians to maintain "impersonal standards" is as meaningless as advising medical doctors to treat all patients the same whether they happen to have cancer or a broken finger. A scholar actively pursuing the answers to the tragic events of the past cannot cut himself into pieces and preserve the political purity of the one piece labeled "historian" while all the other pieces are being consumed by moral outrage against a terrible reality.

Ecological disaster, international arrogance, and economic uncertainty—these are the conditions of life with which the United States faces the future. Political assassinations and official violence at home combined with the brutal war in Indochina and the campaign America's leadership seems to be waging against movements for peace and social justice have demoralized many citizens and undermined the government's credibility. Some historians believe they can no longer afford to celebrate the unbroken consensus that created the American empire or genuflect to the tinseled gods which gave us continual corporate growth.

Radical historians have begun to reassess our past and to rewrite our history books. They are concerned not merely with the ruling forces in our society but with the sources of its discontent. And they have begun to write of people and justice instead of domination and profit.

The following selections juxtapose the best of mainstream and radical history. The fundamental assumptions of the two are opposed to each other. Liberal and mainstream historians affirm the basic correctness of our institutions, although they are willing to reform them. They are, therefore, concerned with continuity. Radical historians seek alternatives to these institutions and focus on sources of social change. While rigid distinctions are not possible, the essays highlight some of the major areas of conflict between the two schools of historiography. In each case, excellence in scholarship and writing, which are essential for the future of humanistic study, have been among the criteria for inclusion in this volume.

farmers and workers: class
and status after the Civil war

Industrialization engulfed America in a generation of frenzied activity. Between 1870 and 1900 furnaces, smokestacks, and factories converted sleepy towns and cities into crowded cogs in a giant entrepreneurial machine. Massive impersonal corporations replaced small manufacturing establishments. Workers no longer socialized with managers; managers were unlikely to be owners; and owners had probably never set foot in the factory. A stream of more than eleven million immigrants in the last thirty years of the century fed the growing industrial system. They were joined by refugees from farms that were no longer productive. Together they crowded into ethnic pockets of rapidly built and rapidly deteriorating cities. Growth stimulated corruption: political license, bribery, and pork-barreling prevailed.

Though 70 percent of the population still lived in rural areas in 1880 they, like their city brothers, could not escape corporate society. Railroads discriminated against small farmers in favor of big ones. Prices for grain storage, milk distribution, and agricultural machinery seemed neverendingly monopolized by powerful groups against whom battle was futile. Even the monetary policies that deprived debtors of the relief inflation brought were created in a national capital dominated by big business. If the farmer was to be victimized not only by the hazards of weather, but also by a corporate economy; if the worker, subject to cyclical economic fluctuations, could lose his job through no fault of his own, what then had happened to the land of opportunity? For many, urban and rural, the promise of America seemed to have died.

When workers struck against wage cuts and farmers rebelled against low corn prices, they were answered with platitudes: responsibility for their destiny was theirs; if they worked hard they would make it; opportunity was open to all. America, rapidly succumbing to its industrial elite, adopted a Social Darwinist ethic—the fittest would survive. Poverty simply provided proof of unfitness. To regulate corporations or to aid any but paupers was to tamper with natural laws and would destroy society's delicate balance. Individualism rose to pedestal heights. Courts viewed collective action by labor as subversive. Aware that economic conditions destroyed any real possibility of success for the majority, workers and farmers became increasingly discontent.

Both mainstream and radical historians who have written about this period sympathize with the plight of what the nineteenth century called the lower orders. They see the twenty years after the Civil War as years in which discontent became increasingly apparent. The tension between dream and reality erupted frequently into major strife. State militia quelled numerous strikes; radical movements grew apace as incipient labor unions foundered. Farmers created the Grange, and then the Alliance and the Wheel.

At this point, radicals part company with their mainstream colleagues. Traditional historians, represented here by Eric Goldman, see the discontent merging into recognizable forms. Workers abandoned the idealism of the Knights of Labor for the bread-and-butter unionism of the American Federation of Labor. The rural south and west created the Populist party. Both were the responses of economic interest groups to threats against their well-being. While neither was particularly successful, mainstream historians present both as constructive attempts to alleviate the worst distress and to restore equality of opportunity to society. Their researches emphasize histories of trade unions, of farmers' organizations, and of abortive political parties. These late nineteenth century social movements foreshadow the wing of the Progressive movement that emerged at the turn of the century convinced that the future of democracy rested in justice for all and special privilege for none.

For radical historians, the period assumes entirely new dimensions. Populism represents the abortive scream of a disaffected class. Some, Norman Pollack for example, see it as a movement that offered serious radical alternatives to capitalism; others like Michael Rogin, whose essay is reprinted here, ask why real discontent never jelled into a viable movement. Most radicals agree that labor unions reflected not the interests of the working class but those of a few skilled members. Progressivism was not a constructive attempt at reform but a consolidation of industrial capitalism. These interpretations lead to new questions. Given the evidence of extraordinary class consciousness, radicals ask: Why was there no revolutionary potential? Concerned with the sources of social change in contemporary society, they wonder out of what forces movements for change emerged in the past. David Montgomery, for example, in *Beyond Equality: Labor and the Radical Republicans, 1862-1872* (Knopf, 1967), points to some of the specific sources of discontent for discrete groups of workers in the period following the Civil War. Why did these movements fail to effect change?

Radical historians like Herbert Gutman have ceased to rely on investigations of labor unions or political parties as fruitful sources of answers and have turned instead to the consciousness of those who participated in the movements. They study the culture and aspirations of working people in an attempt to understand the components of consciousness in the late nineteenth century. They ask what factors encouraged the worker to continue militance? Why did so many workers fight briefly only to return to passive submission to a brutal system? Some of the answers to these questions lie in studies of social mobility. Stephan Thernstrom, for example, in "Notes on the Historical Study of Social Mobility," *Comparative Studies in History and Society* X (June 1968), argues the traditional case that the promise of upward mobility allowed workers to identify with those a notch above them on the social scale. Many historians are now searching for answers in community studies; others search for them in ethnic origins and the role of the family. In both cases, the focus has shifted from questions about movements to questions about people.

# class, status, and community power in nineteenth-century American industrial cities- Paterson, New Jersey: a case study

## HERBERT G. GUTMAN

Herbert Gutman, a leading labor historian, examines community response to working class and radical movements. The article makes two significant contributions to radical history. First, it reveals the central importance of local history to understanding social movements of any kind. Second, in concluding that in the 1870s the power of industrialists in small towns had not yet been legitimized, it raises the issue of the relationship between ideology and political power. Gutman's contention that workers won major victories with community support opens a host of questions about what happened subsequently to alter community attitudes.

Much is known about the early history of New England textile towns, but too much is inferred from this single source about the nineteenth-century American industrial city. Although little is known about the development of the industrial city, urban historians as well as labor and business historians have generalized much about it. Unwarranted assumptions about the social and economic structure of the early industrial city, however, have distorted significant patterns in its early development. Paterson, New Jersey, an industrial city that attracted the attention of men as diverse as Alexander Hamilton, William Haywood, and William Carlos Williams and that had as its official motto *Spe et Labore* (With Hope and Labor), serves as a case study to test some of the generalizations and assumptions.

I

Little is known of the inner history of the nineteenth-century American industrial city. Historians have detoured around Paterson and other nineteenth-century industrial cities for many reasons. Perhaps the landscape seemed unattractive. Perhaps the roadways into and out of the city seemed simple and one-dimensional. Whatever the cause, specialists have built roadblocks that deny access to a rich and hitherto untapped social history. The urban historian apparently finds the large, complex metropolis a greater challenge and a more accessible source for information than the simpler, intensely specialized, and grim factory town. The labor historian learns quickly that industrial cities lacked permanent labor organizations, and since he is by tradition little more than the chronicler of trade union history he just ignores the factory town. And the business historian, anxious to trace the detailed internal development of a particular firm or industry, all too often takes for granted its external relationships to the larger community. These attitudes, among others, have focused attention away from the industrial city as a legitimate subject for detailed and careful inquiry.[1]

Only two events in Paterson's history, for example, have attracted detailed attention: Alexander Hamilton's ill-fated effort to start "the Society for establishing useful Manufactures" in the 1790s and William Haywood's equally troubled effort to organize the immigrant silk workers into the Industrial Workers of the World, in 1913. No less than 120 years separates these two incidents—a period of time that sheds light on the transition from Hamilton to Haywood. But historians have not filled in the void between these two men in ways that make the transition meaningful. Instead, they have too often relied on crude and utterly misleading generalizations about the industrial city, its social order, and its power structure. Here one of these misleading general-izations, perhaps the most important, is subjected to close and critical exam-ination: the widely held view that from the start, industrialists had the social and political power and prestige to match their economic force, and that they controlled the towns. This generalization has several corollaries: industrialists faced ineffective opposition; town politics reflected their interests; other property-owners—particularly small businessmen and professionals—identified with industrialists and applauded their innovations and pecuniary successes. Factory workers enter this version of history only as passive, ineffective, and alienated victims, practically helpless before their all-powerful employers. Stated in another fashion, it is the proposition that from the beginning, there existed a close relationship between economic class, social status, and power and that control over "things"—especially industrial property and machinery— was quickly and easily transformed into authority and legitimized so that industrialists could do little wrong and, better still, quoting Max Weber, "realize their own will in communal action even against the resistance of others who are participating in the action."[2] In place of this common view, another is argued. Through its early years, for at least a generation, the factory and its disciplines, the large impersonal corporation, and the propertyless wage-earners remained unusual and even alien elements in the industrial town. They disrupted tradition, competed against an established social structure and status hierarchy, and challenged traditional modes of thought. In these years, therefore, the factory-owner symbolized innovation and a radical departure from an older way of life. His power was not yet legitimized and "taken for granted." Surely powerful because of his control over "things," the factory-owner nevertheless found it difficult to enforce noneconomic decisions essential to his economic welfare. He met with unexpected opposition from nonindustrial property-owners, did not dominate the local political structure, and learned that the middle and professional classes did not automatically accept his leadership and idolize his achievements. Moreover, the new working class, not entirely detached from the larger community, had significant ties to that community which strengthened its power at critical moments and allowed it, despite the absence of strong permanent labor organizations, often to influence events at the expense of the factory-owner.

Men hold authority in particular setting, Robert M. MacIver has observed, when they possess "the established right to determine policies, to pronounce judgments on relevant issues, or, more broadly, to act as the leaders or guide to other men."[3] The industrial town was too new at the start for the industrialist to command this kind of prestige and to hold this kind of authority. Class position and social status were closely related. But as a new class, the industrialists had not yet achieved high social status. In fact, the absence of the kind of authority described by MacIver shaped much of dramatic early history of the industrial city. The owners of disruptive and radical innovations—power-driven machinery, the factory, and the large corporation—sought to legitimize their economic power in these years. And Paterson is a good illustration of the frustrating search by the industrialist for status and unchallenged authority.


II

By the early 1870s, Paterson ranked as a major American industrial city. Located fourteen miles from New York City, its factories manufactured mainly locomotives, machinery, iron goods of all kinds, and silks and other textiles. Its three locomotive firms contained 25 per cent of the nation's locomotive capacity, and the products of its large ironworks helped construct the Philadelphia Centennial Exposition buildings; many eastern bridges; and New York's Metropolitan Museum of Art, its Lenox Library, and its first elevated railroad. Paterson also stood as America's preeminent silk manufacturing center, and its separate jute, flax, and mosquito net mills were each the largest of their kind in the nation. With a few exceptions, most of the mills came to Paterson after 1850 so that their owners ranked as relative newcomers to the city twenty years later. Older Patersonians saw their small city change radically between 1850 and 1870.[4]

Before 1850 Paterson had grown fitfully. Early in the nineteenth century, small cotton factories started there to take advantage of available water power and the New York market and port nearby. Although the city had twenty cotton mills in 1832, inability to compete with more efficient New England firms caused them to stagnate in the 1840s and 1850s. According to its official industrial historian, as late as 1838 most New Yorkers regarded Paterson as "an upcountry hamlet, chiefly noted for its fine waterfall and valuable water-power."[5]

But the cotton mills attracted machinists to repair and build textile machinery, and the start of the railroad era in the 1830s led one of them, aided by New York capital, to begin locomotive manufacturing in 1836. His pioneer factory grew slowly before 1850, as did a number of smaller machine and iron shops. The great increase in the demand for railroad equipment, iron, and machinery after 1850 stimulated the rapid growth of these industries. Two more locomotive factories opened, and between 1850 and 1873 the three together produced 4,437 locomotives and sold them over the entire nation. In 1873, 3,000 men worked in the locomotive shops. Other iron works grew as quickly. Two

Lancashire millwrights, for example, started a machine works in 1845 with ten hands and employed 1,100 in 1873.[6]

The silk industry grew even more quickly and spectacularly than the iron and locomotive industries. The pattern was quite simple. A declining cotton industry made available water power, cheap mills, and a resident labor force. These first attracted English silk manufacturer John Ryle to Paterson in 1839, after a successful start as a New York silk importer. Small spinning and weaving shops began in the 1840s and 1850s. But the great stimulus came from outside the city in the 1860s, when New York and Boston silk and textile manufacturers and importers moved their mills to Paterson or built new ones there. A few examples suffice. A Coventry Englishman brought his silk mill from New York in 1860. In the next two years, the nation's leading importer of tailor trimmings left Boston for Paterson, as did another Bostonian, a pioneer American silk manufacturer. In 1868, one of New York's great silk importers became a Paterson manufacturer. From the start, these men of wealth con- structed large mills and introduced power machinery, and other innovations. One imported a whole English factory. These men transformed the industry. In 1860 four silk mills employed 590 workers. In 1876, eight silk ribbon and six broad silk factories gave work to 8,000 persons, two thirds of them women. One of every four silk workers was under sixteen years of age. Outside capital also financed other large textile mills in these years. A mosquito net factory came from New York, and Scottish money built the nation's largest jute mill. Eighty one years after its founding in Northern Ireland, in 1865, Barbour Brothers opened a linen factory that quickly became one of Paterson's great mills. Smaller workshops continued, but by the 1870s the large mills dominated the local economy.[7]

Older Paterson residents in 1873 lived in a different city than they had known in 1850. The coming of the large mills, particularly from outside the city, transformed Paterson in many ways. The mill-owners, a new industrial leadership mostly alien to the older city, represented a power unknown in earlier years. More than this, their factories drew in increasing numbers of immigrant and native workers and the city boomed. In 1846 Paterson had only 11,000 inhabitants. In the next twenty-four years, its population increased to 33,000. Immigrants made up more than a third of its residents. French and German skilled silk workers, but especially English skilled hands and an increasing number of unskilled Irish laborers, found work in the rapidly expanding factories. Built on two major industries, iron and textiles, the Paterson economy offered employment to whole families: the iron factories hired only men and textile mills relied mainly on female and child labor. Rapid growth in the 1850s and 1860s illustrated in Paterson all the severe social dislocations incident to quick industrialization and urbanization everywhere, but it also opened new opportunities for small retail businesses. Between 1859 and 1870, for example, the number of grocers rose from 105 to 230 and the number of saloonkeepers from 46 to 270. Paterson's industrial leaders in the early 1870s, mostly new to the city, had innovated boldly and caused a city to change radically in less than twenty years from one characterized by small workshops to one typified by large factories. Between 1873 and 1878 a severe depression halted temporarily this process.[8]

III

It is sufficient to report briefly that this first of modern industrial crises, 1873–1878, crippled the Paterson economy and strained the city's total resources and all its citizens. "Among all classes," it was noted as early as October 31, 1873, "there is a feeling of gloom and intense anxiety in regard to the future." Nearly three years later, a silk worker reported with good reason that "Paterson is in a deplorable condition." The unemployed regularly overtaxed limited public and private charities and occasionally paraded the streets demanding public works. The locomotive workers especially felt the diminished demand for labor. From 1871 to 1873 the three locomotive factories produced 1,185 engines; in 1875, 1876, and 1877 the figure totalled only 195. The 1873 wage bill for 3,172 locomotive workers came to $1,850,000; four years later (1877) the same firms paid 325 workers only $165,000. The silk and other textile workers apparently suffered less unemployment, but recurrent wage cuts between 1873 and 1877 ranged from 10 to 30 per cent and meant exceedingly hard times for nearly 10,000 textile workers. Sporadic silk strikes, particularly in 1876, illustrated the workers' reactions to these deplorable conditions. Despair permeated the city. Its population fell almost 10 per cent between 1875 and 1878. With good reason, a *New York Sun* reporter in September 1876 called Paterson an industrial ghost town comparable to a southern city after Lee's surrender.[9]

In analyzing the consequences of the 1873–1878 depression, historians have argued that the hardship resulting from extensive unemployment and lowered wages shattered labor organizations and immeasurably strengthened employers. But this exclusively economic interpretation ignores the fact that the same cyclical crisis, coming after two decades of radical economic and social change, also tested the status and power of Paterson's new industrialists and workers within the community. The depression created grave economic difficulties for the entire population, and, in trying to solve certain of their problems, the Paterson industrialists sought support and sanction at critical moments from the local community and its leaders. Their successes, but more importantly their failures, revealed much about their status and power in the city, measured the stability and legitimacy of the new industrial order, and gauged the attitudes of shopkeepers and merchants, professionals, politicians, and other prestigious persons in the precorporate city toward the new order and its leaders.

Four incidents between 1877 and 1880 involving Paterson's "public"—two textile strikes and two libel suits against a socialist newspaper editor—will be examined briefly in order to explore the early relationship between economic class, social status, and power.

IV

The first incident illustrated the inability of the new large manufacturers to commit the city government to their interests. It occurred between June and August, 1877 and was an unprecedented general strike of ribbon-weavers, mostly English, French, and German immigrants, against the biggest silk manufacturers. They protested a 20 per cent wage cut and an irksome labor contract and demanded a 10 per cent wage increase and a board of arbitration modeled on English and French precedent. At its peak, the strike—the greatest in Paterson to that time—idled 2,000 workers and closed the mills. After ten weeks, a compromise including restoration of the wage cut took place. What allowed the workers to effect this compromise in the absence of permanent labor organization and after forty-four months of depression? Why did the silk manufacturers fail? In part, the staying power of the weavers frustrated the manufacturers, but even more serious obstacles denied them success.[10]

Important and powerful groups in the community refused to sanction and support the mill-owners. Nonstrikers and elected city officials either supported the strikers or, more significantly, rejected pressure and commands from the mill-owners. Small shopkeepers extended credit and subscribed relief funds to the strikers. A weekly, German-language newspaper also supported them. Although critical of the strikers, the two daily newspapers did not cheer the manufacturers and they even lectured the mill-owners to "put conscience as well as capital" into their enterprises. The local courts displayed their independence of the manufacturers and on several occasions weavers charged with disorderly conduct went free or suffered, at best, nominal fines. After manufacturer William Strange successfully prosecuted two weavers for violating written contracts, pressure from city officials, including the mayor, convinced a local judge to postpone indefinitely forty additional trials.[11]

The Republican mayor, Benjamin Buckley, and the Democratic-controlled Board of Aldermen gave the manufacturers their greatest trouble. The aldermen were mostly self-made men: skilled workmen of independent means and retail shopkeepers. Their number included neither factory workers nor manufacturers. Mayor Buckley personified the precorporate American dream. Born in England in 1808, he had come to Paterson as a young man, worked first in a cotton factory, and then achieved wealth and high status. By 1877, he owned a small spindle factory, headed a local bank, and looked back on a successful career in Republican politics including several terms in the state legislature and the presidency of the state senate. He started the first of his several terms as Paterson's Republican mayor in 1875. Because he viewed his role as maintaining the public peace and little more, Buckley infuriated the silk manufacturers. During the dispute, he used his powers, especially the small police force, with great skill and tact to suppress overt disorders only. This angered the mill-owners. They insisted that inadequate civic authority allowed a few agitators to intimidate hundreds of loyal workers. In the strike's seventh week, therefore, the Paterson Board of Trade, dominated by the largest silk and iron manufacturers, called a special meeting to pressure the city authorities to enlarge the police force and also to declare a state of emergency limiting the strikers' use of the streets and their freedom of action. The Board publicly charged that "the laws of the land are treated with contempt and trampled upon by a despotic mob" led by immigrant radicals and "communists." A silk manufacturer warned that unless the authorities put down these troublemakers Paterson soon would be "a city without manufactories . . . with nothing . . . but the insignificant industries of an unimportant town." Other manufacturers expressed even graver anxieties: one urged that strike leaders be "taken out and shot" and another offered to finance a private militia. Iron manufacturer Watts Cooke admitted their deepest fear—the absence of sufficient status and respect in the city. "All the classes of the community," Cooke lamented, "are coming to lean towards and sympathize with the men rather than the employers." He and the others demanded the protection of the city authorities.[12] But Mayor Buckley and the Board of Aldermen turned a deaf ear toward the complaints and demands of the large manufacturers. Buckley did not issue a proclamation, defended his use of civic authority, and advised the aldermen that the Board of

Trade did "great injury to the credit of the city." He especially commended "the good sense of the working people." The Democratic Board of Aldermen upheld the Republican mayor. It unanimously passed three resolutions: the first tabled without discussion the request for a larger police force; the second applauded Buckley's "wise and judicious course"; and the third, as if to reiterate the independence of the city government from the manufacturers, urged immediate prosecution of mill-owners who violated local fire-escape ordinances. The manufacturers were unable to alter public policies during the strike. City officials—all property-owners—maintained an independence of judgment and explicitly rejected iron manufacturer Watts Cooke's insistence that the Board of Trade was "best able to judge what the city needed to protect it."[13]

After the strike, although the *Paterson Guardian* advised the Board of Trade to get into local politics and "pay the proper attention to the men . . . elected to the city council," the large manufacturers turned away from politics and to the private militia. The Board listened approvingly to a member who found "more virtue in one well drilled soldier than in ten policemen or in one bullet than in ten clubs in putting down a riot." Silk manufacturer Strange led the group that subscribed the first $4,500 for arms and equipment. And of the 120 militiamen signed up by January, 1880, at least 50 per cent were manufacturers, merchants, clerks, salespeople, and professionals. It proved easier to subscribe funds for a militia than to "reform" the city government. The manufacturers had more than enough wealth to finance a private militia but inadequate prestige and power to dominate the city government. In 1877, Paterson had one police officer for every 1,666 residents; ten years later, it had a militia company but the ratio of police to population remained the same. The manufacturers' use of private power indicated weakness, not strength *vis a vis* the body politic and the city government.[14]


V

A year after the ribbon-weavers' strike, a second dispute involving textile workers again illustrated the limited power of the Paterson manufacturers. A third wage cut in less than a year convinced 550 unorganized workers, mostly women and children, to quit the textile mills owned by two brothers, Robert and Henry Adams. One of the East's great textile mills, R & H Adams and Company symbolized the rapid rise of the new industrialism in Paterson. It had moved a small factory there from New York City in 1857 and had thrived in the next twenty years, adding several large and efficient mills to its original plant. By far the largest of its kind in the country and perhaps in the world, the firm exported huge quantities of mosquito netting overseas, especially to Africa and Asia. Two more unequal adversaries than the unorganized Adams strikers and their employer hardly could be found. Yet, after a strike lasting nine months, the company conceded defeat in March 1879, and its senior partner, Robert Adams, who vigorously and publicly combatted the strikers, quit the firm and left Paterson.[15]

Once again, community attitudes toward the dispute shaped its outcome, and Robert Adams, not the striking women, had no allies in this battle. The Board of Trade kept silent. No one publicly protested Adams' recurrent threat to move the mills. The press remained neutral. With one exception noted below, Adams got no overt encouragement from other manufacturers, retail businessmen, or politicians. He even had trouble with his foremen and had to fire a few who defended the strikers. Unlike Adams, the strikers found strength in the community. Many took jobs in other local textile mills. Strike funds gathered mainly from local workers, shopkeepers, and merchants fed the others. Concerts and picnics buoyed their spirits and added to their funds. At least one of every eight Patersonians signed a petition attacking Adams. Frequent street demonstrations indicated additional support. Soon after the trouble began, an outspoken Irish socialist, Joseph P. McDonnell, came to Paterson from nearby New York to encourage the strikers. He organized them into the International Labor Union, an industrial union for unskilled factory workers led by immigrant socialists and Yankee eight-hour reformers. McDonnell stayed on and soon started a socialist weekly newspaper, the Paterson *Labor Standard.* Although its masthead quoted Karl Marx and its columns heaped abuse on local mill-owners and called Adams "Lucifer" and his mills "a penitentiary," its back pages contained numerous local business advertisements. Forty-five retail enterprises, mostly saloons, groceries, and clothing, drygoods, and boot and shoe shops sustained the paper as it railed against manufacturer Adams.[16]

Adams' power against the workers was limited to his firm's income. He sent special agents to Fall River and other New England towns to recruit new workers. Adams hired many new hands but retained few because the strikers made full use of the streets. The strikers and their sympathizers, at one time as many as 2,000 persons, met the new workers at the rail depot or in the streets, urged them to quit Adams, and even financed their way home. This tactic worked: the first time jeers, taunts, and ordinary discourse convinced twenty-two of twenty-five Fall River workers to leave immediately. Although the city authorities arrested a few workers when tempers flared, they quickly released them and made no effort to restrain strikers using the streets peacefully. By carefully separating "peaceful coercion" from "violence," the authorities effectively if unintentionally strengthened the strikers and Adams' wealth gained him no advantage. The freedom to use the streets to persuade outsiders from taking their jobs together with support from shopkeepers allowed the otherwise weak strikers to check Adams' power, thereby revealing his impotence and finally forcing him to surrender and to leave the city.[17]

## VI

The third and fourth events centered on Joseph McDonnell and his socialist newspaper, the *Labor Standard.* Dublin-born McDonnell had crowded much radical experience into his thirty-two years before coming to Paterson in 1878 to aid the Adams strikers. He had edited several Dublin and London Irish nationalist journals, engaged in Fenian "conspiracies," represented Ireland at the 1872 Hague Congress of the First International and sided with the Marxists, organized several huge London labor free-speech demonstrations, and served four prison terms before coming to the United States in January, 1873. Soon after his arrival, McDonnell exposed steerage conditions in indignant letters, edited a New York socialist weekly, and traveled all over the East condemning capitalism, advocating socialism, and organizing weak socialist trade unions. According to traditional historical stereotypes, McDonnell should have been a pariah to all but a few Patersonians and therefore easy game for his opponents. But even though the Irish socialist had serious legal troubles and went to prison, he and his newspaper soon won acceptance as legitimate and useful critics of the new industrial order.[18]

McDonnell's difficulties began in October 1878, before the ink had dried on the *Labor Standard*'s first issue, and continued unabated for eighteen months. The formal complaint of a few loyal Adams workers whom the *Labor Standard* attacked as "scabs" convinced the County Grand Jury to indict McDonnell for libel. A petit jury found him guilty and a judge fined him $500 and court costs. A few months later, McDonnell apparently averted a second libel indictment. But in the fall of 1879, a second Grand Jury indictment did come, for McDonnell had printed a bitter letter by a young worker, Michael Menton, exposing inadequate working and living conditions in a Passaic River brickyard, where Menton had labored and become severely ill. In February, 1880 a jury found McDonnell and Menton guilty of libel and a judge sent them to the Passaic County Jail for three months. Viewed only in these narrow terms, McDonnell's difficulties prove to traditional labor historians only the repressive power of "capital" and the pliancy of the judiciary. Actually, McDonnell's difficulties strengthened him. If these legal troubles were intended to drive him from Paterson, the opposite resulted. Support from workers, mostly nonsocialists, and from other persons prominent in the community assured his survival.[19]

Although new to Paterson, McDonnell was not a complete outcast during his first trial. His lawyer, an old Patersonian, had grown wealthy as a real-estate speculator, fathered the state's first ten-hour law and important banking reforms, organized the city's waterworks, and been a prominent Republican for twenty years before becoming Greenback candidate for New Jersey governor. Despite the county prosecutor's plea to convict McDonnell as a "woman libeler," a "threat" to established order and a "foreign emissary" sent by English manufacturers to "breed discontent" in America, the jury, composed mostly of storekeepers and skilled workmen, remained deadlocked for three days and three nights. Only unusual pressure by the presiding judge finally brought conviction. The $500 fine, substantially less than the maximum $2,000 fine and two-year prison term, told much. A second judge, in the case, himself originally a Lancashire worker and then the owner of a small bobbin pin factory, convinced the presiding judge to go easy on McDonnell. After the conviction, storekeepers and merchants contributed handsomely to McDonnell's "defense fund."[20]

McDonnell's lower-class supporters made known their displeasure with the trial and used the threat of their potential political power. They crowded the courtroom to cheer McDonnell and after the conviction, raised the fine and court costs quickly and carried their hero through the streets. More important, the trial occurred during the bitter 1878 congressional election, and they humiliated the county prosecutor, a Democratic politician. Workers joined by sympathetic storekeepers crowded the annual Democratic election meeting and in a raucous demonstration refused to let it start until the prosecutor left the hall. The meeting ended quickly. McDonnell's supporters then jammed a second meeting and hundreds silently walked out when the prosecutor rose to speak. Politicians competing for labor votes got the point. A Republican argued that only free speech and a free press could preserve American liberty. Fearing the loss of labor votes, the Democrats publicly defended the right to strike and one Democrat declaimed: "Away with the government of the aristocracy! Away with legislators only from the wealthy classes! We have had enough of them!" A nearby newspaper sympathetic to McDonnell concluded: "In Paterson, he

[McDonnell] is stronger than his accusers. Today he has the sympathy of the people, and his paper from this time forth is deeply rooted in Paterson."[21]

The second trial and subsequent imprisonment of McDonnell attracted national attention but only its local significance concerns us. The support McDonnell received this time revealed his growing local prestige and power. Except for the litigants, no one publicly attacked him. His competitor, the Democratic *Paterson Guardian,* found the verdict "to say the least, a great surprise to those who heard or read the testimony." The judge justified sending McDonnell to prison only because he feared that others again would pay a fine. This time, McDonnell's lawyers were the son of a former Democratic mayor and Socrates Tuttle, Paterson's most respected attorney, who had been Republican mayor some years before. Ably defending his client, Tuttle warned that a conviction would endanger the free press and mean that the working classes would "henceforth never be allowed to complain." Three northern New Jersey nonlabor weeklies emphasized the same point. McDonnell's sympathizers were led by two former silk factory foremen, one German and the other English, and both now successful entrepreneurs. Two clergymen, one a Baptist and the other a Methodist (both active in Republican politics and Paterson's most popular clergymen), condemned McDonnell's treatment and counseled the socialist. Several aldermen, former aldermen, and county freeholders visited him in prison. Garrett A. Hobart, a Paterson corporation lawyer, President of the State Senate and that year elected chairman of the Republican State Committee, sent McDonnell ten dollars for his defense, offered "to do his best," and sought to amend the state libel law. Even the son of Henry Adams and nephew of Robert Adams, McDonnell's 1878 adversary, gave the socialist twenty dollars and visited him in jail.[22]

McDonnell's jail experience, surely one of the most unusual in American penal history, depended upon John Buckley, the former mayor's son. He had been a locomotive worker as a young man, a prominent Republican, and warden of the county prison. Apparently distressed over the conviction, Warden Buckley did his best to assure McDonnell's comfort and his freedom while in prison. McDonnell kept a prison diary, and its entries record many surprising amenities. The warden let him edit his newspaper and organize a national and local protest campaign against his imprisonment. McDonnell's supporters visited him daily and often brought their children along. Buckley allowed them to meet in his office. One day as many as twenty-one persons called on McDonnell. Every day his meals arrived from outside, and saloon- and boardinghouse-keepers kept him overstocked with cigars, wines, and liquors. Others brought fresh fruits, cakes, and puddings. On St. Patrick's Day shamrocks came, and on his birthday, two fancy dinners. The day of his release, Warden Buckley publicly commended the good behavior of prisoner Joseph P. McDonnell.[23]

Let out ten days early, McDonnell benefited from a demonstration of popular support unprecedented in Paterson's history. Organized by a committee of seventy-five that was dominated by workers but included twelve saloon- and inn-keepers and five grocers, the demonstration counted between fifteen and twenty thousand persons. After that, few Patersonians doubted the labor agitator's place and power in their city. McDonnell's *Labor Standard* survived until his death in 1908. He founded the New Jersey Federation of Trades and Labor Unions and pioneered in pushing protective labor legislation. Several clues indicate his rapid acceptance as a radical critic. Soon after his imprisonment, the Democratic prosecutor who had called him a "women libeler" and a "foreign emissary" sent by British manufacturers began advertising his legal services in the Labor Standard. The city government regularly bought space to print legal public notices. In 1884, less than six years after he had come to Paterson and four years after his release from jail, socialist McDonnell was appointed New Jersey's first deputy inspector of factories and workshops.[24]

McDonnell never lost feeling for those who helped in the early days. In 1896, although the Labor Standard still carried Karl Marx's words on its masthead, McDonnell printed kind words about Garrett Hobart, then running with William McKinley against William Jennings Bryan. He called Hobart "a rare specimen of manhood in the class in which he moves" and, remembering Hobart's aid in 1880, concluded that "to know him is to like him whether you agree with his opinions or not."[25]


## VII

What general meaning can be inferred from these Paterson events? If they are unique to that city, then only the local historian profits from them. In fact, they typified obstacles encountered by industrialists in other post-Civil War industrial towns and cities during crises similar to the 1877 and 1878 Paterson textile disputes. Time and again, the industrialist found his freedom of action confined by particular local "circumstances." Several examples illustrate his difficulties. A western Pennsylvania jury convicted a mine operator when violence resulted after he brought Italians there. The merchant mayor of an Illinois mining town disarmed Chicago Pinkerton police sent to guard an operator's properties. A sheriff raised a posse to chase special New York police sent to protect railroad repair shops in eastern Pennsylvania. Ohio Valley newspapers condemned iron manufacturers for arming strikebreakers. Northern Pennsylvania merchants housed striking evicted coal miners. A pronounced pattern emerges from these and similar events.[26] Unorganized or poorly organized workers displayed surprising strength and staying power and found sympathy from other groups in the community. Local political officials often rejected or modified the pressures of industrialists. Nonindustrial capitalists— persons with power and prestige locally and persons committed to competitive private enterprise and the acquisitive spirit in their own dealings—responded equivocally or critically to the practices of the new industrialists. Such behavior is quite different from that usually characterized as typical of early industrial America. And yet it occurred frequently in the first decades of the industrial city. How can this pattern of behavior be explained?

Unless two misleading and erroneous conceptions are disregarded, this pattern of response seems anomalous and even meaningless. The first is the idea that the industrialist achieved status and legitimized his power quickly and easily in his local community. The second is the belief that urban property-owners as a group shared a common ideology in responding to the severe dislocations resulting from rapid industrialization and in reacting to the frequent disputes between workers and factory-owners. Because Congress gave huge land grants to railroads, and state governors frequently supplied militia to "settle" industrial disputes, it does not follow that the industrialists in Paterson and other cities so dominated the local political and social structure that their freedom of action remained unchecked. Because a grocer owned his business and a mayor presided over a bank, it does not mean they sympathized with the social policies of a large factory-owner. Because Andrew Carnegie applauded Herbert Spencer, it does not mean that jungle ethics reigned supreme in the industrial city. If we are free of these distorting generalizations, it is possible to look afresh at social behavior and conflict in Gilded Age America. Take the example of the use of state troops in industrial disputes. Such action may have resulted from the low status and power the industrialist had in his local community. Unable to gain support from locally elected officials and law-enforcement groups and unable to exercise coercive power in the community, he reached upward to the state level, where direct local pressures were felt less strongly. If, as E. D. Baltzell writes, "power which is not legitimized tends to be either coercive or manipulative," much is explained by the low status of the new industrialists. Careful examination of particular local industrial conflicts that involved the use of state as opposed to local police might help explain the widespread violence and corruption so often condemned by Gilded Age historians and yet so little understood.

In nineteenth-century America, power and status had meaning on several levels of society. Here the focus is a particular community. If the industrialist is viewed as an innovator in a local context, the Paterson events take on broader meaning. The new industrialist—especially if he came from elsewhere—was a disruptive outsider. He did not create an entirely new social structure, but he confronted an existing one. He found a more-or-less static city, which thrived on small and personal workshops and an intimate and personal way of life. It was hardly ideal, but it was settled and familiar. Making goods and employing people differently, the industrialist abruptly disrupted this "traditional" way of work and life and, as a person, symbolized severe local dislocations. The older residents and the newer workers responded to these changes in many ways. But if the industrialist, in cutting costs and rationalizing production, violated traditional community norms or made unusually new demands upon the citizenry—such as the special use of a police force or the suppression of a newspaper—his decision often provoked opposition.

The size of the industrial city and the particular composition of its population made the industrialist's innovations more visible and his power more vulnerable there than in the larger complex metropolis. Residents of the early factory town had a more direct relationship with one another and with the innovations. Even persons indirectly affected by industrialism could hardly avoid close contact with the large factory, the corporation, and the propertyless wage-earners. The closeness of the middle class and the old resident population to the new industrialism gave such persons the opportunity to judge the industrial city's social dislocations and social conflicts by personal experience, and not simply through the opaque filter of ideologies such as laissez-faire liberalism and Darwinism. In addition, the worker had more power as a consumer and as a voter and could express particular needs more effectively in the factory town than in the metropolis. Street demonstrations had a greater impact in Paterson than in New York or Chicago. In the industrial city, the retail merchant depended heavily on a narrow class of consumers (mostly workers) and the politicians appealed to more homogeneous voting groups. All of these consider-ations contributed to the industrialist's difficulties. So, too, did the rapid growth of the mill-town itself weaken their chances for civic and police control. A number of studies of the mobility patterns of Paterson men (three thousand fathers and sons between 1870 and 1890) show that the more ambitious and able workers found expanding opportunities outside the factories in small retail business, politics, and city employment (including the police force)—the very areas in which the industrialists demanded cooperation or control.[27] Conservative in many ways, these men had a stake in the new society. Some identified entirely with their new class and repressed their origins. But others—a large number in the early years—still had memories, roots, and relatives among the workers. Some had even suffered from the same employers they were now called on to protect. In crisis situations such as those that occurred in the 1870s, their social origins and older community ties may have created a conflict between their fellow-feeling and even family sentiment and their material achievements. The evidence does not make explicit such conflict, but it makes clear that during strikes and other crises the industrialists could not expect and did not get unswerving loyalty or approval from them.

## VIII

Historians have not emphasized sufficiently the subtle and complex patterns of response to social change in nineteenth-century America—particularly to the coming of industrial capitalism. Much has been omitted in these pages: No judgment is passed on working conditions or standards of comfort in the industrial city; nothing is said of the important but little studied working class subculture that thrived in the industrial city, and no attempt is made to precisely measure the strength of the opposing forces of workers and industrialists. The conclusions stated here are that economic power was not easily translated into social and political power, and that the changes resulting from rapid industrialization stimulated sufficient opposition to the industrialist to deprive him of the status and the authority he sought and needed. The theme of this chapter illustrates Dorothy George's (*England in Transition,* 1953) view that "social history is local history" but local history in a larger context that permits the careful examination of grand and sweeping hypotheses. It is finally suggested, indirectly, that knowledge of the early history of American industrialization and urban growth tells much about modern society and the contemporary city: its social structure, its power relationships, and its decision-making process. The nineteenth-century city differed from its twentieth-century counterpart; so much of what "makes" a city has changed in the past seventy years. In *Victorian Cities* (1963), Asa Briggs wisely argued for historical specificity and interdisciplinary approaches to the study of nineteenth-century cities. Free of the nostalgia of those historians who compare the "city" only to the "country" but sensitive to the acute social disorganization that accompanied rapid industrialization and urban development, Briggs showed that different British cities each had a distinct history (shaped by particular inner social patterns) and also that their histories should not be confused with the later city so powerfully affected by radical innovations such as the automobile, the national corporation, and the revolution in communications. All too often, however, social scientists and even historians view the contemporary city in exceedingly ahistorical terms or only study its past by projecting present "trends" backward. For them, as Barrington Moore notes, the past becomes "merely a storehouse of samples," and "facts" are "drawn upon as if they were colored balls from an urn." Stephan Thernstrom's pioneering study of nineteenth-century Newburyport, Massachusetts, *Poverty Progress* (1964), splendidly illustrates the grave pitfalls of an ahistorical view of urban social mobility. It further shows that however carefully the present is studied and however refined the techniques of analysis, the present is not fully comprehended if the past is ignored or distorted.

Class and status altered as the industrial city matured. The industrialist's power became legitimized. The factories and their owners dug deeper into the lives of the mill-towns and became more accepted and powerful. The old middle class, and those who revered the old, precorporate town, lost influence and disappeared. They were replaced by others who identified more fully with the corporate community. The city government became more bureaucratic and less responsive to popular pressures. Why and how these changes occurred remain important subjects for study. But in order to grasp the magnitude of these changes it is necessary to discard the notion that the nineteenth-century factory-owners moved into control of the industrial town overnight. This myth masks reality and prevents us from focusing on the differences between the nineteenth-century city and the contemporary city. If these differences are located and analyzed, "trends" no longer seem timeless, and the "modern condition"—so often tied to the "urban condition"—assumes a meaningful historical dimension because it is rooted in an understandable past.

## NOTES

1. A pioneer study on this subject is Robert K. Lamb, "The Entrepreneur and the Community," in William Miller (ed.), *Men in Business* (New York: Harper & Row, 1952), pp. 91–117. The examples drawn upon in Blake McKelvey's study *The Urbanisation of America* (New Brunswick, N.J.: Rutgers University Press, 1963) show how little attention historians have given to the industrial city. Vera Shlakman's *An Economic History of a Factory Town* (Northampton, Mass.: Smith College, 1936) is the classic in the field but devotes little attention to the factory and the community at large. Any of the numerous labor histories can be consulted for any period of time to notice quickly how little attention labor historians have given to the industrial city.

2. Max Weber, *Max Weber: Essays in Sociology*, trans. and ed. by H. H. Gerth and C. Wright Mills (New York: Oxford University Press, 1946). 180.

3. Robert M. MacIver, *The Web of Government* (New York: The Macmillan Co., 1947), p. 83.

4. Data on the growth of Paterson's manufacturing industries comes from the 1850, 1860, and 1870 unpublished schedules for manufactures of the U.S. Census deposited in the New Jersey State Library, Trenton, New Jersey, and the following works: L. R. Trumbull, *A History of Industrial Paterson* (Paterson: C. M. Harrick, printer, 1882); Charles Shriner, *Paterson, New Jersey: Its Advantages for Manufacturing and Residences* (Paterson: The Press Printing and Publishing Co., 1892).

5. Details on the Paterson cotton industry are found in Trumbull, *History*, pp. 50–69.

6. The locomotive, machinery, and tool and iron industries of Paterson are described in detail in Trumbull, *History*, pp. 72–148. But see also the *Annual Reports* of the Paterson Board of Trade (Paterson: n.p.) that started to appear in 1873. A good early detailed survey on all Paterson industries is found in *Scientific America* 1 (October 29, November 5, 12, 19, 1859).

7. Especially useful information on the early development of the Paterson silk industry is in Trumbull, *History*, pp. 149–157, 176–253; Shriner, *Paterson*, pp. 196–206; William Wycoff, "Report on the Silk Manufacturing Industry," *Tenth Census of the United States, 1880. Statistics of Manufacture* (Washington: U.S. Govt, Printing Office, 1883), 905–35; Victor S. Clark, *History of Manufactures in the United States, 1860–1893*, II (New York: McGraw-Hill Book Co., Inc., 1929), 449–58. The reports of the New Jersey Bureau of Labor Statistics also are filled with much useful but scattered information on the silk manufacture. The 1878–1880 reports have been especially useful in this study.

8. Population data is found in *Tenth Census, 1880, Statistics of the Population* (Washington: U.S. Govt. Printing Office, 1883), 452, 671, 855-59. Information on retail enterprise comes from the 1859 and 1870 *Paterson City Directory* (Paterson: n.p.).

9. The severity of the depression in Paterson is described in *Chicago Times*, October 31, 1873; *New York Sun*, September 3, 1876; *The Socialist* (New York), April 29, 1876; *Chicago Tribune*, August 4, 1877; *New York World*, February 23, 1877; Paterson Board of Trade, *Annual Report, 1877* (Paterson, 1878), 13-17 and *Annual Report, 1880* (Paterson, 1881), 18-19; L. R. Trumbull, *History*, 147-48.

10. Background information on the 1877 ribbon weavers' strike is found in *Labor Standard* (New York), January 20-June 16, 1877; *New York Times*, May 15, June 20-23, 1877; *Paterson Guardian*, June 11, 19, 21, 25, July 10, 14, 1877; *Paterson Weekly Press*, June 21, 1877; Silk Association of America, *Sixth Annual Report, 1878* (New York: n.p., 1878), 15-17.

11. Pertinent editorial comment is in *Paterson Guardian*, June 21, 25, July 10, 14, 25, 30, 1877, and *Paterson Press*, July 5, 11, 12, 21, 1877. Full details on court action against the strikers and the postponement of trials is in *Paterson Guardian*, July 14, 17, 21, 25, 26, 27, 28, 31, 1877; *Paterson Press*, July 14, 16, 20, 1877; *Chicago Tribune*, August 4, 1877.

12. Biographical information on Benjamin Buckley is in E. H. Haines (ed.), *Paterson, New Jersey, 1792-1892. Centennial Edition of the Evening News* (Paterson: Evening News, 1892), 63; the composition of the Paterson Board of Trade is detailed in its *Third Annual Report, 1876* (Paterson, 1877), 88-90; the role of the Board of Trade is described in *Paterson Guardian*, July 31, August 1, 2, 3, 4, 1877; *Paterson Press*, July 31, August 1, 2, 1877.

13. Buckley's response to the Board of Trade is in *Paterson Guardian*, July 28, August 2, 3, 4, 5, 1877; *Paterson Press*, August 7, 8, 15, 1877. The action of the aldermen is in *Paterson Guardian*, August 7, 8, 1877, and *Paterson Press*, August 7, 8, 1877. Biographical information about the aldermen is in the *Paterson City Directory*, 1871-1872, 1877-1878, 1880-1881, 1887-1888.

14. Editorial comment on failure of the Board of Trade is in *Paterson Guardian*, August 16, 1877. Manufacturer talk about a city militia is found in *Paterson Press*, August 15, 1877, and the early history of the Paterson militia is detailed in John Hilton, "Paterson's Militia," in Shriner, *Paterson*, 89-97. Failure by the manufacturers to enlarge the police force can be traced in the *Annual Reports of the City Government for 1877, 1878, 1879, 1880, and 1886* (Paterson: n.p.).

15. A detailed history of the R & H Adams firm is found in Trumbull, *History*, 208-12, and an obituary of Henry Adams appears in *American Silk Journal* (June, 1890), 137-38.

16. Much information on the strike and community attitudes toward it are found in *Labor Standard* (New York), July 7, 14, 21, 28, August 4, 11, 18, 25, September 7, 14, 1878; *Paterson Guardian*, July 23, August 22, September 3, 5, 9, 14, 1878; *Paterson Press*, August 16, 17, 21, 22, 1878; *Irish World* (New York), September 21, 1878. Early issues of the *Paterson Labor Standard* that illustrate support for McDonnell from retail storekeepers are dated November 23, December 7, 1878.

17. The failure of the effort to bring in Fall River workers is found in *Paterson Guardian*, September 9, 10, 11, 12, 1878; *Paterson Press*, September 13, 1878; *New York Sun*, n.d., reprinted in *Labor Standard*, September 14, 21, 1878. The role of city officials and courts is in *Paterson Guardian*, August 14, September 9, 24, October 1, 1878; *Paterson Press*, October 1, 2, 3, 1878; *Labor Standard*, August 18, October 5, 1878. The end of the strike and the defeat of Adams can be traced in *Irish World* (New York), September 28, October 5, 19, 1878; *Paterson Labor Standard*, November 23, December 7, 1878; *Fall River Labor Standard*, October 30, December 14, 1878; *Paterson Press*, October 27, November 22, 1878.

18. Details on McDonnell's career are found in obituaries reprinted in *Paterson Labor Standard*, January 20, 1906, and "Interview with Mrs. J. P. McDonnell, 1908," McDonnell Mss., Wisconsin State Historical Society. Useful background material on the London milieux from which McDonnell came to the United States is found in Royden Harrison, *Before the Socialists. Studies in Labour and Politics, 1861 to 1881* (London: Routledge & Kegan Paul, 1965), 210-45. The Wisconsin Historical Society holds two manuscript lectures that McDonnell delivered in 1873-1875 and other useful information about his career before coming to Paterson is found in *New York Times*, February 17, 1874, and August 8, 1877; *National Labor Tribune*, May 8, August 7, September 28, October 16, 23, 1875, and March 4, 1876; *The Socialist*, April 15, June 19, 1876; *Labor Standard*, August 12, November 11, 1876, January 27, August 4, 1877; *New York Commercial Advertiser*, n.d.,

reprinted in *Labor Standard*, August 19, 1876; *Utica Observer*, n.d., reprinted in *Labor Standard*, March 3, 1877.

19. The author possesses a microfilm copy of McDonnell's 1878 Grand Jury indictment; the original is in the Passaic County Courthouse, Paterson, New Jersey. Detailed reports on his first trial appear in *Paterson Guardian, Paterson Press,* and *Paterson Labor Standard,* October 20–November 10, 1878. The same newspapers contain materials on the 1880 trial in issues published between January 1 and April 5, 1880.

20. A biographical sketch of McDonnell's lawyer, Thomas Hoxsey, appears in Shriner, *Paterson,* 312. See also *Irish World,* November 3, 1877. Occupational information on the jury is found in *Paterson City Directory,* 1877–1878 and 1880–1881. John Daggers, the manufacturer and lay judge, who urged leniency in sentencing McDonnell, had the details of his life recorded in Shriner, *Paterson,* 209–10, and McDonnell later wrote warmly about him in *Paterson Labor Standard,* November 27, 1897, and November 3, 1898. Details on the payment of McDonnell's fine are found in Henry Rose to the editor, *Indianapolis Times,* November 2, 1878; *Paterson Labor Standard,* n.d., reprinted in *The Socialist* (Chicago), November 23, 1878; *Paterson Guardian,* October 26, 1878; *Paterson Press,* October 26, 1878.

21. The political tumult that followed McDonnell's trial is fully described (but in a partisan fashion) in *Paterson Guardian,* October 27, 28, 29, 30, November 1, 4, 5, 1878; *Paterson Press,* October 27, November 2, 4, 5, 1878; *Paterson Labor Standard,* November 23, December 7, 1878; *Passaic City Herald,* n.d., reprinted in *The Socialist* (Chicago), November 23, 1878.

22. McDonnell's prison diary is the most useful source for judging his support while in prison, and the manuscript copy is deposited in the Wisconsin State Historical Society. The names of his visitors have been checked to the *City Directory* for 1880–1881. Much additional information is found in *Paterson Labor Standard,* January 3, 24, 31, March 13, 20, 27, 1880; *Paterson Guardian,* January 30, 31, February 2, 3, 1880; *Paterson Press,* January 30, 31, February 2, 3, 1880; *Fall River Labor Standard,* February 28, 1880; *Irish World,* March 6, 13, 1880; *The Trades* (Philadelphia), March 13, 1880. Details on McDonnell's lawyer, former Republican Mayor Socrates Tuttle, appear in Shriner, *Paterson,* 319–20.

23. Here, again, McDonnell's prison diary offers the most evidence on his jail experiences. But see also the biographical sketch of Warden John Buckley in Haines (ed.), *Centennial Paterson,* 146.

24. McDonnell's release from prison and the celebration that followed are detailed in his manuscript diary, *Irish World,* April 17, 1880, *Patterson Press,* April 2, 1880, and *Fall River Labor Standard,* April 10, 1880. McDonnell's role in the New Jersey Federation of Trades and Labor Unions is detailed in its annual reports, and his work as Deputy Factory Inspector is noted in the *Annual Reports* of the Factory Inspector that appeared between 1884 and 1886.

25. *Paterson Labor Standard,* October 31, 1896.

26. Herbert G. Gutman, "The Buena Vista Affair," *The Pennsylvania Magazine of History and Biography,* 88 (July, 1964), 251–93. "The Workers' Search for Power," in H. Wayne Morgan (ed.), *The Gilded Age; A Reappraisal* (Syracuse: Syracuse University Press, 1963), pp. 38–68. "The Braidwood Lockout of 1874," Illinois State Historical Society, *Journal,* 53 (1960), 5–28. "An Iron Workers' Strike in the Ohio Valley," *The Ohio Historical Quarterly,* 58 (1959), 353–70. "Trouble on the Railroads in 1873–1874," *Labor History,* 2 (1961), 215–35.

27. Drawing from all fathers and sons in three wards as listed in the unpublished 1870 manuscript census, this study traces occupational mobility over a twenty-year period. Males listed in the 1870 census are searched for in the *Paterson City Directory 1887–1888.* Comparisons in the occupation of the father over this period as well as between the fathers and the sons are made. More than thirty per cent of the males listed in 1870 census have been traced and located in the later directory. Careful comparison of the *Paterson City Directory* between 1865 and 1885 makes it possible to trace the social origins of Paterson policemen, politicians, and small businessmen. In 1877–78, for example, the city had twenty patrolmen. Eight had been policemen in 1870. Six others had been workers in 1870. In 1877–78, at least five policemen, all different from the six who had been workers in 1870, had close female and male relatives who worked in the Paterson factories. Similar patterns occur for small retail businessmen.

# populism

## MICHAEL P. ROGIN

To write the history of mass movements is to ask not only about their composition but also about their sources and goals. In the following article, Michael Rogin attacks mainstream historians for examining Populism primarily in terms of its component interest groups. Viewed from that perspective, Populism appears to be merely a composite of the disgruntled, the prejudiced, and the fascist. But, argues Rogin, if one sees Populism as a response to social crisis, one then understands the thrust of the movement as a radical attempt to create a collective conscience. Norman Pollack, in his influential book *The Populist Response to Industrial America,* contends that the Populists heralded later radical movements. Rogin, however, points out that Populism did not become revolutionary because American workers were concerned with bread-and-butter issues and did not perceive industrial capitalism as inimical to their interests.

---

Political movements in a crisis period encompass both ideology and economic demands. Their proposals look to changes in the wider society and are in this sense broader than the proposals of interest groups. Their constituents, in deprived positions in society, require more large-scale changes. Moreover, in the disrupted position in which people find themselves during a crisis, they require some general explanation of the relation between narrow economic demands and their general welfare. Deprived of power, they are not likely to be motivated to act to change their situation by appeals to practical self-interest alone. Because the obstacles to surmount are so great, such appeals seem illusory and in fact often are. Therefore, some emotional appeals are essential; protest movements have crusade characteristics. The movements of farmers in the 1890's, workers in the 1930's, and Negroes in the 1960's have all been crusades. The emotional appeals of these movements transcend rationality defined in terms of Benthamite narrow self-interest. But narrow groups are specifically irrational in a crisis period because their methods can succeed neither in achieving results nor in attracting adherents.

To treat mass movements in pluralist terms is to make them a priori irrational. When they are viewed as responses to social crises, a different picture emerges. Populism must be understood not as a foolish departure from interest group politics but as the product of the widespread and severe stresses of rapid industrialization and a serious depression.

The economic and cultural dislocation brought by industrialization has produced mass movements all over the world. These movements can take several forms. They can reject industrialization entirely and favor direct action and sabotage. This approach often dominated anarchist movements. They can

Reprinted from "Populism," *The Intellectuals and McCarthy: The Radical Specter* by Michael P. Rogin (1967), 168–191, by permission of The M. I. T. Press, Cambridge, Massachusetts. Copyright © 1967 by The M. I. T. Press.

reject any sort of liberal society and seek to resolve economic and cultural problems with totalitarian control. This was the approach of fascism. They can seek to utilize industrialization to solve the problems it itself has created. This was the character of Marxism in Western Europe and Populism in America.

Adam Ulam has suggested that Marxism in Europe, in diverting resentment from the industrial process itself and onto the capitalist, socialized the working class to an acceptance of industrialization. Whereas the Luddites and anarchists fought the industrial work process itself, Marxist workers organized to fight the capitalists. In so doing they took the crucial step of accepting the industrial situation and working to improve their situation within it. Placing anti-industrial feeling in the service of industrial logic, revolutionary Marxism led to reformist trade unionism.[1]

In *The Paradox of Progressive Thought*, David Noble has made a parallel analysis of American progressivism. Hofstadter suggested that the progressives and Populists feared industrialization. But according to Noble, they reinterpreted it as a mechanism for freeing man from the burden of traditions and institutions and for reintroducing agrarian innocence into an advanced civilization.[2] In Ulam's terms, American reformers channeled a potential anti-industrial emotion in the direction of an acceptance of industrialization for the benefits it could bring if properly controlled. The parallel is exact, for the reformers focused their attacks not on the industrial process itself but on the particular bearers of industrialization—in their terms, the plutocrats and the interests.

Populist rhetoric and the Populist program were anti-industrial capitalist not anti-industrial. In the words of one Populist paper, "The people do not want to tear down the railroads nor pull down the factories . . . They want to build up and make better everything." Another explained that the Populists "shall make of this nation an industrial democracy in which each citizen shall have an equal interest." Technology, the Populists argued, could be used to enslave man but also to liberate him.[3]*

True, the Populists opposed capitalists who were industrializing America. Does this make the capitalists progressive, the Populists reactionary? An analogous approach makes Stalinism in Russia into a progressive force because it, too, industrialized. Such overviews ignore the particular issues upon which conflict was joined. Conflict between Populists and conservatives was not about industrialization in the abstract, but about the control of railroads, the power of monopolies, the falling prices of crops, the benefits and dangers of inflation, big business control of politics, and other issues which could all have been met as

*Many Populists, although not anti-industrial, were loath to admit that basic and irreversible changes in American society had caused the problems the farmer faced. Kansas Senator William Peffer began *The Farmer's Side* with a long, realistic description of the effect of industrialization and technology on the self-sufficient farmer. The farm situation, he wrote, had been produced not by the machinations or conspiracies of a few men but by the general development of the society. This evolution could not be reversed; rather the farmers should seek to benefit from it. But Peffer followed this section with another in which he blamed usury for all the farmers' troubles.[4] Here Peffer drew back from the real problems brought by industrialization. Money panaceas became a substitute for the more radical program implied by the earlier analysis. Clearly the two aspects of Peffer's argument are mutually contradictory. If industrialization is the cause of agrarian unhappiness, there is no possibility of going back to an earlier utopia. If usury and the evil actions of a few men explain everything, there is no need to deal with the basic problems brought by industrialization.

the Populists desired without undermining industrialization.*

Had Populism attempted to escape from the problems brought by industrialization it would have relied on finding scapegoats, attacking freedom, and appealing to prejudice. Such a politics could rely—as McCarthyism relied—on the support of local elites. The democratic character of Populism flowed from its willingness to seek concrete, economic solutions to farmer grievances and to challenge local elites in the process.

Because they challenged those in power, Populists could appreciate freedom. They came to see the importance of social relationships rather than individual morality in explaining political attitudes. If conservatives could stress the individual corruption and evil conspiracies of a few men, reformers learned to look deeper.[7] They concentrated on specific economic grievances rather than vague, unfocused resentments. The very existence of agrarian radicals increased the alternatives in rural society, thereby promoting diversity.

Certainly there were aspects of Populism which make the modern observer uncomfortable. Populist leaders appealed to rural suspicion of the city and were unable to suppress their belief in rural superiority. The rural, fundamentalist Populist rhetoric made it difficult to attract urban allies, without which the movement was doomed. Many in the Populist crusade were cranky and narrow-minded. But a total assessment of Populism cannot be made so easily. Let us evaluate the movement in light of the specific pluralist attacks.

Some of these charges have to do with the general Populist ideology. Hofstadter has criticized the movement for its naive belief in a natural harmony of society and a two-sided struggle between the people and the interests. These charges need not long detain us. The Populist rhetoric here derives from Lockean liberalism and was shared by conservatives as well as Populists. Conservatives and Populists attacked each other for interfering with the natural harmony of the world; each saw the other as a special interest. That reality is more complex than political slogans should surprise no one.[8]

More serious is the alleged Populist commitment to a conspiracy theory of history. As a rural movement with religious roots, Populism was especially prone to dramatize experience. It existed at a time when politics as a whole was played at this level. Where Populists saw conspiracies of bankers, conservatives feared anarchist conspiracies. There is little question that many Populist writers exhibited a conspiracy mentality. It is harder to come to an assessment of the importance of that mentality in the movement. Hofstadter argues that Populism was preoccupied with conspiracies. On the other hand, a recent study of Kansas Populism concludes that those who went to "international conspiracy" extremes were a small lunatic fringe of Populism.[9]

More than that, the Populists had been left behind by industrialization, left out of politics by the east and by their own local elites. There were, for example, virtually no farmers in local positions of party leadership in pre-Populist Kansas and Nebraska. But most of the local Populist leaders were

---

*Populists demanded a graduated income tax, government ownership or regulation of the railroads and the telegraph, control over monopoly, a lower tariff, increased education, direct election of senators, the secret ballot, the initiative and the referendum, an eight-hour day on government work, support for the labor movement, the free coinage of silver, a plan for government loans to farmers at low interest rates, and restriction on alien and corporate landholding.[5] If the Populists longed for a "rural utopia,"[6] this longing was not operational.

farmers. Their perception of courthouse "rings" making political decisions was close to the truth.[10] Similarly, on the national level agreements and conspiracies between capitalists were an important part of industrialization. In the legal world, the American Bar Association played an important role in cementing close ties and informal contacts between judges and conservative lawyers.[11] Perhaps Henry Demarest Lloyd paid insufficient attention in *Wealth Against Commonwealth* to the general laws of capitalist development in the creation of Standard Oil. Certainly Sumner and Spencer paid insufficient attention to the illegal acts and conspiracies of particular men.

In part, Hofstadter recognizes this and suggests a distinction between the perception of particular conspiracies and the perception of history as a conspiracy. This is an intellectually impeccable distinction, but one should not overestimate the ease of drawing it in the political practice of the late-nineteenth century.

Perhaps the most serious concrete charges laid against Populist ideology are the charges of nativism and anti-Semitism. According to Hofstadter, Populism activated most of American popular anti-Semitism. Viereck, Bell, Lipset, and Handlin all give currency to the allegation of Populist anti-Semitism.[12] It is particularly important to our argument here because in so far as Populists focused on Jews rather than economic targets they were failing to come to grips with the real problems of industrialization. This failure would have given an authoritarian cast to the movement. Thus Oscar Handlin specifically related Populist anti-Semitism to the movement's fear of the forces brought into play by industrialization—specifically, the Haymarket Affair, the Pullman Boycott, and the western mining strikes.[13]

The fact is, however, that the Populists sympathized with the Haymarket anarchists and were for the Pullman Boycott. The Populist governor of Colorado intervened for the workers in the Cripple Creek strike.[14] It is true that anti-Semitism would have been an alternative to an alliance with a rising labor movement. But while the evidence of Populist support for labor stands out,[15] the evidence of Populist anti-Semitism is very meager. A few Populists like Mary Ellen Lease seem to have been anti-Semitic. Moreover, one can find stereotyping of Jews in some Populist allegorical writing, like Donnelly's *Caesar's Column*.[16] The Jewish theme does not dominate *Caesar's Column*, and stereotyping of immigrant groups was common practice in the late nineteenth century.[17] Donnelly is even sympathetic to the plight of the Jews, but his sympathy is part of an over-all animosity and distrust. Perhaps not unusual in the tawdry romantic novel of the period, Donnelly's portrayal of the Jewish characters is anti-Semitic by modern standards. One Jew heads the plutocracy and another is the evil genius of the revolution. The Jews had survived for hundreds of years under Christian tyranny, writes Donnelly, and now the Christians are paying "for the sufferings inflicted by their bigoted and ignorant ancestors on a noble race."[18]

The anti-Semitism in Donnelly's fantasy can be exaggerated, but if Populist rhetoric in general had been as anti-Semitic as *Caesar's Column*, the case for Populist verbal anti-Semitism would be made. However, the picture of Populist anti-Semitism has been created from slender evidence. Careful examination of tens of thousands of Populist newspapers, pamphlets, and books in Kansas and the other centers of midwestern Populism has uncovered no anti-Semitism in the collections of the state historical societies and only two or three references in the immense production of the Populist press.[19] As for the frequent references in Populist literature to the power of Shylock and the House of Rothschild, it is doubtful if these symbols had specific anti-Semitic connotations. In Kansas Populist literature, the House of Morgan was as frequent a Populist target as the House of Rothschild. The remaining examples of Populist anti-Semitism, such as the charge that Bryan's cross of gold peroration had anti-Semitic intent,[20] are extremely far-fetched. Comparing Populist "anti-Semitism" with the verbal anti-Semitism then common throughout the United States, the restrictions against Jews in respectable eastern society and the riots against Jews in the cities, it is possible to argue that the Populist movement was less anti-Semitic than late nineteenth century America as a whole.

Although much is made of alleged Populist anti-Semitism, little attention is paid to the resistance of southern Populism to anti-Negro rhetoric and activity. Racism was a tool of the conservatives, who sought to discredit and defeat the Populists by arousing the specter of Negro supremacy. Populist supporters in the South may have been anti-Negro, but during the Populist period it was more important to them to ally with Negro farmers along economic lines. In Georgia, Tom Watson attacked Democratic outrages against the Negro. At one point, a number of white Populist farmers rode all night to prevent the lynching of a Negro Populist. Moreover, agrarian reformers like Tillman who remained Democrats were as anti-Negro as their conservative opponents. It was the more radical, ideological, third-party Populists who defended Negro rights.[21]

What of alleged Populist hostility to foreigners? Populism is often interpreted as a revolt of native-born farmers, but outside the South there is virtually no basis for this impression. In the South, Populism tended to be strongest in the hill country of independent, Protestant, native-born farmers and weakest in the black belt. Populists received significant Negro support in some areas but did poorly among Mexicans and others of foreign stock.[22] In Iowa in 1892, the Populists also ran relatively best in the predominantly native-born counties and worse in the German and Scandinavian counties; but Populism generally was weak in Iowa. In Nebraska and the Dakotas, there was no relation between the proportion of native-born and Populism. In Kansas, the Populists scored successes in both native and foreign-born counties. Indeed, a higher percentage of immigrants ran for public office under the Kansas Populist banner than in either of the major parties.[23] Thus to relate the movement to Anglo-Saxon fear of immigration or old-American longing for a distant past is at best questionable.

The support of foreign ethnic groups for Populism varied somewhat from state to state. In Kansas, the Populists ran best in Irish, Bohemian, Welsh, and Danish precincts, and worst in German, Russian-German, and particularly Mennonite and Swedish precincts. In Nebraska, the Populists did poorly in German, Bohemian, and Catholic areas. Over the Plains states as a whole, Norwegians and Danes seem consistently to have given disproportionate support to Populism and Catholics, Germans, and Russian-Germans to have provided a source of opposition.

Populism could have blamed the changes taking place in America on foreigners[24] and sponsored nativist legislation. Indeed, there was some antiforeign sentiment among local Populists in some areas,[25] although research has failed to uncover significant Populist nativism on the Great Plains. That unfriendliness toward immigrants existed in the Populist movement conflicted with the belief that America was and should be the home of the oppressed.[26] Thus Weaver, running for President in 1892, repudiated a restrictionist plank in the 1892 Populist platform. The plank was only there at the request of the Knights of Labor. The Knights feared competition from cheap foreign labor, a fear that led the AFL also to favor immigration restriction. Similarly, in Kansas the Populists only accepted immigration restriction at the behest of the Knights of Labor. Eastern Republicans were much more unambiguously for immigration restriction than were the Populists.[27] The Populist platforms did always include planks calling for a prohibition on alien ownership of land. These planks were not nativist in motivation, but were directed against the ownership of land by large foreign corporations and by nonresidents who held the land for speculative purposes.

Britain was the one country toward which the Populists were hostile. In part, this was antiaristocratic prejudice (which also motivated someone like Carnegie); in part, it was caused by the ties of Wall Street and Grover Cleveland to British bankers.[28] The significance of Irish influence within Populism on this score also should not be discounted.

There is no significant evidence of jingoism in Populist foreign policy. The Populists on the whole favored Cuban liberation but opposed the Spanish American War and the annexation of Cuba and the Philippines.[29] As was the case with nativism, the more moderate progressives were more often jingoist in foreign policy than the "extremist" Populists. Much of the evidence cited of Populist jingoism is perverse indeed. The assertion of an anti-Populist Congressman that McKinley's foreign policy was hurting the Populists (because they opposed it) clearly suggests that the Populists lost support because they were not jingoist. Similarly, to derive Populist jingoism from jingoist attitudes in "Populist areas" is not only to confuse the party with its social base but also to overlook a conservative opposition to Populism that was always either dominant or extremely powerful in "Populist areas." That there is a jingoist tradition in the Middle West is not at issue; the question is the relation of the Populist movement to that tradition.[30]

As for Populist attitudes toward Catholics, Catholics did tend to vote against the Populist party, but this seems as likely to have been due to Catholic characteristics as Populist ones. The Populists often sought fusion with the Catholic party, the Democrats. Moreover, the American Protective Association reached its height in the Populist period. This was an anti-Catholic organization, but it was not involved with the Populists. The APA was strongest in the old Middle West, where Populism was virtually nonexistent. Aside from being anti-Catholic, the APA was strongly anti-Populist. It attacked the Populists with the kind of moralistic language attributed so often to the Populists.[31] The Populists made moralistic attacks on the APA in the name of individual freedom. They accused Republicans in many states of being tools of the APA, and in fact the Republican parties often did have APA connections.[32]

## THE POPULIST CRUSADE

If specific charges of jingoism and anti-Semitism fail, what of the general view of Populism as a moral crusade, destructive of individual differences and privacy? One should not underestimate the elements of a crusade in Populism.

Populism was a Protestant revival in an already intolerant rural setting. There was in rural society little attention paid to the freedom of individuals as individuals. Individual freedom was enforced, if at all, by group power rather than by neutral societal institutions concerned with the protection of individual rights. In practice, the individual Hatfield might be protected by his family against the individual McCoy, the individual Congregationalist by his church against the Anglicans. In theory, there were few institutionalized protections for minority rights. For John Locke, the theorist of rural liberalism, homogeneity seemed to obviate the need for minority safeguards. The major protections entirely altered the relationship between the individual and the society—the right to leave and the right of revolution.[33] With the growth of an urban society, anonymity and individual freedom grew too. Bureaucratic structures concerned with restraints on government arose. Supreme Court interpretations of the Bill of Rights and the Fourteenth Amendment to guarantee individual liberties are strikingly a twentieth-century phenomenon, as is the growth of the American Civil Liberties Union.[34]

Frederic Howe captured the flavor of rural society well when he described his boyhood in Meadville, Pennsylvania:

> One could be sharp in business, possibly corrupt in politics, but one should not forget that life was a serious business, that duty should be always before one's eyes, that one should be diligent in things distasteful, and that self-fulfillment meant getting on in the world, being assiduous to church-going, rather exhibitive in attendance on revivals, the holding to one's particular church denomination, and the avoidance of even the appearance of careless morals, drinking or association with men of questionable opinions.
>
> The other important thing was to live as other men lived, do as other men did, avoid any departure from what other men thought. Not to conform was dangerous to one's reputation. Men who had strange ideas, who protested, who thought for themselves, were quietly ostracized.[35]

As Howe recognized, much of the evangelicalism and intolerance of this rural environment went into the reform movements. Indeed, the roots of Populism in a grass roots, evangelical Protestant mentality cannot be exaggerated. The Populist revolt called forth perhaps the most intense and widespread political involvement in American history. As the historian of the Texas People's Party puts it,

> Populism sprang from the soil. It came into being in many sections of the state within the space of a brief period almost as if by pre-arrangement, yet there was no relation between the various local phases of the movement aside from that provided by the common conditions from which all grew. It was, then, in its incipient stages a spontaneous, almost explosive force.[36]

Progressivism was primarily an elite phenomenon. Populism was a mass uprising. Farmers traveled miles with their families to large camp meetings. They read the immense outpouring of the Populist press, passing the pamphlets and newspapers from hand to hand. They filled local schoolhouses in the evenings, and participated in politics in hundreds of counties throughout the Great Plains and the South. The major parties could count on traditional loyalties, and their local organizations were often moribund. The Populists would have been lost without the remarkable activity of their grass roots supporters.[37]

The revivalist character of this mass uprising is striking. Ministers and ex-ministers were active in the movement; the camp meetings resembled nothing so much as religious revivals. Populist gatherings were sober affairs, suspicious of luxury and full of religious paraphernalia. The party was known as the party of righteousness, and such groups as the Germans feared for their Sunday cards and beer.[38]

Surely this supports the perception of the movement as a dangerous, mass fundamentalist crusade, particularly in light of the Scopes trial, the 1920's Ku Klux Klan, and the more recent manifestations of fundamentalist extremism.

The rural, Protestant Populist environment hardly seems fertile soil for a tolerant, democratic, forward-looking politics. But analyzing the Populist crusade as a product of the intolerance of rural respectability misses a fundamental point. To be an agrarian radical was to challenge respectability. The dominant institutions of nineteenth century rural America—church, press, politicians, local business elites—were all opposed to agrarian radicalism. The established elites owed their political power in part to the cultivation of intolerance; to moralistic appeals to patriotism, Americanism, and the like; to religious fundamentalism; and to the power of conformity. Agrarian radicalism in part participated in this style of politics but in a more basic sense had to combat these methods of political control.

Certain kinds of crusades under certain circumstances destroy privacy and individual differences. But the circumstances in which Populism found itself are important. Because it was a minority movement against powerful elites, because it was in an American tradition of individualism and freedom, the movement could see many of the advantages of free speech and privacy. Thus Populists pushed for the introduction of a secret ballot. Nor did Populist "Americanism" cause them to persecute the opposition. Like agrarian radicals during World War I, Populists were the victims of superpatriotism rather than its perpetrators.

There are three specific areas in which the Populist crusade is alleged to have interfered with freedom. The first of these is in the university. In the Populist and progressive periods there was considerable interference with academic freedom, for academic tenure was not firmly institutionalized as it is today. Although many writers cite Populist interferences with academic freedom,[39] in point of fact there is only one example. In Kansas, the Populists ignored academic tenure in reorganizing the Kansas State Agricultural College. This was not, it should be pointed out, because they were suspicious of "overeducation"; they rather had a somewhat naive faith in what education could accomplish. In Kansas, they desired to introduce a liberal arts curriculum into an exclusively agricultural college.[40] In this case the interference with academic freedom resulted not from anti-intellectualism but from enthusiasm for education. This is not the sort of mentality traditionally associated with attacks on academic freedom. Moreover, the view that the Populist attitudes of the American masses make them anti-intellectual ignores the crucial question of which particular elites (if any) are going to lead anti-intellectual crusades or give in to them. On the whole, in America these functions have been performed by conservative elites, and radical intellectuals like Thorstein Veblen have been the victims. The Populists were not the fathers of modern witch-hunts.

Populist support for prohibition is also cited as evidence for the dangerous effects of the Populist crusade. It is true that Populist voters tended to support prohibition referenda and that prohibition was one of the progressive reforms associated with the initiative, the referendum, and female suffrage.[41] In part, this was because liquor interests played a corrupt role in state politics. In part, it was because temperance, like economic reform, was seen as a necessary precondition for individual advancement. In part, it was out of simple intolerance for the habits of particular ethnic groups and urban classes. However, a proviso should be entered here. In the early days of the prohibition movement, the Prohibition Party platform was generally radical. In the 1890's Prohibition platforms resembled Populist platforms. However, the real cultivation of rural ignorance and prejudice came not in this period, but with the rise of the practical, single-interest, conservative Anti-Saloon League.

Moreover, our concern is not only with the attitude of Populist constituents toward prohibition but the attitude of the movement itself. At the county level, Populists and Prohibitionists often had close relationships. Some state Populist parties, as in North Dakota, endorsed prohibition. It was more common, however, for the movement to steer away from that controversial issue, as it did in South Dakota, Iowa, Texas, and generally in Kansas.[42]

Another charge leveled against the Populist crusade is that it sought to destroy representative democracy. Here again one must measure Populist practice against the claims of its opponents. While many Populists favored the initiative and the referendum, the political reforms most stressed by the Populists were the secret ballot and the direct election of senators. Certainly the Populists sought to challenge the political and economic power of those who dominated American society at the turn of the twentieth century. Certainly the direct election of senators increased the power of the people vis-à-vis the elites. But it is highly dubious that such a Populist reform was a threat to representative democracy. Finally, the Populist attacks on the courts indicate disregard for law and order not so much by the Populists as by the courts themselves. In 1895 alone, the Supreme Court invalidated the income tax and refused to apply the Sherman Act to the sugar monopoly while upholding Debs' conviction under it.[43] This consistent, narrow partiality in interpreting the laws and the constitution explains Populist attitudes better than deductions concerning "plebiscitory democracy."

That Populism was in significant measure a Protestant crusade is impossible to deny. It is also true that the conditions permitting a movement of this sort to focus on concrete economic reforms were fast disappearing. Nevertheless, charges that the Populists were authoritarian are not supported by the evidence. Particularly in contrast to the politics it opposed, Populism was clearly a democratic phenomenon.

Are we required, then, to call Populism an example of class rather than status politics? In the categories of class and status politics, we meet the issue of moralism and pragmatism in another form. For the Beardians, Populism was a pragmatic class movement, representing the special interests of farmers as other groups represented the special interests of their constituencies.[44] The pluralists have seen that Beardian analysis cannot describe the Populist movement successfully. However, in their distinction between "class" and "status" politics they have not transcended Beardian categories. Accepting the narrow Beardian definition of an economic movement and finding that Populism was more than this, they have underplayed its economic character. Rather than transcending the Beardian analysis, they have stood it on its head.

Hofstadter, for example, implicitly interprets Populism as an example of status politics. Distinguishing between the hard and the soft side of the agrarian spirit, he writes,

The farmer's commercial position pointed to the usual strategies of the business world: combination, cooperation, pressure politics, lobbying, piecemeal activity directed toward specific goals. But the bathos of the agrarian rhetoric pointed in a different direction: broad political goals, ideological mass politics, third parties, the conquest of the "money power," the united action of all labor, rural and urban.

Relating this to Populism, Hofstadter explains that in bad times the farmer rejected his role as a capitalist and "withdrew into the role of the injured little yeoman." The Farmers Alliance and the Populist Party had their hard side (business methods, pressure politics), he says, but as the depression deepened the soft Populist rhetoric triumphed and all issues were dropped for the silver panacea.[45]

In order to make the progressive movement an example of status politics, Hofstadter argues that status politics is born of prosperity. This will not do for the Populists; since they flourished during a depression, they would become a class political phenomenon. But Hofstadter reserves class politics for narrow interest groups. The term would place the Populists in an incorrect and—for him—too favorable light. He therefore first treats the Populist Party as an irrational response to crisis; it appears to be an example of status politics. He then turns to the achievements of practical farm organizations with narrow economic goals. According to him these were associated with agricultural prosperity. This was the same period of prosperity that produced progressive status politics.[46]

Hofstadter could overcome the contradiction here explicitly by excepting rural politics from the normal class-status cycle. But this would hardly render his treatment of Populism itself more convincing. For while Populism was certainly more than a narrow pressure group, it was still an economic movement making practical demands. As C. Vann Woodward has pointed out, the Populist demands did not ignore economics but rather were "obsessively economic."[47] The business ventures of the Farmers Alliance were in part examples of farmer unwillingness to come to terms with industrial capitalism. In shifting to politics, the farmers recognized the insufficiency of purely business methods. The politicizing of the Alliance was not simply the result of self-pity; the depression rendered nonpolitical solutions futile. In fact, Hofstadter himself later attributes a measure of success to the third party.[48] Finally, if "the bathos of agrarian rhetoric" produced the free silver panacea as well as the third party, why did free silver destroy both the third party and the general third-party demands? The answer is that free silver did not dominate third-party Populism. It was rather the panacea of the more conservative (and practical?) Democrats like Bryan who were too conservative to make demands for basic changes in American society; they preferred panaceas. Indeed, free silver did not dominate the Populist movement until, in its practical desire to win power, it sought fusion with the Democrats. Here is the ultimate irony; Hofstadter damns Populism for the practical, opportunistic concern for power at the expense of broad, ideological principles—the very politics that wins his praise when practiced by the major parties.

Hofstadter's treatment makes of Populism an irrational, unnecessary movement. This is also the consequence of other pluralist arguments. In Kornhauser's scheme, mass movements arise when the masses are available for mobilization and the elites are accessible to influence from below. In his analysis, the only societies where the masses are available but the elites inaccessible are totalitarian.[49] Surely some finer distinctions are in order. One would like to know which elites are accessible and which inaccessible. To which constituencies are elites accessible, to which inaccessible? By what methods are elites accessible, and what methods will they resist or ignore?

In a basic sense, the elites in America are accessible to popular influence, but mass movements generally arise because of the inaccessibility of elites to the interests of the members of mass movements and in this sense their inaccessibility to the pressure group politics of pluralism. Thus in Populist states, politics was often controlled from outside and the elites that made political decisions were not accessible to the bulk of people. On the national level, the elites were also inaccessible. Particularly important here was the role of the Supreme Court in rejecting legislation that reformers were able to pass. Because the Supreme Court was not accessible to reform influence, it played the role of radicalizing political discontent.[50]

Other factors besides the inaccessibility of elites obviously contribute to the rise of mass movements and determine their character. But whether the movements are democratic or totalitarian, their appearance is related to the inaccessibility of elites.[51] By basing mass movements on the accessibility of elites, Kornhauser denies them the possibility of being a rational response to social crises. For if the elites are accessible, mass movements are unnecessary.

Similarly, when Kornhauser writes that the "objects" of mass movements are "remote" and do not "directly concern the individual,"[52] he again makes mass movements irrational by definition. Interest rates, railroads, corporations, and the money supply certainly concerned the Populist farmers directly. And the Populists were perfectly reasonable in believing that control over railroads, interest rates, corporations, and the money supply was exercised in places remote from the Great Plains. Would they have been more rational to focus their anger on neighboring shopkeepers?

Just as the distinction between moralism and pragmatism cannot contain the Lockean ideology, so the distinctions between proximate and remote concerns, class and status politics, cannot contain agrarian radicalism. As conceived of by the pluralists, class (proximate) politics are concerned with immediate economic group self-interest, status (remote) politics with position in the social structure. Class politics seek gains for the value of the gains themselves (more money, better working conditions, tax benefits, and so forth). Status politics seeks gains because of what they signify (conspicuous consumption, keeping up with the Jones, demonstrating Americanism vis-à-vis the Anglo-Saxons, etc.). Contrary to the pluralist view, periods of prosperity and satisfaction seem to produce both status and class politics in America. As de Tocqueville recognized, in America these are not so different. The group scramble that dominates politics during prosperity involves both "status" concerns and direct, narrow, economic advancement. In a crisis period, however, neither interest-group nor status politics can succeed. In the Populist period, "business methods" were doomed to failure. Similarly, in Wisconsin during the 1930's depression a precursor of McCarthy attempted to win office on the ("status") issue of communism.[53] Ignoring the economic grievances of the people, he was soundly beaten.

Populism, like Marxism, sought to combine a general program for the political control of industrialization with the concrete demands of a significant social force. But the Populist movement was hardly revolutionary. For better or worse, neither the movement nor the farmers it represented wanted to free themselves from the Lockean inheritance.

Marxism was revolutionary; Populism was not. But this was hardly the only difference between them. If agrarian radicalism played a role in America analogous to the role of Marxism in Europe, then in a sense American farmers took the place of European workers.[54] In Europe industrialization uprooted the peasants from the land and brought them to the cities, where they became revolutionary workers. But the uprooted European peasants who settled in American cities remained conservative. In America the farmers who stayed on the land played the role of European workers as the major force challenging industrial capitalism.

How is this to be explained? The absence of feudalism on the one hand hindered the development of working-class consciousness. On the other hand it provided a yeoman farming class instead of a tradition-bound peasantry. The commitment to individual mobility obstructed the rise of socialist consciousness among workers, but it fostered agrarian radicalism. Farmer mobility, farmer experience in self-help, farmer cooperation along the frontier, all enabled farmers to organize politically. They did not require a Napoleonic leader to represent them. Moreover, fascism, feudal in its corporateness and in its attack on individualism, was less likely to appeal to American farmers. And as the class most committed to self-help and individual success, they reacted bitterly against the neofeudal society they saw being created around them.

For three-quarters of a century after the Civil War, there were continual movements of rural protest in the western Middle West. Movements like Populism and 1930's progressivism arose in response to specific agricultural depressions. But depressions alone cannot explain the continual strength of agrarian radicalism in this period. Both farmers and progressives prospered in the decade before World War I. The Non-Partisan League was organized in North Dakota during prosperity and declined during depression. One must look beyond depressions to the long-term structural situation of the American farmer.

The greater exposure of agriculture to international market conditions after the Civil War increased the instability of agricultural life. To compound dependence on the market, newly settled farmers usually produced a single crop; this exposed the farmers not only to market conditions in general but to the widespread fluctuations in the price of a single commodity. Moreover, farming methods had not yet made much impact on the hazards of weather on the Great Plains. Agrarian radicalism has always been stronger in the wheat than in the corn-hog areas. Wheat farming depends more on the weather and on other events over which the farmer has no control. The wheat farmer is traditionally inclined to take the help he can get from outside sources like the government. Corn-hog farming, on the other hand, depends far more on the day-to-day activities of the individual farmer. The conservative, antigovernment commitment to rugged individualism is more meaningful in the corn belt.

The Populist-progressive era was close to the period of settlement. One cannot speak with certainty about the influence of the frontier, but it seems reasonable to suppose that the frontier unsettled tradition and increased the effort to meet problems through political self-help.[55] As the frontier influence declined, these areas became more conservative.

Ethnic traditions also contributed to political protest. The West North Central states plus Wisconsin had far higher percentages of foreign-born in their populations than the states of any other region in the country. This concentration of the foreign-born was particularly striking compared to other rural areas. Early studies showed a tendency for the foreign-born to support protest movements more than native-stock Americans. The research here provides no similar evidence within the progressive states. But if the foreign-born as a whole did not disproportionately support agrarian radicalism at the same time, different groups of foreign-born perpetuated it at different times. Scandinavians and Germans were concentrated in the western Middle West. The Scandinavians consistently supported Populism and progressivism. The Germans, usually resistant to agrarian radicalism, kept it alive during and after World War I.

One might argue, moreover, that ethnic conflict provided a challenge to the political systems in the West North Central states. In the eastern cities, this challenge was met by the machine. In the countryside such a solution was impractical for several reasons—the different character of the ethnic groups, the contrasts in urban and rural political styles, the visibility of economic targets for resentment, the conditions of agriculture, the strength of a tradition of agrarian revolt, the greater isolation within rural areas. Therefore, ethnic dissatisfaction focused on broader class and political goals.[56]

Political conditions added their weight to economic and cultural factors. Politically, the farmers of the Middle West were isolated from the centers of power in the society. This did not mean that they were ignorant of the problems of the larger society so much as it meant that the larger society did not understand their problems. The midwest rural world lacked the power to make the outside political elites sensitive to agrarian demands and moderate on agrarian issues. Political control in the trans-Mississippi West was more nakedly in the hands of railroads and other businesses than was the case in states with a longer political tradition. In many instances, the western states were controlled by outside railroads and corporations. This elite inaccessibility provoked radical demands and radical movements.

Agrarian society, however, was not static. The changes that had produced agrarian radical movements finally undermined them. Consider for the moment only the decline in farm population. In 1860, 59.7 percent of all workers in the country worked on farms. By 1900, the figure was down to 35.7 percent.[57] Farmers were no longer a majority of the population. The decline in the relative number of farmers continued in the twentieth century. From 1920 to 1944, there was a large net migration from the farms. In the West North Central states, where agrarian radical movements had flourished, this decline was especially pronounced. Between 1920 and 1944, the net migration from farms in the West North Central states averaged about 2 percent for each four-year period.[58] By 1950 less than 15 percent of the total United States population lived on farms.* Thus, if farmers in America played the role of workers in Europe, workers were the wave of the industrial future on both continents. A farmer-labor alliance in the 1890's might have altered the course of American development, but labor was turning in a different direction. Workers voted against Bryan in 1896, and Gompers had earlier refused to ally the AFL with the Populist Party. As he

*Moreover, those who have left the farms have been primarily young people. The older rural residents, traditionally more conservative, have therefore become a greater political force.[59] This exodus from the farms to the cities has provided an urban safety valve for rural discontent.[60]

interpreted working-class mentality, it was through with the middle-class radicalism that had permeated the labor movement since Jacksonian days. Before the rise of the AFL, the aim of working-class organizations had been to keep the class structure fluid, to provide for social mobility. This led to alliance with "the people" (farmers and others of the small middle class) rather than to specific class action and specific job-oriented demands. In joining purely class-oriented craft unions, workers accepted the permanency of the wage-earning status for themselves if not for their children. When European workers organized on a class basis, they recognized their wage-earning status only in order to challenge the permanency of a system which had wage-earning statuses in it. But in America, class action was a substitute for a general challenge to the industrial capitalist system.

The class organizations of American workers, then, tended not to participate in broad movements of social change from the Populist period through the 1920's. (However, at certain times and in selected areas some American workers allied themselves with socialism and progressivism.) After the defeat of Populism, agrarian radicalism continued to flourish to the First World War and beyond. But the New Deal and the rise of the CIO reoriented American politics. Workers came to supply the main base of reform, not in alliance with rural areas but against them. Farmer leadership in American radicalism had come to an end.

NOTES

1. Adam B. Ulam, *The Unfinished Revolution* (New York: Random House, 1960), pp. 28–57 and *passim*.

2. David W. Noble, *The Paradox of Progressive Thought* (Minneapolis, Minn.: University of Minnesota Press, 1958), pp. vi–viii, and *passim*.

3. Quoted in Norman Pollack, *The Populist Response to Industrial America* (Cambridge, Mass.: Harvard University Press, 1962), pp. 15–16, 22–25.

4. William A. Peffer, *The Farmer's Side: His Troubles and Their Remedy* (New York: Appleton, 1891), pp. 3–64, 75–123.

5. Populist and Alliance platforms can be found in John R. Hicks, *The Populist Revolt* (Lincoln, Neb.: University of Nebraska Press, 1961), pp. 427–444.

6. Richard Hofstadter, *The Age of Reform* (New York: Knopf, 1955), pp. 62–63.

7. Frederic Howe learned from his environment that individual morality was at the root of politics. His education as a reformer taught him the importance of the system. This was a common experience. Cf. Frederic C. Howe, *Confessions of a Reformer* (New York: Scribner's, 1925); C. Vann Woodward, *Tom Watson: Agrarian Rebel* (New York: Macmillan, 1938), p. 82.

8. See also the excellent and more extended comments by Norman Pollack in "Hofstadter on Populism: A Critique of 'The Age of Reform,'" *Journal of Southern History*, Vol. 26 (November 1960), pp. 482–489.

9. Richard Hofstadter, *The Age of Reform* (New York: Knopf, 1955), pp. 70–81; Walter R. Nugent, "Populism and Nativism in Kansas, 1888–1900" (unpublished Ph.D. dissertation, Department of History, University of Chicago, 1961), pp. 81–83.

10. Stanley Parsons, "Nebraska Populism Reconsidered," Paper delivered at the annual meeting of the American Historical Association, 1962, pp. 3–8; J. Rogers Hollingsworth, "Populism: The Problem of Rhetoric and Reality," *Agricultural History*, Vol. 39 (April 1965), p. 83.

11. Benjamin R. Twiss, *Lawyers and The Constitution* (Princeton, N.J.: Princeton University Press, 1942), pp. 141–146.

12. Richard Hofstadter, *The Age of Reform, op. cit.,* p. 80; S. M. Lipset, *Political Man* (Garden City, N.Y.: Doubleday, 1960), p. 167; Peter Viereck, *The Unadjusted Man* (Boston: Beacon Press, 1956), p. 202; Daniel Bell, *The End of Ideology* (Glencoe, Ill.: Free Press, 1960), pp. 104–107.

13. Oscar Handlin, "American Views of the Jew at the Opening of the Twentieth Century," *Publications of the American Jewish Historical Society,* Vol. 40 (June 1951), p. 338.

14. Leon W. Fuller, "Colorado's Revolt Against Capitalism," *Mississippi Valley Historical Review,* Vol. 11 (December 1934), pp. 355–357.

15. E.g., see Norman Pollack, *The Populist Response to Industrial America, op. cit.,* pp. 43–67; Roscoe C. Martin, *The People's Party in Texas* (Austin, Texas: University of Texas Press, 1933), pp. 217–218.

16. Viereck, however, retells the story to make Jewishness the focal point and then concludes that the vast popular reception for *Caesar's Column* was an example of Populist anti-Semitism at the mass level. Peter Viereck, *The Unadjusted Man, op. cit.,* p. 202.

17. Oscar Handlin, "American Views of the Jew at the Opening of the Twentieth Century," *Publications of the American Jewish Historical Society, op. cit.,* pp. 325–328.

18. Ignatius Donnelly, *Caesar's Column* (Chicago: J. Regan, n.d.), p. 36.

19. Cf. Norman Pollack, "The Myth of Populist Anti-Semitism," *American Historical Review,* Vol. 43 (October 1962), pp. 76–80; Norman Pollack, "Hofstadter on Populism: A Critique of 'The Age of Reform,'" *op. cit.,* p. 500; Walter R. Nugent, "Populism and Nativism in Kansas, 1888–1900," *op. cit.,* pp. 86–89; John Higham, "Anti-Semitism in the Gilded Age," *Mississippi Valley Historical Review,* Vol. 53 (March 1957).

20. Oscar Handlin, "American Views of the Jew at the Opening of the Twentieth Century," *Publications of the American Jewish Historical Society, op. cit.,* p. 338. In the Cross of Gold speech, Bryan used the crucifixion metaphor to attack hard-money advocates. To assume that "gold-bugs" were identified with the Jews (who killed Christ) is to assume just what has not been proved—that the Populists were anti-Semitic.

21. Cf. C. Vann Woodward, "Tom Watson and the Negro in Agrarian Politics," *Journal of Southern History,* Vol. 4 (February 1938), pp. 16–23; C. Vann Woodward, "The Populist Heritage and the Intellectual," *American Scholar,* Vol. 29 (Winter 1959), p. 65; William R. Gnatz, "The Negro and the Populist Movement in the South" (unpublished Master's thesis, University of Chicago, Department of History, 1961), p. 39.

22. On Populist support in the South cf. V. O. Key, Jr., *Southern Politics in State and Nation* (New York: Knopf, 1949), pp. 138–142, 232–237, and 549 for South Carolina, Mississippi, and Georgia; Melvin J. White, "Populism in Louisiana during the Nineties," *Mississippi Valley Historical Review,* Vol. 5 (June 1918), pp. 14–15; Perry H. Howard, *Political Tendencies in Louisiana 1812–1952* (Baton Rouge, La.: Louisiana State University Press, 1957), pp. 90–99; Alex Matthews Arnett, *The Populist Movement in Georgia* (New York: Columbia University Press, 1922), map facing p. 184; C. Vann Woodward, *Tom Watson: Agrarian Rebel* (New York: Macmillan, 1938), pp. 160–161, 217; Roscoe C. Martin, *The People's Party in Texas, op. cit.,* pp. 60–68, 86–111, 136–137. Virginia, where Populism was not strong, is an exception to Populist strength in the hills and weakness in the black belt. Cf. William Du Bose Shelton, *Populism in the Old Dominion* (Princeton, N.J.: Princeton University Press, 1935), pp. 86–87.

23. Cf. Walter Ellsworth Nydegger, "The Election of 1892 in Iowa," *Iowa Journal of History and Politics,* Vol. 25 (July 1927), pp. 442–444; Stanley Parsons, "Nebraska Populism Reconsidered," Paper presented at the annual meeting of the American Historical Association, 1962, pp. 11–13; Walter R. Nugent, "Populism and Nativism in Kansas, 1888–1900," *op. cit.,* pp. 204–215.

24. Richard Hofstadter, *The Age of Reform, op. cit.,* pp. 87–91.

25. Cf. Roscoe C. Martin, *The People's Party in Texas, op. cit.,* pp. 103–111, 132; Donald E. Walters, "Populism in California, 1889–1900 (unpublished Ph.D. dissertation, Department of History, University of California, 1952), pp. 70, 148–150, 289.

26. John Higham, "Anti-Semitism in the Gilded Age," *op. cit.,* pp. 565–566.

27. John Higham, *Strangers in the Land* (New Brunswick, N.J.: Rutgers University Press, 1955), pp. 95–98, 346; Walter R. Nugent, "Populism and Nativism in Kansas, 1888–1900," *op. cit.,* p. 45. Populist and Alliance platforms before 1892 contained nothing about immigration restriction.

28. Nugent writes, "It hardly helped [the farmer's] peace of mind to learn that the Sante Fe railroad was now in the hands of the Barings of London, and that Englishmen alone and in companies owned large tracts of land in Kansas, and that London bankers had close ties with both the eastern bankers, who had bought up their mortgages at bargain-basement prices, and to American statesmen, including John Sheridan and Cleveland, to whom the contraction policy was economic dogma." Walter R. Nugent, "Populism and Nativism in Kansas, 1888-1900," op. cit., p. 34.

29. Walter R. Nugent, "Populism and Nativism in Kansas, 1888-1900," op. cit., pp. 180-182.

30. Richard Hofstadter, The Age of Reform, op. cit., pp. 89-90. Of even more dubiousness as evidence of Populist jingoism are citations from a "west-coast newspaper" (Populist?) and "the silver senator from Nevada." (The Populists ran a ticket against the silver ticket in that state.) Similarly, Hofstadter is more impressed (p. 286) by the unsubstantiated statement that some Klan members supported La Follette in 1924 than by La Follette's forthright attack on the Klan—an attack not matched by Davis and Coolidge.

31. Indeed, the charges against the Populists might better be made against the APA. In Wisconsin the APA was for the rule of the people against the special interests. The workingmen and small businessmen were alleged to be the bulwark of democracy and liberty. "The time is not far distant when class legislation will be a thing of the past, and the workingmen will have as much to say in the making of laws as the millionaire. . . ." This was to be accomplished in a purely "American" way; it would "never come about through the radical methods proposed by Populists or Socialists." Cf. Gerald K. Marsden, "Patriotic Societies and American Labor: The American Protective Association in Wisconsin," Wisconsin Magazine of History, Vol. 41 (Summer 1958), pp. 288-289.

32. Walter R. Nugent, "Populism and Nativism in Kansas, 1888-1900," op. cit., pp. 132-136; John Higham, Strangers in the Land, op. cit., pp. 80-86. In the 1870's anti-Catholicism had been strong among respectable Republicans; ibid., pp. 28-29.

33. John Locke, Of Civil Government (New York: Dutton, Everyman's), pp. 177-179, 183-203.

34. John P. Roche, "The Curbing of the Militant Majority," Reporter, Vol. 29 (July 18, 1963), pp. 34-38.

35. Frederic C. Howe, Confessions of a Reformer (New York: Scribner's, 1925), pp. 17-18.

36. Cf. Roscoe C. Martin, The People's Party in Texas, op. cit., p. 44.

37. In Texas in November 1892, there were 3,170 Populist clubs. Ibid., pp. 142-149.

38. Ibid., pp. 84-85, 166-167; John R. Hicks, The Populist Revolt (Lincoln, Neb.: University of Nebraska Press, 1961), passim.

39. Victor Ferkiss, "Populism: Myth, Reality, Current Danger," Western Political Quarterly, Vol. 14 (September 1961), pp.737-740 and S. M. Lipset, "The Sources of the Radical Right," in Daniel Bell (ed.), The New American Right (New York: Criterion Books, 1955), p. 174, charge that the Populists often interfered with academic freedom. So does Peter Viereck. He cites the example of the removal of Veblen from the University of Minnesota because of the "democratic, egalitarian, Populist milieu." (The Unadjusted Man, op. cit., p. 46.) In fact, the Populists were never close to power in Minnesota. At the time of Veblen's removal, the state was in firm Republican hands.

40. The "overeducation" charge is made by Edward Shils, The Torment of Secrecy (Glencoe, Ill.: Free Press, 1956), p. 99. See the anti-Populist report of G. T. Fairchild, "Populism in a State Agricultural College," American Journal of Sociology, Vol. 3 (November 1897).

41. Prohibition and woman suffrage were allied in part because of fears by Germans and other antiprohibitionists that the women would support prohibition.

42. Cf. Glenn Lowell Brudvig, "The Farmer's Alliance and the Populist Movement in North Dakota (1884-1896)" (unpublished Master's thesis, University of North Dakota, 1956), p. 115; Walter R. Nugent, "Populism and Nativism in Kansas, 1888-1900," op. cit., pp. 53, 118; Herbert S. Schell, History of South Dakota (Lincoln, Neb.: University of Nebraska Press, 1961), p. 232; Herman Clarence Nixon, The Populist Movement in Iowa, reprinted from the January 1926 number of the Iowa Journal of History and Politics (Iowa City, Iowa: State University of Iowa), p. 157; J. Rogers Hollingsworth, "Populism: The Problem of Rhetoric and Reality," op. cit., p. 85; Roscoe C. Martin, The People's Party in Texas, op. cit., pp. 80-81. The North Dakota Populist Party, which supported prohibition, generally fused with the Democrats at election time. In Wisconsin during the 1930's, the

Progressive Party vote was related to the vote for prohibition, as one would expect of a Scandinavian and native-stock movement. But if this was because of the agrarian radical crusade, how to explain the even higher relationship of the Republican vote to prohibition? Cf. H. F. Gosnell, *Grass Roots Politics* (Washington, D.C.: American Council on Public Affairs, 1942), p. 56.

43. Cf. Allan F. Westin, "The Supreme Court, the Populist Movement, and the Campaign of 1896," *Journal of Politics*, Vol. 15 (February 1953), pp. 3–41. "It was in this period (1876–1896) that the Supreme Court created a wide disenchantment with constitutional processes on the part of the Populist Party."

44. Cf. Benton H. Wilcox, "An Historical Definition of Northwestern Radicalism," *Mississippi Valley Historical Review*, Vol. 26 (December 1939), pp. 378–379, 394, and *passim*; Carl C. Taylor, *The Farmers' Movement 1620–1920* (New York: American Book Co., 1953), pp. 49–99 and *passim*.

45. Richard Hofstadter, *The Age of Reform*, *op. cit.*, pp. 46–47.

46. *Ibid.*, pp. 109–112; Richard Hofstadter, "The Pseudo Conservative Revolt," in Daniel Bell (ed.), *The New American Right*, *op. cit.*, pp. 43–44.

47. C. Vann Woodward, "The Populist Heritage and the Intellectual," *op. cit.*, p. 63.

48. Richard Hofstadter, *The Age of Reform*, *op. cit.*, pp. 96–109.

49. William Kornhauser, *The Politics of Mass Society* (Glencoe, Ill.: Free Press, 1959), pp. 39–40.

50. Cf. Allan F. Westin, "The Supreme Court, the Populist Movement, and the Campaign of 1896," *loc. cit.*

51. German fascism owed a real debt to the failure of the German revolution of 1918 to end the inaccessibility and independent power of the army, the police, and the bureaucracy.

52. William Kornhauser, *The Politics of Mass Society*, *op. cit.*, p. 44. Kornhauser adds that not all concern with remote objects is a manifestation of mass behavior, but he insists that all mass behavior has such concerns and that there is a tendency for remote concerns to lead to mass behavior.

53. Karl Ernest Meyer, "The Politics of Loyalty: From La Follette to McCarthy in Wisconsin: 1918–1952" (unpublished Ph.D. dissertation, Department of Political Science, Princeton University, 1956), pp. 79–116.

54. This is not to say that Populists displayed the sophistications of Karl Marx. It is emphatically to deny that the similarities between Marxism and Populism show that America was developing on the European pattern. But cf. Norman Pollack, *The Populist Response to Industrial America*, *op. cit.*, pp. 82–83. For the notion of Populism as a surrogate for socialism, cf. Michael N. Shute, "Populism and the Pragmatic Mystique" (unpublished manuscript, n.d.).

55. Cf. Stanley Elkins and Eric McKitrick, "A Meaning for Turner's Frontier," *Political Science Quarterly*, Vol. 114 (September 1954), pp. 324–339.

56. At the turn of the century, North Dakota, Minnesota, and Wisconsin had higher percentages of foreign-born in their population than any other rural states. In 1920, almost 60 percent of the Swedish farmers in America lived in seven midwestern states. Cf. Carl C. Taylor, "The Evolution of American Rural Society," in Carl Taylor, *et al.*, *Rural Life in the United States* (New York: Knopf, 1949), p. 27. Norwegians were the second-largest ethnic group in the Dakotas and Wisconsin.

Lubell has argued that progressivism in the Middle West served a function for German and Scandinavian immigrants analogous to that served in cities by the machine. This is persuasive in the Scandinavian case, but flies in the face of German opposition to progressivism. Cf. Samuel Lubell, *The Future of American Politics* (New York: Harper, 1952), p. 206.

57. The figures are from Fred A. Shannon, *The Farmer's Last Frontier: Agriculture 1860–1897* (New York: Farrar and Rinehart, 1945), pp. 350–351. Shannon points out that since 1920, when the census began to count farmers and their families as a percentage of the total population, the ratio of those living on farms to total population has been the same as the ratio of farmers to the gainfully employed. Therefore, one can use the latter figures as a measure of the farm population before 1920.

58. Margaret Jarmon Hagood, "The Dynamics of Rural Population," in Carl Taylor, *et al.*, *Rural Life in the United States, op. cit.*, pp. 241–243.

59. Douglas Ensminger, "Rural Neighborhoods and Communities," in *ibid.*, p. 73.

60. The phrase is in Fred Shannon, *The Farmer's Last Frontier, op. cit.*, p. 359.

# the redeemers

## C. VANN WOODWARD

C. Vann Woodward, now teaching at Yale, is one of the most incisive of today's historians, and has long argued that Populism in the south achieved its most radical dimensions. The argument rests in part on evidence that most southerners who still lived in an agrarian world found the political and economic abuses of industrial growth intolerable.

In this excerpt from *The Origins of the New South,* Woodward documents the existence of a dominant Whig coalition that led the south in creating industry and agriculture that would fit into a national economy. Southern businessmen who believed the south's future lay in industrialization are here revealed appealing to northerners. The excerpt, mainstream history at its best, raises some important questions for radicals. How do the emerging industrialists achieve leadership? Benefits to business, and especially to railroads, are assumed, but how useful was the industrialization process for other elements of the south? What does the largely ineffective Populist protest tell us about social class?

---

Any honest genealogy of the ruling family of Southern Democrats would reveal a strain of mixed blood. The mixture sprang from a forced union with the house that had been Democracy's bitter rival for the throne. A Mississippian once whimsically acknowledged this union. "A few years after the war," he wrote, "all lovers of good government in the South concluded to celebrate a marriage. The high contracting parties were Whiggism and Democracy and the ceremony took place in 1875, though the betrothal may antedate that time. . . . As is usual in such cases the parties have now one and the same name, but the Whig party is no more dead than is one of our fair damsels, because she has concluded to cast her lot with the man of her choice for weal or for woe."[1]

The fact was that instead of assuming the submissive role suggested by a change of name, Whiggery often took the dominant position—along with the bulk of desirable offices. A North Carolina editor who described himself as one of the "unterrified Democracy" boasted that "the Democratic nominees for Governor since the war had been Worth, a Whig; Ashe, a Whig; Merrimon, a Whig; Vance, a Whig; and Jarvis, who was too young before the war to have had much political leaning one way or another." The Democrats of the First North Carolina District had in that period nominated five men for Congress, "every one of them former Whigs," and the state supreme court was "composed of three sterling Democrats, all former Whigs." By 1884 it appeared that "the Democrats of today admire Henry Clay just as much as the men of Whig traditions."[2] On the other hand, so repugnant had the marriage with their old enemies been to the Whigs that it was not until eight years after the war that

From C. Vann Woodward, "The Redeemers," *The Origins of the New South: Eighteen Seventy-Seven to Nineteen Thirteen* (Baton Rouge: Louisiana State University Press, 1951), 1–10.

the very name "Democratic" was avowed by the Conservative party of North Carolina.

The Whiggish tendency was widespread. "It is almost impossible to find a disciple of Benton among Southern Democrats," wrote an observer in 1882. The older generation had "apparently determined to adopt the views of the old Whigs," while the younger leaders were uninterested in Jacksonian dogma.[3]

Henry Watterson, thoroughly in accord with all but details of the New Order, took occasion to attack Colonel Arthur S. Colyar, commander of the dominant wing of the Tennessee Democrats. Colyar, he charged, was "in sympathy with the iron, coal, and manufacturing interests of Tennessee exclusively, and, being an old hightariff Whig, has not emancipated himself from the crude opinions which prevailed among the shortsighted and narrow minded political economists among whom he grew to manhood." The reply came promptly from the Nashville *Daily American:* "Better be careful, Mr. Watterson, the Democratic party of Tennessee is made up, at least in part, of old Whigs, and, being now all of the same family, it might hurt the party to establish that the old Whigs were 'short sighted' and 'narrow-minded!' " If the Kentuckian were uninformed, he might make inquiry in his own state concerning the master of all those "narrow minded political economists." "His name was Clay, and no doubt some of the old men will remember him."[4]

All in all the union was a *mésalliance.* With every crossroad hustings and county courthouse the memorial of some battle between the old parties, any semblance of domestic harmony was likely to be forced and artificial. "I despise the very name of Democrat," declared a Democrat of Whig background from the Lower South. "There is not a principle or a tradition belonging to the organization which I approve." Another unwilling adherent described himself as "in principle an Old Line Whig, but, under existing circumstances, in practice and from necessity, a Southern Democrat."[5] Even the name Democrat fell into general disuse in the South during the seventies and eighties. The substitute, "Conservative," though originating in the battle against "Radical" Republicans, proved too appropriate a name to abandon for many years. In some states it was adopted as the official name of the party, sometimes in combination, "Conservative and Democratic Party." "Conservative" was not dropped from the official title of the Democratic party of Alabama for forty years after the war.

The shape and character of salvation promised the South by "Redemption" are in some measure revealed by the extrapolitical concerns of the "Redeemers." The first ex-Confederate state to be restored to Democratic rule, Tennessee had as her first Democratic governor, General John C. Brown, a former Whig and brother of the ante-bellum Whig governor Neill S. Brown. Governor John Brown took prominent part in the ambitious schemes of Thomas A. Scott for a southern transcontinental railroad and served as vice-president of Scott's Texas and Pacific Company. Later he became president of the Bon Air Coal Company, and at the time of his death he was president of the expanding Tennessee Coal, Iron, and Railroad Company. His successor, also a former Whig elected by the Democrats, was James D. Porter, a Confederate veteran. After two terms in office, Governor Porter was elected president of the Nashville, Chattanooga and St. Louis Railroad. He was also a director of the Tennessee Coal, Iron, and Railroad Company, along with several other financial enterprises of Nashville.[6]

The dynamic leader of this Whig-industrialist wing of Tennessee Democrats was Colonel Colyar. There were, according to Watterson, six prominent newspapers in the South that supported every Republican and opposed every Democratic policy. Three of these were published in Tennessee, and the "king" of this whole school of journalists was Colonel Colyar, who controlled the Nashville *American*. Watterson described him as a brilliant captain of industry, "backed by abundant capital of protected industries" issuing orders to his lieutenants throughout the Lower South.[7] His paper fought the free traders and the railroad commissions and defended the policies of the Tennessee Coal, Iron, and Railroad Company, of which Colyar was a director and general counsel. The company leased the convicts of the state penitentiary for an annual rental of $101,000. "One of the chief reasons which first induced the company to take up the system," explained Colonel Colyar, "was the great chance which it seemed to present for overcoming strikes."[8] Governor Albert S. Marks, who succeeded Governor Porter, was a kinsman and former law partner of Colonel Colyar.[9]

Redemption came early in Virginia and was accomplished under peculiar auspices—a combination of Confederate Democrats, conservative Republicans, old-line Whigs, and Negroes. This mongrel group left "Democrat" out of the party name entirely, and for thirteen years was known simply as the Conservative party. "This combination," according to one historian, "was effected by city capitalistic leaders, and to it (and them) was entrusted the inauguration of the new regime." The city man's rule of a countryman's state had as the first Conservative governor a Carpetbagger-Republican and banker from Norfolk, Gilbert C. Walker. The nine men who acted as an executive committee for the state central committee of the Conservatives were all residents of Richmond, and for years all state conventions of the Conservatives were held in that city.[10]

The General Assembly that laid the foundation of the New Order passed two bills of great consequence in quick succession. One of these provided for the sale, at a sacrifice, of the state's valuable holdings in the stock of its own railroads, a sale which proceeded at "immense loss" until virtually all the state roads had fallen into private hands, usually those of expanding Northern railroad systems. The railroads retained the special privileges and exemptions enjoyed under state ownership, but were relieved of state control or regulation— an arrangement which made virtually inevitable "railroad control over the legislature."[11]

The second measure, passed within two days of the railroad bill, was the Funding Act of 1871. The act fastened upon an impoverished, war-broken state an annual interest upon the funded debt almost equal to the entire revenue of the state. The funding and railroad acts were obtained by corrupt pressure methods of a combination of bankers, bondholders, and railroads. To a recent student it is clear that "if ever Virginia bowed to money interests and pressure against the will of her people and contrary to the exigencies of the situation, it was on this occasion."[12] Launched in this manner, the Hamiltonian financial policy of the Conservatives soon occupied such a conspicuous place in the new system that the party members came to be known as the "Funders."

Railroads continued to share honors with bondholders in the degree of influence they exerted over the Conservative party. Whether the Funders or their rivals were in power the railroads were prominently represented. General William Mahone's extensive railroad interests led him to seek power in the Conservative party and to take perhaps the largest individual part in bringing the Conservatives to power.[13] Out-of-state railroads, gaining predominant influence with the Conservatives, then assisted in overthrowing Mahone's schemes and driving him into a political revolt that removed the Conservatives temporarily from office. Even after defeat, subsequent reorganization, and return to power under the name "Democratic," the party remained thoroughly identified with railroad interests. This is clearly indicated by the composition of the state committee of the party in the seventies, eighties, and nineties, during which period nearly every state chairman was a railroad president or director.[14]

Despite Kentucky's failure to secede and join the Confederacy, no state below the Ohio River presented a more solidly Confederate-Democratic front in the decade after Appomattox. For a short time after the fear of Radical and Negro votes was quieted, a rift in the ranks opened between a weak "Bourbon" wing led by J. Stoddard Johnson's Frankfort *Kentucky Yeoman,* and a powerful "New South" or businessman's wing, whose spokesman was Henry Watterson's Louisville *Courier-Journal.* The struggle was uneven and short-lived.[15]

Watterson's policy called for "an intelligent appeal to the business interests and conservative elements of Northern society" and a firm alliance of those elements against radicals of all sorts. He demanded a program of subsidies, tax exemptions, and privileged franchises in order to accommodate Eastern capital and encourage its flow into the state. The constant theme of New-South editors and orators was cheap resources, business opportunities, railroad developments, and commercial enterprise.[16] "Even though they might look like Southern colonels," writes one student of the new leaders of Kentucky, "with goatee and moustaches, and speak like Southern orators, retaining these outer trappings of the olden days, the program of the 'New Departure' was a program of surrender."[17] The "Bourbon" opposition soon faded into the past. By September 7, 1880, Watterson could write in the *Courier-Journal* of the old secession leaders that "not one of them remains upon the stage of active political life."

A multitude of interests, both in and out of the state, were served by the New Order in Kentucky, and joined in loyal support of its leaders. The railroads, the great wholesale merchants, the liquor and tobacco interests—none should be overlooked. It would be a mistake to identify the new structure with any one of its pillars and buttresses. However, the Louisville and Nashville Railroad should be singled out for special notice, not only because of its unique importance in Kentucky, but because of its remarkable influence in the affairs of other states to the southward into which it penetrated. By process of aggression, colonization, city building, and acquisition, the "L and N" gained predominance in Kentucky, and established connections with Memphis, New Orleans, Mobile, Atlanta, and Savannah. "Having here in Louisville a Railway Emperor and a Railway Bismarck," Watterson wrote, celebrating the latest "coup de chemin de fer" of the L and N, it was not to be wondered at that they were "making a 'United Germany' of the Southern railways which were lying about loose . . . instead of leading to Louisville as they should."[18]

It was characteristic of the times that in its battles to achieve monopoly, which differed in no essential from similar struggles the nation over, the L and N managed to identify its cause with that of the downtrodden South. This is the more curious in view of the road's service to the Union army during the war, the passage of control and ownership to Northern and European capital, and the appearance in the lists of its directors of the names Jay Gould, Thomas Fortune Ryan, Jacob Schiff, and August Belmont.[19] As chief lobbyist and leading light of its legal staff, however, "General Basil W. Duke, C.S.A.," as he described himself in the title of his *Reminiscences,* served the L and N for twenty years.

Not only in his Confederate military record, but in his family connections, his striking appearance (including the standard mustache and goatee), his literary service to the Confederate memories, and his chivalrous and attractive personality, General Duke was all that the age expected in the Kentucky colonel of the old school.[20]

"The only inducement for railroad companies to enter politics—become parties to the dirty work—is to protect their property," remarked Milton H. Smith, president of the L and N. He was the first to admit that this inducement alone was considerable. It was found necessary to retain "legislative agents" in various states, lawyers in all county seats through which the road ran, and in strategic places friendly judges, legislators, and officeholders of all sorts with passes in their pockets or relatives on the L and N pay roll.[21]

Revealing light is shed upon the nature of Redemption and of the Redeemers of Alabama by following the course of the Louisville and Nashville empire builders in that state. Albert Fink, one of the ablest railroad superintendents of his time, foreseeing the immense potentialities of the undeveloped mineral resources of northern Alabama, began soon after the war to make large investments in that region for the L and N, subsidizing numerous developments and encouraging the building of new towns. In this manner there were affiliated with the fortunes of the L and N many of the new industries, along with a rising class of industrialists. In the front ranks of these men was James W. Sloss, said by the Birmingham *Iron Age* to be "identified with the development of the industrial interests of Alabama to a greater extent than any other man in the State."[22] Sloss was closely associated, in business as well as in politics, with the most prominent leaders of the Democratic party in Alabama. Although the Panic of 1873 resulted in the transfer of ownership to Northern and European capital, the L and N continued as in the past to work in close co-operation with the state Democratic organization.[23]

Behind the fury of partisan conflict during Reconstruction there proceeded a struggle between the L and N and a rival system for access to the riches of the mineral region of northern Alabama. The opposing system, the Alabama and Chattanooga Railroad, seeking to divert ore shipments from Louisville to Chattanooga for smelting, was linked in its fortunes with the Republican party through the investments of such men as Henry Clews, Russell Sage, and William D. ("Pig-Iron") Kelley. During Reconstruction both railroads were beneficiaries of extravagant state-government aid that virtually bankrupted the state. Liabilities assumed for these two railroad systems alone, in the form of loans and endorsements of bonds, accounted for $17,000,000 of the total estimated $25,000,000 "debt" incurred after the war. That the system of state aid was inaugurated by the provisional Democratic government and manipulated to the advantage of a number of prominent party leaders did not deter the Democrats from playing up the state debt as the most sensational charge against the Carpetbag government.[24]

The election of 1874 had more than a racial or political significance, for it would determine not only the fate of the Republican party and Reconstruction in Alabama but also which of the financial interests involved would be able to make the best possible settlement with a state government they had both brought to the point of bankruptcy. Walter L. Fleming wrote that "the campaign fund was the largest in the history of the state," and mentioned especially the contributions of "northern Democrats and northern capitalists who had invested in the South or who owned part of the legal bonds of the state."[25] It should be remembered, however, that it was just this question of the "legality" of bonds that would be determined by the outcome of the campaign to which the Northern capitalists contributed. The Conservatives won by a large majority. The L and N was by this time firmly identified with the downtrodden South and the victory of White Supremacy in Alabama.

George S. Houston, Redeemer governor of Alabama, described in campaign literature as "the Bald Eagle of the Mountains," won his office with the usual slogans of "White Supremacy" and "home rule." A northern Alabama lawyer with industrial interests, he was a leader of the Unionists of the state. "How much will the young men . . . be enthused by H[ouston]'s nomination?" demanded one Alabama Democrat. "Can it be expected that they will vigorously exert themselves for a man selected because he is supposed to be strong with that element which in all this region is known in common parlance as Tories?"[26] Houston was a close associate of Sloss and the L and N, for one of whose affiliated lines he was a director.[27]

Houston hastened to bring about a settlement with the state's bondholders and the railroads. His friend Rufus W. Cobb, who framed the plan later adopted with modifications, was a local attorney of the L and N and president of the Central Iron Works at Helena, which was subsidized by that railroad.[28] Governor Houston served as ex-officio chairman of the debt commission. Levi W. Lawler, one of the commissioners and director of a railroad competing with the Alabama and Chattanooga, confessed privately that in view of his party's complicity in the railroad bond legislation, "we, the commissioners, and the party, are environed with embarrassments of no ordinary magnitude."[29] The settlement agreed upon was satisfactory to some bondholders and highly advantageous to those railroad systems favored by the Redeemers, particularly L and N affiliates with which Sloss and Houston were in one way or another associated. Since the debt was always a potential debt, and would have become an actual debt only by the state's becoming the owner of the railroads endorsed, the "debt settlement" took the form of relieving the state of its potential debt and relieving the railroads of the threat of foreclosure on mortgages held by the state. The "settlement of 1876 left the residual obligations of the State Government . . . at approximately $12,000,000."[30]

## NOTES

1. Jackson *Clarion*, September 19, 1883.

2. Raleigh *News and Observer*, February 23, 1884.

3. Henry L. Nelson, "The Political Situation in the South," in *International Review* (New York), XII (1882), 415.

4. Nashville *Daily American*, January 19, 1883.

5. Letter to editor, dated Washington, February 27, 1877, in New York *Tribune*, March 3, 1877; and "an ex-Confederate officer," quoted *ibid.*, June 20, 1881.

6. William S. Speer, *Sketches of Prominent Tennesseans* (Nashville, 1888), 37–40.

7. Quoted in Daniel M. Robison, *Bob Taylor and the Agrarian Revolt in Tennessee* (Chapel Hill, 1935), 19. This book has the best account of the Tennessee Redeemers.

8. Knoxville *Daily Chronicle*, July 7, 1883; Nashville *Daily American*, August 23, 1892.

9. Speer, *Sketches of Prominent Tennesseans*, 74–75.

10. Charles C. Pearson, *The Readjuster Movement in Virginia* (New Haven, 1917), 22–23. See also, Allen W. Moger, *The Rebuilding of the Old Dominion* (Ann Arbor, 1940), 4–5.

11. Pearson, *Readjuster Movement*, 28–31; Nelson M. Blake, *William Mahone of Virginia, Soldier and Political Insurgent* (Richmond, 1935), 120, 136.

12. Moger, *Rebuilding of the Old Dominion*, 7. See also, Pearson, *Readjuster Movement*, 30, 32; and Blake, *William Mahone*, 136, 160.

13. Blake, *William Mahone*, 108–109, 135. Governor Gilbert C. Walker acknowledged his obligation to Mahone handsomely.

14. George M. McFarland, "The Extension of Democracy in Virginia, 1850–1895" (Ph.D. dissertation, Princeton University, 1934), 154–55. See also, Ralph C. McDanel, *The Virginia Constitutional Convention of 1901–1902*, in Johns Hopkins University *Studies in Historical and Political Science*, XLVI (Baltimore, 1928), 304–305.

15. Thomas D. Clark, *A History of Kentucky* (New York, 1937), 585–86.

16. Henry Watterson, *"Marse Henry", An Autobiography"* (New York, 1919), I, 183. See also, Louisville *Courier-Journal*, May 9, 1880; August 6, 1881; October 5, 1882.

17. Edward F. Prichard, Jr., "Popular Political Movements in Kentucky, 1875–1900" (Senior thesis, Princeton University, 1935), 16–17.

18. Louisville *Courier-Journal*, January 19, 1880.

19. John L. Kerr, *The Story of a Southern Carrier . . . The Louisville and Nashville* (New York, 1933), 45, 49–51; George R. Leighton, "Louisville, Kentucky: An American Museum Piece," in *Harper's Magazine* (New York), CLXXV (1937), 409–10.

20. See Thomas M. Spaulding, "Basil Wilson Duke," in Allen Johnson, Dumas Malone, and Harris E. Starr (eds.), *Dictionary of American Biography* (New York, 1928–1944), V, 495–96; *Reminiscences of General Basil W. Duke, C.S.A.* (Garden City, 1911), *passim*.

21. Interstate Commerce Commission, *Hearings Relative to the Financial Relations, Rates, and Practices of the Louisville & Nashville Railroad Co., The Nashville, Chattanooga & St. Louis Railway, and other Carriers* (Washington, 1916), *Senate Documents*, 64 Cong., 1 Sess., No. 461, pp. 407–10, 430–31, 439, 447–48.

22. Birmingham *Iron Age*, December 24, 1879. See also, Albert B. Moore, "Railroad Building in Alabama during the Reconstruction Period," in *Journal of Southern History* (Baton Rouge), I (1935), 421–41.

23. Ethel M. Armes, *The Story of Coal and Iron in Alabama* (Birmingham, 1910), 245, 249.

24. Horace M. Bond, *Negro Education in Alabama; A Study in Cotton and Steel* (Washington, 1939), 42–50; Walter L. Fleming, *Civil War and Reconstruction in Alabama* (New York, 1905), 589–604.

25. Fleming, *Civil War and Reconstruction in Alabama*, 792.

26. Rufus K. Boyd to Robert McKee, April 29, 1874, in Robert McKee Papers (Alabama Department of Archives and History, Montgomery).

27. Armes, *Story of Coal and Iron in Alabama*, 245; Bond, *Negro Education in Alabama*, 55.

28. Rufus W. Cobb to McKee, September 8, 1874, in McKee Papers; Bond, *Negro Education in Alabama*, 54–55.

29. Levi W. Lawler to McKee, June 12, 1875, in McKee Papers. A most revealing letter on Democratic responsibility for policies ordinarily attributed to Negroes and Carpetbaggers. Lawler wrote from New York City, where he was in touch with bondholders.

30. Bond, *Negro Education in Alabama*, 55–62; Fleming, *Civil War and Reconstruction in Alabama*, 583–86; also memorandum on stationery of "Executive Office, State of Alabama," dated May 15, 1883, presumably by McKee, private secretary to Governor, in McKee papers.

# from the bottom up

## ERIC F. GOLDMAN

Instead of examining the tensions that existed in the American past, liberal historians have preferred to look at the way in which emerging discontent was absorbed into traditional political channels. Most view past protest movements as ineffective in themselves but useful because they articulate programs and ideas ahead of their time. When the nation's mood changes, visionary programs are incorporated into the platforms of major political parties. Eric Goldman illustrates this pattern in the following selection. Discontent results when economic cycles and a nonresponsive government create undue hardship. Government help is demanded; when it is not forthcoming, workers and farmers separately and together seek other ways of creating opportunity. Frightened and outraged, liberals, as Goldman reveals, respond with progressive reforms that incorporate some of the most important demands of earlier protesters. Like other mainstream historians, Goldman sees protest as a means of inducing a somewhat reluctant, but well-intentioned system to respond to the needs of some within it.

---

Early on a September afternoon, 1873, a newsboy yelled an extra about the failure of Jay Cooke's bank, and a policeman promptly arrested the boy. Jay Cooke was one of the most successful of all the new successes, the renowned financier of the war against Rebellion, a man who could sit in his seventy two room mansion and casually discuss with "Ulysses" the way to raise children; businesses run by Jay Cookes simply did not close their doors. With the confirmation of the news and the rapid spread of bank failures, people still consoled one another that this was only a panic. Bustling America, guided by tough-minded businessmen, was much too strong to be laid low very long. A few stupefying weeks, banks and businesses going down like dominoes, and the word "panic" lost its power to console. The United States had to face the depression of 1873.

The country had known hard times before, but only when it was overwhelmingly agricultural. Now it learned how much more serious depression could be in a rapidly industrializing society. The years of economic distress from 1873 to 1879 threw a garish light on the whole structure of opportunity. Military control was removed from the South during the depression, but the former Confederacy returned to a nation almost as frustrated by hard times as the South had been by defeat. Millions of industrial workers, confident of a golden future a short while ago, were unemployed or desperately worried about holding their jobs. Many a small investor, once so sure of a brownstone and a carriage, found his life's savings wiped out overnight. Farmers' gilt-edged mortgage certificates turned from bright symbols of hope to nagging reminders of overconfidence. If the hard times boomed migration westward, the new pioneers passed covered wagons dragging east like whipped animals, their covers chalked with "Going back to our wife's folks" or "In God we trusted, in Kansas we busted."

No less disturbing were the large-scale corporations that rose above the shambles of hard times. The industrialization of the United States had been marked by the steady combination of businesses, and the depression rendered small entrepreneurs still less able to resist the consolidators. Before the crash came, the people of Ohio had begun hearing about the son of an itinerant medicine-seller who was gathering into his Standard Oil Company one after another of the state's oil firms. During the depression John D. Rockefeller's combine spread far outside Ohio. By the end of the hard times, the Standard Oil Company had achieved a substantial monopoly of oil refining in the United States, was reaching out for a monopoly over distribution, and was being taken as a model by ambitious men in every basic industry. The spindly, mild-mannered Rockefeller, who rarely missed a week teaching his Baptist Sunday-school class, was also well on his way to being one of the most feared and hated men in American history. In some respects Rockefeller was a good deal more ethical than the usual businessman of his day. He never watered his stock, he kept the quality of his product high, he treated his employees comparatively well. But Rockefeller had built the first American trust, and trusts, a good many of his countrymen were sure, meant a severe squeezing of opportunity for the small entrepreneur.

Still more disturbing, the depression of 1873 gave the United States its first taste of widespread violence caused by economic hardship. At the blackest period of the depression the country was swarming with "tramps," who were usually factory or farm hands looking vainly for a livelihood and drifting into gang life. Here and there bands of these men allied with professional criminals, drinking, stealing, raping, and murdering.

No large city entirely escaped bitter strikes, and in the summer of 1877 the first nationwide strike produced the first labor rioting that reached into many states. The trouble started when the principal railroads, refusing to decrease high dividends on watered stocks, decreed a ten per cent cut in wages. First on the Baltimore & Ohio lines in West Virginia, then north and west all the way to Canada and California, the workers hit back. Their violent strikes provoked the use of troops by business-minded governments, and the use of troops provoked more violence.

The turbulence reached a climax in Pittsburgh. Twenty-five people were killed and many more wounded when soldiers came into collision with a mob of strikers and strike sympathizers. Disorder ricocheted across the city. Barrels of liquor were tapped and drunk on the spot; stores were broken into for food, clothing, and furniture; long lines of freight cars were looted and set on fire. The incendiarism spread until the four-story Union Depot, two thousand cars, the railroad machine shops, a grain elevator, and two roundhouses with 125 locomotives had been destroyed. Two days later the city awoke to its hangover of ashes and caskets. Railroad executives and storekeepers wrathfully estimated their losses at five to ten millions; railroad workers sullenly went back to work with the wage cut intact. The nation, uneasy and irritated, wondered what America was coming to.

In San Francisco a pale, tense young man wrote some more bitter words on his yellow foolscap. For Henry George, the depression was the last straw. As a boy he had listened to Uncle Thomas proclaim that any lad who worked hard was sure to get ahead swiftly in America. From his thirteenth year George had worked hard, as a delivery-boy, seaman, typesetter, gold prospector, clerk, salesman, and editor, only to find himself still an impoverished nobody. In the late Sixties he managed to acquire some standing as a newspaperman and was sent to New York to arrange telegraphic news for a struggling San Francisco paper; the near-monopolistic Associated Press saw to it that he went home once more a failure. A few years later the depression of 1873 engulfed San Francisco, and Henry George had enough. Far into the night, in his rugless, ill-heated room, he piled up the sheets of foolscap, pounding into them the angry eloquence of *Progress and Poverty*.

"The present century," the book began, "has been marked by a prodigious increase in wealth-producing power. . . . It was natural to expect, and it was expected, that . . . the enormous increase in the power of producing wealth would make real poverty a thing of the past." But "disappointment has followed disappointment. . . . We plow new fields, we open new mines, we found new cities; we drive back the Indian and exterminate the buffalo; we girdle the land with iron roads and lace the air with telegraph wires; we add knowledge to knowledge, and utilize invention after invention. . . . Yet it becomes no easier for the masses of our people to make a living. On the contrary, it is becoming harder. . . . The gulf between the employed and the employer is growing wider; social contrasts are becoming sharper; as liveried carriages appear, so do barefooted children."

This situation was made worse by depression, George went on, but hard times were not the basic explanation. The United States had been a wondrous land of opportunity only because of its vast area of public lands. "The child of the people, as he grows to manhood in Europe, finds all the best seats at the banquet of life marked 'taken,' and must struggle with his fellows for the crumbs that fall. . . . In America, whatever his condition, there has always been the consciousness that the public domain lay behind him. . . . The general intelligence, the general comfort, the active invention, the power of adaptation and assimilation, the free, independent spirit, the energy and hopefulness that have marked our people, are not causes, but results—they have sprung from unfenced land. This public domain has given a consciousness of freedom even to the dweller in crowded cities, and has been a well-spring of hope even to those who have never thought of taking refuge upon it." But now the United States had used up much of its public domain. With industrialization helping to speed up the concentration of wealth and power, the New World was beginning to repeat the Old World's dismal story. It was re-enacting the European experience not only, as Samuel Tilden had said, by creating a corrupt ruling class; it was headed toward rigid economic and social stratification and a consequent narrowing of opportunity for the masses.

*Progress and Poverty*, published in 1879, was not out a year before its author was a national figure. Across the country, farmers squinted over the book's fine print. "Tens of thousands of industrial laborers," the economist Richard Ely noted, "have read *Progress and Poverty* who never before looked between the covers of an economics book." Troubled Americans who were neither factory hands nor farmers helped make *Progress and Poverty* one of the ten or so most widely selling non-fiction works in the history of the United States. The young man who had wanted to get ahead so fervently and had been stopped so often, with his moving arraignment of his times, his warning that America was moving down the weary road of Europe, his summons to recreate opportunity, had caught the mood with which thousands of Americans left the depression of 1873.

II

The Eighties lumbered ahead, now prosperous, now dragging through months of economic upset. In good years and in bad, sometimes even more so during the stretches of general prosperity, the sense of frustrated opportunity continued to gnaw at large numbers of Americans.

During the Eighties huge corporations kept rising like so many portents of a Europeanized future. In the decade after the depression more than five thousand firms were wrought into giant combines, virtually all of which were pushing toward monopolies in their fields. At the end of the decade United States Senator John Sherman, whose basic friendliness to business could not be questioned, spoke the worry of a good many of his countrymen. "If we are unable or unwilling [to take action against the trusts]," Sherman told the Senate, "there will soon be a trust for every production and a master to fix the price for every necessity of life."

For most industrial workers of the Eighties, real wages were rising with aggravating slowness, and each year extremes of wealth jutted out more irritatingly. A titan like Marshall Field made five hundred to seven hundred dollars an hour; his nonexecutive employees were paid twelve dollars a week or less for a fifty-nine-hour week. Quickly made fortunes were lavished with infuriating conspicuousness—on a mansion in red, yellow, and black bricks, the purchase of a titled husband for the daughter, banquets where the cigarettes were wrapped in hundred-dollar bills, or a poodle was draped with a fifteen-thousand-dollar collar. Just around the corner, slums were sprawling out, filthy, heatless, so dark their corners could not be photographed until flashlight photography was invented in 1887.

Along with extremes of wealth came walls of impersonality. By the Eighties a large percentage of factory hands worked in big plants, where the owner was as remote as any feudal lord had ever been from his serfs. The dry-goods shop was becoming the department store, and in department stores the clerk did not first-name the boss or presume to take his daughter to church. Without the familiar relations, callousness was easy, almost inevitable. An inventor remarked that he could sell a time-saving device in twenty places and a lifesaving invention scarcely at all. Doctors thought nothing of charging two dollars a visit to workingmen whose wages were a dollar-and-a-half a day. The first move to protect children from the vice and disease of the slums came from the president of New York's Society for the Prevention of Cruelty to Animals, who, as a kind of afterthought, founded the Society for the Prevention of Cruelty to Children. "Land of opportunity, you say," a Chicago worker snarled at a spreadeagle speaker. "You know damn well my children will be where I am—that is, if I can keep them out of the gutter."

The newest immigrants, the millions pouring into the United States from southern and eastern Europe, were finding that America was no longer in a come-one, come-all mood. Many of the older settlers, feeling crowded and cornered, had little welcome for any newcomer, and every prejudice in the American collection was roused by immigrants who were predominantly impoverished and unskilled, short and dark in appearance, Catholic or Jewish in religion. Rapidly the national speech was acquiring phrases that carried as much sneer and hiss as any in the language—"wop" and "dago" for the Italian, "bohunk" for the Hungarian, "grease-ball" for the Greek, and "kike" for the Jew.

A member of a Congressional committee, questioning a railroad-construction boss in 1890, asked: "You don't call . . . an Italian a white man?"

The construction boss was surprised that a United States Congressman should ask so silly a question. "No, Sir," the construction boss said. "An Italian is a Dago."

Organized anti-Catholicism, dormant since the Know-Nothing movement of the 1850's, flared up again in the form of the American Protective Association; anti-Semitism, which had scarcely appeared previously, spread widely. Lincoln Steffens never forgot his introduction to what opportunity could mean in the new immigrant slums. A Russian-Jewish woman pulled him up the tenement stairs to point out how her three little girls were watching a prostitute across the airway serve a customer. *"Da se'en Sie,* there they are watching, always they watch. They count the men who come of a night. . . . My oldest girl says she will go into that business when she grows up; she says it's a good business . . . and you can dress and eat and live."

For all the discontented of the cities, the frontier was losing much of its ability to keep hopes high. It was not simply that most of the best acres had passed into private hands; Americans were beginning to realize that the land might be cheap or even free, but transporting yourself and the family to the homestead, buying essential tools, and sustaining a wife and children during a season or two of sodbusting cost a sum beyond the resources of the usual urban employee. One Fall River worker, asked why he did not go west, expressed the new attitude toward homesteading with savage simplicity. "Well," he said, "I never saw over a $20 bill. . . . If someone would give me $1,500 I will go."

Out among those who had managed to go, in all agricultural areas of the nation, times were hard and growing harder. For the farmer, the Eighties differed from the unbroken depression years of the Seventies only in leaving him worse off economically. The price of manufactured articles the farmer had to buy and the cost of shipping his crop were sky-high; the amount he received for his products was plummeting down; and the policies of a creditor-minded Washington made it more and more difficult for him to escape his mortgage. Often the farmer lost money by shipping and selling, and for want of a profitable market, apples lay under the trees, milk was fed to the hogs, corn or cotton was used for fuel. "Many a time," Vernon Parrington remembered from his boyhood near Pumpkin Ridge, Kansas, "have I warmed myself by the kitchen stove in which ears were burning briskly, popping and crackling in the jolliest fashion. And if while we sat around such a fire watching the year's crop go up the chimney, the talk sometimes became bitter . . . who will wonder?"

In both the South and the Midwest, special circumstances increased the difficulties of the farmer. By clinging to the one-crop system, Southerners were making themselves prisoners of the price of cotton. Midwesterners were discovering that methods of agriculture learned in the East were unsuited to the Great Plains. Worse yet, the reckless destruction of the forests brought a succession of droughts and floods, and periodically the Midwest was ravaged by chinchbugs, corn borers, or, most destructive of all, plagues of grasshoppers. The bugs swirled down in pelting hordes, ruining the heads of grain, chirping and flaring around the helpless farmers, covering everything with brown disaster.

Noneconomic facts thickened the pall over rural America. As urbanization accelerated and the farm regions sank more deeply in debt, the whole prestige of agricultural life skidded down. Once the tiller of the soil, his head raised high in prickly independence, had been the very symbol of the American way. Now the sneer word "hayseed" was coming into common usage and farmers had to watch their own sons and daughters maneuvering to be off to the city.

Life in the less settled regions of the West brought additional aggravations. Many a pioneer had sung his way to a homestead only to settle into an existence of dreary grubbing. Log-cabin living, a long buckboard ride from the nearest town, meant a nagging loneliness and lack of comforts. Not one farmer in three hundred could get a daily newspaper, and families that lived five miles from the village post office were lucky to receive mail once a week. Women especially paid the price of isolation; for want of the simplest medical care, thousands died in childbirth or lost their babies in infancy. Hamlin Garland, a product of the North Dakota frontier, set out to describe the life of backcountry women but confessed, when his book was done, that he had stopped far short of the truth. "Even my youthful zeal," Garland wrote, "faltered in the midst of a revelation of the lives led by the women. . . . Before the tragic futility of their suffering, my pen refused to shed its ink."

In Kansas, a handsome Irish woman, grown sad-eyed watching the blighting of dreams, caught the mounting national restlessness in five volcanic words. What was needed, said Mrs. Mary Ellen Lease, was to raise "less corn and more HELL."


III

The hell was raised. The immediate result of the discontent was an enormous increase in the support for liberalism. Reformers of the 1872 type, coming up out of their storm cellars after the Greeley debacle, found a far more receptive audience for their assaults on Grantism. By the Eighties, liberal triumphs were becoming common on the municipal, state, and federal levels. In 1885 and again in 1893, the White House itself was taken over by Grover Cleveland, a liberal's liberal complete with an abhorrence of corruption and a zeal for local rule, decreased tariffs, governmental economy, and economic liberty.

Yet all the while that lower-income discontent was strengthening liberalism against Grantism, more and more of the discontented were thinking along non-liberal lines. Theoretically, liberalism of that day offered an honest, efficient government, holding its activities to a policing minimum, which would leave all citizens free and equal in their drive to get ahead. But liberal politicians had to function amid endless pressures, agrarian, laborite, and capitalist, and the pressure from large-scale business interests was easily the most potent. The liberals, moreover, were predisposed by the very origins of their doctrine toward the more successful groups. Increasingly liberalism became a pro-corporation credo.

Liberal-minded jurists might applaud local rule and uphold it rigidly when the federal regulation of business was proposed; they reacted differently when a state legislature passed a law controlling the activities of corporations. President Cleveland might be all for keeping the government out of economic life and he did keep it out so far as most legislation benefiting low-income groups was concerned. He also heartily approved maintaining a gold standard, which favored creditors over debtors, he assumed a tax system that kept the burden off corporations, and he used federal troops to help the Pullman Company defeat a strike of its pitifully squeezed workers. It was all honest enough; no one would have thought of offering Grover Cleveland a bribe. The more important point was that a good many Americans were wondering whether honesty was enough. "Cleveland might be honest," the agrarian leader William Jennings Bryan snapped, "but so were the mothers who threw their children in the Ganges."

Even if liberalism had been able to preserve an exact governmental impartiality toward all groups, it could hardly have satisfied the new discontent. A twelve-dollar-a-week worker dependent on a twelve-million-dollar corporation for his livelihood, or a small farmer desperate about a mortgage owed to a J. P. Morgan bank, was hardly interested in having an impartial government. He wanted a government that would be on his side, helping him fight what seemed to him unfair and overwhelming odds. In 1887 Congress appropriated ten thousand dollars to aid drought sufferers in buying new grain seed, and Cleveland vetoed the item with a declaration that "though the people support the Government the Government should not support the people." It was a perfect statement of liberal doctrine, and a perfect illustration why liberalism seemed irrelevant or downright evil to thousands who were quite sure that, even if the government should not support them, it should certainly help them support themselves.

With a curse for Grover Cleveland, farmers and workingmen were hurrying into organizations that spoke neither the tone nor the program of liberalism. Three "Farmers' Alliances"—a Western and a Southern organization and a separate Negro Alliance in the South—were growing at a phenomenal rate, and taking on an emotional intensity that recalled the days of the crusade against slavery. The agrarian bitterness came closest to a call for armed revolution in the South, where the farmers' poverty was deepest and where rule by manufacturers and bankers smacked of another Yankee invasion. The official history of the Southern Alliance had the title, The Impending Revolution, and the Arkansas author of the book explained: "Thousands of men who have already lost all hope of a peaceable solution of the great question of human rights are calmly waiting the issue."

A wide variety of non-liberal movements churned the lower-income districts of the cities. The Eighties had scarcely begun when Terence Powderly, a deaconish machinist who turned to labor organizing only after he was blacklisted during the depression of 1873, found himself the head of half a million belligerent "Knights of Labor." By 1885 the railroad workers in the Knights were powerful enough to force representatives of the mighty Jay Gould to sit down at the same table and discuss a strike settlement, the first such demonstration of union power in American history. When the Knights won something that could be called a victory, their membership leaped another hundred thousand and encouraged union activity throughout the country.

Urban agitations that had been present even in the halcyon late Sixties took on added impetus—especially the drive for an eight-hour day and the "Greenback—Labor" demand to break the control of banks over the currency. A new agitation, the single-tax movement, was having a pervasive effect. To remedy the curse of poverty amid progress, Henry George's book had called for a "single tax" on the increase in the value of land as communities grew up around it. This increase, George argued, was totally unearned; taxing it one hundred per cent would smash concentrated wealth and spread the national wealth around in a way that would reopen opportunity. Few farmers could be attracted by a program of heavy land taxes, but for the urban discontented here was a plan of alluring simplicity. "No man," the official Knights of Labor organ testified in 1887, "has exercised so great an influence upon the labor movement of to-day as Henry George."

The immigrant slums were finding their single-taxism in the old-country doctrines of anarchism and socialism. Anarchism looked as if it might rival the European successes of the "Black International" until a bomb went off during an eight-hour demonstration in 1886 and killed the movement by associating it with black-bearded horror. Socialism showed no such signs of demise. Led by Daniel De Leon, a fiery if highly dialectical immigrant, it was gaining a wide and tenacious hold in the sweatshops of the big cities. Before the Eighties were done, socialism, in a Utopian form, was even trickling through to the middle classes. A raft of novels advocating some variety of Utopian socialism appeared, and in 1888 one of these novels, Edward Bellamy's *Looking Backward,* swept together the collectivist yearnings into a far from negligible movement. Soon *Looking Backward* was selling at the rate of ten thousand copies a week and ardent Bellamy clubs were gathering in professors, ministers, and tradesmen as well as farmers and industrial workers.

With dissidence permeating both the urban and rural regions, reformers naturally dreamed of a national union of the discontented. There were certainly plenty of encouraging facts. Whatever their doctrinal differences, the Farmers' Alliances, Knights of Labor, socialists, single-taxers, even the anarchists, were united by a fear of big business and by an impatience with liberalism's refusal to sanction governmental action in behalf of the poor. Two local elections of the Eighties sent a special thrill of hope through the coalitionists. In 1886, single-taxers, socialists, union members, and thousands of citizens who were just plain irritated supported Henry George with such fervor that he barely missed winning the mayorship of New York; a rising young liberal named Theodore Roosevelt ran third. Then, in the state and national elections of 1890, candidates backed by the Alliances scored a series of striking victories in the South and West. Five United States Senators, six Governors, and forty-six Congressmen championing bold new economic legislation, a single-taxer almost mayor of the nation's metropolis—weren't these facts sure harbingers of a new national party of urban and rural discontent, which would take power as the coalition Republican Party had triumphed in 1860? With the approach of the Presidential election of 1892, more than thirteen hundred delegates converged on Omaha to get under way just such a coalition, the "People's" or "Populist" Party.


IV

Hour after hour anger swept through the cavernous old Coliseum Building. July 1892 brought as wilting a heat as Omaha had ever known, the city frolicked in a Fourth-of-July mood, near-by saloons had laid in an extra supply of liquor. But nothing could distract the delegates from their rounds of furious speeches, wild applause, and fierce resolutions. From all parts of the United States, some bumping along hundreds of miles in buckboards, others using their last folding money for train fare, the Populists had gathered to launch an all-out assault on the political and economic masters of America. They did it with the dedicated wrath of a camp meeting warring on the Devil himself.

Any delegate who strayed from the mood of the convention was promptly hurled back on a wave of emotion. Midway in the proceedings a member of the Resolutions Committee, pointing out that the Union Pacific had not provided the reduced rates usually granted for convention delegates, proposed that the railroad be asked to rectify this "oversight." Instantly Marion Cannon, of California, was on his feet, his face livid. An oversight? Ask a corporation to be fair? Cannon shouted. The "customary courtesy was denied deliberately and with insolence. I do not want this Convention . . . to go back to the railroad company, hat in hand, and ask for any privileges whatever. The Democrats and Republicans secured half-fare, but we—not connected with railroads, but producers of the earth—have been refused equal terms." The delegates thundered approval as Cannon concluded: "We can stand the refusal."

On the afternoon of July 4, a plump, genial Irishman with a reputation for quips and politicking mounted the rostrum and this day he sounded like a prophet out of the Old Testament. "We meet in the midst of a nation brought to the verge of moral, political, and material ruin," Ignatius Donnelly cried. ". . . Corruption dominates the ballot-box, the Legislatures, the Congress, and touches even the ermine of the bench. . . . Our homes [are] covered with mortgages. . . . The urban workmen are denied the rights of organization for self protection, imported, pauperized labor beats down their wages; a hireling standing army, unrecognized by our laws, is established to shoot them down, and they are rapidly degenerating into European conditions. A vast conspiracy against mankind has been organized. . . . If not met and overthrown at once it forebodes terrible social convulsions . . . or the establishment of an absolute despotism."

This was the kind of language the delegates wanted to hear. When the specific proposals of the platform continued in the same tone, the convention exploded into a demonstration unprecedented in all the turbulent history of American political gatherings. With the last thrust at "tyranny and oppression," the delegates rose in a cheering, stomping, marching mass. Hats, coats, papers, fans, umbrellas went up in the air, leaders were bounced from shoulder to shoulder, every state tried to outdo the next in noise and movement. Texans whooped and beat on coffee cans. Nebraskans chanted: "What is home without a mortgage? Don't all speak at once." New Yorkers hoisted a beaming old man to the platform, thrust a baton in his hand, yelled wildly while he pretended to lead the musicians in hymns and marching songs. "Good-Bye, My Party, Good-Bye," the delegates sang. Then, to the tune of "Save a Poor Sinner, Like Me," they shouted how "the railroads and old party bosses together did sweetly agree" to deceive and exploit "a hayseed like me." And, breaking through the bedlam time and again, came the "People's Hymn," sung to the consecrated music of the "Battle Hymn of the Republic":

They have stolen our money, have ravished our homes;
With the plunder erected to Mammon a throne;
They have fashioned a god, like the Hebrews of old,
Then bid us bow down to their image of gold.

Edwin Godkin read the reports from Omaha and erupted in an editorial that was all anger and foreboding. Carl Schurz, proclaiming the Republic near "the precipice," poured out a thirty-four-page letter pleading for Cleveland's re-election. In free-trade clubs, in universities, at soirées, wherever liberals gathered, the news from Omaha left men furious and frightened. Here was a drastically, alarmingly different reformism, bursting up from the bottom.

The leaders at Omaha made it emphatically plain that they intended to base their movement on the groups which the Best People were sure represented the worst people. Populism, almost the first words of the Omaha platform declared, was to be a "permanent and perpetual . . . union of the labor forces of the United States. . . . The interests of rural and civic [urban] labor are the same; their enemies are identical." Since the convention was predominantly agrarian, Populist leaders were careful to emphasize their interest in labor's problems, and resolutions adopted by the convention supported the most important labor demands of the day. The delegates warmly backed a shorter work week and roundly condemned both the use of Pinkerton men in strikes and unlimited immigration, which "crowds out our wage earners."

Another resolution provoked a debate which showed that these pro-labor statements were no mere contrivances on the part of leaders, slipped by an indifferent rank and file. A Knights of Labor union was engaged in a hard-fought strike against Rochester clothing manufacturers, and the resolution not only expressed support of the strikers but called on "all who hate tyranny and oppression" to boycott the goods of the manufacturers. Sympathy for strikers was one thing; a secondary boycott was going far (so far that its legality was decidedly in question). A secondary boycott was going much too far for a Texas delegate, who wanted to table the resolution, and for a New Yorker, who proposed dividing it so that he could vote for the sympathy and against the boycott.

Promptly, two of the most unmistakably agrarian delegates were on their feet in defense of the boycott. "There is no such thing as a boycott," roared "Cyclone" Davis, of Texas. "It only consists in letting your enemies alone and staying with your friends."

Then Ignatius Donnelly, from agricultural Minnesota, took up the fight. "This resolution," Donnelly declared, "is a declaration that free men will not clothe their limbs in the goods of manufacturers of this slave-making oligarchy. [Loud cheers.] It is war to the knife and the knife to the hilt. [Loud cheers.] I trust that those who have staggered away from this resolution because of the opprobrium that a hireling press has applied to the word boycott, will withdraw their opposition, and that the resolution may be adopted by a rising vote. [Tremendous applause.]" A motion to strike out the boycott clause was overwhelmingly defeated, and the whole resolution was adopted by acclamation.

Among the delegates conspicuous in the uproar was a coal-black Negro, marching about the Coliseum Building with an American flag fluttering from a cane and apparently feeling gaily at home. A number of important Populist leaders not only aimed to unite the discontented of the cities and the countryside. They sought something that no American party has achieved before or since: a political coalition of the poor whites and the poor blacks of the South. The Southern Farmers' Alliance was conspicuously friendly to the Colored Farmers' Alliance. Committees of white Southern Populists ceremoniously met with black colleagues, joint platforms were adopted, and Negro delegates were named to local and national Populist conventions. The most important Southern Populist leader, Tom Watson of Georgia, regularly held mixed meetings, despite violent attempts to prevent them. When Georgians threatened to lynch a Negro Populist leader, the state witnessed an unprecedented sight. At Watson's call, two thousand white Populists assembled to protect the Negro. For two days and nights, their arms stacked on Watson's veranda, the white men grimly carried out the Populist doctrine that the issue was poverty, not color.

The groups on which Populism was depending for support, so different from the most ardent followers of liberalism, were offered an appropriately different program. The Populists took over the liberal demand for honest, efficient political leaders, but the reformed government was to be no reflection of upper-income, better-educated America. Civil-service reform was not emphasized at Omaha; it smacked too much of establishing a permanent ruling group and contradicted the Jacksonian faith that any well-intentioned American was good enough to carry on government for his fellows. Populist government was to be by and for "the people," or, to use a more revealing phrase that the Populists borrowed from pre-Civil War reformers, by and for "the producers." The Populist reversion to the practice of dividing the population into producers and nonproducers was the surest indication of their view of America. It indicated their belief that "producers"—those who worked with their hands—were the men who really created the wealth of the nation. In the Populist view, the producers should run the country and should receive a value from their labor which gave little or no return to men whose chief function was providing capital.

In their eagerness to increase the political power of the producers, the Populists urged the secret ballot and endorsed three adventurous techniques for direct democracy: the popular election of United States senators; the initiative, giving the voters the right to legislate over the heads of their representatives; and the referendum, providing the voters with a veto over the actions of the legislature. The initiative and referendum proposals seemed so radical in 1892 that their chief advocate at Omaha, a representative of a New Jersey working-men's organization, had to argue vigorously for including them in the platform, but he was ultimately successful. Populists could not resist any idea that promised to end the political control of corporations. In fact, so intense was the Populist hatred of politics as it was being practiced that the Omaha gathering whooped through a resolution unique in the history of American conventions, conservative or radical. No one who held a federal, state, or municipal office, the delegates decreed, could sit in a future Populist convention.

And all politics or political machinery was but a means; the end was economic and social reform. The Populists swept together the discontent with both Grantism and liberalism into a bold doctrine of continuous state intervention in behalf of the producers. Governments were to stop aiding the corporations, directly or indirectly, and were to start passing legislation beneficial to Americans who had little or no capital. The issue that excited liberals and old-style Republicans so much—the tariff—was just a "sham battle" to the Populists. "We believe," the Omaha platform emphasized, "that the powers of government should be expanded . . . as rapidly and as far as the good sense of an intelligent people and the teachings of experience shall justify, to the end that oppression, injustice and poverty shall eventually cease in the land."

The Populist eye was on the Interstate Commerce Act of 1887, which put controls over railroads, and the Sherman Anti-Trust Act of 1890, which declared combinations in restraint of trade illegal. These the Populists wanted to strengthen and, in strengthened form, to make the models for state and federal interferences in economic life that would regulate all corporations and would splinter into small units those which had reached the monopoly stage. For years the Populists had watched extremes of wealth piling up, unchecked by legislation; the Omaha platform proposed to reverse, or at least halt, the trend by a graduated federal income tax. In the minds of most Populists, one of the chief enemies of the farmer was a rigid currency system, and the delegates demanded "a national currency, safe, sound, and flexible, issued by the general government only." Government-operated postal savings banks were to take the savings business out of the hands of private bankers. Federal subtreasuries, "or some other system," should be established to lend money to farmers at no more than two per cent interest and to see to it that the supply of currency fluctuated with the demand for agricultural credits. "All land now held by railroads and other corporations in excess of their actual needs," the Omaha convention added, ". . . should be reclaimed by the government and held for actual settlers only." On the general subject of the railroads, those prime ogres of the farmers, the Populists were ready for the most drastic kind of governmental power. The United States was to own and operate the railroads. It was, moreover, to own and operate the telegraph and telephone systems, which were approaching the monopoly stage and which the Populists felt were being run with an arrogant disregard of the consumer's interest.

The obvious socialism of these last proposals brought the most anguished of all cries from liberals. They were startled and outraged that free men could seriously propose handing over such great powers to the state, and their vehemence underlined the fundamental difference in the liberal and Populist approaches. The liberal, however much his practices might deviate from his doctrine under the pressure of the corporations, kept his principal emphasis on liberty, the freedom of the individual in political, economic, and social relations. The Populist did not forget liberty, but in the troubled Nineties the essence of liberty to a large number of Americans was the freedom to escape poverty and to rise in economic and social status. The Populists stressed opportunity rather than sheer liberty.

Most of the Populists, like so many of the liberals, found their hero in Thomas Jefferson. This may have been a tribute to the many-sided Jefferson, but it was also an example of the confusion that results from applying a man's thought in a different age. Liberals looked to the Jefferson who feared centralized power; Populists, to the Jefferson who considered capitalist power the chief enemy of the aspiring masses. Tom Watson, ardent Jeffersonian and bitter opponent of liberalism, caught the heart of Populism when he spoke of the movement's "yearning, upward tendency." Populism's central target, Watson continued, was "monopoly—not monopoly in the narrow sense of the word—but monopoly of power, of place, of privilege, of wealth, of progress." Its battle cry was: "Keep the avenues of honor free. Close no entrance to the poorest, the weakest, the humblest." Re-create an America that said to ambition: "The field is clear, the contest fair; come, and win your share if you can!"

V

In the elections of 1892 the Populists became the first third party to carry a state since the GOP started on its way in 1856. The contingent of Populist-minded United States Senators rose to five; the number of Representatives to ten. Populist governors were elected in Kansas, North Dakota, and Colorado, while the number of sympathetic state legislators and county officials mounted to fifteen hundred. In the important Illinois election the Democrats swept the state, but the result was more a defeat for the Populist Party than for reform. At the head of the victorious state ticket was John P. Altgeld, who agreed substantially with every important plank in the Omaha platform.

The next year the dissenters acquired a powerful ally. Hard times settled over the country again, bringing all the jolting effect of a second severe depression in one generation. The twelve months that began in the middle of 1894 have been called the *"année terrible"* of the post-Civil War period and the phrase is not overly dramatic for the record of savage strikes and brutal labor repression, deepening agricultural distress, and a national atmosphere of foreboding at the top and bitterness at the bottom.

1894 made labor history, with nearly 750,000 workingmen out in militant strikes. The leader of the Pullman strikers, sent to jail by Cleveland's liberalism, sat mulling over the situation and came out a full-blown socialist. "We have been cursed with the reign of gold long enough," Eugene Debs told wildly cheering crowds. ". . . We are on the eve of a universal change." In the clay hills of the South, across the scorched prairies, the farmer's agitation was rapidly becoming, as one supporter described it, "a religious revival, a crusade, a pentecost of politics, in which a tongue of flame sat upon every man." It was "a fanaticism like the crusades," a Kansas observer added. "At night, from ten thousand little white schoolhouse windows, lights twinkled back hope to the stars. . . . They sang . . . with something of the same mad faith that inspired the martyr going to the stake. Far into the night the voices rose, women's voices, children's voices, the voices of old men, of youths and of maidens rose on the ebbing prairie breezes, as the crusaders of the revolution rode home, praising the people's will as though it were God's will and cursing wealth for its iniquity." Hamlin Garland, watching the Populists flail away in Congress, was sure that the country was approaching "a great periodic upheaval similar to that of '61. Everywhere as I went through the aisles of the House, I saw it and heard it. . . . The House is a smoldering volcano."

In Indianapolis, a ruche-collared lady measured the political situation and went off to see the cathedrals of Europe. "I am going to spend my money," she said, "before those crazy people take it."

# bibliography

The history of American workers is now beginning to be written in the manner of E. P. Thompson, *The Making of the English Working Class* (Pantheon, 1963). Together with Eric Hobsbawm, *Laboring Men* (Anchor, 1967), this book provides a superb introduction to the working class. In America, Herbert Gutman has been the most prominent historian to follow Thompson's lead. Among the most useful of his essays are "The Reality of the Rags to Riches 'Myth': The Case of the Paterson, New Jersey Locomotive, Iron and Machinery Manufacturers, 1830–1880," in Stephan Thernstrom and Richard Sennett (eds.), *Nineteenth Century Cities: Essays in the New Urban History* (Yale University Press, 1969), pp. 98–124 and "The Negro and the United Mine Workers of America: The Career and Letters of Richard L. Davis and Something of Their Meaning, 1890-1900," in Julius Jacobson (ed.), *The Negro and the American Labor Movement* (Anchor, 1968). Norman Ware's *The Labor Movement in the United States, 1860-1895.* (Peter Smith, 1959), though old, explores the process through which industrial capitalism alters traditional values. Studies in labor violence include Wayne Broehl, *The Molly Maguires* (Harvard University Press, 1964), Robert V. Bruce, *1877, Year of Violence* (Bobbs-Merrill, 1959), and Melvyn Dubofsky, *We Shall Be All: A History of the IWW* (Quadrangle, 1969). For those who want to pursue the subject further, John Evansohn, *et al.* have compiled a comprehensive bibliography on the working class which appeared in *Radical America* (March–April, 1969). See also Robert Zieger, "Workers and Scholars: Recent Trends in American Labor Historiography," *Labor History*, 13 (Spring 1972), 245–266.

While family studies are still in the early stages, they reveal much about working class life. Virginia Yans McLaughlin, "Patterns of Work and Family Organization: Buffalo's Italians," *Journal of Interdisciplinary History*, 2 (Autumn 1971), 299–314, shows what can be done with statistics. In *Families Against the City* (Harvard University Press, 1970), Richard Sennett traces changing family patterns in a Chicago neighborhood. Stephan Thernstrom, *Poverty and Progress: Social Mobility in a Nineteenth Century City* (Harvard University Press, 1964), places the family in the context of the American myth.

On the Populists, the reader would do well to consult Frank Le Rond McVey, *The Populist Movement* (American Economics Association, 1896), who raised some of the issues which are now being re-examined by radical historians. Chester McArthur Destler, *American Radicalism, 1865-1901* (Quadrangle, 1946), remains the single best treatment of the Populists as a radical movement. Norman Pollack, *The Populist Response to Industrial America* (Norton, 1962), has been justly criticized by Ann J. Lane, *Science and Society* (Summer 1964), 326–329, for taking the rhetoric of the Populists too seriously and therefore seeing them as more radical than they in fact were. Finally, though not radical history, C. Vann Woodward's *Tom Watson: Agrarian Rebel* (Oxford University Press, 1963) deserves study for its attempt to place a significant movement in a racial context.

# the origins of
# American imperialism

Traditional historians used to speak of the Spanish-American War and the acquisition of Hawaii and the Philippines as an aberration, a temporary exception to the progressive role of the United States as an anti-imperialist nation. Ernest R. May writes that American leaders in the 1890s "were at most only incidentally concerned about real or imagined interests abroad." The American acquisitions occurred unintentionally; the United States "had greatness thrust upon it."

This "greatness" supposedly resulted from a series of motives: the human-itarian concern to save the Cubans from oppressive Spanish rule; the subtle ravings of William Randolph Hearst and other members of the "yellow journalism" press; the crisis in society and the "status revolt," which led the populace to assuage its frustrations by supporting acts of imperialist acqui-sition; and, of course, the need of the United States to act to protect the Monroe Doctrine and prevent European incursions into the Western Hemisphere.

All of these explanations have one theme in common; as Philip S. Foner points out, they minimize or ignore the existence of the real economic interests that led business leaders and statesman alike to seek markets for trade and commerce from Latin America to Asia. America's form of expansion differed from the traditional path taken by European imperialism. During the crisis of the 1890s, American business and government leaders posited the solution to new domestic overproduction: continued expansion abroad as the sole vehicle for maintenance of domestic prosperity.

The strategy chosen was the Open Door policy of overseas economic expansion. The demand for equal access and fair treatment for United States economic power in China issued by John Hay in 1899 became the particular American form of noncolonial imperialist expansion—the American version of informal empire, or the imperialism of free trade. The Open Door notes, as Thomas McCormick shows, departed from British policy, since the British version called for spheres of influence in China. Rather, as David Horowitz has stated, they were "the natural policy of a newly great economic power, recognizing . . . that competition in foreign as in domestic markets was merely the most efficient way of ensuring victory, and subsequent privilege, to the strongest."

Mainstream historians continue to confuse imperialism with old style European colonial acquisition. They refuse to acknowledge the American pattern of imperialism: economic expansion and domination of world markets carried out under the banner of opposition to political expansion and dom-ination. The policy of a new empire was most visible, as radical historian Walter LaFeber has pointed out, in America's treatment of Cuba at the end of the Spanish-American War. Although Cuba was nominally independent, it signed a reciprocal trade treaty with the United States, which increased American economic penetration of the Cuban market. At the same time the United States obtained a ninety-nine-year lease for a naval base at Guanta-namo—the very lease by which the United States today maintains this base. Finally, the United States reserved the right to intervene militarily in case of instability or disorder.

The United States had no need of a formal colonial empire. It worked instead to increase its power by reliance upon its superior economic position. The goal was to secure an Open Door world—to create an international liberal capitalist empire that was safe for the markets and commercial interests of American business. This effort produced conflict. The most fundamental threat to the position of American commerce was that posed by the rise of Bolshevism after 1917, since Bolshevism posited formal expropriation of private property. This development eventually led Woodrow Wilson to seek a "road away from revolution" by building an international association of nations that would create the successful preconditions for maintenance of the international Open Door.

Before World War I, plans for economic domination of other countries were not disguised. American leaders then, like many mainstream historians today, did not consider the American form of imperialism to be imperialism. Liberals like Woodrow Wilson did not recognize that investment in and ownership of other nations' raw materials, transport industry, and financial apparatus constituted imperialist exploitation.

British historian Gareth Stedman Jones has aptly pointed out that Open Door expansion appeared to them

unproblematically as a natural division of labor between industrialized and agrarian nations; it meant mutually beneficial business relationships and 'trade; it meant the assumption by the United States of its natural place in the world economy through the elimination of artificial impediments to the operation of the laws of competitive commerce. In the words of President Truman, "the Open Door policy is not imperialism, it is free trade."

Truman's claim has been asserted again by Arthur M. Schlesinger, Jr., in a recent issue of *Commentary*. He asks why reciprocal trade is a "sinister and vicious" arrangement and why American membership in the International Trade Organization supposedly expresses "the imperialist will of the American business system." Schlesinger attacks Noam Chomsky for accepting the thesis that "the Open Door . . . economic multilateralism—has been the chosen instrument of American business in its presumed quest for world economic domination." To Schlesinger, as to other mainstream historians, the Open Door is merely a liberal response to old style "economic nationalism"; a "conventional and even routine argument in the spirit of Cordell Hull, Will Clayton and the Reciprocal Trade Agreements Act for economic multilateralism and a freely trading world."

Radical historians answer that concepts of a "freely trading world" and the Open Door have long been the disguise behind which the reality of American imperialism is masked. The empire has for too long been invisible, since American imperialist interests have been concealed behind different organizations that shield the strength of American power and through which informal economic domination is carried out. By obscuring the reality of American imperialism, mainstream historians such as Ernest R. May help to defend the existence of the empire itself. Radical historians, by shedding light on the origins of American imperialism and by affirming its true nature and its very existence, provide a new open door for those who seek to topple the long life of the awesome yet vulnerable leviathan.

# the seventh power

## ERNEST R. MAY

Ernest R. May, perhaps the most influential of the mainstream historians writing on American imperialism, argues that the American government at the turn of the century sought no "new role in world affairs."

According to William Appleman Williams, May's major failure was his inability to "see that the domestic political pressures involved grew out of very clear and vigorous conceptions of real and imagined interests abroad, and out of arguments about the intimate connection between those interests and the situation in Cuba." Williams presents the radical answer to May by noting that Americans "defined their ideological and economic interests in ways that converged upon a demand for forceful action in the arena of foreign affairs."

Undoubtedly May's writings make up the most subtle presentation of imperial apologia coming from the academic community.

---

Had the President and the Senate acted otherwise, foreign observers might have been bewildered. As it was, they saw the United States behaving as a great power was expected to—taking what it could and keeping it.

The result was that Europeans kept their new conception of America. The continental press did find it mildly amusing that Aguinaldo and his cohorts rejected annexation, declared a war for independence, and kept the American army busy for nearly three years in intermittent guerrilla warfare. Apropos of American press attacks on Germany, the *Berliner Volkszeitung* snapped in 1899 that the Yankees would do well to "beat the Filipinos first." Then in 1902 when the United States belatedly granted independence to Cuba, Europeans interpreted the act less as the honoring of a promise than as an effort to avoid repetition of the Philippine experience. Nevertheless, neither the long-drawn-out contest with Aguinaldo nor the nominal surrender of Cuba diminished by much the reputation which the United States had acquired.

After 1899 writings on the "American peril" used the present, not the future tense. Octave Noël warned readers of the Paris *Correspondant* in March, 1899, that the threat from America was as real and immediate as that from Germany. Ugo Ojetti declared in the Milan *Corriere della Sera* that while Italy could probably defend herself against "victorious America," her colonies might well go the way of Spain's. The editors of *Russkoe Bogatstvo* advised Russians to regard English and American imperialisms as twin phenomena, equally dangerous for their own country. In Germany, Max Goldberger, Wilhelm Polenz, and Otto, Count Moltke, published books in effect declaring that America was working day and night to achieve dominion over the world.[1] To

From "The Seventh Power," in *Imperial Democracy: The Emergence of America as a Great Power,* © 1961 by Ernest R. May, 263–270, 299. Reprinted by permission of Harcourt Brace Jovanovich, Inc.

many such students of international politics and trade, the "American menace" had become, not a prospect, but a reality.

Though these writers were significant, they were not altogether representative; the chronicles and periodic commentaries in major newspapers and journals actually touched upon the subject infrequently. Indeed, after Cuban and Philippine affairs passed off the front pages, references to the United States appeared only a little more often than before 1898.

The real change was not in the amount of attention given America but in the attitude which journalists and diplomats now tended to adopt. In the summer of 1900 the periodicals of Europe were full of writings about navies. The German Reichstag was debating the government's thirty-eight-battleship budget, and analysts everywhere were examining its possible impact on the balance of power. The best statistics available indicated that the American fleet ranked just ahead of Germany's and just behind Russia's and France's. This had been its relative standing for some time. Earlier, however, commentators tended to leave it out when computing the potential strength of conceivable combinations. Now, they almost invariably included it.

The idea of the United States as a factor in the balance of power cropped up frequently. A. Maurice Low predicted flatly in the *National Review* for October, 1899, "If the United States is not an ally of England, then most assuredly she will be of Russia. It is a very simple proposition." A writer in *Questions diplomatiques et coloniales* interpreted the re-election of McKinley in 1900 as foreshadowing a bid for alliance with one bloc or another. A French socialist asserted that the great task for Europe was to build a makeweight against the Anglo-Saxon bloc, and an editorialist in the thoroughly antisocialist *Novoe Vremya* declared: "The Americans have discarded the Monroe doctrine and have allied themselves with their traditional enemy and with Japan. A counterpoise to American power is needed."[2]

In the spring of 1899 the St. Petersburg *Vedomosti* suddenly came out editorially for a Russo-American alliance. Prince Ukhtomskii, who was the *Vedomosti*'s editor, made a similar proposal through the columns of an American magazine. He and his newspaper were among the leading advocates of Russian expansion in the Far East. The reason for their unexpected declarations was undoubtedly the fact that negotiations were in progress with Britain for a Chinese railway agreement. The English seemed to be stalling. Ukhtomskii and his collaborators hoped that the threat of a Russian deal with America would make them more businesslike. Perhaps it did, for the agreement was promptly signed, and Ukhtomskii and the *Vedomosti* dropped their American alliance campaign. Nevertheless, it was significant that they had even momentarily broached such a project, for their words not only indicated that they thought a pact conceivable but that they would evaluate it as the equivalent of one with Great Britain.

It was also significant that right-wing German newspapers read importance into Ukhtomskii's suggestion. The agrarian *Kreuzzeitung* copied the *Vedomosti* editorial and published a long commentary on it. Misinterpreting it as evidence that Russia feared an Anglo-American alliance, this thoroughly conservative journal remarked that the interests of England and the United States were actually dissimilar. Germany itself, said the *Kreuzzeitung*, might do well to seek closer relations with the Americans. And this thought was then echoed in the almost equally conservative *Grenzboten*.

In the past such journals as the *Petersburgskaya Vedomosti* and the

*Kreuzzeitung* had, like English Tory organs before 1895, viewed the United States at worst as a symbol of liberalism. Their bias was unchanged. They continued to condemn things American. At the same time, however, they began to speak of possible combinations with or against the American republic just as coldly as of possible combinations with or against England or any other power.

When Chamberlain spoke at Leicester in November, 1899, suggesting an Anglo-American-German alliance, many commentators thought his project unlikely to materialize; none thought it impossible. Newspapers speculated from time to time on whether there actually did exist a secret compact between Britain, the United States, and Japan. Like the editorial writer for *Novoe Vremya,* some Russian statesmen believed that it did. And Bülow, Holstein, and Muraviev all at one time or another committed to paper speculations on possible international combinations including the United States.[3]

In no European capital, including London, were such thoughts more than fitful. Dealing chiefly with issues in Europe, Africa, and the Near East, diplomats still concerned themselves mainly with other European states. Even when confronted with crises in the Far East, they did not always take the United States into account. When they did, however, it was as a major power rather than as a minor one.

Perhaps the cartoons in continental humor magazines were in this case worth several thousand words. Some writers speculated on the possibility that there were two classes of great powers. "Diplomaticus" in the *Fortnightly Review,* for example, observed that there were only three "world powers"—Britain, Russia, and the United States. A Swiss political scientist asked if Europe in its old sense could even be said to exist any more. *Kladderadatsch* expressed this uncertainty by picturing the street of the great powers, with quaint national dwellings for the Europeans and a towering skyscraper for America.[4]

On the other hand, *Kladderadatsch* still at times represented the powers as five or six figures in European costumes. In August, 1899, it was inspired, as other journals were, to comment on the beginnings of the Boxer disturbances in China. It portrayed figures dashing from a burning pagoda. The Vienna *Floh* showed hands and long spoons dipping into a soup bowl labelled "China." In both pictures Uncle Sam was missing. He was also absent from a group pictured in the *Humoristicke Listy* of Prague. But he appeared in comparable cartoons in the Berlin *Ulk,* the Paris *Silhouette,* and the Turin *Fischietto.*[5] Like statesmen, caricaturists did not always think of the United States in connection with the states of Europe. When they did, however, they thought of it as one of the great powers.

This changed conception of America rested in part on misunderstanding. Many Europeans believed that the United States had deliberately chosen to throw itself into competition for colonies, economic concessions, and the other current gauges and emblems of international status. Not everyone was deceived. The *Journal des Débats* remarked astutely on July 3, 1899, "Let us remember how McKinley, who has no will of his own, came to annex the Philippines. Public opinion demanded it, and he was about as much master of the situation as a log drifting downstream." On the other hand, when McKinley was re-elected, nearly every major journal in Europe including the *Journal des Débats* interpreted the event as affirmation of an imperialist policy.

Europeans were impressed, to be sure, with America's population, navy, and industrial output. Especially was this so when figures for 1900 showed America leading in coal, iron, and steel. At about the same moment, it was revealed that the British and German governments had both gone to New York banks to borrow money. Data of this kind had been in evidence for years. The loans were not necessarily more significant than the first sales of American steel in European markets. The difference was that in the meantime Europeans had also been impressed by America's apparent resoluteness and combativeness in foreign relations. They thought they saw in Washington a government not only commanding great resources but also having the will to use them.

This was, of course, a delusion. The American government had rarely displayed any purposefulness whatever. When Hawaii offered itself for annexation in 1893, the Harrison administration moved to accept the gift only when persuaded that the public wanted it. Cleveland reversed the decision and refused the islands. So far as the evidence shows, he did so not from conviction that annexation was against the national interest but merely because the transaction seemed tainted. He thought it *morally* obligatory to make res- toration.

Cleveland's demands upon Britain in 1895 were bolder. In them there was some element of national self-assertion. But the President probably would not have acted had he not been under heavy pressure from the Republican opposition and from dissident elements in his own party. And he almost certainly would not have moved had he not seen in the frivolous Venezuelan- Guianan dispute a grave *moral* issue.

The virtual ultimatum that Cleveland presented to Lord Salisbury's govern- ment had far-reaching effects. It excited a hostile reaction at home that virtually broke politicians of their habit of electioneering by appealing to hatred for Britain. In England it shocked statesmen and opinion leaders into realization that the United States was a power with whom Britain should come to terms. In effect, Cleveland and Olney startled England and the United States into one another's arms. It cannot be said, however, that they had any such expectation at the time. Even with all the evidence in, indeed, it is hard to divine just what they did have in mind.

In dealing with Cuba, Cleveland and McKinley had a purpose in view. It was to avoid any international complications that might upset business. They wanted the Cuban problem to go away.

When it would not do so, McKinley found himself faced with a terrible choice. He could embark on a war he did not want or defy public opinion, make himself unpopular, and risk at least the unseating of the Republican party if not the overthrow of what he conceived to be sound constitutional government. He was influenced, as Cleveland had been, by moral revulsion against cruelties in Cuba. He was also affected by indications of approaching trouble in Asia and possibly in the Western Hemisphere. But he was occupied most by domestic considerations. When public emotion reached the point of hysteria, he succum- bed.

Neither the President nor the public had any aim beyond war itself. The nation was in a state of upset. Until recently its people had been largely Protestant and English; its economy predominantly rural and agricultural. Men in their forties could remember it that way. Now, however, the country was industrialized and urbanized. Catholics were numerous and increasing. People of older stock found themselves no longer economically or even socially superior to members of immigrant groups or to others without family, background, or education who had won success in business or industry. The panic of 1893 made this new condition even more visible by depressing agricultural prices, rents, investment income, professional fees, and white-collar salaries. Movement into and within cities had cut ties with families and churches. Young men and women were thrown together more than they had been, yet economic conditions forced them into later and later marriages. The young also heard old men talking on and on of the great war between the states and of the great men, great deeds, and great ideals that had been. In some irrational way, all these influences and anxieties translated themselves into concern for suffering Cuba. For the people as for the government, war with monarchical, Catholic, Latin Spain had no purpose except to relieve emotion.

The taking of Hawaii and the Philippines was more deliberate. There is even evidence that President McKinley thought Hawaii's annexation desirable. But his preoccupation was still with domestic public opinion. In contemplating the Philippine problem he evidently considered little else. The conservative senators who served as his lieutenants in the treaty fight showed no more conviction than he that the policy they advocated was necessarily the right one. They and their kind had simply been scared by the public's earlier convulsion. Like the President, they wanted to do whatever seemed necessary to prevent its recurring.

From first to last, the makers of American policy and the presumed leaders of American opinion concerned themselves either with abstract morality or with conditions inside the United States. They scarcely thought of proclaiming to the world that America was a power. They were at most only incidentally concerned about real or imagined interests abroad. They gave no sign that they meant the United States to become a factor in the international balance.

In 1899 and later the government was to proclaim an "Open Door" policy for Asia, stake out a security zone in the Caribbean, and even assist in ending a war in the Far East and resolving a European crisis over Morocco. In initiating these steps, McKinley may still have been thinking mainly about the domestic danger of seeming to be insufficiently aggressive toward foreigners. The same thought may have oppressed even Theodore Roosevelt. A certain number of journalists and business, professional, and church leaders may have endorsed the later policies of the government, as they endorsed the annexation of the Philippines, because it seemed the safest rather than the wisest course. Spaniards were to speak in retrospect of a disillusioned "generation of ninety-eight." Perhaps Americans also had a generation of ninety-eight—a generation of public leaders so frightened by the outbursts of mass emotion they had witnessed that their thoughts were dominated by dread of witnessing it again. But that is a question for some other book.

In the 1890's the United States had not sought a new role in world affairs. Issues in Hawaii, China, Turkey, Venezuela, and Cuba had intruded almost of their own accord. Statesmen and politicians dealt with them according to their judgment of domestic, not foreign, conditions. Cleveland and McKinley had showed more intense preoccupation with matters at home than even the most isolationist advocate of national solipsism in the 1920's and 1930's. Unconcernedly and almost unthinkingly, these statesmen ran the risk of precipitating Europe into a coalition against America. Yet their actions had the paradoxical effect of convincing people abroad that the United States possessed not only the might but also the will to be a force among nations. Some nations achieve greatness; the United States had greatness thrust upon it.

# NOTES

1. Octave Noël, "Péril américain," *Le Correspondant*, CXCIV (March 25, 1899), 1083–1104, CXCV (April 10, 1899), 116–144; Ugo Ojetti, *L'America vittoriosa* (Milan, 1899); *Russkoe Bogatstvo* (Nov., 1900), 151–154; Max Goldberger, *Das Land der unbegrenzten Möglichkeiten* (Berlin, 1903); Wilhelm Polenz, *Das Land der Zukunft* (Berlin, 1903); Otto, Graf Moltke, *Nord-Amerika: Beiträge zum Verständnis seiner Wirtschaft und Politik* (Berlin, 1903).

2. Louis Paul, "L'imperialisme Anglo-Saxon," *Revue socialiste*, XXIX (March, 1899), 257–274; *Novoe Vremya* quoted in *Literary Digest*, XVIII (March 11, 1899), 289.

3. On reactions to Chamberlain's speech, see *Questions diplomatiques et coloniales*, VIII (Dec. 15, 1899), 504–505; *Grosse Politik*, XIII, No. 3566, XIV, Nos. 3778, 3941, 4035; *Documents diplomatiques français, première série*, XIV, Nos. 528, 578. See also A. Dobrov, *Dal'nevostochnaya politika S.Sh.A. v period russko-yaponskoi voiny* (Moscow, 1952), 237; and my commentary on Dobrov in the *American Historical Review*, LXII (Jan., 1957), 345–351; *Das Echo*, XVIII (April 13, 1899), 566; *North American Review*, CLXIX (July, 1899), 6–7.

4. *Fortnightly Review*, LXXII(Sept., 1899), 545; Marc Debrit quoted in *Public Opinion*, XXIX (Nov. 15, 1900), 619; *Kladderadatsch*, LI (Feb. 5, 1899).

5. *Ibid.*, LII (Aug. 5, 1900); others in *Questions diplomatiques et coloniales*, XXXIV (Aug. 1, 1900), 340, (Aug. 15, 1900), 450–451, (Sept. 15, 1900), 674–675.

# why the United States went to war with Spain in 1898

## PHILIP S. FONER

Philip S. Foner, an orthodox Marxist historian, is completing a multivolumed history of United States–Cuban relations. Foner's article summarizes mainstream and radical literature on the Spanish-American War. Foner reveals that in the 1950s many historians were quick to buy the thesis that American business opposed the war. He shows how this assumption fit in with the political need to attack the views of those whom William Leuchtenberg referred to scornfully as "Leninist historians." Mainstream history, it turns out, is not as value-free as its practitioners would like readers to believe.

Foner concludes by presenting a strong case for the "predominance of economic factors" in the events leading up to the Spanish-American War, a war that he concludes was clearly "imperialist."

In the *New York Times Book Review* of January 29, 1961, Frank Friedel, the author of *Splendid Little War,* a pictorial history of the Spanish-American War, wrote: "Today, when Fidel Castro and his claque are screaming epithets at the United States and charging that the Spanish-American War was fought only for imperialistic reasons, it is heartening to be reminded of the fundamentally humanitarian motives that took America into the war." The reminding was done by Ernest R. May's *Imperial Democracy: The Emergence of America as a Great Power,* which Friedel was reviewing. But Friedel did not quote from May the following sentences which subvert his thesis: "An imperialist movement had come into being and was not to be demolished. . . . Its leaders had discerned that public opinion could be captured for an imperialist cause, if only that cause could be clothed in the rhetoric of piety. They were stubborn, willful men. . . ."[1]

As Professor Friedel must know, the thesis that the Spanish-American War was an imperialist war, fought for imperialist reasons, did not originate with Fidel Castro. Long before Castro and the Revolutionary Army ousted the dictator Fulgencio Batista and later set up the first socialist government in the Western hemisphere, this thesis was already advanced. Keir Hardie, the British labor and socialist leader, wrote shortly after the Spanish-American War

Philip S. Foner, "Why the United States Went to War with Spain in 1898," *Science and Society,* XXXII, (winter 1968), 39–65.

This article is a chapter from Professor Foner's book, *History of Cuba and its Relations with the United States,* Volume III, 1895–1898, published spring 1968 by International Publishers.

began: "Personally all my sympathies are with the Cubans—that they are entitled to self-government is not to be denied—but I cannot believe in the purity of the American motive. . . . The American man in the street is doubtless honest and sincere in his zeal for Cuban freedom, but he is simply shouting—without knowing it, of course—at the prompting of others." The "others," he made it clear, were the trusts and Wall Street financiers who were intent on extending American economic dominance over Cuba, Latin America, and the Far East. Hardie concluded: "Desiring as I do to see Cuba freed, I frankly declare that I have not the slightest sympathy with this American-made war, nor do I believe in the motives which inspire it."[2]

In France, too, the United States' profession of humanitarian motives as a basis for intervention was ridiculed. Socialists and non-socialists alike empha-sized that humanitarian motives were merely a disguise for commercial desires—the major cause being the desire for commercial conquest of all the Caribbean Islands and Latin America. Paul Louis, the socialist, declared that the United States, a great capitalist power, was simply following the example of France, England, Germany, and Italy in its desire for expansion.[3]

In the United States, of course, there were many who questioned that the war was caused by the humanitarian desire to obtain Cuban freedom, and none more effectively than *The People*, official organ of the Socialist Labor Party, edited by Daniel DeLeon. *The People* challenged the sincerity of the capitalists' pretended sympathy for the struggling Cubans by pointing to the multitude of oppressions and injustices at home. In America, too, "the 'Reconcentradoes' [sic] are seen all around . . . famishing figures of all ages and all sexes, premature corpses, bearing either the marks of slow and gradual starvation, or the marks of sudden death by bullet and bayonet, or mutilation by factory machine."[4] Cuban freedom was only a ruse to justify war.

War, *The People* argued, was necessary as a result of economic conditions in the United States where "good times" had failed to materialize and external conflict was always a good way of diverting attention from social evils at home. War was necessary "to protect American commercial interests in Cuba." War was necessary because American capitalism was finding it necessary to "spread out and fight for markets," and capitalism had to expand in order to survive. "The capitalist class needs markets. It needs them because it has on hand more goods than the people can buy." Not only would the war provide markets in Cuba for American capitalism, but it would open the vast new markets of the Far East. "To make any attempt to capture part of that new market for the capitalists of this country requires a larger naval force and army than we now have. We will need ships to take territory, and men to hold the territory when taken. To attempt to do that in time of peace has failed; let us therefore raise trouble with some back-numbered country—Spain, for instance, and during the excitement get what we want. Presto, it is done."[5]

On October 26, 1907, the Socialist weekly *Appeal to Reason,* published in Girard, Kansas, carried an answer to a question sent in by a reader, inquiring what were the causes "which brought about the war with Spain." The answer read in part:

Cuba was the prize for which the Spanish-American war was fought. The island was rich in natural resources, the development of which would yield profits to the capital invested as well as supply a market for the growing surplus of American manufac-ture. . . . The capital of the United States was under the necessity of finding new fields in which to operate. Visions of Havana franchises and fertile sugar plantations rose before the profit-hungry ruling class of this country. . . .

The adherents of the theory that the war was caused solely by humanitarian factors dismissed these socialist interpretations as reflecting "the Marxist Machiavellian analysis of history." But they could not so easily dismiss the analysis presented by Frederick Emory, chief of the Bureau of Foreign Commerce of the Department of Commerce, who wrote in *World's Work* of January, 1902:

Underlying the popular sentiment, which might have evaporated in time, which forced the United States to take up arms against Spanish rule in Cuba, were our economic relations with the West Indies and the South American republics. So strong was this commercial instinct that had there been no emotional cause, such as the alleged enormities of Spanish rule or the destruction of the *Maine,* we would have doubtless taken steps in the end to abate with a strong hand what seemed to be an economic nuisance. . . . The Spanish-American War was but an incident of a general movement of expansion which had its root in the changed environment of an industrial capacity far beyond our domestic powers of consumption. It was seen to be necessary for us not only to find foreign purchasers for our goods, but to provide the means of making access to foreign markets easy, economical and safe.

Commenting editorially on this analysis, the New York *Tribune* concluded: "The war in which we intervened was pre-eminently an economical war, provoked by commercial, financial and industrial forces."[6]

This interpretation of the forces that produced American intervention in Cuba was endorsed in the same year, 1902, by the noted British economist J. A. Hobson in his book, *Imperialism: A Study:* "It was this sudden demand for foreign markets for manufactures and for investments which was avowedly responsible for the adoption of Imperialism as a political policy and practice by the Republican Party to which the great industrial and financial chiefs belonged, and which belonged to them. . . ." Hobson warned his readers not to be deceived by such slogans as "humanitarianism," "manifest destiny," and "mission of civilization," raised by politicians and propagandists. They were merely the spokesmen for the monopolists. "It was Messrs. Rockefeller, Pierpont Morgan, and their associates who needed Imperialism and who fastened it upon the shoulders of the great Republic of the West. They needed Imperialism because they desired to use the public resources of the country to find profitable employment for their capital which otherwise would be superfluous." Hobson concluded that the Spanish-American War was an imperialist war, and that "American Imperialism was the natural product of the economic pressure of a sudden advance of capitalism which could not find occupation at home and needed foreign markets, for goods and investments."

In his classic work, *Imperialism: The Highest Stage of Capitalism,* written in 1917, V. I. Lenin paid tribute to Hobson's analysis as "an excellent and comprehensive description of the principal economic and political characteristics of imperialism." Although Lenin differed with Hobson on basic issues,[7] he agreed with the British economist in characterizing the Spanish-American War as an imperialist war, fought by the United States for imperialist reasons.[8]

During the 1920s and early 1930s, several American historians also characterized the Spanish-American War as an imperialist war, although their description of imperialism was closer to Hobson than to Lenin. Harold U. Faulkner stated in 1924 that the cause for the war with Spain was to be found in the fact that by 1898 the United States was "sufficiently advanced for financial imperialism," and that the war was fought for markets and fields for investments.[9] Professor Harry Elmer Barnes wrote in 1930 "that the passing of the frontier in 1890 produced the necessity of discovering a field for expansion and investment elsewhere than within the boundaries of the United States. The dispute with Spain over Cuba provided but a welcome pretext and provided a moral issue which allowed the formal and systematic initiation of a process which had long been in preparation."[10] Likewise, Charles A. Beard, in his study *The Idea of National Interest,* published in 1934, wrote: "Within a few years the movement for territorial expansion, conforming to the commercial type, was renewed in the Caribbean direction, with the Cuban Revolution of 1895 as the occasion for action." Beard acknowledged that American concern about Cuba came under the heading of "the national interest," but that "supplementary interests were plainly economic."[11]

The 1930s also saw the publication of several historical works which challenged the interpretation of the Spanish-American War as having been caused by United States imperialism in need of markets, sources of cheap raw materials, and new fields for investment. Writing in 1930, Louis Hacker suggested that the war resulted from an attempt by the Republican Party "to take men's minds off vexing domestic concerns."[12] Several historians designated the "yellow press" as the primary cause of the war. Marcus M. Wilkinson in 1932 concluded that the press drove McKinley, Congress, and the people into war. He declared that the war marked a triumph of the sensational press which, led by the New York *Journal* and *World,* "left the American public reeling from a bombardment of half-truths, misstatements of facts, rumors, and faked dispatches," and that the McKinley administration, "sensing the popular tide . . . and egged on by a 'jingo' Congress, proposed war."[13] Two years later, Joseph E. Wisan singled out one sensational newspaper publisher, William Randolph Hearst, and accorded him first place in promoting the war. He concluded that fighting would not have started "had not the appearance of Hearst in New York journalism precipitated a bitter battle for newspaper circulation."[14] This school of interpretation received an additional adherent in 1940, George W. Auxier, Jr., who published a study of the Midwestern press in which he noted that while sensationalism was not particularly well represented in the area, the newspapers caused the war.[15]

But so far as the vast majority of American historians was concerned, the decisive blow to the interpretation of the Spanish-American War as an imperialist war was delivered by the appearance in 1934 of Julius W. Pratt's "American Business and the Spanish-American War," and in 1936 of his work, *Expansionists of 1898: The Acquisition of Hawaii and the Spanish Islands.* After a study of financial and commercial journals, Pratt stated that the vast majority of business and financial interests of the country until the last moment "strongly opposed action that would lead to war with Spain," and the few who did support it did so solely "on humanitarian grounds." While he does not exonerate the entire American business community of any responsibility for the Spanish crisis, this is clearly implied in his thesis that American business did not favor, but rather actively opposed, the Spanish-American War, and in his statement that "business interests in the United States were generally opposed to expansion or indifferent to it until after May 1, 1898." Not the business community, Pratt argued, but strategically placed intellectuals (with non-economic motives) were responsible for American imperialism.[16] But once the war started, and once the expansionists had begun to press for the retention of the Philippines, the attitude of the business community changed. Then the arguments of the expansionists about the commercial possibilities in the new Pacific acquisition brought a significant number of businessmen over to the expansionist side.[17]

Now American historians, taking their cue from Wilkinson, Wisan, and especially from Pratt, began to construct the thesis that the Spanish-American War was the result of mass hysteria produced by the propaganda of the "yellow press," aided and abetted by the Cuban *Junta;* the "self-assertive egoism and altruistic idealism" of the American people, apart from business leaders, who wanted war and got it after a "popular clamor for war"; the rise of Social Darwinism with its insistence that a struggle for existence "among the nations and peoples would result in the survival of the fittest," e.g., the United States and white Anglo-Saxons; the result of the influence of "a little group of young Republicans" who sought "National power for its own sake." The latter—the "original imperialists"—were motivated (according to this theory) solely by the "political possibilities of imperialism," and they forced a weak and indecisive President McKinley, who displayed "no interest in international politics" and had "no policy of imperialism on which to stand or fall" to lead the country into war.[18]

In the rush to present the new picture of the causes of the Spanish-American War, economic factors were cast aside. Charles A. Beard joined the group of American historians who emphasized that emotional and psychological factors were largely responsible for the war. In 1939, he advanced the theory that the war was sold to the country by politicians who were frightened by the "specter of Bryanism," and were seeking to divert the attention of the people from the grave problems that lay beneath the revolt of the farmers expressed in the populist movement. His earlier emphasis on territorial expansion and economic interests that stood to gain from the war was now abandoned.[19] Twenty-seven years after he had first stressed the prominence of economic causes for the war, Harold U. Faulkner stated in 1951 that "the point of view taken by certain economic historians that the United States went to war with Spain primarily for economic reasons seems not warranted by the evidence."[20] In *Politics, Reform and Expansion, 1890–1910,* published in 1959, Professor Faulkner found that the business interests in 1898 were worried about the possibility of war, and were definitely on the side of peace.[21] Also influenced by Pratt, Foster R. Dulles rewrote his earlier works on American imperialism to lay added emphasis upon psychological and political factors while virtually eliminating previous allusions to economic causes for the conflict between the United States and Spain.[22]

The non-economic interpretation of the causes of the war was reflected in nearly all historical works dealing with this period. Matthew Josephson emphasized that opposed to the "war party" was a group strong for peace, the "Big Business faction."[23] Arthur M. Schlesinger wrote that there can be no question that McKinley was for peace and that his desire "was ardently backed by Big Business and Wall Street."[24] Thomas A. Bailey stated that during the hectic months before the actual intervention, "perhaps the most important single restraint on the jingoistic spirit was big business. Except for a relatively small group . . . the financial and commercial interests of the United States were almost solidly opposed to war."[25] Samuel Flagg Bemis called the charge that American business desired intervention "a legend once eagerly accepted in academic circles." But now it was clear that rather than desiring intervention, "business interests in the United States were to the last opposed to any war with Spain."[26] Nor, states A. Whitney Griswold, did commercial groups interested in the Far East desire a war, and he goes on to say that "it is safe to say that the handful of Americans engaged in commerce with the Far East at first saw no connection between *Cuba Libre* and the open door in China. Neither did the American people as a whole."[27]

If economic forces did appear as a factor in the agitation for the war, they appeared in a strangely inverted way. "The threat to peace came from a new quarter," writes W. E. Leuchtenberg, "from the South and the West, the strongholds of Democracy and Free Silver." The Bryanites had hoped that the war would put a strain on the currency so that the opponents of free silver would collapse. Since they saw that Wall Street opposed the war, they claimed that the Administration's "peace policy" was the product of a bankers' conspiracy to deny free silver to the American people and independence to the people of Cuba. This theory, Leuchtenberg concedes, can be questioned, but there can be no doubt that, in the main, the business interests of the country opposed the war.

McKinley came to power as the "advance agent of prosperity" and business interests were almost unanimous in opposing any agitation of the Cuban Question that might lead to war. Contrary to the assumption of Leninist historians, it was Wall Street which, first and last, resisted a war which was to bring America its overseas empire.[28]

Richard Hofstadter summed up the position of the dominant school of American historians when he wrote that "since Julius W. Pratt published his *Expansionists of 1898* . . . it has been obvious that any interpretation of America's entry upon the path of imperialism in the nineties in terms of rational economic motives would not fit the facts and that the historian who approaches the event with preconceptions no more supple than those, say, of Lenin's *Imperialism,* would be helpless." While uncritically accepting Pratt's thesis, Hofstadter, in accounting for the Spanish-American War, advances what he calls "The Psychic Thesis." He concedes that a number of factors, in varying degrees of intensity, were responsible for the war, including economic factors. But he argues that war finally came because at the moment these war-producing factors came to a head, the country was undergoing what he calls a "psychic crisis." The depression which followed the Panic of 1893 frustrated the American people, Hofstadter argues, and they responded to their frustrations with aggression in all directions. Imperialism followed naturally from the psychic—not basically economic—necessities of the moment. For their own selfish purposes, the "manufacturers of inevitability," the "yellow press" and the imperialist "junto" around Theodore Roosevelt and Henry Cabot Lodge, were thereby able to pervert the sympathies of the American people for the suffering Cubans into a palatable argument for a war and an empire against the basic interests and traditions of the American people. Pointing to McKinley's war message to Congress, Hofstadter notes that the Spanish had actually capitulated and that war was unnecessary. "Evidently," he writes, "McKinley had concluded that what was wanted in the United States was not so much the freedom of Cuba as a *war* for the freedom of Cuba."[29]

The first critical analysis of the Pratt thesis was made by Arthur Barcan in his unpublished Master's thesis presented to the graduate faculty of Columbia University in 1940, entitled "American Imperialism and the Spanish American

War." Beginning by noting that big business controlled the government of the United States under McKinley, Barcan observed that it was inconceivable "that the administration's decision to enter a war was supposedly unfavorable to big business." He then proceeded to a detailed analysis of business, financial, and industrial journals for the period 1895 to 1898, a number of them ignored by Pratt, and concluded that he was convinced from this study that the Spanish-American War was "no more the freak—a non-imperialist venture in an imperialist setting, a war opposed by business men in a country controlled by them—but it now becomes a more plausible account of how the United States was forced into war to satisfy her new imperialist appetites, aided and abetted by business men who were in it to gain directly or indirectly from the war." He found nothing in his research to justify the conclusion of "mass business opposition to war" in commercial, business, and financial journals, or the concept that "the United States did not find its imperialist urge until the war was under way, as if a country can, within the space of one month, develop the necessary resources and needs that produce imperialism." He showed in his study that the rapid economic growth of the United States had developed an increasing need for markets for surplus goods and capital. By 1898, these expanding American capitalists found themselves in discouraging, and even precarious straits. In Cuba, the Revolution had for three years disrupted economic activity, destroyed valuable capital investments, and held back further exploitation of the island's great resources, while Spain had proven herself impotent to restore order, a condition highly necessary for continued imperialist activity in the "Pearl of the Antilles." In Hawaii, Americans had already assumed control, but their desire and need for annexation to the United States was balked by persistent efforts of domestic beet and cane sugar growers, aided by anti-imperialist elements in the country. In China, American capitalists found profitable fields for trade and capital increasingly menaced by the monopolistic encroachments of European imperialisms. American capitalists, Barcan discovered from his research,

now turned covetous glances in the direction of the Philippines, which were sufficiently close to the Asiatic mainland to serve as an excellent base for American navy and ships, thus bolstering the American position in China. It was the need to acquire the Philippines, and the inability to annex Hawaii except under extreme conditions as a "war measure" that bolstered and gave impetus to the war drive in March and April, 1898, supposedly concerned merely with the desire to free the Cubans from the Spanish "yoke." . . . Nor is it mere accident that the first important step in the fight to drive Spain out of Cuba was Admiral Dewey's victory in Manila Bay.

Barcan concluded his study with the statement that while the war cannot be explained only in terms of economic factors, "the business imperialist interests were dominant."[30]

Since Barcan wrote his study—in many ways a limited analysis of the whole problem because of a failure to examine many available sources which would have further buttressed his conclusion—the Pratt thesis has come under increasing criticism. In 1953, in an unpublished doctoral dissertation at the University of Pittsburgh, Ralph Dewar Bald, Jr., proved that the journals of the leading industries and businesses in the United States repeatedly emphasized, beginning with 1885, "that the country was faced with the necessity of securing overseas markets for industrial surpluses." These journals published and endorsed the call by Mahan, Roosevelt, Lodge, and other imperialist-minded intellectuals and politicians, demanding overseas expansion, and giving special attention to the value of annexing Cuba as a source for trade and investment of capital. Rather than remaining indifferent to imperialism, as Pratt had asserted, the organs of the business community in the early 1890s "contributed importantly to the creation of an atmosphere of opinion favorable to expansion."[31] Since Pratt relied heavily on a few trade journals in reaching his conclusions, Bald's more intensive study of these periodicals showed that the Pratt thesis was in need of revision.

A more direct critical analysis of the Pratt thesis appeared in 1958 in Nancy Lenore O'Connor's article, "The Spanish American War: A Re-evaluation of Its Causes," published in *Science & Society*. Miss O'Connor emphasized that "economic considerations had much more to do with the coming of the [Spanish-American] War than has generally been acknowledged by American historians." Challenging Pratt, she notes that his conclusion is based on inadequate evidence, since he relied mainly on "eastern and coastal opinion." Then too, Pratt underestimated the role played by American bankers, merchants, manufacturers, steamship owners, and agents engaged in the export and import trade to Cuba who favored intervention. Miss O'Connor finds, moreover, that even in the East there was "a strong split in business opinion" over the question of war with Spain, with a substantial group calling for military intervention. She challenges Pratt's contention that "American business had been either opposed or indifferent to the expansion philosophy which had arisen since 1890," citing specific examples where "industrial and commercial interests demanded new bases of operation." She concludes:

Thus, on the eve of the conflict with Spain, business interests accepted war as a necessary extension of the American Policy. To assume that the foment of mass ideology, *real politik*, and lust for power can explain away the operation of economic factors which led the business community to support different forms of expansion in accord with their own best interests is convenient, but misleading. . . . Given the milieu of the expansionist philosophy of the eighteen-nineties, the notion that American business opposed the Spanish-American War is subject to considerable revision.[32]

Another challenge to Pratt's thesis was presented by Martin J. Sklar in *Science & Society* a year later in an article entitled, "The N.A.M. and Foreign Markets on the Eve of the Spanish-American War." Analyzing the proceedings of the National Association of Manufacturers, founded in 1895, Sklar points out that

. . . for more than two years, at least, prior to the Spanish-American War, a significant body of U.S. industrialists was convinced of the necessity of expanding their trade into foreign markets. The continued depression following the Panic of 1893 had demonstrated to them that the domestic market had finally passed the stage of indefinite elasticity capable of accommodating the growing productive capacity of the nation's industrial plant;[33] that the crisis required for its solution "the conquest of foreign markets" in order to "make room for the further expansion of our industries," not to mention the mere restoration of current production to full capacity; that unless something were done in this direction *post haste*, not only economic but social and political disaster for the capitalist way of life as they so fondly knew it might result.

Although Sklar does not discuss the attitude of this large and influential body of U.S. businessmen toward the Cuba crisis, he effectively demolishes Pratt's thesis that the American business community was either opposed or indifferent to the expansionist ideology of the 1890s. He proves that, on the contrary the leading businessmen were among the foremost advocates of this philosophy, and pointed repeatedly to Latin America and Asia as promising "the most glittering market opportunities for U.S. manufactures"—markets needed to "absorb glutted commodities, renew demand, and permit profitable expansion of productive capacity as an investment outlet for accumulated capital." Moreover, it was becoming clear to U.S. industrialists just prior to the Spanish-American War that in order to obtain "their 'share' of world markets," they had to throw themselves into the struggle for these markets, "and do so without further delay, before the world had been too hopelessly divided by the other industrial nations without U.S. participation. . . ."[34] Sklar demonstrates that for at least two years prior to the war, the U.S. industrialists embarked upon an aggressive struggle against the business interests of other industrial nations in competition for the markets of the world, and spheres of influence and control. This they did with the full cooperation and support of the business-minded McKinley administration. The implication thus is clear that United States industrial and financial capital viewed war with Spain as part of the aggressive drive to gain a dominant place in the markets of the world.[35]

Over a half-century before Sklar presented this thesis, the National Executive Committee of the Socialist Labor Party pointed to the proceedings of the N.A.M. convention in late December, 1897, as throwing "valuable light . . . upon the purpose of the Spanish-American War." It described the event as "a Congress of the owners of the United States to decide what their Government should do about expansion." It quoted Warren Miller, chairman of the convention, as telling the delegates: "Wars to-day are for commerce. The killing of a missionary furnishes the excuse for opening up of a market." Charles Emory Smith, Postmaster General in McKinley's cabinet, and a leading Republican spokesman for big business, told the delegates: "The economic problem of the world to-day is the distribution of the surplus. . . . Under this stress the nations of Europe are struggling for empire and trade. . . . We have come to the point in our national development where we must decide. . . . Why should we not obtain our legitimate share of the great stake? . . . The United States must not be counted out in determining the fate even of the coast of Asia." Less than four months later, the Socialist Labor Party pointed out, war was declared against Spain, and the first step taken was to seize its Pacific possessions. The current of events had been started, "under capitalist guidance," by the businessmen and their representatives in Washington. It was "to issue forth like a Gulf Stream, and operate 'way around on the other side of the world on the shores of China. . . ."[36]

Pratt's thesis has also been criticized by Professor William Appleman Williams. He contends that in 1898 many businessmen were convinced that recovery from the recession had been due to overseas economic expansion and thus became advocates of an "active foreign policy." Like Sklar, he cites the president of the N.A.M. as having asserted that "many of our manufactures have outgrown or are outgrowing their home markets, and the expansion of foreign trade is the only promise of relief." And like Miss O'Connor, he criticizes Pratt for underestimating the role of American businessmen whose interests in Cuba were being threatened with destruction by the continued fighting. The Cuban situation had to be stabilized in order to protect these interests, and American investors, looking for new areas for investing capital, did not welcome the prospect of continued strife in Cuba. Moreover, the need to "pacify the island" was supported by businessmen who agreed with McKinley that continued war in Cuba "injuriously affects the normal functions of [American] business, and tends to delay the condition of prosperity to which this country is entitled." Then again, Williams stresses, many businessmen in the United States feared the victory of the radical revolutionaries—"the troublesome adventurers and non-responsible class"—whose attitude toward American interests in Cuba was considered unreliable. By 1898, many businessmen favored American intervention in order to secure the ascendency of conservative elements (many of them Spaniards) in a Cuba free from Spain. Finally, Williams stresses "the clear and increasing interest in acquiring the Philippines as a base for winning a predominant share in the markets of China," an interest shared by many businessmen and not only by "Theodore Roosevelt and his imperialist cronies. . . ." Williams then concludes that American business, though preferring not to go to war as long as it could attain its objectives peacefully, had no objection to war "as the court of last resort." President McKinley "did not go to war simply because the businessmen ordered him to do so; but neither did he lead the nation to war against their economic wishes, as is so often asserted."[37]

Writing in 1960 and again in 1963, Thomas McCormick demonstrated the tremendous interest on the part of American businessmen and the McKinley administration in "the penetration, and, ultimately, the domination of the fabled China market," and clearly showed the link between the Cuban crisis and expansion in the Far East.[38] During this same period, Walter La Feber's research in materials related to American foreign policy confirmed the findings of other critics of Pratt's thesis. He proves in his study, *The New Empire: An Interpretation of American Expansion, 1860–1898*, published in 1963, that the American business community considered foreign markets, especially those of Latin America and Asia, a solution to the domestic depression of 1893 (although he notes that even after 1873 there were signs of excess capacity in major segments of the American economy). Translating this viewpoint into action, businessmen after 1893 not only began systematically opening Latin American markets, but prodded the State Department to assist them in formulating Latin American policies. By 1897–98, they were beginning to move in the same way toward Asian markets and calling upon the McKinley administration to act diplomatically in behalf of their interests in the Far East.

American business, in short, was not a passive onlooker while Roosevelt, Mahan, Lodge, and the other "young imperialists" shouted for American expansion abroad, but was the initiator of the expansionist policy, and urged government officials to adopt the necessary strategy to advance the interests of a business community urgently seeking new markets. Many businessmen, La Feber points out, supported intervention against Spain not only because it would open the Cuban market for further U.S. economic penetration, but also because they had their eyes on Spain's possessions in the Far East. "It is possible to suggest," he writes with specific reference to Pratt's thesis, ". . . that by the middle of March important businessmen and spokesmen for the business community were advocating war. It is also possible to suggest that at the same time a shift seems to be occurring in the general business community regarding its over-all views on the desirability of war." In short, businessmen and leading politicians thought alike on the need for foreign markets and acquisition of colonies, and the foreign policy of the U.S. government flowed from this state of affairs.[39]

My own research confirms recent conclusions that the thesis advanced by

Julius W. Pratt and accepted uncritically by so many historians is not tenable. For one thing, there is ample evidence that businessmen were just as concerned about foreign markets and exports as the only feasible way of overcoming the industrial glut at home as were the imperialist-minded politicians and intellectuals. The Caribbean area and Latin America were frequently mentioned in trade journals and meetings of manufacturers as a field for American investment and trade expansion, but expansion in the Pacific was also increasingly being mentioned and linked with the others. On November 5, 1897, Francis B. Loomis, a leading spokesman for American business, wrote in a "confidential" letter to William R. Day, Assistant Secretary of State:

> *Above all,* let me say in conclusion I would send a commercial attaché to the Orient to operate in China and Japan. It is in that direction the great markets of the immediate future will be found. I happen to know that England sees this with distinctness and is acting promptly on her foresight. This administration can make a powerful and lasting impression upon the imagination and the welfare of the whole business world in the United States, and a richly deserved prestige for originality and progressiveness by taking up and exploiting the idea of trade in the Orient. . . .
>
> If you have not done so, let me suggest to you to read the article by Cpt. Mahan in the October number of Harper's Monthly. It is a strategic "Study of the Caribbean sea," and the writer is the foremost of authorities on that subject.[40]

Captain Mahan's article emphasized the need for naval bases, particularly in the strategically important Caribbean area and in Hawaii, as a major step toward expansion of American economic activity in Latin America and Asia. The prophet and apostle of sea power argued that the U.S. must begin to look outward. Deploring the country's self-imposed isolation in the matter of markets and the decline of its shipping, Mahan asserted that the growing production of the country would necessitate new markets, and this, in turn, would require facilities for their protection—a powerful navy dominated by an aggressive spirit, a healthy merchant marine, and secure bases and coaling stations from which they could operate. Strategically, the Caribbean area was crucial; Mahan considered control of the Isthmus of Panama by the United States vital. Such control was in turn contingent upon control of its approaches and of the bases that dominated them. Nothing less than American supremacy in the Caribbean would suffice. With the Caribbean and Hawaii, the United States could dominate Latin American commerce and move aggressively into the markets of the Far East. Mahan saw a clear relationship between the Caribbean and the vast market of China—via Cuba and Puerto Rico, the Isthmus, Hawaii, the coaling and cable station system in the Ladrones and Samoa, the Philippines to the Asian mainland. Appraising the value of all the Caribbean islands, Mahan directed American attention to Cuba as offering the best position for the United States in that area.[41]

As Loomis' letter to Day indicates, Mahan's outlook was shared by leading business interests. On February 3, 1898, the New York State Chamber of Commerce sent a memorial to President McKinley urging the government to pay careful attention to the opportunities for the expansion of trade with China and the danger that this might be affected by "the changes now going on in the relation of the European powers with the Empire of China." In other words, the American businessmen faced the threat of being cut out of that potentially great market. The memorial was referred to Secretary of State John Sherman, who replied as follows to A. E. Orr, President of the Chamber of Commerce:

This Government having been the first to bring about the opening of the ports of China to foreign commerce, and the commercial relations of the United States with the Chinese Empire having been of large and growing importance during the forty years since its treaties with that Empire went into effect, this Department necessarily feels a deep interest in conserving and expanding the volume of trade with that country. I have pleasure, therefore, in assuring the Chamber of Commerce of the State of New York that this subject is being given the most careful consideration.[42]

The letters and memorials quoted above are only a few examples of many that could be cited to demonstrate that the important business interests were deeply concerned with the need for foreign markets before the outbreak of the Spanish-American War, and were concerned, too, at the danger of pre-emption of these markets by European interests. In this connection, John J. McCook's report of a meeting with the heads of the Standard Oil Company, America's leading trust, in the fall of 1896, is significant. McCook wrote that the Standard Oil people were extremely interested in "Manifest Destiny in Asia," and added: "Mr. [Henry M.] Flagler thought that the increase of Russian influence in China after the railway [being constructed by Russia] was completed would be hurtful to them as Russia would of course use all its power to have their petroleum, which has become a large article of commerce with them, used in China and in all countries coming under their influence."[43]

Not long after the start of the Spanish-American War, Henry Cabot Lodge, in a letter to Theodore Roosevelt, expressed the conviction that the McKinley administration had committed itself to the "large policy we both desire."[44] By this Lodge meant using intervention in Cuba as the stepping stone for expansion in the Far East through the acquisition of Spain's Pacific possessions. Many American businessmen were fully committed to the "large policy" long before May 1, 1898. They prodded the government and the government responded. On October 14, 1900, the *Daily People* reminded the American people that "in 1895, the American capitalists organized the American Manufacturers Association, later the American Asiatic Association, etc., to reach into foreign trade." Later, with the cooperation of the McKinley administration, "they proceeded with the further formation of Trusts at a terrific rate, in order better to encounter the world's markets.[45] By 1898 they were ready, and determined to aid in forcing open the Chinese market, the last considerable unexploited market in the world. Hence occupation of the Philippines as a base at the doorway of China." It continued:

Hence the Spanish-American War, whereby while fighting Spain in the Antilles, the color of plausibility could be given to the seizure of the Philippines as belonging to the same power. Observe that Manila, so absolutely disconnected from the Cuban question that it lies almost directly straight through the earth from us and Cuba, 8000 miles beneath our feet, was where the first battle was fought! Cuba was simply the fulcrum of the lever used by the capitalists in prying the "Open Door" of China.

The *Daily People* ignored the fact that there were American businessmen who had direct economic interests in Cuba, and, as we have seen, had for three years prior to the war been repeatedly calling attention to the losses they were sustaining because of the government's refusal to intervene. Most of them were elated by the steps taken by McKinley for intervention, and they urged prompt and efficient measures to restore peace in the island, which would mean the restoration of a most valuable field for investment and trade. To what degree were they joined by other business interests? My own research demonstrates that while much business sentiment, especially in the East, opposed war with Spain in the early months of 1898, primarily because "it would endanger our currency stability, interrupt our trade and threaten our coasts and commerce,"[46] numerous business spokesmen began to emphasize that uncertainty, generated by the Cuban Revolution, was holding back business recovery. By mid-March many began to feel that even war was better than continued suspense, and that war would not seriously affect American business, for after the first shock, "things would whirl as usual."[47] Senator Proctor's speech had a marked effect upon the business community. The *Wall Street Journal* declared: "Senator Proctor's speech converted a great many people in Wall Street who had heretofore taken the ground that the United States had no business to interfere in a revolution on Spanish soil." For one thing, the men in Wall Street and other business areas had been skeptical of sensational reports in the "yellow press" about terrible conditions in Cuba, and Proctor, who had a reputation for being a moderate, convinced them that these reports were not exaggerated. Then again, Proctor did much to allay conservative fears that if Spanish domination was removed, "the people of Cuba would be revolutionary." The fact that the white population of Cuba was growing more rapidly than the decreasing Negro population, the fact that many educated and intelligent people lived on the island, and "the large influx of American immigration and money," Proctor assured conservatives, "would all be strong factors for stable institutions."[48]

With the stock market moving from one level to another, there was an increasing cry from the business community for an immediate solution. Such business giants as John Jacob Astor, William Rockefeller, Stuyvesant Fish, Thomas Fortune Ryan, and John Gates declared themselves for a more belligerent policy toward Spain, and J. Pierpont Morgan joined the group in late March, 1898, when he declared that nothing more could be obtained by arbitration.[49] At the same time, a leading New York journalist sent a telegram to a friend of McKinley which was passed on to the President: "Big corporations here now believe we will have war. Believe all would welcome it as relief to suspense. . . ."[50] On the declaration of war, *American Banker* noted, "call loan rates which had averaged about 2 percent in February rose sharply during March and touched 5 percent at the opening of hostilities."[51] The approach of war, in other words, had had a highly stimulating effect on American capital!

With the support of a substantial section of, if not the entire, business community, McKinley moved to war. Thus it is clear that Pratt's conclusion that most big businessmen opposed the declaration of war in 1898 requires a thorough re-evaluation. Likewise in need of re-evaluation is the concept in many historical works that the President moved hesitantly and fearfully under the impact of a popular clamor too great for him to withstand.[52] As Ernest R. May puts this thesis, "mass hysteria" compelled President McKinley to lead his country "unwillingly toward a war that he did not want for a cause in which he did not believe."[53] A corollary to this thesis is that McKinley moved to war without being aware of, to say nothing of being influenced by, the requirements of expansion to meet the needs of American business for foreign markets. McKinley, like most American leaders, May argues, was "at most only incidentally concerned about real or imagined interests abroad."[54]

McKinley moved resolutely to war, following a course mapped out months before, and in so doing contemptuously ignored the overwhelming popular and

Congressional demand for recognition of the independence of the Cuban Republic. In fact, he was so indifferent to popular clamor that he steadfastly refused to yield to almost universal popular demand to recognize Cuban belligerency, much less Cuban independence.

A study of what McKinley did and said reveals that the demands of the business community and of the political and intellectual expansionists met a very favorable response from the President.[55] McKinley delivered the keynote address at the organizational meeting of the National Association of Manufacturers in 1895, and he pointed out to these leading industrialists, organized to push trade overseas, that industry as a whole "cannot be kept in motion without markets." Foreign markets were essential "for our surplus products." As President, McKinley gave the featured address at the 1897 meeting of the Philadelphia Commercial Museum, also organized to push overseas economic expansion. "No worthier cause [than] the expansion of trade," he declared, ". . . can engage our energies at this hour."[56]

Like all advocates of the "large policy," McKinley called for a big navy and an increase in the American merchant marine. Like them, too, he advocated the immediate annexation of the Hawaiian Islands, recommending it as soon as he assumed office on the grounds of inevitable destiny. When the treaty was first submitted to the Senate, he referred to annexation as the "inevitable consequence" of history and the following year, he observed that annexation was "manifest destiny." McKinley worked to implement other parts of the expansionist program. Upon becoming President, he moved toward the ownership and construction of an Isthmian canal. He also tried to purchase Cuba, and he would have annexed the island or placed it under a protectorate if the Spanish had been willing to sell. As John D. Offner writes in his study of McKinley's foreign policy: "McKinley's naval ideas and his interest in acquiring Hawaii, Cuba, and an American canal appear to form a well-rounded plan of expansion and development of American power . . . [and]his acts indicate that he was aware of the currents of expansionism behind a more comprehensive foreign policy."[57]

These "currents of expansionism" played a crucial part in the decision to go to war. McKinley was aware of the relationship between military action against Spain over Cuba and the establishment of an American base of operation in the Philippines from which to venture into the lucrative Far Eastern markets. He talked about this connection with Theodore Roosevelt and others as early as September, 1897, and he was involved in the plans which readied the entire Pacific campaign for immediate action even before the war was officially declared. Timothy G. McDonald puts it well in his article, "McKinley and the War with Spain":

McKinley had his eyes on the Philippines as well as Cuba and wished to wage war on both fronts if war came. . . . Exactly when McKinley began to take an interest in the Philippines is uncertain. We do know, however, that strategic discussions involving those islands were underway not later than September 21, 1897. Quite possibly, Spain's Far Eastern possessions occupied the thoughts of Washington strategists from the moment McKinley's diplomatic offensive commenced. . . . In September of 1897, McKinley and his advisors were discussing both operations, but only the attack on the Philippines was carried out. Further, virtually everyone concerned knew the importance of the Philippines and there was general knowledge within and without the government that Americans had better hasten the coming of their Asian base, given the development of China.

American business leaders, increasingly concerned with world markets, heard disquieting reports in the fall of 1897. European nations, it appeared, were plotting to restrict the potentially vast Far Eastern markets for American staples. Washington shared this concern—on December 24, 1897, European efforts to dismember the Chinese Empire provided the principal topic at a Cabinet meeting in the White House. One of the participants told reporters that the President intended to keep a watchful eye upon the situation in order that full protection be given to the interests of the United States in China. Again, toward the end of January in 1898, McKinley assured American businessmen, in a speech before the National Association of Manufacturers in New York City, that America must reoccupy the fields temporarily lost to her and go on to peaceful conquests of new and greater fields of trade and commerce. American naval power, based in the Philippines, would be able to protect present and future American interests in East Asia. Keeping these factors in mind, it would appear that the decision to attack the Philippines was crucial. As a matter of fact, McKinley planned the American conquest of the Philippines almost before the echoes of gunfire at Manila Bay had ceased. . . .

To put the matter briefly, eliminating Spain from both Cuba and the Philippines were equal objectives. . . .[58]

To put it again briefly: the Cuban policy of the United States culminating in the use of force against Spain had its root in the rise of monopoly capitalism and its drive for markets. There were political, social and psychological roots, too, and no analysis of the road to war can ignore humanitarian sentiments, the role of the press, the sinking of the *Maine,* the influence of the ideologists of expansionism. But these reinforced economic factors. The predominance of economic factors in the sequence of events which led to the outbreak of conflict between the United States and Spain has been sufficiently demonstrated in recent historiography to warrant the conclusion that the Spanish-American War was indeed an imperialist war.

## NOTES

1. New York, 1961, pp. 23–24. Later in his book, Professor May forgets this statement and contradicts himself, emphasizing only that mass hysteria, developed over the Cuban situation in 1896 and again in 1897, compelled President McKinley to lead his country "unwillingly toward a war which he did not want for a cause in which he did not believe" (*ibid.,* p. 237). But he himself pictures McKinley in December, 1897, a period not marked by "mass hysteria," as having concluded that if Spain's reforms should not have brought peace to Cuba by the opening of the rainy season in the spring, intervention would be necessary. Certainly, then, when McKinley asked Congress for intervention, he was only carrying into effect a program decided upon months before.

2. *Labour Leader,* June 4, 1898.

3. James Louis Whitehead, "French Reaction to American Imperialism, 1895–1908," unpublished Ph.D. thesis, University of Pennsylvania, 1943, pp. 77–79.

4. *The People,* April 24, 1898.

5. *Ibid.,* April 17, 24, May 1, 8, 15, 22, 29, 1898.

6. *World's Work,* January, 1902, p. 224; New York *Tribune,* March 23, 1902.

7. While Hobson focused on symptoms of trustified expansionism, Lenin concentrated on the whole system of capitalism in its imperialist stage, showing the inevitable path which imperialism must follow. Again, whereas Hobson found it possible to reform capitalism, Lenin called for its abolition, insisting that imperialism was inevitable in capitalism and could not be reformed.

8. J. A. Hobson, *Imperialism, A Study,* London, 1938, pp. 77–78; V. I. Lenin, *Imperialism: The Highest Stage of Capitalism,* New York, 1939, p. 15.

9. Harold U. Faulkner, *American Economic History,* New York, 1924, pp. 624–25.

10. Harry Elmer Barnes, *World Politics in Modern Civilization,* New York, 1930, p. 233.

11. Charles A. Beard, *The Idea of National Interest,* New York, 1934, pp. 65–70, 78–83.

12. Louis M. Hacker, "The Holy War of 1898," *American Mercury*, XXI (November, 1930), 326.

13. Marcus M. Wilkinson, *Public Opinion and the Spanish-American War: A Study in War Propaganda*, Baton Rouge, La., 1932, p. 132.

14. Joseph E. Wisan, *The Cuban Crisis as Reflected in the New York Press, 1895-1898*, New York, 1934, p. 458.

15. George W. Auxier, Jr., "Middle Western Newspapers and the Spanish-American War, 1895-1898," *Mississippi Valley Historical Review*, XXVI (1940), 528-29. Yet in his unpublished doctoral dissertation, which is a much more careful survey of Midwestern opinion, Dr. Auxier notes that "especially from about the middle of March 1, 1898 . . . the economic motive stands out in relief as the administration papers gradually gave way to the war sentiment and the opposition editors more readily admitted the Marxian implication of our purposes." He concludes that editors of a representative cross-section of the press, though divided in their attitudes regarding Cuban belligerency, "seemed primarily interested in assisting the President bring back domestic prosperity." ("The Cuban Question as Reflected in the Editorial Columns of Middle Western Newspapers, 1895-1898," unpublished Ph.D. thesis, Ohio State University, 1938, pp. 21, 209, 295-99.)

16. These influential politicians and intellectuals were Alfred T. Mahan, Theodore Roosevelt, Henry Cabot Lodge, Henry Adams, and his younger brother Brooks. They formed a loose coterie that vigorously sought a policy of expansion. Mahan selected the commercial needs of a great power as the foundation of his theory, and argued that a large navy and foreign bases were necessary to protect markets and a sizable merchant fleet. Applying his general theory to the United States, he pointed out that basic to American growth were annexation of Hawaii, construction and ownership of an Isthmian Canal, and control of Cuba. Lodge and Roosevelt accepted Mahan's ideas as the basis for their "large policy," which called for expansion of national interests. They set out to make their country the leading power in the Western hemisphere, "possessed of a great navy, owning and controlling an Isthmian canal, holding naval bases in the Caribbean and the Pacific, and contesting on at least even terms with the greatest powers, the naval and commercial supremacy of the Pacific Ocean and the Far East." (Julius W. Pratt, "The 'Large Policy' of 1898," *Mississippi Valley Historical Review*, XIX [1932], 223.)

Brooks Adams, related to Lodge through marriage and a friend of Roosevelt, published a volume in 1895, *The Law of Civilization and Decay*, in which he contended that an imperialistic nation was healthier than one content with its own borders, and advocated American control of the Western hemisphere and economic dominance of Asia. His brother, Henry, worked actively in Washington in favor of intervention in Cuba.

17. Julius W. Pratt, "American Business and the Spanish-American War," *Hispanic American Historical Review*, XIX (May, 1934), 163-201. See also his *Expansionists of 1898: The Acquisition of Hawaii and the Spanish Islands*, Baltimore, 1936, pp. 22, 230-316. Actually, this thesis had been somewhat casually advanced as early as 1928 by Leland H. Jenks: "If ever there was a war which the people of the country, as distinguished from their political and business leaders demanded, it was the war which the United States began on April 21, 1898." (*Our Cuban Colony: A Study in Sugar*, New York, 1928, p. 57.)

18. Cf. Oscar Handlin, *Chance or Destiny: Turning-points in American History*, Boston, 1945, pp. 121-42; John D. Hicks, *The American Nation*, Boston, 1949, p. 113; Sidney Hook, *The Hero in History*, Boston, 1955. pp. 53-54.

19. Charles A. Beard, *Giddy Minds and Foreign Quarrels: An Estimate of American Foreign Policy*, New York, 1939, p. 236.

20. Quoted in Foster R. Dulles, *America's Rise to World Power*, New York, 1955, p. 41.

21. New York, 1959, p. 223.

22. Compare Dulles, *America in the Pacific*, New York, 1932, pp. 227-35, with *China and America*, Princeton, N.J., pp. 101-04; *The Imperial Years*, New York, 1956, pp. 165-83; and *America's Rise to World Power*, pp. 40-41. In 1965 Dulles wrote that "economic considerations had little to do with the popular sentiment" that led to war in 1898. (*Prelude to World Power: American Diplomatic History, 1860-1900*, New York, 1965, p. 89.)

23. *The President Makers*, New York, 1940, p. 79.

24. *The Rise of Modern America, 1865-1951*, New York, 1951, p. 185.

25. *A Diplomatic History of the American People*, New York, 1950, p. 504.

26. *A Diplomatic History of the United States*, rev. ed., New York, 1936, p. 437.

27. *The Far Eastern Policy of the United States*, New York, 1938, pp. 8–9.

28. "The Needless War with Spain," in *Times of Trial*, edited by Allan Nevins, New York, 1958, pp. 179–86.

29. "Manifest Destiny and the Philippines," in *America in Crisis*, edited by Daniel Aaron, New York, 1952, pp. 188–89.

30. Arthur Barcan, "American Imperialism and the Spanish American War," unpublished M.A. thesis, Columbia University, 1940, pp. 5, 11, 81, 100–01, 108–10.

31. Ralph Dewar Bald, Jr., "The Development of Expansionist Sentiment in the United States, 1885–1895, As Reflected in Periodical Literature," unpublished Ph.D. thesis, University of Pittsburgh, 1953, pp. 121–25, 215–16.

32. *Science & Society*, XXII (Spring, 1958), 129–43.

33. Sklar does not mention it, but in connection with this important point, it is necessary to add that a change occurred in the thinking in the business community on the cause of the Panic of 1893 and the ensuing depression. Originally it was explained as resulting from dangerous or outmoded monetary theories and policies but by 1895 there was increasing emphasis on overproduction and lack of markets as the basic cause. (See, in this connection, Thomas McCormick, " 'A Fair Field and No Favor': American China Policy during the McKinley Administration, 1897–1901," unpublished Ph.D. thesis, University of Wisconsin, 1960.)

34. The New York *Journal* complained in 1896 that "the areas of the world" were being "taken over by naval powers," and that the world's trade routes were falling into the hands of other nations. The United States was in danger, the *Journal* felt, of being entirely excluded from its "rightful share" (February 29, 1896).

35. *Science & Society*, XXIII (Spring, 1959), 133–62.

36. New York *Daily People*, October 14, 1900.

37. William Appleman Williams, *The Tragedy of American Diplomacy, 1750–1955*, New York, 1959, pp. 31, 32–33, 34; *The Contours of American History*, Cleveland & New York, 1961, pp. 349, 363–68; *The United States, Cuba and Castro*, New York, 1962, pp. 5–6. See also Williams' review of Ernest R. May's "Imperial Democracy: The Emergence of America as a Great Power" in *Studies on the Left*, III (1963), 94–99.

38. Thomas McCormick, *op. cit.*, pp. 145–46, 153–54; "Insular Imperialism and the Open Door: The China Market and the Spanish American War," *Pacific Historical Review*, XXXII (May, 1963), 155–69.

39. Ithaca, New York, 1963, pp. 385–406.

40. Francis B. Loomis to William R. Day, November 5, 1897, William R. Day Papers, Library of Congress.

41. Alfred T. Mahan, "Strategic Features of the Caribbean Sea and the Gulf of Mexico," *Harper's New Monthly Magazine*, XCV (October, 1897), 680–91. Mahan's article and his other writings of this period show how inaccurate is Morris Levy's conclusion that Mahan had no interest in the Philippines or other Asian areas before the war with Spain. (Morris Levy, "Alfred Thayer Mahan and United States Foreign Policy," unpublished Ph.D. thesis, New York University, 1964, pp. 163–64.)

42. A. E. Orr, President of the New York State Chamber of Commerce, to William McKinley, enclosing memorial, February 3, 1898, William McKinley Papers, Library of Congress; John Sherman to A. E. Orr, February 11, 1898, John Sherman Papers, Library of Congress.

43. John J. McCook to James H. Wilson, November 17, 1896, James H. Wilson Papers, Library of Congress. Henry M. Flagler was, with John D. Rockefeller, the founder of the Standard Oil Company. "It is generally agreed that, next to Rockefeller himself, Flagler was the strongest man in the organization" (*Dictionary of American Biography*, New York, 1946, VI, 451).

John J. McCook was a New York businessman and banker who was deeply involved in Cuban affairs, especially in the floating of bonds for the Cuban *Junta* in the United States. He was also interested in the development of investments and trade in the Far East.

44. Henry Cabot Lodge to Theodore Roosevelt, May 24, 1898, *Selections from the Correspondence of Theodore Roosevelt and Henry Cabot Lodge, 1884–1918*, New York, 1925, I, 278.

45. During 1898 gigantic mergers took place in copper refining, lead, sugar, salt, tobacco, cans, whiskey, baking, street railways, cigar-making, steel, and other industries.

46. The New York *Financial Record*, however, argued that war with Spain would not depress securities nor injure business but would rather vastly increase the net earning power of every security sold on the market (November 4, 1897). The Chicago *Economist* called fallacious the argument that war would seriously hurt business (Vol. XIX, February 26, 1898). The Chattanooga *Tradesman* stated that a small prospect of war had already stimulated the iron trade in certain lines (March 1, 1898). The *Manufacturers' Record*, organ of Southern industrialists, declared in late March, 1898, that war would open vast new markets for American industry and would have no serious effect on the securities market (reprinted in *The State*, Columbia, South Carolina, March 26, 1898). On April 23, 1898, *Bradstreets'* declared: "For nearly two months the New York banks, and the money market of the country generally, have been preparing for the events of the present week" (p. 257). On the same day, the New York *Journal of Commerce* observed: "Naturally, the business sentiment of the country has not protested with any unqualified earnestness against the influences under which we have drifted into war." On April 25 President McKinley asked Congress for a joint resolution recognizing a state of war with Spain. Both the House and the Senate passed the resolution by a voice vote the same day.

47. *Commercial and Financial Chronicle*, LXVI (February 12, 1898), 308; *Bankers' Magazine*, LVI (March, 1898), 358; John C. Spooner to Frank Bigelow, March 8 1898, John C. Spooner Papers, Library of Congress.

48. *Wall Street Journal*, March 19, 1898; *Congressional Record*, 55th Congress, 2nd Session, pp. 5916–19; Russell Hastings to William McKinley, March 27, 1898, William McKinley Papers, Library of Congress.

49. Washington *Post*, March 27, 1898; Washington *Evening Star*, April 6, 1898.

Thomas Beer in his biography of Mark Hanna writes that his (Beer's) father "heard in Washington that Wall Street was solidly lined up against a war with Spain. He retired to New York and men grabbed his arm . . . asking what this insane Hanna meant by trying to head off the war? He noted that John Jacob Astor, John Gates, Thomas Fortune Ryan, William Rockefeller, Stuyvesant Fish, John Pierpont Morgan, and many others in Wall Street were avidly for war" (Thomas Beer, *Hanna*, New York, 1929, p. 200).

50. William C. Reick to John Russell Young, March 25, 1898, telegram in William McKinley Papers, Library of Congress.

51. *American Banker*, LXIV (1898), 9.

52. Margaret Leech, *In the Days of McKinley*, New York, 1959, p. 180.

53. May, op. cit., p. 269.

54. *Ibid.*, p. 270. See also Pratt, *Expansionists of 1898*, pp. 326–27.

55. Williams, *The Contours of American History*, p. 363.

56. *American Naval Policy as Outlined in Messages of the Presidents of the United States from 1790*, Washington, D.C., 1922, p. 22; Pratt, *Expansionists of 1898*, pp. 326–27; *Senate Report 681*, 56th Congress, 2nd Session, pp. 65–67.

57. John L. Offner, "President McKinley and the Origins of the Spanish-American War," unpublished Ph.D. thesis, Pennsylvania State University, 1957, p. 81.

58. Timothy McDonald, "McKinley and the Coming of the War with Spain," *The Midwest Quarterly*, VII (April, 1966), 233–35.

# insular imperialism and the open door-the China market and the Spanish American war

## THOMAS J. McCORMICK

Thomas J. McCormick, author of *China Market: America's Quest for Informal Empire,* shows that the acquisition of the Philippines and Hawaii was the result of a conscious policy of insular imperialism.

   The Open Door expansionists in the McKinley administration saw the newly acquired areas as strategic stepping stones toward the conquest of the heralded China market. McCormick contradicts those mainstream historians who proclaim that, since no further possessions were acquired, the Philippines and Hawaii were only temporary excursions into imperialism. He concludes that their acquisition was part of an overall commitment to informal empire and thus served the larger purpose of American neocolonialism.

---

Territorial expansion, in fact, has been but an incident of the commercial expansion. . . . The recent acquisitions are but outposts of our future trade, and their chief importance consists not in their own resources or capabilities, but in their unquestionable value as gateways for the development of commercial intercourse with . . . the Far East. —*Frederic Emory,* 1899[1]

Amerian policy in the Pacific, immediately before and during the war with Spain, wrote the final ending to the "Cobdenized" expansionism that had flourished under Grover Cleveland. The new appróach was significantly different. To be sure, Cleveland's "free-trade imperialism" and McKinley's "pragmatic expansionism" shared in common a great deal of intellectual real estate. Both accepted the industrial overproduction analysis and the corollary commitment to marketplace expansionism. Both opposed formal, administrative colonialism in heavily populated, major market areas (such as China), regarding it as materially and spiritually too burdensome for the potential rewards involved. Instead, both chose commercial open doors over closed colonies or spheres of influence. Both accepted (with some reluctance on Cleveland's part) the government's responsibility to act energetically to open new doors and

Thomas J. McCormick, "Insular Imperialism and the Open-Door—The China Market and the Spanish American War." *Pacific Historical Review,* © 1963 by the Pacific Coast Branch, American Historical Association. Reprinted from Volume XXXII, Number 2 (May 1963), pp. 155–169, by permission of the Branch.

prevent old ones from being closed. Both favored an isthmian canal as America's shortcut to Pacific markets. Both favored a better consular service to aid and advise American businessmen abroad. Both favored an enlarged battleship Navy to keep the main trade routes open. Both favored tariff revision (whether freer trade or reciprocity) to stimulate the export trade.

Yet for all these important points of identity, the McKinley era marked an important change in the tone and tactics of American expansionism—a change characterized by a more non-ideological, pragmatic approach; by more utilitarian, businesslike methods of doing a necessary job efficiently, but at the least possible cost. McKinley's policies were, in other words, essentially those of "pragmatic expansionism."

Specifically, the most obvious and vital difference centered on the question of insular imperialism. Among Democrats of the Cleveland ilk (as with Republicans of the Carl Schurz variety) anti-colonialism was an article of faith. Cleveland's rejection of Hawaiian annexation in 1893 and his later opposition to retention of the Philippines bore witness to that. But to Republicans like McKinley, weaned on the recent heritage of Seward, Grant, and Blaine, anti-colonialism was relative rather than absolute. One's right hand might affirm it in continental market areas, while one's left hand qualified it with a limited dose of "insular imperialism" in islands and enclaves that were potentially useful as strategic stepping-stones to those very same market areas. Such pragmatic niceties reflected the perceived realities that rapid communications necessitated oceanic cables and cable relay points; that an enlarged Navy demanded operational bases; that market penetration could be facilitated by nearby possessions; that steam technology required coaling stations. (As the New York Tribune put it in March 1898, "Coal Is King"—a fact that "The United States has begun to consider . . ." apparently in relationship to "Chinese waters.")[2] In the Pacific, Seward's purchase of the Aleutians and the occupation of Midway Island, Harrison's attempt to annex Hawaii, and McKinley's revival of that project in 1897 and again in early 1898 all manifested a conscious, rational effort to foster and protect American trade in an "open" Asia through effective control of the Kiska-Honolulu axis (an early nineteenth-century geopolitical idea of Russian origin).

Analyzed against this backdrop, America's insular acquisitions of 1898 were not products of "large policy" imperialism. Hawaii, Wake, Guam, and the Philippines were not taken principally for their own economic worth, or for their fulfillment of Manifest Destiny, or for their venting of the "psychic crisis." They were obtained, instead, largely in an eclectic effort to construct a system of coaling, cable, and naval stations for an integrated trade route which could help realize America's overriding ambition in the Pacific—the penetration and ultimate domination of the fabled China market.

From the very beginning of the Spanish-American War, the McKinley administration intended to retain a foothold in the Philippines as an "American Hong Kong," a commercial entrepot to the China market and a center of American military power. Formulation of this policy commitment began seven months before hostilities with Spain, when McKinley examined a Navy Department memorandum written by Assistant Secretary Theodore Roosevelt. This multipurpose paper made one especially bold suggestion: in the event of war with Spain, the Asiatic Squadron "should blockade, and if possible take Manila." Historical myth notwithstanding, it was a suggestion that fell on already prepared ground, for the influential Senator from Connecticut, Orville Platt, had earlier taken pains to impress upon the President "that Manila had become one of the most important ports of the Orient and that the importance of that station demanded most careful attention."

Temporarily put in abeyance by a short-lived détente with Spain in late 1897, the proposal was revived and made the basis of Roosevelt's famous February 25 orders instructing Commodore George Dewey to "start offensive operations in the Philippines" after eliminating the Spanish fleet. The view that this was simply a conspiratorial effort by "large policy" extremists misses two more significant facts: first, Roosevelt's superiors accepted his orders for the Philippine operations even though they unceremoniously countermanded nearly two-thirds of the other miscellaneous orders issued concurrently by the Assistant Secretary; second, the administration had already accepted the substance of Dewey's orders in principle and thereafter permitted the Naval War Board to incorporate the February 25 orders into overall strategy plans for the Pacific. Clearly, while Roosevelt's actions may have been precipitate, they fell within the main lines of the "large policies" of the administration. Of these, Roosevelt, as he privately admitted, was largely "ignorant."[3]

With the outbreak of war the McKinley administration rushed (with almost unseemly haste) to implement its designs upon the likeliest entrepôt, Manila, by determining to send an army of occupation to the Philippine capital. It made this decision on May 2 *before* fully credible news of Dewey's victory at Manila Bay reached Washington and it formally issued the call for Philippine volunteers on May 4, three days *before* an anxious, jittery Secretary of the Navy received authoritative word that the Asiatic Squadron was safe—not immobilized by heavy damages, as he feared. The size of the Army force was to be "not less than twenty thousand men"—quadruple the number recommended by Dewey "to retain [Manila] and thus control the Philippine Islands." It was a move that confirmed Roosevelt in his belief that "the Administration is now fully committed to the large policy." It also persuaded the *San Francisco Chronicle,* on May 4, to splash across its front page the prophetic headline: "We Will Hold the Philippines."

On May 11, in one of the most important (and overlooked) decision-making sessions in American history, McKinley and his cabinet gave definite form to their war aims in the Pacific by approving a State Department memorandum calling for Spanish cession to the United States of a suitable "coaling station," presumably Manila. The islands as a whole, however, were to remain with Spain. Acting within the framework of this decision, McKinley on May 19 endowed the commander of the expeditionary force with sufficiently broad powers to effect "the severance of the former political relations of the inhabitants and the establishment of a new political power." Simultaneously, he instructed his Secretary of the Treasury to undertake a study of the islands with an eye "to substitut[ing] new rates and new taxes for those now levied in the Philippines." The stated purpose of both orders, as well as a similar one to Dewey (which he was to "interpret . . . liberally"), was to "[give] to the islands, while in the possession of the United States, that order and security which they have long since ceased to enjoy." Shortly thereafter, on June 3, when it became apparent that the great distance between Manila and Honolulu demanded an intermediate coaling and cable station, the President broadened the American position to include "an island in the Ladrones" (Marianas). The choice made was Guam, and the United States Navy promptly seized it.[4]

As of early June, then, the administration envisioned postwar control only of Manila and Guam as way stations to the orient. But dramatic events swiftly undercut this limited resolve and for a critical fortnight set American policy aimlessly adrift. First of all, as the State Department itself noted, the emergence of the Philippine "insurgents" as "an important factor" made it increasingly doubtful that the islands—minus Manila—could be returned to effective Spanish sovereignty. What then—bestow the largess of Philippine independence but with the stipulation of American control in Manila? Certainly it was within American power to impose such a solution upon the insurgents, by force if necessary. Moreover, the revolutionaries might even have accepted it peacefully, especially since they themselves had offered (as far back as November 1897) to turn over "two provinces and the Custom House at Manila" in exchange for an alliance against Spain (though theoretically these would not be permanent cessions but simply collateral pledges against eventual Filipino repayment for American aid). Nevertheless, relinquishing the rest of the islands ran counter to the administration belief that "if we evacuate, anarchy rules"; that (as Dewey later noted) "The natives appear unable to govern."

This presumption that an independent Philippines would be strife-ridden and unstable raised, in turn, the most frightening spectre of all: European intervention, especially by Germany, who considered herself heir-apparent to Spain's insular empire in the Pacific. Actually, the threat was not to American designs on Manila—notwithstanding the Continental feeling that an American foothold in the islands would "complicate the Eastern Question" or the seemingly hostile presence of the German squadron in Manila harbor. Given Germany's diplomatic isolation, Europe's divisiveness, and England's pro-American stance, there was little likelihood of another 1895-type intercession to deprive the victor of his spoils.[5] Germany herself made this clear on several fronts by mid-July. In Berlin one high-ranking German official assured Ambassador White "that Germany does not want large annexations and could not afford to take the Philippine Islands if they were offered her." And in London the German Ambassador told Hay that his government had "no disposition to interfere with, or deprive [the United States] of [her] rights of conquest in any direction." It was on the basis of this and other collaborating evidence that Hay advised the President that he could "now make war or make peace without danger of disturbing the equilibrium of the world."[6]

The real and continuing danger was German intervention against a weak, fledgling republic that might well render the isolated American position in Manila more vulnerable than useful. This was no chimera! By mid-June, Andrew White had already confirmed what the State Department feared: that Germany would use the expected "anarchy, confusion and insecurity under a 'Philippine Republic'" as an excuse "to secure a stronghold and centre of influence in that region." Less than a month later, Germany informed White (and Hay as well) that she expected "a few coaling stations" and "a naval base" in the Philippines (not to mention control of the Carolines and "predominant" influence in Samoa). Nor did the passage of time and the solidification of American intentions eliminate such German ambitions. Even after the armistice with Spain, rumors flowed freely that Germany still sought "the Sulu islands" in the southern Philippines—rumors given great credence by Assistant Secretary of State John Bassett Moore. And in late October the State Department continued to receive "trustworthy information" that if the United States failed to take all the Philippines, Germany has "every intention to establish a foothold there."[7]

Rival intervention or nationalistic revolution: either could undermine American plans for Manila. Unable to decide on a course of action, American policy lay momentarily immobilized—at a time when the growing crisis in China itself least afforded the luxury of prolonged indecision. On the one hand, intensified rumors that Russia would close Talienwan to foreign commerce and that she regarded her southern Manchurian leases as "integral portions of Russian territory" weakened the already shaky underpinnings of the open door in that key commercial area. At the same time England's extension of her Hong Kong settlement and her monopolistic approach to Yangtze Valley developments seemed to indicate that nation's growing estrangement from her traditional open door approach, and threatened to leave American policy in China diplomatically isolated.[8] In this deteriorating framework, any sustained impasse over Philippine policy incurred the risk of letting American hopes in China go by default. Against the formidable hosts of Philippine insurgency, German antagonism, and crisis in China, the limited American policy commitment of June 3 (for Manila and Guam) seemed an ineffectual one indeed. Realizing the situation, the McKinley administration in mid-June made a determined effort to break the bind by initiating three dramatic and interrelated moves in Hawaii, China, and the Philippines, designed to increase American influence and leverage in the western Pacific.

On June 11, 1898, the administration once more reactivated the sagging debate on Hawaiian annexation. First proposed by McKinley a year earlier, that venture had floundered amidst diplomatic complications with Japan—complications that produced in Navy circles much anxiety as well as grand proposals for naval construction, but which elicited from most administration officials the calmer conviction that firmness, candor, and patience would resolve matters satisfactorily. (Even Roosevelt, for all his agitation about "the Japs . . . feeling decidedly ugly about Hawaii," was "very sure their feelings will not take any tangible form.") When American diplomacy did successfully hurdle the Japanese obstacle, the administration revived the project and placed an annexationist treaty before the Senate in early 1898. There the partitioning crisis in China proved to be *nearly* decisive, as sentiment grew (in the words of Senator Frye) "that the state of affairs in China makes the annexation of Hawaii to the United States a necessity." Nevertheless, the treaty barely failed of the necessary two-thirds ratification, apparently killing any prospects of annexation for at least a year.[9]

By early June, however, the Philippine question and the general Far Eastern situation made it both propitious and imperative that the Hawaiian project be revived in the hope of strengthening America's hand in the Pacific basin (on the long-standing belief held by Mahan and many Americans that Hawaii was the key to "commercial and military control of the Pacific").[10] The ensuing debate on the joint congressional resolution was something of a dress rehearsal for the "great debate" that lay seven months ahead. It was predicated clearly on the assumption that passage of the Hawaiian annexation resolution made retention of the Philippines both possible and likely, while a defeat might foreshadow a similar fate for any territorial aspirations in the oriental archipelago. Congressman William Alden Smith made these and other links explicit with his statement, "If we will take the Hawaiian Islands, hold on to the Philippines, and cultivate good neighborship with the Orient, to which they are the key, the expansion of our commerce will be augmented a thousandfold."[11]

In the actual debate, administration spokesmen hammered the same theme: "we must have Hawaii to help us get our share of China." America needed Hawaii not only for its own economic or cultural worth but also for its commercial and military value as a stepping-stone to the China market. The influential Iowa Representative, William P. Hepburn, captured the theme best when he declared: "I can distinguish between a colonial policy and a commercial policy. I can distinguish between the policy that would scatter colonies all over the islands of the sea and the lands of the earth and that policy which would secure to us simply those facilities of commerce that the new commercial methods make absolutely essential."

Other annexationists offered their own variations. Hawaii, they exclaimed, would give the United States "strategic control of the North Pacific"; "a permanent share in the mighty commerce which beats its wings in the waves of the broad Pacific"; "this half-way house to the great markets of the East"; "a harbor which will enable us to protect with out fleet our commerce in the Far East"; and a necessary "crossroads" for "our rapidly increasing commerce with the mighty hordes with whom we shall trade . . . across the Pacific." Even former opponents of annexation found such ideas persuasive. For example, Frederick H. Gillett, Republican Representative from Massachusetts, who earlier regarded Hawaii as "useless and unnecessary," now defined it as "our essential stepping-stone and base." And why? Simply because the triumph at Manila had given the United States the potential capacity to retard the "partitioning . . . in that vast and populous East, which is just entering into the commercial current of the world." Such expressions were mainly Republican (often midwestern), but a few Democrats and one Populist helped to swell the chorus.

Strikingly, even the opposition accepted the annexationists' chief premise that America needed commercial expansion into Asia. As one Democratic opponent on the House Foreign Affairs Committee put it, he favored "as earnestly as any man can the legitimate extension of our commerce"; nor was he "unmindful that the excessive production of our fields and factories must have an outlet." Some even admitted the modern necessity of commercial-military bases as accoutrements to marketplace expansionism, but they argued that the Pearl Harbor lease of 1886 and the Kiska holding in the Aleutians already gave "all the advantages, everything required." Most, however, stressed the laissez-faire, free-trade approach that "commercial expansion" could best be realized "by competition of quality and price," not by "annexation of territory"; in the words of the Minority Report of the House Foreign Affairs Committee: "Political dominion over the islands is not commercially necessary." But the point did not carry. On June 15 the House passed the annexation resolution by an overwhelming vote, 209 to 91. Three weeks later, after redundant and one-sided discussion (annexationists remained silent to hurry the process), the Senate affirmed the measure by a similar ratio.[12] Thus, on July 8, with McKinley's signature, America acquired her halfway house to the Philippines and China. The acquisition followed by only four days the American occupation of Wake Island, a move intended to meet the technological necessities of an additional cable base between Hawaii and Guam.

Synchronous with the push on Hawaiian annexation, the administration initiated the first step in an American economic offensive in China itself by proposing a government commission to China to recommend measures for trade

Thomas J. McCormick    **97**

expansion. Secretary of State William R. Day's supporting letter to Congress made it pointedly clear that an industrial production "of large excess over home consumption" demanded "an enlargement of foreign markets." He also made clear his conviction that "American goods have reached a point of excellence" which made fulfillment of that demand quite feasible. Analyzing the world market situation, he concluded that underdeveloped areas offered the best export outlets and that "nowhere is this consideration of more interest than in its relation to the Chinese Empire." Aware that "the partition of commercial facilities" in China threatened America's "important interests," the Secretary still contended that "the United States . . . is in a position to invite the most favorable concessions to its industries and trade . . . provided the conditions are thoroughly understood and proper advantage is taken of the present situation."

Congress failed to appropriate the necessary monies for the China commercial commission—as it would again fail in 1899 and 1900. But the chief reason was most revealing. Most who opposed the measure did so because they considered such one-shot missions to be ineffectual and an inadequate substitute for a thoroughgoing reform of our consular representative in China (and elsewhere as well). Nevertheless, the administration proposal—when coupled with subsequent prodding of Minister Conger to gain more "Precise knowledge . . . of the large and grave questions of commercial intercourse," and with intensive questioning of American consuls as to specific means to expand the China trade—served clear notice of American intent to take "proper advantage . . . of the present situation" in order to play a more active role in China.[13]

Simultaneously, on June 14 the administration capped its trio of dramatic moves by shelving the earlier decision to return the Philippines to Spain, thus opening the disposition of the islands to further examination. Thereafter, despite uneasiness over increased military and administrative burdens, there began a progressive redefinition of the desired area of American sovereignty: from Manila, to Luzon, and finally to the entire group. Significantly, this redefinition involved no real change in the focus of political power; those who influenced and made policy in June 1898 still did so at year's end. What changed was men's minds. As the powerful Mark Hanna put it, from the vantage point of late September, "conservative, far-seeing and thinking men in this country" who initially favored only retention of "a naval base and coaling station" were, "for the most part," the "same men . . . advocating the termination of Spanish rule in the whole group." It was an apt generalization that nicely mirrored the whole transformation of attitudes among the "prag-matic expansionists"—whether in Hanna's own mind, the editorial pages of the *Chicago Inter-Ocean,* or the foreign policy of William McKinley.[14]

For two months after the June 14 shift, American policy remained seemingly ambivalent on the vexing problem of what to retain in the Philippines. Even the armistice agreement of August appeared to beg the question by reserving the issue of "control, disposition, and government" for final peace negotiations. But the ambiguity was more apparent than real. Spain certainly sensed this and regarded the terms (especially in their original wording) as clear indication that "the United States intends to take the Philippine Islands group."[15] McKinley's refusal to entertain a Spanish proposal to cede only "a station or commercial base" simply confirmed this view. So did his initial evasiveness and his final out-of-hand rejection of repeated Spanish efforts to secure (in the President's words) "inadmissable reservations" to the effect that peace negotiations would consider only the problem of "administrative reforms," without questioning the "permanent sovereignty of Spain" in the Philippines. Failing at every such corner, Spain could only wait for the "veiled . . . intentions of the federal government" to reveal themselves in their anticipated fullness.[16]

McKinley's own cabinet already knew what Spain only feared. Confronted with a nearly even, three-way split between departmental secretaries (Manila, Luzon, or the whole prize?), the President—in the calculating but affable manner that was his trademark—simply maneuvered his subordinates into accepting a position he had already predetermined. The policy glossed over internal differences; gave him the flexibility to move in whatever direction changing circumstances might dictate; and allowed him the time and opportunity both to test and educate public opinion. In the process he crushed a move headed by "Judge Day" (and backed by the Secretaries of the Treasury and the Navy) to limit American commitment to "a hitching-post," simply by declining to put the proposal to a vote. (". . . I was afraid it would carry," he said, only half-facetiously.) In sealing this extremity, he left open only the question of how far to journey toward the other—Luzon or the entire group? The beginning of the final peace negotiations in early October found this question still unresolved. While the American commissioners were instructed to demand only Luzon, they were also to "accumulate all possible information" on the possible necessity of controlling the whole archipelago. And since three of the five commissioners already favored the latter possibility publicly, it seemed likely that the information accumulated would lend itself to their interpretation. Whatever, less than a month later, on October 25, McKinley himself finally cut the knot by broadening his instructions to include all the Philippines.[17]

In this evolution of Philippine policy, America's commercial stake in China played the primary role in the thinking of the business and government elite that chiefly shaped and supported McKinley's decisions. It also played a significant, though not paramount, part in the outlook of the military advisers who exercised a more limited but still crucial influence upon the President's policies.

Between June and October, economic and political leaders united vigorously in support of retaining all or a large part of the Philippines. But they de-emphasized the intrinsic worth of the islands and stressed instead their strategic relationship to China—both as a commercial stepping-stone and a political-military lever. Moreover, they increasingly affirmed that Manila alone would not suffice for these purposes, that the United States would have to take Luzon and perhaps the whole group. In part this support for enlarged control reflected the already pervasive fear that native revolution or European penetration might undermine the viability of American power in Manila. But it also indicated a growing belief, born of newly accumulated information, that the economic interdependence of the archipelago made efficient division most difficult. Charles H. Cramp, that renowned Philadelphia shipbuilder, aptly illustrated the impact of all these factors upon influential Americans when he asserted: "[Manila] is the emporium and the capital of the Philippines . . . and it exists because of that fact. . . . Can anyone suppose that with Manila in our hands and the rest of the Philippine territory under any other Government, that city would be of any value?"[18]

In the business world many associations, journals, and prominent individuals accepted and propagated the analysis that commercial ambitions in China *demanded* American control in the Philippines. Led by the NAM and the

American Asiatic Association, special business organizations urged retention of the islands "for the protection and furtherance of the commercial interests of our citizens in the Far East." In a survey of the trade journals of the country, the *Chicago Inter-Ocean* found it "remarkable with what unanimity they have advocated the retention of the Philippines." Even more remarkable was the unanimity of their reasoning: that (in the words of the *Insurance Advocate*) it would encourage "the teeming millions of the Middle Kingdom" to "buy largely from us"; that with "one-third of the human race within easy distance of us, coaling stations on the road, and Manila as the Hong Kong of Uncle Sam's alert and keen merchant trader," the result was preordained. Finally, save for a few prominent dissenters like Andrew Carnegie and Chauncey Depew, McKinley's many personal friends in the corporate world espoused similar viewpoints.[19] Typical in both its analysis and conclusion was the advice of Irving M. Scott, manager of the Union Iron Works, that America needed the Philippines as "a point of observation at or near the centre of activity." Predicting that "the world is ours commercially" if the United States preserved peace and the open door, Scott urged that "the implements must be on hand, the position must be secured, and a vigilant watch kept on every encroachment." He noted that "the first move has been made in China" and concluded that "nothing has so effectually stopped it as the occupation of Manila."

Most of McKinley's close associates in the federal government (many of whom were themselves products of the business community) pressed similar views upon their chief. There were exceptions, of course. Worthington C. Ford, head of the Bureau of Statistics, appeared to feel (like former Minister to China George F. Seward) that *"We do not want the Philippines at any price or under any circumstances."* A few others like Judge Day held largely to the position (as Carl Schurz summarized if for the President) that "all desirable commercial facilities" and "all naval stations needed could be secured without the annexation of populous territories," without "dangerous political entanglements and responsibilities." But most thought and counseled otherwise. The redoubtable Mark Hanna, State Department economic expert Frederic Emory, Charles Denby and his successor Edwin Conger, Comptroller of the Currency Charles G. Dawes, Assistant Secretary of the Treasury Frank A. Vanderlip, to name a few, all shared in general the conviction (as Vanderlip stated) that an American-controlled Philippines would be "pickets of the Pacific, standing guard at the entrances to trade with the millions of China and Korea, French Indo-China, the Malay Peninsula, and the islands of Indonesia." By October, McKinley's cabinet—led by his new Secretary of State, John Hay—was nearly as one in voicing that sentiment. Like Hanna two months earlier, they had apparently decided that "we can and will take a large share of the commerce of Asia . . . and it is better to strike for it while the iron is hot." Likewise, the dominant triumvirate on the peace commission—Whitelaw Reid, Cushman K. Davis, and William P. Frye—primarily saw "the great importance of the Philippines with reference to trade in China" and predicted that "if to [Hawaii] we now added the Philippines, it would be possible for American energy to . . . ultimately convert the Pacific Ocean into an American Lake."

Exerting a more narrow influence upon McKinley's Philippine policy was a third group, the military. In general the President's military advisers shared the widespread concern over the strategic relationship of the archipelago to the Asian mainland. Yet, attracted by the siren's call of *imperium* (in which they would play a prominent role), many military spokesmen also promoted retention of the Philippines as the first step toward an expansive territorial imperialism. These hopes were dashed as McKinley refused to heed their advice for a general American advance into Micronesia and the islands of the South China Sea. But military advice could claim one significant result: it resolved the President's ambivalence (shared by the business and government elite) between taking Luzon or the entire group by convincing him that the islands were an indivisible entity; that strategically and economically they were interdependent and inseparable. Especially persuasive were the lengthy and articulate reports of Commander R. B. Bradford and General Francis V. Greene. Coming in late September and early October, they were a decisive factor in broadening McKinley's instructions.[20]

The great repute of these business and government groups, coupled with their ready access to a like-minded Chief Executive, gave much weight to their contention (shared in part by the military) that American interests in China necessitated American sovereignty in the Philippines. But this view gained a powerful ally in the twin crisis in China itself during the fall of 1898. One side of the crisis was intensified partitioning of railroad concessions by the European powers. Explicit British modification of the open door by Acting Foreign Secretary Lord Balfour ("a concession must be given to someone, and when someone has got it, other people must be excluded . . ."), and the Anglo-German railroad accord of September delineating exclusive concessions spheres, in the Yangtze and Shantung areas respectively, both confirmed beyond doubt that the open door had no current relevance to the world of railroad invest-ments. From the McKinley administration's point of view, none of this helped American economic interests. True, it caused no consternation about the immediate future of American railroad investments, for the government still regarded such concessioneering (with some justification) as both inept and speculative. (For example, the State Department refused to protect the American China Development Company's newly acquired Hankow-Canton concession against "prejudice from foreign . . . interference," and it declined to support the company's half-interest option agreement with the British and China Corpo-ration as "a binding engagement upon the imperial Chinese Government.")[21] But the carving out of railroad spheres did further threaten the important American export trade by requiring American goods to travel from treaty port to market over European railroads. And as noted before, the prospect was not inviting, for these products might well encounter railroad rate discrimination which would render them less competitive.

Meanwhile, America's economic dreams faced another menace from a different quarter in China. In September 1898 a successful *coup d'état* by conservative, anti-foreign elements, headed by the Empress Dowager, managed to crush the pro-Western reform party surrounding the young Chinese Emperor. The new government immediately initiated administrative measures viewed by the United States as inimical to "commercial development" and the "pendulum of progress." Not only did conservative forces fail to control anti-foreign uprisings inspired by their own *putsch,* but Chinese troops and militiamen joined in them. Centered along projected Manchurian railroads, the violent demonstrations offered Russia an excuse for intervention to save her great railroad interests. The mere suggestion of such a prospect was sufficient to conjure up visions of a further fragmented China and a vitiated open door. Indeed, it probably explains the speed with which the McKinley administration met Conger's urgent request for gunboats and Marines. (The reinforcements came—and quickly—from Manila, offering an early illustration of the uses to which the Philippines could be put.)

These developments in China spawned first alarm, then action in Washington. The first move came in September with official renewal of inquiries to Russia and Germany concerning foreign trade policies in their spheres. Germany's replies seemed satisfactory and her action in opening Kiaochou as a "free port" even more so. But Russian refusal to give any "details of the completed lease" and her admission that she had not "as yet fully decided upon the administrative regulation" on foreign trade appeared to be foreboding retreats from earlier positions. State Department concern was translated in October into favorable action upon a textile industry petition concerning the Russian threat in China. Noting that half of America's cotton textile exports to China went to Russian-dominated areas, the petitioners demanded a "vigorous policy" to prevent "these markets" from being "eventually closed to our trade." Immediately the Department responded by instructing its embassy in St. Petersburg to "use every opportunity to act energetically" against Russian adoption of discriminatory trade policies in Manchuria.[22] Quite obviously, the American government regarded the crises in China as dangerous enough to warrant substantial reaction, and as further argument for control of the Philippines.

There can be no doubt that the Chinese question, illuminated by the opinions of business, government, and the military and by the growing crises in China, had a progressive impact upon the shaping of America's Philippine policy.[23] Nowhere is this more dramatically apparent than in the private, candid, and lengthy exchange between McKinley and his peace commissioners at a White House meeting on September 16. The President, speaking somberly and with none of his frequent evasiveness, explained his reasons for retaining all or part of the islands. Almost all of them were negative, embraced with obvious reluctance. The *only* positive and assertive determinant was his conviction that "our tenure in the Philippines" offered the "commercial opportunity" to maintain the open door, a policy which McKinley defined as "no advantages in the Orient which are not common to all." "Asking only the open door for ourselves," he told his commissioners, "we are ready to accord the open door to others." Explaining further, he made it clear that retention of the Philippines was no first step in an orgy of imperialism and jingoism, but simply a limited though important accoutrement to commercial expansion. "The commercial opportunity . . . associated with this opening," he declared, "depends less on large territorial possessions than upon an adequate commercial basis and upon broad and equal privileges."[24]

This last statement was more than mere rhetoric, and nothing proved it more than the President's policy in Micronesia during the last stages of peace negotiations with Spain. Acting on the advice of the Pacific Cable Company that Wake Island had certain technical drawbacks, the administration instructed its peace commissioners to negotiate for the purchase of "one of the Caroline Islands"—preferably Ualan (Kusaie)—"for cable purposes." Despite strong German protests that "Kusaie lies in the midst of German sphere" and that "Germany regards herself as the only competitor for the acquisition of the Carolines," the United States pressed on with its effort, offering Spain $1 million for the island and "cable-landing rights in other Spanish territory" (an offer which, in turn, provoked an even stronger German denunciation of the American "policy of seeking islands all over the world for coaling stations").

What happened next is most revealing. Declining the American offer, Spain made an even more dramatic counterproposal—the cession of *all* the Carolines and *all* the Marianas in exchange for open door status for Spain in Cuba and Puerto Rico. In so doing, Spain appeared to be playing directly into the hands of the Reid-Frye-Davis group (and some of the American military) who had favored total American control in those islands all along. (Indeed, Reid and Frye implied at one juncture a hope that Spain would break off peace negotiations, giving America an excuse to take the islands.) These three commissioners gave their enthusiastic endorsement to the project and asked for permission to negotiate along the lines of the Spanish proposal (though perhaps with a time limit on the open door for Spain). But McKinley and Hay refused to pay such a price for something they neither needed nor desired. Seeking only individual cable and coaling stations for limited purposes, they were in no way disposed to exercise indiscriminate sovereignty over numerous, widely dispersed islands; to plant the Stars and Stripes on every ocean-bound rock and pebble they could get. Hay rejected the Spanish offer out-of-hand by return cable on December 4, and there the matter died. The whole episode further illustrated that commercial needs, not Manifest Destiny, guided American decision-making in the Pacific basin; that the Open Door, not colonialism on a vast scale, was to remain the chief vehicle of American expansion.[25]

Thus the peace negotiations with Spain, initiated in September within the conscious framework of the Chinese question, concluded three months later on an identical note. Article IV of the treaty made clear the intimacy that bound Philippine and China policy: McKinley would keep his earlier promise to accord the open door in the Philippines, provided the United States received reciprocal treatment elsewhere in the orient. In actuality, this American open door was limited in time and scope, and it later vanished in the midst of emerging American economic aspirations in the Philippines themselves. But for the moment administration spokesmen regarded the proviso as key to future American policy in the Far East. Assistant Secretary of State A. A. Adee, that permanent fixture in the Department, stated unequivocally that "the open door paragraph is the most important"; and Whitelaw Reid, the peace commission's most powerful figure, insisted the open door for the Philippines "enables Great Britain and the United States to preserve a common interest and present a common front in the enormous development in the Far East that must attend the awakening of the Chinese Colossus."[26]

The final treaty arrangements on the Philippines were the outgrowth of an evolving set of circumstances dating back to 1895, when the combined impact of the American depression and the Sino-Japanese War offered both the need and the hope that China might become the great absorber of America's industrial surplus. Subsequent developments, culminating in the partitioning of late 1897 and early 1898, critically threatened the hope but in no way dissipated the need. They did, however, dictate the desirability of finding some vigorous means of safeguarding America's present and future commercial stake in the Chinese Empire. Fortunately, the Spanish-American War provided just such an opportunity, and the McKinley administration was quick to exploit it. The result was the effective thrust of American influence into the far Pacific. From Honolulu through Wake and Guam to Manila stretched a chain of potential coaling, cable, and naval stations to serve as America's avenue to Asia. Only the construction of an isthmian canal remained to complete the system.

The grand scheme was not imperial—in the narrow sense of the word. The insular possessions in the Pacific were not pieces of empire, per se, but stepping-stones and levers to be utilized upon a larger and more important stage—China. Paradoxically, American expansion was designed in part to serve an anti-imperial purpose of preventing the colonization of China and thus preserving her for open door market penetration: *the imperialism of anti-imperialism* ("neo-colonialism" in today's parlance). All this McKinley captured in his Presidential Message of December 5, 1898, when he declared that our "vast commerce . . . and the necessity of our staple production for Chinese uses" had made the United States a not "indifferent spectator of the extraordinary" partitioning in China's maritime provinces. Nevertheless, he continued, so long as "no discriminatory treatment of American . . . trade be found to exist . . . the need for our country becoming an actor in the scene" would be "obviated." But, he concluded, the fate of the open door would not be left to chance; it would be, he said, "my aim to subserve our large interests in that quarter by all means appropriate to the constant policy of our government."[27] Quite obviously, the fruits of the Spanish-American War had enormously multiplied the "appropriate . . . means" available to American policy-makers and had completed the setting for America's illusory search after that holy commercial grail—the China market.

## NOTES

1. Frederic Emory, "Our Commercial Expansion," *Munsey's Magazine*, XXII (1899), 544. Emory, as noted earlier, was chief of the State Department's Bureau of Foreign Commerce.

2. *New York Tribune*, March 22, 1898, 6.

3. Theodore Roosevelt to Henry Cabot Lodge, September 21, 1897, Letterbook, Roosevelt MSS; National Archives, Reference Group, hereafter NA, RG 59, *Consular Despatch*, enclosed clipping, O. F. Williams to William R. Day; George Dewey, *Autobiography of George Dewey*, New York, 1913, 179; Margaret Long, ed., *The Journal of John D. Long*, Ridge, N.H., 1956, 217; Margaret Leech, *In the Days of McKinley*, New York, 1959, 162, 195; Roosevelt to B. F. Tracy, April 18, 1898, Letterbook, Roosevelt MSS.

4. Russel A. Alger, *The Spanish-American War*, New York, 1901, 326; Leech, *Days of McKinley*, 210; George Dewey to John D. Long, May 13, 1898, McKinley MSS; Henry C. Lodge, ed., *Selections from the Correspondence of Theodore Roosevelt and Henry Cabot Lodge, 1884–1918*, New York, 1925, I, 299; *San Francisco Chronicle*, May 4, 1898, 1; State Department memorandum, May 9, 1898, John Bassett Moore MSS; John Bassett Moore memorandum, undated, Moore MSS; McKinley to the Secretary of War, May 19, 1898, McKinley MSS; McKinley to the Secretary of the Treasury, May 19, 1898, McKinley MSS; Charles H. Allen, Assistant Secretary of the Navy, to John Bassett Moore, undated, Moore MSS; State Department draft letter to Secretaries of the Treasury, War, and Navy, May 18, 1898, Moore MSS; NA, RG 59, *England Instructions* 32, strictly confidential, telegram, Day to John Hay, June 3, 1898; Leech, *Days of McKinley*, 212, 261.

5. NA, RG 59, *England Instructions* 32, strictly confidential, telegram, Day to Hay, June 14, 1898; NA, RG 59, *Consular Despatch* 19, Rounsevelle Wildman to Day, No. 19, November 8, 1897; *ibid.*, O. F. Williams to Day, September 5, 1898; Hay to Day, telegram, October 15, 1898, Moore MSS; NA, RG 59, *France Despatches* 115, No. 272, Horace Porter to Sherman, June 10, 1898; Thomas A. Bailey, "Dewey and the Germans at Manila," *American Historical Review*, XLV (1939), 59. For example, Joseph Chamberlain's famous "Birmingham speech" of May 13, 1898, was widely interpreted as a warning to other European powers to avoid any interference in the Spanish-American War. Tyler Dennett,

*John Hay: From Poetry to Politics,* New York, 1934, 219. See also relevant portions of Charles S. Campbell, Jr., *Anglo-American Understanding, 1898-1903,* Baltimore, 1957.

6. NA, RG 59, *Germany Despatches* 66, telegram, Andrew White to Day, July 12, 1898; Hay to Day, July 14, 1898, Moore MSS; Walter Millis, *The Martial Spirit,* Boston and New York, 1931, 333. Also Hay to Day, July 14, 1898, Moore MSS.

7. Andrew White to Day, June 18, 1898, Moore MSS; NA, RG 59, *Germany Despatches* 66, telegram, White to Day, July 12, 1898; Hay to Day, July 14, 1898, Moore MSS; Moore to Day, September 3, 1898, Moore MSS; Hay to Day, October 29, 1898, Moore MSS. Complica-tions with Germany must be placed within the context of general American distrust of Germany everywhere in the world by 1898—in Asia, Central and South America, the Caribbean, and Europe itself. For a good summary of this view, see Andrew White to Day, August 10, 1898, Moore MSS.

8. NA, RG 59, *China Despatches* 104, No. 2929, Denby to Sherman, May 15, 1898; *ibid.,* No. 2939, June 6, 1898; Joseph, *Foreign Diplomacy in China,* 337, 357-358. This uncertainty over British policy may have been the motivating factor in Hay's attempt to renew discussion of the earlier proposal for joint support of the Open Door Policy. Though McKinley discouraged the attempt, he did try to encourage the British to hold the line on their China policy by obliquely prophesying that "the outcome of our struggle with Spain" might develop "the need of extending and strengthening our interests in the Asiatic Continent." Day to Hay, July 14, 1898, Hay MSS.

9. Roosevelt to Mahan, May 3, 1897, Letterbook, Roosevelt MSS; *ibid.,* Roosevelt to Long, September 30, 1897. For a good summation of the Japanese views see NA, RG 59, *Notes from Japanese Legation* 6, No. M163, Hoshi to Sherman, July 10, 1897. Roosevelt to Long, June 23, 1897, Letterbook, Roosevelt MSS; *Chicago Inter-Ocean,* January 6, 1898, 6. As late as mid-May 1898 the New York Times quoted one Senator that "there is not the slightest probable chance for the House joint resolution to annex the Hawaiian Islands to pass Congress at this session." *New York Times,* May 17, 1898, 2. For a general discussion of the Hawaiian issue in 1897 and early 1898, see Walter LaFeber, *The New Empire: An Interpretation of American Expansion, 1860-1898,* Ithaca, N.Y., 1963, 362-370.

10. Alfred T. Mahan, "Hawaii and Our Future Sea Power," *Forum,* XV (1893), 7. Also Henry Cabot Lodge, "Our Blundering Foreign Policy," *Forum,* XIX (1895), 17. Presumably Japan was given prior notification of the annexationist move, in line with an American promise in early May that "no decisive action would be taken in regard to the Hawaiian matter without duly informing [Japan]." Memorandum of conversation with Japanese Minister, May 6, 1898, Moore MSS.

11. *Congressional Record,* 55th Cong., 2nd Sess., 6006-6007.

12. George F. Hoar, *Autobiography of 70 Years,* New York, 1903, II, 308; *Congressional Record,* 55th Cong., 2nd Sess., 6017; *ibid.,* 5772, 5775, 5879, 5895, 5897, 5916, 5988, 5899, 5782-5783, 5904, 5780, 5924, 5925, 5904, 6016, 6019, 6712. According to the *New York Times,* "The advocates of annexation say they will make no speeches, leaving the opponents to occupy all the time to be consumed in debate."*New York Times,* June 20, 1898, 3.

13. *House Document* 536, 55th Cong., 2nd Sess; NA RG 59, *China Instructions* 5, No. 22, John Bassett Moore to Edwin H. Conger, August 30, 1898; NA RG 59, *China Despatches* 105, No. 65, Conger to Hay, October 12, 1898.

14. NA, RG 59, *England Instructions* 32, strictly confidential, telegram, Day to Hay, June 14, 1898; *New York Times,* October 1, 1898, 1. According to John Bassett Moore, even Theodore Roosevelt, a so-called "large-policy" imperialist, went through the same evolution of attitudes as Hanna and other pragmatists. In his uncompleted, unpublished autobiography, Moore recalled a "brief conversation" with Roosevelt, after the latter's resignation as Navy Assistant Secretary, in which Roosevelt "warned me against the acquisition of the Philippines, which lay far beyond what we had considered to be our sphere of government." Moore MSS. The editorial pages of the *Chicago Inter-Ocean* offer a beautiful micro-illustration of the transformation that Hanna described. Ambivalent and cautious in the beginning, by August the paper was ridiculing the idea that America could settle for "that insignificant thing—a coaling station in the East." Indeed, by mid-September it was concerned about McKinley's apparent indecision on the Philippines—until it deciphered that indecision as simply McKinleyite cunning in announcing only for Luzon while letting the realities of circumstance maneuver Spain into giving up the whole lot. See the editorial page (p. 6) of the *Inter-Ocean* for these dates in 1898: May 3,

May 30, June 8, June 11, June 27, July 16, July 30, August 8, August 17, September 12, September 17, and October 17.

15. *Spanish Diplomatic Correspondence and Documents, 1896–1900* (translation), Washington, D.C., 1905, 213–214; Day to McKinley, November 18, 1898, McKinley MSS; Memorandum of a McKinley interview with the French Ambassador, July 30, 1898, Moore MSS. The initial American draft of the armistice agreement used the word "possession" instead of "disposition." Spain regarded the choice as indicative of American designs against Spanish sovereignty in the islands. *Spanish Diplomatic Correspondence*, 213–214.

16. Day to McKinley, November 18, 1898, McKinley MSS; *Spanish Diplomatic Correspondence*, 215–216; *Papers Relating to the Foreign Relations of the United States, 1898*, lxiv (hereafter the short title, *Foreign Relations*, will be used); *ibid.*, 823.

17. Charles G. Dawes wrote McKinley that his "postponement of an immediate decision" on the Philippines "makes the right solution certain," because it would give time for further study and reflection—both by the administration and the people. Dawes to McKinley, August 10, 1898, McKinley MSS. Similarly, see Seth Low to McKinley, August 6, 1898, McKinley MSS. Charles S. Olcott, *The Life of William McKinley*, II, Boston and New York, 1916, 61, 63; Moorfield Storey and Marcial P. Lichauco, *The Conquest of the Philippines by the United States*, New York, 1926, 66–67; Leech, *Days of McKinley*, 286; Reid Diaries, September 16, 1898, Reid MSS. As early as June 6, Senator Frye had confessed that "The only fear I have about this war is that peace will be declared before we can get full occupation of the Philippines and Puerto Rico." Frye to James H. Wilson, Wilson MSS. Whitelaw Reid's public statements before his appointment to the peace commission led the *Inter-Ocean* to conclude that "the appointment indicates that the administration . . . is inclined to hold the Philippines." *Chicago Inter-Ocean*, September 6, 1898, 6. Similarly, Cushman K. Davis said in a Minneapolis speech on September 7 that "This government will secure from the situation in the Orient and in those waters whatever American courage, American honor and American valor have gained." *Chicago Inter-Ocean*, September 9, 1898, 6. For a firsthand account of the commissioners' views, see Reid Diaries, September 16, 1898, Whitelaw Reid MSS. The other two members dissented from the majority view of taking all the islands. Senator George Grey of Delaware opposed any political control but felt himself bound by the President's instructions to seek the island of Luzon. Judge Day, former Secretary of State, favored retention of Luzon only, coupled with a non-alienation pledge and an economic open door for the rest of the islands. Later, in a last-ditch effort to head off absorption of all the islands, he broadened his position to include most of the islands in the northern half of the archipelago. Undated Memorandum, Moore MSS. McKinley to Day, Letterbook, October 25, 1898, McKinley MSS; *Foreign Relations 1898*, 935.

18. See especially Benjamin H. Williams, *Economic Foreign Policy of the United States*, New York, 1926, 325–326. For example, when the Philadelphia Commercial Museum announced the sending of a trade commission to the Philippines on September 20, 1898, the *New York Times* concluded still that "in the view of many persons who have given the subject considerable study, the interests which the United States will retain in the Philippines will be chiefly valuable as a stepping-stone toward the extension of American commerce with the Orient . . ." *New York Times*, September 20, 1898, 2. Charles H. Cramp to Charles Emory Smith, undated, Reid MSS.

19. See especially Campbell, *Special Business Interests*, 16; *Journal of the American Asiatic Association*, I (1898), 1; *Chicago Inter-Ocean*, September 16, 1898, 6. For example, one prominent Chicago financier wrote Hay that almost all business "opinion here favors keeping all the territory won by war and the expansion of trade" following such a policy. W. B. Bliss to Hay, October 31, 1898, Hay MSS. And a West Coast friend wrote him that "We are all expansionists here-away, for we know that the prosperity resulting from the annexation . . . will make itself manifest first on our coast." W. W. Norris to Hay, October 17, 1898, Hay MSS.

20. Irving M. Scott to Charles A. Moore, August 4, 1898, McKinley MSS; "Notes on China," undated, W. C. Ford, Ford MSS; George F. Seward to Hay, November 7, 1898, Hay MSS; Carl Schurz to McKinley, September 22, 1898, McKinley MSS; Campbell, *Special Business Interests*, 16; Memorandum, September 16, 1898, McKinley MSS; Reid Diaries, September 15, 1898, Reid MSS; NA, RG 59, *China Despatches* 104, No. 31, Conger to Day, August 26, 1898; Charles G. Dawes to McKinley, August 10, 1898, McKinley MSS; Storey and Lichauco, *Conquest of the Philippines*, 38; *Foreign Relations 1898*, Hay to Day, telegram, October 28, 1898, 938; Campbell, *Special Business Interests*, 16; Reid Diaries, September 15,

1898, Reid MSS. See especially Leech, *Days of McKinley*, 339-341, and Earl S. Pomeroy, *Pacific Outpost: American Strategy in Guam and Micronesia*, Stanford, 1951, 3-19; Leech, *Days of McKinley*, 327, 330, 334-336, 339-341. Dewey's advice, however, was extraordinarily ambivalent and could be (and was) interpreted as favoring retention of Luzon only or of all the Philippines. In General Wesley Merritt's opinion (as expressed to the peace commission), Dewey "did not wish to express any opinion which would make him unavailable as a candidate for the Presidency." Reid Diaries, October 4, 1898, Reid MSS.

21. Joseph, *Foreign Diplomacy in China*, 346-347, 363-364. Conger, for example, reported that the American China Development Company had bungled a golden contract opportunity because it had no permanent agents on the scene "with authority to act," and because it would only act where contractual terms were so liberal as to insure a quick profit. NA, RG 59, *China Despatches* 105, No. 109, Conger to Hay, December 7, 1898. Campbell, *Special Business Interests*, 39-40.

22. See Lim Boon Keng, *The Chinese Crisis from Within*, London, 1901, 48-67; Meribeth E. Cameron, *The Reform Movement in China, 1898-1912*, Stanford, 1931, 23-55; George Nye Steiger, *China and the Occident: Origin and Development of the Boxer Movement*, New Haven, 1927, 87-106. NA, RG 59, *China Despatches* 105, No. 49, Conger to Day, September 24, 1898; *ibid.*, No. 71, Conger to Hay, October 14, 1898; *ibid.*, telegram, Hay to Conger, October 10, 1898; *ibid.*, telegram, Conger to Hay, November 5, 1898; *ibid.*, telegram, Hay to Conger, October 10, 1898; *ibid.*, No. 36, Conger to Day, September 6, 1898; NA, RG 59, *Russia Despatches* 53, No. 158, Hitchcock to Day, September 29, 1898; Campbell, *Special Business Interests*, 47-48.

23. This is not meant to deny that McKinley's tour "around the circuit" and the impact of public opinion did not also play important roles in the President's final decision. But several qualifications should be noted. McKinley's tour of the country cut both ways: it not only sounded out public opinion but also tended to mobilize it. Second, public opinion never acted as more than a veto factor: it could not dictate; it could only permit the President to do—or prevent him from doing—what he wanted to do anyway. Finally, even among those who saw "popular opinion" as the decisive factor in McKinley's decision, the term was defined sometimes rather narrowly: "popular opinion" equals "men conspicuous in public, professional, and business life." *Chicago Inter-Ocean*, October 10, 1898, 6.

24. Reid Diaries, September 16, 1898, Reid MSS; *Foreign Relations 1898*, 907-908.

25. Edmund L. Baylies to Reid, September 9, 1898, Reid MSS; Hay to Day, November 1, 1898, Letterbook, Hay MSS; American Chargé d'Affaires in Berlin to Hay, November 27, 1898, McKinley MSS; *Foreign Relations 1898*, 962; Reid Diaries, December 3, 1898, Reid MSS; *Foreign Relations 1898*, 939; Reid to McKinley, October 28, 1898, Letterbook, Reid MSS; Reid Diaries, December 3, 1898, Reid MSS; *ibid.*, December 4, 1898. The two works most specifically concerned with America's relations to the Carolines, Marianas, Marshalls, and so on, are Pomeroy, *Pacific Outpost*, and David N. Leff, *Uncle Sam's Pacific Islets*, Stanford, 1940. The latter is useful mainly for its maps. The former, while more scholarly and ambitious, is somewhat deficient in the 1898-1900 period.

26. Williams, *Foreign Economic Policy*, 325-326; A. A. Adee to Hay, December 13, 1898, Hay MSS; Whitelaw Reid, *Problems of Expansion*, New York, 1900, 18.

27. *Foreign Relations 1898*, lxxii.

# bibliography

A good starting point for a radical summary of the origins of American imperialism is Gareth Stedman Jones, "The Specificity of US Imperialism," *New Left Review*, no. 60, (March-April 1970), 59–86. Another highly useful synthesis, which puts American expansion in the context of global imperialism and Marxist theory, is David Horowitz, *Empire and Revolution* (Random House, 1969).

The tradition of expansion from the Revolution to the age of Woodrow Wilson is developed in Richard W. Van Alstyne, *The Rising American Empire* (Oxford University Press, 1960). Similar themes on the nature of expansionist ideology are to be found in the provocative work by Henry Nash Smith, *Virgin Land* (Harvard University Press, 1950), and in Charles Vevier, "American Continentalism: An Idea of Expansion, 1845–1910," *American Historical Review*, LXV (January 1960), 323–335.

As readers are already aware, the various works of William Appleman Williams are particularly important. Most significant for this topic are *The Tragedy of American Diplomacy* (Delta, 1962) and *The Roots of the Modern American Empire* (Random House, 1969). Williams' themes are developed further in the work of many of his students. Of importance are Walter LaFeber, *The New Empire: An Interpretation of American Expansion, 1860–1898* (Cornell University Press, 1963); Thomas McCormick, *China Market: America's Quest for Informal Empire, 1893–1901* (Quadrangle Books, 1967); and LLoyd C. Gardner, *A Different Frontier* (Quadrangle Books, 1966). Also of importance is John W. Rollins, "The Anti-Imperialist and Twentieth Century American Foreign Policy," *Studies on the Left*, III (1962), 9–24; Martin J. Sklar, "The N.A.M. and Foreign Markets on the Eve of the Spanish-American War," *Science and Society*, XXIII, no. 2 (Spring 1959), 133–162; Nancy Lenore O'Connor, "The Spanish-American War: A Re-Evaluation of its Causes," *Science and Society*, XXII, no. 2 (Spring 1958), 129–143; and Ronald Radosh, "American Labor and the Anti-Imperialist Movement," *Science and Society*, XXVIII, no.1 (Winter 1964), 91–100. An approach different from that taken by radicals trained by Williams is that of Harold Baron, "Anti-Imperialism and the Democrats," *Science and Society*, XXI (Summer 1958), 222–239.

Perhaps the most comprehensive treatment of United States–Cuban relations is in the volumes published and those under way by Philip S. Foner, *The History of Cuba and Its Relations with the United States* (International Publishers, 1962, . . . ).

The relationship between progressivism and imperialism is taken up in Padraic Colum Kennedy, "LaFollette's Imperialist Flirtation," *Pacific Historical Review*, XXXIX (May 1960), 131–144; Barton J. Bernstein and Franklin Leib, "Progressive Republican Senators and American Imperialism, 1898–1916: Re-Appraisal," *Mid-America*, L (July 1968), 163–205; and Jerry Israel, *Progressivism and the Open Door: America and China, 1905–1921* (University of Pittsburgh Press, 1971).

liberal reform:
change on a treadmill

Perhaps the most fundamental assumption regarding the nature of liberal reform is that the history of America is characterized by a struggle between liberals and conservatives, between the forces of equality and privilege. Reformers supposedly waged a battle against the people's enemies, particularly those in the business community. Out of this struggle emerged a movement opposed to large corporate business, whose participants demanded federal regulation of business.

According to mainstream historians, the extension of the welfare state and government intervention in business were evidence of progress. Liberal reform supposedly developed out of government's response to pressure from the people. This thesis was most succinctly stated by Arthur M. Schlesinger, Jr., in his classic study, *The Age of Jackson.* "Liberalism in America," he wrote, "has been ordinarily the movement on the part of the other sections of society to restrain the power of the business community."

Radical historians have sharply challenged this assumption. Gabriel Kolko, James Weinstein, Murray N. Rothbard, and William Appleman Williams, among others, have argued that liberalism has actually been the favored ideology of dominant corporate business groups, and that they have supported intervention by the state to supervise corporate enterprise.

Radical analysis of liberal reform begins with a reevaluation of the "Progressive" era. In *The Triumph of Conservatism,* Gabriel Kolko argues that large corporate business played a key role in developing the regulatory legislative measures of the Progressive era. Businessmen wanted to escape the rigors of competition via federal regulation of their own industries. The legislation they developed was meant to preserve "existing power and economic relations in society." According to Kolko, regulation was initiated and controlled by leaders of the regulated industry, and directed toward ends they deemed acceptable or desirable. More important, industrial leaders believed in the justice of private property, and their proposed regulatory measures were always framed within safe limits.

Kolko's thesis was given added dimension by James Weinstein's *The Corporate Ideal in the Liberal State, 1900–1918.* While reforms developed impetus from the needs of those on the bottom of the social structure, few of them were enacted without the approval or guidance of large corporate interests. Weinstein concentrates on the National Civic Federation, a corporate "peak" group organized in 1900, which stressed recognition of conservative trade unionism and which began to change the consciousness of large corporation leaders. Since they had a commitment to use the power of the state to rationalize the system, NCF members in the early 1900s proposed reforms that envisioned and forecast the entire New Deal. These men, Weinstein writes, had the sophistication "to move to the left in the face of real, imminent, or anticipated threats" from anticorporation radicals.

It was possible, Weinstein shows, for liberal administrations to respond to business needs without being antilabor. Laissez-faire capitalism was replaced by a statist and cartelized capitalism, which sought to enhance its legitimacy by merging into its structure potentially dissident groups. While workers, farmers, and small businessmen had *less* real strength at the end of the Wilsonian era, they gained recognition as "legitimate social forces." However, the reforms initiated, as Martin J. Sklar shows, were always limited to those that would allow corporate capitalism to function more efficiently.

Liberal reform culminated in the New Deal. The variety of reforms instituted during the first hundred days has been a focus of analysis and debate since the 1930s. Most recently, historians of the New Left such as Barton J. Bernstein have argued that the changes merely buttressed the corporate capitalist order. The vaunted New Deal reforms did not address themselves to the social needs of the 1930s, nor to the structural causes of poverty, racism, and war.

In a recent attack on this radical interpretation, Arthur M. Schlesinger, Jr., asserted that F.D.R. will "survive this assault from the left, as he has survived the earlier assault from the right." Like many others of his generation, Schlesinger views the reforms, particularly the Social Security Act, as measures that meant "a tremendous break with the inhibitions of the past," since the "federal government was at last charged with the obligation to provide its citizens with a measure of protection from the hazards and vicissitudes of life."

To mainstream historians, the New Deal continued and extended the liberal past. They see the New Deal as a movement that rejected dogmatic ideologies of the right and the left and that enabled Roosevelt to bring new confidence to the nation. The New Deal, writes Schlesinger, was a practical and successful movement that showed how a "managed and modified capitalist order achieved by piecemeal experiment could combine personal freedom and economic growth."

The validity of this analysis rests on the view that the forces of organized wealth fought projected New Deal programs, while F.D.R. and his administra- tion responded to the needs of the people. Hence Schlesinger writes that "organized business had long warned against such pernicious notions" as social security, and that "Republicans in the House faithfully reflected the business community."

Mainstream arguments are based on the mythology that business opposed social reform. Schlesinger does not account for the support given the Social Security Act by the Business Advisory Council, which included a represen- tative group of the most powerful bankers and industrialists in the nation. Men like Gerard Swope of General Electric and Walter Teagle of Standard Oil not only supported the Act but visited the White House to endorse it and to counter the opposition emanating from small businessmen in the National Association of Manufacturers.

The result of the New Deal reforms, as sociologist G. William Domhoff points out, was that the system was stabilized. It put a floor under consumer demand, raised people's expectations for the future, and directed political energies back into conventional channels. But the chasm between rich and poor remained. The distribution of wealth did not change, and decision-making power remained in the hands of upper-class leaders. Reform eased tension, created stability, and undermined movements for fundamental structural change.

Historians of the New Left do not argue that the reforms were merely incremental gestures. They admit that the reforms worked, but they point out that they simply bolstered the existing political economy and, moreover, that the sponsors of the reforms often came from the large corporate community itself. But the reforms encouraged the illusion that the United States had transcended traditional capitalism and that now big labor balanced and countered the influence of big industry. America had become, supposedly, a new pluralist democracy.

Radical historians agree with Charles LeRoy Brown, a conservative Republi- can Chicago lawyer who wrote in 1933 that the New Deal was just a "new set of plans" meant to "preserve the conservative order of things." The New Deal as Arthur A. Ekirch, Jr., suggests, was the sophisticated corporate liberal's answer to the crisis of the new order that had emerged in the 1900s. The deep problems stemming from corporate capitalism were not transcended. The recognition of their very existence helped in developing a more realistic assessment of *the nature of liberal reform.*

# the golden day

## ARTHUR M. SCHLESINGER, Jr.

As the introduction to this chapter indicates, Arthur M. Schlesinger, Jr., typifies the response of those mainstream historians who view liberal reform as the outcome of a progressive response by democratic administrations to popular need. In this selection, an excerpt from *The Crisis of the Old Order,* Schlesinger traces what he argues is the continuity of the reform impulse, beginning with "the Populist challenge to business rule in the 1890s" and ending with Woodrow Wilson's adoption of the New Nationalism, which Schlesinger interprets as the adoption of "affirmative federal action aimed to produce equality of opportunity."

---

THE NEW NATIONALISM

Out in America the universal element still burned in the soul. There the hope of 1919 was no sudden impulse of enthusiasm. "Democracy is infectious," the *New Republic* had proclaimed in 1917. "It is now as certain as anything human can be that the war . . . will dissolve into democratic revolution the world over."[1]

In the United States the democratic revolution had been gathering strength for thirty years. The Populist challenge to business rule in the 1890's had ushered in a new stage in American reform. Breaking sharply with the Jeffersonian past, the Populists renounced the old faith that that government was best which governed least. "We believe," their platform declared in 1892, "that the powers of government—in other words, of the people—should be expanded . . . to the end that oppression, injustice, and poverty shall eventually cease in the land."[2] The Populist uprising had its ambiguous elements. In part a justified protest by poor farmers against excessive levies by banks, railroads, and processors, it was in part too an irrational upsurge of frustration and spite, tending to interpret the world in terms of a conspiracy of international bankers controlled by Wall Street and the House of Rothschild. But, for all the rancor of Populism, the Populist platform was rich in political and economic invention. The Populist demands—a rudimentary farm-price support system, a graduated income tax, the secret ballot, the direct election of senators, the initiative and referendum, and the government ownership of railroads, telephone, and telegraph—defined the objectives of reform for the next generation.

In 1896 the Populist spirit captured the Democratic party and created William Jennings Bryan. In the later nineties the rise in farm prices diminished the radicalism of the countryside; but the reform impulse only took other forms,

From Arthur M. Schlesinger, Jr., "The Golden Day," Chapters 3, 4, and 5, *The Crisis of the Old Order,* Volume I of *The Age of Roosevelt* (Boston: Houghton Mifflin, 1957), 17–36, 491–494. Copyright © 1957 by Arthur M. Schlesinger, Jr. Reprinted by permission of the publisher, Houghton Mifflin Company.

the cities becoming the new source of reform energy. Where Populism was driven by a sense of panic over what the farmers took as conspiratorial business domination, Progressivism emerged rather from the feelings of distress experienced by settled community leadership now threatened by a crude and grasping class of *nouveau riche*. Middle-class in its outlook, moralistic in its temper, moderate and resourceful in its approach to problems of policy, Progressivism originated less than Populism. But it executed much more.

The Progressive era was an unprecedented time of popular education. The muckrakers in press and magazines disclosed the techniques of political and business corruption. And political leaders sought to show how honesty and intelligence might provide the remedy. Thus there arose Robert M. La Follette of Wisconsin, Charles Evans Hughes of New York, Hiram Johnson of California, James M. Cox of Ohio—typical Progressive governors, some Republicans, some Democrats, but all standing for the enforcement of middle-class standards of civic decency against greedy wealth and crooked politics. The greatest of them all in his public impact was Theodore Roosevelt of New York.


II

Roosevelt transfixed the imagination of the American middle class as did no other figure of the time. With his squeaky voice, his gleaming teeth, his overpowering grin, and his incurable delight in self-dramatization, he brought everything he touched to life. His capacity for moral indignation was unlimited; his energy cascaded everywhere. He gathered into himself the mounting discontent with which Americans were contemplating business rule. By offering this discontent release in melodrama, he no doubt reduced the pressure behind it for accomplishment. La Follette and others complained of his "rhetorical radicalism." His cannonading back and forth, La Follette said, filled the air with noise and smoke, but, when the battle cloud drifted by, little had been achieved.[3] Yet Roosevelt's personality gave the reform movement a momentum it could hardly have obtained from economics alone. He stirred the conscience of America. Young men followed him in the service of the commonweal as they had followed no American since Lincoln.

Theodore Roosevelt, indeed, was more complicated than he sometimes seemed. He sensed with brilliant insight the implications of America's new industrial might. At home, the industrial triumph had rendered acute the problems of economic justice and social peace. Abroad, it was thrusting America irrevocably into world power politics. With all the boisterousness of his personality, Roosevelt sought to awaken the nation to a recognition of new responsibilities. And the only way these responsibilities—domestic or foreign— could be met, he deeply believed, was by establishing a "powerful National government" and thus affirming national purpose as the guiding force in public policy.

Ancestry and outlook equipped Roosevelt peculiarly for this revival of a sense of national purpose. Coming from a well-born family in New York, inheriting wealth and independence, he considered himself above class allegiances. In particular, he looked with disdain on the business community. "I do not dislike," he wrote, "but I certainly have no especial respect or admiration for and no trust in, the typical big moneyed men of my country. I do not regard them as furnishing sound opinion as regards either foreign or domestic

policies." There was absolutely nothing to be said, he continued, for "government by a plutocracy, for government by men very powerful in certain lines
and gifted with 'the money touch,' but with ideals which in their essence are
merely those of so many glorified pawnbrokers." He stood equally, he declared,
against government by a plutocracy and government by a mob.[4]

He was fortified by the conviction that he was restoring an older tradition of
national purpose—the tradition of the Federalists, about which he had written
with such ardor as a young historian. His admiration for Hamilton's conception
of government was qualified only by regret over Hamilton's skepticism toward
democracy. Jefferson, even though he was right about the plain people, was
hopelessly wrong about the role of the state. As Roosevelt's younger friend
Henry L. Stimson liked to put it, government was not "a mere organized police
force, a sort of necessary evil, but rather an affirmative agency of national
progress and social betterment."[5]

For national government to do its job, it had to be stronger than any private
group in society. Instead of regarding the state as a possible tyrant, "as Jefferson
did," said Stimson, "we now look to executive action to protect the individual
citizen against the oppression of this unofficial power of business."[6] From very
nearly the start of his presidency, Roosevelt was engaged in battles to vindicate
the national will against its boldest domestic challengers—the trusts and
combines, the court favorites of earlier Republican rule.


III

Roosevelt's warfare against the trusts was neither very consistent nor very
effective. But his uncertainty derived less from political expediency than from
the fact that he had a more complex vision of the problem than the old-
fashioned trust busters. For a man like La Follette, with his ruthless simplicities,
the Sherman Antitrust Act remained "the strongest, most perfect weapon
which the ingenuity of man could forge for the protection of the people against
the power and sordid greed of monopoly."[7] But for Roosevelt, who discerned an
evolutionary necessity in economic concentration, the Sherman Act was an
exercise in nostalgia.

Herbert Croly's *The Promise of American Life*, published in 1909, the year
when Roosevelt left the Presidency, added little to Roosevelt's program. But it
gave his instinct for national assertion a persuasive setting in political
philosophy. In a thoughtful reconsideration of the national experience, Croly
saw the essence of the American faith in the careless belief that the nation was
"predestined to success by its own adequacy." The promise of American life
had been too long considered somehow self-fulfilling; the same automatic
processes which had taken care of the past would take care of the future. Croly
sharply challenged this whole spirit of optimism and drift. The traditional
American confidence in individual freedom, he said, had resulted in a morally
and socially undesirable distribution of wealth under which "the ideal Promise,
instead of being automatically fulfilled, may well be automatically stifled." The
only hope was to transform the national attitude toward social development, to
convert the old unconscious sense of national destiny into a conscious sense of
national purpose, to replace drift by management. What this meant, Croly said,
was that the national state would have to take an active and detailed
responsibility for economic and social conditions. It meant a "more highly

socialized democracy," a "new nationalism." The theory of the Sherman Act, he added, operated as a "fatal bar" to national planning.[8]

Croly was more interested in affirming a viewpoint than in designing a program; but others were ready to give the New Nationalism its economics. George W. Perkins of J. P. Morgan and Company, himself one of the great trust organizers, felt that modern technology had revolutionized the world and rendered old-style competition obsolete. "What underlies ruthless competitive methods?" Perkins asked. "The desire to supply the public with better goods at a lower price? Is that the moving, impelling force behind it? Nonsense!" Competition, he said, was simply a struggle for power at the expense of everything else. "The entire path of our industrial progress is strewn with the white bones of just such competition." What had given us exploitation, evil working conditions, unemployment, low wages? Competition! "The Congressman who stands for a literal enforcement of the Sherman Act," declared Perkins, "stands for the sweat shop and child labor." Competition had become "too destructive to be tolerated. Co-operation must be the order of the day."

The national government, Perkins said, had first undertaken the supervision of the states, then of the banks, then of the railroads; now, he said, it must undertake the supervision of big business. Let the government license all interstate corporations; and let the licensing system enforce federal standards with respect to capitalization, trade practices, prices, and labor policy. As for corporations, they must recognize that they had obligations to labor and to the public as well as to their stockholders. Let them work out plans for co-partnership; let them, as he put it in a clumsy but expressive phrase, "people-ize" modern industry; let them devise plans for profit-sharing, for social insurance, for old-age pensions. In true co-partnership, said Perkins, there would be "socialism of the highest, best and most ideal sort"—socialism, in other words, which preserved the right of private property.[9]

Perkins was sincerely impressed by the advantages of the German cartel system—for social security, for economic stability, for industrial growth, for national unity—and he wanted to propel American economic development in the same direction. In 1910 he left Morgan's and went up and down the country, preaching the gospel to any group that would listen. In 1912 he gave over $250,000 to Roosevelt's campaign. As for T.R., he valued Perkins's ideas as much as his money.

T.R. discovered further stimulus in a book published in the spring of 1912— *Concentration and Control: A Solution of the Trust Problem in the United States,* written by Charles R. Van Hise, a classmate of La Follette's at the University of Wisconsin and later the university's president. Agreeing with Perkins about the inevitability of concentration, Van Hise asserted even more strongly the indispensability of control. "If we allow concentration and co-operation," he wrote, "there must be control in order to protect the people, and adequate control is only possible through the administrative commission."[10]

As his own thought clarified, and as his resentment of William Howard Taft, his successor in the Presidency, grew, Roosevelt became increasingly specific. Trust busting seemed to him madness—"futile madness." "It is preposterous to abandon all that has been wrought in the application of the cooperative idea in business and to return to the era of cut-throat competition." But acceptance of bigness could not be allowed to mean surrender to bigness: this was the test of democratic government. "The man who wrongly holds that every human right is secondary to his profit," Roosevelt declared, "must now give way to the advocate of human welfare, who rightly maintains that every man holds his property subject to the general right of the community to regulate its use to whatever degree the public welfare may require it."[11] *To whatever degree:* this was strong language, even for Teddy Roosevelt.

## IV

One other force contributed vitally to Roosevelt's developing philosophy. Mastery of private bigness was only half the job; the other half was help for the individual cast adrift in the great society. Here the New Nationalism absorbed the new experience of social work as well as the new teachings of the Social Gospel.

Both the Social Gospel and social work had arisen in the late nineteenth century as nonpolitical responses to the miseries and injustices of the industrial order. Socially-minded ministers began to remind their parishioners that Christians had duties toward their fellow men, that Christian morality was relevant to slums and sweatshops, and that the Christian task would not be completed until the social order itself had been Christianized. "The Christian law," said Dr. Washington Gladden, "is meant to live by, to do business by, to rule politics." When society was transformed by Christian faith, "rotten politics and grinding monopolies would shrivel and disappear; under its banner light and beauty, peace and plenty, joy and gladness would be led in."

This goal, the advocates of the Social Gospel reckoned, could be achieved within history; the Kingdom of God would, in due time, realize itself on earth. But it could not be achieved by the churches alone. "There is a certain important work to be done," wrote Gladden, "which no voluntary organization can succeed in doing—a work which requires the exercise of the power of the state." Nor was this likely to be the existing state, controlled as it was by the business class. "If the banner of the Kingdom of God is to enter through the gates of the future," said Walter Rauschenbusch, the most searching theologian of the Social Gospel, "it will have to be carried by the tramping hosts of labor."[12]

Gladden and Rauschenbusch, in rousing the conscience of modern Protestantism, thus predisposed it both toward an affirmative theory of the state and toward a belief that the power of business must be offset by the power of labor. The formation of such organizations as the Methodist Federation for Social Service in 1907 and the Federal Council of Churches in 1908 signaled the spread of the Social Gospel through the Protestant churches.

## V

What was faith for the apostles of the Social Gospel became works for the men and women of the settlement houses. The first heroine of social work was Jane Addams of Hull-House on Halsted Street in Chicago. Soon after, Lillian Wald set up the Henry Street Settlement in New York. Hull-House, Henry Street, and their counterparts in other cities gave the middle class its first extended contact with the life of the working class—with the sweatshops, the child labor, the unsanitary working conditions, the long hours, the starvation wages, the denial of the right to organize. Relinquishing comfortable middle-class homes, the social workers moved to the city slums and labored to create a breathing-space of hope for the poor, the immigrant, and, above all, for the slum-born children.

This middle-class mission to the poor coincided with the release of energy which came from the new emancipation of women. Hull-House and Henry Street, in particular, produced an extraordinary group of women whose vitality and compassion reshaped American liberalism. From Hull-House came Florence Kelley, who became the driving force in the National Consumers' League. The idea of the United States Children's Bureau was Lillian Wald's, and its first two chiefs—Julia Lathrop and Grace Abbott—were from Hull-House. The same hopes and ideals fired many younger women—Josephine Goldmark, Frances Perkins, Mary Dewson, Mary Anderson, Edith Abbott. These were the "dedicated old maids." Social work not only relieved their middle-class conscience. It also provided an outlet for their energy in a field which women could make their own.

More than anyone else, Florence Kelley devised the new techniques of social reform. The daughter of W. D. ("Pig-Iron") Kelley, the protectionist congressman, she was a socialist, a friend of Friedrich Engels, and a whirlwind of courage, vigor, and, in Frances Perkins's phrase, "blazing moral indignation." The National Consumers' League had been established in 1899 on the belief that the customer who bought sweatshop goods was as much the employer of sweated labor as the boss of the shop. Under Florence Kelley's direction, the League battled against home manufacturers in tenements, against child labor, against night work and excessive hours for women. The League's investigations turned up facts to stir the public conscience. Then the League's lawyers drafted bills, and the League's lobbyists sought to push them through legislatures. The League thus initiated the fight for minimum-wage laws and worked out a model statute, soon enacted in thirteen states and the District of Columbia. When the law was challenged in the courts, Florence Kelley rushed up to Boston to ask Louis D. Brandeis to argue its constitutionality. For this purpose Brandeis invented the famous "Brandeis brief," which introduced the heresy that the facts as well as the law were relevant to determinations of community health and welfare.

Organizations like the Women's Trade Union League and the Association for Labor Legislation carried on other aspects of the fight for decent labor standards. It was from these middle-class groups, and not from the trade unions, that the first demand came for the abolition of child labor, for maximum-hour and minimum-wage laws, and for social insurance. And the opposition these reformers met from many businessmen—an opposition camouflaged as solicitude for the "freedom" of women to work twelve hours a day or of seven-year-old children to strip tobacco leaves or twist artificial flowers in slum tenements—deepened suspicion of business motives.

Hull-House, Henry Street, the Consumers' League, and the other organizations educated a whole generation in social responsibility. Henry Morgenthau, Jr., Herbert Lehman, and Adolf A. Berle, Jr., all worked at Henry Street; Frances Perkins, Gerard Swope, and Charles A. Beard at Hull-House (where John Dewey was an early member of the board of trustees); Sidney Hillman at both Hull-House and Henry Street; Joseph B. Eastman at Robert A. Woods's South End House in Boston; an Iowa boy coming east from Grinnell College in 1912 went to work at Christadora House on the lower East Side of New York; his name, Harry Hopkins. Through Belle Moskowitz the social work ethos infected Alfred E. Smith; through Frances Perkins and others, Robert F. Wagner; through

Eleanor Roosevelt, active in the Women's Trade Union League and a friend of Florence Kelley's and Lillian Wald's, Franklin D. Roosevelt.

And, for all the appearance of innocence and defenselessness the social workers' apparatus wielded power. "One could not overestimate," observed Wagner, "the central part played by social workers in bringing before their representatives in Congress and state legislatures the present and insistent problems of modern-day life." The subtle and persistent saintliness of the social workers was in the end more deadly than all the bluster of business. Theirs was the implacability of gentleness.[13]

## VI

Among politicians, no one responded more alertly than Theodore Roosevelt. In the early eighties he had led the fight in the New York legislature against cigar-making in tenement houses. As President, he hailed the Consumers' League as early as 1907; and his White House conference on children gave social work, said Jane Addams, "a dignity and a place in the national life which it never had before." Nor was the alliance unnatural. The inner logic of social work was, to a considerable degree, *noblesse oblige* and paternalistic; the bias was more toward helping people than toward enabling them to help themselves. The caseworker often felt she knew best. T.R. always knew best too.

In the meantime, the Progressives in the Republican party were pressing their battle against the Taft administration. La Follette had been their original candidate; but early in 1912 Roosevelt announced his availability. When the Republican convention renominated Taft, Roosevelt decided to quit the party. Before his own convention, he met with a group of leading social workers and adopted a program recently drawn up by the National Conference of Social Work. "Our best plank," he later wrote of the Progressive platform, "the plank which has really given our party its distinctive character, came from them. . . . [The social workers] are doing literally invaluable work." At the convention, Jane Addams was among those seconding his nomination.[14]

Roosevelt's movement reached its climax at Chicago in August. Before a crowd gone mad, T.R., strong as a bull moose, challenged his followers to stand at Armageddon and battle for the Lord. Across the nation young men rose to his call: Gifford Pinchot of Pennsylvania; Harold Ickes and Donald Richberg of Illinois; William Allen White and Alfred M. Landon of Kansas; George W. Norris of Nebraska; Frank Knox of Michigan; Henry A. Wallace of Iowa; Felix Frankfurter and Norman Thomas of New York; Francis Biddle of Pennsylvania; John G. Winant and Charles W. Tobey of New Hampshire; Dean Acheson of Connecticut.

## THE NEW FREEDOM

For their part, the Democrats in 1912 nominated Woodrow Wilson, the governor of New Jersey. Wilson brought qualities as unusual as those of Theodore Roosevelt to American politics. The two men had much in common: cultivation, knowledge, literary skill, personal magnetism, relentless drive. But, where Roosevelt was unbuttoned and expansive, Wilson was reserved and cool; no one known to history ever called him "Woody" or "W.W." Both were lay preachers, but where Roosevelt was a revivalist, bullying his listeners to hit the sawdust trail, Wilson had the severe eloquence of a Calvinist divine. Roosevelt's egotism overflowed his personality; Wilson's was a hard concentrate within. Roosevelt's power lay in what he did, Wilson's in what he held in reserve.

Erect in bearing, quick in movement, tidy in dress, with sharp eyes and a belligerent jaw, Wilson, when not overcome by self-righteousness or moral fervor, had humor and charm. For all his professorial background, he showed considerable aptitude for politics. He was, in particular, a powerful orator—as the nation discovered in 1912 when he outlined his alternative to the New Nationalism in a series of notable speeches. Declaring "a new social age, a new era of human relationships . . . a new economic society," Wilson summoned his countrymen to the task of liberating the nation from the new tyranny of concentrated wealth. "When we undertake the strategy which is going to be necessary to overcome and destroy this far-reaching system of monopoly," he said, "we are rescuing the business of this country, we are not injuring it; and when we separate the interests from each other and dismember these communities of connection, we have in mind . . . that vision which sees that no society is renewed from the top but that every society is renewed from the bottom." This was the New Freedom.

Wilson vigorously rejected theories of the paternal state. Hamilton had no charm for him: "a great man, but, in my judgment, not a great American." The philosophy of America was equal rights for all and special privileges for none—"a free field and no favor." "I do not want to live under a philanthropy," Wilson said. "I do not want to be taken care of by the government. . . . We do not want a benevolent government. We want a free and a just government."

He cherished the Jeffersonian dream. Yet he began to give his Jeffersonianism significant new inflections. As he had read the "spirit of Jefferson" as late as 1906, it had enjoined him to eschew nearly all forms of public intervention in the economy. But the very goal of dismantling the system of special privilege called for action by the state. In the end, he set the Jeffersonian theory of the state on its head: "I feel confident that if Jefferson were living in our day he would see what we see. . . . Without the watchful interference, the resolute interference of the government, there can be no fair play." And his experience as governor soon increased his tolerance of governmental power. Political ambition at the same time sharpened his sensitivity to popular discontents; and contacts with William G. McAdoo and Louis D. Brandeis in the 1912 campaign completed the transformation of his Jeffersonianism from a counsel of inaction to a doctrine with a cutting edge. Under the pressure of responsibility, he was coming to see that if he aspired to Jeffersonian ends he might have to relinquish Jeffersonian means.[15]

II

In McAdoo, Wilson found a businessman with a free-wheeling operator's animus toward Wall Street and with developed ideas about business reform. A Georgian by birth, a New Yorker by residence, a lawyer by training, a promoter by temperament, McAdoo, who was forty-nine years old in 1912, had built the first tunnel under the Hudson and was now president of the Hudson and Manhattan Railroad Company. Tough and energetic, he observed insistently to the business community that corporations must be the servants, not the masters, of the people; that "the public be damned" approach had to be replaced by "the public be pleased." His reading of America's economic development was diametrically opposite to that of George W. Perkins. Where Perkins wrote that the modern corporation's underlying cause was "not the greed of man for wealth and power, but the working of natural causes—of evolution," McAdoo rejoined, "These great combinations are not the *natural* outgrowth of new economic conditions and complex civilization. They are more likely the artificial product of the unrestrained activities of ambitious men of highly-developed acquisitive power."

What could be done about them? "For my part," replied McAdoo, "I believe that all the powers of the nation should be exerted to preserve competitive conditions." Regulation could be attempted; but regulation was only possible through commissions; and the real question was, Who would control the commissions? "Unregulated competition is better than regulated monopoly," said McAdoo early in 1911, thrusting some new phrases into the controversy, "but regulated competition is better than either."[16]

Louis D. Brandeis carried the analysis a few steps farther. Born in 1856 in Louisville, Kentucky, Brandeis had graduated from the Harvard Law School and then settled down to an immensely successful law practice in Boston. His analytical brilliance and his tenacious advocacy won him the clients who could pay most for these talents. By 1907 Brandeis was a millionaire. But, for an idealist, bred in the tradition of the Revolution of 1848, material success was hardly enough. Beginning in the nineties, he had developed a second career—this time as a "people's lawyer," working without fee in the public interest, moving from local problems (streetcar franchises) to state (savings bank life insurance) and then to regional (the New Haven railroad). Starting in 1907, he came to national attention as counsel for the Consumers' League in a series of notable tests of hours and wages legislation.

He was a tall, stooped figure, with longish gray hair, deep-set eyes, a face of melancholy nobility and brooding wisdom, and something of the aspect of a Jewish Lincoln. In combat, his wrath aroused, he displayed the stern righteous-ness of an Old Testament prophet; this sometimes made it hard for him to believe that his opponents, too, had honest motives. But, in relaxation, talking among friends, a tinge of Kentucky drawl still in his voice, he had rare serenity of spirit.

For Wilson, Jeffersonianism had been a faith; Brandeis seemed to transform it into a policy. He bluntly denied the major premise of the New Nationalists. Economic bigness, he said, was not inevitable. It did not come from the necessities of the machine age. It was not the inescapable result of the movement toward efficiency. It was the creation, not of technology, but of finance. It sprang from the manipulations of the bankers, eager to float new securities and water new stocks.

The mania for consolidation, Brandeis believed, could end only in the strangling of freedom: J. P. Morgan was the socialists' best friend, because, after he was through with his work, socialism would have so little left to do. "Just as Emperor Nero is said to have remarked in regard to his people that he wished that the Christians had but one neck that he might cut it off by a single blow of his sword, so they say here: 'Let these men gather these things together; they will soon have them all under one head, and by a single act we will take over the whole industry.' "

Where Croly was concerned with the morale of the nation, Brandeis was concerned with the morality of the individual. The curse was bigness: "we are now coming to see that big things may be very bad and mean." For, though business and government might increase indefinitely, men would always remain the same size. Excessive power was the great corrupter. To bestow more power on men than they could endure was to change the few into tyrants, while it destroyed the rest. Centralization enfeebled society by choking off experiment and draining talent from the community into the center. Nor could one pin faith on government regulation: "remedial institutions are apt to fall under the control of the enemy and to become instruments of oppression." In the end responsibility was the only developer—the institutions of the state and the economy must be proportioned to the capabilities of man. The growth of the individual, Brandeis concluded, was "both a necessary means and the end sought."[17]

## III

Here was the reformulation of Jeffersonianism toward which Wilson had been groping. His first meeting with Brandeis in August 1912 was an instant success. The problem, Wilson agreed, was not to regulate monopoly but to regulate competition; and he soon asked Brandeis for a program. Competition, Brandeis replied, could and should be maintained in every branch of private industry. Where monopoly could not be avoided, industry should be "owned by the people and not by the capitalists." Government regulation of monopoly, he continued, was a delusion; either break the power up or take it over. The nation must choose between industrial absolutism, tempered by government control, and industrial liberty.[18]

Thus the New Freedom, and to this summons, too, young men rallied—W. G. McAdoo and Franklin Delano Roosevelt of New York, Cordell Hull of Tennessee, John N. Garner and Sam Rayburn of Texas, Homer Cummings of Connecticut, Dan Roper of South Carolina, Joseph E. Davies of Wisconsin.

## NATIONALIZING THE NEW FREEDOM

The partisans of 1912 had no doubt that they were debating fundamentals. To the followers of Wilson, the New Nationalism was a menacing tyranny, in which the twin giants of business and government would grind the individual to sand. To the followers of Roosevelt, the New Freedom harked back impotently to the Jeffersonian past—Jeffersonianism restated, to be sure, in terms of finance capitalism, but obsolete nonetheless in the assumption that the system, once reformed, could run by itself. Wilson and Roosevelt thus raged at each other over the trust issue as if they stood on opposite sides of an impassable abyss.

"This difference in the economic policy of the two parties," declared Brandeis in 1912, "is fundamental and irreconcilable."[19] The New Nationalists could not agree more. Nor did Wilson's election and his initial policies reassure them. As late as 1914 Croly dismissed Wilson's program as a mere "revival of Jeffersonian individualism," lacking in a sense of national purpose, oblivious to the fact that "the nationalism of Hamilton, with all its aristocratic leaning, was more democratic, because more constructively social, than the indiscriminate individualism of Jefferson." The young historian Charles A. Beard, fresh from his bold researches into the origins of the Constitution, concurred: agrarian democracy had been Jefferson's futile ambition, "just as the equally unreal and unattainable democracy of small business is Wilson's goal." The acute and fluent journalist Walter Lippmann, only lately resigned from the Socialist party, contrasted the Wilsonian policy of drift with the Rooseveltian policy of mastery. As George Perkins summed it up with scorn, the "New Freedom had better be called the Old Bondage."[20]

But the gap soon turned out to be less impassable than it had first appeared. Roosevelt did not—as Wilson charged—want to make monopoly universal, any more than Wilson—as Roosevelt replied—wanted to break up every corporation in the country. In abusing each other and misrepresenting each other's views, they obscured the fact that their agreements were actually greater than their differences. Whether the objective was to regulate monopoly or competition, the method was to meet the power of business by expanding the power of government. The New Nationalism and the New Freedom alike affirmed the necessity of active intervention in economic life by the state.

Wilson had already accepted this as the logic of twentieth-century Jeffersonionism when he had shifted from his do-nothing position of 1906 to his activism of 1912. "The program of a government of freedom," he said, "must in these days be positive."[21] Even Brandeis, for all his fear of bigness, wanted the state not only to break up the trusts but to carry out an extensive program on behalf of labor and social security.

Others of Wilson's associates looked even more genially on the state. Colonel E. M. House, the quiet and self-effacing Texan, soon to become the new President's confidential adviser, had published in 1912 Philip Dru, Administrator, a utopian fantasy in which the hero, fearful in the year 1920 that organized wealth was about to end American freedom, seized power and proclaimed himself dictator. Dru had to divest himself, House noted, of early states-rights predispositions; but he quickly established a strong central regime, put corporations under stringent national control (while declining to limit their size), abolished holding companies, socialized the telephone and telegraph, enacted full employment legislation, decreed federal old-age and unemployment insurance, and in general set up a nationalism so comprehensive that it might even have given Theodore Roosevelt pause.[22] Yet, by 1918, Franklin K. Lane, Wilson's Secretary of the Interior noted, "All that book has said should be, comes about slowly, even woman suffrage. The President comes to Philip Dru in the end."[23]


II

Still, it was less advice than circumstance which caused Wilson to begin to bridge the abyss. The first pressure came from the radical wing of the southern Democrats. Southerners of a more genteel stripe, like Carter Glass of Virginia and Oscar W. Underwood of Alabama, were well satisfied with the New Freedom of 1912. But some of their colleagues had a more active conception of government. Congressman Cordell Hull wanted a federal income tax. Congressman Sam Rayburn, with Brandeis's assistance, had drawn up a bill to control the marketing of railroad securities. And, for the agrarian Democrats of the Bryan school, champions of the cracker and the redneck, haters of Wall Street, the first New Freedom seemed especially meager. It was not enough they felt, to whittle down class legislation for the business community. The Wilson administration, they believed, had a positive obligation to the poor. It must balance Republican favoritism for big business by doing something itself for small business and the farmers. The southern radicals had their first triumph when they helped Bryan, Brandeis, and McAdoo force a basic revision of Carter Glass's bill for a Federal Reserve system. Then they made another breach in the conservative conception of the New Freedom by tacking on to the Federal Reserve bill provisions for short-term credits for farmers. Wilson soon found himself accepting what was, by his theory of 1912, class legislation.[24]

At the same time, Wilson began to move in strange new directions in the critical field of antitrust policy. Brandeis, who in 1912 had felt regulation to be worse than useless, now took up the New Nationalist idea of a federal commission to supervise corporations. As a result came the laws of 1914 establishing the Federal Trade Commission and giving it regulatory powers. Worse, Brandeis soon recommended for appointment as chairman of the Commission on Industrial Relations the same Charles Van Hise whose *Concentration and Control* had been T.R.'s bible two years earlier. The "fundamental and irreconcilable" differences of 1912 had lost their sting by 1914.

As the election of 1916 approached, Wilson completed his acceptance of the main lines of the Progressive program of 1912. He now stood clearly for strong government, for administrative regulation, for some intervention on behalf of the farmer and the worker—in short, for affirmative federal action aimed to produce equality of opportunity. In a basic respect, Roosevelt seemed to have been right: the people's government had to be stronger than business if popular rule were to be effective.


III

While Wilson was appropriating its platform, the Progressive party, already set back by the elections of 1914, was fighting for its life. Its adored leader callously showed his new opinion of his old crusade by suggesting that it might make Henry Cabot Lodge its candidate in 1916. George W. Perkins, the party's angel, had also come to feel that the Bull Moose had outlived its usefulness. Whether the party was killed by Perkins, as Harold Ickes believed, or by Wilson, its 1916 convention showed that its time had passed.

As for the men and women who had battled for the Lord, many now found to their surprise that the New Nationalism was fulfilled in the New Freedom. As Walter Lippmann put it, Wilson's Democratic party was "the only party which at this moment is national in scope, liberal in purpose, and effective in action." Herbert Croly, repenting his earlier skepticism, announced his support for Wilson. Progressives like Bainbridge Colby and Frederic C. Howe, Edward P. Costigan and Amos Pinchot, Jane Addams, Lillian Wald, and Washington Gladden turned to Wilson.[25]

And Roosevelt? "Like you, I am a radical," he wrote to Harold Ickes in December 1915. "I stand for every particle of our platform in 1912; but overwhelmingly my chief interest at present is in the relationship of the United States to the present European situation." The old radicalism still had moments of life. In March 1918, T.R. moved far ahead of the Wilson administration and set new goals for American liberalism in demanding a system of old-age, sickness, and unemployment insurance, public housing, and other reforms. But more and more in these years foreign policy consumed and, in the end, exhausted him. Bitter because Wilson refused to use him in the war, bitter more essentially because of wasted years since 1908, sick, tired, and unhappy, he died in the first month of 1919.

"Something went out of my life that has never been replaced," Ickes said a quarter-century later of the moment when he heard of Roosevelt's death. "I could only press my face into the pillow," wrote Donald Richberg, receiving word on a sickbed in Chicago, "and cry like a child."[26]

## NOTES

1. "The Great Decision," *New Republic*, April 7, 1917.

2. Edward Stanwood, *History of the Presidency* (Boston, 1898), 509–13; Richard Hofstadter, *The Age of Reform* (New York, 1955), Ch. 2.

3. Robert M. La Follette, *La Follette's Autobiography* (Madison, Wisc., 1913), 478, 479.

4. Theodore Roosevelt, *An Autobiography* (New York, 1913), 67; Roosevelt to F. S. Oliver, Aug. 9, 1906, in Theodore Roosevelt, *Letters*, E. E. Morison, ed., 8 vols. (Cambridge, 1951–54), V, 352; Roosevelt to Sir Edward Grey, Nov. 15, 1913, in Theodore Roosevelt, *Works* (Memorial ed.), XXIV, 409.

5. H. L. Stimson and McGeorge Bundy, *On Active Service in Peace and War* (New York, 1948), 63; Roosevelt to F. S. Oliver, Aug. 9, 1906, in Theodore Roosevelt, *Letters*, V, 351, to F. J. Turner, Nov. 4, 1896, I, 504, to W. H. Moody, Sept. 21, 1907, V, 803.

6. Stimson and Bundy, *On Active Service*, 60.

7. La Follette, *Autobiography*, 478, 686–87.

8. Herbert Croly, *The Promise of American Life* (New York, 1909), 12–13, 17, 20–21, 25, 169, 274.

9. G. W. Perkins, *Copartnership: Address . . . [before] the Canadian Club, Ottawa, February 4, 1911* (n.p., n.d. [1911]), 3; *Address . . . Before the Quill Club of New York, December 20, 1910* (n.p., n.d. [1911]), 5; "Business and Government," *Saturday Evening Post*, March 16, 1912; *Wanted—A Constructive National Policy: Address . . . [before] Michigan College of Mines . . . August 7, 1911* (n.p., n.d. [1911]), 12; *A Constructive Suggestion: Address . . . Youngstown, Ohio, December 4, 1911* (n.p., n.d. [1912]), 4–5, 9; *Copartnership*, 15; *Efficiency in Business and What It Must Stand For: Address . . . Before . . . the Massachusetts Institute of Technology, Boston, January 4, 1911* (n.p., n.d. [1911]), 15; *Modern Industrialism: Address . . . [before] Southern Commercial Congress, Atlanta, Georgia, March 8, 1911* (n.p., n.d. [1911]), 7.

10. C. R. Van Hise, *Concentration and Control* (New York, 1912), 278.

11. Theodore Roosevelt, Introduction to S. J. Duncan-Clark, *The Progressive Movement* (Boston, 1913), xix; Theodore Roosevelt, *The New Nationalism* (New York, 1910), 23–24.

12. Washington Gladden, *Social Salvation* (Boston, 1902), 229 30, 61; Walter Rauschenbusch, *Christianizing the Social Order* (New York, 1912), 449.

13. Frances Perkins, "A Method of Moral Progress," *New Republic*, June 8, 1953; Florence Kelley, *Minimum Wage Boards* (New York, [1911]); Lillian Wald, *Windows on Henry Street* (Boston, 1934), 45. See also the *Annual Reports* of the Consumers' League; Florence Kelley, "Twenty-five Years of the Consumers' League Movement," *Survey*, Nov. 27, 1915; Paul Kellogg, "Semi-Centennial of the Settlements," *Survey Graphic*, Jan. 1935; Josephine Goldmark, "50 Years—The National Consumers' League," *Survey*, Dec. 1949; speech by Paul H. Douglas at the Fiftieth Anniversary Dinner of the Consumers' League, Dec. 9, 1949; Jane Addams, *The Second Twenty Years at Hull-House* (New York, 1930); Josephine Goldmark, *Impatient Crusader: Florence Kelley's Life Story* (Urbana, Ill., 1953); R. L. Duffus, *Lillian Wald* (New York, 1938); Frances Perkins, *People at Work* (New York, 1934), Sec. II.

14. Theodore Roosevelt to Mrs. Frederick Nathan, Jan. 20, 1907, National Consumers' League, *Eighth Annual Report* ([New York, 1907]), 15; Addams, *Second Twenty Years*, 18–27; Roosevelt to G. W. Perkins, Aug. 23, 1913, in Theodore Roosevelt, *Letters*, VII, 742–43.

15. Woodrow Wilson, *The New Freedom* (New York, 1913), 7–8, 55, 190, 198, 218, 221, 284; "Ideals of Public Life" (1907), quoted by A. S. Link, *Wilson: The Road to the White House* (Princeton, 1947), 115; "The State and the Citizen's Relation to It" (1909) and "Spirit of Jefferson" (1906), quoted by William Diamond, *The Economic Thought of Woodrow Wilson* (Baltimore, 1943), 73, 78.

16. W. G. McAdoo, *Crowded Years* (Boston, 1931), 104–5; G. W. Perkins, *The Modern Corporation: Address . . . [at] Columbia University, February 7, 1908* (n.p., n.d. [1908]), 2; W. G. McAdoo, *Decent Treatment of the Public by Corporations and Regulation of Monopoly: A Speech . . . Before the Chamber of Commerce, Boston, Mass., January 30, 1911* (n.p., n.d. [1911]), 8, 9.

17. Senate Interstate Commerce Committee, *Control of Corporations, Persons and Firms . . . Hearings*, 62 Cong., 2 Sess. (1911), I, 1258, 1278; A. T. Mason, *Brandeis and the Modern State* (Princeton, 1933), 96; A. T. Mason, *Brandeis: A Free Man's Life* (New York, 1946), 585.

18. Link, *Wilson*, 492.

19. Brandeis to Wilson, Sept. 30, 1912; A. S. Link, *Wilson: The Road to the White House* (Princeton, 1947), 492.

20. Herbert Croly, *Progressive Democracy* (New York, 1914), 16–17, 54; Charles A. Beard, "Jefferson and the New Freedom," *New Republic*, Nov. 4, 1914; Walter Lippmann, *Drift and Mastery* (New York, 1914), 136–37; George W. Perkins, *National Action and Industrial Growth* [New York], 1914, 9, address at Lincoln Day Dinner of the Progressive Party, Feb. 12, 1914.

21. Woodrow Wilson, *The New Freedom* (New York, 1913), 284.

22. It is an odd and stilted book. At one point Dru muses about Russia and wonders when her deliverance will come. "There was, he knew, great work for someone to do in that despotic land." As the book ends, Dru has resigned his dictatorship, learned "Slavic," and sailed with his preternaturally patient girl friend from San Francisco to an unknown destination, presumably to start the Russian revolution. See [E. M. House], *Philip Dru, Administrator* (New York, 1912). House's original version of the book, I am informed by B. W. Huebsch, its publisher, and Harry E. Maule, was rewritten by Mr. Maule in order to bring it up to minimum standards of readability. The revision had to do only with style, however, not with content or form. Colonel House was apparently unhappy about the changes and gave only grudging approval to the final version.

Students of the occult, noting the resemblance between some of Dru's domestic program and the New Deal, take pleasure in pointing out that the first two letters of Dru's names spell F [Ph] DR. Roosevelt actually called the novel to a friend's attention in 1932, shortly before the Democratic convention; and a year later, toward the end of the Hundred Days, Miss LeHand wrote Huebsch, "The President desires to obtain a copy of . . . 'Philip Dru, Administrator.'" (F.D.R. to W. H. MacMasters, June 8, 1932, M. A. LeHand to B. W. Huebsch, June 1, 1933, Roosevelt Papers.)

23. F. K. Lane, *Letters*, A. W. Lane and L. H. Wall, eds. (Boston, 1922), 297.

24. A. S. Link, "The South and the 'New Freedom,'" *American Scholar*, Summer 1951.

25. Walter Lippmann, "The Case for Wilson," *New Republic*, Oct. 14, 1916; Herbert Croly, "The Two Parties in 1916," *New Republic*, Oct. 21, 1916; A. S. Link, *Woodrow Wilson and the Progressive Era* (New York, 1953).

26. H. L. Ickes, *Autobiography of a Curmudgeon* (New York, 1943), opposite 164, 217; Roosevelt's speech of March 28, 1918, in Theodore Roosevelt, *Letters*, E. E. Morison, ed., 8 vols. (Cambridge, 1951–54), VIII, 1294; Donald Richberg, *Tents of the Mighty* (Chicago, 1930), 97.

# Woodrow Wilson and the political economy of modern United States liberalism

## MARTIN J. SKLAR

With this essay, Martin J. Sklar virtually began the reinterpretation of Wilsonian democracy. Mainstream historians had largely accepted the analytical breakdown of Wilson's administrations into two separate periods: a laissez-faire period of the New Freedom from 1912 through 1914 and a post-1914 period when Wilson adopted commission regulation and supposedly moved toward the New Nationalism first proposed by Theodore Roosevelt.

Sklar posits instead a consistent Wilsonian vision: the desire to adopt new methods that would further extend American export markets and that would revise the law to correspond to the needs of large-scale corporation capitalism. Wilson's progressive reforms, Sklar argues, affirmed corporate capitalism and were meant to result in an easier acceptance by the populace of the new economic structure.

Unlike mainstream historians, Sklar does not view Wilson's candid defense of corporate interests as an example of immoral behavior on Wilson's part. Only mainstream liberals, Sklar claims, divorce politics and economics. Sklar notes that Wilsonian policy took place in the context of commitment to corporate capitalism. Hence the defense of the system was considered to be the highest morality. Sklar does not confuse his own opposition to capitalism with the charge that Wilson was hypocritical. He charges that the work of liberal historians is actually ahistorical as well as misleading.

---

Most persons are so thoroughly uninformed as to my opinions that I have concluded that the only things they have not read are my speeches. —Woodrow Wilson, 1912

Perhaps the greatest source of historical misconception about Woodrow Wilson is the methodological compartmentalization of his mentality into two distinct components, the "moralistic" and the "realistic" or "commercialistic," as if they were discrete and mutually exclusive. From this point of departure, if one thinks or acts "moralistically," he can not be considered capable at the same time of thinking and acting "realistically," at least not consistently: if one is a "moralist," his political behavior can be considered as deriving only secondarily, if at all, from an understanding of, or a serious concern for, the affairs of political economy.

Martin J. Sklar, "Woodrow Wilson and the Political Economy of Modern United States Liberalism, " Studies on the Left, I (1960), 17–47.

According to this approach, wherever Wilson is perceived to have spoken or acted for the "little man," "democracy," "liberty," "individual opportunity," and the like, he was "liberal" and moralistic; wherever he is perceived to have spoken or acted for corporate interests, economic expansion abroad, and the like, he was "conservative," "commercialistic," "expedient," or realistic. Where Wilson supported measures promoting large corporate interests at home or abroad, he is considered to have forsaken his moralism, to have been driven by political expediency, personal egoism, or implacable social and economic forces, or to have gathered the unintended consequences of a misdirected moralism. In this view, Wilson the moralist is generally considered the true type, and Wilson the realist, the deviant.

Aside from objections that may be raised against the naiveté and theoretical deficiencies of such an approach to social thought and ideology in general,[1] certain specific objections may be raised against such an approach to Wilson, particularly should the main ideological components generally attributed to Wilson's mentality be granted at the outset, and their implications accorded a modicum of examination.

First, the "Puritan ethic," to which students of Wilson have attached fundamental importance as basic to his mentality, made no such mutually exclusive distinction between a transcendent morality and the world of political economy. Puritanism embraced a morality applicable not merely to the world beyond, but as well to the living individual and existing society; it sanctioned, indeed posited, capitalist social and economic relations. The affirmation of capitalist society was therefore implicit in Wilson's Protestant morality. From the straightest-laced New England Puritan of the seventeenth century to Poor Richard's Benjamin Franklin, to Gospel-of-Wealth Andrew Carnegie, to New Freedom Woodrow Wilson, religious conviction and "market-place materialism" were each practical, each the uplifting agent of civilization and Providence, each the necessary condition for personal salvation and general human improvement, each a function of the other, mutually interdependent and interwoven like the white and purple threads of the single holy cloth. To the extent, then, that Puritanism entered significantly into Wilson's world-view, the affirmation of the capitalist system in the United States (and throughout the world) was a function of his morality, not merely an auxiliary prepossession.

Second, Wilson's moral affirmation of capitalism sanctioned by Puritan conceptions found powerful confirmation in the economic writings of Adam Smith (himself a professor of moral philosophy), John Bright, and Richard Cobden; as student and professor he had become firmly grounded in their theories of political economy, which he admired and enthusiastically espoused, and it is not difficult to perceive that such writings would strongly appeal to one reared on Puritanism. In Smith, Bright, and Cobden, Wilson found secular moral sanction for the bourgeois-democratic political economy as well as indefeasible economic principles. Private, competitive enterprise manifested natural law in the realm of political economy, and went hand in hand with republican institutions, comprising together the essential conditions of democracy, individual liberty, and increasing prosperity. To Wilson, much of whose economic thinking was based upon the assumption of the growing superiority of United States industry, the arguments of Smith, Cobden, and Bright were compelling: they, in their day, spoke for an industrially supreme Great Britain, and recognizing Britain's position, argued that the optimum condition for the nation's economic growth and expansion rested upon the "natural" flow of trade, a "natural" international division of labor, uninhibited by "artificial" hindrances.

Taken together, Puritanism and Smithian-Manchestrian economics instilled Wilson with the compulsion to serve the strengthening and extending of the politico-economic system he knew in the United States as a positively moralistic commitment, since that would strengthen and extend the sphere of liberty, democracy, prosperity, and Providence, and accorded with natural law. As William Diamond observes, such assumptions were to become "basic" to Wilson's "thought on foreign policy."[2]

Third and finally, the organismic view of society that Wilson derived from Edmund Burke and Walter Bagehot provided him with the concept that whatever social phenomena or social system evolved "naturally" from the traditions and customs of the past, from the working of natural law through "irresistible" social forces, were not only inevitable as prescriptively ordained but morally indisputable. They represented both the evolution of the genius of human custom and institutions and the assertion of God's will in human affairs. To Burke, whom Wilson revered and assiduously studied, the market economy manifested the working of natural law, which in turn manifested divine law. In Burke, Wilson could find a reverence for the market economy akin to religious awe: "the laws of commerce . . . are the laws of nature, and consequently the laws of God," Burke had said.[3] American Puritan doctrine, as developed by Johnathan Edwards, had itself become firmly anchored in the natural law of Newton and Locke; it required the intensive study of society's concrete development and condition, in order to comprehend God's work in the universe. In this respect, Puritanism and Burke stood on common ground. Here both religious and secular morality converged upon the affirmation of things as they were and as they appeared to be evolving. That which was "natural" was moral. The part of wisdom, morality, and statesmanship was to comprehend, affirm, and work for the necessary institutional adjustments to "natural" evolution and "the well-known laws of value and exchange."[4] This evolution-ary-positivist or conservative-historicist[5] approach to society served to modify whatever predilections Wilson may have had for atomized economic relations; it provided him with philosophical ground for rejecting the doctrine of unrestricted competition, as did the institutional economists he encountered at Johns Hopkins in the 1880's, and for affirming, as an inevitable result of the laws of commerce and natural social evolution, the demise of the freely competing entrepreneur at the hands of the large corporation. As Wilson once remarked, explaining his approval of large-scale industrial corporations, "No man indicts natural history. No man undertakes to say that the things that have happened by operation of irresistible forces are immoral things. . . ."[6]

To the extent that the characterization of Wilson's mentality as "moralistic" connotes Sunday school platitudes or pollyanna ingenuousness, therefore, it is not only irrelevant, but fundamentally misleading. Since Wilson's writings, speeches, policy decisions, and actions simply do not correspond with such "moralism," the tendency of those who view his mentality in this manner is to judge both Wilson's utterances and actions, and the great events with which he was concerned, either in terms of a Faustian personality torn between the forces of high idealism and gross materialism, or less charitably, in terms of a sophisticated hypocrisy: "Beneath the layer of Christian moralism is the shrewdness of the Puritan merchant. . . ."[7]

But Wilson's moralism was not simply a veneer "beneath" which lurked supposedly amoral "commercialism." It was a genuine and basic component of his ideological framework, though, it is submitted, no more so than in that of William Howard Taft, Philander C. Knox, Theodore Roosevelt, or Huntington Wilson. Woodrow Wilson's "wrung heart and wet hanky," we may be sure, were "real enough."[8] His thought in matters of political economy embraced a body of moralistic concepts, just as his moralism presumed certain principles of political economy and corresponding social relations. Whether or not in human thought and ideology the two have often failed to be inextricably interrelated, in Wilson they certainly were. A view of ideology that cast morality and ethics into one realm and political economy into another, that sees history as a struggle between the "ethical" men and the "materialistic" men, between the lofty and the commercialistic, suffers from an inverted economic determinism that overlooks the possibility that commitment to an economic way of life may go hand in hand with the most intense and highly systematized morality; with respect to Wilson, it forgets that just as classical political economy, "despite its worldly and wanton appearance—is a true moral science, the most moral of the sciences";[9] so Puritanism, as the works of R. H. Tawney and Max Weber suggest, despite its heavenly concern, is a truly worldly doctrine.

For Wilson, like Burke, ideals and principles, to the extent that they validly applied to society, arose from and satisfied, not rationally deduced abstract precepts, but practical experience with the concrete conditions of society drawn in the light of "the inviolable understandings of precedent."[10] "Will you never learn this fact," he lectured Boston real estate men in January, 1912, "that you do not make governments by theories? You accommodate theories to the circumstances. Theories are generalizations from the facts. The facts do not spring out of theories . . . but the facts break in and ignore theories . . . and as our life is, as our thought is, so will our Government be."[11] Accordingly, Wilson insisted upon the necessity of adjusting legal institutions to the changed circumstances of economics and politics: ". . . if you do not adjust your laws to the facts, so much the worse for the laws, not for the facts, because law trails after the facts. . . . we must [adjust the laws to the facts]; there is no choice . . . because the law, unless I have studied amiss, is the expression of the facts in legal relationships. Laws have never altered the facts; laws have always necessarily expressed the facts; adjusted interests as they have arisen and have changed toward one another."[12] It was the necessity, the "facts," which Wilson recognized that determined his world view.

Time and again Wilson emphasized that the facts of modern life to which adjustment was most urgent were economic in character. Indeed, Wilson viewed economic relations as basic to all other social relations. He analyzed conditions in the United States, its troubles and opportunities, as essentially the result of rapid industrialization aggravated by the passing of the continental frontier. He conceived the major issues of his time as "questions of economic policy chiefly," and defined in this manner not only the tariff, coinage and currency, trust, and immigration questions, but also, significantly, "foreign policy" and "our duty to our neighbors."[13] The life of the nation, he declared in 1911, was not what it was twenty, even ten, years before: economic conditions had changed "from top to bottom," and with them "the organization of our life."[14] As New Jersey governor-elect Wilson noted, "the world of business [has changed], and therefore the world of society and the world of politics. . . . A new economic society has sprung up, and we must effect a new set of adjustments. . . ." And as candidate for the Democratic presidential nomination in 1912, he declared, ". . . business underlies every part of our lives; the foundation of our lives, of our spiritual lives included, is economic." Business, he emphasized, "is the foundation of every other relationship, particularly of the political relationship. . . ."[15]

Wilson's view of economic relations as basic to social, political, and spiritual life, fit altogether consistently into his conservative-historicist, natural law approach to society. Understood in these terms, Wilson's "idealism" arose, therefore, from his conception of practical experience, of "natural" social evolution, of the genius of evolved social institutions, custom, habit, and traditions, of "irresistible" social forces, and the laws of commerce. It was that mixture of classical nineteenth century liberalism with conservative-historicism that made Wilson the Progressive he was: rational adjustments, determined by enlightened men concerned with the general welfare, were made to irrational processes, that is, to processes not determined by men but evolving irresistibly in accordance with supra-human natural law or predetermination.

Wilson's position on the "trust" question cannot be accurately understood apart from his firm conviction that law must correspond with the facts of economic life, must accommodate the people, their habits and institutions to, *and facilitate,* natural economic development, and in the process achieve the general welfare or national interest.

He defined the general welfare or national interest not in terms of abstract reasoning or visionary dreams, or from "pure" moral principles, but historically in terms of the "facts" of the existing economic structure and business organization. To Wilson, the "facts" were that the large corporation and large-scale industry had replaced the individual entrepreneur and small producing unit as the central and dominant feature of modern capitalism. Accordingly, the adjustments to be made, in Wilson's mind, involved not an attempt to restore the entrepreneurial competition of by-gone days nor the dissolution of large corporations, but on the contrary, "the task of translating law and morals into terms of modern business. . . ."[16] More precisely, the problem to be defined was that ". . . Our laws are still meant for business done by *individuals;* they have not been satisfactorily adjusted to business done by great *combinations,* and we have got to adjust them. . . . there is no choice."[17] What was needed were "open efforts to accommodate law to the material development which has so strengthened the country in all that it has undertaken by supplying its extraordinary life with necessary physical foundations."[18]

Usually overlooked in discussions about the great "anti-trust" debates of the pre–World War I period is that the leading participants were concerned not so much with the abstract idea of "competition versus monopoly" as with the role of the corporation in the new industrial order and its relation to the state. This was as true of Wilson as it was of Roosevelt, Taft, George W. Perkins, Elbert H. Gary, and Herbert Croly. In his writings and speeches on the "trusts," Wilson placed particular emphasis upon "the extraordinary development of corporate organization and administration,"[19] as the dominant mode of modern capitalist enterprise, upon the corresponding decline of unrestricted competition and the growth of "cooperation," and furthermore, of particular importance, consistent with his over-all view, upon the legitimacy of the process, the need to affirm and adjust to it. Large corporations were "indispensable to modern business enterprise"; "the combinations necessarily effected for the transaction of modern business"; "society's present means of effective life in the field of industry" and its "new way of massing its resources and its power of enterprise"; "organizations of a perfectly intelligible sort which the law has licensed for the convenience of extensive business," neither "hobgoblins" nor "unholy inventions of rascally rich men."[20]

As institutions that had developed "by operation of irresistible forces," large corporations could not be considered "immoral"; ". . . to suggest that the things that have happened to us must be reversed, and the scroll of time rolled back on itself," Wilson declared in 1912, '. . . would be futile and ridiculous. . . ."[21] On more than one occasion during the campaign of 1912, as he had in the past, Wilson declared: "I am not one of those who think that competition can be established by law against the drift of a world-wide economic tendency; neither am I one of those who believe that business done upon a great scale by a single organization—call it corporation or what you will—is necessarily dangerous to the liberties, even the economic liberties, of a great people like our own . . . I am not afraid of anything that is normal. I dare say we shall never return to the old order of individual competition, and that the organization of business upon a great scale of co-operation is, up to a certain point, itself normal and inevitable."[22] Or, as he put it on another occasion, ". . . nobody can fail to see that modern business is going to be done by corporations. . . We will do business henceforth when we do it on a great and successful scale, by means of corporations. . . ."[23]

With respect to remedies in the matter of "trusts," the task according to Wilson was "not to disintegrate what we have been at such pains to piece together in the organization of modern industrial enterprise"; a program of dissolution of the large corporations would only calamitously derange the economy; it would "throw great undertakings out of gear"; it would "disorga- nize some important business altogether."[24] Rather, the task was to prevent the misuse of corporations by individuals, make guilt and punishment individual rather than corporate, prescribe in law those practices corporations might and might not undertake, prohibit unfair and coercive methods of competition, require reasonable competition among the large corporations, and assure that corporations operate in the public interest.[25]

Historians have argued over when it was that Wilson first declared in favor of commission regulation of business, as if this were of fundamental importance to his over-all view of the trust question.[26] To Wilson, however, the question of commission regulation did not involve that of *laissez-faire* versus "positive" government, or regulation of monopoly versus enforcement of competition. It involved instead, the question of whether the ground rules of the new corporate system were to be left to arbitrary decisions of executive officers, subject to change with each administration, and possibly productive of both interference with personal and property rights and irrational attacks upon corporations, or whether, as he advocated, they were to become institutionalized in law. As had the corporate leaders themselves who testified before congressional committees, what Wilson wanted was "the certainty of law." Within that context, he favored "as much power as you choose."[27]

Whether one examines Wilson's thought before or during his "New Free- dom" years, it is evident that what is thought of as *laissez-faire* Jeffersonianism is not one of its characteristics. In 1908, for example, pointing to "the necessity for a firm and comprehensive regulation of business operations in the interest of fair dealing," Wilson stated, "No one now advocates the old *laissez-faire* . . ."[28] As if to emphasize his conviction that the popular notion of Jeffersonianism bore little direct relevance to the problems of modern times, Wilson took the occasion of the Democratic party's Jefferson Day Banquet in 1912 to assert, "We live in a new and strange age and reckon with new affairs alike in economics and politics of which Jefferson knew nothing."[29] With respect to the government's role in particular, as William Diamond summarizes the record, "Throughout his political life . . . [Wilson] was willing to use the government as a positive instrument in the economic life of the nation. . . ."[30]

In two most basic areas of policy and thought, then, that of the extent of government intervention in the economy and that of the "trust" question, Wilson was no more a "Jeffersonian" than was Theodore Roosevelt, Edward D. White, Oliver Wendell Holmes, George W. Perkins, or Herbert Croly. If "Jeffersonian" is meant to connote a return to an agrarian yeoman republic, or to the regime of unrestricted competition among independent entrepreneurs or small business units, or a government policy of *laissez-faire,* then much as it obscures more than clarifies in applying the term to any leading twentieth century figure in United States history, it certainly fails even allegorically to characterize, or provide much insight into, Wilson's thought or policy positions.

Accordingly, Wilson's "New Freedom" years, 1912-1914, may be more accurately comprehended not as a break with his past, just as his decision to make commission regulation the core of his "trust" program may be better understood not as a break with his "New Freedom" views. Before, during, and after 1914, Wilson's views on the "trust" question, like those of large corporate spokesmen within the Chicago Association of Commerce, National Civic Federation, and the United States Chamber of Commerce, and like those of Roosevelt and Bureau of Corporations chiefs James R. Garfield and Herbert K. Smith, embodied the common law-Rule of Reason doctrine ultimately handed down by the Supreme Court in its American Tobacco and Standard Oil decisions of 1911. Like the others, Wilson had opposed the Court's earlier decisions prohibiting both "reasonable" and "unreasonable" restraints of trade; like them his approach affirmed large-scale corporate organization, sought the institutional legitimization of reasonable restraints of trade and the prohibition of unreasonable restraints or "unfair" competition, as determined at common law and by judicial precedent, with the public interest as the central consideration.

Wilson's position on the "trust" question as of 1912–1914 may be looked upon as a synthesis of the positions of Taft and Roosevelt: on the one hand, acknowledgement of the demise of *individualistic, entrepreneurial* competition, but the affirmation of and insistence upon reasonable *intercorporate* competition; on the other hand, the prevention of "unfair competition" and affirmation of "reasonable" combination and intercorporate arrangements consistent with the "public interest" or "general welfare," under a government regulatory policy rooted in the settled precedents and practices of common and civil law jurisprudence, whether enforced by the courts or by an administrative commission or by a combination of both.

To cite the fact that Louis D. Brandeis exerted decisive influence in Wilson's acceptance of the trade commission bill as evidence of a basic alteration in Wilson's views on the trust question, is either to overlook Brandeis' public utterances at the time and the program he advocated, or to disregard Wilson's previous writings and statements. Brandeis' position avowedly embodied the Supreme Court's Rule of Reason decisions of 1911; he advocated "reasonable" restraints of trade (including limitations upon competition by trade associations) and the prohibition of "unfair practices."[31] The issue involved in Wilson's abandoning the Clayton bill was primarily the impracticality of specifying every unfair practice to be proscribed, and the severity with which, in its original form, it threatened to interfere with corporate practices. The Rule of Reason decision, on the other hand, provided the general term, "unfair competition," with a recognized meaning at common law as evolved over the past decades in court decisions. And after its establishment, when the Federal Trade Commission sought to define "unfair methods of competition," it began by cataloguing all practices that had been found by the courts to be unreasonable or unfair at common law.[32] The trade commission act, while not providing full certainty of law, as Wilson had wished, satisfied the basic elements of his position in removing regulatory powers from the arbitrary decisions of commissioners and grounding them in judicial precedent.

It should also be noted, within the context of the community of agreement on the "trust" question between Wilson and large corporate spokesmen, that the circumstances surrounding the writing of the bill bear no anomaly. As Arthur S. Link shows, Brandeis and George L. Rublee worked closely together and in consultation with Wilson in drafting the legislation; Rublee actually wrote the bill.[33] Generally unknown, however, is that at the time Rublee worked in Washington writing the measure, he was serving as a member of a special committee on trade commission legislation of the United States Chamber of Commerce. (Brandeis had been an initial member of the Chamber's committee, but retired in favor of Rublee under the press of other affairs.)[34]

But all this is not to imply that Wilson "sold out," that he was obliged reluctantly to submit to "implacable" forces, or that his views or policies had undergone any basic change. Rather, it is to suggest that, viewed within the context of Wilson's over-all thought and programmatic approach, the "New Freedom" years are not best understood as a distinctive period in his intellectual or political life, nor as "anti–Big Business" in nature or intent.

This view may be all the more forcefully substantiated if the interrelationship between the "New Freedom" legislation of 1913–1914 and promotion of United States economic expansion abroad is appreciated. Here again, it may be seen that, consistent with Wilson's previous and subsequent views, the "New Freedom" was not directed against large corporate developments at home or abroad.[35]

That prior to 1912–1914 Wilson had been a firm advocate of United States economic expansion abroad is a matter of record upon which there is general agreement by historians. His views in this respect have been sufficiently observed and analyzed elsewhere.[36] The main elements of his thought may be briefly summarized here. As an early adherent of Turner's frontier thesis Wilson defined the nation's natural political-economic development and its prosperity as a function of westward expansion. With the end of the continental frontier, expansion into world markets with the nation's surplus manufactured goods and capital was, in his view, indispensable to the stability and prosperity of the economy. It was also no more than a natural development in the life of any industrial nation, and, to him, in no way morally invidious since in his view, the nation's economic expansion was a civilizing force that carried with it principles of democracy and Christianity as well as bonds of international understanding and peace. Given the United States' superior industrial efficiency she would assume supremacy in the world's markets, provided artificial barriers to her economic expansion were eliminated. Accordingly, Wilson admired and championed Hay's open door policy and advocated vigorous government diplomacy and appropriate government measures to attain the ends in view.

Within this broad framework of thought, the application of the expanding-frontier image to economic expansion abroad, assumed a significance more fundamental than the invocation of a romantic metaphor: the West had been developed by the extension of railroads, the opening of mines, the development of agriculture—in short by the extension of the sphere of enterprise and investment that resulted in the widening of the internal market and fed the growth of large-scale industry. Markets for manufactured goods were in this way actively *developed, created,* in the West, by the metropolitan industrial and finance capitalists, and not without the significant aid of the federal government. Similarly with such markets abroad: foreign investments and industrial exports were seen by the corporate interests most heavily involved and by like-minded political leaders, such as Wilson, as going hand in hand, centered as their concern was on the needs of an industrial capitalist system in general and heavy industry in particular. Accordingly, the idea of "development" of agrarian areas in other parts of the world, and "release of energies," is prominent in Wilson's approach to economic expansion abroad.

Wilson's emphasis on exports of manufactures, his belief in their indispensability to the nation's prosperity, and his conception that the government should play a leading role in these matters, coincided in every essential respect with the views of the so-called Dollar Diplomatists, and of large corporate spokesmen within the U.S. Chamber of Commerce, the American Asiatic Association, the Pan-American Society, the American Manufacturers Export Association, and the National Foreign Trade Council. In like manner his advocacy of appropriate government measures to encourage an effective merchant marine and adequate international banking facilities flowed from this common concern for expanding the economic frontier; and his support of a low tariff was in large part informed by his belief that it was necessary to the nation's assumption of its proper role in world economic affairs.

But these were not merely the views of a supposedly "early" Wilson, later to be abandoned by the "New Freedom" Wilson; on the contrary, he carried them most emphatically, along with programmatic proposals, into his presidential campaign of 1912. Wilson's consistent theme, in this respect, during his bid for the presidency, is summarized in his address accepting the Democratic Party's presidential nomination: "Our industries have expanded to such a point that they will burst their jackets if they cannot find a free outlet to the markets of the world . . . Our domestic markets no longer suffice. We need foreign markets. . . ." The alternative, as he had previously put it, was "a congestion that will operate calamitously upon the economic conditions of the country." The economic imperatives, therefore, required institutional adjustments on the governmental and private business levels to break an outmoded "chysalis," in order to "relieve the plethora," and "use the energy of the [nation's] capital." They also pointed to "America's economic supremacy" (a phrase which Wilson shared with Brooks Adams): ". . . if we are not going to stifle economically, we have got to find our way out into the great international exchanges of the world"; the nation's "irresistible energy . . . has got to be released for the commercial conquest of the world," for "making ourselves supreme in the world from an economic point of view." He stressed three major reforms to meet the new necessities of the time—the downward revision of the tariff, the development of a strong merchant marine ("The nation that wants foreign commerce must have the arms of commerce"), and laws permitting foreign branch banking tied to a commercial-acceptance system (". . . this absolutely essential function of international trade . . .").[37]

Wilson's concern for the promotion of foreign trade and investment found expression in some of his key appointments upon assuming the presidency. To China, for example, he sent Paul S. Reinsch, long a prominent spokesman for economic expansion abroad. He appointed his intimate friend, Walter H. Page, as ambassador to Great Britain; as editor of *World's Work,* Page had published series of articles on such topics as "the industrial conquest of the world," to which Reinsch contributed.[38] Wilson's appointments of Edward N. Hurley and George L. Rublee to the newly formed Federal Trade Commission proved decisive, in its first few years, in making it a leading agency of foreign trade promotion, an aspect of its activities that was not then widely anticipated nor since been sufficiently appreciated.[39]

Wilson appointed William C. Redfield to head the Department of Commerce, which, with its Bureau of Foreign and Domestic Commerce, shared with the State Department the central responsibility within the federal government for promoting foreign economic expansion. It is a mistake to dismiss Redfield, as Link does with the remark that "perhaps his chief claim to fame was the fact that he was the last man in American public life to wear side whiskers. . . ."[40] For Redfield was a prominent member of the corporate community, enjoying the respect and confidence of corporate leaders. As a New York manufacturer of iron and steel products he spent many years abroad developing markets and as a "business statesman" much of his time expounding the theme of expansion and downward revision of the tariff. Like Wilson he had been a gold-Democrat, and the views of the two men were strikingly similar in matters of trade expansion and the tariff. Indeed, Wilson, in January, 1912, acknowledged that "I primed myself on Mr. Redfield's [tariff] speeches."[41] Of greater significance, indicating Redfield's prominence in the corporate community and the degree to which he represented corporate opinion, Redfield had been president of the American Manufacturers Export Association (organized in 1910), which, to use Robert A. Brady's terminology, was a peak association of large corporate interests. As Secretary of Commerce, with Wilson's support and approval, he immediately undertook to reorganize the Bureau of Foreign and Domestic Commerce for more efficient service in promoting foreign trade, and submitted a bill to Congress for the creation of a system of commercial attachés and agents, and trade commissioners, which Congress passed in 1914. Between the two of them, Redfield and Hurley, again with Wilson's approval, instituted many of the mechanisms of business-government cooperation in domestic and foreign trade, including the encouragement of trade associations, that are usually regarded as initially introduced by Herbert Hoover while Secretary of Commerce during the 1920's. Finally, it is important to note that while Wilson permitted Secretary of State William Jennings Bryan to make many ambassadorial appointments on the basis of patronage obligations, he refused to permit Bryan to disturb the consular service.

Against this background, the attitude of corporation leaders toward the three major pieces of "New Freedom" legislation of 1913–1914 (Underwood Tariff, Federal Reserve, and Federal Trade Commission acts), as well as the extent to which that legislation affected foreign trade expansion and to which, in turn, the nature of the legislation was determined by considerations relating to such expansion, may be more clearly understood.

Between 1910 and 1914, corporate leaders, particularly those connected with the large corporations and banking houses, were unusually active in organizing themselves for the promotion of their interests and programmatic objectives in domestic and foreign affairs. In 1910 industrial corporations organized the American Manufacturers Export Association (AMEA); in 1912, these corporations, along with other business organizations, such as the American Asiatic Association (AAA), established the United States Chamber of Commerce; and in 1914 the AMEA, the AAA, and the Pan-American Society joined together to form the National Foreign Trade Council (NFTC). These were all what might be called "peak associations" of large corporate interests; but the NFTC may be legitimately considered a peak association of peak associations. The officers and memberships of these associations interlocked as intricately as did the directors of the huge industrial corporations and finance houses of the time.

Of the more significant manifestations of the Wilson administration's concern for the promotion of foreign trade and of the community of agreement between large corporate interests and that administration, therefore, one was its endorsement of the purposes of the first National Foreign Trade Convention, convened in Washington, D. C., May 27 and 28, 1914. The Convention, presided over by Alba B. Johnson, and the National Foreign Trade Council subsequently established, with James A. Farrell as its president, were led and dominated by men representing the nation's greatest industrial, mercantile, and financial corporations.[42] As Johnson related, "This Convention had its inception at a meeting in New York some time ago" with Secretary of Commerce Redfield. He gave the idea for such a convention "his most cordial approval, and, therefore, it is fair to say" that he "is in a sense the Father of this Convention. . . ."[43] Edward N. Hurley, the first vice-chairman and later chairman of the Federal Trade Commission, also played a leading role in the organization of the Convention and in the Council's subsequent affairs.[44]

The Convention met in the afterglow of Secretary of State Bryan's appearance, in January, 1914, as guest of honor at the annual dinner of the American Asiatic Association, of which Willard Straight was then president.[45] At that time, the Underwood Tariff and Federal Reserve acts, measures most closely associated with the "New Freedom," had been passed by Congress. The Association's expressed purpose for inviting Bryan to the dinner, which was attended by leaders of the corporate community, was to exchange views with him on, and have him clarify, the administration's foreign policy. Emphasizing that the "era upon which we are entering is not only that of the Pacific Ocean, it must be one of Pacific development as well," Straight cited the new tariff as a stimulant for "carrying the war into the enemies' camp and competing abroad with those who will now invade our own market. . . ." And to the cheers of the diners, he observed that with the Panama Canal and the opportunity provided by the reserve act for the extension of foreign banking and investment, ". . . we are in a better position than at any time in our history aggressively to undertake the development of our export trade."[46] In response, Bryan pointed out that his duties as Secretary of State kept him "in touch with the expansion of American Commerce and the extension of American interests throughout the world," with which both he and the President were in "deep sympathy," and he assured the business men that the administration "will see that no industrial highwayman robs you. This government stands committed to the doctrine that these United States are entitled to the greatest possible industrial and commercial development." In this respect, like Straight, he singled out the tariff and reserve acts as decisive instrumentalities for giving the doctrine practical effect.[47]

The administration's endorsement of the National Foreign Trade Convention the following May assumed tangible forms. Secretary of Commerce Redfield delivered the opening address of the Convention on the morning of May 27, and he served as toastmaster at its banquet that night; Secretary of State Bryan delivered the main after-dinner speech at the banquet; and Wilson the next day received the delegates at the White House for a short interview.

As the Council later announced, the national importance of the Convention was "attested by the fact that its purpose [to promote foreign trade and a coordinated national foreign trade policy based upon the cooperation of government and business] was cordially indorsed by the President of the United States, who received the delegates at the White House; by the Secretary of State, who delivered, at the banquet, an outline of the administration's policy toward American business abroad; and by the Secretary of Commerce, who opened the convention. . . ."[48]

In his address to the delegates in the East Room of the White House, after having been introduced to them by Edward N. Hurley, Wilson declared his "wish to express . . . the feeling of encouragement that is given by the gathering of a body like this for such a purpose." For, he said, "There is nothing in which I am more interested than the fullest development of the trade of this country and its righteous conquest of foreign markets." Referring to Secretary Redfield's address of the previous day, Wilson confided: "I think that you will realize . . . that it is one of the things that we hold nearest to our heart that the government and you should cooperate in the most intimate manner in accomplishing our common object." He expressed the hope that this would be "only the first of a series of conferences of this sort with you gentlemen." In reply, Alba B. Johnson assured the President that as business men they realized "the deep interest which this government takes in promoting legitimate foreign trade. . . ."[49]

Bryan delivered two addresses at the banquet on the night of May 27, 1914, the first a short, prepared statement for release to the press, the second a lengthier extemporaneous speech. In the prepared speech Bryan declared the administration "earnestly desirous of increasing American foreign commerce and of widening the field of American enterprise. . . ." He reiterated its intention to cooperate with the business community to this end, and speaking for his own department he emphasized its "earnest purpose" to "obtain for Americans equality of opportunity in the development of the resources of foreign countries and in the markets of the world." Accordingly it was his "intention to employ every agency of the Department of State to extend and safeguard American commerce and legitimate American enterprises in foreign lands," consistent with the "sovereign rights of other governments."[50]

In his extemporaneous remarks, Bryan explained to the men of capital that his department's policy was Wilson's policy—what it "does in foreign affairs is but what the President desires." This meant, he said, "policies which will promote our industry abroad as well as home"; already, in the short time of the administration's existence, it had taken measures that would "tend directly and necessarily to promote commerce," such as the tariff and reserve acts. But "more than that," Bryan continued, the administration's efforts to win friends for the United States, safeguard the peace, and conclude commercial treaties constituted a broad contribution to the stabilization and extension of foreign economic expansion. "One sentence from President Wilson's Mobile speech has done a great deal to encourage commerce." When he there renounced territorial conquest as an object of United States policy in Latin America, ". . . he opened the doors of all the weaker countries to an invasion of American capital and American enterprise. (Applause.)"[51] As Bryan had put it at the Asiatic Association dinner, ". . . The doctrine of universal brotherhood is not sentimen- talism—it is practical philosophy . . . The government could not create trade, but it was its 'duty' to "create an environment in which it can develop."[52] He looked forward with "great expectations" to the extension of United States trade and investment abroad; the Convention itself provided "evidence that we are going forward," and the statistics showing the increase in exports of manufactured goods left "no doubt" that the United States could compete successfully with the European industrial nations "in the newer countries that are awaiting complete development," and that the United States would thus become "an increasing factor in the development" of such countries.[53]

Bryan's approach to economic expansion exemplifies a unified world view, embracing "moralism" and "commercialism" as interdependent and mutually consistent elements, that was so common to the expansionists of the time; the underlying assumptions of the "Good Neighbor" policy of later administrations were not basically different; and like the policy of Wilson or Straight it emphasized not merely trade but also "development" of agrarian countries, and the government's responsibility to foster those operations.

Promising the complete support of his Department for the extension of markets and investments abroad, and inviting the close cooperation between the business men and the State Department, Bryan told the corporate leaders, "I promise you that the State Department—every agency of it—will be back of every honest business man in pushing legitimate enterprise in all parts of the world. (Applause.)" To emphasize the community of purpose between the Department and the corporate interests, he continued by extending a colorful analogy: "In Spanish-speaking countries hospitality is expressed by a phrase, 'My house is your house.'. . . I can say, not merely in courtesy—but as a fact— my Department is your department; the ambassadors, the ministers and the consuls are all yours. It is their business to look after your interests and to guard your rights." If any of them failed to fulfill his responsibility, advised Bryan, "we shall be pleased to have you report them." For his part, the Department would "endeavor to open all doors to you. We shall endeavor to make all people friendly to you . . ."[54]

Given the general approach to expansion shared by men such as Wilson, Straight, Bryan, and corporate spokesmen, the question of "inner" motive is somewhat irrelevant. For example, what may be said of Straight's "inner" motive when he spoke of trade as the means to peace; or of the Steel Corporation's president, James A. Farrell, when he told the Convention: ". . . there is no factor which is so much involved in . . . [the nation's] material prosperity as the export trade," and then proceeded to say that "due to its great significance with respect to the economic conditions of our financial relations with the markets of the world, the export trade is likewise a vital factor in international affairs . . . The contest today is for supremacy in the trade of the world's markets, because that country which is a commercial power is also a power in other respects."?[55] The important point is that they held in common the assumption that expansion of markets and investment abroad was indispensable to the stability and growth of the political economy. As Redfield had put it at the banquet while introducing Bryan as the next speaker, the mission of his fellow diners was "to make this land of ours one of continual increasing prosperity." For, he continued:

. . . we have learned the lesson now, that our factories are so large that their output at full time is greater than America's market can continuously absorb. We know now that if we will run full time all the time, we must do it by reason of the orders we take from lands beyond the sea. To do less than that means homes in America in which the husbands are without work; to do that means factories that are shut down part of the time. And because the markets of the world are greater and steadier than the markets of any country can be, and because we are strong, we are going out, you and I, into the markets of the world to get our share. (Applause.)[56]

The record leaves no reason to doubt that the knowledgeable corporate leaders understood and accepted as genuine the administration's policy statements.[57] The difficulty in their view, lay not with the administration, but with the people. In this respect, upon closer examination, it is apparent that many of the pronouncements by business men in this period that have been interpreted as directed against the Wilson administration were more often directed against an "unenlightened" public and/or hostile senators or con-gressmen. As one business man put it, the public must realize "that governmen-tal assistance to American shipping and the American export trade is not only a business but a patriotic policy, pertaining to national defense as well as to our industrial welfare."[58] Or as Willard Straight phrased it, under current conditions of public opinion, "any administration may be attacked if it utilizes the power of the Government for the profit of private interests, no matter what indirect advantage might accrue to the country as a whole." The problem was to educate the people to accept government support of private foreign investments as action not on behalf of a special, but of the national, interest.[59]

In the context of Wilson's approach to both foreign trade and the "trust" question, and of the community of views between large corporate interests and his administration in these areas, the significance for foreign trade of the Federal Trade Commission Act, as the legislative embodiment of the Rule of Reason, may be better comprehended.

It was generally recognized in business circles that the large industrial corporations were most suited to successful export trade, and that the rapid rise in exports of manufacturers from the late 1890's to 1914 had been due largely to the operations of these corporations. The large corporations enjoyed low unit costs necessary for competition in world markets, particularly in the capital and durable goods industries. Their superior reserves and intimate connections with the great financial institutions enabled them to carry the expense of foreign sales promotion, offer attractive foreign credit facilities, and reap the benefits of foreign loans and concessions, all indispensable to an expanding and stable export trade. It was these corporations that were most intimately involved in the "development" of agrarian nations. Since the export of manufactured goods was considered primary in maintaining the nation's international exchanges, in liquidating foreign debts, and in guaranteeing domestic prosperity, the success of any business or governmental policy looking to the promotion of export trade and the achievement of these related objectives appeared to stand or fall with the large corporation. A domestic policy, therefore, designed to atomize large corporations could only prove self-defeating.

These were the points emphasized by such prominent spokesmen for large corporate interests as John D. Ryan, president of the Amalgamated Copper Company, M. A. Oudin of General Electric, and Alba B. Johnson of the Baldwin Locomotive Works.[60] As Johnson put it, "To attack our business interests because by reason of intelligent management they have grown strong is to cripple them in the struggle for the world's trade."[61] But their views, in so far as they related to the maintenance of large business units, were in no essential respect different from those of Wilson, whose attitude, as already indicated, may be summed up by the declaration in his Acceptance Speech: ". . . I am not afraid of anything that is normal."[62]

It is important to note, therefore, that the criticisms of "antitrust" bills pending in Congress by speakers at the 1914 National Foreign Trade Convention were leveled not against Wilson and his administration, but against "radicals" in Congress and what was considered misguided and dangerous public opinion. They particularly applied to the policy of the previous Taft administration, which in its last year and a half had "mined the Sherman Act for all it was worth."[63] But Wilson's position on the "trust" question was clear to all who read or heard his speeches, at any rate by early 1914; indeed, in his special address on the "trusts" to Congress in January, 1914, he had specifically declared, ". . . no measures of sweeping or novel change are necessary. . . . our object is not to unsettle business or anywhere seriously to break its established courses athwart."[64] Programmatically his position centered upon the legislative proposals advanced since the Hepburn amendments of 1908–1909, by large corporate interests through such organizations as the Chicago Association of Commerce, the National Civic Federation, and later the Chamber of Commerce. And by the end of 1914, large corporate interests found that they could look with satisfaction upon the status of the nation's "antitrust" laws.[65]

The "New Freedom" legislation on "trusts" bore upon matters of foreign trade expansion in a more overt way. In February, 1914, the Chamber of Commerce devoted its principal session, in which Secretary Redfield participated, to a discussion of the administration's trust program.[66] It was here that the Chamber appointed its special committee on trade commission legislation, of which William L. Saunders and Rublee were members. Other members included president of the Chamber R. G. Rhett, Professor Henry R. Seager of Columbia University, Charles R. Van Hise, president of the University of Wisconsin, and Guy E. Tripp, chairman of the board of directors of the Westinghouse Electric Manufacturing Company. One of the committee's recommendations, issued in the spring of 1914, urged that Congress "direct the Commission [when established] to investigate and report to Congress at the earliest practicable date on the advisability of amending the Sherman Act to allow a greater degree of cooperation" in the export trade. By a vote of 538 to 67 the Chamber's membership approved this specific recommendation (as did the National Foreign Trade Convention in May, 1914), along with the broader one supporting a trade commission act.[67] Accordingly, in the drafting of the act, which Rublee wrote, it was this Chamber committee that inserted word for word section 6(h), which authorized the trade commission to investigate world trade conditions and submit appropriate recommendations to Congress.[68] With Rublee and Hurley appointed by Wilson as two of the agency's five commissioners, the FTC undertook and completed in its first year of operation four investigations, three of which dealt with foreign trade conditions.[69] One of these resulted in the two volume *Report on Cooperation in American Export Trade*, which recommended that Congress pass what was to become the Export Trade

(Webb-Pomerene) Act of 1918 permitting cartels in the export trade, a bill which Wilson strongly supported.

The requirements of foreign trade promotion also influenced, in a negative way, the nature of the Clayton Act. As Oudin reported to the Foreign Trade Convention of May, 1914, ". . . the Committee on the Judiciary of the House . . . has reported a bill containing strict prohibitions against discriminations in prices for exclusive agencies, but providing that such prohibitions shall apply only in respect to commodities sold within the jurisdiction of the United States. This emphatic recognition of the distinction between domestic and export commerce reflects the growing disposition of the Government to render sympathetic assistance to American exporters. . . ."[70]

Just as the character of "New Freedom" legislation concerning the regulation of business related to the requirements of foreign trade promotion and reflected a community of views between the corporate community and the Wilson administration, the same was true, as already indicated of the two most important "New Freedom" laws passed in 1913, the Underwood Tariff and the Federal Reserve acts.

When Bryan, in his banquet address to the Foreign Trade Convention delegates, cited the tariff and reserve acts as measures taken by the administration for the promotion of foreign trade, he was not assuming the posture of protesting too much, nor was he merely waxing politically expedient to please his audience: the large corporate spokesmen among the delegates analyzed the two laws in precisely the same way. The two laws, it should be noted, were passed against the background of a trend among large industrial and financial interests, which had visibly emerged at least a decade before, toward tariff and banking structures oriented (inter alia) to their foreign trade and investment requirements. Bryan pointed to the elementary principle underlying the new tariff: "if we are to sell abroad, we must buy from people beyond our borders." The reserve act "will do more to promote trade in foreign lands than any other one thing that has been done in our history"; it had "set a nation free."[71] From no less a figure in large corporate circles than John E. Gardin, vice-president of the National City Bank of New York, came a similar view. Complaining of the nation's immaturity in matters of international finance, Gardin found encouragement in the tariff and reserve acts. 'The administration . . . certainly has given us two things of which we might be proud: one, the reduction of the tariff . . . opening up the markets of the world—if we want to sell we have got to buy; and the other is the Federal Reserve Law, which relieves us from the bondage" of an outmoded banking law, providing "relief just as important as the emancipation of the slaves. . . ." In view of these laws, Gardin looked forward to the projected program of the NFTC, as working "for the benefit of all those who wish to partake . . . of the new freedom."[72]

Among those spokesmen of industrial and financial interests who praised the Underwood Tariff, representatives of smaller interests were conspicuously absent. It is a mistake to view the Underwood measure as part of a "New Freedom" crusade against large corporations. It was part of the "New Freedom" program; but the heathens were not necessarily the large corporations. It was part of an attack on "special privilege" conceived to be in conflict with the national interest understood in terms of the conditions of modern times; but it was the special privilege cherished by smaller and by non-industrial interests, no longer needed by the larger interests as export trade became increasingly more important to them.

Aside from its immediate intent to stimulate export trade, the tariff, consistent with Wilson's views, sought to enforce industrial efficiency by inviting world-wide competition, which would result in making United States industry and finance a more formidable competitor in world markets. The larger industrial interests could withstand, and expect to fatten on, such competition, but not the smaller. Those items placed on the free list by the tariff were, in the majority, articles of food, clothing, and raw materials, industries occupied by the "little man." Large corporations engaged in the capital and durable goods industries, and most heavily involved in the export trade so far as manufactures were concerned, could approve this provision, because should the tariff have the intended effect, it would operate to keep wage levels down, reduce costs of materials, and in the process enable more effective competition in world markets, aside from increasing the profit rate. The issue was analogous to the great Corn Law debates in England during the previous century, where the industrialists sought to abolish import duties at the expense of producers of food and raw stuffs. Wilson, after all, had learned well from Cobden and Bright, the apostles of what has been aptly termed the "imperialism of free trade."[73]

At the same time, those items of heavy industry placed upon the free list, such as steel rails and agricultural machinery and implements, were already produced by the larger United States corporations with an efficiency and at a cost of production sufficient to permit not only successful competition in world markets in general, but within the national markets of the European industrial nations as well, a point Wilson frequently made. Of further aid to such competition, moreover, the Underwood Tariff granted drawbacks on exported items comprised in part or in whole of imported materials subject to import duties.[74]

In effect, the Underwood tariff strengthened the position of the larger corporations as against the smaller, and as against producers of agricultural materials. In this case, legal reform served the interest of those seeking to buttress the socio-economic status quo, while adherence to established law and institutions rallied those whose interest lay in forestalling the onward rush of that status quo. Accordingly, the greatest danger to the Underwood bill's downward revisions while pending in Congress "came from a horde of lobbyists," among whom the "owners and managers of industries that produced the great bulk of American industrial products were unconcerned and took no part. . . ." As Link concludes, the Underwood duties assumed their greatest significance "in so far as they reflected a lessening of the pressure from the large industrial interests for a McKinley type of protection."[75] It is understandable, therefore, that among the Congressional critics of the Underwood Tariff, as with the reserve law and the trade commission and Clayton acts, were "radical" and insurgent Democrats and Republicans claiming to represent the smaller and agrarian interests. In so far as the tariff, perhaps more dramatically than other issues, brought into unified focus the elements of efficiency, bigness in business, foreign trade, and an expanding sphere of enterprise—the last holding out the promise of more room for the "little man"—it may be accurately described as one of the high points of Wilsonian reform.

It is not meant to imply that the corporate community had no criticisms of the Underwood Tariff or Federal Reserve Act; but large corporate interests in particular viewed the new tariff either as a worthwhile experiment or more positively as sound policy, and business opinion overwhelmingly viewed the reserve law as basically sound, in need of perfecting amendments, rather than as a measure directed against their interests. The conflict over the reserve system bill during 1913 had not revolved so much around the provisions of the bill as around the question of how and by whom those provisions should be administered, except in so far as the "radical" and agrarian Republicans and Democrats insisted upon provisions that Wilson rejected. Otherwise, with respect to the manner of administering the system, the division lay not between Wilson and the "small" interests on the one side and "big business" on the other: the large corporate interests themselves were divided, particularly, the evidence indicates, along industrial and financial lines. As Link notes, the great mass of non-banking business opinion approved the bill, and in October, 1913, for example, both the Merchants Association of New York and the United States Chamber of Commerce (the latter by a vote of 306–17) endorsed it.[76]

The Federal Reserve Act may be interpreted, with respect to the issues raised here, in terms of a movement of large finance and industrial corporate interests, extending back to and before the National Monetary Commission, for branch banking, a commercial acceptance market for the facilitation of foreign trade and investment, and a reserve system that would protect the gold stock from foreign and domestic runs; a movement that, by expanding the credit structure, would reduce industrial corporations' dependence upon the money markets for investment capital, and insulate industrial operations from stock market fluctuations and speculators; a movement that Wilson approved and responded to favorably without himself being in any way responsible for its initiation, just as in the case of the movement for the Federal Trade Commission Act.

Indeed, upon his election, Wilson had no well-defined specific program; he had a general approach, and even his "specific" proposals were couched in general terms. He had identified himself with, and then given ideological and political leadership to, those movements with which his general approach corresponded, and which therefore corresponded with the concept of national interest embraced by that general approach. These movements—what are known as the Progressive reform movements (and they were reforms)—were movements led by and consisting of large corporate interests and political and intellectual leaders affirming the large corporate industrial capitalist system, and convinced of the necessity of institutionalized reforms, legal and otherwise, to accommodate the nation's law and habits, and the people's thinking, to the new corporate business structure and its requirements, domestic and foreign. As Wilson had put it, laws "meant for business done by individuals" had to be "satisfactorily adjusted to business done by great combinations," requiring "open efforts to accommodate law to the material development which has so strengthened the country."

Wilson's careful and emphatic distinction between the large corporation and the "trust" may be cited as one of the more forceful illustrations substantiating this formulation. A corollary of his evolutionary historicism, this distinction, in terms of Wilson's programmatic proposals, was decisive to his approach to the "trust" question, just as it was to that of the Bureau of Corporations under Garfield and Smith, and to that of Roosevelt, Taft, Perkins, Gary, and Croly. The large corporation, in this view, and the restriction of competition by correspon- ding forms of "cooperation," were the inevitable product of natural economic development. The "trust," however, was an artificial contrivance of predatory design, deliberately created by unscrupulous business men for undue ends. Accordingly, Wilson believed that while ". . . the elaboration of business upon a great co-operative scale is characteristic of our time and has come about by the natural operation of western civilization," this was different from saying that the "trusts" were inevitable. "Big business is no doubt to a large extent necessary and natural. The development of business upon a great scale, upon a great scale of cooperation, is inevitable, and, . . . is probably desirable. But that is a very different matter from the development of trusts, because the trusts have not grown. They have been artificially created; they have been put together not by natural processes, but by the will, the deliberate planning will, of men who . . . wished to make their power secure against competition." On the other hand, ". . . any large corporation built up by the legitimate processes of business, by economy, by efficiency, is natural; and I am not afraid of it, no matter how big it grows. . . ."[77]

Conservative-historicism, with Edmund Burke as one of its more prominent spokesmen, regards the politico-economic sphere of society "as a completely irrational one which cannot be fabricated by mechanical methods but which grows of its own accord. This outlook relates everything to the decisive dichotomy between 'construction according to calculated plan' and 'allowing things to grow.'" "A mode of thought is. thus created which conceives of history as the reign of pre- and super-rational forces."[78] This mode of thought, transmitted to Wilson in particular from Burke, may be traced as a central thread winding not only through the early twentieth century liberalism (Progressivism) of Theodore Roosevelt, Croly, et al., as well as Wilson, but also through the liberalism of such presently prominent bourgeois ideological leaders as Adolf A. Berle, Jr., who states: "Unlike the socialist commissariat, the American corporation is not a product of doctrine and dogma; it is an organic growth. . . ."[79] With respect to the basic structure of society, modern liberalism regards as legitimate only those institutions that it conceives as emerging independently of and beyond the deliberate, conscious determination of men; the underlying principle is submission to natural law, as distinguished, for example, from Marxism, which demands the understanding of objective laws of social development operating independently of man's will precisely in order to subject social development to man's conscious will; and as distinguished also from French Enlightenment social thought, which assumed that man could determine his society in accordance with Reason.[80] Conscious determination by men assumes its legitimate and proper function, from the modern liberal standpoint, only in facilitating natural evolution (as manifested in the basic structure of society as it is), and devising appropriate adjustments to it through parliamentary means (reforms).

The sharp and protracted ideological and social conflicts of the late nineteenth and early twentieth century, revolving around the corporate reorganization of the economy and erupting in the great "anti trust" debates of that period, suggest that the growth of the corporation was not so "organic" as modern United States liberals insist; that capitalists and like-minded political and intellectual leaders fought hard and consciously, with "doctrine and dogma" and with economic, political, and legal strategem, to establish the large corporation, in an historically short period of time, as the dominant mode of business enterprise, and to attain popular acceptance of that development. Nevertheless, the "allowing-things-to-grow" doctrine achieves a triumphant renaissance, as the unifying conception, in twentieth century United States liberalism, which may be accurately referred to as corporate-liberalism (though now Burke is left neglected backstage and Croly given the curtain calls). It is the fundamental element that makes modern United States liberalism the bourgeois Yankee cousin of modern European and English social-democracy.[81]

Within this essentially natural-law framework, while consistently holding that the large industrial corporations were natural and beneficent products of social evolution, Wilson attributed much of the evils with which they were popularly associated to financiers, *dei ex machina,* manipulating corporate securities and practices for speculative profit and creating artificial corporate structures for monopolistic advantage.[82] At the same time, by tying credit and currency mechanisms to the "natural laws" of commerce, that is, by basing the banking system upon commercial paper rather than upon government bonds, and building up a reserve system, measures long sought by large financial and industrial corporate interests, the federal reserve law corresponded with Wilson's view that trade and investment should be set "free" to pursue their "natural" course, unhindered by the arbitrary will of a few financiers; in theory, it would encourage greater competition (through greater opportunities for investment borrowing), and permit "little men" to obtain credit with which to start or maintain a business enterprise of their own, though no longer in the central areas of production, transportation, or communication. *Mutatis mutandis,* Wilson's position on the tariff flowed from similar considerations: the govern-ment's role was to provide business with the "environment" best suited to the assertion of its "natural" course.

Wilson held no dogmatic views on the question of the extent of government intervention in economic affairs—he had long believed that the state should intervene so far as "experience permits or the times demand"—and with respect to the reserve law, he had by June, 1913, firmly decided upon government control of the central reserve board, in the face of stiff banker opposition. The compromise that resulted constituted a concession to the large banking interests. After the bill's passage, and the announcement of Wilson's appointments to the central reserve board, the large banks' spokesmen, as well as spokesmen for large industrial corporations, expressed widespread satisfaction,[83] just as they had in the case of the Underwood Tariff and Federal Trade Commission acts.

In this way, Wilson emerged as a foremost ideological and political leader of a social movement affirming industrial corporate capitalism, and as the pre-eminent personality in the nation's public life acting as a bridge of communica-tion between that movement and the public (or, the electorate to which the movement appealed), popularizing the movement's ideology and program, and making them understandable and acceptable to the' people in terms of the nation's traditions, evolutionary development, and "destiny." The ideology embraced a neo-Comtean positivism that (in European terms) Wilson, the conservative-historicist and modified Manchestrian liberal, was eminently qualified to serve. Wilson's position was not that of a representative of the "little man," or the "middle class," *against* "big business"; but that of one who, affirming the large corporate industrial capitalist system, was concerned with establishing the legal and institutional environment most conducive to the system's stability and growth, while at the same time preserving some place within the system for the "little man." His formula was fair competition and impartial access to credit at home, and expansion of the economic frontier abroad, upon the assumption that the wider the market and the more impersonal its conditions, the more room and opportunity for the "little man" to coexist side by side with the big. The very conditions of industrial production and of foreign economic expansion, however, made the "little man," as an independent entrepreneur, increasingly irrelevant to the national economy, except in peripheral spheres of services and distribution. Theodore Roosevelt sought to meet this disturbing reality by acknowledging it and insisting upon equal opportunity for every young man to rise within the established corporate structures. While similarly insisting upon such equality, Wilson refused to concede the irrelevance of the "little man"; but his refusal was not a matter of sentimentality: it stemmed from his fear that given a growing irrelevance of "little men" in the nation's economy, fewer and fewer people would retain a stake in the capitalist system, and more and more would lose hope for betterment under capitalism and turn toward socialism or other forms of radicalism.[84] As such, the Wilsonian and Rooseveltian variants of Progressivism signified, if not the birth, then the coming of age, of twentieth century United States liberalism, whose present-day fundamentals, converging upon large-scale corporate capitalism at home and economic expansion abroad, remain genetically true to the components of Wilson's world view, their immediate parental source.

According to the generally accepted interpretation offered by Arthur S. Link, Wilsonian Progressivism, as applied and developed during Wilson's two terms as president from 1913 to 1921, can be divided into two periods: the first, the period of the "New Freedom," characterized by government attempts to regulate and stand in hostile posture apart from "big business," and directed at restoring some semblance of a *laissez-faire*, free-competition social order; the second, characterized by a government policy of cooperation with "big business" and active regulatory intervention in the economy. The divide, according to this view, lay somewhere around November, 1914 (though at points the divide is rolled back to early 1914, as a response to the continuing depression, leaving scarcely a year to the "New Freedom" phase). Thus, it is argued, the "New Freedom" was capable of serving the cause of Progressivism for only a short time; Progressivism gained new life after November, 1914, through the abandonment of the "New Freedom" and the move toward Herbert Croly's and Theodore Roosevelt's "New Nationalism."

If Wilson is properly understood in terms of the widely current evolutionary-positivistic world view that he shared alike with leading industrial and finance capitalists and with prominent politicians and intellectuals within the bi-partisan Progressive movement, and if the approaches taken by his administration to both foreign and domestic affairs are viewed as basically interrelated, rather than compartmentalized, as affecting each other, rather than operating in isolated spheres, then it is of greater analytical value to view the attitude assumed by Wilson and his administration toward "business" before and after November, 1914, as undergoing consistent development, rather than fundamental change. That attitude corresponded with a world view that affirmed large-scale corporate industrial capitalism as the natural and inevitable product of social evolution, and that regarded foreign investments and exports, defined in terms of the needs of industrial and finance capital, as indispensable to the nation's prosperity and social well-being. Beneficence at home and abroad, in this view, was a function of necessity. Large corporate production appeared as the vehicle of domestic material progress; foreign economic expansion, considered a decisive condition of such production, promised to carry "civilization," bourgeois-liberal ideas and institutions, and a better way of life, to the agrarian areas of the world, particularly as "development" of natural resources in those areas was considered essential to such expansion.

It no more occurred to such liberals as Wilson than it did to the so-called Dollar Diplomatists before him, or than it does today to the "internationalist" liberals, that investment in, and ownership of, other nations' resources, railroads, and industry, by United States capitalists, constituted imperialism or exploitation. Imperialism to them meant British- and European-style colonialism or exclusive spheres of interest; exploitation meant unscrupulous gouging, exorbitantly profitable concessions gained by undue influence with corrupt government officials, and the like, in short, "unfair practices" analoguous to those characteristics that distinguished the "trust" from the large corporation in domestic affairs. Open door expansion, on the other hand, appeared to them as simply the implementation of the natural international division of labor between the industrialized and agrarian nations; it meant mutually beneficial (and beneficent) business relationships and trade; it meant the assumption by the United States of its natural place in the world economy vis-à-vis the other industrial nations, by the elimination of "artificial" impediments to the operation of the laws of competitive commerce; it meant "free trade."[85]

In the Wilsonian manner, former president Truman recently remarked, "The Open Door policy is not imperialism; it is free trade." Unfortunately, the bourgeois-liberal mind seems unable to understand how any transaction that involves the exchange of equivalent for equivalent can carry with it any quality of injustice or exploitation. In the economic realm, morality and justice are defined as exchange at value, so long as it is devoid of any element of extra-pecuniary coercion; in more sophisticated ideological terms, morality and justice correspond with natural law. But it is precisely in the relationship defined by natural law, precisely in the exchange of equivalent for equivalent (assuming the free and competitive exchange of equivalents in the first place, though this is often not the case), that the exploitation, the injustice, the immorality, from the point of view of the agrarian peoples, resides. For, while the relationship is reified by the liberal mind as purely an exchange of goods, a confrontation of things, of private properties, what is really involved is a relationship between human beings. Concern for the nicely balanced exchange of things according to their market value—"a fair field and no favor"—blinds the liberal mind to the real relationship between people, of which the exchange of goods is but a consequence, and to the resulting conditions of life (the "human relations" and "individual dignity" with which the liberal is so articulately preoccupied.)[86] Hence, the innocent shock consistently evinced by liberals at anti-Americanism and resentment in the agrarian areas of the world regardless of whether United States foreign policy is of the "Dollar Diplomacy" or the "Good Neighbor" variety.

For, the essence of open door expansion involved an international system of economy identical to that established by England and the European industrial nations with their colonies and other agrarian areas. The latter were to become increasingly familiar with modern relations of capital and labor, but with capital appearing in the form of the foreigner and labor in the form of the indigenous population; they were assigned the role of suppliers of raw materials and markets for industrial goods and capital investment; and, of particular importance, control over, and investment decisions affecting, decisive sectors of their economies were to be transferred from their determination to that of capitalists in the United States. Those sectors of their economies were to become "complementary" to, and integrated with, the United States corporate economy, each an *imperium in imperio* within its respective nation, with all the implications of economic dislocation, political instability, and restriction of national economic and political independence. To Wilson, such implications were no necessary part of open door expansion, but rather of imperialism and exploitation as he narrowly conceived them; as for the rest, it all appeared as only natural in relations between "capital surplus" and "capital deficient" nations, and as the mode of progress in international affairs.[87]

It was the part of statesmanship to make law the expression of the necessities and facts of the time: to institutionalize the ground rules of the corporate economy at home and the mechanisms of economic expansion abroad, so that day to day business, the laws of commerce, and the government's role with respect to them, might flow smoothly along settled paths, rather than by the fits and starts of fire-brigade policy or executive fiat. As Wilson had put it in 1907, ". . . an institution is merely an established practice, an habitual method of dealing with the circumstances of life or the business of government. . . ."[88] In Wilson's view, it was this, with respect to modern circumstances of the modern industrial order, that the legislation of 1913–1914 promised to do.

Historians who have studied Wilson appear to harbor guilt-feelings about capitalism: a policy based upon considerations of the economic imperatives of capitalism is sordid, immoral, or amoral; a policy based upon non-economic principle is moralistic. The corporate and political policy-makers of the United States, Wilson included, have had no such guilt-feelings or compulsion to make such a division in their thinking. To them there was (and is) nothing immoral about capitalism; it embraces the highest morality. The strength and spread of morality appear as the function of the strength and spread of capitalism. Historians, however, disregarding the imperatives of modern capitalism, while assuming its existence all the same, seem to have created an ideal construct of what liberalism ought to be, arbitrarily imputing to it certain characteristics of a transcendent nature and withholding from it others, particularly those relating to the affairs of political economy. It is an academic, idealized liberalism, not the responsible political liberalism as it operates as a functional ideology outside the university walls; it is a liberalism from which historians have written history in the manner of advice, consent, and dissent, rather than history that analyzes the nature of liberal ideology as it operates and appears in the hurly-burly of political economy. Accordingly, historians have tended to appraise the nature of the Wilsonian liberal (or Progressive) movement by deduction from, and in comparison with, the supposed nature of its ideology, instead of basing their analyses on an empirical study of the movement and comprehending the ideology of its leaders as emerging from and interacting with that movement and its adversaries. Particularly is the latter approach essential to an analysis of Wilson, to whom the great issues of his day turned upon concrete economic interests and questions.

Finding that Wilson's thought and policies often deviated from the ideal model, many historians have concluded superficially that Wilson was a "hypocrite" or a conservative in liberal's clothing. The point raised here, however, is not a quarrel as to whether Wilson was in fact a liberal or Progressive; on the contrary, it is submitted that a successful, comprehensive effort at analyzing precisely what Wilsonian liberalism or Progressivism was (and modern United States liberalism in general) has yet to be made.

It would be conducive to a more impartial and comprehensive understanding of Wilson and Wilsonianism to discard as a tool of analysis both the "New

Freedom"–"New Nationalism" formula and the "Moralism"-vs.-"commercial-ism" presumption. This approach sees behind the "New Freedom" the shadow of a misconstrued Brandeis, who is taken inaccurately to symbolize an anti-"big business" program for the restoration of some sort of *laissez-faire,* free-competition society; more accurately, it sees behind the "New Nationalism" the shadow of Croly as represented in his book, *The Promise of American Life.* At the outset, and only at the outset, it may be more pertinent and analytically suggestive to a re-evaluation of Wilson and Wilsonianism, to see instead the shadow of Croly-the-adolescent behind the earlier years of Wilson's pres-idency, Croly-the-strapping-young-man behind the later (and lingering into the 1920's), with Croly-the-nearly-mature biding his time until the advent of the New Deal. In view of the present "national purpose" campaign of corporate spokesmen, liberal political and intellectual leaders, the Luce publications and the New York *Times,* short of a basic reordering of United States society, Croly-the-mature may yet arrive, and then the nation will surely be in need of a new freedom.

## NOTES

1. See Karl Mannheim, *Ideology and Utopia* (Harvest Book edition), 59–70. Mannheim here distinguishes between the "particular conception of ideology" and the "total conception of ideology"; it is in terms of the latter that Wilson's world view is comprehended in this essay.

2. William Diamond, *The Economic Thought of Woodrow Wilson* (Balt., 1943), 29. As revealed by his life, speeches, and writings, Wilson's concern was to protect the private enterprise system, as beneficent in itself and in its effects, from those dishonest, un-scrupulous men who threatened to misuse and pervert it (and from socialists who threatened to abolish it). It was in keeping with his intense commitment to his moral principles that Wilson, early and late in his life, viewed an activist political career as his "heart's first—primary—ambition and purpose," as opposed to pure academic pursuits. Wilson to Ellen Axson, Feb. 1885, cited in Arthur S. Link, *Wilson: The Road to the White House* (Princeton, 1947), 19 (hereafter cited as Link, *Wilson,* I). Emphasis in original. *Cf. ibid.,* 20, 23, 97, 123, 130; and Ray S. Baker, *Woodrow Wilson, Life and Letters* (8 vols., N.Y., various dates), I, 229, II, 98. It was therefore only natural that in the 1880's and 1890's and thereafter, far from being a head-in-the-clouds "idealist," Wilson made himself in-timately conversant with the concrete political and economic issues of the day.

3. Burke, *Thoughts and Details on Scarcity* (World Classics edition), VI, 22, also 6, 9, 10.

4. See, e.g., Wilson's "The Making of the Nation," *Atlantic Monthly,* LXXX (July 1897), in Ray S. Baker and William E. Dodd (ed.), *The Public Papers of Woodrow Wilson* (4 vols., N.Y., 1925, 1926), I, 328 (hereafter cited as *P P W W*); and "Democracy and Efficiency," *Atlantic Monthly,* LXXXVII (March 1901), *ibid.,* 400.

5. The term conservative-historicist is used in the technical sense defined by Mannheim, *op. cit.,* 120, 121, and is not meant here to denote "conservatism" as against "liberalism" as those terms are conventionally used.

6. "Richmond Address," delivered before the General Assembly of Virginia and the City Council of Richmond, Feb. 1, 1912, *P P W W,* II, 377.

7. Richard W. Van Alstyne, "American Nationalism and Its Mythology," *Queen's Quarterly,* LXV, 3 (Autumn 1958), 436.

8. For this reference to Wilson by D. H. Lawrence, see his *Studies in Classic American Literature,* 1922 (Anchor edition: N.Y., 1951), 32–33, which contains a valuable insight into the morality showed by Wilson in the chapters on Benjamin Franklin and Hector St. John de Crevecoeur, pp. 19–43.

9. Karl Marx, *Economic and Philosophic Manuscripts of 1844* (Foreign Languages Publishing House, Moscow, n.d.), 119.

10. "The Ideals of America," *Atlantic Monthly*, XC (Dec. 1902), *P P W W*, I, 422; Baker, *Wilson, Life and Letters*, II, 104.

11. "Efficiency" (Jan. 27, 1912), *P P W W*, II, 361.

12. *The New Freedom* (N. Y., 1914), 33, 34, 35; "Richmond Address" (Feb. 1, 1912), *P P W W*, II, 376. For an interesting comparison worth noting here, see Karl Marx, *The Poverty of Philosophy* (1847): "Indeed, an utter ignorance of history is necessary in order not to know that at all times sovereign rulers have had to submit to economic conditions and have never been able to dictate laws to them. Both political and civil legislation do no more than recognize and protocol the will of economic conditions. . . . Law is nothing but the recognition of fact." Translation is that found in Franz Mehring, *Karl Marx, the Story of His Life* (London, 1951), 123. (*Cf. The Poverty of Philosophy* [For. Lang. Pub. House, Moscow, n.d.], 83). For a present-day view that regards law as subordinate to economic fact, specifically with respect to the rise of the corporation as the predominant form of business organization, *cf.* Edward S. Mason (ed.), *The Corporation in Modern Society* (Cambridge, Mass., 1959), 1, where Mason, in his Introduction, states: ". . . law in a major manifestation is simply a device for facilitating and registering the obvious and the inevitable. . . ."

13. "Leaderless Government," address before Virginia State Bar Association, Aug. 4, 1897, *P P W W*, I, 354.

14. "Issues of Freedom," address at banquet of Knife and Fork Club of Kansas City, Mo., May 5, 1911, *P P W W*, II, 285; *The New Freedom*, 3.

15. Inaugural Address as gov.-elect of New Jersey, Jan. 17, 1911, *P P W W*, II, 273; "Government in Relation to Business," address at Annual Banquet of the Economic Club, New York, May 23, 1912, *ibid.*, 431, 432. In 1898, Wilson had observed, "For whatever we say of other motives, we must never forget that in the main the ordinary conduct of man is determined by economic motives." Quoted in Diamond, *op. cit.*, 52 n.

16. "Politics (1857–1907)," *Atlantic Monthly*, C (Nov. 1907), *P P W W*, II, 19.

17. "Richmond Address" (Feb. 1, 1912), *ibid.*, 376.

18. *The New Freedom*, 117–118.

19. "The Lawyer and the Community," annual address delivered before the American Bar Association, Chattanooga, Aug. 31, 1910, *P P W W*, II, 253.

20. *Ibid.*, 254–257, 262; "Bankers and Statesmanship," address before the New Jersey Bankers' Association, Atlantic City, May 6, 1910, *ibid.*, 229; *The New Freedom*, 5; Inaugural Address as gov.-elect of New Jersey (Jan. 17, 1911), *P P W W*, II, 271.

21. "Richmond Address," *ibid.*, 376–377.

22. Address accepting Democratic party presidential nomination, Aug. 7, 1912, *Official Report of the Proceedings of the Democratic National Convention*, 1912, 407. The "certain point" referred to by Wilson was the point of diminishing returns. The enterprise that made money in the market without recourse to coercive or "artificial" practices was normal, its size justified by its pecuniary success.

23. "The Tariff and the Trusts," address at Nashville, Tenn., Feb. 24, 1912, *P P W W*, II, 410–411. In this connection, more than a decade before Theodore Roosevelt denounced the "rural tories" as reactionaries whose passion for unrestricted competition and small business units would turn back the clock of progress, Wilson, in December, 1900, had applied the same criticism to Populists and Bryan-Democrats: "Most of our reformers are retro-reformers. They want to hale us back to an old chrysalis which we have broken; they want us to resume a shape which we have outgrown. . . ." "The Puritan," speech before the New England Society of N.Y.C., Dec. 22, 1900, *ibid.*, I, 365.

24. "The Lawyer and the Community" (Aug. 31, 1910), *ibid.*, II, 254.

25. "You cannot establish competition by law, but you can take away the obstacles by law that stand in the way of competition, and while we may despair of setting up competition among individual persons there is good ground for setting up competition between these great combinations, and after we have got them competing with one another they will come to their senses in so many respects that we can afterwards hold conference with them without losing our self-respect." Wilson, Jackson Day Dinner Address, Jan. 8, 1912, *ibid.*, 348.

26. See, e.g., John W. Davidson (ed.), *A Crossroads of Freedom: The 1912 Campaign Speeches of Woodrow Wilson* (New Haven, 1956), 80.

27. "The Vision of the Democratic Party" (New Haven Address, Sept. 25, 1912), *ibid.*, 264–265. Davidson points out (see fn 26 above) that Wilson declared for commission regulation at his Buffalo speech of September 2, 1912, at least three weeks prior to the New Haven address, but the point Wilson made on these occasions was in no essential respect different from that which he made more than four years earlier, when insisting "everywhere upon definition, uniform, exact, enforceable," he stated (in criticism of the pending Hepburn amendments to the Sherman Act), "If there must be commissions, let them be, not executive instrumentalities having indefinite powers capable of domineering as well as regulating, but tribunals of easy and uniform process acting under precise terms of power in the enforcement of precise terms of regulation." "Law or Personal Power," address delivered to the National Democratic Club, N. Y., April 13, 1908, *P P W W*, II, 28.

28. *Ibid.*, 25.

29. "What Jefferson Would Do," *ibid.*, 424.

30. Diamond, *Econ. Thought of Wilson*, 130.

31. See, e.g., Brandeis' testimony before House Comm. on the Jud., *Trust Legislation* (Ser. No. 2)—*Patent Legislation* (Ser. No. 1), *Hearings on H. R. 11380, H. R. 11381, H. R. 15926, and H. R. 19959*, Jan. 26, 27, and Feb. 19, 1912, 62d Cong., 2d Sess. (Wash., 1912), 13–54 (Brandeis testified on Jan. 26, 1912); and Brandeis, "The Solution of the Trust Problem," *Harper's Weekly*, LVIII (No. 2968), Nov. 8, 1913, 18–19.

32. *Memorandum on Unfair Competition at the Common Law* (printed for office use only by the Federal Trade Comm., 1915), cited and discussed in Thomas C. Blaisdell, Jr., *The Federal Trade Commission* (N.Y., 1932), 21–23.

33. Link, *Wilson: The New Freedom* (Princeton, 1956), 436–438, 441 (hereafter cited as Link, *Wilson*, I). See also, George Rublee, "The Original Plan and Early History of the Federal Trade Commission," *Proceedings of the Academy of Political Science*, XI, 4 (Jan. 1926), 114–120.

34. Senate Comm. on Interstate Commerce, "Promotion of Export Trade," *Hearings on H. R. 17350*, 64th Cong., 2d Sess., Jan. 1917 (Wash., 1917), 10–12.

35. For a characteristic formulation of the conventional interpretation of the "New Freedom," particularly with respect to foreign relations, see Charles A. Beard, *The Idea of National Interest* (N.Y., 1934), 121, 122, 464. In this valuable theoretical work designed to demonstrate that United States foreign policy has historically been based not upon abstract ideals, but upon the pursuit of national interest as defined by the realities of political economy, Beard felt obliged to classify Wilson as an exception to the rule. According to Beard, Wilson "turned a cold shoulder" to the great economic interests that had "on the whole, supported and benefited by dollar diplomacy." "From the turn of the century," Beard explains, "the practice of giving aggressive support to the interests of American citizens abroad grew until it appeared to attain almost world-wide range and received the authority of a positive official creed in the conception of dollar diplomacy. . . . After a brief setback during the Wilson regime, the pattern was restored again with the return to power of a Republican administration in 1921. . . ." But, "in the main, the policies of President Wilson, both domestic and foreign, ran counter to corporate development and commercial expansion under the impulse of dollar diplomacy, with their accompanying interpretations of national interest. . . ."

36. Diamond, *op. cit.*, 131–161.

37. See in particular his speeches, "Efficiency" (Jan. 27, 1912), *P P W W*, II, 357–360, 372–375, 380; "The Tariff and the Trusts" (Feb. 24, 1912), *ibid.*, 407–409; and "Speech of Acceptance" (Aug. 7, 1912), *ibid.*, 471–472.

38. See, e.g., Walter H. Page to Paul S. Reinsch, Aug. 13, Nov. 15, Dec. 10, Dec. 28, 1900, in *Paul S. Reinsch Papers, Correspondence, 1892–1908*. Collection owned by State Historical Society of Wisconsin (Madison).

39. As a member of the Chamber of Commerce's special committee on trade commission legislation, Rublee played a leading role in the Chamber's campaign to authorize the Commission to investigate world trade conditions and make appropriate recommendations to Congress. Hurley was a prominent Illinois industrialist who had introduced the pneumatic tool industry to the United States, had been an active member and president of the Illinois Manufacturers Association, and, as an articulate advocate of economic expansion abroad, had played a leading role in the organization of the National Foreign Trade Council. In 1913 he toured Latin America as an official trade commissioner for

Wilson's Department of Commerce to investigate market and investment opportunities for United States industry and finance.

40. Link, *Wilson*, II, 139. It might also be noted that Link errs in stating (*Woodrow Wilson and the Progressive Era, 1910-1917*, N.Y., 1954, 74) that Rublee was prevented from serving on the Federal Trade Commission due to the Senate's refusal to confirm his nomination in deference to Senator Jacob H. Gallinger (Repub.—N.H.), who declared Rublee "personally obnoxious." Actually, Rublee served, under a recess appointment by Wilson, for about eighteen months, from March 16, 1915, to Sept. 8, 1916, before he was obliged to retire. See *Federal Trade Commission Decisions* (March 16, 1915, to June 30, 1919), Wash., 1920, I, p. 4; and Rublee, *op. cit.*, 120.

41. "The Tariff" (Jan. 3, 1912), *P P W W*, II, 330.

42. *Official Report of the National Foreign Trade Convention* (1914), 15, 16, 457–458 (hereafter cited as NFTC, *Proceedings*). Johnson was himself president of the Baldwin Locomotive Works, and Farrell the president of the United States Steel Corporation.

43. *Ibid.*, 203–204.

44. *Ibid.*, 15, 17, 457.

45. Straight had served as agent of the American Banking Group in China during the days of the Six-Power Consortium, was associated with the House of Morgan, and was a leading participant in the organization of the NFTC.

46. The reserve act, as Straight noted, permitted "the establishment of branches of American banking institutions abroad," and with its provision for a commercial-acceptance system promised to "free vast sums for use in an international discount market and for the purchase of desirable foreign securities." *Journal of the American Asiatic Association*, XIV, 1 (Feb. 1914), 8 (hereafter cited as *AAA Jour.*).

47. The reserve act, according to Bryan, as a law the nation "long needed," would stimulate foreign trade "not only in the Orient but also throughout South America"; the new tariff meant "a larger commerce between our nation and the world, and in this increase the Orient will have her share," to the advantage not only of the public in general, but "especially" of "those merchants and manufacturers now turning their eyes to the Far East." McKinley's advocacy of tariff reduction "as a means of extending . . . our exports," was "a prophetic utterance": we "must buy if we would sell." *Ibid.*, 12–13.

48. NFTC, *Proceedings* (1914), 8.

49. *Ibid.*, 392–393.

50. *Ibid.*, 206, 207. That this represented administration policy, not merely edifying rhetoric to win the favor of corporate interests, is corroborated, *inter alia*, by the exchange of notes during the summer of 1913 between Bryan and E. T. Williams (U. S. Chargé d'Affaires at Peking). Williams requested instructions "as to the attitude to be taken by this Legation towards financial transactions between American capitalists and the Chinese Government," in view of President Wilson's statement of March 18, 1913, repudiating the Six-Power Consortium and the Reorganization Loan. Referring to the passages in that statement that the American people "wish to participate . . . very generously, in the opening . . . [of] the almost untouched and perhaps unrivaled resources of China," and that the U. S. government "is earnestly desirous of promoting the most extended and intimate trade relationship between this country and the Chinese Republic," Williams suggested as his understanding of the administration's policy that the State Department would support "industrial" loans and investments for the development of railways and mineral resources, secured upon the assets and earnings of such enterprises, but not "financial loans" to the Chinese provincial and central governments secured upon government revenues. Bryan replied that ". . . the Legation is right in assuming that the Department is extremely interested in promoting, in every proper way, the legitimate enterprises of American citizens in China and in developing to the fullest extent the commercial relations between the two countries." He continued, "It may be stated, in general, that this Government expects that American enterprise should have opportunity everywhere abroad to compete for contractual favors on the same footing as any foreign competitors, and this implies also equal opportunity to an American competitor to make good his ability to execute the contract. . . . [This Government] stands ready, if wrong be done toward an American citizen in his business relations with a foreign government, to use all proper effort toward securing just treatment for its citizens. *This rule applies as well to financial contracts as to industrial engagements.*" (Emphasis added). Dept. of State,

*Papers Relating to the Foreign Relations of the United States*, 1913, 183–187, 170–171. It is essential to note that the conditions outlined by Bryan in this note and in one cited by him from Secretary of State Richard Olney to Minister Charles Denby in 1896 (*ibid.*, 1897, 56), delimiting the extent of government support for U. S. enterprise abroad (*i. e.*, refusing special support for one U.S. firm to the exclusion of others, refusing to guarantee the execution of contracts or the success of an enterprise, and renouncing any commitment to intercede forcibly in the internal affairs of foreign nations on behalf of U.S. capitalists), were all well established principles affirmed alike by the Dollar Diplomatists (such as Taft, Knox, H. Wilson, Calhoun, Straight, Warren, Mark) in their public statements and diplomatic notes, and by their predecessors. These delimiting principles were in no way peculiar to the Wilson administration, and cannot be considered as distinguishing its policy from that of Taft and Knox.

51. NFTC, *Proceedings* (1914), 208–210. Along with the Mobile speech, the statement repudiating the Six-Power Consortium is most often cited to substantiate the view that Wilson repudiated Dollar Diplomacy. If this is meant as a repudiation of government support of corporate interests in expanding investments and exports abroad, then as already indicated in the immediately preceding text and in footnote 50, above, neither the Mobile speech nor the consortium statement is amenable to such interpretation. Wilson's consortium statement not only emphasized the government's intention to promote United States participation in the development of China and the closest of commercial relations between the two countries, but also specifically declared, ". . . The present administration will urge and support the legislative measures necessary to give American merchants, manufacturers, contractors, and engineers the banking and other financial facilities which they now lack and without which they are at a serious disadvantage as compared with their industrial and commercial rivals. This is its duty. This is the main material interest of its citizens in the development of China. . . ." *Foreign Relations*, 1913, 171. *Cf.* the versions of and references to the statement in George H. Blakeslee (ed.), *Recent Developments in China* (N.Y., 1913), 159–160; John V. A. MacMurray (ed.), *Treaties and Agreements with and concerning China, 1894–1919* (N. Y., 1921), II, 1025; Charles Vevier, *The United States and China, 1906–1913* (Rutgers Univ. Press, N. J., 1955), 210. All these versions include the reference to banking and other financial facilities needed for effective competition in Chinese markets. (These facilities were regarded as essential by corporate interests to foreign economic expansion and were provided in 1913 by sections 13, 14, and 25 of the Federal Reserve Act, which permitted branch banking abroad and the establishment of a domestic discount market for foreign trade commercial acceptances). Unfortunately, in the widely used *Documents of American History*, edited by Henry S. Commager, the consortium statement, there entitled "The Repudiation of 'Dollar Diplomacy,'" is entirely reproduced, except for the passage referring to the banking and other financial facilities (5th ed., 1949, Doc. 390). For further evidence regarding the Wilson administration's intentions in repudiating the consortium, see Secretary of State Bryan's address before the Asiatic Association in January, 1914, where he explained, ". . . The new administration in withdrawing approval from the Chinese loan did not question the good faith or good intent of those who had seen in it a means of increasing our influence, prestige and commercial power in China. The President believed that a different policy was more consistent with the American position, and that it would in the long run be more advantageous to our commerce. . . ." See also Willard Straight's remark on the same occasion that though many business men ". . . have interpreted the announcement . . . to mean that the American Government would not extend to our bankers the support which those familiar with trade conditions in China consider necessary . . . I personally feel assured that this impression . . . is not justified. . . ." *AAA Jour.*, XIV, 1 (Feb. 1914), 12, 8–9; *cf.* editorial in *ibid.*, 2. The present author examines this question in greater detail in his master's thesis.

52. *AAA Jour.*, XIV, 1 (Feb. 1914), 13. *Cf.* Straight's remark: "The true armies of world peace . . . are the merchants engaged in international trade. In this army, the Secretary of State is a Chief of Staff, and the Ambassador a Corps Commander. We of this [Asiatic] Association are the rank and file. . . ." *Ibid.*, 8. Also, that of M. A. Oudin, manager of the Foreign department of General Electric Co., that while the government could not create trade, it could "point the way to private enterprise." NFTC, *Proceedings* (1914), 366,367, 379–380.

53. *Ibid.*, *Proceedings* (1914), 207, 208.

54. *Ibid.*, 210–211.

55. *Ibid.*, 35, 36.

56. *Ibid.*, 205. For similar expressions on the indispensability of exports to the nation's prosperity by business and political leaders, see *Ibid.*, 6, 7, 70, 74, 80, 86, 117, 140, 141, 214, 218, 230–231, 285.

57. See, e. g., the remark of M. A. Oudin of General Electric, *Ibid.*, 366, 367, 379–380.

58. P. H. W. Ross, president of the National Marine League, *Ibid.*, 143.

59. *Ibid.*, 174–187.

60. See their remarks in *Ibid.*, 167, 168, 375–378, 327–328.

61. *Ibid.*, 327–328.

62. *P P W W*, II, 464; *ibid.*

63. Robert H. Wiebe, "The House of Morgan and the Executive, 1905–1913," *American Historical Review*, LXV, 1 (Oct. 1959), 58. *Cf. The Federal Antitrust Law with Amendments, List of Cases Instituted by the United States, and Citations of Cases Decided Thereunder or Relating Thereto*, Jan. 1, 1914, in Sen. Comm. on the Jud., *Hearings . . . together with Briefs and Memoranda . . . Compiled for Use in Consideration of H. R. 15657*, 63d Cong., 2d Sess. (Wash., 1914), 164–183.

64. *P P W W*, III, 82, 83. Emphasis in original.

65. See, e.g., the report of William L. Saunders to the second National Foreign Trade Convention in January, 1915. Chairman of the board of the Ingersoll-Rand Company, Saunders was also a charter member of the National Foreign Trade Council, and had served with Rublee on the Chamber of Commerce's special committee that played a leading part in drafting the trade commission act. Saunders observed that the Sherman Law prohibited only those restraints of trade that were "unreasonable or contrary to the public welfare," and that there was "no likelihood" of its becoming "any more drastic." The Clayton Act "defines a monopoly and . . . announces certain moral principles to which we all agree;" while the trade commission act "prevents unfair methods of competition," and as such "is the most wholesome legislation . . . that has been passed recently" in the matter of trusts. Saunders criticized *opponents* of the trade commission act for not seeing that "cooperation among business men—cooperation and concentration—is wholesome business and a good economic condition." NFTC, *Proceedings* (1915), 54, 56.

66. See *La Follette's Weekly*, VI, 8 (Feb. 21, 1914), 1–2.

67. Sen. Comm. on Interstate Commerce, "Promotion of Export Trade," *Hearings*, 64th Cong., 2d Sess., 11.

68. FNIIbid., 10–12.

69. *Annual Report of the Federal Trade Commission for the Year Ended June 30, 1916*, 18.

70. NFTC, *Proceedings* (1914), 379; *cf.* House Comm. on Jud., *Hearings on Trust Legislation* (2 vols.), 63d Cong., 2d Sess., Serial 7, 1914, II, 1960–1963.

71. NFTC, *Proceedings* (1914), 208–209.

72. *Ibid.*, 249, 250–251. See also the remarks of Fred Brown Whitney, chairman of the board of directors of the Lake Torpedo Boat Co., Alba B. Johnson, Clarence J. Owens, managing director of the Southern Commercial Congress (at whose convention in 1913 Wilson had delivered his Mobile address), Herbert S. P. Deans, manager of the foreign exchange department of the Merchants Loan and Trust Company Bank of Chicago, Edward N. Hurley, representing the Illinois Manufacturers Association. *Ibid.*, 251, 22–23, 90–91, 304, 291. Whitney: the reserve act represented the people's "mandate—eternal and omnipotent—that the United States shall become a World Power in international finance and trade. . . ." Johnson: the new tariff was "part of the preparation . . . for this great forward movement in the world's market;" the reserve act "is designed particularly to facilitate exchange transactions with other nations. . . ." Owens: along with the Panama Canal the reserve act "announced the beginning of a period of direct financial relations" with Latin American markets, "giving America the chance, for the first time, to compete in this regard with Great Britain and Germany."

73. See John Gallagher and Ronald Robinson, "The Imperialism of Free Trade," *The Economic History Review*, VI, 1, Second Series (Aug. 1953), 1–15. This is not meant to imply that the Underwood Tariff was a free trade tariff; it was, in Taussig's terms, a "competitive tariff." F. W. Taussig, *The Tariff History of the United States* (8th edition: N.Y., 1937), 418–422.

74. Federal Trade Commission, *Report on Cooperation in American Export Trade* (2 vols.), June 30, 1916, I, 162; Taussig, *op. cit.*, 425–449.

75. Link, *Wilson*, II, 186, 196. The lobbyists included representatives of such interests as wool, sugar, textile manufacturers, citrus fruits.

76. Link, *Wilson and the Progressive Era*, 51.

77. *The New Freedom*, 163–165, 166.

78. Mannheim, *Ideology and Utopia*, 120, 121.

79. In his Foreword to Mason (ed.), *The Corporation in Modern Society*, p. ix. In the same way, and characteristically, Wilson anticipated the downward revision of the tariff not "because men in this country have changed their theories," but because "the condus of America are going to bust through [the high tariff]. . . ." "Efficiency" (Jan. 27, 1912), *P P W W*, V, 360.

80. In this connection, Wilson's conservative-historicism was reinforced by his adaptation of Darwin's theory of biological organic evolution to social evolution, though not in the form of survival-of-the-fittest "Social Darwinism" associated with Spencer, Sumner, and Fiske. See *Constitutional Government in the United States* (N. Y., 1908), 56–57, 199–200, and *The New Freedom*, 46, 47–48, where Wilson describes his view of government and social life as organic, Darwinian, as distinguished from the mechanistic, Newtonian conception of Montesquieu, the Enlightenment thinkers, and Jefferson. *Cf.* also, Diamond, *Econ. Thought of Wilson*, 39, 47, and Link, *Wilson*, I, 21–22.

81. Herbert Marcuse, *Reason and Revolution* (2nd edition: N.Y., 1954), 398–401. Since completing this essay the author's attention has been drawn to Arnold A. Rogow's "Edmund Burke and the American Liberal Tradition," *The Antioch Review* (Summer, 1957), 255–265, which analyzes the decisive relevance of Burke to Wilsonian liberalism in particular and modern U.S. liberalism in general.

82. See, e. g., "Law or Personal Power" (Apr. 13, 1908), *P P W W*, II, 29.

83. See annual address of American Bankers' Association president Arthur Reynolds at the 1914 convention, and his later remarks at the same convention. *Proceedings of the Fortieth Annual Convention of the American Bankers' Association*, Richmond, Va., Oct. 12–16, 1914, pp. 57–68, 312–315. See also letters expressing approval of the Federal Reserve Act from George M. Reynolds, president of Continental and Commercial National Bank of Chicago, A. Barton Hepburn, chairman of the board, Chase National Bank, and A. J. Hemphill, president of Guaranty Trust Company of N.Y., to F. H. Goff (president of Cleveland Trust Co.), president of Bankers' Association's Trust Company Section, dated Sept. 23, Oct. 9, Oct. 5, 1914, respectively, in *ibid.*, 305–308. *Cf. La Follette's Weekly*, VI, 4 (Jan. 24, 1914), 3, where Jacob H. Schiff of Kuhn, Loeb & Co., is quoted praising the reserve law as "legislation highly pleasing to me." La Follette, who opposed the measure, remarked, "The published reports that Wall Street banking interests were fighting the Administration's currency bill tooth and nail now appear somewhat pale in the light of the enthusiastic approval Wall Street is bestowing upon this law." See also, Link, *Wilson*, II, 451–452, 454–455.

84. As Wilson advised leading business men in his address at the Annual Banquet of the Economic Club in New York, May 23, 1912 (*P P W W*, II, 446, 449–451): "How would it suit the prosperity of the United States, how would it suit the success of business, to have a people that went every day sadly or sullenly to their work? How would the future look to you if you felt that the aspiration has gone out of most men, the confidence of success, the hope that they might change their condition, if there was everywhere the feeling that there was somewhere covert dictation, private arrangement as to who should be in the inner circle of privilege and who should not, a more or less systematic and conscious attempt to dictate and dominate the economic life of the country? Do you not see that just as soon as the old self-confidence of America, . . . as her old boasted advantages of individual liberty and opportunity are taken away, all the energy of her people begins to subside, to slacken, to grow loose and pulpy, without fibre, and men simply cast around to see that the day does not end disastrously with them."

"What is the alternative, gentlemen? You have heard the rising tide of socialism. . . . Socialism is not growing in influence in this country as a programme. It is merely that the ranks of protestants are being recruited. . . . If it becomes a programme, then we shall have to be very careful how we propose a competing programme . . . the programme of socialism would not work; but there is no use saying what will not work unless you can say what will work.

". . . If you want to oust socialism you have got to propose something better. It is a case, if you will allow me to fall into the language of the vulgar, of 'put up or shut up.'. . . It is by constructive purpose that you are going to govern and save the United States. . . .

"Very well, then, let us get together and form a constructive programme, [that posterity will say that after America had passed through a simple age] . . . when the forces of society had come into hot contact, . . . there were men of serene enough intelligence, . . . of will and purpose to stand up once again . . . [and who found out] how to translate power into freedom, how to make men glad that they were rich, how to take the envy out of men's hearts that others were rich and they for a little while poor, by opening the gates of opportunity to every man. . . ."

85. See, e. g., Wilson's "Be Worthy of the Men of 1776," July 4, 1914, *P P W W*, III, 142–143: "The Department of State . . . is constantly called upon to back up the commercial . . . and the industrial enterprises of the United States in foreign countries, and it at one time went so far in that direction that all its diplomacy came to be designated as 'dollar diplomacy.'. . . But there ought to be a limit to that. There is no man who is more interested than I am in carrying the enterprise of American business men to every quarter of the globe. I was interested in it long before I was suspected of being a politician. I have been preaching it year after year as the great thing that lay in the future for the United States, to show her wit and skill and enterprise and influence in every country in the world. . . . [But if] American enterprise in foreign countries, particularly in those . . . which are not strong enough to resist us, takes the shape of imposing upon and exploiting the mass of the people . . . it ought to be checked and not encouraged. I am willing to get anything for an American that money and enterprise can obtain except the suppression of the rights of other men. I will not help any man buy a power which he ought not to exercise over his fellow beings."

86. " . . . we are told that free trade would create an international division of labor, and thereby give to each country the production which is most in harmony with its natural advantages. You believe perhaps, gentlemen, that the production of coffee and sugar is the natural destiny of the West Indies. Two centuries ago, nature, which does not trouble herself about commerce, had planted neither sugar-cane nor coffee trees there." "If the free-traders cannot understand how one nation can grow rich at the expense of another, we need not wonder, since these same gentlemen also refuse to understand how within one country one class can enrich itself at the expense of another." ". . . the protectionist system is nothing but a means of establishing large-scale industry in any given country, . . . of making it dependent upon the world market, and from . . . [that] moment . . . there is already more or less dependence upon free trade. . . ." Marx, "On the Question of Free Trade," public speech delivered before the Democratic Association of Brussels, Jan. 9, 1848, in *The Poverty of Philosophy*, 22–223, 224.

87. See, e. g., the report of Edward E. Pratt, chief of the Bureau of Foreign and Domestic Commerce under Wilson, for the fiscal year July 1, 1914, to June 30, 1915: ". . . we can never hope to realize the really big prizes in foreign trade until we are prepared to loan capital to foreign nations and to foreign enterprise. The big prizes . . . are the public and private developments of large proportions, . . . the building of railroads, the construction of public-service plants, the improvement of harbors and docks, . . . and many others which demand capital in large amounts. New countries are generally poor. They look to older and richer countries to supply them with the capital to make their improvements and to develop their resources. The country which furnishes the capital usually sells the materials and does the work . . . there is no doubt that the loans of one nation to another form the strongest kind of economic bond between the two. It is commonly said that trade follows the flag. It is much more truly said that trade follows the investment or the loan." "A foreign commercial policy . . . is gradually taking shape under a wise and careful administration. American investments abroad are being encouraged. The fact that investment must precede trade and that investments abroad must be safeguarded is fully recognized." *Reports of the Department of Commerce*, Oct. 30, 1915 (Wash., 1916), 247, 249. *Cf.* the more recent statement of the prominent liberal spokesman, Dean Acheson: '. . . in the nineteenth century an international system of sorts not only kept the peace for a century but also provided highly successful economic working arrangements. It brought about the industrialization of Europe and of many other parts of the world—our own country, for one. It stimulated production of raw materials and led to a great, though

unevenly distributed, rise in the standard of living. This was accomplished by the export of capital, primarily by Great Britain, but also by all of Western Europe." ". . . a system for the export of capital, much greater than our present . . . efforts, is necessary. The system has been destroyed which expanded the power of Western Europe. . . . One to replace it will be devised, managed, and largely (but not wholly) financed by the United States; otherwise, it is likely to be provided by the Soviet Union, under circumstances destructive of our own power. . . ." "Foreign investment can provide wider opportunity for use of national energies. This can well enhance pride in national achievement and relieve frustrations among members of the populace now denied opportunity to use their full capabilities and training. This should tend to lessen xenophobia, strengthen social fabric and political stability, and bring new meaning to national independence. . . ." Acheson, *Power and Diplomacy* (Cambridge, Mass., 1958), 18, 19–20, 22. The first chapter of the book includes a subsection entitled, "The Collapse of a World Order," referring to the disintegration of the imperial system of the 19th century, and argues the necessity of replacing it with one similar to it, in its economic aspects, led by the United States. Acheson prefaces the chapter with lines of verse from Alfred Noyes: "When his hundred years expire / Then he'll set hisself a-fire / And another from his ashes rise most beautiful to see!"

88. Wilson, *Constitutional Government*, 14.

# the new deal:
# the conservative achievements
# of liberal reform

## BARTON J. BERNSTEIN

Barton J. Bernstein's essay presents both a summary of the New Deal and a radical critique of its accomplishments. Unlike historians writing in the 1940s and 1950s, Bernstein argues that the New Deal was not a revolution, or even, as historian William Leuchtenburg once wrote, a "half-way revolution." Rather, it was a political movement in which liberal reforms "conserved and protected American corporate capitalism," and in which no "significant redistribution of power in American society" took place.

Bernstein points out how very limited liberal reform actually was, even during the era of its greatest accomplishments. He also points out what many contemporaries failed to understand—that the New Deal reforms actually worked to bolster the capitalist political economy. It is harder to understand how Roosevelt won the everlasting gratitude of many members of the dispossessed classes, since the New Deal reforms did so little to change their actual position in American society. Bernstein fails to grapple with this question, attributing Roosevelt's popularity to the "power of rhetoric." Radical scholars have yet to show how reform could yield both significant change and the stabilization of corporate capitalism.

---

Writing from a liberal democratic consensus, many American historians in the past two decades have praised the Roosevelt administration for its nonideological flexibility and for its far-ranging reforms. To many historians, particularly those who reached intellectual maturity during the depression,[1] the government's accomplishments, as well as the drama and passion, marked the decade as a watershed, as a dividing line in the American past.

Enamored of Franklin D. Roosevelt and recalling the bitter opposition to welfare measures and restraints upon business, many liberal historians have emphasized the New Deal's discontinuity with the immediate past. For them there was a "Roosevelt Revolution," or at the very least a dramatic achievement of a beneficent liberalism which had developed in fits and spurts during the preceding three decades.[2] Rejecting earlier interpretations which viewed the New Deal as socialism[3] or state capitalism,[4] they have also disregarded theories of syndicalism[5] or of corporate liberalism.[6] The New Deal has generally commanded their approval for such laws or institutions as minimum wages, public housing, farm assistance, the Tennessee Valley Authority, the Wagner Act, more progressive taxation, and social security. For

Barton J. Bernstein, "The New Deal: The Conservative Achievements of Liberal Reform," from *Towards a New Past: Dissenting Essays in American History*, edited by Barton J. Bernstein (New York: Pantheon, 1968), 263–288. Copyright © 1967, 1968 by Random House, Inc. Reprinted by permission of the publisher.

most liberal historians the New Deal meant the replenishment of democracy, the rescuing of the federal government from the clutches of big business, the significant redistribution of political power. Breaking with laissez faire, the new administration, according to these interpretations, marked the end of the passive or impartial state and the beginning of positive government, of the interventionist state acting to offset concentrations of private power, and affirming the rights and responding to the needs of the unprivileged.

From the perspective of the late 1960s these themes no longer seem adequate to characterize the New Deal. The liberal reforms of the New Deal did not transform the American system; they conserved and protected American corporate capitalism, occasionally by absorbing parts of threatening programs. There was no significant redistribution of power in American society, only limited recognition of other organized groups, seldom of unorganized peoples. Neither the bolder programs advanced by New Dealers nor the final legislation greatly extended the beneficence of government beyond the middle classes or drew upon the wealth of the few for the needs of the many. Designed to maintain the American system, liberal activity was directed toward essentially conservative goals. Experimentalism was most frequently limited to means; seldom did it extend to ends. Never questioning private enterprise, it operated within safe channels, far short of Marxism or even of native American radicalisms that offered structural critiques and structural solutions.

All of this is not to deny the changes wrought by the New Deal—the extension of welfare programs, the growth of federal power, the strengthening of the executive, even the narrowing of property rights. But it is to assert that the elements of continuity are stronger, that the magnitude of change has been exaggerated. The New Deal failed to solve the problem of depression, it failed to raise the impoverished, it failed to redistribute income, it failed to extend equality and generally countenanced racial discrimination and segregation. It failed generally to make business more responsible to the social welfare or to threaten business's pre-eminent political power. In this sense, the New Deal, despite the shifts in tone and spirit from the earlier decade, was profoundly conservative and continuous with the 1920s.


I

Rather than understanding the 1920s as a "return to normalcy," the period is more properly interpreted by focusing on the continuation of progressive impulses, demands often frustrated by the rivalry of interest groups, sometimes blocked by the resistance of Harding and Coolidge, and occasionally by Hoover.[7] Through these years while agriculture and labor struggled to secure advantages from the federal government, big business flourished. Praised for creating American prosperity, business leaders easily convinced the nation that they were socially responsible, that they were fulfilling the needs of the public.[8] Benefitting from earlier legislation that had promoted economic rationalization and stability, they were opponents of federal benefits to other groups but seldom proponents of laissez faire.[9]

In no way did the election of Herbert Hoover in 1928 seem to challenge the New Era. An heir of Wilson, Hoover promised an even closer relationship with big business and moved beyond Harding and Coolidge by affirming federal responsibility for prosperity. As Secretary of Commerce, Hoover had opposed unbridled competition and had transformed his department into a vigorous friend of business. Sponsoring trade associations, he promoted industrial self-regulation and the increased rationalization of business. He had also expanded foreign trade, endorsed the regulation of new forms of communications, encouraged relief in disasters, and recommended public works to offset economic declines.[10]

By training and experience, few men in American political life seemed better prepared than Hoover to cope with the depression. Responding promptly to the crisis, he acted to stabilize the economy and secured the agreement of businessmen to maintain production and wage rates. Unwilling to let the economy "go through the wringer," the President requested easier money, self-liquidating public works, lower personal and corporate income taxes, and stronger commodity stabilization corporations.[11] In reviewing these unprecedented actions, Walter Lippmann wrote, "The national government undertook to make the whole economic order operate prosperously."[12]

But these efforts proved inadequate. The tax cut benefitted the wealthy and failed to raise effective demand. The public works were insufficient. The commodity stabilization corporations soon ran out of funds, and agricultural prices kept plummeting. Businessmen cut back production, dismissed employees, and finally cut wages. As unemployment grew, Hoover struggled to inspire confidence, but his words seemed hollow and his understanding of the depression limited. Blaming the collapse on European failures, he could not admit that American capitalism had failed. When prodded by Congress to increase public works, to provide direct relief, and to further unbalance the budget, he doggedly resisted. Additional deficits would destroy business confidence, he feared, and relief would erode the principles of individual and local responsibility.[13] Clinging to faith in voluntarism, Hoover also briefly rebuffed the efforts by financiers to secure the Reconstruction Finance Corporation (RFC). Finally endorsing the RFC,[14] he also supported expanded lending by Federal Land Banks, recommended home-loan banks, and even approved small federal loans (usually inadequate) to states needing funds for relief. In this burst of activity, the President had moved to the very limits of his ideology.

Restricted by his progressive background and insensitive to politics and public opinion, he stopped far short of the state corporatism urged by some businessmen and politicians. With capitalism crumbling he had acted vigorously to save it, but he would not yield to the representatives of business or disadvantaged groups who wished to alter the government.[15] He was reluctant to use the federal power to achieve through compulsion what could not be realized through voluntary means. Proclaiming a false independence, he did not understand that his government already represented business interests; hence, he rejected policies that would openly place the power of the state in the hands of business or that would permit the formation of a syndicalist state in which power might be exercised (in the words of William Appleman Williams) "by a relatively few leaders of each functional bloc formed and operating as an oligarchy."[16]

Even though constitutional scruples restricted his efforts, Hoover did more than any previous American president to combat depression. He "abandoned the principles of laissez faire in relation to the business cycle, established the conviction that prosperity and depression can be publicly controlled by political action, and drove out of the public consciousness the old idea that depressions must be overcome by private adjustment," wrote Walter Lippmann.[17] Rather than the last of the old presidents, Herbert Hoover was the first of the new.

## II

A charismatic leader and a brilliant politician, his successor expanded federal activities on the basis of Hoover's efforts. Using the federal government to stabilize the economy and advance the interests of the groups, Franklin D. Roosevelt directed the campaign to save large-scale corporate capitalism. Though recognizing new political interests and extending benefits to them, his New Deal never effectively challenged big business or the organization of the economy. In providing assistance to the needy and by rescuing them from starvation, Roosevelt's humane efforts also protected the established system: he sapped organized radicalism of its waning strength and of its potential constituency among the unorganized and discontented. Sensitive to public opinion and fearful of radicalism, Roosevelt acted from a mixture of motives that rendered his liberalism cautious and limited, his experimentalism narrow. Despite the flurry of activity, his government was more vigorous and flexible about means than goals, and the goals were more conservative than historians usually acknowledge.[18]

Roosevelt's response to the banking crisis emphasizes the conservatism of his administration and its self-conscious avoidance of more radical means that might have transformed American capitalism. Entering the White House when banks were failing and Americans had lost faith in the financial system, the President could have nationalized it—"without a word of protest," judged Senator Bronson Cutting.[19] "If ever there was a moment when things hung in the balance," later wrote Raymond Moley, a member of the original "brain trust," "it was on March 5, 1933—when unorthodoxy would have drained the last remaining strength of the capitalistic system."[20] To save the system, Roosevelt relied upon collaboration between bankers and Hoover's Treasury officials to prepare legislation extending federal assistance to banking. So great was the demand for action that House members, voting even without copies, passed it unanimously, and the Senate, despite objections by a few Progressives, approved it the same evening. "The President," remarked a cynical congressman, "drove the money-changers out of the Capitol on March 4th—and they were all back on the 9th."[21]

Undoubtedly the most dramatic example of Roosevelt's early conservative approach to recovery was the National Recovery Administration (NRA). It was based on the War Industries Board (WIB) which had provided the model for the campaign of Bernard Baruch, General Hugh Johnson, and other former WIB officials during the twenties to limit competition through industrial self-regulation under federal sanction. As trade associations flourished during the decade, the FTC encouraged "codes of fair competition" and some industries even tried to set prices and restrict production. Operating without the force of law, these agreements broke down. When the depression struck, industrial pleas for regulation increased.[22] After the Great Crash, important business leaders including Henry I. Harriman of the Chamber of Commerce and Gerard Swope of General Electric called for suspension of antitrust laws and federal organization of business collaboration.[23] Joining them were labor leaders, particularly those in "sick" industries—John L. Lewis of the United Mine Workers and Sidney Hillman of Amalgamated Clothing Workers.[24]

Designed largely for industrial recovery, the NRA legislation provided for minimum wages and maximum hours. It also made concessions to pro-labor congressmen and labor leaders who demanded some specific benefits for unions—recognition of the worker's right to organization and to collective bargaining. In practice, though, the much-heralded Section 7a was a disappointment to most friends of labor.[25] (For the shrewd Lewis, however, it became a mandate to organize: "The President wants you to join a union.") To many frustrated workers and their disgusted leaders, NRA became "National Run Around." The clause, unionists found (in the words of Brookings economists), "had the practical effect of placing NRA on the side of anti-union employers in their struggle against trade unions. . . . [It] thus threw its weight against labor in the balance of bargaining power."[26] And while some far-sighted industrialists feared radicalism and hoped to forestall it by incorporating unions into the economic system, most preferred to leave their workers unorganized or in company unions. To many businessmen, large and independent unions as such seemed a radical threat to the system of business control.[27]

Not only did the NRA provide fewer advantages than unionists had anticipated, but it also failed as a recovery measure. It probably even retarded recovery by supporting restrictionism and price increases, concluded a Brookings study.[28] Placing effective power for code-writing in big business, NRA injured small businesses and contributed to the concentration of American industry. It was not the government-business partnership as envisaged by Adolf A. Berle, Jr., nor government managed as Rexford Tugwell had hoped, but rather, business managed, as Raymond Moley had desired.[29] Calling NRA "industrial self-government," its director, General Hugh Johnson, had explained that "NRA is exactly what industry organized in trade associations makes it." Despite the annoyance of some big businessmen with Section 7a, the NRA reaffirmed and consolidated their power at a time when the public was critical of industrialists and financiers.


III

Viewing the economy as a "concert of organized interests,"[30] the New Deal also provided benefits for farmers—the Agricultural Adjustment Act. Reflecting the political power of larger commercial farmers and accepting restrictionist economics, the measure assumed that the agricultural problem was overproduction, not underconsumption. Financed by a processing tax designed to raise prices to parity, payments encouraged restricted production and cutbacks in farm labor. With benefits accruing chiefly to the larger owners, they frequently removed from production the lands of sharecroppers and tenant farmers, and "tractored" them and hired hands off the land. In assisting agriculture, the AAA, like the NRA, sacrificed the interests of the marginal and the unrecognized to the welfare of those with greater political and economic power.[31]

In large measure, the early New Deal of the NRA and AAA was a "broker state." Though the government served as a mediator of interests and sometimes imposed its will in divisive situations, it was generally the servant of powerful groups. "Like the mercantilists, the New Dealers protected vested interests with the authority of the state," acknowledges William Leuchtenburg. But it was some improvement over the 1920s when business was the only interest capable of imposing its will on the government.[32] While extending to other groups the benefits of the state, the New Deal, however, continued to recognize the pre-eminence of business interests.

The politics of the broker state also heralded the way of the future—of continued corporate dominance in a political structure where other groups agreed generally on corporate capitalism and squabbled only about the size of the shares. Delighted by this increased participation and the absorption of dissident groups, many liberals did not understand the dangers in the emerging organization of politics. They had too much faith in representative institutions and in associations to foresee the perils—of leaders not representing their constituents, of bureaucracy diffusing responsibility, of officials serving their own interests. Failing to perceive the dangers in the emerging structure, most liberals agreed with Senator Robert Wagner of New York: "In order that the strong may not take advantage of the weak, every group must be equally strong."[33] His advice then seemed appropriate for organizing labor, but it neglected the problems of unrepresentative leadership and of the many millions to be left beyond organization.[34]

In dealing with the organized interests, the President acted frequently as a broker, but his government did not simply express the vectors of external forces.[35] The New Deal state was too complex, too loose, and some of Roosevelt's subordinates were following their own inclinations and pushing the government in directions of their own design.[36] The President would also depart from his role as a broker and act to secure programs he desired. As a skilled politician, he could split coalitions, divert the interests of groups, or place the prestige of his office on the side of desired legislation.

In seeking to protect the stock market, for example, Roosevelt endorsed the Securities and Exchange measure (of 1934), despite the opposition of many in the New York financial community. His advisers split the opposition. Rallying to support the administration were the out-of-town exchanges, representatives of the large commission houses, including James Forrestal of Dillon, Read, and Robert Lovett of Brown Brothers, Harriman, and such commission brokers as E. A. Pierce and Paul Shields. Opposed to the Wall Street "old guard" and their companies, this group included those who wished to avoid more radical legislation, as well as others who had wanted earlier to place trading practices under federal legislation which they could influence.[37]

Though the law restored confidence in the securities market and protected capitalism, it alarmed some businessmen and contributed to the false belief that the New Deal was threatening business. But it was not the disaffection of a portion of the business community, nor the creation of the Liberty League, that menaced the broker state.[38] Rather it was the threat of the Left—expressed, for example, in such overwrought statements as Minnesota Governor Floyd Olson's: "I am not a liberal . . . I am a radical. . . . I am not satisfied with hanging a laurel wreath on burglars and thieves . . . and calling them code authorities or something else."[39] While Olson, along with some others who succumbed to the rhetoric of militancy, would back down and soften their meaning, their words dramatized real grievances: the failure of the early New Deal to end misery, to re-create prosperity. The New Deal excluded too many. Its programs were inadequate. While Roosevelt reluctantly endorsed relief and went beyond Hoover in support of public works, he too preferred self-liquidating projects, desired a balanced budget, and resisted spending the huge sums required to lift the nation out of depression.

IV

For millions suffering in a nation wracked by poverty, the promises of the Left seemed attractive. Capitalizing on the misery, Huey Long offered Americans a "Share Our Wealth" program—a welfare state with prosperity, not subsistence, for the disadvantaged, those neglected by most politicians. "Every Man a King": pensions for the elderly, college for the deserving, homes and cars for families— that was the promise of American life. Also proposing minimum wages, increased public works, shorter work weeks, and a generous farm program, he demanded a "soak-the-rich" tax program. Despite the economic defects of his plan, Long was no hayseed, and his forays into the East revealed support far beyond the bayous and hamlets of his native South.[40] In California discontent was so great that Upton Sinclair, food faddist and former socialist, captured the Democratic nomination for governor on a platform of "production-for-use"— factories and farms for the unemployed. "In a cooperative society," promised Sinclair, "every man, woman, and child would have the equivalent of $5,000 a year income from labor of the able-bodied young men for three or four hours per day."[41] More challenging to Roosevelt was Francis Townsend's plan monthly payments of $200 to those past sixty who retired and promised to spend the stipend within thirty days.[42] Another enemy of the New Deal was Father Coughlin, the popular radio priest, who had broken with Roosevelt and formed a National Union for Social Justice to lead the way to a corporate society beyond capitalism.

To a troubled nation offered "redemption" by the Left, there was also painful evidence that the social fabric was tearing—law was breaking down. When the truckers in Minneapolis struck, the police provoked an incident and shot sixty-seven people, some in the back. Covering the tragedy, Eric Sevareid, then a young reporter, wrote, "I understood deep in my bones and blood what fascism was."[43] In San Francisco union leaders embittered by police brutality led a general strike and aroused national fears of class warfare. Elsewhere, in textile mills from Rhode Island to Georgia, in cities like Des Moines and Toledo, New York and Philadelphia, there were brutality and violence, sometimes bayonets and tear gas.[44]

Challenged by the Left, and with the new Congress more liberal and more willing to spend, Roosevelt turned to disarm the discontent. "Boys—this is our hour," confided Harry Hopkins. "We've got to get everything we want—a works program, social security, wages and hours, everything—now or never. Get your minds to work on developing a complete ticket to provide security for all the folks of this country up and down and across the board."[45] Hopkins and the associates he addressed were not radicals: they did not seek to transform the system, only to make it more humane. They, too, wished to preserve large-scale corporate capitalism, but unlike Roosevelt or Moley, they were prepared for more vigorous action. Their commitment to reform was greater, their tolerance for injustice far less. Joining them in pushing the New Deal left were the leaders of industrial unions, who, while also not wishing to transform the system, sought for workingmen higher wages, better conditions, stronger and larger unions, and for themselves a place closer to the fulcrum of power.

The problems of organized labor, however, neither aroused Roosevelt's humanitarianism nor suggested possibilities of reshaping the political coalition. When asked during the NRA about employee representation, he had replied that workers could select anyone they wished—the Ahkoond of Swat, a union, even the Royal Geographical Society.[46] As a paternalist, viewing himself (in the words of James MacGregor Burns) as a "partisan and benefactor" of workers, he would not understand the objections to company unions or to multiple unionism under NRA. Nor did he foresee the political dividends that support of independent unions could yield to his party.[47] Though presiding over the reshaping of politics (which would extend the channels of power to some of the discontented and redirect their efforts to competition within a limited framework), he was not its architect, and he was unable clearly to see or understand the unfolding design.

When Senator Wagner submitted his labor relations bill, he received no assistance from the President and even struggled to prevent Roosevelt from joining the opposition. The President "never lifted a finger," recalls Miss Perkins. ("I, myself, had very little sympathy with the bill," she wrote.[48]) But after the measure easily passed the Senate and seemed likely to win the House's endorsement, Roosevelt reversed himself. Three days before the Supreme Court invalidated the NRA, including the legal support for union-ization, Roosevelt came out for the bill. Placing it on his "must" list, he may have hoped to influence the final provisions and turn an administration defeat into victory.[49]

Responding to the threat from the left, Roosevelt also moved during the Second Hundred Days to secure laws regulating banking, raising taxes, dissolving utility-holding companies, and creating social security. Building on the efforts of states during the Progressive Era, the Social Security Act marked the movement toward the welfare state, but the core of the measure, the old-age provision, was more important as a landmark than for its substance. While establishing a federal-state system of unemployment compensation, the government, by making workers contribute to their old-age insurance, denied its financial responsibility for the elderly. The act excluded more than a fifth of the labor force leaving, among others, more than five million farm laborers and domestics without coverage.[50]

Though Roosevelt criticized the tax laws for not preventing "an unjust concentration of wealth and economic power,"[51] his own tax measure would not have significantly redistributed wealth. Yet his message provoked an "amen" from Huey Long and protests from businessmen.[52] Retreating from his promises, Roosevelt failed to support the bill, and it succumbed to conservative forces. They removed the inheritance tax and greatly reduced the proposed corporate and individual levies. The final law did not "soak the rich."[53] But it did engender deep resentment among the wealthy for increasing taxes on gifts and estates, imposing an excess-profits tax (which Roosevelt had not requested), and raising surtaxes. When combined with such regressive levies as social security and local taxes, however, the Wealth Tax of 1935 did not drain wealth from higher-income groups, and the top one percent even increased their shares during the New Deal years.[54]

V

Those historians who have characterized the events of 1935 as the beginning of a second New Deal have imposed a pattern on those years which most participants did not then discern.[55] In moving to social security, guarantees of collective bargaining, utility regulation, and progressive taxation, the government did advance the nation toward greater liberalism, but the shift was exaggerated and most of the measures accomplished far less than either friends or foes suggested. Certainly, despite a mild bill authorizing destruction of utilities-holding companies, there was no effort to atomize business, no real threat to concentration.

Nor were so many powerful businessmen disaffected by the New Deal. Though the smaller businessmen who filled the ranks of the Chamber of Commerce resented the federal bureaucracy and the benefits to labor and thus criticized NRA,[56] representatives of big business found the agency useful and opposed a return to unrestricted competition. In 1935, members of the Business Advisory Council—including Henry Harriman, outgoing president of the Chamber, Thomas Watson of International Business Machines, Walter Gifford of American Telephone and Telegraph, Gerard Swope of General Electric, Winthrop Aldrich of the Chase National Bank, and W. Averell Harriman of Union Pacific—vigorously endorsed a two-year renewal of NRA.[57]

When the Supreme Court in 1935 declared the "hot" oil clause and then NRA unconstitutional, the administration moved to measures known as the "little NRA." Reestablishing regulations in bituminous coal and oil, the New Deal also checked wholesale price discrimination and legalized "fair trade" practices. Though Roosevelt never acted to revive the NRA, he periodically contemplated its restoration. In the so-called second New Deal, as in the "first," government remained largely the benefactor of big business, and some more advanced businessmen realized this.[58]

Roosevelt could attack the "economic royalists" and endorse the TNEC investigation of economic concentration, but he was unprepared to resist the basic demands of big business. While there was ambiguity in his treatment of oligopoly, it was more the confusion of means than of ends, for his tactics were never likely to impair concentration. Even the antitrust program under Thurman Arnold, concludes Frank Freidel, was "intended less to bust the trusts than to forestall too drastic legislation." Operating through consent degrees and designed to reduce prices to the consumer, the program frequently "allowed industries to function much as they had in NRA days." In effect, then, throughout its variations, the New Deal had sought to cooperate with business.[59]

Though vigorous in rhetoric and experimental in tone, the New Deal was narrow in its goals and wary of bold economic reform. Roosevelt's sense of what was politically desirable was frequently more restricted than others' views of what was possible and necessary. Roosevelt's limits were those of ideology; they were not inherent in experimentalism. For while the President explored the narrow center, and some New Dealers considered bolder possibilities, John Dewey, the philosopher of experimentalism, moved far beyond the New Deal and sought to reshape the system. Liberalism, he warned, "must now become radical. . . . For the gulf between what the actual situation makes possible and the actual state itself is so great that it cannot be bridged by piecemeal policies undertaken *ad hoc*."[60] The boundaries of New Deal exper-imentalism, as Howard Zinn has emphasized, could extend far beyond Roosevelt's cautious ventures. Operating within very safe channels, Roosevelt not only avoided Marxism and the socialization of property, but he also stopped far short of other possibilities—communal direction of production or the organized distribution of surplus. The President and many of his associates were doctrinaires of the center, and their maneuvers in social reform were limited to cautious excursions.[61]

## VI

Usually opportunistic and frequently shifting, the New Deal was restricted by its ideology. It ran out of fuel not because of the conservative opposition,[62] but because it ran out of ideas.[63] Acknowledging the end in 1939, Roosevelt proclaimed, "We have now passed the period of internal conflict in the launching of our program of social reform. Our full energies may now be released to invigorate the processes of recovery in order to preserve our reforms. . . ."[64]

The sad truth was that the heralded reforms were severely limited, that inequality continued, that efforts at recovery had failed. Millions had come to accept the depression as a way of life. A decade after the Great Crash, when millions were still unemployed, Fiorello LaGuardia recommended that "we accept the inevitable, that we are now in a new normal."[65] "It was reasonable to expect a probable minimum of 4,000,000 to 5,000,000 unemployed," Harry Hopkins had concluded.[66] Even that level was never reached, for business would not spend and Roosevelt refused to countenance the necessary expend-itures. "It was in economics that our troubles lay," Tugwell wrote. "For their solution his [Roosevelt's] progressivism, his new deal was pathetically insuffi-cient. . . ."[67]

Clinging to faith in fiscal orthodoxy even when engaged in deficit spending, Roosevelt had been unwilling to greatly unbalance the budget. Having pledged in his first campaign to cut expenditures and to restore the balanced budget, the President had at first adopted recovery programs that would not drain government finances. Despite a burst of activity under the Civil Works Administration during the first winter, public works expenditures were frequently slow and cautious. Shifting from direct relief, which Roosevelt (like Hoover) considered "a narcotic, a subtle destroyer of the human spirit," the government moved to work relief.[68] ("It saves his skill. It gives him a chance to do something socially useful," said Hopkins.[69]) By 1937 the government had poured enough money into the economy to spur production to within 10 percent of 1929 levels, but unemployment still hovered over seven million. Yet so eager was the President to balance the budget that he cut expenditures for public works and relief, and plunged the economy into a greater depression. While renewing expenditures, Roosevelt remained cautious in his fiscal policy, and the nation still had almost nine million unemployed in 1939. After nearly six years of struggling with the depression, the Roosevelt administration could not lead the nation to recovery, but it had relieved suffering.[70] In most of America, starvation was no longer possible. Perhaps that was the most humane achievement of the New Deal.

Its efforts on behalf of humane *reform* were generally faltering and shallow, of more value to the middle classes, of less value to organized workers, of even less to the marginal men. In conception and in practice, seemingly humane efforts revealed the shortcomings of American liberalism. For example, public housing, praised as evidence of the federal government's concern for the poor, was limited in scope (to 180,000 units) and unfortunate in results.[71] It usually meant the consolidation of ghettos, the robbing of men of their dignity, the treatment of men as wards with few rights. And slum clearance came to mean "Negro clearance" and removal of the other poor. Of much of this liberal reformers were unaware, and some of the problems can be traced to the structure of bureaucracy and to the selection of government personnel and social workers who disliked the poor.[72] But the liberal conceptions, it can be argued, were also flawed for there was no willingness to consult the poor, nor to encourage their participation. Liberalism was elitist. Seeking to build America in their own image, liberals wanted to create an environment which they thought would restructure character and personality more appropriate to white, middle-class America.

While slum dwellers received little besides relief from the New Deal, and their needs were frequently misunderstood, Negroes as a group received even less assistance—less than they needed and sometimes even less than their proportion in the population would have justified. Under the NRA they were frequently dismissed and their wages were sometimes below the legal minimum. The Civilian Conservation Corps left them "forgotten" men—excluded, discriminated against, segregated. In general, what the Negroes gained—relief, WPA jobs, equal pay on some federal projects—was granted them as poor people, not as Negroes.[73] To many black men the distinction was unimportant, for no government had ever given them so much. "My friends, go home and turn Lincoln's picture to the wall," a Negro publisher told his race. "That debt has been payed in full."[74]

Bestowing recognition on some Negro leaders, the New Deal appointed them to agencies as advisers—the "black cabinet." Probably more dramatic was the advocacy of Negro rights by Eleanor Roosevelt. Some whites like Harold Ickes and Aubrey Williams even struggled cautiously to break down segregation. But segregation did not yield, and Washington itself remained a segregated city. The white South was never challenged, the Fourteenth Amendment never used to assist Negroes. Never would Roosevelt expend political capital in an assault upon the American caste system.[75] Despite the efforts of the NAACP to dramatize the Negroes' plight as second-class citizens, subject to brutality and often without legal protection, Roosevelt would not endorse the antilynching bill. ("No government pretending to be civilized can go on condoning such atrocities," H. L. Mencken testified. "Either it must make every possible effort to put them down or it must suffer the scorn and contempt of Christendom.")[76] Unwilling to risk schism with Southerners ruling committees, Roosevelt capitulated to the forces of racism.[77]

Even less bold than in economic reform, the New Deal left intact the race relations of America. Yet its belated and cautious recognition of the black man was great enough to woo Negro leaders and even to court the masses. One of the bitter ironies of these years is that a New Dealer could tell the NAACP in 1936: "Under our new conception of democracy, the Negro will be given the chance to which he is entitled. . . ." But it was true, Ickes emphasized, that "The greatest advance [since Reconstruction] toward assuring the Negro that degree of justice to which he is entitled and that equality of opportunity under the law which is implicit in his American citizenship, has been made since Franklin D. Roosevelt was sworn in as President. . . ."[78]

It was not in the cities and not among the Negroes but in rural America that Roosevelt administration made its (philosophically) boldest efforts: creation of the Tennessee Valley Authority and the later attempt to construct seven little valley authorities. Though conservation was not a new federal policy and government-owned utilities were sanctioned by municipal experience, federal activity in this area constituted a challenge to corporate enterprise and an expression of concern about the poor. A valuable example of regional planning and a contribution to regional prosperity, TVA still fell far short of expectations. The agency soon retreated from social planning. ("From 1936 on," wrote Tugwell, "the TVA should have been called the Tennessee Valley Power Production and Flood Control Corporation.") Fearful of antagonizing the powerful interests, its agricultural program neglected the tenants and the sharecroppers.[79]

To urban workingmen the New Deal offered some, but limited, material benefits. Though the government had instituted contributory social security and unemployment insurance, its much-heralded Fair Labor Standards Act, while prohibiting child labor, was a greater disappointment. It exempted millions from its wages-and-hours provisions. So unsatisfactory was the measure that one congressman cynically suggested, "Within 90 days after appointment of the administrator, she should report to Congress whether anyone is subject to this bill."[80] Requiring a minimum of twenty-five cents an hour ($11 a week for 44 hours), it raised the wages of only about a half-million at a time when nearly twelve million workers in interstate commerce were earning less than forty cents an hour.[81]

More important than these limited measures was the administration's support, albeit belated, of the organization of labor and the right of collective bargaining. Slightly increasing organized workers' share of the national income,[82] the new industrial unions extended job security to millions who were previously subject to the whim of management. Unionization freed them from the perils of a free market.

By assisting labor, as well as agriculture, the New Deal started the institutionalization of larger interest groups into a new political economy. Joining business as tentative junior partners, they shared the consensus on the value of large-scale corporate capitalism, and were permitted to participate in the competition for the division of shares. While failing to redistribute income, the New Deal modified the political structure at the price of excluding many from the process of decision making. To many what was offered in fact was symbolic representation, formal representation. It was not the industrial workers necessarily who were recognized, but their unions and leaders; it was not even the farmers, but their organizations and leaders. While this was not a conscious design, it was the predictable result of conscious policies. It could not have been easily avoided, for it was part of the price paid by a large society unwilling to consider radical new designs for the distribution of power and wealth.

VII

In the deepest sense, this new form of representation was rooted in the liberal's failure to endorse a meaningful egalitarianism which would provide actual equality of opportunity. It was also the limited concern with equality and justice that accounted for the shallow efforts of the New Deal and left so many Americans behind. The New Deal was neither a "third American Revolution," as Carl Degler suggests, nor even a "half-way revolution," as William Leuchtenburg concludes. Not only was the extension of representation to new groups less than full-fledged partnership, but the New Deal neglected many Americans—sharecroppers, tenant farmers, migratory workers and farm laborers, slum dwellers, unskilled workers, and the unemployed Negroes. They were left outside the new order.[83] As Roosevelt asserted in 1937 (in a classic understatement), one third of the nation was "ill-nourished, ill-clad, ill-housed."[84]

Yet, by the power of rhetoric and through the appeals of political organization, the Roosevelt government managed to win or retain the allegiance of these peoples. Perhaps this is one of the crueller ironies of liberal politics, that the marginal men trapped in hopelessness were seduced by rhetoric, by the style and movement, by the symbolism of efforts seldom reaching beyond words. In acting to protect the institution of private property and in advancing the interests of corporate capitalism, the New Deal assisted the middle and upper sectors of society. It protected them, sometimes, even at the cost of injuring the lower sectors. Seldom did it bestow much of substance upon the lower classes. Never did the New Deal seek to organize these groups into independent political forces. Seldom did it risk antagonizing established interests. For some this would constitute a puzzling defect of liberalism; for some, the failure to achieve true liberalism. To others it would emphasize the inherent shortcomings of American liberal democracy. As the nation prepared for war, liberalism, by accepting private property and federal assistance to corporate capitalism, was not prepared effectively to reduce inequities, to redistribute political power, or to extend equality from promise to reality.

NOTES

1. The outstanding examples are Arthur Schlesinger, Jr., Frank Freidel, Carl Degler, and William Leuchtenburg. Schlesinger, in *The Crisis of the Old Order* (Boston, 1957), emphasized the presence of reform in the twenties but criticized the federal government for its retreat from liberalism and condemned Hoover for his responses to the depression. The next two volumes of his *The Age of Roosevelt*, *The Coming of the New Deal* (Boston, 1958) and *The Politics of Upheaval* (Boston, 1960), praise the New Deal, but also contain information for a more critical appraisal. His research is quite wide and has often guided my own investigations. For his theory that the New Deal was likely even without the depression, see "Sources of the New Deal: Reflections on the Temper of a Time," *Columbia University Forum*, II (Fall 1959), 4–11. Freidel affirmed that the New Deal was a watershed (*American Historical Review*, October 1965, p. 329), but in *The New Deal in Historical Perspective* (Washington, 1959), he has suggested the conservatism of the New Deal as a reform movement. Degler, in *Out of Our Past* (New York, 1959), pp. 379–416, extolled the New Deal as a "Third American Revolution." But also see his "The Ordeal of Herbert Hoover," *Yale Review*, LII (Summer 1963), 565–83. Leuchtenburg, *Franklin D. Roosevelt and the New Deal, 1932–1940* (New York, 1963), offers considerable criticism of the New Deal, but finds far more to praise in this "half-way revolution." He cites Degler approvingly but moderates Degler's judgment (pp. 336–47). The book represents years of research and has often guided my own investigations.

2. Eric Goldman, *Rendezvous with Destiny* (New York, 1952); Henry Steele Commager, "Twelve Years of Roosevelt," *American Mercury*, LX (April 1945), 391–401; Arthur Link, *American Epoch* (New York, 1955), pp. 377–440. In his essay on "Franklin D. Roosevelt:

the Patrician as Opportunist" in *The American Political Tradition* (New York, 1948), pp. 315-52, Richard Hofstadter was critical of the New Deal's lack of ideology but treated it as a part of the larger reform tradition. In *The Age of Reform* (New York, 1955), however, while chiding the New Deal for opportunism, he emphasized the discontinuity of the New Deal with the reform tradition of Populism and Progressivism.

3. Edgar E. Robinson, *The Roosevelt Leadership, 1933-1945* (Philadelphia, 1955), the work of a conservative constitutionalist, does accuse the administration of having objectives approaching the leveling aims of communism (p. 376).

4. Louis Hacker, *American Problems of Today* (New York, 1938).

5. William Appleman Williams, *The Contours of American History* (Chicago, 1966), pp. 372-488; and his review, "Schlesinger: Right Crisis—Wrong Order," *Nation*, CLXXXIV (March 23, 1957), 257-60. Williams' volume has influenced my own thought.

6. Ronald Radosh, "The Corporate Ideology of American Labor Leaders from Gompers to Hillman," *Studies on the Left*, VI (November-December 1966), 66-88.

7. Arthur Link, "What Happened to the Progressive Movement?" *American Historical Review*, LXIV (July 1959), 833-51.

8. James Prothro, *The Dollar Decade* (Baton Rouge, La., 1954).

9. Louis Galambos, *Competition and Cooperation* (Baltimore, 1966), pp. 55-139; Link, "What Happened to the Progressive Movement?"

10. Joseph Brandes, *Herbert Hoover and Economic Diplomacy* (Pittsburgh, 1962); Hofstadter, *American Political Tradition*, pp. 283-99.

11. William S. Myers, ed., *The State Papers and Other Writings of Herbert Hoover* (New York, 1934), I, 84-88 (easier money), 137, 411, 431-33; II, 202 (public works); I, 142-43, 178-79 (lower taxes). The Commodity Stabilization Corporation was created before the crash.

12. Lippmann, "The Permanent New Deal," *Yale Review*, XXIV (June 1935), 651.

13. Myers, ed., *State Papers*, II, 195-201, 214-15, 224-26, 228-33 (on the budget); II, 405, 496-99, 503-5 (on relief).

14. Gerald Nash, "Herbert Hoover and the Origins of the Reconstruction Finance Corporation," *Mississippi Valley Historical Review*, XLVI (December 1959), 455-68.

15. W. S. Myers and W. H. Newton, eds., *The Hoover Administration: A Documentary History* (New York, 1936), p. 119; "Proceedings of a Conference of Progressives," March 11-12, 1931, Hillman Papers, Amalgamated Clothing Workers (New York).

16. *Contours of American History*, p. 428.

17. Lippmann, "The Permanent New Deal," p. 651.

18. For an excellent statement of this thesis, see Howard Zinn's introduction to his *New Deal Thought* (New York, 1966), pp. xv-xxxvi. So far historians have not adequately explored the thesis that F.D.R. frequently acted as a restraining force on his own government, and that bolder reforms were often thwarted by him and his intimates.

19. Bronson Cutting, "Is Private Banking Doomed?" *Liberty*, XI (March 31, 1934), 10; cf. Raymond Moley, *The First New Deal* (New York, 1966), pp. 177-80.

20. Moley, *After Seven Years* (New York, 1939), p. 155; Arthur Ballantine, "When All the Banks Closed," *Harvard Business Review*, XXVI (March 1948), 129-43.

21. William Lemke, later quoted in Lorena Hickok to Harry Hopkins, November 23, 1933, Hopkins Papers, Franklin D. Roosevelt Library (hereafter called FDRL).

22. Baruch to Samuel Gompers, April 19, 1924, Baruch Papers, Princeton University; Schlesinger, *Coming of the New Deal*, pp. 88-89; Gerald Nash, "Experiments in Industrial Mobilization: WIB and NRA," *Mid-America*, XLV (July 1963), 156-75.

23. Gerard Swope, *The Swope Plan* (New York, 1931); Julius H. Barnes, "Government and Business," *Harvard Business Review*, X (July 1932), 411-19; Harriman, "The Stabilization of Business and Employment," *American Economic Review*, XXII (March 1932), 63-75; House Committee on Education and Labor, 73rd Cong., 1st Sess., *Thirty Hour Week Bill, Hearings*, pp. 198-99.

24. *Ibid.*, pp. 884-97; Hillman, "Labor Leads Toward Planning," *Survey Graphic*, LXVI (March 1932), 586-88.

25. Irving Bernstein, *The New Deal Collective Bargaining Policy* (Berkeley, Cal., 1950), pp. 57-63.

26. Quotes from Hofstadter, *American Political Tradition*, p. 336. "It is not the function of

NRA to organize . . . labor," asserted General Hugh Johnson. "Automobile Code Provides for Thirty-Five Hour Week," *Iron Age*, CXXXII (August 3, 1933), 380.

27. Richard C. Wilcock, "Industrial Management's Policy Toward Unionism," in Milton Derber and Edwin Young, eds., *Labor and the New Deal* (Madison, Wis., 1957), pp. 278–95.

28. Leverett Lyon, *et al.*, *The National Recovery Administration* (Washington, 1935).

29. The characterization of Berle, Tugwell, and Moley is from Schlesinger, *Coming of the New Deal*, pp. 181–84, and Johnson's address at the NAM is from NRA press release 2126, December 7, 1933, NRA Records, RG 9, National Archives.

30. "Concert of interests" was used by F.D.R. in a speech of April 18, 1932, in Samuel Rosenman, ed., *The Public Papers and Addresses of Franklin D. Roosevelt* (13 vols.; New York, 1938–52), I, 627–39. (Hereafter referred to as *FDR Papers*.)

31. M. S. Venkataramani, "Norman Thomas, Arkansas Sharecroppers, and the Roosevelt Agricultural Policies," *Mississippi Valley Historical Review*, XLVII (September 1960), 225–46; John Hutson, Columbia Oral History Memoir, pp. 114ff.; Mordecai Ezekiel, Columbia Oral History Memoir, pp. 74ff.

32. Quoted from Leuchtenburg, *F.D.R.*, p. 87, and this discussion draws upon pp. 87–90; John Chamberlain, *The American Stakes* (Philadelphia, 1940); James MacGregor Burns, *Roosevelt: The Lion and the Fox* (New York, 1956), pp. 183–202.

33. Quoted from House Committee on Education and Labor, 74th Cong., 1st Sess., *National Labor Relations Board Hearings*, p. 35.

34. For a warning, see Paul Douglas, "Rooseveltian Liberalism," *Nation*, CXXXVI (June 21, 1933), 702–3.

35. Leuchtenburg, *F.D.R.*, p. 88, uses the image of "a parallelogram of pressures."

36. For example see the Columbia Oral Histories of Louis Bean, Hutson, and Ezekiel.

37. *New York Times*, January 30, 1934; House Interstate and Foreign Commerce Committee, 73rd Cong., 2nd Sess., House Report No. 1383, *Securities Exchange Bill of 1934*, p. 3; "SEC," *Fortune*, XXI (June 1940), 91–92, 120ff.; Ralph DeBedts, *The New Deal's SEC* (New York, 1964), pp. 56–85.

38. Frederick Rudolph, "The American Liberty League, 1934–1940," *American Historical Review*, LVI (October 1950), 19–33; George Wolfskill, *The Revolt of the Conservatives* (Boston, 1962). Emphasizing the Liberty League and focusing upon the rhetoric of business disaffection, historians have often exaggerated the opposition of the business communities. See the correspondence of James Forrestal, PPF 6367, FDRL, and at Princeton; of Russell Leffingwell, PPF 886, FDRL; of Donald Nelson, PPF 8615, FDRL, and at the Huntington Library; and of Thomas Watson, PPF 2489, FDRL. On the steel industry, see *Iron Age*, CXXXV (June 13, 1935), 44. For very early evidence of estrangement, however, see Edgar Mowrer to Frank Knox, November 8, 1933, Knox Papers, Library of Congress.

39. Quoted from Donald McCoy, *Angry Voices: Left of Center Politics in the New Deal Era* (Lawrence, Kan., 1958), p. 55, from *Farmer-Labor Leader*, March 30, 1934.

40. Long, *My First Days in the White House* (Harrisburg, Pa., 1935).

41. Quoted from Sinclair, *The Way Out* (New York, 1933), p. 57. See Sinclair to Roosevelt, October 5 and 18, 1934, OF 1165, FDRL.

42. Nicholas Roosevelt, *The Townsend Plan* (Garden City, N.Y., 1935). Not understanding that the expenditures would increase consumption and probably spur production, critics emphasized that the top 9 percent would have received 50 percent of the income, but they neglected that the top income-tenth had received (before taxes) nearly 40 percent of the national income in 1929. National Industrial Conference Board, *Studies in Enterprise and Social Progress* (New York, 1939), p. 125.

43. Sevareid, *Not So Wild a Dream* (New York, 1946), p. 58.

44. Sidney Lens, *Left, Right and Center* (Hinsdale, Ill., 1949), pp. 280–89.

45. Quoted in Robert Sherwood, *Roosevelt and Hopkins*, rev. ed. (New York, 1950), p. 65.

46. Roosevelt's press conference of June 15, 1934, *FDR Papers*, III, 301; cf., Roosevelt to John L. Lewis, February 25, 1939, Philip Murray Papers, Catholic University.

47. Burns, *The Lion and the Fox*, pp. 217–19; quotation from p. 218.

48. Perkins, Columbia Oral History Memoir, VII, 138, 147, quoted by Leuchtenburg, *F.D.R.*, p. 151.

49. Irving Bernstein, *The New Deal Collective Bargaining Policy*, pp. 100–8; Burns, *The Lion and the Fox*, p. 219.

50. Margaret Grant, *Old Age Security* (Washington, 1939), p. 217. Under social security, payments at sixty-five ranged from $10 a month to $85 a month, depending on earlier earnings.

51. Roosevelt's message to Congress on June 19, 1935, *FDR Papers*, IV, 271.

52. *New York Times*, June 20 and 21, 1935; *Business Week*, June 22, 1935, p. 5.

53. John Morton Blum, *From the Morgenthau Diaries: Years of Crisis, 1928–1938* (Boston, 1959), pp. 302–4.

54. Simon Kuznets, *Shares of Upper Income Groups in Income and Savings*, National Bureau of Economic Research, Occasional Paper 35 (New York, 1950), pp. 32–40.

55. Otis L. Graham, Jr., "Historians and the New Deals: 1944–1960," *Social Studies*, LIV (April 1963), 133–40.

56. *New York Times*, November 19, 1933; May 1, September 30, November 17, December 23, 1934; May 1, 3, 5, 28, 1935; "Chamber to Vote on NIRA," *Nation's Business*, XXII (December 1934), 51; "Business Wants a New NRA," *ibid.*, XXIII (February 1935), 60; "Listening in as Business Speaks," *ibid.*, XXIII (June 1935), 18, 20; William Wilson, "How the Chamber of Commerce Viewed the NRA," *Mid-America*, XLIII (January 1962), 95–108.

57. *New York Times*, May 3, 4, 12, 1935. On the steel industry see L. W. Moffet, "This Week in Washington," *Iron Age*, CXXXV (March 21, 1935), 41; *ibid.* (April 18, 1935), 49; "NRA Future Not Settled by Senate Committee's Action for Extension," *ibid.* (May 9, 1935), 58.

58. Ellis W. Hawley, *The New Deal and the Problem of Monopoly* (Princeton, 1966), pp. 205–86.

59. Freidel, *The New Deal*, pp. 18–19. On Arnold's efforts, see Wendell Berge Diary, 1938–1939, Berge Papers, Library of Congress; and Gene Gressley, "Thurman Arnold, Antitrust, and the New Deal," *Business History Review*, XXXVIII (Summer, 1964), 214–31. For characteristic Roosevelt rhetoric emphasizing the effort of his government to subdue "the forces of selfishness and of lust for power," see his campaign address of October 31, 1936, his press conference of January 4, 1938, and his message of April 29, 1938, in *FDR Papers*, V, 568–69 and VII, XI, 305–32.

60. Dewey, *Liberalism and Social Action* (New York, 1935), p. 62.

61. Howard Zinn, in *New Deal Thought*, pp. xxvi–xxxi, discusses this subject and has influenced my thought. Also consider those whom Zinn cites: Edmund Wilson, "The Myth of Marxist Dialectic," *Partisan Review*, VI (Fall 1938), 66–81; William Ernest Hocking, "The Future of Liberalism," *The Journal of Philosophy*, XXXII (April 25, 1935), 230–47; Stuart Chase, "Eating Without Working: A Moral Disquisition," *Nation*, CXXXVII (July 22, 1933), 93–94.

62. See James T. Patterson, "A Conservative Coalition Forms in Congress, 1933–1939," *Journal of American History*, LII (March 1966), 757–72.

63. Hofstadter, *American Political Tradition*, p. 342; cf., Freidel, *The New Deal*, p.20.

64. Roosevelt's annual message to the Congress on January 4, 1939, *FDR Papers*, VIII, 7.

65. Fiorello LaGuardia to James Byrnes, April 5, 1939, Box 2584, LaGuardia Papers, Municipal Archives, New York City.

66. Hopkins, "The Future of Relief," *New Republic*, XC (February 10, 1937), 8.

67. Tugwell, *The Stricken Land* (Garden City, N.Y., 1947), p. 681.

68. Roosevelt's speech of January 4, 1935, *FDR Papers*, IV, 19.

69. Hopkins, "Federal Emergency Relief," *Vital Speeches*, I (December 31, 1934), 211.

70. Broadus Mitchell, *Depression Decade: From New Era Through New Deal* (New York, 1947), pp. 37–54.

71. Housing and Home Finance Agency, *First Annual Report* (Washington, 1947), pp. 24–25. Timothy McDonnell, *The Wagner Housing Act* (Chicago, 1957), pp. 53, 186–88, concludes that the Wagner bill would have passed earlier if Roosevelt had supported it.

72. Jane Jacobs, *The Life and Death of Great American Cities* (New York, 1963). Racial policy was locally determined. U.S. Housing Authority, *Bulletin No. 18 on Policy and Procedure* (1938), pp. 7–8; Robert C. Weaver, "The Negro in a Program of Public Housing," *Opportunity*, XVI (July 1938), 1–6. Three fifths of all families, reported Weaver, were

earning incomes "below the figure necessary to afford respectable living quarters without undue skimping on other necessities." (p.4)

73. Allen Kifer, "The Negro Under the New Deal, 1933–1941" (unpublished Ph.D. dissertation, University of Wisconsin, 1961), *passim*. The National Youth Agency was an exception, concludes Kifer, p. 139. For Negro protests about New Deal discrimination, John P. Davis, "What Price National Recovery?" *Crisis*, XL (December 1933), 272; Charles Houston and Davis, "TVA: Lily-White Construction," *Crisis*, XLI (October 1934), 291.

74. Robert Vann of the *Pittsburgh Courier*, quoted in Joseph Alsop and William Kintner, "The Guffey," *Saturday Evening Post*, CCX (March 26, 1938), 6. Vann had offered this advice in 1932.

75. See Eleanor Roosevelt to Walter White, May 2, 29, 1934, April 21, 1938, White Papers, Yale University; Frank Freidel, *F.D.R. and the South* (Baton Rouge, La., 1965), pp. 71–102.

76. Quoted from Senate Judiciary Committee, 74th Cong., 1st Sess., *Punishment for the Crime of Lynching, Hearings*, p. 23. Cf. Harold Ickes, "The Negro as a Citizen," June 29, 1936, Oswald Garrison Villard papers, Harvard University.

77. Roy Wilkins, Columbia Oral History Memoir, p. 98; Lester Granger, Columbia Oral History Memoir, p. 105, complains that Wagner had refused to include in his labor bill a prohibition against unions excluding workers because of race. When Wagner counseled a delay, Negroes felt, according to Granger, that the New Deal "was concerned with covering up, putting a fine cover over what there was, not bothering with the inequities."

78. Ickes, "The Negro as a Citizen." Ickes had said, "since the Civil War."

79. Schlesinger, *Politics of Upheaval*, pp. 362–80; quotation from Tugwell, p. 371.

80. Martin Dies, quoted by Burns, *Congress on Trial* (New York, 1949), p. 77.

81. The law raised standards to thirty cents and forty-two hours in 1939 and forty cents and forty hours in 1945. U.S. Department of Labor, BLS, *Labor Information Bulletin* (April 1939), pp. 1–3.

82. Arthur M. Ross, *Trade Union Wage Policy* (Berkeley, Cal., 1948), pp. 113–28.

83. Leuchtenburg, *F.D.R.*, pp. 346–47. The Bankhead-Jones Farm Tenancy Act of 1937 provided some funds for loans to selected tenants who wished to purchase farms. In 1935, there were 2,865,155 tenants (about 42 percent of all farmers), and by 1941, 20,748 had received loans. *Farm Tenancy: Report of the President's Committee* (Washington, February 1937), Table I, p. 89; *Report of the Administrator of the Farm Security Administration, 1941* (Washington, 1941), p. 17.

84. Roosevelt's Inaugural Address of January 20, 1937, FDR Papers, VI, 5.

# from new deal
# to new war

## ARTHUR A. EKIRCH, Jr.

Arthur A. Ekirch, Jr., cannot be classified as a radical or as part of the New Left. But with his affirmation of parts of the American tradition, values, and institutions that were discarded as America moved toward empire abroad and statism at home, Ekirch has developed a critical perspective toward American corporate liberalism.

   In this chapter from Ekirch's important book, *The Decline of American Liberalism,* Ekirch captures the manner in which New Dealers were able to use the principle of planning to implement a war economy and illuminates how an increased state power led to resurgent totalitarianism at home. Ekirch particularly shows the acquiescence of American liberal intellectuals to state power, bureaucracy, and war—an accommodation accepted because the "threat" was Nazi Germany, but one that set the pattern for the Cold War liberalism of the 1950s.

---

The threat of a second world war, never wholly absent in the post-Versailles world, showed new signs of becoming a reality by the middle of the 1930's. After the onset of the depression, the halting efforts to achieve a stable, peaceful world order crumbled rapidly. Although nationalism was rampant in all countries, it reached extremes of chauvinism and militarism in Italy, Germany, and Japan. Each of these nations was dissatisfied with the work of the Paris Peace Conference and was thus all the more ready to resort to war as an instrument of change. Even though World War I had hardly accomplished a victory for the liberal ideals of peace and democracy, these ideals were unfavorably linked with the peace settlement. And as the feeling toward the Versailles Treaty grew more bitter, much of Europe turned against the liberal values that it unfairly associated with the verdict of the war.

   In the United States disillusionment took the somewhat different form of a reaction, not only against the World War I experience but also against possible American participation in any future war. The traditional pacifism of liberal thinking was reinforced by the widespread development of strong isolationist sentiments, which were further deepened in the 1930's by the Nye Committee's investigation of the role of the munitions industry in connection with American entrance into World War I. Revelations of business unneutrality and profiteering uncovered by this committee of the United States Senate were paralleled by the publication of critical historical works on the origins of the war. To many Americans, therefore, World War I became an object lesson in the economic interpretation of history, a lesson which they attempted to apply in the neutrality legislation from 1935 to 1937.

Coming into power in the midst of this swelling antiwar and isolationist feeling, the Roosevelt administration shared the general public attitude. In the 1932 elections, foreign affairs had not been a major issue although Roosevelt, despite his earlier identification with the Wilson administration and the League of Nations, tended to be regarded as the isolationist candidate. It was true that a few liberals, including Oswald Garrison Villard, called attention to Roosevelt's lifelong interest in the navy and the danger that in office he might pursue a militarist course.[1] But such fears seemed to lose their point as the depression compelled the New Deal to concentrate on domestic affairs. With adequate natural resources and no apparent need for more territory, the American people did not envisage war or the abandonment of isolationism as a possible solution to the grave economic problems facing them at home. The early thinking of the New Deal, instead, emphasized the necessity of positive planning to achieve a balance between domestic production and demand. Foreign trade, which had declined to the vanishing point, was largely ignored in favor of developing a stronger consumer economy.

For many liberals the New Deal's program of a balanced economy served as a guarantee that the United States would be able to avoid the dangers of overseas imperialism and foreign wars. Thus Secretary of Agriculture Henry Wallace, in his widely read pamphlet America Must Choose, offered planning "to build up consumption per capita at home, as a substitute for the continual search for new consumers abroad." Stressing intelligent planning as a middle ground between nationalism and internationalism, and as a step toward "new dealing with the world," Wallace wrote: "Our New Deal seeks to promote consumption more soundly. It directs purchasing power to those in need, by wage advances and alleviations of debt. It lessens the need to force exports. It looks toward balancing production with consumption at home."[2]

Planning as a substitute for war was also the thesis advanced by Charles Beard in his realistic studies of the economic mainsprings of American foreign policy. Beard, a supporter of the early New Deal, believed that national interest in the twentieth century had come to mean an increasingly intensified struggle on the part of industrial nations for world markets. Swelling armaments and resort to war had become concomitant features of modern industrial statecraft. Glorious little wars, however, were not always available, and any war once started was not easy to control or bring to a close. While force and war had hitherto been powerful factors in world history, in themselves they had not provided solutions to world economic problems or to maintaining "any culture save that of the barracks." Historically, Beard found that "in cruel truth, internationalism may be a covering ideology for the aggressive nationalism of one or more countries," and he turned therefore to an advocacy of what he called "the open door at home." This Beard hoped to see achieved under the planned economy of the New Deal. "Offering to the world the strange sight of a national garden well tended, the United States," he wrote, "would teach the most effective lesson—a lesson without words."[3]

Beard's vision was reminiscent of the old American dream, looking to the peaceful advance of democracy through adoption by the rest of the world of America's beneficent example of orderly self-government. What most liberals overlooked, however, in their initial enthusiasm for the New Deal's economic planning was the ease with which such planning could be diverted from peace to war. Also forgotten in the popular concentration upon the New Deal's efforts to fight the depression, was the fact that the dividing line between domestic economic recovery and military preparedness was never too clearly drawn. Despite the prevailing pacifist isolationism of the early thirties, with which the Roosevelt administration went along, there was never any reason to doubt the President's own personal sympathy for a big army and navy program. At first, however, campaign promises of economy, and the political dangers inherent in a too sudden adoption of a larger military budget, resulted in a program of rearmament by indirection.

As early as June 1933, the President allocated over two hundred million dollars from the NRA appropriation to the construction of new battleships. Funds intended for the Public Works Agency also were used to bolster up the army and navy, and aircraft carriers, military airplanes, airports, highways, wind tunnels, and hospitals were constructed from PWA money. In 1935 public opposition to this policy persuaded Congress to state the specific purpose for which appropriations were made. But in the case of some agencies of the New Deal little change resulted. As the biographer of Harry Hopkins has noted, "despite the prohibitions against any military activities which had been written into the Work Relief Bill, W.P.A. accomplished a great deal of construction— airports, highways, bridges, etc.—that had deliberately strategic importance."[4]

As the public became conditioned to large-scale New Deal expenditures, economy and indirection in the military budget was less necessary. For example, conservative businessmen, though hostile to outlays for domestic reform, were willing to accept government spending for military purposes. But the major factor behind increasing New Deal appropriations for the army and navy was the administration's growing concern over world affairs and the diversion of its primary interest from domestic to foreign policy. By late 1936 the President, according to Under Secretary of State Sumner Welles, was already "obsessed" with the dangers to the United States stemming from the threat of war in Europe and Asia.[5]

The most dramatic expression of the New Deal's changed emphasis came in Roosevelt's famous "quarantine" speech attacking aggressor nations, which he delivered at Chicago in October 1937. Although the President's words were general in nature, the address implied the possibility of some sort of collective action to deter the ambitions of Germany and Japan. Supporters of the President's abandonment of isolation argued that the best pathway to peace lay in United States encouragement of a strong collective security stand by the nonfascist nations of the world. On the other hand, widespread fears that such a policy, if carried beyond mere words, might presently involve the United States in another world war were probably responsible for the generally unfavorable public reaction to the Chicago speech. The popular neutrality laws, designed to keep America out of war, rather than to try to prevent war from breaking out overseas, were obviously not in harmony with the President's now evident desire to use American power and influence to curb the expansionist aims of Germany and Japan. While the President and the State Department wanted a flexible law that would enable the United States to withhold war supplies from any belligerent deemed an aggressor nation, Congress and the country were determined that the neutrality legislation should apply equally to all warring nations.

Although President Roosevelt, aware of the extent of isolationist sentiment, and with an eye to his own re-election in 1940, continued to maintain a precarious balance between peace and war, such administration measures as repeal of the embargo and enactment of lend lease pointed clearly to eventual American involvement. Even though America was not a belligerent in the first two years of the war, Roosevelt did not believe that the country could be neutral or indifferent to Nazi war aims. On the other hand, former President Hoover was convinced that his successor was leading the United States into a foreign war despite the desire of the majority of the people for peace. Modern war, Hoover warned, "means that our country must be mobilized into practically a Fascist state. It would be so organized. It went some distance in the last great war, although we did not use that term at the time."[6]

Echoing Hoover's gloomy prediction, Senator Arthur H. Vandenberg, Republican of Michigan, in the midst of the Congressional debate over repeal of the embargo, charged that sending munitions to the Allies would be the prelude to further intervention in their behalf, until ultimately the United States would enter the war as an avowed cobelligerent. If this came true, the senator warned, "we would get such a regimentation of our own lives and livelihoods, 20 minutes after we entered the war, that the Bill of Rights would need a gas mask, and individual liberty of action would soon become a mocking memory."[7]

To many American liberals the now-changing situation at home was almost as disheartening as the menace of totalitarianism and war from abroad. An aggressive United States foreign policy, they realized, spelled the end of domestic reform. Already the New Deal had lost much of its initial allure. Its evident failure to achieve any real prosperity was highlighted by estimates of ten million workers still unemployed at the close of the thirties. With the road to recovery via planning and reform seemingly at a dead end, some critics wondered whether the administration's growing attention to foreign affairs was entirely a result of the worsened international situation. Viewed in such a light, much of the New Deal's nationalism and centralization, and its vast expenditures, could be reconsidered as steps in preparedness for an impending war.[8]

Among the first to argue such a thesis was Albert Jay Nock, an intransigent and uncompromising individualist who had no doubt about the eventual direction of the New Deal's planned economy. "What we and our more nearly immediate descendants shall see," he wrote in 1935, "is a steady progress in collectivism running off into a military despotism of a severe type. Closer centralization; a steadily growing bureaucracy; State power and faith in State power increasing, social power and faith in social power diminishing." Three years later, Nock confided to a correspondent: "I see that Franklin is playing what is usually the jobholder's last card—'National defence.' " And after America entered the war, Nock, as unreconciled as ever, observed publicly: "At any time after 1936 it was evident that a European war would not be unwelcome to the Administration at Washington, largely as a means of diverting public attention from its flock of uncouth economic chickens on their way home to roost, but chiefly as a means of strengthening its malign grasp upon the country's political and economic machinery."[9]

Particularly among those liberals who resisted the administration's foreign policy, war was feared as a prelude to totalitarianism. The answer to the problem of fascism, they believed, depended on more than the defeat of Italy, Germany, or Japan. Like communism, fascism was viewed as part of a world revolt against many of the values of liberalism and democracy. And the United States, by concentrating its attention on the danger of a fascist or nazi aggression from abroad, overlooked the more real threat of an approaching totalitarianism at home. This threat, however, did not come primarily from some of the more blatant, radical demagogues of the right who encouraged such profascist organizations as the German-American Bund. Rather, as Huey Long, one of the first and most able of their number, explained, if fascism ever took hold in America it would arrive in the guise of antifascism.

Lawrence Dennis, the leading American exponent of intellectual fascism, underlined Long's point with his thesis that a purely American fascism would not have to include all the undesirable features of Hitler's nazi state. In his *Coming American Fascism,* published in 1937, Dennis maintained that neither economic planning nor the use of force was un-American. Liberal capitalism, he argued, was doomed and could no longer be made to work short of the economic incentives supplied by war. The latter, in turn, would automatically, and of necessity, result in the imposition of some kind of fascist state and economy.

Although most Americans had little sympathy with avowed fascist-type organizations or leaders, there was a growing fear, especially in liberal circles, that fascism and the totalitarian collectivist state were symptomatic of a deeply rooted malaise striking at the heart of Western civilization. Fascism, according to this view, was part of a Machiavellian or managerial revolution that sought to overthrow the remnants of an already declining liberal society. It fed on the craving of the masses, not only for economic security but also for the type of psychological security found in authoritarian institutions. The so-called revolt of the masses was thus actually more an apathetic resistance to the initiative that a free liberal society entrusted to the individual—a "flight from freedom," or a retreat from reason. Catering to the psychological and social needs of the people by offering them all sorts of nationalistic and militaristic flourishes, the fascist states were able to stir the patriotism of the masses. In this way, too, the state gained acceptance for the cutting back of consumers' goods and could devote the savings to war preparations. In Karl Mannheim's dire words, "The less bread, the more circuses."[10]

The role of fascist ways of thinking in American life provoked continued commentary in the months before American entrance into World War II. Noting that many of those who had formerly deplored the fascist tendencies of the domestic program of the New Deal now "accepted the inevitability of the Fascist impact in a period of preparedness," Edgar Kemler, a young journalist, chronicled what he called *The Deflation of American Ideals.* "We have reduced a rich heritage of hopes and dreams to the bare endeavor to make the system work," Kemler wrote, but he added: "I, for one, am willing to pay this price." Others also noted that the multiplicity of New Deal laws, even though they had promised some social good, in no way changed the fact that they were often gained at the price of individual liberty.[11]

Most cynical, perhaps, was James Burnham, who argued in his well-known book *The Managerial Revolution* that United States hostility to totalitarianism was merely resentment of its foreign aspects—"a 100% American totalitarianism would not be objectionable." While the United States was the most primitive of the managerial states, it tended in the same direction as its European counterparts. American liberals were naturally confused by the mixture of aims and purposes put forth under the New Deal banner. Such old-fashioned liberal individualists as Oswald Garrison Villard, for example, whom both Kemler and Burnham regarded as typical, were especially bewildered because "the New Deal's liberalism and progressivism are *not* liberalism and progressivism in the historical meaning of these terms."[12] Villard, despite his admiration for much of the early New Deal and his approval of Roosevelt's stand against fascist aggression, could not reconcile growing American militarization or Roosevelt's Supreme Court plan and third-term ambitions with his own liberal philosophy. Believing that New Deal liberalism was being slain by preparations for war, Villard unhappily continued to protest that he was still a New Dealer as well as a staunch pacifist.[13]

As the United States moved ever closer to war, American liberals, already at odds over the issues at stake, were still further divided by charges that the scholars and writers among them had been notably indifferent to the totalitarian advance threatening the free world. In an earlier view of this question, the so-called treason of the intellectuals was regarded as not to the state but to their responsibilities as intellectuals. Their treason therefore was not a lack of patriotism but their renunciation of the philosophy of liberalism for the favors and dictates of the state. It followed from this that "One of the gravest responsibilities of the modern State is that is has not maintained (but could it do so?) a class of men exempt from civic duties, men whose sole function is to maintain non-practical values."[14] The New Deal, with all its emergency WPA aid to art and letters, had been able to avoid political censorship because the criterion was the individual's need for relief and not the content of his work. But now, with the approach of war, the old conservative refrain of "rights without duties" was revived as a whip to lash the hesitant, nonconformist liberal intellectuals into line.

After the fall of France in the late spring of 1940, Archibald MacLeish led a group of American intellectuals in accusing their fellows of a "failure to understand what it is that is happening to their world," and of failing to oppose soon enough the fascist destruction of scholarship and humane values. Having seen "the crisis of our time" in France, MacLeish charged that American intellectuals continued to think and write of it in a detached way as a purely European phenomenon. This criticism, as it was later developed and enlarged in the course of the war, was basically a charge that many American liberals and intellectuals, imbued with the disillusionist and critical viewpoint of the twenties and early thirties, had not responded with sufficient enthusiasm to the stimulus of American nationalism and patriotism. Presumably guilty of this charge of having been overly critical in their writings were such authors as Sinclair Lewis, H. L. Mencken, and Charles Beard. According to the MacLeish school of thought, these writers, "The Irresponsibles," had undermined the confidence of American youths in American institutions and had thus weakened their will to fight the battle of democracy against fascism.[15]

This indictment was a natural outgrowth of the new spirit of nationalism that had begun to develop in the thirties. In part, a result of the support that the New Deal gave to various intellectual and cultural projects, this cultural nationalism was also related to the search for positive values in the midst of a deteriorating world order. In such a time of stress, the kind of liberalism that indulged in a critical view of accepted institutions and beliefs was likely to be subordinated to a philosophy of emotional affirmation and uncritical faith. Accordingly, two days after Pearl Harbor, the Writers' War Board was organized to meet the need for a wartime propaganda agency. This Board had as its "basic function . . . the fulfillment of requests from governmental agencies for all kinds of writing required to win the war."[16]

The very virulence of the MacLeish attack on the writers and intellectuals of the interwar period, in a sense, provided its own explanation for much of their pessimistic and critical spirit. But, as a later defender of the accused authors was to point out, it never occurred to their wartime detractors that the bitterness of the writings they attacked was rooted in the fact of one world war and was in the process of being justified by another even greater global conflict.[17]

In the midst of these final intellectual preparations for possible war, important changes were overtaking American democracy. Almost unnoticed, Congress passed what was in effect the first peacetime sedition law in the United States since the unhappy Federalist Act of 1798. Serious interest in such a law had its origins in the period immediately after World War I, when Wilson's attorney general, A. Mitchell Palmer, tried unsuccessfully to persuade Congress to transpose the wartime sedition legislation into a permanent statute. In the twenties most of the illiberal war legislation, except in some of the states, became a dead letter, and then in the 1930's the Supreme Court began to bolster liberals' confidence in the matter of civil liberties. The Court, under Chief Justice Charles Evans Hughes, became a zealous defender of the right of free speech, and Justices Holmes and Brandeis, formerly in a minority on such cases, now found their views accepted by a majority of their colleagues.

But, while the Court was thus giving the country more liberty, toward the end of the decade Congress and state legislatures began giving it less. Fears of communism revived and soon resulted in state laws interfering with freedom of speech, press, and teaching. In 1935 Congress called for hearings on a peacetime sedition law, and three years later the Dies Committee began its investigation of un-American activities. Concerned with ferreting out subversive nazi and communist activity in the United States, the Dies Committee also had the effect of intimidating left-wing and radical sentiment within the New Deal administration and in the labor movement.[18] The drive for a peacetime sedition law, accordingly, seemed based on more than a foreign threat to America.

A month before Hitler moved his army into Poland, the House of Representatives after weeks of thorough discussion passed a sedition bill by an overwhelming majority. Less than a year later, in June 1940, the bill became law, but the brief final debate made no reference to the collapse of France that spring or to the danger of a nazi attack on the United States. Indeed, the chief connection of the bill with events in Europe seemed to rest in its misleading title of Alien Registration Act. The impression that most Americans had of the act was that it was a statute for the registration and fingerprinting of foreigners. Zechariah Chafee, an authority on the history of legislation pertaining to freedom of speech, has admitted: "Not until months later did I for one realize that this statute contains the most drastic restrictions on freedom of speech ever enacted in the United States during peace." Chafee added that the law commonly called the Smith Act "is no more limited to the registration of aliens than the Espionage Act of 1917 was limited to spying." The comparative liberal silence regarding the Smith Act at the time of its passage, he felt, was probably a result of the rush of legislation that spring, the lessened critical feeling of the country in the face of impending war, and finally the false stress on the bill as a measure dealing chiefly with aliens.[19]

This latter emphasis was true of the bill as originally drawn up, when Congress, in a mood of bitter and vindictive antiforeign feeling almost akin to nazism in Germany, was ready to pass any kind of restrictive measure dealing with aliens. Justified at first on the grounds that it applied only to the alien deemed guilty of subversive activities, the bill was then, in turn, criticized because it did not apply equally well to suspect citizens. Congress suddenly seemed panic-stricken by the realization that the country had existed for almost one hundred fifty years with no law governing sedition in time of peace. Accordingly, the bill was amended so that citizens as well as aliens were prohibited from such activities as interfering with the loyalty of the armed forces. This antisubversive section put into effect again the terms of the World War I Espionage Act. Finally, the whole bill was broadened not only to include activity involving the army or navy but to forbid anyone from teaching or advocating the "overthrow or destruction of any government in the United States by force or violence; or to be or become a member of, or affiliate with, any such society, group, or assembly of persons . . . ."[20]

This last provision contained the "guilt by association" clause that provided a foundation for the antiradical campaign following World War II. Thus it was evident that the Alien Registration Act included far more than its title indicated and that it carried sedition legislation beyond the World War I example. The only precedent in all American history for its insistence that guilt was not necessarily personal but could be determined by membership or association was in the alien deportations of 1919. "Neither the Sedition Act of 1798 nor the Espionage Acts of 1917 and 1918 included such a conception. We got safely through the Civil War and the World War without finding it necessary to create group guilt outside the limits of an actual conspiracy."[21]

The general aim of the 1940 sedition legislation, like that of the more limited laws of 1798 and 1918, was, of course, to suppress the dissemination of opinions and beliefs deemed subversive, but which nevertheless could not be prosecuted as treasonable within the meaning of the Constitution and the courts' interpretation of treason as dependent on some overt activity. The danger in all such legislation was not its actual provisions dealing with subversion of the armed forces or overthrow of the government—practices which almost all would accept as undesirable—but the way the law could be used to threaten free speech and nonconformist activity. "The truth," as Chafee has pointed out, "is that the precise language of a sedition law is like the inscription on a sword. What matters is the existence of the weapon. Once the sword is placed in the hands of the people in power, then, whatever it says, they will be able to reach and slash at almost any unpopular person who is speaking or writing anything that they consider objectionable criticism of their policies."[22]

Although at least one congressman warned that the Smith Act could also be used to prevent conservatives from agitating against a type of government they deemed radical and un-American, in practice, legislation of this type was more liable to operate "as a device to keep down the agitation of discontented workmen."[23] Thus the Smith Act was largely unworkable in World War II when it was invoked in the mass sedition trial of a group of alleged nazi sympathizers, but it was used effectively in 1941 against a number of Trotskyist labor leaders. Eighteen men and women members of the Socialist Workers party and the Minneapolis Motor Transport Workers Union, a CIO local, were the first to be convicted under the Smith Act's provisions against any conspiracy to overthrow the government by force or violence. Wartime liberals who ignored the Minneapolis case and were willing to enforce the doctrine of guilt by association against members of the pro-nazi German-American Bund, were later to reap a heavy harvest of retribution when the Smith Act was found to be susceptible of use against left-wing and radical groups in the period after the war.[24]

In the same month in which Congress passed the Alien Registration, or Smith, Act, it began serious consideration of another measure also unprecedented in American peacetime history—military conscription. Some form of military training in peace as a preparation for universal service in war had long been desired in military circles. This enthusiasm, however, was not shared by the American people or the Congress, and all such plans looking toward compulsory training or drill were rejected after World War I. Although such a New Deal measure as the Civilian Conservation Corps of the 1930's provided a degree of military training and preparedness, there had been no real opportunity to revive the draft issue until after the coming of the war in Europe.

Presented to the people as legislation for the better defense and protection of the United States by a system of peacetime military training, the Selective Service Act of 1940 was in reality a war measure. Despite the emphasis on training for defense, the law forecast the sending of an American army to Europe or Asia as soon as the United States might become an actual belligerent. Conscription, widely denounced as the sure path to war, held out far-reaching implications for American foreign policy. And, at the same time, as Senator Norris pointed out in the debate over the measure, a permanent system of compulsory military training would go far to transform the domestic pattern of life in the United States as he and his colleagues had known it.[25]

With its potentiality for heightening nationalist and militarist sentiment, conscription was obviously inimical to the ideals of peace and individual liberty long prized by all liberals. In conflict with traditional liberalism, conscription was also at odds with democracy, except in an interpretation of the latter from an extreme equalitarian or collectivist point of view. This conflict between conscription and democratic ideals was immediately pointed out in a statement signed by some three hundred prominent educators, authors, clergymen, business and professional leaders, who denounced the impending draft as totalitarian and unworthy of the spirit of American democracy.[26]

Liberals, with a respect for the historic tenets of their principles, could justify conscription only to the extent that they viewed United States entrance into the war as necessary and desirable. It was again the old World War I confusion over ends and means. The dilemma of the prowar liberals lay in the fact that they could not logically refrain from acceding to the militarism that might be needed to back up the President's interventionist foreign policy. Thus Freda Kirchwey, editor of the Nation, wrote somewhat reluctantly, "There Is No Alternative." And the New Republic, which at first believed that the United States should limit its efforts to continuing as the arsenal of democracy, announced in September 1940: "It is with heavy hearts that the editors of the New Republic endorse the principle of compulsory service at this time."[27]

In contrast to the tortured consciences of the editors of the liberal journals, some conservative spokesmen, who did not join in the general military and business enthusiasm for conscription, were able to suggest that the draft was basically a New Deal totalitarian measure. For example, the Commercial and Financial Chronicle, which had greeted the Burke-Wadsworth selective service bill with the caption "Involuntary servitude must not be restored," asked: "Does not this defense program in some of its aspects take on the appearance of another New Deal project tainted with the philosophy of totalitarianism and heavy with risk of further infringement of individual liberty?"[28]

After the passage of the Selective Service Act, the problem of the conscientious objector to military service thrust itself upon all those liberals who were not completely captivated by the war spirit. While the small number of actual CO's was to prove disappointing to the many liberals who had taken seriously the antiwar pledges of college youths in the 1930's, the prospect of even a few thousand objectors was disquieting to the government. Although Selective Service procedures in regard to the CO came to represent a considerable advance over World War I legislation and practice, Congress in 1940 refused to follow Britain's liberal example and accept as sincere those objectors who were motivated by other than religious beliefs. Liberal and pacifist spokesmen at the first draft hearings therefore warned the congressmen that they were enacting a measure which, in providing insufficient protection for the cause of conscience, would again fill Federal jails with objectors to war. This prediction was in part realized as many CO's were either denied such a classification on technical grounds or themselves refused to comply with the strict provisions of the act.[29]

In the course of the war, some six thousand CO's, including four thousand Jehovah's Witnesses denied classification as ministers, were convicted of Draft Act violations and sentenced to prison terms of as much as five years. Twice this number, or some twelve thousand men, were assigned to the civilian work camps or to special units on farms or in mental hospitals. A much larger number of CO's, variously estimated at from twenty-five to one hundred thousand men, were granted noncombatant status in the army. For the CO in general there had been a significant change since World War I. Although not in agreement with his views, most people seemed to feel that the sincere objector had a right to his convictions. Many of the churches, for example, though they again followed the populace in giving their sanction to war, coupled this stand with resolutions affirming support of the individual whose conscience compelled him to stand aside.[30]

In the light of the comparative toleration extended at least to the religious objector, the most serious victims of wartime hate and hysteria were the Japanese Americans living along the Pacific coast and in the Hawaiian Islands. Although there was no case of espionage or sabotage by a single Japanese, citizen or noncitizen, all Americans of Japanese descent were evacuated from the Pacific coast, and military government was imposed upon the Hawaiian Islands, where Japanese Americans formed the largest single element in the population. Later, after the close of the war, the Supreme Court declared the army rule of Hawaii to have been an illegal invasion of the rights of the inhabitants. But, in the case of the removal of the West Coast Japanese Americans, the Court refused to intervene.

On the authority of a presidential order allowing the commanding general on the Pacific coast to designate military areas from which any or all civilians could be excluded, General John L. DeWitt gave more than one hundred thousand Japanese Americans, two-thirds of whom were citizens of the United States, five days in which to leave their homes and be transferred to government relocation or detention centers. As a staunch advocate of evacuation, General DeWitt played the key role in the affair, but his decision enjoyed the approval of both President Roosevelt and Secretary of War Stimson. In the post-Pearl Harbor mood of anti-Japanese feeling, no attempt was made to distinguish between citizen and alien or between the loyal and disloyal. The protests emanating from such organizations as the Fellowship of Reconciliation and the American Civil Liberties Union were ignored, and even the latter organization at first approved, or at least condoned, the evacuation.[31]

Gradually, however, liberals perceived the falsity of the blanket charges of disloyalty directed against the Japanese Americans, and the harsh injustice of depriving them of their homes, property, and means of future livelihood. In 1943 the Supreme Court, although refusing to rule against the army decision, nevertheless expressed its grave suspicion of the necessity of the evacuation. And after the war the Court decided that the evacuees must be permitted to return to their Pacific coast homes. Still another judicial criticism of the army's procedure was handed down by the Circuit Court of Appeals in 1949. Affirming the restoration of citizenship to those Japanese Americans who had renounced it during their incarceration in the wartime relocation centers, Judge William Dunham wrote a decision which the New York Times described as "a blistering denunciation of Lieut. Gen. John L. DeWitt." The judge likened the relocation centers to German concentration camps and denounced the general's doctrine of enemy racism as similar to the Nazi philosophy.[32]

Except for the glaring instance of the treatment of the West Coast Japanese Americans, there was no concerted official violation of the civil liberties of the citizen in World War II. Though the Roosevelt administration and Attorney General Francis Biddle deserved much credit for this record, the improvement could also be explained, at least in part, by the lack of any real opposition to the war. This almost universal acquiescence helped to account for the improved record of the government in the matter of civil liberties as compared with World War I. Assured of general support, the Roosevelt administration could afford to be tolerant of its few academic and intellectual critics. The sensational raids and vindictive prosecutions of World War I were, on the whole, avoided, and the attempt to prosecute a group of American pro-nazi sympathizers resulted in a mistrial. Aside from a few disloyal individuals, the alien population of the United States proved no great problem, and only a few hundred were interned besides the Japanese Americans.[33]

Whatever the reason, liberals could hardly complain over the comparative absence of serious infringements upon civil liberties. Of more immediate concern to many liberals therefore were some of the trends in the United States which, however normal and expected in wartime, gave indications that they would continue far beyond the period of actual hostilities. This was particularly true in the matter of the increasing concentration and control of the economic life of the nation by the joint forces of big business and big government. When the Temporary National Economic Committee, created back in 1938 to investigate just this problem, submitted its final report in 1941, it was embarrassed to find on every side fresh evidence of the concentration of economic power. Later, in the midst of the war, a special committee appointed by the Senate to study the status of the smaller business and industrial plants, reported an alarming rate of wartime casualties so that there were one-half million fewer enterprises in 1943 than in 1941. Other figures showed that a high proportion of government contracts were being awarded to the largest corporations, which naturally were thereby placed in a close relationship with the army and navy. Even allowing for the considerable amount of subsequent subcontracting to smaller firms, an important feature of the war economy seemed to be a strengthening of big business.[34]

During the war the military did its best to direct the allocation of all industrial output, engaging in a long struggle over this issue with the civilian

War Production Board headed by Donald Nelson. One of the important matters in dispute, and a vital factor in the early resumption of a normal peacetime economy, was setting a date for the relaxation of government controls so that civilian production could be resumed. In general, this was a problem of greater concern to smaller businesses without sizable government orders. In any case, by 1944 Nelson believed that the state of war production was sufficiently healthy to make possible the gradual reconversion of American industry to postwar peacetime needs. This change-over the army, however, was able to block, thus maintaining for a longer period Federal authority over prices, production, and raw materials.[35]

By the middle of the war the army, in conjunction with those business leaders who favored closer ties between industry and the armed forces, also attempted to secure full control over the nation's manpower through a labor draft. Liberal and labor sentiment, however, regarded such a war service bill as equivalent to slavery. They rejected the timeworn contention that conscription for the army justified a labor draft in industry—an argument that overlooked the fact that the worker in private industry was also making possible profits for his employer. As William Green, president of the American Federation of Labor, was quick to point out, there could be no fair draft of labor without a correspondingly drastic levy on capital.[36] This overambitious effort to regiment all American manpower occasioned much bitterness and resulted further in widespread charges of totalitarianism. In the ensuing reaction against the whole scheme of a labor draft, strong public sentiment also developed against proposals to turn the wartime system of selective service into a permanent peacetime plan for compulsory military training. This question was accordingly postponed until after the war.

Although Congress refused to sanction either peacetime conscription or a labor draft, in almost all other respects the war period was one of tremendous expansion in the powers of government over the individual. Allocation of raw materials and industrial capacity was carried down to the average citizen through a system of rationing and price control of consumers' goods. The long time trend toward greater concentration and centralization of the political and economic life of the nation had never before been so explicitly institutionalized and brought home to each and every person. Imitative of big business was now big government, full of grave problems and implications for the future of liberalism and democracy.

In the midst of wartime regimentation of the national economy, the argument that centralized economic planning would result in some sort of permanent, totalitarian, collectivist order increased in intensity. This thesis attracted the attention of a wide variety of economists, publicists, and scholars, who depicted the United States as marching toward fascism or returning to serfdom. Of all this wartime literature, the book that had the greatest impact was probably Friedrich Hayek's *The Road to Serfdom,* published in 1944. The work of an Austrian economist teaching in England, Hayek's volume was a far more sensitive and modest book than either its disciples or critics made out. In essence it advanced the contention that the United States and England, though not resembling the Germany of Hitler and World War II, did bear a close analogy to the Germany of World War I and after. The progressive abandonment of freedom in economic affairs, Hayek feared, was leading to a similar destruction of political and personal freedom. Political democracy in itself was no guarantee against arbitrary power, and in the advance of economic collectivism under centralized state planning Hayek saw a new despotism and reversion to a feudal type of social order.[37]

In angry rejoinder to Hayek's book, Herman Finer, one of his former English colleagues who was teaching at Harvard University, hastily published *Road to Reaction,* pointing out some inconsistencies and confusion of purpose in Hayek's writing, but in no sense refuting his major thesis. Instead, Finer resorted to personal invective, berating Hayek as one of the company of men who failed to distinguish between the Fascists and Nazis, and "the pro-popular impulse of the Soviet system." According to Finer, Hayek was also one of a small group of liberals, some of whom had "decided against America's entry into World War II before Pearl Harbor."[38] Undoubtedly, Hayek's book was used by certain reactionary groups to serve a dubious ulterior purpose, out of keeping with the author's own reasonable point of view, but this did not contradict the essentials of his argument that the United States was witnessing a decline of economic freedom that would affect all liberty. Especially interesting, in the light of his own vast influence on New Deal economic thought, was the judgment of John Maynard Keynes, who, without disavowing planning, nevertheless wrote to Hayek that he agreed morally and philosophically with his controversial book.[39]

*The Road to Serfdom,* published in the middle of World War II, marked a critical break between two eras of national planning. It also illustrated the confusion of individualist liberals caught between the waning New Deal and the waxing war economy of the 1940's. These liberals could not help but feel a growing concern lest modern government degenerate into a species of arbitrary and tyrannical rule administered by a swollen bureaucracy. The emergency powers granted to the New Deal in the crisis of the depression were constantly being expanded in the course of the war. As President Roosevelt told Congress after Pearl Harbor, in announcing his intention to arrogate authority regarding price controls if desired legislation was not passed, "I cannot tell what powers may have to be exercised in order to win this war."[40]

Despite the many precedents for the wartime assumption of authority by the President of the United States, there was the ever-present danger that Congress, as Senator Taft put it, in reply to the President, would be reduced to "a mere shell of a legislative body." Doctrines of presidential power and responsibility, illustrated by Roosevelt's disregard of the third-term tradition in 1940, and again in 1944, and the whole theory of military necessity, as argued in the case of the Japanese Americans, raised the question of whether the government was outrunning both constitutional law and American traditions. The peril was not that of an explicit fascism or a demagoguery of the old Huey Long type but rather, as one writer expressed it, "Our danger is that we are drifting away from the secure anchorage of constitutional government, with little thought as to where the winds of expediency will carry us." Hopeful that trends toward collectivism might be absorbed in the democratic system, various reformers suggested plans for the modernization and reorganization of the Federal government, especially in the field of legislative-executive relationships. At the same time, fearful of the wartime shift of power to the President and the executive bureaucracy, liberals began to take a new interest in preserving the legislative branch of the government as a bulwark of democracy. "The difference between an authoritarian and a democratic state centers on the position of the representative body. If the Legislature is free and strong, authoritarian rule cannot exist."[41]

Liberals' growing concern and criticism, however unwelcome in the midst of a wartime emphasis on undivided national loyalty and unity, nevertheless served the useful and important function of calling attention to problems and trends that transcended even the impact of the war. Looking ahead to the postwar world, American liberals had little basis for an optimistic confidence. A period of total war, characterized by indiscriminate bombing of civilian populations and flagrant violation of neutral rights, was not likely to be the prelude to a coming era of peace and international understanding. Nor was it easy to see how, after a period of severe war destruction and state control of economic life, there could be any quick return to a free economy on either a national or an international scale. Instead, as in the era of World War I, there was every indication that wartime methods and patterns of thinking would continue to hold their own in the years immediately ahead.

## NOTES

1. "The Pot and the Kettle," *Nation*, CXXXV (Oct. 26, 1932), 390.

2. *World Affairs Pamphlets No. 3* (1934), 31.

3. C. A. Beard and G. H. E. Smith, *The Open Door at Home* (New York: Macmillan, 1934), 44–45, 99, 111, 131, 319.

4. Dixon Wecter, *The Age of the Great Depression* (New York: Macmillan, 1948), 78; R. E. Sherwood, *Roosevelt and Hopkins* (New York: Harper, 1948), 75–76.

5. *Where Are We Heading?* (New York: Harper, 1946), 0.

6. Feb. 1, 1939, quoted in *Congressional Record*, 76 Cong., 1 Sess., Appendix, 402–404.

7. Oct. 4, 1939, *ibid.,* 76 Cong., 2 Sess., 97.

8. Broadus Mitchell, *Depression Decade*, chap. 11 "War to the Rescue."

9. *Our Enemy the State* (New York: Morrow, 1935), 205–206; *Letters from Albert Jay Nock 1924–1945* (Caldwell: Caxton, 1949), 103; *Memoirs of a Superfluous Man* (New York: Harper, 1943), 247–248.

10. *Man and Society in an Age of Reconstruction* (New York: Harcourt, Brace, 1940), 135. The literature on the impact of fascism is extensive, but especially provocative is Peter Drucker, *The End of Economic Man* (New York: John Day, 1939).

11. (Washington: American Council on Public Affairs, 1941), 6–7, 66ff. See also Mauritz Hallgren, *Landscape of Freedom* (New York: Howell, Soskin, 1941), 426.

12. *The Managerial Revolution* (New York: John Day, 1941), 152, 196–197, 257–258.

13. See Villard's letters to William T. Evjue, Aug. 8, 1937; Frederick H. Allen, Oct. 17, 1937; Frank E. Gannett, Sept. 17, 1938; Franklin D. Roosevelt, Oct. 5, 1938; E. P. Adler, Aug. 2, 1939; Van Wyck Brooks, Sept. 27, 1940, Villard Papers. See also Villard, "Credo of an Old-Fashioned Liberal," *American Mercury*, LV (October 1942), 464–470.

14. Julien Benda, *The Treason of the Intellectuals* (New York: Morrow, 1928), 104, 158–159.

15. *The Irresponsibles* (New York: Duell, Sloan and Pearce, 1940), 3, 9, and *passim*. See also Lewis Mumford, *Faith for Living* (New York: Harcourt, Brace, 1940); Herbert Agar, *et al.,* *The City of Man* (New York: Viking, 1940).

16. Writers' War Board, *Third Annual Report,* January 1945.

17. Philip Rahv, *Image and Idea* (Norfolk: New Directions, 1949), 161–164.

18. A. R. Ogden, *The Dies Committee* (Washington: Catholic U. Press, 1950), chap. 1, and 152.

19. Chafee, *Free Speech*, 441, 443, chap. 12.

20. "Alien Registration Act," June 28, 1940, Title I, *U.S. Statutes at Large*, LIV, 670–671.

21. Chafee, *Free Speech,* 470.

22. *Ibid.,* 467.

23. *Ibid.,* 465, 484.

24. See, however, as examples of contemporary concern: "Civil Liberties in Minneapolis," *New Republic*, CV (July 28, 1941), 103–104; "The Issues at Minneapolis," *Nation*, CLIII (Dec. 13, 1941), 602; American Civil Liberties Union, *The Bill of Rights in Wartime* (New York, 1942), 27–28.

25. Aug. 12, 1940, *Congressional Record*, 76 Cong., 3 Sess., 10114.

26. *New York Times*, July 9, 1940, p. 4, col. 1.

27. *Nation*, CLI (Aug. 3, 1940), 81, 85–86; *New Republic*, CIII (July 1, Sept. 2, 1940), 6–7, 294–295.

28. CL (June 29, 1940), 4027–4029; CLI (Aug. 3, 1940), 591–593.

29. Mulford Sibley and Philip Jacob, *Conscription of Conscience (Ithaca: Cornell U. Press, 1952), Part 3.

30. *Ibid.*, 83ff., 313–319. See also American Civil Liberties Union, *Conscience and the War* (New York, 1943).

31. Morton Grodzins, *Americans Betrayed* (Chicago: U. Chicago Press, 1949); Caleb Foote, "Have We Forgotten Justice?" *Fellowship*, VIII (May 1942), 79–81; A. C. L. U., *Military Power and Civil Rights* (New York, 1942), 4; and *Freedom in Wartime* (New York, 1943), 29.

32. *Federal Reporter*, 2d ser., CLXXVI, 953ff.; *New York Times*, Aug. 27, 1949, p. 5, col. 4.

33. The reports of the American Civil Liberties Union, published under various titles from 1941 to 1944, provide a good summary.

34. "Economic Concentration and World War II: Report of the Smaller War Plants Corporation," *U. S. Senate Doc. No. 206*, 79 Cong., 2 Sess. (Washington, 1946), vii–viii, and *passim*.

35. Donald Nelson, *Arsenal of Democracy* (New York: Harcourt, Brace, 1946), xvii, 363, and chaps. 19–20. See also the excellent summary by Jack W. Peltason, "The Reconversion Controversy," *Public Administration and Policy Development*, ed. Harold Stein (New York: Harcourt, Brace, 1952), 228ff.

36. Senate Comm. on Military Affairs, "National War Service Bill," *Hearings*, 78 Cong., 2 Sess. (Washington, 1944), 184. *Christian Century*, LX (March 24, 1943), 356–359.

37. (Chicago: U. Chicago Press, 1944), 2, 13, 71, 206, 215.

38. (Boston: Little, Brown, 1945), 106.

39. R. F. Harrod, *The Life of John Maynard Keynes* (New York: Harcourt, Brace, 1951), 436.

40. Sept. 7, 1942, *Public Papers and Addresses*, XI, 364–365. See also Roosevelt's "Fireside Chat on Cost of Living," Sept. 7, 1942, *ibid.*, 372–373.

41. Sept. 7, 1942, *Congressional Record*, 77 Cong., 2 Sess; 7, 2 Sess., 7046–7047; Merlo Pusey, *Big Government: Can We Control It?* (New York: Harper, 1945), 48ff., 96, 111ff.; T. K. Finletter, *Can Representative Government Do the Job?* (New York: Reynal and Hitchcock, 1945), 13, 18.

# bibliography

The thesis that government reform was instituted by big businessmen to escape competition is developed by Gabriel Kolko in *Railroads and Regulation, 1877–1916* (Princeton University Press, 1965) and *The Triumph of Conservatism* (Free Press, 1963). Kolko's thesis is modified and supported in the work by James Weinstein, *The Corporate Ideal in the Liberal State, 1900–1918* (Beacon Press, 1968).

Although not considered a radical, historian Samuel P. Hays has helped in the radical reassessment of progressivism. In *Conservation and the Gospel of Efficiency* (Harvard University Press, 1959), Hays argued that progressive era conservation was the result of businessmen and scientists who favored rational use of natural resources. In his widely reprinted essay, "The Politics of Reform in Municipal Government in the Progressive Era," *Pacific Northwest Quarterly*, LV (October 1964), 157–169, Hays looked at the progressive support for municipal government reform. He found that reform did not arise because of a fight between business and the masses. Rather, businessmen in local areas wanted reform so that the upper classes could retain control over political life and usurp the influence of the lower classes. One of Hays' students, K. Austin Kerr, brings a similar approach that is generally supportive of Kolko's work to a study of the railroads and shippers, *American Railroad Politics, 1914–1920: Rates, Wages and Efficiency* (University of Pittsburgh Press, 1968). Further confirmation for the effect of government intervention on industry along the lines taken by Kerr is Melvin I. Urofsky, *Big Steel and the Wilson Administration* (Ohio State University Press, 1969).

General reevaluation of progressivism, carried on through an analysis of the New Deal, is to be found in Arthur A. Ekirch, Jr., *The Decline of American Liberalism* (Longmans, Green, 1955). Ekirch argues that the progressives were nationalists who abandoned traditional liberalism on behalf of statism.

The nature of organized labor and its relation to government is taken up in a new fashion by Robert H. Zieger in *Republicans and Labor, 1919–1929* (University Press of Kentucky, 1969). Zieger argues that Herbert Hoover attempted to improve labor's condition through voluntary cooperation of workers at the plant level and by support for union demands backed by public opinion. A similar article, stressing the integration of organized labor and its leadership into the corporate capitalist system, is Ronald Radosh, "The Corporate Ideology of American Labor Leaders from Gompers to Hillman," *Studies on the Left*, VI, no. 6 (1966), 66–87.

Liberalism in the 1920s and the emergence of corporate state policies are taken up in a seminal article by Martin J. Sklar, "On the Proletarian Revolution and the End of Political-Economic Society," *Radical America*, III, no. 3 (May–June 1969), 1–41. The further development of state intervention in the economy during the 1920s and a reevaluation in particular of Herbert Hoover's role is to be found in the writings of Murray N. Rothbard. Two of his essays, on Hoover and business collectivism in the 1920s, are to be found in Ronald Radosh and Murray N. Rothbard, eds., *A New History of Leviathan* (Dutton, 1972). Also to be found in this collection is Ronald Radosh's essay "The Myth of the New Deal."

Much work has recently been done by radicals on the New Deal era. New insights and suggestions of importance to historians are to be found in G. William Domhoff, *The Higher Circles: The Governing Class in America* (Random House, 1970), particularly in Chapter 6, "How the Power Elite Shape Social Legislation."

Other seminal radical articles on the New Deal include Howard Zinn's introductory essay to his anthology *New Deal Thought* (Bobbs-Merrill, 1966), in which he juxtaposes the ideas of mainstream liberals and radicals, emphasizing the limited nature of New Deal reform. Paul Conkin, a traditional historian teaching at Wisconsin, has written a brief book on the era in which he argues that the New Deal was the best friend of business and that the Welfare State it created was eminently conservative. Conkin's argument is to be found in *The New Deal* (Thomas W. Crowell, 1967). A major challenge to New Left historiography on the New Deal is the essay by Jerold Auerbach, "New Deal, Old Deal or

Raw Deal: Some Thoughts on New Left Historiography," *Journal of Southern History*, XXXV (February 1969), 18–30, in which he argues that the radical historians writing on the New Deal are ahistorical and emotional.

# from World war II
# to World war III

The desire of America's corporate governing class to create a world-wide Open Door empire continued after the Spanish-American War.

As historian Stephen E. Ambrose points out, America's desire to avoid another depression after World War II and to counter Russia's domination of eastern Europe increased United States efforts to seek new markets abroad. "Politicians looked for areas in which American influence could dominate; the businessmen looked for profitable markets and new sources of raw materials; the military looked for overseas bases," and America began a "program of expansion that had no inherent limits."

American policy, Gabriel Kolko has argued in his monumental study, *The Politics of War*, can be understood as an attempt to create a postwar world structure that would maintain United States hegemony throughout the world. The interaction between broad economic goals and politics was reflected most clearly in United States policy toward eastern Europe. The United States did not object to sovietization on moral grounds such as lack of "democracy" or a refusal to hold "free elections." Rather, as Kolko writes, United States policy was based first on the assumption that "Americans could make future investments only within the context of a capitalist economy at least some of which the eastern European nations might not wish to continue," and second on "tangible demands for an open door to the eastern European economies."

United States policy at Yalta was thus economic in context, calling for multilateral trade patterns, equality of opportunity, and freedom to invest for United States corporations. While the State Department gave lip service to Russian security needs, those needs were not to interfere with American economic opportunities or involve a change in prewar economic relations. Hence, in eastern Europe the United States opted for a conservative restoration of the prewar status quo. Rejecting either a move toward the left or neutrality, the United States government worked with the right because its own economic objectives dovetailed with those of American corporations. Hence, as Kolko puts it, American leaders objected to any changes that would have "impinged on American freedom to invest and trade along traditional lines."

The United States desired restoration of old trade patterns so that eastern Europe would maintain its old semicolonial status as breadbasket to the industrial west. American political goals were vague in nature, stressing containment of Russian influence. But economic goals were precise. The United States wished to maintain the industrial strength of Europe, to prevent Russia from obtaining United States–owned oil, and to end all restrictions on United States business in eastern Europe.

Primarily, the United States opposed nationalization. Eastern European oil was considered crucial to the economic restoration of western Europe. Thus the State Department worked for incorporation of the Danube River states into a Europe-wide inland waterway system under United States control. Fearing a Russian monopoly in the former Axis satellites, the United States worked to preserve eastern Europe as an area that would sell its raw materials primarily to Germany.

This radical assessment, shared in varying degrees by William Appleman Williams, Gabriel Kolko, David Horowitz, Water LaFeber, and Stephen Ambrose, defines the gap with the mainstream or orthodox liberal view of the Cold War, which saw postwar "containment" as a valid and necessary response to Soviet expansionism and to the decline of western power in eastern Europe. The radical historians point out that Soviet policy was actually conservative and often bolstered America's position in such areas of the globe as Greece, France, and China. The revisionist historians stress actual Russian weakness following World War II and note Russian conciliatory efforts to reach some modus vivendi with the west. American leaders ignored Russian efforts and used United States economic and military predominance as a lever to gain its political ends.

One element of mainstream thinking implicitly challenged by radical historians is the conception that United States foreign policy merely responded to the aggressive and self-interested actions of rival powers. The United States is itself an expansionist power and the rhetoric of internationalism has functioned as a cloak for intervention. The selections in this chapter trace the line of continuity in American policy from the 1930s—when the United States assumed a globalist stance and moved toward intervention in the European war—to Korea and Vietnam. Many myths are exposed as it is made clear to the reader that the old assumptions upon which policy has been formulated still exist.

Mainstream historians claimed that American foreign policy before World War II was disinterested and uninvolved. The United States was pushed to accept responsibility by the aggression of totalitarian nations like Germany and Japan. When World War II ended, the views and assumptions of policy remained the same, but the "enemy" changed. Now the United States was prevented from building a peaceful world because of the threat posed by Soviet Russia. The outline of the mainstream view remains the same: the United States is somehow viewed as a uniquely pacifistic power whose only interest is attaining a peaceful world structure and whose professed goals happen to coincide with the best interests of other nations and peoples.

By examining the actual interests the United States has in building an informal empire, in containing and limiting the spread of social revolution, and in replacing declining British and French rule with American power and investments, the radical historian reveals the nature of the power that keeps the United States on an interventionist course. The radical historian provides the knowledge necessary for understanding the vast effort that will be needed before a fundamental change can actually take place in the direction of American foreign policy.

# the embroilment of the United States in Asia as a consequence of the cold war, and the prospects for the future

## LOUIS J. HALLE

Louis J. Halle, a noted member of the 'realist' school of diplomatic historians, sought to move beyond crudely assigning guilt for the Cold War solely to the Russians. He argues that misconceptions by both east and west led to myths of an ideological nature: the American myth of a monolithic Communist conspiracy, and the Communist myth of a world divided between capitalist imperialists and the victims of their exploitation.

Halle, however, assumes that Soviet perceptions of postwar American policy were entirely fallacious. Like other mainstream historians, he argues that the "original Cold War had been set off by the sudden expansion of Russia in Europe," and that "there could be little doubt in any impartial mind that, when the West rallied under American leadership to halt that expansion, it was acting in its own legitimate defense rather than in a spirit of aggression."

Similarly when writing about Vietnam and Asia, Halle argues that American intervention was based on "misconceptions," since the United States obviously was "without expansionist ambitions, in Asia or anywhere else"—a statement that serves to obscure the actual expansionist goals of the United States in Asia and explain Vietnam as a result of the purely ideological desire to contain China.

---

All nations cultivate myths that endow them with dignity and, when occasion arises, give nobility to the causes in which they fight. A simple view would have it that myths, being fictional, must therefore be false. In a more sophisticated view, myths belong to the conceptual world by which, alone, we are able to interpret the existential world that constitutes our raw environment. This conceptual world, even if fictional, provides interpretations of the existential world that we must assume to be true in some degree. Most of us would agree that Shakespeare's *Hamlet* is a piece of fiction that represents truth in a high degree. Einstein's special theory of relativity is also a piece of fiction that, we suppose, represents truth in a high degree.[1]

We men have to live, then, in two worlds at once, the conceptual and the existential, and our central problem is to maintain the correspondence between them. It is when these two worlds diverge excessively that we find ourselves in serious trouble.[2]

Under circumstances of conflict between individuals or societies, and to the degree that conflict becomes passionate, the respective conceptual formulations of the parties tend to diverge from the existential realities they ostensibly represent. Fear, hatred, and the need for self-justification find their expression in conceptual falsification, whether innocent or deliberate.

Whenever an international conflict breaks out, each side is impelled to construct what we might call an advocate's account of the existential circum-stances by which to identify itself with righteousness and its opponent with evil. At its crudest this takes the form of deliberately fabricated propaganda. More commonly it takes forms that are, at least in a subjective sense, less corrupt. When a people is called on by its national leadership to sacrifice all comfort and happiness for the sake of victory, the leadership is driven to create a mythology (in which it generally believes itself) that will serve to justify such sacrifices in their eyes. So it creates, for example, the myth of a proletarian struggle against wicked capitalists that is destined to bring about, at last, a classless society in which universal justice and happiness will be established forevermore; or it creates the myth of a worldwide contest between "peace-loving" and "aggressor" nations; and so the divergence between the existential and the conceptual is widened, with potentially tragic results. The false myth that inspires a people to fight successfully may obviate the possibility of crowning its success by the conclusion of a peace. This tragedy, represented in the two World Wars and their consequences, was not to be spared mankind altogether in the conclusion of the Cold War.

At the outset of the Cold War, the specific objective of the Western allies, however it was generalized for rhetorical purposes, had been to contain Russia's westward expansion at the line it had already reached in Europe. The specific objective of the Russians had been to prevent the restoration, on the western side of this line, of a strength they regarded as menacing. In the event, Western strength was restored in spite of the Russian opposition, and so the Russian empire expanded no farther. This result, however, left the two sides still at grips with each other in a conflict with diminishing relevance to the particular issues over which it had begun. Like all great conflicts, it had become its own reason for being; it had taken on implications of life and death for each side. On each side voices rose to proclaim the necessity of finally eliminating the menace that the other represented. What this history exemplifies is the tendency in any great conflict for the issues to become generalized and unlimited. The conflict called the Cold War quickly expanded until it encircled the globe—as has been the case with both World Wars, each of which had at first been confined to Europe. Generalization, expansion, and intensification gave increased scope to the conceptual corruption that, as we have seen, is an element in every conflict.

From the beginning the West was governed by the myth of a single conspiracy for world conquest under the direction of a satanic band in the Kremlin to whom all who called themselves Communists, the world over, gave blind obedience. On the basis of this myth the United States, especially, identified the triumph of a native uprising on the mainland of Asia in 1949 as the extension of the Kremlin's empire to include China, whose 600 million people were, accordingly, thought to have fallen captive to the conspiracy. Under Washington's leadership, then, the line of containment was extended, from the Middle East across South Asia and north to Korea, in order to embrace what was regarded as the enlarged Russian empire. Along the 38th parallel in Korea, along the line of islands from Japan to the Philippines, in the Straits of Formosa, and along the 17th parallel in Viet Nam, the United States deployed its military strength. So it was that, even after it had become clear that China was, in fact, independent of Moscow, the United States found itself committed to the siege it had already mounted.

If there was misapprehension on the part of the United States that led to this new Asian conflict, there was more extreme misapprehension on the part of China. When Mao Tse-tung and his collaborators came to power in 1949 they were as ignorant of the international world, in its existential reality, as Lenin and his collaborators had been when they came to power in 1917. In both cases, an ideological myth that had almost no correspondence to that world, standing for it in their minds, had misled them. It had led Lenin to expect that the workers and peasants of the countries that were neighbors to Russia, if not the workers and peasants of the whole world, were ready to rally behind the revolutionary banner that he held aloft, to overthrow the bourgeois states of the day at his signal, and to establish the international dictatorship of the proletariat that the prophets, Marx and Engels, had foreseen. Over thirty years of disillusioning experience had, by the 1950's, taught first Lenin and then his successors that the existential reality did not correspond to the conceptual vision on which this expectation had been based.

In the winter of 1949–1950 Mao and his associates had been at the same stage of innocence as Lenin and his associates in the winter of 1917–1918. Their ideological preconception presented to them a world divided between the evil capitalist-imperialists and the victims of their exploitation, the peasants and workers who, at this stage in history, stood increasingly ready to fulfill the hundred-year-old prophecy of the *Communist Manifesto* by breaking the chains that bound them, destroying the slave states of the capitalist-imperialists, and establishing forever the ultimate society of mankind in which all men were free and equal.[3] The United States, in this entrancing vision, was the leader of the imperialist camp in the worldwide struggle that was now reaching its climax. Therefore, by *a priori* conception, the United States was the chief enemy of the new China, which represented the peasants and workers of the world in their historic movement of liberation.

The fact that over the years the United States had become so closely identified with the *ancien régime* of Generalissimo Chiang Kai-shek served to confirm this view. Washington's intention of disengaging itself from this regime, when it had clearly lost the Chinese civil war, had been frustrated by an access of ideological passion among the American people and the consequent prevalence over their minds of concepts that misrepresented the existential circumstances in China. The final and inescapable commitment of the United States to the losing side had occurred, then, at that nocturnal meeting in Blair House when the unpondered decision had been taken to intervene with military force in the Straits of Formosa.

Even before this decision had been taken, however, the new Chinese regime had embarked on a campaign of anti-American propaganda and of atrocities against American citizens who fell into its hands. It is evident that, in addition to the ideological motive, what this represented was the need that every revolutionary regime feels, upon its acquisition of power, to create the bogy of a monstrous external enemy as a basis for enforcing on its own population the discipline without which it could not survive. The Sino-American conflict had already attained a considerable intensity, then, before the decision was made to intervene in the Straits of Formosa. That decision, however, made the conflict irresolvable, perhaps for a generation to come. Self-deception on both sides, in 1949–1950, must be held accountable for the extension of the Cold War to the Far East in a form in which it could not be brought to an end when the original conflict in Europe had at last reached the point of resolution.

At the same time that the United States committed itself to the defense of the defeated Chinese regime in its Formosan refuge it also began to commit itself, by a more gradual process, to the defense of the regime in Viet Nam that had been improvised largely by the French and that, although possessing question-able authority in the country, qualified for American support by its identifica-tion as anti-Communist. Just as the United States had committed itself to the containment of China in the belief that it was thereby containing the Russian empire, so it committed itself to the containment of the Vietnamese liberation movement under the impression that it was thereby containing the Chinese (or the Russo-Chinese) empire.

The original Cold War had been set off by the sudden expansion of Russia in Europe. Consequently, there could be little doubt in any impartial mind that, when the West rallied under American leadership to halt that expansion, it was acting in its own legitimate defense rather than in a spirit of aggression. But China, when the United States undertook its containment, had not expanded beyond its traditional boundaries.[4] To anyone familiar with the dynamics of revolution a theoretical danger of expansion did exist, and this justified vigilance on the part of its neighbors and of those powers that bore a responsibility for the maintenance of international order. Because it had not in fact expanded, however, and because the United States was in the position of denying the new Chinese Government's right to govern even in China proper, the United States was, in this case, the party that appeared to be playing the role of aggressor in Asia. In Viet Nam, as everyone could see, the foreign forces were not Chinese; they were those of the United States and its allies, and the forces opposing them in the field were native Vietnamese. This represented an essentially false position into which the United States, acting on the miscon-ceptions that conflict engenders, had got itself; for it was in fact without expansionist ambitions, in Asia or anywhere else. By the middle of the 1960's, however, its essential commitments in Asia had become inescapable—just as its ancient commitment to the defense of China, however unwise in its origins, had become inescapable by the 1930's.

The position that the United States was in with respect to China and Viet Nam was only superficially similar to the position it had been in with respect to Russia when it embarked, with Russia's European neighbors, on the original policy of containment. A better parallel was that of the period from 1918 to 1920 in Russia, when Britain and the United States had refused to recognize Lenin's revolutionary new regime and had deployed their military forces against it.[5]

By the middle of the 1960's both sides in the original Cold War were disposed to discontinue the contest and to seek the development of more rewarding relations between them. Although far from ready to swear friendship, the powers that had been led by Moscow and those that had been led by Washington were ready to make peace. Unless the international situation got altogether out of control, eventuating in some wide catastrophe, such a peace would gradually be achieved, although its achievement would be delayed by all the repercussions of the American involvement in Asia. The time would come, then, when the division of Europe that had characterized the period immediately after World War II would have faded away, when new combinations and new conflicts had established new divisions across the world. And, all the time, the inexorable pressure of technological development would be enforcing a constantly growing association of the European states, and more widely of the states opening on the Atlantic, just as the once independent and sovereign Swiss cantons had been forced into the increasing association that had at last taken the form of their confederation. In such an association the boundary between the two Germanies would lose its importance, and so the Berlin problem, without ever being solved, would disappear. All this, it might be expected, would come about imperceptibly, like the movement of the hour-hand on a watch.[6]

What one could not foresee the end of, as yet, was conflict. In the constant recombinations of international society there would be new and sometimes alarming confrontations of power. Formerly, conflicts between societies had always been subject to the dynamics of escalation, which led to their resolution, at last, by the test of military combat. Since 1945, however, the presence on the scene of weapons that could, presumably, destroy the greatest societies in one blow, had had a major inhibiting effect on this tendency. What was historically unique about the Cold War was the restraining influence of the new weapons, which had prevented a conflict on the grand scale from culminating in general war. In the new weapons, then, lay the hope of the world, no less than its peril, as it moved on into an unknown future.

NOTES

1. "Physical concepts are free creations of the human mind, and are not, however it may seem, uniquely determined by the external world. In our endeavor to understand reality we are somewhat like a man trying to understand the mechanism of a closed watch. He sees the face and the moving hands, even hears its ticking, but he has no way of opening the case. If he is ingenious he may form some picture of a mechanism which could be responsible for all the things he observes, but he may never be quite sure his picture is the only one which could explain his observations." (Albert Einstein and Leopold Infeld, *The Evolution of Physics*, Cambridge, 1961, p. 31.)

2. I have developed this thesis in my *Men and Nations*, and have exemplified it in *The Society of Man*.

3. Marx and Engels had had only industrial workers (the proletariat) in mind. Lenin had discounted the peasants as a revolutionary force. Mao, raised in a peasant country with few industrial workers, had in effect given them the role that Marx and Engels had reserved for the proletariat. (This had been his heresy in Moscow's eyes after 1927.) So the authority of the prophets was maintained for a prophecy that had been conveniently transmuted.

4. The occupation of Tibet in 1959 was the occupation of a land that had traditionally belonged to the Chinese empire. The occupation in 1962 of certain areas on the Himalayan frontier with India was the occupation of areas to which India had no clearer title than China.

5. This involvement in Russia had been a by-product of Anglo-American belligerency in World War I, just as the American involvement with China and Viet Nam, now, was a by-product of America's struggle in the Cold War.

6. All prediction is based on the perception of some order that has extension in time.

Every order, however, is subject to disruption by unpredictable accidents. I can predict of a child that it will, in a certain number of years, be a man, but my prediction assumes that it will not be killed by an automobile first. Our world may be in evolution toward a more complete order than exists at present, but accident still plays a major role in it.

Louis J. Halle   **201**

# from Korea to Vietnam: the failure of a policy rooted in fear

## STEPHEN E. AMBROSE

The continuity of American policy from Korea to Vietnam is brilliantly described by military historian Stephen E. Ambrose, an editor of *The Eisenhower Papers* and author of *Rise to Globalism,* a book which expands upon the themes discussed here.

Many Americans feel that the war in Korea differed from the reprehensible war in Indochina. Ambrose reveals their basic similarity and shows that the Korean war was a political, economic, and social boon to American imperialism. The assumptions behind Korea are those behind Vietnam. Ambrose convincingly relates the nature of those basic "American assumptions about the nature of the world," which will have to be changed if war is ever to end.

---

On June 24, 1950, American foreign policy in the Pacific was remarkably close to what some of the doves of 1970 want it to be today. At its heart, the policy of 1950 was one of maintaining positions of strength on Asia's offshore islands, especially Japan, Okinawa, and the Philippines, avoiding all entanglements on the mainland, and recognizing the fundamental fact of Asian politics—the emergence of Communist China.

American troops had been withdrawn from South Korea, so there were no American combat units anywhere on the Asian mainland. Mao Tse-tung's troops were preparing an amphibious operation against Chiang Kai-shek's remnants on Formosa, and President Harry Truman and Secretary of State Dean Acheson had warned American ambassadors around the world to be prepared for the repercussions stemming from the final fall of the Chinese Nationalist government.

In Indochina, the French were struggling, without much success, to eradicate the Communist Ho Chi Minh and his Vietminh, while in the Philippines the government faced a serious challenge from the Communist Huks. The United States was giving tidbits of aid to both counterrevolutionary efforts but, in view of the budget restraints at home and what was felt to be the overwhelming need to rearm Europe (not to mention the United States itself), scarcely enough to affect the outcome in Indochina. America's overall policy remained one of holding to its offshore bases, protected by the world's most powerful navy, staying out of the Chinese civil war, and avoiding any involvement on the mainland.

Stephen E. Ambrose, "From Korea to Vietnam: The Failure of a Policy Rooted in Fear." Reprinted and © from the November 1960 (pp. 14–20) issue of *The Progressive* magazine, Madison, Wisconsin.

There had been two recent statements by Truman Administration spokesmen making this policy clear. On January 12, 1950, at the National Press Club, Secretary Acheson had drawn a line on a map to indicate the American defensive perimeter—the line excluded South Korea and Formosa. And on May 2, Senator Tom Connally of Texas, chairman of the Senate Foreign Relations Committee, said he was afraid South Korea would have to be abandoned. He thought the Communists were going to overrun Korea when they got ready, just as they "will overrun Formosa." Connally said he did not think Korea was "very greatly important. It has been testified before us that Japan, Okinawa, and the Philippines make the chain of defense which is absolutely necessary."

That remained the American position until June 25, 1950, the day hostilities began in Korea. Then, after only a few hours of meetings with Acheson and a select group of top advisers, without consulting Congress or the United Nations or America's European allies, Mr. Truman announced that he was sending supplies to South Korea, immediately increasing aid to the French in Indochina and to the Philippine government, and ordering the United States Seventh Fleet to sail between the Chinese mainland and Formosa to prevent the expected invasion of the island by the Communists. Mr. Truman had, in short, involved the United States in four civil wars at once, and, except in the Philippines, all in areas the Americans had previously regarded as outside their sphere of influence. The United States was *on* the Asian mainland.

These were sweeping policy decisions, among the most important of the entire Cold War, carrying with them enormous long-term implications. They were hardly the kind that a government ordinarily makes without deliberation. Yet Mr. Truman later claimed that he made them solely as a result of the Korean War, the outbreak of which astonished him—as it supposedly did General Douglas MacArthur's headquarters in Tokyo—as much "as if the sun had suddenly gone out." For a man who had been surprised, Mr. Truman had recovered with amazing speed.

Actually, as I. F. Stone has shown in his book, *The Hidden History of the Korean War*, there was no surprise. The Americans had a good general idea of what was coming and had their countermeasures prepared. Intelligence reports on North Korean intentions had been specific enough to allow the United States State Department, days before the attack, to prepare a resolution to submit to the Security Council of the United Nations condemning North Korea for aggression.

At the time, the Soviet Union was boycotting the United Nations for its refusal to seat Red China; the State Department was prepared to take its resolution to the General Assembly if the Russians came back to the Security Council and exercised their veto. But the Soviets did not return, for they had been caught off guard. Stalin, in fact, seems to have been the most surprised by the outbreak of hostilities; certainly the Americans were much better prepared to move for United Nations action than the Russians were. The resolution the Americans pushed through the Security Council on the day of the attack branded the North Koreans as aggressors, demanded a cessation of hostilities, and requested a withdrawal behind the thirty-eighth parallel. The resolution was a brilliant stroke, for without any investigation at all it established war guilt and put the United Nations behind the official American version.

The speed and scope of the American response to the Korean War were truly impressive. So were the Cold War advantages that accrued. America eventually established a costly hegemony over non-Communist Asia, gained gigantic (and strategically invaluable) military bases for itself in South Korea, Formosa, Indochina, and Thailand, aroused public support for an enormously increased Department of Defense budget (from $13 billion in 1950 to $50 billion the next year), made possible European, including West German, rearmament, and in general put the United States on a permanent Cold War footing. In addition, the Americans saved the governments of Chiang in Formosa and Syngman Rhee in South Korea from certain extinction. After a thorough examination of these and other pieces of circumstantial evidence, Stone, and historian D. F. Fleming, in his work *The Cold War and Its Origins,* have charged that the South Koreans—with American support—began the war.

Before that accusation can be examined, however, it is necessary to understand the basis of the Truman policy. How did it come about that the United States became committed to the containment of Communism everywhere whatever the cost? Which is only another way of asking, "How did we get on the Asian mainland?" and "How did we get to Vietnam?"

The United States fights in Vietnam for many reasons, but the chief reason is a set of assumptions about the nature of the world, assumptions given wide currency by our policy-makers. These views were formed largely by the events preceding the Korean War and by the interpretation of the origins of that war. It is to that conflict we must look if we are to understand American policy today.

When Harry Truman became President of the United States, he led a nation anxious to return to traditional civil-military relations and the historic American foreign policy of noninvolvement. The public, as it demonstrated by electing a Republican Congress in 1946, wanted an up-dated version of Harding's return to normalcy, with the emphasis on a speedy demobilization from World War II, lower taxes, less Government interference in the economy, and a foreign policy that would rely on the atomic bomb and/or the United Nations to keep the peace. There was no general perception of a threat to America's vital interests.

Mr. Truman and his senior advisers were adamantly opposed to the budding isolationism, primarily because they had a different set of assumptions. They did see a threat, one posed by monolithic Communism directed from the Kremlin, that aimed at world conquest and whose tactics—in the words of George Kennan, a State Department planner and one of the authors of the containment of Communism concept—would be "to make sure that it has filled every nook and cranny available to it in the basin of world power." The Truman Administration was convinced that only the United States could prevent the Kremlin from achieving its victory, but to do so it would have to swing American public opinion to a more "realistic" view of the nature of the world.

In March, 1947, Mr. Truman led the way when he called on Congress to provide aid to the Greek government, the rather shabby rightist monarchy which was threatened by an indigenous guerrilla movement. Mr. Truman assumed that the Greek Communists were directed and aided by Stalin (a judgment almost no historian would accept today). As the then Under Secretary of State Dean Acheson put it, if Greece were lost, Turkey would be untenable. Russia would move in and take control of the Dardanelles, with the "clearest implications" for the Middle East. Morale would sink in Italy, Germany, and

France. Acheson was describing what would later be called the domino theory, although—as always—he was more colorful in his choice of symbols. One rotten apple, Acheson said, would infect the whole barrel.

The biggest apple of them all, the United States, would not escape, the theory contended. The American economy had become so intimately related to the rest of the world, especially Europe and Latin America, that it could not survive on a hostile globe. "The whole world should adopt the American system," Mr. Truman declared in a speech of March 6, 1947. "The American system can survive in America only if it becomes a world system."

To persuade the American people, and the economy-minded Republican Congress, to pay the cost of containing Communism and spreading the American economic system, Mr. Truman needed a cause more inspiring than one of providing support for the Greek monarchy. He provided it. "We must assist free people to work out their destinies in their own way," he declared on March 12, 1947, in asking for aid to Greece, thereby making an unlimited and consequently indiscriminate commitment. "At the present moment in world history every nation must choose between alternative ways of life," he asserted, thereby creating a sense of permanent and universal crisis.

The critics, ranging from Walter Lippmann and publications like *The Progressive,* to Senator Robert Taft, warned that such globalism would eventually erode American political institutions, subvert domestic efforts at reform, and ruin the economy, but Mr. Truman ignored them, for he pursued a greater goal. America's mission was "to insure the peaceful development of nations, free from coercion . . . to make possible lasting freedom and independence for all."

The messianic hope of redeeming history drove President Truman. "I believe that it must be the policy of the United States to support free peoples who are resisting attempted subjugation by armed minorities or by outside pressures," he declared, which amounted to a definition of what was to become American policy for the next twenty years. It was a brilliant political speech and it worked, as Congress gave the President the money he wanted.

The following year, 1948, Mr. Truman got the Marshall Plan through the same Republican Congress, thereby starting Western Europe on the road to recovery and insuring that France, Britain, and West Germany would stick to the United States in any confrontation with the Soviet Union. Communism in Europe had been contained, or so it seemed.

The trouble was that aside from the millions given to Greece and Turkey, and the extensive Marshall Plan aid, Congress was unwilling to provide the funds needed for containment. Mr. Truman could not get Universal Military Training; he could not save the draft; America's armed forces continued to dwindle; the American stockpile of atomic weapons was by no means sufficient to deter the Red Army if it chose to march across the Elbe River; and the Europeans showed no inclination to tamper with their budding prosperity by assuming the cost of rearming. America had a policy in Europe—containment—but it did not have the military muscle to implement it if the 175 Russian divisions marched; nor did the American or Western European peoples show the slightest inclination to pay the heavy costs involved in building that muscle. By June, 1950, the Truman Administration had reached an impasse in Europe.

At home, Truman faced criticism of his earlier foreign policy. The West had lost Czechoslovakia, but Mr. Truman boasted that he had saved Greece, Turkey,

Italy, and Western Europe. The use of such concepts as "won" or "lost," however, had serious repercussions. The Republicans had not made an issue of foreign policy in the 1948 elections (only third-party Presidential candidate Henry Wallace did), and by 1950 they tended to believe that their failure to do so was a key factor in their defeat. They began, almost gleefully, to charge the Truman Administration with having "lost" China and with losing the Philippines, Formosa, South Korea, and Indochina. The Republicans, led by Senator Joseph McCarthy, began to insist that the Truman Administration, and most notably Secretary Acheson, was soft on Communism, or worse.

The Democrats were bewildered and angry. With some justice, they wondered what more they could have done to stand up to the Soviets, especially in view of the funds available, funds drastically limited by the very Republicans who now demanded blood for the State Department's shortcomings. Mr. Truman desperately wanted to extend containment to Asia, but he could not even implement it in Europe.

Mr. Truman's frustrations, in the spring of 1950, were great. Foreign and military policy were moving in opposite directions. While Acheson advocated ever greater commitments to the non-Communist world, Louis Johnson, a curious kind of Secretary of Defense, was scuttling the Navy's super-carrier and doing everything he could to keep the Defense Department budget under $13 billion, all in accord with Mr. Truman's own policy of balancing the budget. Mr. Truman had commissioned a major study of America's strategic position; the final result reached his desk in early June, 1950, as National Security Council paper number 68 (thereafter known as NSC 68). Still classified and unpublished twenty years later, it was one of the key historic documents of the Cold War. NSC 68, as Senator Henry Jackson, Washington Democrat, observed, was "the first comprehensive statement of a national strategy."

NSC 68 advocated, in the words of one of its authors, "an immediate and large-scale build-up in our military and general strength and that of our allies with the intention of righting the power balance." It did so on the basis of an analysis of the Soviet Union which held that the Soviets were not only dedicated to preserving their own power and ideology but to extending and consolidating power by absorbing new satellites and weakening their enemies. Implicit in the analysis was the idea that whenever the West lost a position of strength, whether it be a military base or a colony undergoing a war of national liberation, the Kremlin was behind it. This came close to saying that all change was directed by the Communists and should be resisted. The analysis also assumed that if America were willing to try, it could stop change.

The paper was realistic in assessing what it would cost America to become the world policeman. Instead of the $13 billion the Truman Administration was planning on spending annually on defense, NSC 68 wanted to start with $35 billion in fiscal year 1951 and move up to $50 billion a year later. Politically, this was impossible. Truman recognized, as he later wrote, that NSC 68 "meant a great military effort in time of peace. It meant doubling or tripling the budget, increasing taxes heavily, and imposing various kinds of economic controls. It meant a great change in our normal peacetime way of doing things." He refused to allow any publicity about NSC 68 and indicated that he would do nothing about revising the budget until after the Congressional elections in November, 1950. He knew that without a major crisis there was no chance of selling the program to the Congress or to the country.

The contradictory pressures on foreign policy, meanwhile, were almost maddening. While President Truman and Acheson defended themselves from charges of having given China to Mao, they simultaneously had to prepare for even more embarrassments, most notably the expected loss of Formosa and South Korea.

In Korea, all was tension. Postwar Soviet-American efforts to unify the country, where American troops had occupied the area south of the thirty-eighth parallel, and Russia the area to the north, had achieved nothing. In 1947 the United States had submitted the Korean question to the United Nations General Assembly for disposition. Russia, fearful of the implications, had refused to go along. The Soviets reasoned that if the question of Korea could be given to the General Assembly, where the United States controlled a voting majority, nothing would prevent the United States from giving the problem of divided Germany to the Assembly too. The Soviets therefore refused to allow the U.N. Commission on Korea to enter North Korea.

Elections were held in South Korea in May, 1948; Syngman Rhee became president. The Russians set up a government in North Korea. Both the United States and the Soviets withdrew their occupation troops; both continued to give military aid to their respective zones, although the Russians did so on a larger scale.

Rhee was a petty dictator and an embarrassment to the United States. In January, 1950, Philip C. Jessup, U.S. Ambassador-at-large, told the Korean National Assembly that the United States was dissatisfied with the severe restraints on civil liberties which it had imposed. In April, Acheson told Rhee flatly that he either had to hold previously scheduled but consistently delayed elections or lose American aid. Rhee gave in, although on the eve of the elections he arrested thirty of his leading opponents in anti-Communist raids. Still his party collected only forty-eight seats, with 120 going to other parties, mostly on the left. The new Assembly then began to indicate that it wanted to consider unification with the North. Rhee was faced with the total loss of his position.

There was a curious incident shortly after the South Korean elections, one that none of the historians of the Korean War has examined in depth. On June 9 the radio at Pyongyang, North Korea's capital, denounced the recent elections in the South as fraudulent and called for a general election throughout Korea. The North Koreans proposed an election on August 5 of a general legislative organ that would meet in Seoul, capital of South Korea. Rhee, his prime minister, and the U.N. Commission in Korea would all be barred.

Rhee scoffed at the call for elections, dismissing it as "poppycock propaganda" but the U.N. Commission indicated that it was interested, and on June 11, John Gaillard, an American member of the Commission, crossed the thirty-eighth parallel to talk to three North Korean representatives. They gave him copies of the appeal for an election, then crossed the parallel themselves with hundreds of copies of the appeal, which they intended to distribute to the South Koreans. Rhee's police immediately arrested them. There appears to be no evidence that Washington ever explored Pyongyang's suggestion for general elections, and this raises interesting questions about the entire U.S. policy regarding Korea.

Events everywhere in Asia were moving towards a crisis. The British were out of India, revolt was stirring in Malaya, and the Dutch had been forced to leave Indonesia. In Indochina, the French were barely able to hold on. Nearly all the independent Asian governments were hostile to the West. The substitution of native leaders, usually radical, for the white rulers in Asia carried with it terrifying implications for Washington. There was a real possibility that American corporations would lose both their access to the raw materials (especially metals) and to the markets of Southeast Asia. Strategically, none of the new governments would be able to serve as an effective counter to the Chinese, which meant an end to the balance of power in Asia. Only Rhee in South Korea and Chiang in Formosa swam against the powerful tide, and the West did not have the military means available at that time to keep either of its proxies in power. What the Americans liked to call "stability in Asia" was threatened.

The crisis was most acute in China, for if the Chinese Communists drove Chiang off Formosa they would complete their victory and eventually the United States would have to recognize the Communists as the legitimate government of China, which would mean—among other things—giving Chiang's seat on the U.N. Security Council to Mao. The United States would no longer be able to regard Chiang as head of a government or maintain the fiction that he would someday return to his rightful place as ruler of all of China. This in turn would require a new definition of the economic and political relations between China and the United States.

Since late 1949, President Truman had consistently refused to provide aid to Chiang, who had proved to be a poor investment at best. The President insisted—rather late in the game—that the United States would not be drawn into the Chinese civil war. This policy was consistent with the European orientation of the Truman Administration and, in terms of the money Congress had made available for foreign aid, it was realistic. Its only possible outcome, however, was an end to Chiang's pretensions and an American acceptance of the Chinese Communists among the family of nations.

The domestic political results for the Democrats of such a course of events were frightening to contemplate. Already former President Herbert Hoover had joined with Senator Taft in demanding that the U.S. Pacific Fleet be used to prevent an invasion of Formosa, while other Republicans advocated using the fleet to carry Chiang's forces back to the mainland for the reconquest of China. If Mr. Truman wished to quiet the McCarthyites at all, he would have to rethink his China policy.

By June, 1950, a series of desperate needs had come together. Mr. Truman had to have a crisis to sell the NSC 68 program of a huge U.S. military build-up. Chiang could not hold on, nor could Rhee, without an American commitment; the U.S. Air Force and Navy needed a justification to retain their bases in Japan; the Democrats had to prove that they could get tough with the Communists. Most of all, the Americans had to establish themselves on the mainland before the white man was driven out of Asia and its islands forever.

The needs were met on June 25, 1950. The outbreak of the Korean War came as a godsend to Chiang, Rhee, and the Truman Administration. Since it "proved" the aggressiveness of international Communism, the war enabled Mr. Truman to push through the NSC 68 program with its vastly increased military budgets, American aid for European rearmament, and an enormously expanded American military presence in Asia.

When President Truman announced that the Seventh Fleet was going to the Formosan Straits, Peiping immediately charged that the Pentagon was seeking to establish a military base on Chinese territory and asked the United Nations to order the Americans to withdraw. Warren Austin, U.S. Ambassador to the United Nations, refuted the charge indignantly, while Mr. Truman declared that the United States "would not seek any special position or privilege on Formosa." Jakob Malik, the Russian delegate, then accused the United States of lusting for bases in Formosa and supported his charge by quoting General MacArthur's statements to the effect that America intended to establish and hold air fields on the island. Mr. Truman rejoined that MacArthur did not speak for the Administration. Yet, as everyone knows, the United States now has enormous air bases on Formosa. By the same token, the Americans declared throughout the Korean War that they had no intention of maintaining troops there once the conflict ended. Lyndon Johnson was to say the same thing about Vietnam.

For more than a decade and a half after the Korean War began, almost no one seriously questioned the Truman Administration's interpretation of the cause of the war, which held that it began because Stalin told the North Koreans to go ahead and attack South Korea. This interpretation strengthened the notion that there was an international Communist conspiracy, centered in the Kremlin, and that therefore all wars of national liberation were carried out by Russian proxies solely to serve the interests of the Soviet Union. This view in turn allowed the Americans to dash into Lebanon at President Eisenhower's orders, to attempt by force, with President Kennedy's approval, to overthrow Castro, to intervene in the Dominican Republic at President Johnson's command, and most of all to involve this country in Vietnam.

The interpretation of the causes of the Korean War, in short, has helped shape American assumptions about the nature of the world. The interpretation may conceivably be correct, but there are questions concerning it that must be asked, and answered, before it can be fully accepted. The standard explanation, for example, as to why the Russians were not in the United Nations during the critical period when the Korean War began, is that Stalin simply made a mistake. He did not think the Americans would return to the Korean peninsula, nor did he expect the United States to go to the United Nations and ask for a condemnation of aggression by North Korea. But Stalin was ordinarily a cautious man who made few mistakes.

The explanation that he was surprised by the American reaction, even if he was, is clearly unsatisfactory, for it leaves unanswered a further query: why did not Stalin send his ambassador back to the Security Council after the first U.S. resolution went through on June 25, the day war broke out, branding North Korea as the aggressor?

The importance of the second question lies in the fact that not until June 27— two days after the outbreak of hostilities—did the United States introduce the second resolution—passed that day—which recommended to the members of the United Nations that they aid South Korea in restoring peace. It was the June 27 resolution which gave the United States U.N. cover for its essentially unilateral action in Korea. Those who wish to maintain that the Russians started the North Koreans on their way south must explain why the Soviets were not in the United Nations to protect their own interests in that world body.

The second mystery about the Soviets is why they took no action elsewhere. President Truman and Acheson assumed from the start that the Korean War was a feint. They reasoned that Stalin wanted them to put America's strength into the Pacific so that he could then march against a defenseless West Europe. The Americans countered this expected strategy by concentrating their military build-up in Europe, not Korea (much to General MacArthur's disgust; indeed, this was a basic cause of the Truman-MacArthur controversy).

Administration supporters have argued that Stalin did not move in Europe only because the United States beat him to the punch. The trouble with that view is that it took months for the Americans to get any strength into Europe; in the meantime, Stalin did nothing. If he started the Korean War as part of a worldwide offensive, as Mr. Truman argued, where was the rest of the offensive?

Finally, if the Russians started the whole thing, where were they at the critical moment? The North Koreans pushed the South Koreans and the small American contingent steadily south until early August, when MacArthur's forces were pinned into a beachhead around Pusan. But the North Koreans were incapable of delivering the final blow and had to watch, more or less helplessly, as MacArthur built up his strength and made his position invulnerable.

Red Army officers must have watched from afar with anguish, for their experience against the Germans only five years earlier had made them the world's leading experts on knocking out defensive positions. If Russia did indeed urge the North Koreans to attack, and if Stalin's aim was in fact to conquer the peninsula, why were no Red Army advisers sent to the North Koreans at the decisive moment? MacArthur himself testified later that no Russians had ever been seen anywhere in the Korean peninsula during the war. Once the Americans had intervened, but before they arrived in great strength, why did not the Russians send a few "volunteer" units to Korea to insure the final push of MacArthur's forces into the sea?

The idea that Russia and China acted in concert in starting the war has, fortunately, long since disappeared. A 1960 RAND Corporation study, *China Crosses the Yalu,* by Allen S. Whiting, concluded that the Chinese were the most surprised of anyone by the outbreak of hostilities in Korea. Mao's two major priorities in June, 1950, were to use his army to reconstruct China and to invade Formosa. His troop dispositions reflected these priorities, and were about as bad as they possibly could have been to support a war in Korea. Indeed, the big losers in the war—aside from the Korean people—were the Chinese, who lost their chance to grab Formosa and who had to divert desperately needed human and material resources from reconstruction and the building of a new society to keep American troops from the Yalu River at China's southern door. The Russians lost too, for Stalin's worst fears were realized as a direct result of the war—West Germany was rearmed and integrated into an anti-Soviet military alliance, and the United States began a massive rearmament program.

The big winners were Chiang, Rhee, and the Truman Administration, which extended containment to Asia, gained additional military bases in the Far East, unilaterally wrote the Japanese peace treaty, retained American markets and access to the natural resources of Southeast Asia, proved to the public that it was not "soft on Communism," and in general reversed the tide of change—at least for a time—that had been running so strongly against the white man in the Far East.

As noted earlier, I. F. Stone and D. F. Fleming have carefully examined the problem of whose needs were met by the Korean War, and who won and who lost, and concluded that the North Koreans were merely responding to aggression by Rhee, an aggression encouraged by Chiang and the United States. But while the circumstantial evidence is strong, these charges almost certainly go too far. The North Korean offensive was too strong, too well coordinated, and too successful to be simply a counterattack.

But granting that the North Koreans were the aggressors does not automatically make the Truman Administration interpretation of the origins of the war correct. There are too many questions that must be answered before it can be accepted.

The most reasonable tentative conclusion is that the North Koreans took matters into their own hands. They decided they could over-run the peninsula before the Americans could reinforce the South Koreans—an assessment that was not far wrong—and they moved. They probably expected that the United States would not intervene at all. Certainly we have had sufficient evidence in the late 1960s of North Korean independence from the Kremlin to make this judgment reasonable.

For our time, the important point is that Mr. Truman seized the opportunity to extend containment to the Asian mainland, thereby reversing entirely—and evidently permanently—America's Pacific policy, on the basis of a highly dubious interpretation of the causes of the conflict, based in turn on a belief in an international Communist conspiracy that never existed. The irony is that of all Mr. Truman's dramatic actions in the last week of June, 1950, the least noticed turned out to be the most important—the increase in U.S. aid to the French in Indochina that demonstrated his determination to prevent Ho Chi Minh from gaining control of Vietnam.

The seeming inevitability of American foreign policy in the postwar period the Russians act, we react to preserve freedom—rests, in its essentials, on one basic assumption. President Truman, Acheson, and the other architects of the policy of containment (which was never more than a euphemism for the expansion of American influence and dominance) believed—or at least professed to believe—that the Kremlin had a "strategy" for world conquest.

For those who demanded proof of Stalin's intentions, the Administration pointed above all to the supposed Russian influence on and support for the Greek rebels, Ho Chi Minh, and the North Koreans. Historians, however, are finding it extraordinarily difficult to come by any solid evidence of Russian involvement on a significant scale in Greece, Indochina, or even North Korea (after 1948).

The obsessive American fears, in short, not to mention the violent American reaction, were based on assumptions that were almost surely wrong. Taking into account all that flowed from those assumptions—McCarthyism, the Cold War, ABMs, Indochina, and so on—this is the major tragedy of our times.

# the conquest of history: America's long dream in Asia

## WALTER LaFEBER

Walter LaFeber, the distinguished Professor of History at Cornell University, is author of *The New Empire* and the revisionist *America, Russia and the Cold War*. In the following two short articles, LaFeber attempts to correct America's ignorance of its own history. He reveals America's sustained interest in Asian expansion and the manner in which the original commitment to empire developed.

This commitment has led to the belief that Japan would function in the Far East as a junior partner of American imperialism and do the bidding of the United States in exchange for recognition of limited Japanese interests. In tracing the unique and strained relationship between the United States and Japan, LaFeber reveals how the fallacious view of Japan once led to war and how contemporary strains and developments might once again create the possibility of severe conflict. LaFeber presents a realistic account of the ways in which imperialist rivalry might produce the very end that the Open Door was meant to prevent.

---

There are many ways to explain the catastrophe in Vietnam, and as George Romney has rather unwittingly observed, many of them have been offered to the American people. Perhaps the most dangerous and popular of these explanations has been to call Vietnam the end result of an "accidental" American empire or a policy of "drift," or to suggest that here is another case of "greatness thrust upon the United States," without Americans having sought it.

Such explanations are convenient. They preserve a cherished image of American innocence, greatly simplify the complexities of the Vietnamese involvement, and exonerate past Presidents and diplomats whose reputations we would rather misunderstand than question.

As explanations, however, they are also totally inaccurate, providing the most disastrous basis on which to plan policy. Secretary Rusk recently offered an example of the confusion. When challenged privately that American policies must work less successfully in Asia than in Europe where strong cultural, political and economic affinity exists, Rusk shot back that he did not buy "this master-race theory." In a phrase, he blurred 2,500 years of history, and also accused his critics of resembling Nazis. President Johnson demonstrated a more sophisticated misuse of the past when he appealed to the policies of Theodore Roosevelt as a reason for escalation in Southeast Asia. Unfortunately, the President or the "intellectuals" who help write his speeches apparently did not know that Roosevelt denounced American intervention in Asia within two years of leaving the White House.

Walter LaFeber, "The Conquest of History: America's Long Dream in Asia," *The Nation*, Vol. 205, no. 15 (November 6, 1967), 456–459.

But Administration critics also suffer from historical myopia. Diagnosing "the Great Society" as a "sick society," Senator Fulbright believed that "we are proving the strength of the American dream by resisting the dream of an imperial destiny." This assumption forced him to explain that Asian conquest "is being thrust upon us, not by history but by our policy makers in the Department of State and the Pentagon." As a conservative, Fulbright sincerely wishes to understand and invoke the past in order to return to what he likes to call "our traditional values." Such a return, however, could be dangerous because in practice "our traditional values" have not been what either Johnson or Fulbright assumes them to have been.

Uncovering these traditional values requires an analysis of the historical web which Americans have spun around themselves. That might begin by remembering that Americans have always thought of themselves as missionaries to the world. Hubert Humphrey's warning of April, 1966, that the United States alone upholds "the whole fabric of international law and order" is not a new idea in American annals. Only the present incredible power of the United States makes Humphrey's righteousness different from or more ominous than many similar announcements in the past. For a nation with a historic mission the U.S. has become painfully ignorant of that history.

This was not always the case. The founding fathers comprehended the past as well as their own ledger books (one reason why they so easily reconciled the two). James Madison helped persuade the citizens of New York and other states to vote for the new Constitution in 1787 with three long newspaper articles explaining why ancient confederations rose and fell. Madison's feat may be contrasted with the lead sentence of a special article in *Look* of May 30 on Vietnam: "The East is the new American West." The use of the word "new" not only reveals how far removed the opinion makers of the 20th century are from the historical knowledge held by those of the 18th but illustrates a primary reason for the disaster in Asia.

For the idea that East was West appeared early in American history—about the time of Christopher Columbus in fact—and has been a driving principle in that historical development ever since. Contrary to Senator Fulbright's hopes, Americans were planning for an "imperial destiny" as soon as they were free of the British restraints that had threatened to stunt that destiny. In perhaps the first 4th of July address in American history, Dr. David Ramsay, a South Carolinian who was also a gifted historian, remarked in 1778 that "We have laid the foundations of a new empire" which will not only "give happiness to a great continent" but will allow us to have "our turn to figure on the face of the earth, and in the annals of the world." Ramsay was confident, moreover, that "ever since the flood," empire and riches "have taken a slow and gradual course from east to west." Shortly thereafter, George Washington boasted of "our rising empire"; he devoted his life to insuring that Benjamin Franklin was correct in his observation to the Constitutional Convention that the sun was rising, not setting, on the American destiny. The era of the founding fathers is an appropriate place to begin a re-examination of the "accidental-empire" thesis.

Driven by the land hunger of farmers, the get-rich-quick schemes of speculators, and the cultural-religious ideology which made many businessmen missionaries (and vice versa), Americans exploded out of the thirteen original colonies to conquer a great continent. Washington officials provided all necessary governmental aid, whether for fighting in European wars (as in 1812 and the quasi-war with France in 1798–1800) or for inciting or encouraging revolutions in foreign-held Florida, Texas and California. With the continent won by the 1850s, Washington's "rising empire" had reached its first stage. Those who believe that this was accomplished in either innocence or absent-mindedness can find instruction in the private writings of Jefferson and Polk, or read the accounts of the French, Spanish, Mexicans, Russians and, of course, Indians, who were shot, bought, or pushed out of the way. The American empire was not immaculately conceived.

Control of the continent gave the United States access to the Pacific. The conquest had opened at last the fabled "passage to India"—and points northeast. When John Quincy Adams acquired the first American foothold on the Western coast in 1819, he considered it his greatest achievement—a not inconsiderable boast, since he is still considered to be our greatest Secretary of State. True to his mercantile and Puritan background, Adams fully realized how this vantage spot could lead to the fulfillment of America's supposed manifest destiny in Asia. In the 1850s, William Henry Seward of New York, a disciple of Adams and the leading Republican in Congress, called the Pacific "the chief theatre of events in the world's great hereafter." Seward set out as Senator and as Lincoln's Secretary of State to maintain by force an open door for American interests in China, and to blast open the markets (for both businessmen and missionaries) in Korea.

A leading historian of American Far Eastern policy, Tyler Dennett, observed in 1922 that the United States had never had to move beyond Seward's strategies and tactics in the Far East. That view remains tenable today, with one major addendum: as he negotiated the SEATO arrangements in 1954, John Foster Dulles observed that American objectives in the East had moved up a notch. Instead of an open-door-for-all policy, the United States, Dulles announced, had expanded the Monroe Doctrine to Asia. He was confident that this move slammed the door on any Communist-oriented entity hoping to compete in the area.

During the 1890 to 1910 period, the era which President Johnson has used as a reference point, Seward's policy accelerated—and then crashed. The acceleration occurred because of problems in American domestic society that were little short of traumatic.

Religious groups exemplified the dilemma. Confronted with apparently declining missionary opportunities in a rapidly settling American West, and challenged by a Darwinian-scientific upsurge that shook Protestantism to its foundations, missionaries sought escape in the traditional manner: move farther west—this time across the Pacific to Asia. The rallying cry of the leading missionary group, "The Evangelization of the World in this Generation," neatly summarized the objective. Nor is that slogan unrelated to recent, more secular proclamations pledging an instant Great Society in the Mekong Delta. The evangelism of the 1890s did indeed prove fruitful, but not as planned. Despite Secretary Rusk's implications to the contrary, missionaries discovered that Asia was not like the West. But Chinese revolutionaries quickly learned how the foreign missionaries and businessmen hoped to transform China, and used them as scapegoats to intensify Chinese nationalism.

A second trauma of the 1890s occurred in the American business community. A twenty-five-year depression began in 1873, spawning what one Secretary of

State called in late 1893, "symptoms of revolution" from Brooklyn to California. This crisis forced the business community to face a most unpleasant alternative: either radically reorient its ideology and economic structure, or restore maximum employment and production by waging economic and, if necessary, military war for the fabled and apparently bottomless markets of Asia.

Put another way, the question that starkly confronted Americans was whether they would reorganize their economy and attack the roots of the growing crises in the industrialized urban areas, or wage war against major world powers for control of the markets—and of secondary but related importance, the strategic points—of Asia. Both Democratic and Republican administrations between 1893 and 1910 chose the second alternative. To implement this crucial decision, the United States annexed the Philippines in order to possess strategic bases close to the Asian markets. This move quickly paid off: within two years of annexation, American ships and soldiers moved out of Manila to check Chinese nationalist attacks on American officials and interests on the mainland.

Of course, such a convenience demanded a price. Within weeks after annexing the Philippines, thousands of American troops became bogged down in crushing a revolutionary movement which wanted the Philippines governed only by Filipinos. We wanted no land, President William McKinley kept assuring the doubting revolutionaries, just defensive positions from which we could guarantee American interests in Asia. About 5,000 Filipinos died in the revolution. Within five years after the United States had restored order on the islands, President Theodore Roosevelt was lamenting in 1907 that their cost and exposed position made them the Achilles' heel of the burgeoning American empire.

Roosevelt nevertheless deepened the American commitment to empire in Asia. He updated the McKinley approach by moving directly onto the mainland and trying to protect Chinese-American trade from Chinese nationalism—and for American traders—in 1904 and 1905. Roosevelt next attempted—in 1908—to deny the rich Manchurian market and raw materials to the Russians and Japanese for the sake of American trade and oil interests. That policy failed. Russia and Japan cooperated to defeat American infiltration, and T. R.'s sending of the United States Navy to intimidate the Japanese had no effect on the Far Eastern power balance. (In 1958, *Time* called the sending of the fleet Roosevelt's greatest act because it demonstrated how to use credible deterrence. *Time* never investigated how the story turned out.)

After leaving office, Roosevelt candidly warned his picked successor, William Howard Taft, that U.S. policy in Asia rested on sand. Inasmuch as President Johnson has referred to Roosevelt's policies in the Pacific, T. R.'s letter of 1910 might be quoted in part:

> I do not believe in our taking any position anywhere unless we can make good; and as regards Manchuria, if the Japanese choose to follow a course of conduct to which we are adverse, we cannot stop it unless we are prepared to go to war. . . . The "open-door" policy in China was an excellent thing, and will I hope be a good thing in the future, so far as it can be maintained by general diplomatic agreement. . . .

Instead of pressuring Russia and Japan to bend to American interests in Asia, a course which could—and did—lead to a Russian-Japanese alliance against the United States and ultimately to an American-Japanese war, Roosevelt suggested that Taft concentrate his attention on such pressing domestic problems as Japanese immigration into California.

The suggestion was not followed. From 1910 through World War I, the United States increased its interests in Asia, more often through unilateral actions than by the "general diplomatic agreements" that Roosevelt had advised. When the Chinese Revolution erupted in full force after 1911, Woodrow Wilson tried to manipulate it between 1913 and 1915 by supporting the most available conservative group. This policy collapsed when Wilson's favorite warlord died. Centuries of Western intervention and the nationalism generated by the World War accelerated the revolution in 1919.

Against this and the Russian revolutionary backgrounds, the United States sat down with the leading European powers at the Washington Conference in 1921 to establish a proper kind of Far East. The lessons of 1900 to 1915 had convinced American officials that they badly needed allies to restore a stable, safe and open Orient. Assured that the Japanese shared American feelings about the Chinese Revolution and the desirability of the open door, the United States gave Tokyo dominance in the western Pacific. As for the Chinese themselves, when they requested control over their own tariffs and the foreigners within China, the Western powers refused to listen. Instead, American delegate Elihu Root substituted a series of regulations which kept Chinese trade and a large amount of political power within China in Western hands.

This made the West a perfect target for the expanding Chinese Revolution of the mid-1920s. Within a decade after the Washington Conference, that upheaval had severely reduced American missionary and business interests inside China, and had so confused the Hoover administration that when Japan struck against Manchuria in 1931, United States officials could make no effective response.

Such failure did not convince those officials to reduce our Asian commitments, however. The two central policies, control of nationalist revolutions and the use of force to maintain a balance conducive to the expansion of the American West into the East, finally ended in war with Japan. When that conflict ended, the Asia of 1946 made the situation of 1905 or 1910 attractive by comparison. The West now had no chance to control the Chinese revolutionary forces which were in full rebellion against those historical Western influences. Despite its position as the greatest power the world has ever known, the United States by 1949 had failed in Asia. Not even its immense power could repeal a century of mistakes.

But the original dream never died. Gen. Douglas MacArthur told Washington officials that Europe was the "dying system," and that the Pacific would "determine the course of history in the next 10,000 years." Japan, the General admonished, stood as the "western outpost of our defenses," and he described the American fight for the future in vivid images: the struggle against communism was comparable to Christ's struggle at Gethsemane, for "Christ, even though crucified, nevertheless prevailed."

And indeed a second chance did seem to be arising as the French attempted to regain their control over Indo-China. In the spring of 1950, before any intimation of conflict in Korea had appeared, the Truman administration committed itself to helping the French war effort. The United States was once again becoming a dominant factor in domestic Asian affairs. A State Department release in 1951 told why: the United States must retain in Western hands the "much-needed rice, rubber, and tin," and "perhaps even more important would be the psychological effect of the fall of Indo-China. It would be taken by many as a sign that the force of communism is irresistible and would lead to an attitude of defeatism." Therefore, "Communist forces must be decisively conquered down to the last pocket of resistance." This policy of total military victory required large amounts of American aid, for without such help "it is doubtful whether [the French and the Bao Dai regime installed by the French] could hold their ground."

The Korean War marked the re-entry of the United States into Asian affairs with its full, fantastic power. The growth of the American commitments in those affairs since the early 1950s has been detailed elsewhere. What should be noted here is how American officials continued to make policies based upon mistaken historical assumptions and analogies. Foremost among these officials in the early 1950s was the Assistant Secretary of State for Far Eastern Affairs, Dean Rusk.

On May 18, 1951, Rusk made a speech to 800 guests of the China Institute of America, perhaps the foremost lobbying group for the interests of Chiang Kai-shek. John Foster Dulles shared the platform with Rusk, and Henry Luce was master of ceremonies. Rusk's words were widely interpreted to mean that he agreed with MacArthur (who had just been recalled and repudiated by President Truman) that the Korean War might be widened until the Chinese Communists were overthrown by an internal revolution fueled with American aid. Rusk proceeded to read history in a way that would for him justify such a revolution. He predicted that China might be ruled by "a colonial Russian Government—a Slavic Manchukuo on a larger scale. It is not the Government of China. It does not pass the first test. It is not Chinese."

He repeated the misreading of history six months later. On November 19, 1951, Rusk spoke of the "new nations" in Asia: "If we are true to our past, we shall establish a right relationship with the peoples of Asia because of themselves." Rusk did not give a single example when in "our past" the United States had established such a relationship. And with good reason—it had never occurred.

Asian and American interests have been dissimilar historically and are even more dissimilar now. The Republican Policy Committee's White Paper, issued in May, 1967, was historically correct—that is, it presented a tenable ground upon which to construct effective policy—when it observed: "Vietnam is basically Buddhist and Confucian, both ethical religions without a personal god. Thus, Asiatic communism as espoused by Asiatics can masquerade as an ally in the older, more familiar struggle against Western theism, Western colonialism, and Western capitalism." (One might add that this no doubt also partly explains why the State Department works through Roman Catholic political regimes in Saigon.) "These accidents of culture, history, and geography," the White Paper continues, "for better or for worse, carry equally as much weight in the Vietnamese conflict today as, say, the effective fire power of the Seventh Fleet on a given day." The Senate Republican leadership disavowed the White Paper, but it could not repeal historical facts.

The development of the United States as an imperial power since the 18th century, the failure of that power to come to terms with Asian culture and the revolutions to which that culture has given birth, are primary reasons why the United States is trapped in Southeast Asia. American society as a whole, and its policy makers in particular, have been ignorant of past involvements. At that point, Isaac Asimov's dictum applies: "Violence is the last refuge of the incompetent."

When, therefore, Hubert Humphrey asked Americans to remake Southeast Asia because "there is a tremendous new opening here for realizing the dream of a great society of Asia, not just here at home," the Vice President ignored a double historical lesson: two centuries of American expansion into Asia have not created the Great Society at home, nor could the United States easily transfer its Great Society into Asian cultures even if there were such a society at home. It is also possible that Asian leaders would not want an American-style society.

And when, therefore, Dean Rusk condemned "those who have not revised their thinking in the light of the realities of modern weapons and communica-tions, who cling to the obsolete notions of a bygone age," and who consequently cannot see the importance of Southeast Asia because "the Pacific is too broad for them," the Secretary of State ignored certain facts:

Americans have not only been able to see the importance to them of Asia extremely well but have moved across the Pacific since the 18th century; the United States has involved itself in internal Asian politics since at least the "bygone age" of the 1860s and the 1890s; and the only "obsolete notions" in American history are the tragic policies of Washington officials who succeeded Seward and believed they could jump across divergent cultures, control foreign revolutions, and thus carry the American empire into Asia.

Erik Erikson has written that our history should teach us "deeper humility before the processes which govern us, and the ability to live through them with greater simplicity and honesty." In Asia, Americans have tried to escape from their own imperial history by ignoring, misreading or—especially—believing themselves superior to it.

And yet, when their history has caught up with them, as it did in the 1890s and as it has done in the 1960s, they have ironically sought escape by repeating that tragic history—by seeking an empire in the Far East in order to escape to a New West.

# fifty-year flirtation:
# our illusory affair with Japan

## WALTER LaFEBER

In this article, Walter LaFeber traces Japanese-American economic and political relations in the context of this continuing discussion of America's interest in Asian expansion.

Once again anti-American riots have bloodied Japanese streets. And for the third time in seventy years important American spokesmen look hopefully to the Japanese as partners in stabilizing and developing Asia. The Fourteen Scholars writing from Freedom House in December observed: "No concern of the United States in the Pacific is more vital than that Japan's emerging initiative in foreign policy should be exercised in such a way as to utilize her enormous potentials in support of world peace and prosperity." Praising Japan's economic growth as "extraordinary" (one of the few understatements in the entire document), the scholars nevertheless deeply regretted that "in political affairs abroad, she has remained largely inactive if not frankly isolationist." But this situation was improving: "Today, however, reviving self-confidence is moving Japan increasingly to a reassertion of an independent stance in world politics."

To anyone with a knowledge of 20th-century American history, these words have a familiar and ominous ring. They have been sounded at least twice before, in the 1895–1910 period and again during the 1920s and early 1930s. In each case American diplomats failed to find a proper spirit of partnership in their Japanese counterparts, and the second time the denouement was marked by a World War. Particularly since the Fourteen Scholars have urged a discussion of America's position in the Far East, the time is not too early to analyze briefly Japan's recent resurgence, the state of Japanese-American relations, and the unavoidable questions which arise about that relationship.

There are two bases for present American interest in Japanese affairs. First, the appalling costs of Vietnam have forced even the most outspoken proponents of American power overseas to wish that they had some respectable Asians to help pacify Asia. Second, the fantastic upsurge of the Japanese economy since 1961, and the resulting extension of Tokyo's influence into Korea, Thailand, Burma, the Philippines, Malaysia, China and Asiatic Russia, have rebuilt Japan into a political power throughout the Far East. This record should make historians, government officials and the Fourteen Scholars more cautious in their use of the term "isolationist," for in Japan as in the United States, expansion in the domestic economy has proved over a period of time to be

Walter LaFeber, "Fifty-Year Flirtation: Our Illusory Affair With Japan," *The Nation*, Vol. 206, no. 11 (March 11, 1968), 330–338.

inseparable from expansion of economic and political power abroad. To the Fourteen Scholars and many others, "isolationism" means: "You do not agree with my hopes for American (or Japanese) power." Only in that sense, indeed, are the Japanese "isolationist."

## ELECTRONIC BOOTSTRAP

The Japanese are developing and using their power in their own way. Their economic growth has made a world-wide impact. Japan's shipbuilding has led the world for a decade; in late 1967 it had twice the orders of its three closest rivals. Its automobile factories, producing more than 2 million units a year, challenge Germany for second place in the world market. Only the United States outranks Japan in electronics and computers. Its involvement in these two fields will increase, for Japan is superbly equipped in these key industries: it trains a large number of highly skilled technicians and engineers, and the industries have relatively little need for ground space and raw materials, items the Japanese lack in comparison with the United States.

Japan's ability to produce and market transistors is legendary, in part, no doubt because President de Gaulle once referred to a Japanese Premier as "that transistor salesman." The country has a chemical complex second only to that of the United States in the production of synthetic rubber, plastics and resin, rayon and acetate, noncellulosic fiber and caustic soda.

Twenty years ago the Japanese were a defeated people fingering the rubble of burned-out and atomically bombed cities which were 80 per cent destroyed. An explanation for their success since then might begin with an observation by the editor of *Forbes*: the Japanese "work like hell." When they began to modernize in the late 19th century, the Japanese did not destroy their feudal institutions but tended to shift them into the industrial sector. Plants are consequently organized around a family concept of mutual obligation, with wages providing only a relatively small portion of worker incentive. This arrangement also means that unions are, in the Western sense, company unions. These characteristics not only explain Japanese craftsmanship and productivity, but create obstacles which prevent American capital from penetrating that country as it has Europe.

Japan has perhaps the most thoroughly rationalized and integrated business-government relationships in the non-Communist world. Its government bureaucracy is highly trained and efficient, and members move between business and government with a rapidity exceeding even that in the United States. This movement is particularly noticeable among some bureaucrats who upon reaching their 50s often move into key executive jobs in industry and banking. The economy's efficiency is further increased by close links between banks and industries. Japanese tend to invest their money in savings rather than in stocks which, in marked contrast to Western economies, make up less than 30 per cent of total business capital. This allows the banks to channel funds quickly and in volume into priority sectors of the economy.

## GLITTER AND SQUALOR

Efficiency also results from concentration, a characteristic which Gen. Douglas MacArthur and other occupation authorities tried to purge from Japan in the immediate postwar years. By the mid-1960s, pro-Japanese observers admitted that the consolidation movement appeared to be evolving toward the situation of pre–World War II. A 1956 recession hurried this process. In 1966 a record 11,058 companies became bankrupt, and the giants sought help through mergers. The second largest auto producer, Nissan, merged with the fourth largest, Prince Motors, to become number one; this triumph was short-lived because the former number one, Toyota, merged with number eight, Hino, to regain the top position. In steel the two largest producers began to cooperate in scheduling sales. Some aggregations, such as Mitsubishi and Mitsui, carry the names of the 1930s. The economic power of these combines is unquestionable; their political power in the area of foreign affairs is a lesser known quantity.

That latter power now rests on total overseas assets of approximately $8 billion. Only the United States, Great Britain and West Germany claim more. In 1966 Japan was one of the few nations to export more capital than it imported. The economy as a whole is dependent upon overseas trade, particularly imports of raw materials and fuels.

The economic picture glitters in Japan, but beneath the surface are uneven development, squalor and disturbing political instability. Japan's economy was shaken by a recession in 1965–66 which cut its growth to 2.7 per cent for that fiscal year. One major channel of escape from this downturn was the Vietnamese conflict. Japanese growth jumped back to a 7.5 per cent rate after being stoked by $1 billion of American spending for Vietnam. This war-generated income not only spurred a general recovery but raised foreign trade, particularly imports, with the United States to a record high. Wars in Asia have recently occurred at opportune moments for the Japanese. During the Korean conflict $2 billion of American spending brought Japan's economy into full postwar recovery. The Vietnamese conflict has now stopped another skid. What that economy will do, and specifically what will happen to Japanese-American trade—the key to general relations with Japan—if the Vietnamese struggle tails off are vital questions.

The Japanese social structure is showing the strains of this economic resurgence. The country has become pockmarked by a mass movement of population from countryside to urban areas. This influx of cheap labor fuels the industrial renaissance, but it also creates severe problems of pollution, crime, juvenile delinquency and general resettlement, which not even the Japanese with their tradition and efficiency have been able to solve.

## LIBERALISM, SOCIALISM, MYSTICISM

These failures have caused political ripples. The Liberal-Democratic coalition, ruler of Japan for twenty years, has within the past year been severely challenged from within and without. The Liberal-Democrats themselves form factions which have to be carefully balanced by Premier Eisaku Sato. Such juggling was difficult even in a period of economic expansion, few foreign policy problems, and relatively minor social maladjustments. In January, 1967, the time of reckoning seemed to be approaching. For the first time in two decades the Liberal-Democrats won less than 50 per cent of the popular vote in the general elections. They continued to control a majority in the Diet, but had to do considerably more bargaining with opposition parties.

That opposition was also undergoing change. The Socialists have moved closer to Peking as the Communists have split and then tended toward Moscow. The Socialists paid for this reorientation by losing large numbers of votes which were picked up by two minor parties, the Democratic Socialists and the Komeito (the political apparatus of the Soka Gakkai, a mystical religious sect based on Buddhism which has expanded tremendously in Japan during the last seven to ten years). They won thirty and twenty-five seats respectively in the lower house. Komeito has been an especially interesting phenomenon. Meaning literally the "Clean Government Party," its rise has been remarkable, but this can be explained in part by the movement from countryside to city and in part by its mysticism. Soka Gakkai's numbers are largely comprised of agrarians newly resettled in the cities, shopkeepers, workers and women who want a political voice in a traditionally male-dominated society. For these reasons it is conservative enough socially so that it has been compared with the Poujadists in France, but it also is vocally anti-American and urges diplomatic recognition of Communist China. Robert Scalapino, one of the Fourteen Scholars, has precisely summarized the significance of these political changes: "Clearly, Japan lacks a consensus on foreign policy, now or for the foreseeable future."

## TEDDY ROOSEVELT'S PARTNER

The United States is now urgently asking this rapidly changing Japan for help in staving off Asian revolutions and stabilizing the Far East so that both Japanese and American interests can prosper. The central question is whether American and Japanese interests coincide to the extent that policy makers assume. History provides some instruction, for on two other occasions, Washington urged Japan to do much the same thing, and each time the affair ended disastrously because the key assumption was wrong.

In 1900, after annexing the Philippines and announcing its great-power status in Asia through the open-door notes, the United States looked to Japan as its partner. The Japanese had been the one people to accept the notes with some enthusiasm, agreeing with Secretary of State John Hay that China and Manchuria must be maintained as a "fair field" with no unequal "favors" to any power. Japan was also the single nation which possessed the location, determination and resources to block America's number-one enemy in the area, Russia.

Alfred Thayer Mahan, the famous naval strategist who deeply influenced Theodore Roosevelt's views of Asia, heavily counted upon the Japanese to help the United States. Mahan—a 1900 version of the Fourteen Scholars as a one-man band—argued that the Japanese were "Teutonic by adoption" and comprised "the grain of mustard seed" which would regenerate all of Asia. Mahan and Roosevelt consequently did nothing to stop Japan from going to war with and defeating Russia in 1904–05. At the point when Japanese resources seemed to be reaching their limit, Roosevelt interceded to mediate the peace.

By 1907 Russia was indeed no longer a major threat in Asia. The United States had helped make Japanese power dominant. The Japanese proceeded to exercise that power. They conquered and closed off Korea. Roosevelt did not object. The Japanese next moved into southern Manchuria, shutting out the large amounts of American petroleum and textiles which had found rich markets there. Roosevelt thought this was going too far, and when on top of it the Japanese began to act up about American immigration legislation which discriminated against the "yellow peril," he sent the Great White Fleet on a show of force to the western Pacific. The Japanese received the fleet cordially, but their smiles hid a renewed determination not to be overawed or placed at the mercy of that fleet.

Roosevelt and his successor, William Howard Taft, both attempted to use American economic power to reopen Manchuria. T.R. soon realized the futility of the venture and retreated, but Taft persisted. The result was a surprising but easily formed partnership in 1910 between the two former enemies, Japan and Russia. Japan would control south Manchuria, Russia the north, and the United States would be largely excluded from both. Not for the last time Japan reached agreement with its old enemy in an attempt to exclude American power from Asia. By 1913 round one had ended with the collapse of United States policy.

## LINE DOWN THE PACIFIC

Mahan now displayed the insight and courage to change his mind. In publications during 1910 and 1911, he no longer termed Japan "Teutonic by adoption" but a "problem state." He argued that a line should be drawn down the Pacific, with Japan controlling the western portion and the United States retreating to the area east of Hawaii-Samoa-Australia. Although continuing to argue that American might made right in the Western Hemisphere and Europe, Mahan had learned that Asian power politics were quite another matter.

Woodrow Wilson and the Republican administrations of the 1920s did not listen to Mahan's advice. As other powers focused their attention on World War I, Japan had tightened its control by forcing concessions within China and conquering the former German colonies on the periphery of Asia. After Wilson had failed to loosen the Japanese grip at the Versailles Peace Conference in 1919, the new Republican foreign policy, formulated by Charles Evans Hughes and Herbert Hoover, tried another approach. At the Washington Conference of 1921, Japan, over the strong protests of our Navy Department, was given naval superiority in the western Pacific. This arrangement was written into the Five-Power Pact. In return, Japan signed a Nine-Power Treaty in which it guaranteed that the door to Chinese markets would remain open equally to all.

Or, to phrase the American policy in contemporary terms, the Japanese, in return for a supposed minimum build-up in armaments, promised to use their economic and military power to moderate the revolution raging in China, contain the Bolsheviks in Russia (whom the United States refused to recognize), and keep the entire area open for Western democracy and Western goods. The second round had now begun, and as it progressed it began to resemble the first. After trying to contain and exploit the Soviets by occupying parts of Siberia in 1919-20, Tokyo by 1925 had reached an accord with Moscow in which diplomatic relations were restored, trade resumed, and a division of labor implicitly worked out between the two powers. These agreements lasted for two decades, enduring through the hectic 1930s because the United States between 1932-34 rejected Stalin's requests for help against Japanese aggression in Manchuria. For the second time in a quarter century, Japanese and Russian interests proved not irreconcilable. They conveniently renewed their pledge of benevolent neutrality in April, 1941, on the eve of Hitler's attack on Russia and the Japanese strike against Pearl Harbor.

## JOURNEY TO PEARL HARBOR

With Soviet relations in order, the Japanese could take advantage of the turmoil within revolution-torn China. The major step occurred with the invasion of Manchuria in 1931. This move was caused by political pressures and instability in Tokyo and the need for markets and raw materials by Japanese industry, particularly that part producing increased amounts of military goods.

The United States was trapped. It had supported Japan since 1921 in the belief that the Japanese would contain and ultimately stabilize the revolution in the Far East, while, at the same time, acting properly toward American economic and political interests. When the Japanese struck Manchuria, President Hoover and Secretary of State Henry Stimson could not call on either the Russian or Chinese revolutionaries for help; the United States refused to admit officially that the former existed and could not bring itself to trust the latter. Hoover refused to use force against the Japanese. That could escalate into full-scale war, would be an admission of the failure of American policy and, besides, was no way to treat your major partner in the area. The Japanese moved on, renouncing the Five-Power Treaty in 1934, attacking China proper in 1937, and announcing an "East Asian Co-Prosperity Sphere" in which Japanese economic power would stretch into and ultimately dominate Southeast Asia.

By 1939 American officials had begun drawing the line. They admitted that their Japanese policy in round two had been a failure. Vital exports to Japan were stopped and demands made that Tokyo withdraw its troops from China and Southeast Asia. Instead, the Japanese attacked Hawaii.


## THIRD TIME AROUND

After four years of bloodshed, round three opened with the United States determined to restructure Japanese society from the Emperor down. Under Gen. Douglas MacArthur's consulship, Hirohito was divested of his divinity, Shintoism banned, American-style farms mistakenly given to agrarians, the zaibatsu supposedly broken up, war criminals and Communists purged, and the famous Article IX, stating that Japan renounced war and would never again maintain armed forces for offensive purposes, inserted in the new Constitution.

These policies lasted for two years. In February, 1948, the Social Democratic government of Tetsu Katayama fell from power, and with it fell the reform program. That same year George Kennan returned from an official visit to Japan to recommend that the reforms and purges be slowed down so that the Japanese could control their own government. He suggested that American forces in Japan be reduced to "tactical" elements, with bases left for future negotiations. By early 1949 many American controls had been loosened.

Then came the fall of China to Mao and the explosion of the Russian atomic bomb in the autumn of 1949. In September, 1949, Secretary of State Dean Acheson and British Foreign Secretary Ernest Bevin agreed that Japanese-American relations must be regularized through a formal peace treaty. American bases in Japan would be retained and guaranteed through a separate security pact. The Russians bitterly complained that although they had been among the victors in the Pacific war, they were not included in the treaty negotiations.

Kennan evidently objected strongly to the militarization of Japan, but given his own premise that Japan was potentially the most potent power base in Asia and therefore necessary for American security, he had little room to maneuver. The treaty negotiations were placed in the hands of John Foster Dulles, and to make the new policy doubly clear, Washington signed assistance agreements with the French forces fighting in Indo-China in May, 1950. As the famed NSC-68 memorandum explained that spring, the United States would now have to lead a global war against communism. Containment was extended in detail to the Far East.

These American policies, particularly with regard to Japan, were doubtless a major reason why Stalin encouraged North Korea to attack across the 38th Parallel in June, 1950. The Soviets tried to strike at what they feared would be a NATO of the Pacific with a remilitarized Japan serving as the linchpin of the alliance. That attack, however, simply confirmed Washington's estimate of the Far Eastern situation. Japan once again would have to serve as the Asian bulwark against the Russian advance into Korea and China, just as the Japanese were to have been the bulwark in 1900 and 1921. This third time, we hoped to escape the distasteful side effects.


FORTRESS AGAINST THE DOMINOES

The peace treaty was rushed to completion in 1951 and the Japanese were free to repeal MacArthur's reforms if they wished. The islands prospered as the advance base for the American effort in Korea. Allies in Australia, New Zealand and the Philippines, however, had longer memories. They demanded American guarantees against future Japanese aggression. The State Department responded with the ANZUS and U.S.-Philippine security treaties.

Japan was now the American fortress in the western Pacific. A former Japanese possession, Okinawa, had become the key logistics base in the deployment of United States power around the southern rim of Asia. And as Japan became ever more important as a critical segment of the containment policy, the French effort in Vietnam began to weaken.

President Eisenhower described the relationship between the struggle in Indo-China and Japan in his famous news conference of April 7, 1954, when he first announced the theory of the "falling dominoes." In the response which contained the domino allusion (or illusion, as some would have it), Eisenhower outlined the economic value of Southeast Asia, its strategic importance, and then neatly summarized and concluded his remarks: "It [any "Communist" success in Indo-China] takes away, in its economic aspects, that region that Japan must have as a trading area or Japan, in turn, will have only one place in the world to go—that is, toward the Communist areas in order to live. So, the possible consequences of the loss are just incalculable to the free world."

This thesis became a controlling assumption: the loss of Vietnam would mean the economic undermining and probable loss of Japan to Communist markets and ultimately to Communist influence if not control. At the NATO Foreign Ministers' meeting in Paris on May 10, 1955, Secretary of State John Foster Dulles warned that "the stakes are too high" to give up the fight against Communist China, for "Japan represents an industrial capacity, which if combined with the manpower and raw material resources of the Continent would be formidable." A month earlier, Dulles had announced a major change in American policies toward South Vietnam. Our aid would henceforth move directly from Washington to the Vietnamese, instead of through French colonial officers. This effectively terminated French influence in the area, but Dulles also explained its significance for Japan: the new policy undercut French monopolies and created "a competitive situation" in which "there is a good chance of Japanese textile goods, for instance, moving into Indo-China. The French are somewhat concerned about that . . . ."

## SCRAMBLE FOR MARKETS

If, however, the United States hoped to keep the Japanese away from traditional markets in China and safe for the Western world, Washington, as in 1921, would have to provide a *quid pro quo*. Now, however, unlike 1921, Japanese forces were to be increased, and under American pressure Article IX was to become a dead letter. In 1954 Japan promised to increase its force of 110,000 men. So-called "depurges" returned many pre-1945 officials to public life. By the end of the 1950s Japanese war industries produced arms for Southeast Asian markets and, at one point, 200 Lockheed F-104 jets. Highly sophisticated anti-missile defenses appeared in the home islands, and Japan possessed a "defensive" missile capacity. It now seems safe to say that during this period the majority of Japanese did not want to rearm. The Tokyo Foreign Office shrewdly used these feelings to persuade the United States that Japan could rearm, but would have to do so in its own way and without undue American interference.

Despite all that Dulles was doing for them in Southeast Asia, the Japanese nevertheless wanted to resume trade with China, and trade did begin, despite the absence of any formal diplomatic relationship. In 1958, however, this link broke and Japan began avidly searching for Western markets. A large influx of Japanese textiles and steel, among other items, met with a request from Washington that Japan place so-called "voluntary" restrictions upon these imports. Western European nations followed the American lead. The Japanese rightly denounced these moves as a violation of the General Agreement on Tariffs and Trade, a pact which in happier days was an American-developed lever to increase free trade in the non-Communist world. Japan retaliated more directly by restricting imports of American goods. For this it was roundly denounced by the United States. In the midst of this economic warfare occurred the renegotiation in 1960 of the security treaty, the terrible riots preventing Eisenhower's visit, and the arrival of Hayato Ikeda as Prime Minister.

## RETURN OF "CO-PROSPERITY"

Ikeda's economic "miracle" has been accompanied by increased Japanese activity throughout Asia. In early 1967 Japan had under way in Southeast Asia 400 major construction projects totaling more than $100 million. Five Japanese automobile companies control more than half the Thai market, and Tokyo-based textile and steel companies have begun extensive operations in that country. In Korea, a Japanese possession from 1905 until 1945, the former rulers have installed large machine tool companies and banks, and are increasing trade through the 1965 normalization agreement. One economic weapon has been the Asian Development Bank, strongly supported by President Johnson to develop the countries surrounding China. The Japanese matched the American contribution of $200 million to the bank, each nation's contribution being carefully tied so that the donor's money had to be spent on goods in the donor's country. Tokyo is stepping up its foreign aid program, again tying it to Japanese trade. Outside Asia, Japanese investors are moving large amounts of capital into Brazil, Saudi Arabia, and particularly Alaska and Canada, where Japan hopes to find badly needed oil.

Premier Sato, who displaced Ikeda in 1964, has said that his country's economy "has now evolved to the point where we can—and must—take a more active role in assisting in the development of Asia." Others use different terms. *U.S. News & World Report* outlined Japan's economic upsurge under the title: "New Idea for 'Co-Prosperity Sphere.'" Repeated references to the infamous Co-Prosperity Sphere of the 1930s have led Foreign Minister Takeo Miki and other officials to insist upon the term "Asia-Pacific Concept" to describe present Japanese plans.

Japanese relations with China have meanwhile moved away from the days when Dulles persuaded Japan not to sell steel pipe, machine tools and chemical fertilizers to Mao's regime. Shortly after Ikeda assumed power, negotiations began to regularize trade with the mainland. In 1962 the "L-T" agreement (named after the initials of the two key negotiators) initiated five years of government-sponsored trade which reached a peak of $621 million in 1966. This sagged to $560 million in 1967 when the agreement expired, but some of the loss has been made up through the operations of so-called "friendly companies" (Japanese companies acceptable to Peking) which accounted for 70 per cent of Sino-Japanese trade in 1967. In 1966 the Chinese ranked fourth among Tokyo's trading partners. This was abetted by a constant increase of tourism; some 1,000 Japanese visited China in 1966. The Red Guards and Mao's dislike of heavy Japanese trade with Formosa and Vietnam have strained relations. Indeed, the Soviets have replaced China as Japan's main source of trade within the Communist bloc. China recently replaced the Soviets at the bottom of a popularity poll conducted in Japan.

## CONTAINMENT OR TRADE

The Japanese nevertheless continue to regard China as a great potential market, and Tokyo is less interested in "containing" China than Washington could wish. Former State Department official George R. Packard III, recently quoted a member of Japan's Defense Agency as complaining: "It seems that the Pentagon wants us to play the infield while you play the outfield against the Chinese." The Japanese prefer to penetrate the Chinese market, not contain it.

This attitude carries political overtones. In a Cabinet reshuffle in November, Sato moved into key positions men who were leading exponents of peaceful coexistence and trade with China. Sato's government did not rush to join the Asian and Pacific Council, becoming a member only after the Koreans and Thais promised that ASPAC would not concentrate upon the containment of China. After encouraging Japan to enter ASPAC, the State Department found Tokyo preventing the council from taking strong anti-Peking positions.

While attempting to restore historic ties with China, the Japanese also are improving relations with Russia. The two nations have not yet signed a formal peace treaty, but a consular agreement has taken effect and there are now direct commercial air flights between Moscow and Tokyo. In March, 1967, the two nations agreed to increase mutual trade by 16 per cent. Most important, the

Soviets are asking the Japanese to work jointly in the development of immense natural resources, including oil, copper, timber and coal, in Sakhalin and Siberia. A sore point is the Russian refusal to return southern Sakhalin and the Kurile Islands, taken by Stalin in 1945. It is not a minor irritant, but as the Soviets point out, Japan can import their coal at nearly one-third the cost of American coal. Soviet oil resources also attract the Japanese, who must import 99 per cent of their petroleum, 65 per cent of it from the unstable Middle East. It also might well be that, made anxious by Vietnam, Japanese officials are beginning to view the Asian balance of power anew and, like their ancestors of the 1905–10 era, are turning toward cooperation with Russia.

## NUCLEAR ALLERGY

Historical analogies must of course be used with great care, and particularly in this instance, for in the 1905–10 and 1921–40 periods Japan enjoyed a freer hand than now. No equivalent of the U.S. Seventh Fleet roamed the western Pacific. But this distinction must also be made with care. Do Japanese-American relations really rest upon overwhelming American military power instead of upon common economic and political interests? If so, the United States must step up its investment of military resources in the Pacific, not only to contain China and Russia but, in the long run, Japan as well. This is a peculiar type of "partnership," but it does have disturbing historical precedents.

A rearmed, nuclear-equipped Japan is no longer wholly imaginary. Article IX has become a convenient cover for the rebuilding of the image and power of the Japanese military. The Cabinet considers raising the Defense Agency to full ministerial rank; Sato urges the use of the terms "army," "navy" and "air force" instead of "self-defense forces"; and a forty-minute feature film has been made of military programs in West Germany, France, England, Switzerland and NATO headquarters to be shown in commercial movie theatres in Japan. The "self-defense" force itself has grown into a quarter-million-man army, and is still expanding.

Most significant, however, has been the development of Japan's nuclear power. It already employs advanced space and nuclear research programs for peaceful purposes, but these have been so developed that they can quickly be converted to military ends. The Chinese test explosions are having a marked effect on public opinion, and the Sato government is using brilliantly the strong Japanese desire to repossess Okinawa as a club to keep anti-nuclear politicians on the defensive. Sato has gained support rapidly in the past year with the argument that if Japan wants Okinawa, it must accept as permanent fixtures United States bases and the attendant nuclear weapons.

Interesting variations are being played on this theme. Takeo Fukuda, the most probable successor to Sato, announced in late December that Japan "must get away from the nuclear allergy." No street demonstrations erupted. Instead, Nobuhiko Uchiba, the parliamentary Vice Minister for Foreign Affairs expanded the argument to declare: "if we insist only that Japan will not possess nuclear weapons and will not permit their entry, it will be impossible to debate the future foreign policy and defense of our country." The Japanese ambassador in Washington announced that Japan should not surrender the possibility of controlling its own nuclear weapons, and Foreign Minister Takeo Miki refused to define or limit what the ambassador meant. Most ominously, Education

Minister Hirokichi Nadao has proposed that primary and junior high school teachers be taught "defense consciousness," and that textbooks be rewritten so that Japanese children will appreciate future military programs.

## KEEPING JAPAN "SWEET"

The growing centralization of Japanese education, expansion of the military, and Sato's apparent rush to make nuclear weapons politically acceptable form a combustible mixture. But the Japanese can ask whether these steps are not imperative if they are truly to end their supposed "isolationism." This question has become more urgent in the aftermath of Britain's announced military withdrawal from the Far East. Throughout much of this century England has cooperated closely with Japan along lines first indicated in the 1902 Anglo-Japanese agreement: Japan would respect Great Britain's primary Asiatic interest in India, and in turn London would not disturb Japanese expansion in Manchuria and parts of China. Together they would keep open the vital trade routes of the Indian Ocean and South China Sea. Britain kept its part of the bargain even when it had to assume an anti-American position as, for example, in the 1907–11 years. Now that the British have retreated, vacuums will appear, particularly in the vital Malacca Straits through which Japanese oil imports flow from the Middle East. Japan can no longer depend on British help, and given the historical record, may legitimately wonder whether it has enough common interests with the United States to work out a division of labor comparable to that developed with Great Britain. Japan will have to fend for itself militarily.

How the United States thinks it can keep Japan "sweet" (as Franklin D. Roosevelt liked to say), is not clear. The Japanese are not repeating the European mistake of allowing American corporations to enter and dominate their economy. Last May, George Ball called for an end to the traditional American open-door policy in Africa, to be replaced by a policy which would allow European politicians to worry about the political enigmas of Africa, and European corporations to develop African resources. He could do this with the confidence that American businessmen are so firmly entrenched in Europe that they will get their share even if Europe becomes politically dominant in Africa. No such easy view can be taken toward Japan's development of Asia.

## FIGHTING OFF THE DOLLAR

Only $750 million of American money is invested in joint ventures within Japan. This is not expanding rapidly. Most Japanese agree that, generally speaking, American capital should be excluded. They can do this, moreover, because with the high rate of internal savings, Japanese banks can find the necessary funds and do not have to rely upon foreign money. In addition to the factor of control, the Japanese fear that an influx of American capital would bring with it a unionism which, because of its payment for production rather than for seniority, would undermine the traditional and highly fruitful Japanese labor-management relationship. When Tokyo did relent slightly and allow Nestles and General Foods to enter the retail market, the two firms immediately took 80 per cent of the instant coffee market from Japanese retailers. No similar mistakes have been made in more vital areas. In July, 1967, when it appeared that American investors were quietly buying up gilt-edged shares of Sony Corporation, the Japanese Finance Ministry stepped in to stop all further purchases by foreigners.

After intense American pressure, Tokyo finally announced last July that it would allow American money into fifty types of businesses. The announcement was deceiving, for the seventeen types in which Americans were permitted to have 100 per cent interests included steel, shipbuilding and motorcycles, fields in which Japanese ownership is so solid that American money cannot compete. At the September meeting of the Joint U.S.-Japan Committee on Trade and Economic Affairs, the American delegation politely called the Japanese announcement of July "somewhat disappointing" and expressed "the hope that liberalization be accelerated as soon as possible." The Americans also complained about "recent measures which appear adversely to affect the operations of existing United States businesses in Japan."

In his January 1 announcement that curbs would be placed upon the flow of U.S. dollars abroad, Mr. Johnson specifically exempted Great Britain, Canada, Australia and Japan, as well as the "developing countries." Why Japan was so favored is a fascinating question, the more so because the President immediately sent Under Secretary of State Eugene Rostow and Rostow's top deputy on a flying trip to Tokyo to explain the new measures personally to Premier Sato. Obviously, the United States has not given up on the Japanese market, but one may doubt whether Japan appreciates being lumped in with Great Britain, Canada and Australia, three nations which have become dependent upon American capital for development of many of their critical industries. These problems have not been offset by easing trade relations. Foreign Minister Miki complained to Secretary Rusk in September of "some visible tendencies in the United States and among American industry toward protectionist movements." Miki singled out textiles and steel as items requiring particular "cooperation" between Tokyo and Washington. It is extremely doubtful if that "cooperation" will be forthcoming. American steel imports in early 1968 are running 13 million tons above the comparable 1967 period, and Japan controls 45 per cent of that market.

"CONFRONTATION" OR "INTERPLAY"

In sum, the Japanese economy is booming, but the causes and results of this expansion should give pause, particularly when Japan's political instability seems to be increasing and its urban problems are becoming dangerous. The historical record gives no one the right to assume that Japanese-American interests in the Far East are compatible or even, in the long run, reconcilable. Tokyo's views of China and Russia, as well as its recent determination to overcome its "nuclear allergy," gravely compound the historical problems. Nor is there any reason to suppose that over a period of time American money and business management practices can bring those interests together. Sen. Mike Mansfield recently hoped that Japan would not rearm, but would instead concentrate on developing its economic power, so that "military confrontation" in Asia might be transformed into "economic interplay." This is only a wish, not a set of assumptions on which policy can be based. A more accurate view was provided by a delegation of Japanese businessmen and politicians who told visiting American dignitaries last September in Shimoda that the future political position of Japan "is obviously going to be different from what it is now," and then warned that over the next few years Japanese foreign affairs would become increasingly independent.

## BLOODSHED FOR MOTORCYCLES

Given the current American determination to save Asia from Asians, there are apparently only two broad policy alternatives. First, the United States can continue to rely upon military intervention to "contain" China. That is the course the Johnson Administration thinks it is pursuing in Vietnam. It is ironic that despite the impetus Vietnam has given the Japanese economy, Tokyo differs with the United States on fundamental aspects of that conflict. Foreign Minister Miki has publicly called the struggle "a civil war." Japanese public opinion is such that when President Johnson hoped to visit Tokyo after the Manila Conference of October, 1966, the Japanese Government immediately rejected the President's plans. Sato refused to be connected publicly in such a manner to the American war effort.

The State Department says that Japanese officials express in private appreciation for the American military involvement since it has kept Asian Communists off balance and protects the key Japanese raw material and market areas in the southwestern Pacific. But if such views are stated, they inevitably raise a further question, which Prof. Thomas McCormick has phrased precisely: is the United States sacrificing more than 16,000 of its young men "in order to make Southeast Asia safe for Japanese economic interests"?

No State Department spokesman has tackled that question, although it has been circumvented numerous times since Eisenhower first outlined the Vietnam-Japan relationship in 1954. The former President recently suggested that it would perhaps be better not to discuss this particular aspect of the war at the present time. If indeed American blood is not being shed for Japanese motorcycle manufacturers, a second policy alternative appears: the United States has committed more than half a million men to Southeast Asia in order to advance its own strategic and economic interests. Given the rising political and economic stake in the area (including the recent establishment of American branch banks which want, as one of their officials phrased it, to be in on the "ground floor" when Vietnam is reconstructed), this seems the more enlightened alternative for Washington "realists." It and the increased exhortation that the Japanese end their supposed "isolation" mean that, given a "fair field" (that is, a field without Communist or left-wing nationalist agitation to interrupt the play), the United States and Japan could truly form the partnership and have the "economic interplay" for which the Fourteen Scholars and Senator Mansfield have such high hopes.

The prospect may look rosy, but we should be aware that we have already visited where the Fourteen Scholars and Senator Mansfield now want to take us. They are not pioneers. Some years ago another Democratic politician proclaimed that Americans and Japanese would march "shoulder to shoulder" to develop Asia. That was Franklin D. Roosevelt in 1923.

# bibliography

The bibliography of works concerning World War II is immense; some of the most extensive revisionist and radical works were completed in the 1940s. Rather than reiterate these well-known works here, we will list only those sources written by contemporary historians whose perspective is radical and probing.

On World War II and its origins, readers should consult the thoughtful and questioning study by Bruce M. Russett, *No Clear and Present Danger: A Skeptical View of the U.S. Entry into World War II* (Harper & Row, Harper Torchbooks, 1972). Russett makes cogent comparisons between the policies of Franklin D. Roosevelt prior to United States entry in World War II and those pursued by Lyndon B. Johnson during the escalation of the war in Vietnam. Also critical is the essay by Robert F. Smith, "American Foreign Relations, 1920–1942," in Barton J. Bernstein, ed., *Towards a New Past: Dissenting Essays in American History* (Pantheon, 1968).

For American foreign policy in the 1920s, one should begin with the background of Wilsonian diplomacy, covered in N. Gordon Levin, Jr., *Woodrow Wilson and World Politics* (Oxford University Press, 1968), and Joan Hoff Wilson, *American Business and Foreign Policy, 1920–1933* (University Press of Kentucky, 1972).

By 1972, the appearance of numerous revisionist and radical works evaluating the nature of American Cold War policy has been overwhelming. Perhaps a good introduction to the literature is Christopher Lasch, "The Cold War Re-Visited and Revisioned," *New York Times Magazine* (January 14, 1968). After reading Lasch, readers should turn to the seminal works by William Appleman Williams. His books pertaining to the Cold War and American foreign affairs include *The Tragedy of American Diplomacy*, rev. ed. (Delta, 1972), *The United States, Cuba and Castro* (Monthly Review Press, 1962), and an edited collection, *From Colony to Empire* (Wiley, 1972).

The works of Gabriel Kolko take off from the general framework provided by Williams and provide a wealth of detail on the nature of United States foreign policy in the war and postwar years. Of prime importance are *The Politics of War* (Random House, 1968), *The Roots of American Foreign Policy* (Beacon Press, 1969), and Joyce and Gabriel Kolko, *The Limits of Power* (Harper and Row, 1972).

Readings of importance on different themes appear in several notable collections of essays. Articles by Williams, Lloyd C. Gardner, David Eakins, G. William Domhoff, Henry Berger, Todd Gitlin, and others appear in two collections edited by David Horowitz, *Containment and Revolution* (Beacon Press, 1967) and *Corporations and the Cold War* (Monthly Review Press, 1969). Horowitz's own works carry out a powerful revisionist and Marxist indictment of United States foreign policy. See his first essay, *The Free World Colossus*, rev. ed. (Hill & Wang, 1971), and *Empire and Revolution* (Random House, 1969). Another group of important essays revealing contemporary early criticisms of the Cold War is Thomas G. Paterson, ed., *Cold War Critics* (Quadrangle Books, 1971). Included in this collection are essays by Barton J. Bernstein on Walter Lippmann; Ronald Radosh and Leonard Liggio on Henry A. Wallace; Henry Berger on Robert Taft; and others.

Some of William Appleman Williams' students have published major works taking up various themes pertaining to Cold War ideology and policies. Lloyd C. Gardner develops the points of view of different Cold War policy-makers in *Architects of Illusion: Men and Ideas in American Foreign Policy 1941–1949* (Quadrangle Books, 1970). Additional major works are Walter LaFeber, *America, Russia and the Cold War, 1945–1971*, 2nd ed. (Wiley, 1972); LaFeber, *The Origins of the Cold War, 1941–1947* (Wiley, 1971); and LaFeber, *America in the Cold War* (Wiley, 1969).

A work by an early student of Williams' that assumed major proportions was Gar Alperovitz, *Atomic Diplomacy: Hiroshima and Potsdam* (Simon and Schuster, 1965). Alperovitz argued that the atomic bomb did not have to be used to end World War II against Japan and that it was used to frighten the Soviet Union into making diplomatic concessions in the Far East.

Other general works of revisionist scholarship that should be consulted include Richard J. Barnet, *Intervention and Revolution* (New American Library, 1968), and Ronald Steel, *Imperialists and Other Heroes* (Random House, 1971). The best general summary is Stephen E. Ambrose, *Rise to Globalism: American Foreign Policy since 1938* (Penguin, 1972). A scathing critique of the foreign policy of John F. Kennedy, particularly taking up the favorable estimates of Kennedy's foreign policy made by Schlesinger, Theodore Sorenson, and others is Richard J. Walton, *Cold War and Counter-Revolution* (Viking, 1972).

racism, sexism, and nativism
in the twentieth century

As we approach issues relating to our own era, a great variety of historians are beginning to ask about the effect of racism, sexism, and nativism on the quality of American life. Each of the articles in this chapter addresses itself in a new way to those issues born out of the crises of our recent past. Their contributions to radical history lie in their explorations of dissenting movements and the responses they evoked.

Europeans who immigrated to the United States in the twentieth century were greeted by restrictions that made it easy to deport unwanted aliens. As William Preston's article makes clear, immigrants became scapegoats for many of the economic and social evils which accompanied America's transformation from a debtor to a creditor nation. During World War I, for example, Woodrow Wilson crusaded against "disloyal hyphenates" and "duped" Americans involved in the "sinister intrigue" for peace. In 1916 Wilson proclaimed Flag Day a national holiday to honor the "sacredness of the flag," paraded through Washington with one draped across his chest, and announced that loyalty to the flag was "the first test of tolerance in the United States."

Opposition to fundamental economic reform and social change was so intense that various acts of official violence accompanied the activities of organizations such as the Industrial Workers of the World that sought to unite the working class. The goal of the I.W.W. was to organize everybody who worked regardless of class, sex, or race. During World War I the I.W.W. was prosecuted as a threat to national security under the Alien and Sedition Acts, even though they did not officially oppose the war. But the I.W.W. went beyond the narrow economic concerns of "bureaucratic pro-capitalist" trade unionism and hoped to expose the class antagonisms they considered intrinsic to the corporate structure. As James Weinstein's article indicates, the I.W.W.'s "sedition" consisted of its belief that revolutionary change would follow the organization of a militant labor union.

During World War I racial violence accompanied the government's attacks on "hyphenate-Americans" and radical workers. In "The Wilson Administration and the Wartime Mobilization of Black Americans," (Labor History, Summer 1969), Jane Lang and Harry Scheiber note that 100,000 blacks voted for Wilson in 1912 because he promised "to deal fairly with the Negroes." Instead he segregated Washington, stripped black officials appointed by his predecessors of their functions, and removed them from their offices to an unused broom closet because he resented the fact that they gave dictation to white stenographers. Even William Monroe Trotter and W. E. B. DuBois had supported Wilson, and DuBois suspended his work for the newly organized NAACP to recruit black servicemen for a war in which they were segregated and humiliated. The war also resulted in domestic racial strife, which Wilson did nothing to prevent or alleviate. In the East St. Louis riots, for example, a white mob attacked and burned a black community, killing or wounding between fifty and five hundred men, women, and children. The Woman's Peace Party reported Wilson's attitude to this massacre in the August 25, 1917, issue of its journal, Four Lights:

Six weeks have passed since the East St. Louis riots and no public word of rebuke, no demand for punishment of the offenders, has come from our Chief Executive. These American Negroes have died under more horrible conditions than any non-combatants who were sunk by German submarines. But to our President their death does not merit consideration.

Our young men who don their khaki are thus taught that, as they go out to battle under the flag of the United States, they may outdo Belgian atrocities without rebuke if their enemies be of a darker race. And those who guard our land at home have learned that black men and women and little children may safely be mutilated and burned while they stand idly by.

Wilson's betrayal of the black vote and his hostility to "ethnic" Americans was paralleled by the policies of Franklin Delano Roosevelt's administration during World War II. The removal of all Japanese Americans to concentration camps while the fighting Nisei achieved more military decorations than any other unit is well documented in such works as Captain Allan R. Bosworth's *America's Concentration Camps*. Less well known is the United States' restriction of Jewish immigrants to 4,705 in 1943 while the total annual immigration quota was undersubscribed by 125,000. In 1939 Roosevelt and Secretary of State Cordell Hull opposed the Wagner-Rogers Refugee Children's Bill aimed at rescuing 20,000 Jewish children. Within one day after the announcement of the bill 4,000 American families offered to adopt the children through a program supervised by Quakers. But Congress was not interested in refugees and had at that time sixty anti-alien bills before it. When Congresswoman Caroline O'Day of New York queried Roosevelt about the bill, he put her memo aside: "File, No Action. F.D.R." For an index of man's inhumanity, Roosevelt's administration provides many examples and Harvard Sitkoff's article indicates some of its grimmest moments.

Sitkoff describes the brutality toward and degradation of black soldiers during World War II, the military's refusal to protect its black members from white mobs, and Roosevelt's total disregard for violent race riots. Like Wilson's southern advisers, Roosevelt's southern advisers refused to alleviate or prevent the numerous lynchings and vicious race riots which occurred throughout the country. In Los Angeles, for example, when white mobs stripped and attacked black youths who wore "zoot suits," the police arrested the victims. When black organizations protested the lynchings and beatings of black citizens, they were called disloyal.

In 1944 J. Edgar Hoover proposed to round up Communist Party agitators who, he said, caused racial unrest. As Harold Cruse points out, however, the Communist Party was no particular friend to the black community, and its activities were generally motivated by its own self-interests. By dismissing black nationalism, the Party cut itself off from many of the very people it had hoped to work with. Cruse's bitter opposition to the Communist Party, to which he was attracted in his youth, is rooted in what he considered the Party's opportunism. But Cruse's current appeal for black nationalism and his acceptance of black capitalism is not entirely satisfying. Nationalism in corporate or state capitalist environments has a generally pernicious history. If, as Frantz Fanon asserted, the goal is human liberation, the creation of "a new history of Man," the old oppressive forms will not do.

When you look at the history of black people in the United States, at the unbroken continuum of inhumanity, physical brutality, psychological violence— all designed to deny the dignity of a people—you have to begin to wonder why. Why was it necessary for white people to establish a class of people they considered man-machines to do their work, and why after the Civil War was it necessary to keep black people in a state of economic deprivation? The United States is the only nation to free its subject class without providing them any land or property with which to survive economically. The former slaves were expected to remain the serfs of America. For James Boggs, at least, the answer is obvious. In "The Myth and Irrationality of Black Capitalism," a lecture he gave to the Black Economic Conference in April 1969, he said: "When we talk about the system, we are talking about capitalism. . . . And when we talk about capitalism, we are talking about the system that has created the situation blacks are in today. . . . Black underdevelopment is a product of capitalist development."

Just as the racist mythology considered blacks biologically inferior to whites and therefore "suited" to servility, so the sexist mythology regarded women as biologically inferior to men and their political and economic roles "ordained" by their biological condition. In the end, both groups were degraded and kept outside the circle of influence and power. Within the past five years a renewed interest in feminism has resulted in a spate of books which reveal a concern for women, but most of the old biases persist and they are limited to elitist feminist activities. The feminist movement was isolated from, if not contemptuous of, working-class women and had almost no contact with black and immigrant women. Nancy Schrom's article is one of the few attempts to deal with those neglected groups of women.

The trade union movement also ignored the problems of unskilled and migrant workers, black and white. One of the most enduring contributions of the I.W.W. is that it pointed out how it was in the interests of corporate capitalism for workers to hate blacks and immigrants. If trade unionists did not have such scapegoats, they might have directed their attention toward the institutions which exploited them all.

As Lenin observed in *What Is To Be Done*: "Working class consciousness cannot be genuine political consciousness unless the workers are trained to respond to *all* cases of tyranny, oppression, violence, and abuse, no matter *what* class is affected." At least one representative of a constituency of ethnic workers, Barbara Mikulski, a member of Baltimore's City Council, addressed herself to that issue in 1971: "There was no racial prejudice in our hearts when we came to the United States. The elitists who now smugly call us racists are the ones who taught us the meaning of the word." It is now time, she concluded, to tell blacks and whites to stop competing for the same slice of the pie and work instead for "a whole new bakery."

# the immigrant
# as scapegoat

## WILLIAM PRESTON, Jr.

The absurd belief that radical ideas were imposed on the United States by the foreign born resulted in immigration restrictions and laws that made deportation a simple administrative function. By the 1920s America's intolerance was manifested in wholesale roundups of thousands of immigrants, most of whom had no radical credentials. The Palmer Raids and the "deportation delirium" of the Wilson era was followed by resistance to the immigration of people in flight from Hitler during World War II and an intense campaign to achieve 100 percent Americanism during the Cold War. Anti-communist hysteria resulted in McCarran's Internal Security Act of 1950 and the Immigration Act of 1952. Dalton Trumbo, the author of *Johnny Got His Gun*, called the McCarthy era "the time of the toad." The period featured continued persecution of alien Americans in its relentless search for "communists" in labor unions, in the professions, in government, and finally, in the armed forces, which ultimately ended McCarthy's reign. That most immigrants were conservative was irrelevant. The nativist repression of the twentieth century helped break the back of the radical wing of the labor movement, and all activities on behalf of social justice were postponed.

In the following article, William Preston, a liberal mainstream historian, explores the connection between the activities of radical groups and the government's response, a legal crusade against immigrants.

---

The Immigration Bureau brought to the deportation of radicals the same abusive tactics used in the apprehension and removal of all aliens. Contemporary observers were aware of the excessive and devious violations of fundamental rights. The roundup of many innocent people, detentions incommunicado, excessive bail, and denial of counsel until confessions had been extorted were not the product of an unusual nationwide postwar hysteria that denied due process to "reds"; the processing of aliens had been growing more and more summary for years. Yet many of the procedures had remained unchallenged, the powers untested, until they were exposed to public scrutiny during the red scare and fully debated for perhaps the first and last time in immigration history.

Due process in deportation was smashed on the rock of judicial decision in 1893, never to be put together again. In *Fong Yue Ting v. United States*, the Supreme Court determined the future pattern of expulsion in one simple interpretation: Deportation was not a punishment for crime but merely an administrative process for the return of unwelcome and undesirable alien residents to their own countries.[1] The United States deported aliens on the grounds of expediency not of crime, not as punishment, but because their presence was "deemed inconsistent with the public welfare."[2]

Some years later, the high court in the *Japanese Immigrant Case* reaffirmed the absolute power of Congress to deport aliens summarily and by administrative fiat if it chose. Because of the "extremely informal and summary character of the proceedings which were followed therein," this case remained "the most emphatic decision" limiting the rights of aliens.[3] An alien resided in the United States at the entire sufferance of Congress and became deportable whenever that body classified him as such. It could do so for any reason at any time as "an inherent and inalienable right of every sovereign and independent nation."[4]

Once deportation had been defined as noncriminal, all else followed. The guaranties of the Bill of Rights applied only to persons charged with crime. Expulsion often involved, therefore, long detention, excessively high bail, unreasonable searches and seizures, the denial of counsel, self-incrimination, and trial without jury. It was difficult for an alien under arrest to realize that he was not undergoing a cruel banishment from a country where he had lived for many years. It was even less comprehensible that few of the rights he had come to associate with American judicial practice were available to him. The Fourth, Fifth, Sixth, and Eighth amendments and section 9 of Article I prohibiting ex post facto laws afforded him no protection.

These considerations did not sway the decisions of more than a minority of the Supreme Court justices. Conceivably, the Court might have decided that deportation *was* punishment. In the 1893 case Mr. Justice Brewer's famous dissent flatly asserted: "Deportation is punishment. It involves first an arrest, a deprival of liberty; and second, a removal from home, from family, from business, from property." He presumed that "everyone knows that to be forcibly taken away from home and family, and friends . . . and sent across the ocean to a distant land, is punishment; and that oftentimes the most severe and cruel."[5] Rejecting the concept that the United States has the inherent power to deport aliens in any manner, Mr. Justice Field once said, "Brutality, inhumanity, and cruelty cannot be made elements in any procedure for the enforcement of the laws of the United States."[6] Although the Department of Labor itself had considered deportation *"more severe punishment* than imprisonment," it never allowed this belief to influence its procedure.[7] It stood by the Court.

Supreme Court decisions have sometimes concealed the true nature of reality. For many years a legal fiction absolved the deportation rites of their penal character. If the act of expulsion was not punishment, then almost any administrative implementation of the act was legal. The Court's interpretation has thus opened the way to practices basically at odds with its own definition of due process. Deportation has been "a system of executive justice, with a maximum of powers in the administrative officers, a minimum of checks and safeguards against error and prejudice, and with certainty, care and due deliberation sacrificed to the desire for speed."[8] In a field largely free from judicial and congressional dictation, immigration officials have evolved procedures that guarantee results rather than rights, deportation rather than due process.

Four techniques came to predominate: arrest without warrant; telegraphic application for a warrant of arrest; preliminary hearing; and denial of counsel until a relatively late stage. Adopted informally, these practices became a normal, if not essential, part of deportation. A generation of officials so trained found it difficult to function any other way. Perhaps they could not even remember there was another way.

Both detention without warrant and telegraphic application came into being out of real necessity in certain unique cases. These procedures then became common practice, the immigration inspectors apparently being unable to regulate such contagiously useful devices. According to the rules, the Washington office issued a warrant only when an inspector had made out a prima facie case against the alien under the immigration law and accompanied the application with "some substantial supporting evidence."[9] Yet this was entirely too involved and lengthy in cases involving Chinese aliens and immigrants crossing the border. The Chinese were required to produce documentary evidence of their right to be in the country, yet aliens found without this certificate often disappeared while the inspectors awaited legal authority to hold them. It became customary, therefore, to detain Chinese without a warrant of arrest. Similarly in border-crossing cases aliens caught in the act were arrested without warrant.[10]

Telegraphic warrants took root in much the same way. Originally the immigration rules cautioned subordinate officials that "telegraphic application may be resorted to *only in case of necessity*" or "when some substantial interest of the government would thereby by served."[11] There was a justifiable fear that the telegraphic warrant might prove the instrument of local hysteria and lawlessness or the cloak for individual incompetence. Yet the terminology was broad enough to tolerate the expansion that began in 1908. The Immigration Bureau was then a part of the Department of Commerce and Labor, and its solicitor approved telegraphic warrants for aliens with criminal records. The government feared that the police might release deportable alien criminals before a written application for a warrant of arrest was received at Washington and returned to the local inspector.[12] In the same year Secretary of Commerce and Labor Oscar Straus endorsed telegraphic applications for anarchists "in rare instances" of certain deportability.[13] In so doing the department made possible an irresponsible autonomy susceptible to local pressure for the roundup of radicals. The Washington office could only hope that probable cause for telegraphing a warrant existed, and that the immigration inspector knew what he was doing.

Very early in the history of deportation the alien himself began to supply the "substantial supporting evidence" required by the rules for the warrant of arrest. While local authorities (when possible) "detained" the immigrant, the inspector conducted a "preliminary hearing," at which the individual was encouraged to tell all. This extralegal interview soon overshadowed all other deportation practices. Evidence secured there was usually sufficient to obtain the warrant and to accomplish the deportation as well. No lawyer was present at the "preliminary hearing."[14]

At one time the Bureau of Immigration had considered the interrogation of aliens before their arrest a questionable practice.[15] Doubts as to its legality, however, disappeared in the self-assurance induced by the Supreme Court. Immigration officials relied increasingly on the authority of the *Japanese Immigrant Case* decision, which upheld proceedings "of an extremely informal and summary character."[16] The Court had decided that the hearing reserved to the alien should be "not necessarily an opportunity upon a regular set occasion and according to the form of judicial procedure, but one that will secure the prompt, vigorous action contemplated by Congress."[17]

Immigration officials could hardly be expected to be self-critical when sustained by such high authority. The average inspector pictured himself as the heroic protector of the public welfare, with the immigrant lawyer cast as villain. While the myth of the dishonest counsel may certainly have had some basis in the fact of immigrant exploitation, it was all too easy a rationale for developing a self-incriminating procedure. The hypocrisy and smugness implicit in this stereotype were depicted in a bureau memorandum of 1910. "The reason for holding a preliminary hearing without the presence of counsel," it explained, "is to enable the immigration authorities to ascertain in their own way the true facts without the intervention of the dilatory tactics which some counsel are disposed to employ, including advice often given the alien not to answer questions put by the immigration authorities." After noting that the proceedings were noncriminal and designed "only to determine whether the alien has the right to be in the United States," the report concluded, "It is appropriate to ask him any relevant questions calculated to throw light on the situation, and if he refuses to reply to any such question the fact may be noted and in the discretion of the immigration authorities taken strongly against him."[18]

Once the warrant of arrest had been served, the Immigration Bureau officially took the alien into custody, notified him of the charges, and gave him an opportunity to be heard. According to rule 22 of bureau procedure, at some time during this hearing the inspector had to notify the immigrant of his right to have counsel. Although rule 22 had changed over the years on this point, its most generous stipulation afforded the immigrant legal aid "preferably at the beginning of the hearing under the warrant of arrest or at any rate as soon as such hearing has proceeded sufficiently in the development of the facts to protect the government's interests."[19] The Supreme Court again upheld this procedure, being unable to find it "so arbitrary and so manifestly intended to deprive the alien of a fair, though summary hearing" as to be unconstitutional.[20] The Immigration Bureau, reading the high court's endorsement as moral approval, saw no need to introduce greater justice on its own authority but instead simply avoided gross abuse.[21] As for the alien's attorney, the bureau suggested that his role might be "to correct any possible error or oversight on the part of the immigration authorities."[22]

The hearings themselves were reminiscent of the Star Chamber and the Inquisition. The examining inspector, often legally unqualified, was detective, prosecuting attorney, interpreter, stenographer, and judge. In his bias, eagerness to win a confession, and desire to make a case, the immigration officer played most enthusiastically and convincingly the role of prosecutor. There was no attempt to conform to the rules of courtroom procedure. Thus the file forwarded to Washington for action might contain unsworn statements, ex parte affidavits, inspectors' reports, personal letters, statements of informers, hearsay or opinion evidence, and extraneous material not related to the charges. The examination itself was a fishing expedition into the alien's life, often an abusive and hostile interrogation characterized by vague or leading questions. In defense the immigrant could insist that there be no flagrant misuse of discretion, and that his lawyer be able to cross-examine government witnesses, introduce those of his client, and submit a written brief. At the end of the hearing, the inspector prepared a recommendation for his superiors. This summary might not be based on evidence in the record, and all too frequently indicated a willingness to deport aliens solely on grounds of their general undesirability.[23]

From the detention by local authorities to the transmission of the file for final approval, the alien faced dangers that Judge Learned Hand found "inherent in a system where prosecutor and judge are one and the ordinary rules which protect the accused are in abeyance." It is an easy road, warned the distinguished jurist, "to the disposition of cases without clear legal grounds or evidence which rationally proves them."[24]

The alien could rarely expect his exit from the country to be interrupted by executive or judicial review. While the file sent to Washington passed from a law examiner to the commissioner general of immigration to the Assistant or Acting Secretary of Labor, theirs was a perfunctory review. This rubber-stamping was routine unless a well-contested case came to their attention through a personal appeal. The deportation of aliens thus remained largely the prerogative of the local inspector.[25]

The federal courts usually supported the government and frequently confused the alien by substituting their own judgment about the meaning of the law for that of the Immigration Bureau. The judges construed individual rights narrowly and broadly upheld the rights of sovereignty and public welfare.[26] If there was any evidence at all under any part of the immigration code, expulsion was certain to follow. As to the fairness of the proceedings, the courts required "only the loosest kind of procedural safeguards," and insisted merely that there be no gross abuse of discretion or due process.[27] Furthermore, a successful habeas corpus action by the alien might be only a prologue to a second arrest. Since the proceedings were not criminal, a dismissal did not operate as res adjudicata. The Immigration Bureau could and did issue new warrants, while the court often delayed the discharge of the alien until these had been served.[28]

There were few openings and many dead ends in the deportation maze. Most aliens succumbed during the preliminary hearing; those who carried the fight further did so with the odds against them. One historian of deportation has insisted that "the present procedure affords opportunity for deprivation of rights considered fundamental to Anglo-Saxon law where personal liberty is involved."[29] The immigrant arriving at New York City suffered from a delusion. The statue he might have admired did not symbolize the rights and justice afforded aliens by the Constitution and courts of his adopted country.

In the years before World War I, Immigration Bureau customs became steadily more repugnant to normal judicial procedures and to commonsense notions of fair play. There was neither mystery nor conspiracy behind this trend. It was the natural growth of an administrative technique unrestrained by publicity or opposition.

The government tested and applied its malpractices against a steadily increasing group of outcasts—prostitutes, procurers, lunatics, idiots, paupers, persons likely to become a public charge, professional beggars, individuals suffering from a loathsome or dangerous contagious disease, polygamists, epileptics, persons convicted of felony, crime, or misdemeanor involving moral turpitude, and Chinese and Japanese.[30] These were in the main friendless, despised, ignorant, defenseless people, and, more important, *unorganized*. While anarchists were deportable after 1903, they only had the semblance of organization. As the Immigration Bureau discovered later, "Real anarchists are usually associated together, if at all, simply in groups or gatherings which have no constitution . . . and no officers other than a Secretary and Treasurer."[31] And for various reasons there were very few anarchist cases that might possibly have called into play a vigorous defense by these semiorganized radicals. Thus, the Department of Commerce and Labor and the local inspectors operated almost without check and largely without public notice in the development of the distasteful methods that caused such an outcry after the war. The aliens rounded up had failed to make the protests that might have advertised the procedure and forced its reconsideration by the government.

The alien fared better in the prewar period than he would after 1917. Despite ever-increasing administrative inflexibility, the law itself provided some protections that were later abandoned. Immigration legislation still possessed a minimum number of vague standards and terms. It was quite certain whether an immigrant was or was not a prostitute, a pauper, or an individual afflicted with a loathsome contagious disease. An alien was therefore aware of what brought him within the law. "Liable to become a public charge" and "crimes involving moral turpitude" were the only clauses that defied clear and consistent interpretation.

Furthermore, specific time limits defined the duration of the alien's liability. No one could be wrenched from family and friends if he survived one-, then two-, and later, three-year probation. This minimized as well the menace of nebulous phrases. The later abolition of all time restrictions and the increase of indefinite standards placed immigrants on permanent parole, the conditions of which are not fully disclosed.[32]

The immigration inspector also preferred the calmer and less complicated prewar years. Dealing with resigned, docile individuals whose deportability was easily established, he had relatively few administrative problems. Armed with a signed confession, he firmly believed that deportation could be prompt and vigorous. He had but slight familiarity with the interpretation of vague standards, and he had not dealt with many aliens of long residence. He was thus singularly ill-equipped by training and experience for the coming struggle with radicals.

Often without legal background, the inspector was not prepared to appreciate either the fine distinctions within the same radical philosophy or the distinguishing features among different radical beliefs. If he could, he still had to decide which were legal actions or thoughts according to the law. The few scattered anarchist cases before 1917 supplied him with little practical knowledge of the operations of radicals under fire.

By 1917 a procedure and a state of bureaucratic mind had developed within the Immigration Bureau. When government officials so oriented met radicals, always sensitive to persecution and tenacious of their rights, it was not surprising that the struggle should be poisoned by misunderstanding, fear, and hatred on both sides. Only the time of the contest remained in doubt.

That it came at the end of World War I was a result of numerous factors. Among them the most important was probably the radical's growing estrangement from his fellow Americans. They had not always singled him out for such hostile attention. But beginning in the late nineteenth century, the tide of repression seemed to surge more forcefully and ebb less completely at each succeeding phase of reaction. Had this development been directed solely against the radical, it would have been unnecessary and unfortunate enough. But contrary to the realities of American life, the foreigner became identified as extremist. Nativism thus tended to focus federal policies on immigration, and the alien began to carry the double burden of his foreign birth and of his trumped-up radicalism.

*　　*　　*

## NOTES

1. *Fong Yue Ting v. U.S.*, 149 U.S. 698, 709; Milton R. Konvitz, *Civil Rights in Immigration* (Ithaca, 1953), 97–98.

2. *Fong Yue Ting v. U.S.*, 149 U.S. 698, 709.

3. F. H. Larned to Commissioner of Immigration, San Francisco, April 10, 1914, IN File 53244/1. See also *Japanese Immigrant Case*, 189 U.S. 86, 97.

4. Konvitz, 40–44, 97–98, 102; *Fong Yue Ting v. U.S.*, 149 U.S. 698.

5. *Fong Yue Ting v. U.S.*, 149 U.S. 698, 737, 740–741. Justice Brewer also quoted with approval James Madison, who said, "If a banishment of this sort [deportation] be not a punishment, and among the severest of punishments, it will be difficult to imagine a doom to which the name can be applied."

6. Quoted in Jane Perry Clark, *Deportation of Aliens from the United States to Europe* (New York, 1931), 48. Other justices have objected to the idea that deportation is not punishment. Chief Justice Fuller dissented in the Fong Yue Ting case. More recently Justices Black, Douglas, Murphy, and Rutledge have criticized or challenged the historic position of the court (Konvitz, 103–106).

7. E. J. Henning to Hon. Charles Nagel, July 30, 1923. IN File 54616/42.

8. William Cabell Van Vleck, *The Administrative Control of Aliens: A Study in Administrative Law and Procedure* (New York, 1932), 224.

9. Rule 22, subdiv. 3, of Immigration Bureau regulations, IN File 54549/622D; Van Vleck, 83.

10. IN File 53775/139, *passim*; Anthony Caminetti to the Assistant Secretary, August 28, 1920, Alfred Hampton to Commissioners of Immigration, Seattle, El Paso, Montreal, September 30, 1920, and October 6, 1920, J. A. Flukey to Commissioner General, October 14, 1920, IN File 53244/1.

11. Rule 22, subdiv. 3, IN File 54549/622D. Author's emphasis.

12. Solicitor Charles Earl to A. Warner Parker, March 19, 1908, IN File 51924/30.

13. Oscar Straus and F. P. Sargent to all Commissioners of Immigration and Immigrant Inspectors in Charge, March 23, 1908, *ibid.*

14. Clark, 331–332, Van Vleck, 228; Reuben Oppenheimer, *The Enforcement of the Deportation Laws of the United States: Report to the National Commission on Law Observance and Enforcement* (Washington, 1931), 26–27.

15. F. H. Larned (Acting Commissioner General) to Inspector in Charge, St. Louis, July 31, 1908, IN File 53244/1.

16. Larned to Commissioner of Immigration, San Francisco, April 10, 1914, *ibid.*

17. *Japanese Immigrant Case*, 189 U.S. 86, 101. Author's emphasis. Much the same viewpoint was upheld in *Pearson v. Williams*, 202 U.S. 281.

18. William Williams to Commissioner General, May 21, 1910, IN File 53244/1. On the latter point the case of *U.S. v. Lee Huen*, 118 F. 442, 456, is relevant.

19. Anthony Caminetti to the Acting Secretary, July 24, 1919, IN File 54645/378; Oppenheimer, 43.

20. *Low Wah Suey v. Backus*, 225 U.S. 460, 471–472.

21. See the attitude expressed in Caminetti to Francis Garvan, July 27, 1919, IN File 54235/85C. Commissioner General Caminetti testified before a congressional committee that, if anything, the immigration hearings had been too fair (IN File 54549/662D). Examples may be found generally in almost any case history where the defense lawyer has challenged the procedure for lack of due process. See F. H. Larned to Inspector in Charge, Denver, May 17, 1914, IN File 53244/1B.

22. Williams to Commissioner General, May 21, 1910, IN File 53244/1.

23. Clark, 331–338, 361–386, 391, 422–423, 487–488; Konvitz, 107–109; Oppenheimer, 26–52, 59, 72, 80–92; Van Vleck, 83–89, 91–111, 172, 219–220, 224–228.

24. *U.S. ex rel. Iorio v. Day*, 34 F. 2d 920, 922.

25. Clark, 303–304, 377–382; Oppenheimer, 50–52, 86; this was true of the I.W.W. cases also until their defense became well organized.

26. Caminetti to Garvan, June 27, 1919, IN File 54235/85C.

27. Clark, 318.

28. The paragraphs on judicial review are based on a summary of Caminetti to Garvan, June 27, 1919, IN File 54235/85C; H. S. Ridgely to Solicitor General, Memorandum of November 23, 1920, DJ File 39-O-11x; Clark, 315–320; Van Vleck, 150–160, 171–173, 176, 180, 186, 193–197, 201–202, 208.

29. Clark, 487.

30. *Ibid.*, 41–54; Roy L. Garis, *Immigration Restriction: A Study of the Opposition to and Regulation of Immigration into the United States* (New York, 1927), 83–116.

31. Caminetti to Garvan, June 27, 1919, IN File 54235/85C.

32. Clark, 43–44, 51–53; Garis, 104, 107, 112, 134–135; Konvitz, 130–131.

# the IWW and American socialism

## JAMES WEINSTEIN

The I.W.W. intended to unite all working people in a massive labor organization which would expose capitalism's faults and gradually cause its overthrow. Until Caesar Chavez, the I.W.W. was the only organization to recruit migrant farm workers and lumber workers. It also recruited unskilled, skilled, and professional workers. It was one of the first unions to use women organizers; such women as Elizabeth Gurley Flynn and Anna Louise Strong, one of the leaders of Seattle's 1919 general strike, were among the best organizers anywhere.

The Wobblies opposed violence, but to destroy the organization, the government resorted to the kind of *agent provocateur* activity which resulted in intense violence, familiar to students of the 1970s. In the following article James Weinstein, a radical historian, explains that despite the I.W.W.'s recruiting successes, a combination of government brutality, postwar repression, and the organization of a large number of workers who abandoned revolutionary fervor for more immediate bread-and-butter issues destroyed its appeal.

---

I

The relationship between workplace organizing (trade unionism) and a revolutionary movement (some form of party) was the central problem of socialist politics in the United States from the founding of the Socialist Labor Party in 1877 until after World War II. For most of the last century socialists have seen the industrial working class as the historic agent of revolution, and have focused on the ways in which the "economic" activity of workers could become "political" (revolutionary). Both in Europe and in the United States, the early Social Democratic parties and the later Leninist parties viewed trade unions as natural defensive organizations, the spontaneous creation of workers to defend their immediate interests as workers, in contrast to the party, which was created self-consciously by revolutionaries to end the domination of the working class by the capitalist class. While the unions sought to improve conditions within a class society, the party was organized not simply to help workers improve their lot as workers, but to destroy capitalism and create a society in which there would be no working class.

Although this view of trade union activity has been the dominant one in revolutionary politics both in Europe and in the United States, revolutionary syndicalism has existed side by side with the socialist tendencies and has been present in some degree in the thinking and practice of socialist (which includes

James Weinstein, "The IWW and American Socialism," *Socialist Revolution,* Vol. I, no. 15, 3–41.

"communist") parties. Revolutionary syndicalists believed that union activity would bring the workers to a revolutionary consciousness in the course of fighting for their own immediate interests. For the revolutionary syndicalist, the party is either unnecessary, or at best secondary to the union. Syndicalists envisioned greater and greater struggles at the point of production, leading to a general strike (in which the state would become helpless and unable to carry on production), and then to the reorganization of society around the factories.

Both the traditional socialist and the revolutionary syndicalist perspectives derived from Marx, who argued that although the first aim of workers' resistance was merely to maintain wages, the unions that they formed were compelled to move beyond that narrow purpose because of repression by an organized capitalist class. Marx believed that "a veritable civil war" would develop in the course of workers' struggles to defend their unions. In this fight, "all the elements necessary for a coming battle unite and develop," he wrote. And once the struggle reached that point, "association takes on a political (socialist) character." Capitalism creates a common situation and common interests among workers; it creates a "class as against capital, but not yet for itself." In these defensive struggles "this mass becomes united, and constitutes itself as a class for itself. The interests it defends become class interests." And the struggle against capitalists is a political struggle.[1]

Marx's theory of competitive capitalism furnished the basis of this perspective. According to Marx, the accumulation of capital (reinvestment of profit to expand production) meant and increasing industrial work force and growing immiseration—which Marx meant both in the sense of keeping the workers at a bare subsistence level, and also in the sense of turning people's 'life-time" into "working-time." Marx pointed out that the development of capitalist industrialization meant domination over and exploitation of more and more propertyless workers, who had less and less control over their lives. Further, competitive capitalism, as an anarchic system of production, entailed cycles of increasingly severe economic crisis.

This analysis encouraged an evolutionary and determinist view among socialists and revolutionary syndicalists alike—a view that persisted on the left in the United States long after capitalism had passed from its competitive into its corporate phase. The industrial working class was expected to increase steadily; immediate material conditions were expected to get worse; trade union struggles by more and more workers against worsening conditions were expected to lead to a socialist or revolutionary syndicalist consciousness. A revolutionary movement would develop as a matter of course following militant struggles or the experience of a sharp depression. For parliamentary socialists this meant a mass party that would recruit more and more members and also educate workers to assert their right to power primarily through the electoral process. For revolutionary syndicalists this scenario meant that workers would be involved in larger and larger strikes until a general strike occurred and power could be seized.[2]

In Germany, where the largest and most influential socialist movement existed, the party established the unions, rather than emerging from struggles to maintain them. But Socialists still accepted Marx's view that union activity would necessarily lead to political struggle against capitalism. The unions were seen as recruiting stations for the party, and actually functioned in this way for thirty or more years after they were established in the 1860s. As auxiliaries of the party, the unions were expected to make revolutionaries of the workers. As time went on, however, the unions developed their own independent perspective. While the party leaders viewed union successes as part of the process of the organization of the proletariat for revolutionary action, the new union bureaucracy saw their gains as victories in and for themselves. Gradually socialist trade unionists ceased to see the unions primarily as recruiting stations for the party and began to insist on political neutrality within the unions in order to maximize union membership. Within the party the perspective—and the balance of forces—gradually shifted. Those with a narrow trade union perspective became more and more powerful, and the party increasingly subordinated itself to the immediate needs of the trade unions. This process also strengthened the narrowly parliamentary tendencies in the German party, since the winning of votes involved the same kind of "practical" concern with immediate reforms that was characteristic of trade unionism. Both increasingly focused on ameliorative reforms within the existing system. Since most socialists shared the view that the industrial working class would continue indefinitely to grow in numbers, and that the process of politicization was naturally evolving, those who stood for disruptive tactics such as the political strike were substantially disarmed. Why risk "adventures" when the majority of the population was not yet with you but was inexorably moving to the left?

The outcome of this process was increasing reformism and bureaucracy, and eventually, once World War I started, cooperation with the capitalist governments in fighting an imperialist war.[3]

In the United States the trade union movement was never socialist, although socialist influence was strong in the formative period of the American Federation of Labor (AFL). When the Socialist party was formally organized in 1901 the AFL was thirteen years old, and was already firmly committed to "pure and simple" unionism—to the improvement of wages and working conditions within the existing framework of corporate capitalism. Even so, the perspective of the American Socialist party was similar to that of the German. It believed that the unions could be won to socialism, and it directed its activity primarily toward winning the support of organized workers, particularly those in the major unions. Left-wing and right-wing socialists shared this perspective, which was partially successful. By 1912 almost one-third of the unions in the AFL had elected Socialists to leadership.[4] Having a parliamentary perspective, and viewing all workers as natural recruits, the party tried to win the votes and general support of AFL members even though it did not directly intervene in union affairs.

The major difference between the German and American parties was that the Socialist unionists did not have a bloc within the American party. Individual trade union leaders were party members, but there was no group of trade union Socialists distinct from other party members or officials. This gave the American party greater flexibility, and is one of the important reasons that it was able to retain a socialist perspective and oppose American participation in World War I, even though the trade unions supported the war.

European social democracy collapsed as a potentially revolutionary movement with the coming of World War I and the participation of the major parties of Western Europe in wartime governments. Similarly, for somewhat different reasons, the American Socialist party broke up and declined shortly after the war. The failure of European and American parties was at the time, and has often since been, attributed to their parliamentary perspectives and to their cooperation with conservative trade unions. To the critics of the old

Socialist movement, the Industrial Workers of the World (IWW), as a rev-olutionary syndicalist union, was an heroic exception, both because of its anti-parliamentary perspective and because of its alleged refusal to subordinate its revolutionary perspective to the narrowly economic needs of trade unionism.

The IWW consistently engaged in direct action, opposed reformist politics, shunned bureaucracy and encouraged maximum participation and initiative from its members. Furthermore, it consistently supported the struggles of the most oppressed. It organized immigrants in the East, blacks in the South, and Chinese and Japanese in the West at various times, and opposed racism within the union at all times. In its own mind (if an organization as loose and diverse as the IWW can be said to have a single mind), as well as in the romantic vision of artists and young intellectuals of its day, the IWW came to represent not only the most downtrodden, but also the most "natural" or "primitive" instincts and virtues. Particularly among the young writers and artists in Greenwich Village, the IWW stood for raw courage (personified by William D. Haywood, the IWW's most commanding and best-known figure), simplicity, and an opportunity to serve the underprivileged. The myth of the unspoiled, heroic proletarian, which the IWW came to embody, was the cultural counter-part of the theory of increasing polarization between a small capitalist ruling class and an increasingly unskilled and undifferentiated working class. As such, it reinforced the idea of the proletariat as a mass of brawny workers (as presented in IWW cartoons) even while it exhalted heroic individualism—the Bunyanesque worker.

For novelists, poets, and folksingers the IWW was the model of proletarian heroism from 1910 until the Great Depression. From the 1930s through the 1960s the IWW almost disappeared from public consciousness—first because of the absorption of the left, dominated by the Communist party, in the activities of the CIO (which, like the IWW, was organized along industrial lines), and then in the early days of SNCC and SDS because of the new left's disenchant-ment with the industrial working class, with the cult of proletarianism, and with old left sectarianism in general. In the last several years, however, the IWW has enjoyed a revival, both in the "movement" and among historians—in the "movement" because militancy, opposition to racism, and commitment to direct action provided a tradition with which to associate, and among historians because the IWW appeared in some ways a predecessor of the "movement."[5] Thus, although it was in the public eye for only some ten years (1909–1919), and although it never developed a stable mass following, the IWW has been well remembered if not well understood.


II

The appearance of several new histories of the IWW in the last few years, especially Melvyn Dubofsky's We Shall be All and Joseph R. Conlin's Big Bill Haywood and the Radical Labor Movement, makes possible a re-evaluation of that organization stripped of the mythology that has surrounded it. None of the recent books is adequate in itself, but together they provide all the information about the IWW's successes and failures that is necessary to understand its meaning as part of the history of American revolutionary movements.

The founders and organizers of the IWW generally agreed that it was to be a revolutionary union organized along industrial lines—that it would organize all workers in various industries, regardless of their skills or craft, with the explicit ultimate purpose of gaining control of industry for the workers. The delegates to the Founding Convention of the IWW, June 1905, represented a fairly wide range of tendencies within the American left; they had in common a deep-seated hostility to the American Federation of Labor, which they viewed as too narrow and as hopelessly corrupt. They also tended to see in mass industrial organizing a more or less automatic corrective to AFL conservatism. Eugene V. Debs asserted that the AFL had "long outgrown its usefulness," that it was "not only in the way of progress" but, because it retained a craft form of organizing and limited its goals to those of "pure and simple unionism," it had become "positively reactionary, a thing that is but an auxiliary of the capitalist class." In contrast, Debs stated, the IWW was formed "for the purpose of uniting the working class" to struggle against capitalism.[6] Similarly, Big Bill Haywood declared at the opening session of the Founding Convention that there was no labor organization that had the same purpose as the IWW—"to put the working class in possession of the economic power, the means of life, in control of the machinery of production and distribution, without regard to capitalist masters."[7]

There were differing opinions among the initial members about the relation-ship of the revolutionary union and the revolutionary party, as we shall see, but in 1905 these were submerged in a shared understanding of the limits of the AFL as an organizer of the working class. This understanding centered on the craft form of organization that was predominant among AFL affiliates. A few AFL unions were organized along industrial lines—most notably the Brewery Workers, the United Mine Workers (partially), the Western Federation of Miners (which helped organize the IWW, but returned to the AFL in 1911), and later, the Amalgamated Clothing Workers (organized by Socialists in 1914)—but these were exceptions. Most AFL unions organized only a narrow stratum of workers in any given industry—and these on the basis of their craft (plumbers, carpenters, etc.), rather than the industry in which they worked.

This form of organization was least regressive in the building trades, where there was the least mechanization and erosion of the traditional skill cat-egories—and where the industry consisted of a large number of small contrac-tors who were generally less well organized than the workers.[8] But in the rapidly developing manufacturing industries where the unskilled were replac-ing the skilled at a steady and rapid rate, craft unionism protected only a small elite group of workers. Since the skilled union members were usually native Americans and the unskilled usually immigrants, this meant that craft unions divided workers along lines of national origin.

The craft form of organization was a carry-over from the old pre-industrial guilds and was inappropriate as a defensive organization for workers in mechanized industry. But craft unionists had been able to build stable unions during the period of rapid mechanization because skilled workers had pride in their crafts and confronted an immediate attack on their status and their income—both of which they consciously but unsuccessfully defended.

Organizing all workers in a given industry into the same union made much more sense both as a means of defense against the increasingly degrading and oppressive working and living conditions of the early twentieth century and as a means of preparing the workers to carry out the revolution. In his initial remarks to the Founding Convention, Haywood called the gathering the Continental Congress of the working class, and declared that the IWW would "open wide its doors to every man that earns his livelihood either by his brain or his muscle." This intention was widely shared by those present, regardless of their politics. Debs asserted that the IWW was formed "for the purpose of uniting the working class," and would be "broad enough to embrace every honest worker." And Charles O. Sherman, the IWW's first (and only) president, said the IWW did not propose "to organize only the common man with the callous hands," but also the clerical force: "We want the soft hands that only get $40.00 a month, those fellows with the No. 10 cuffs and collars."[9]

The founders of the IWW did not think of themselves as organizers of a union with no existing support. The Western Federation of Miners (WFM) and its offspring, the American Labor Union, were instrumental in establishing the new union, and even though the WFM's 27,000 membership made it by far the largest affiliate, it participated in the hope of finding allies and of creating a coalition of powerful unions. The IWW intended to organize the unorganized, but it hoped to include not only the WFM and the ALU, but also the Socialist-led and industrially organized Brewery Workers Union, which was still affiliated with the AFL in 1905. The Brewery Workers Union had long been an irritant within the Federation because it insisted on organizing the coopers (barrel makers), firemen, engineers, and teamsters in the brewing industry in the face of claims of the unions in each craft to jurisdiction over these workers. By 1907 the issue had come to a head and the Brewery Workers were expelled from the AFL. Even then, however, the Brewers did not seriously consider joining the IWW. This was because they, like the WFM, needed support from organized workers—specifically for the union label on beer, and for their boycott of non-union beer—and most organized workers were in AFL affiliates. Instead of joining the IWW when they were expelled from the AFL, the Brewers sought and reached a compromise with the Teamsters and other craft unions, and won readmission in 1908.[10]

The inability to win over the Brewers was indicative of IWW weakness. Part of the difficulty lay in the diversity of political tendencies and in the resulting factional squabbling with which the IWW was saddled. That the two strongest tendencies were an "anti-political" syndicalism (opposition to all political parties) and the Socialist Labor Party group led by Daniel De Leon made matters worse. Both these groups were anathema to the Socialist-led Brewers, and also to the Socialist-led Western Federation. Partly because of the weakness of the IWW, symbolized by the Brewers' return to the AFL, and partly because of developing anti–Socialist party attitudes (at the 1906 IWW convention, the IWW instructed its Denver local to withdraw support from Big Bill Haywood, who was the Socialist party candidate for governor of Colorado while he was on trial for the murder of ex-governor Steunenberg in Idaho), the Western Federation of Miners quickly lost interest in the IWW and withdrew in 1908.[11]

The failure to win over the Brewers and then the loss of the WFM reduced the IWW to minor importance as a potential rival to the AFL. From 1905 to 1909 the new union met with almost unrelieved failure and appeared moribund. Debs and Algie M. Simons, another leading Socialist, had dropped out by 1908 for the same reasons that prompted the WFM to quit. Debs had hoped that Socialist trade unionists would help swing their respective unions into the IWW and that it could start out with substantial organized support as well as some success at organizing. But most Socialists, particularly those active in the unions of their craft, greeted the IWW with hostility. The most vociferous opponents of the IWW within the Socialist party were Victor Berger of Milwaukee (whose political base was among Brewers) and Max Hayes, a Typographical Union leader in Cleveland. The opponents viewed the IWW simply as a dual union—one that sought to disrupt the existing AFL unions by competing for their members. Their perspective was to work within the AFL and eventually to convert it to the industrial form of organization.

Just as the IWW appeared headed for oblivion it got involved, almost fortuitously, in the first of the series of spectacular strikes that made it famous. This was the Pressed Steel Car Company strike in McKees Rocks, Pennsylvania, in 1909. The Pressed Steel Car Company was organized in 1899 in a merger of the two leading American railroad car building firms. It introduced assembly-line mass production into the industry, which it dominated, and was militantly anti-union. The strike was initiated over long-standing grievances by the unskilled immigrants who made up the bulk of the labor force. Wages had been cut during the 1907 panic but had not been restored by 1909 to pre-1907 levels. Piecework rates and continual speed-up, as well as a punitive wage-pooling system (which limited wage rates to that of the slowest and least efficient worker in the pool), further reduced pay. Some workers received less than a dollar a day. In addition, living conditions in the company-owned houses were extremely bad.

The workers belonged to no union and there were no organizers in McKees Rocks, but conditions were so intolerable that the unskilled workers simply walked off their jobs on July 13, 1909. They were joined by the native-born skilled workers, who although they were unaffected by the wage-pooling arrangement also had grievances against the company. Public sympathy for the strikers was widespread at first. Even respectable and influential sectors of the Pittsburgh community supported the strikers with funds. But public support was tied to the participation in the strike of the skilled native-born workers, whose grievances were fewer and more limited than the immigrants'. The company soon perceived that it could deal with the skilled workers while ignoring the more expensive demands of the unskilled. In turn, the native-born workers were more conservative. When the company brought in strike breakers the unskilled formed mass picketing corps and prepared to fight the scabs—and the state police. At this the skilled workers balked. They quickly accepted the terms offered them by the company and on July 31, two weeks after the strike started, the leaders of the skilled workers announced that they had settled with the company.

Only then, when the mass of unskilled immigrants had been abandoned by the native-born skilled workers and had no other outside resources, did the IWW enter the strike. Until August 5, three weeks after the strike began, there had been no sign of the IWW in McKees Rocks, and no reference to the strike in the *Industrial Worker,* the IWW newspaper. The IWW had been called upon only after the better-organized skilled workers had settled with the company, and other unions had refused help. Its entrance into the situation increased the distance between skilled and unskilled, native and foreign born. IWW organizers helped to unify the immigrants—its organizers spoke in ten languages to the strikers. Its presence, and the possibility of a mass revolutionary union that its presence conjured up, spurred the company to reach a compromise with the unskilled workers that at first appeared to be a victory for them and the IWW.

But in early September the workers returned to their jobs only to discover that conditions remained substantially unchanged.

In the face of this betrayal, the IWW general organizer, William Trautmann, prepared to hold mass meetings to revive the strike and ensure solidarity. To prevent this, the leader of the skilled workers filed a complaint against Trautmann and had him jailed; but another IWW organizer quickly replaced Trautmann and on September 15, four thousand workers walked off their jobs. This time the company quickly mobilized its skilled workers to defeat the strike. They heckled strike meetings and demanded that the immigrants act like American citizens. On September 16, the leader of the skilled workers headed a march of some two thousand workers, behind a giant American flag, toward the plant gate and the massed pickets. When the procession approached, the picket line parted and the marchers peacefully entered the factory, ending the strike.

The strike was over, but the IWW claimed to have gained five thousand members in the newly created Car Builders Industrial Union No. 229. Joe Ettor, an IWW organizer, was enthusiastic about IWW prospects in Western Pennsylvania. By late October Ettor reported success in organizing among Poles, Slovenians, Germans, Czechs, Hungarians, Croatians, and other nationalities. "If I am not mistaken," he declared, "things and men will move around here. History will be made, and, let's hope, so fast that we shall have no time to write about it." And quickly there were strikes in New Castle and Butler steel plants. But just as quickly these were squelched and ended in total failure. So, too, did IWW organizing efforts in the area. Three years later, in August 1912, when Trautmann tried to reorganize the McKees Rocks local he could get only twenty signatures on a local charter application.

The pattern established at McKees Rocks was repeated often during the next four years, sometimes with success—in the sense of an immediate victory for the workers—more often not. The most famous of these strikes, which was also the greatest victory, occurred in the textile mills of Lawrence, Massachusetts, in 1912. Once again, the strikers were overwhelmingly unskilled immigrants of several nationalities, and again the cause of the strike was a wage cut in the face of already intolerably low pay. The specific incident that set off the strike was the enactment of a fifty-four-hour maximum work week by the state of Massachusetts, reducing the then current week in the mills by two hours. The workers expected that wages would be raised proportionately so that take-home pay would remain the same, but the companies retained the old wage rate, thereby cutting the workers' income.

The first workers to stop work were a group of Polish women. They were followed by a group of Italians, who not only quit work but proceeded to march through their own mill and then others, calling workers off their jobs. The day before this happened—January 10, 1912—the Italian branch of the small IWW local in Lawrence had invited Joe Ettor to come and to help organize a protest. Ettor arrived after the first walkout (on Saturday, January 13) and immediately started agitating for a full-scale strike. His success was clear on Monday morning when an immense crowd stormed City Hall. Ettor and Arturo Giovanitti, a poet, syndicalist, and Wobbly organizer, were the main leaders of the strike in its initial stage.

When Ettor and Giovanitti were jailed on trumped-up murder charges (of a young woman striker who was probably shot by the police), Big Bill Haywood and Elizabeth Gurley Flynn were called in. They then led the strikers to a startling victory—one that was achieved in the face of constant provocation, by the repudiation of violence and a reliance on a disciplined unity thought impossible with such a diverse work force.

The Lawrence strike was not the first textile strike in New England in which the IWW had participated. In 1907 the union had led a walkout in Skowhegan, Maine; in 1910 it sparked a strike in New Bedford; and in 1911 Local No. 20 of the National Industrial Union of Textile Workers, IWW, had engaged in several strikes in Lawrence itself. For several years the IWW had tried to organize Lawrence textile workers, and had succeeded to the extent of establishing a small local with Italian and French-Canadian branches. But on the eve of the big strike no stable union existed; while the IWW was known to many workers, it had no significant following. As in McKees Rocks, the IWW became a major force in Lawrence only after the strike had begun and the workers needed the organizing skills and experience of people like Ettor, Haywood, and Flynn.

The Lawrence strike was the first major IWW strike in the textile industry and its most famous victory. It was unusual in the large number of women and children involved, and in the degree of cooperation between the IWW and the Socialist party. As always, the IWW, in contrast to the AFL, did not seek union recognition or a contract with the employers. But standard trade union demands were made. Under IWW leadership, the strike committee demanded a fifteen per cent wage increase, double pay for overtime, the elimination of objectionable aspects of a piecework premium system, and no discrimination or retaliation against strikers or strike leaders. Nor, contrary to its general stance, did it introduce revolutionary propaganda during the strike. The IWW sought simply to help the workers win a victory on their own terms, although most IWW members did believe that the experience of the strike would lead to the development of revolutionary consciousness among the workers.

The existence of an IWW local in Lawrence for some time before the strike helped the union by providing some experienced leadership already on the scene, particularly in the Italian branch. And it may also have helped the strikers in a negative sense. IWW presence may have helped to disarm the mill owners and managers, since early IWW agitation had produced such meager results. In any case, the companies did not expect the strike to last long and therefore did not bring in strikebreakers, as the corporation at McKees Rocks had done. Interestingly, one of the reasons given by the employers for believing that the workers had no deep-seated grievances was the fact that so many workers had savings accounts—even though many were earning less than a dollar a day. What this reflected, of course, was not satisfaction but a deeply held ethic among workers, and particularly among the newly proletarianized immigrants. Many workers starved and skimped in order to accumulate enough money to return to Europe and buy land; others did so in order to escape the working class by becoming petty entrepreneurs of one kind or another.

For the first several weeks of the strike the mill owners consistently underestimated the depth of the workers' discontent as well as their ability to continue a disciplined unity. Attempts were made to provoke the strikers, and also to smear them as violent. Early in the strike, police found several caches of dynamite, and the newspapers immediately proclaimed a conspiracy of immigrant Wobblies, intent on revolution. But much to the authorities' dismay, it turned out that a local businessman and school board member had planted the dynamite to turn public sentiment against the strikers—and later a contractor for the American Woolen Company admitted that the scheme had been the idea of the president of the company.

It was true that the strike had begun with violence. On the first day the Italian workers in the Wood mill of the American Woolen Company had damaged machinery, and other strikers had smashed windows in other factories. There were also early clashes with the police, including the one in which a woman striker was killed. But when Ettor was called in, he exerted his influence to reduce the violence. "By all means make this strike as peaceful as possible," he advised. "In the last analysis all the blood spilled will be your own." Haywood, too, insisted that the workers keep their hands in their pockets.

Despite Ettor, Haywood, Flynn, and the other IWW organizers, violence continued in Lawrence. But it was violence directed against the strikers by the local police and the state militia—and it won for the strikers and for the IWW a widespread and decisive public support.

For the IWW, as a self-proclaimed revolutionary organization, violence and public support had a different meaning than they did for the AFL and other unions that accepted the prevailing framework of large-scale corporate capitalism. Although various IWW leaders and sympathizers often spoke and acted as if public support were irrelevant, and although they enjoyed advocating sabotage—especially in debates with more cautious socialists—in practice the IWW was much less likely to use violent means than were the conservative trade unionists. The reasons for this are not hard to find. The trade unions accepted the system and sought union recognition, collective bargaining, and time contracts (under which they accepted part of the responsibility for disciplining the work force). They represented no profound threat to the employers, particularly in the less competitive industries, and so whether or not an AFL union won out was often a matter of what was more expensive (or disruptive) to the employer. AFL unions publicly repudiated violence, but at times resorted to dynamite and other clandestine destruction in order to coerce recognition (particularly in the building trades). This form of coercion was not as readily available to the IWW, precisely because it presented itself as revolutionary and refused to cooperate once an agreement with the employer was reached.

The mere presence of the IWW in a community gave rise to widespread fears of "revolution"—fears shared in and also promoted by the employers—and in that situation, violence, except when clearly used against the strikers, quickly created an atmosphere in which the IWW could be suppressed, legally or extra-legally, by local authorities or company police. Thus, for the IWW, the only forms of coercion available were disciplined unity among the workers and the pressure of favorable public opinion, both of which it consistently sought.

At Lawrence, the nature of the work force helped to inspire the IWW's main public relations scheme, one that also had the virtue of helping to reduce the heavy burden of providing relief to the strikers as the weeks wore on. At the end of January (three weeks after the strike began), Italian Socialists in New York suggested that strikers' children (some of whom were also strikers) be sent away from Lawrence to be cared for by sympathetic comrades. The *New York Call,* Socialist party New York daily, promoted the idea and hundreds of Socialists offered to take children for the duration of the strike. Children were then selected and given new clothes and a medical examination. On February 11 Margaret Sanger, then a Socialist, picked up 119 children, aged five to fifteen, and brought them to New York, where they were greeted by a huge crowd of working people and reformers. The result was nationwide publicity and sympathy for the strikers, and so children's pilgrimages were arranged by other groups of sympathizers in New York, Philadelphia, Jersey City, and Barre, Vermont (headquarters of the Socialist-led Quarry Workers Union).

The success of the children's evacuation embarrassed and enraged company officials in Lawrence. As a result, the militia commander declared that no children would be allowed to leave without the written consent of their parents. When this was obtained by the strike committee, the city marshal ruled on February 22 that no more children would be allowed to leave under any circumstances. The strikers ignored this ruling, but two days later when a group of Philadelphia Socialists came to pick up two hundred children they were brutally attacked by the local police. The spectacle of policemen clubbing and trampling children and their mothers was too much, however. Victor Berger, Socialist congressman, demanded a congressional investigation, which gave the strikers more favorable publicity, and the governor of Massachusetts joined in, apologizing for the brutality of Lawrence's officials. At this point, with the strikers' ranks still solid, the companies gave in and came to terms with the strikers by granting most of their demands. On March 14 the strike ended in victory.

Immediately after the strike at Lawrence things looked good for the IWW. The local had sixteen thousand members and the IWW itself had gained a national reputation and won the cooperation of many outside the union, including the New York Socialists and Victor Berger. But the cooperation was soon to deteriorate, and it became clear that leading strikes, no matter how successful during the time of intense combat, was not the same as establishing a sustained and growing organization.

As at McKees Rocks, so at Lawrence the local soon dissipated, in this case to a few hundred members within a few months. Because the IWW had not sought union recognition through a contract, its members and other militants had no protection after they had gone back to work and things had settled back to normal. The Lawrence textile companies systematically retaliated against strike activists, both as individuals and by nationality. Nationalities loyal to the IWW (mostly Italians, Franco-Belgians, Syrians, and Poles) were laid off in large numbers, those more loyal to the companies (mostly Irish, but also French-Canadians) were not. The companies also singled out the militants and within two years not a single local strike leader remained at work in the mills.[12]

The Lawrence strike brought the IWW to its high point as a revolutionary organization, both because the strike itself was spectacular, massive, and successful, and because of the apparently unambiguous support given the strikers by Socialists and other radicals. But the success of Lawrence was never repeated. In the next year similar strikes occurred at Paterson, New Jersey, silk mills and in Akron, Ohio, rubber plants. Both were tenaciously and brutally opposed by the corporations and by state and local government authorities who feared the IWW not simply as a union but as a revolutionary force. The Paterson strikers attempted to reproduce the impact of the Lawrence children's evacuation by staging a giant pageant of the strike at Madison Square Garden. The pageant was a dramatic success but a financial failure and a drain on the energies of the strikers, who acted their own parts in the strike. After a long and often bloody struggle both the Paterson and Akron strikes were lost. They were to be the last of the IWW's major strikes in Eastern industrial centers.

Within the Socialist party, the Lawrence strike and other IWW activity forced a reconsideration of relations between party and union. Even before the Paterson and Akron strikes, party leaders who were oriented toward working within the AFL took steps to dissociate the party from the IWW. This was done in two steps. The first was the adoption of section two, article six of the Socialist party constitution at the convention in May 1912. This was the notorious "anti-sabotage" clause which called for expulsion from the party of any member who advocated crime, sabotage, or other methods of violence as weapons in the class struggle. The second, taken in 1913, was the recall of Haywood from his position as a member of the party's national executive committee. From the time of his acquittal in the Steunenberg murder trial, Haywood had devoted most of his time to the party. His prominence in the Lawrence strike brought him much closer to the center of the IWW, and the events in the party in 1912 and 1913 ended his career as a Socialist. From 1913 on, Haywood would devote all his considerable energies to the IWW.

The meaning of these events has been the subject of much factional infighting ever since 1912. IWW members believed that Haywood's recall proved that the Socialist party opposed industrial unionism and direct action. Many Socialists believed that Haywood was recalled because of his advocacy of violence. There was some truth in each belief, but the more important issues ran along different lines—and these have been obscured by the ideological writings of historians. On one side, Communist historians have taken the IWW side of the debate, while on the other, liberal historians have opposed violence and sided with the Socialists on this basis.[13] Violence was an issue in 1912, particularly because of the recent nationwide publicity given to the confession of John and James McNamara, two leaders of the conservative AFL Bridge and Structural Iron Workers, to the dynamiting of the *Los Angeles Times* building in which twenty workers were killed. But most Socialist leaders had other reasons for opposing an identification of the Party and the IWW, and these had been expressed vigorously since 1905.

That reason was dual unionism, and the fear that Socialists would become isolated from the main stream of organized labor. Victor Berger and Max Hayes were invited to the founding convention of the IWW, but refused to attend because they saw the IWW as sectarian. As Hayes explained, he did not wish to "cut loose and flock by ourselves" in new "secession movements and fratricidal wars" between workers' organizations. Hayes preferred to "agitate on the inside of the organizations now in existence," so as to "dump conservatism overboard." Other socialists argued that the Party should concentrate on winning over AFL unions and central labor councils, as the Socialists had done in Milwaukee.[14]

The prominence of Daniel De Leon in the newly formed IWW also raised fears of dual unionism, since he had created the Socialist Trades and Labor Alliance as the Socialist Labor Party's own dual union in opposition to the AFL. Indeed, many Socialists, including Hayes, Morris Hillquit and others, had split with De Leon on this issue in 1899, at which time they had quit the SLP and moved to form the Socialist party. These Socialists had successfully worked within the AFL and had even made some progress toward building industrial unions affiliated with it—such as the Western Federation of Miners, the Brewery Workers, and later the Amalgamated Clothing Workers. They did not support Gompers or the AFL relationship to the large corporations as symboli-zed by its membership in the National Civic Federation. They understood the AFL as a battleground on which the Socialists could contest for leadership of organized labor against the conservatives in control. As Victor Berger wrote just after the 1912 convention, the time to fight Gompers was "all the time, because the American labor movement will remain ultrareactionary as long as he has any influence."[15]

Socialists had fought over the IWW in 1905 when it was formed, but it became less of an issue within the party in the following years because of IWW weakness. The revival of concern about the IWW followed from its success at Lawrence and in the free speech fights on the West Coast,[16] along with an increasing number of incidents in which the IWW competed with existing unions, especially the United Mine Workers and the Western Feder-ation of Miners, for control of various locals. One of the strongest statements in opposition to this activity of the IWW came from Debs after he dropped his membership. In 1913, during a bitter coal strike in the Cabin Creek area of West Virginia, Debs had helped to settle the strike and had thereby gotten involved in a dispute with the IWW, which criticized him for his role. In a sharp retort, Debs reaffirmed his belief in industrial unionism, but declared that he was "not an industrial bummeryite." In West Virginia, he charged the IWW with "magnifying every petty complaint against the United Mine Workers and arousing suspicion against everyone connected with it." The IWW, said Debs, were "the real enemies of the working class," who had "never done one particle of organizing" in the "dangerous districts" of the state, though the UMW had "been on the job for years." The UMW was a stable organization "steadily evolving into a thoroughly industrial union." In contrast, Debs concluded, "never in a thousand years" would these "disrupters" succeed in unionizing the miners of West Virginia, or of "any other state."[17]

At stake immediately after Lawrence, in short, was not violence or non-violence, but whether Socialists would be able to continue working within the AFL. As long as the IWW appeared moribund this was no problem. With its apparent emergence as a growing union things became more difficult, especially as long as Haywood remained the central figure in the IWW while being a member of the party's national executive committee. Haywood's recall was the result partly of opposition to the advocacy of sabotage, and partly of hostility to dual unionism—of an intention not to be cut off from access to AFL unions, with their three million organized workers.

There was reason for preferring to retain access to the AFL. From 1909 through 1913 the IWW had led hundreds of thousands of strikers, yet in 1914—less than a year after the Paterson strike—the entire IWW had only thirty thousand members in good standing, and of these, twenty-five thousand were part of the newly affiliated Marine Firemen, Oilers, and Water Tenders' Union. This situation prompted long-time IWW executive board member Ben Wil-liams to complain that the IWW was to the labor movement "what the highdiver is to the circus. A sensation, marvelous and ever-thrilling." But that "as far as making Industrial Unionism fit the everyday life of the workers" it had "failed miserably."[18]

Williams' complaint was essentially accurate. While the IWW correctly perceived the pitfalls of collective bargaining and time contracts, it provided no alternative to AFL trade unionism other than the idea of industrial, as opposed to craft, organization. Years later—in 1936—the CIO would recreate the AFL along industrial lines, but the IWW could not realize its ideal because it provided no form of organization that allowed for a sustained relationship between the union and the workers in any industry. The exception to this was among the lumber workers in the Northwest and the migratory agricultural workers in the Central states—industries in which the work was seasonal and the work force transitory. And even there IWW success was limited to the early war years when the labor market was exceptionally tight and wartime repression had not yet begun.

The seasonal nature of the work provided the opportunity for prolonged periods of contact with the workers during the winter, when they gathered in the cities with little to do. Most cities in the Northwest provided no social services. In their place, IWW halls became social centers, served as libraries, and in other ways serviced the temporarily unemployed lumber workers. It was away from the place of work, in these various headquarters, that scores of workers heard and discussed IWW lectures for weeks or months at a time, and came to absorb the union's revolutionary ideal. But in their actual organizing work, and especially in the strikes that made the IWW famous, the union gradually replaced a revolutionary outlook with militant but narrow actions in support of immediate demands.

After Haywood assumed direction of the IWW in 1914 (he succeeded Vincent St. John as general secretary) the separation of the union's revolutionary outlook from its day-to-day organizing increased. Just as the Socialists were unable to devise a program that allowed them to go much beyond the liberal reforms of the Progressive Era while retaining popular support, so were the Wobblies unable to go beyond traditional trade union demands when they finally began to organize large numbers of workers into relatively stable unions in 1916 and 1917. Starting in 1915, the Agricultural Workers Organization of the IWW organized tens of thousands of migratory workers in the Great Plains states, while the Lumber Workers Industrial Union had similar success in the Northwest. But as Dubofsky notes, the IWW under Haywood "increasingly addressed itself to higher wages and shorter workdays, to improved conditions of life and job security; and it said less and less about revolutions to come and utopias to be."[19] Believing that revolution would come about simply by fighting for the immediate interest of workers as workers (rather than as revolutionaries whose purpose was to destroy class society), the IWW under Haywood's leadership concentrated on developing tactics that would provide the greatest unity in the struggle at hand. Such an approach inevitably required a concentration on immediate economic issues and a subordination of more general political questions—such as the war, or the nature of capitalism as a social system.

As Dubofsky and Conlin each point out, Haywood centralized and more efficiently organized the IWW. This bureaucratic internal administration did not strengthen the union in the two years following the Paterson defeat in 1913. Indeed, in these two years of severe depression the IWW declined even more sharply than the Socialist party (whose post-1912 slump has been attributed by most historians to the recall of Haywood from the party's national executive committee in 1913). When the IWW began its rebirth in late 1915–1916 it was not on the basis of spectacular strikes or free speech fights, but was the result of the business-like organizing of migratory agricultural workers and lumber workers. In these years the severe labor shortages of the wartime boom forced employers to deal with the hated IWW or cease operations, and so the union grew to some one hundred thousand—a figure never before approached.

If the heyday of the IWW—1916-1917—was the result of wartime labor shortages, so, too, was the war the union's undoing. Even though it did not follow the Socialist party's lead in opposing American involvement, the government moved to smash the IWW soon after the United States entered the European conflict (April 1917). Like the Socialists, most IWW's understood the war as an imperialist contest in which workers had no interest. But Haywood, in a manner somewhat paralleling that of the trade union socialists in Europe, refused to condemn the war and even modified the IWW's pre-war songs and pamphlets so as to eliminate their anti-war sentiments. Nevertheless, the Wilson administration seized the wartime opportunity to smash the IWW by prosecuting the entire union leadership under the wartime Espionage and Sedition acts. Anathema because of its militancy and revolutionary rhetoric, the IWW could neither expect nor find protection by staying within the law. As a result it got the worst of it both ways. It surrendered the political struggle and was destroyed by the government acting under the cloak of the law.

The IWW declined to oppose the war because it thought that such "political" action would divert it from the class struggle—by which it meant the fight to improve immediate conditions of workers. IWW experience in the Northwest, however, clearly illustrated the limitations of its understanding. There an apparently successful fight by the IWW for the eight-hour day in the lumber industry was turned into disaster for the union when the federal government stepped in, imposed an eight-hour day on the industry, and set up its own "union"—the Loyal Legion of Loggers and Lumbermen—while another arm of the federal government was busy arresting and trying scores of IWW leaders for sedition. In contrast, precisely because it based its politics on opposition to the capitalist war, the Socialist party gained in popular support and in strength during the war, despite similar repression at the hands of the government.[20]

III

At the founding convention of the IWW in 1905 those present had expected to win substantial affiliates away from the AFL and then to organize the mass of unskilled industrial workers, including lumber workers, into stable revolution-ary unions. In his major address to the convention, Haywood declared that the new organization proposed to provide a decent livelihood for every working man and woman, and that in struggling toward that goal it would recognize neither race nor creed, color nor sex. Initially, the IWW stood for the organization of "every man and woman, and, if necessary, child, that is working for wages with either brain or muscle." This included not only "the men who worked in sewers," Haywood insisted, but even "our journalistic friends here on this platform who think they are professional men."[21]

Haywood's emphasis, however, was on the organization of industrial workers. Increasingly, he explained, work was coming to consist of a series of machine-like operations that required little or no thought, but more and more unskilled workers. "Today," Haywood declared, "there are no skilled mechan-ics," while "in the packing house there are no butchers. There is a train of specialized men that do just their part, that is all."[22] Unlike the craft unions, which organized only the contracting sector of skilled workers, Haywood and others in the IWW intended to organize the increasing sector of the working class along with the contracting. For the revolutionaries in the IWW, industrial unionism appeared to be an essential means of developing a revolutionary class consciousness. Craft unionism increased competition among different groups of workers within a factory, mine, or railroad; industrial unionism would break down such differences, and, it was believed in a jump of logic, unite workers on a class-wide basis. Indeed, many Socialists and almost all IWW's believed that the experience of industrial unionism alone would be sufficient to create a successful proletarian revolutionary movement.

Neither the experience of the IWW nor the later experience of the CIO bore out these expectations, although when the IWW was organized there were substantial reasons for thinking that it might. In the latter half of the nineteenth century (the period of rapid industrialization) the process of capital accumulation had meant a steady relative and absolute increase in the industrial work force, a spontaneous opposition to the conditions of work and low wages by the newly proletarianized workers, and many bitter and violent strikes and insurrections. The depth of this spontaneous anti-capitalism among the farm boys, artisans, and others entering the rapidly expanding industrial work force became clear during the great railroad strikes of 1877. During the riots tens of thousands of railroad and factory workers poured out of their shops to attack company property, the police, and anyone or thing that threatened to stifle the expression of their anger. In Pittsburgh, where almost the entire city supported the workers, 104 locomotives, 2154 railroad cars, roundhouses, sheds, the depot, offices, and other railroad property were burned to the ground, along with the city's grain elevator and other buildings. When the elevator was under attack, an official of the elevator company argued that it was not railroad property and should be spared. But a striker yelled out: "It's owned by a damned monopoly—let it burn." And it did. The *Pittsburg Leader* quoted a striker as saying that even if "so-called law and order" should beat them down, "we would at least have our revenge on the men who have coined our sweat and muscle into millions for themselves" while leaving the workers to starve. And a militiaman reported that he could find but a single spirit and purpose among the strikers: "that they were justified in resorting to any means to break the power of the corporations."[23]

During this period of explosive, chaotic development, the granting of wage increases or other ameliorative improvements was usually understood by individual entrepreneurs and small corporations as a threat to their competitive positions, and therefore to their continued existence as capitalist enterprises. In this situation a wage increase could not be overcome by a price increase, unless all competing companies in a given industry simultaneously granted the same increase—which was virtually impossible given the large number of widely scattered competitors. Increases in wages could only come out of profits. That meant a slower rate of expansion and therefore a competitive disadvantage and possible bankruptcy. No wonder then that employers viewed unions as threats to their class position and resisted unionization so fiercely. And no wonder that radicals and revolutionaries saw the fight for union recognition and contractual agreement as inherently revolutionary.

These struggles, broadened and exacerbated by periodic economic collapses, were expected to lead to revolution. Instead they led to liberal corporate capitalism. The process of change was prolonged and not clearly apparent, even with hindsight, until the reforms of the Progressive Era. But even by the time of the Haymarket riots in 1886, the early spontaneous anti-corporatism was coming under control and the large corporation and conditions of quasi-monopoly, on which the political economy of corporate liberalism was based, were developing. With the rise of the large corporation, and particularly after the merger movement of 1897–1904, the meaning of trade unionism, at least to the larger manufacturers, began to change. By the early 1900s several of the basic industries were eliminating price competition by agreement among the major producers (as in the famous "Gary dinners" in the steel industry, at which Elbert H. Gary of United States Steel would announce the price of steel to be charged by his company, thereby setting prices for the coming year), or through federal regulation of rates, as in the railroad industry. In these industries increases in wages, either as a result of union organization or as a means of keeping the union out, could be and were passed on to the customers.

At the same time, as a result of the technological and policy changes that accompanied large-scale corporate manufacturing, the overall trends in the make-up of the labor force shifted. The proportion of factory wage earners did not continue to rise until it became a majority of the work force. New sectors grew rapidly. These trends did not become pronounced until the 1920s. That decade showed a movement of workers out of agriculture, fishing, lumbering and mining; a leveling off of the number of manufacturing workers, and a sharp increase in the number of workers in retailing, finance, education, other professions, domestic service, and government. Between 1920 and 1930 the number of manual workers rose only 7.9 per cent, while non-manual workers increased by 38.1 per cent—by 1930 there were 30.7 million manual and 14.5 non-manual workers. Agricultural and other extractive workers declined from 12.1 to 11.9 million; industrial workers remained at about 10.9 million; retailing, service, professional, and government workers increased from 11.5 to 16.7 million.[24]

These shifts were a consequence of rapid changes in technology involving the development of new machinery as well as new techniques of production. The increasing complexity of industrial production and of the means of distribution and sales promotion led to the need for larger and larger numbers of engineers and technicians of one kind or another. And as this process went on, the ability to continue expanding production became more and more integrally related to mass education, the development of new ethics of consumption, and problems of social control. The meaning of these changes as they affected the composition of the work force and the possibilities for revolution was, at best, but dimly understood by contemporaries.[25]

No one in the IWW perceived these developments, but Haywood did express an understanding that the increase of the unskilled industrial work force was not a one-way process. He saw machines taking the place of workers at an increasing rate. "There is not an employing capitalist," Haywood said, who, if possible, "would not operate his entire plant or factory by machines and dispose of every human being employed." This implied, as Haywood insisted, that the machine was rapidly taking the worker's place—"It will have you entirely displaced pretty soon." And it brought to the fore the underlying revolutionary purpose: once the machine had replaced workers, "who is going to own and control and manipulate and supervise that machine."[26]

But the organizing opportunities that actually were available to the IWW reinforced a narrow conception of the working class. More and more, it came to view the unskilled industrial and migratory workers as the only true proletarians and their primary needs—for a living wage and physically tolerable working conditions—as the central struggle. For example, the early free speech demonstrations came increasingly to be seen by the IWW as diversionary, rather than complementary activity. By 1917 the dominant tendency in the IWW was to ignore the war and to concentrate on immediate economic demands.

For revolutionary syndicalists (both in and outside of the IWW) all questions were subordinate to "the class question," which meant the immediate interests of workers on the job. And all problems would be solved once this sole revolutionary agent took power and established the cooperative commonwealth. These attitudes were most common among the syndicalists of the IWW and other splinter groups who increasingly combined them with anti-parliamentary attitudes. Thus Haywood in his "Blanket Stiff Philosophy" of late 1912 declared that the "scum proletariat" consisted of "lawyers, preachers, authors, lecturers, and intellectual non-producers generally" and was an "even more dangerous element than the lumpen proletariat."[27] One aspect of this "orthodox Marxist" outlook that continued to be important among revolutionaries was that movements that did not center in the workplace, such as the women's movement and the post–World War I black nationalist movements (particularly Garveyism), were seen as subordinate or contradictory to a developing revolutionary movement. Another aspect was that the increasing number of white collar workers, technicians, service workers, and the like were generally seen as middle class.

Long before the changes in the composition of the working class became apparent, other changes in the political economy combined to change the attitude of corporations toward "the labor question." By 1900 the AFL had consolidated its position as the first stable trade union federation by accommodating itself to the new corporate system and by restricting its activity to the narrow confines of "a fair day's pay for a fair day's work." But the corporatist outlook of Gompers and his supporters within the AFL was under attack by the Socialists within the AFL, as well as by the IWW on the outside. The organization of the Socialist party in 1901 and its rapid growth thereafter posed a threat to the continued conservatism and cooperation of the unions, raising the specter of a militant socialist, rather than a bureaucratic pro-capitalist, trade union movement. This awakened many businessmen to the advantages of a non-revolutionary union movement. At the same time, either through mergers or new technology, various corporations became able to make concessions that would reduce tensions on the job and social discontent in society at large. One form of these concessions was the development of welfare programs and voluntary wage increases or improvements of other kinds—usually in the face of agitation by the workers for improved conditions and union recognition, but sometimes for more directly political reasons.

International Harvester Company (producing eighty-five per cent of the country's harvesting machinery), for example, retained a strong anti-union policy from the time of its organization by J. P. Morgan in 1902 until the 1940s. Yet, as it had done in earlier labor disputes, the company made sweeping concessions on wages and hours during a strike in 1916. The work day was reduced from ten to nine hours and hourly rates were increased 11.1 per cent;

piece rates were increased in the same proportion; the minimum wage rate was increased five cents, to twenty-five cents per hour; and time-and-one-half was granted for overtime work. Three years earlier, the company had reduced hours of work for women in all its plants to fifty-five, after it had been forced to do so in its New York plants by a state law; it had also eliminated night work for women. At the same time, in the face of an investigation by the Illinois legislature into women's wages, the company instituted an $8 minimum weekly wage as "a humanitarian move voluntarily instituted."[28] At the time, International Harvester was being prosecuted under the Sherman Anti-Trust Law.

The United States Steel Corporation, another Morgan firm, also instituted welfare programs and maintained or voluntarily increased wages in order to prevent strikes and unionization—and to ward off anti-trust action by the government. Similarly, although without fear of government prosecution (the automobile industry was still highly competitive in the early 1900s), the Ford Motor Company voluntarily instituted an eight-hour day and a $5 daily minimum wage in 1914.

International Harvester, US Steel, and Ford were each in their own way pioneers in "welfarism," while pursuing strongly anti-union policies. US Steel changed its approach in 1936 when the CIO was organized, but Ford and International Harvester resisted unionism even after the great wave of organization by the CIO in the later 1930s. Nevertheless, by a combination of concessions and vigilant repression of pro-union workers within their plants, these companies and many others were able to keep their workers pacified, if not satisfied, until the mid-1930s.

Unions were accepted and viewed as beneficial in some industries where skills remained relatively unchanged or where for particular reasons there were strong union traditions. As the senior vice president of the New York Central Railroad wrote in 1908, "organized labor has done a tremendous work for labor," and at the same time, "by raising the standard of intelligence," was "beneficial to all interests." Certainly, he concluded, "this is true so far as it relates to organized railroad labor."[29] Similarly, in the brewing industry the employers used the union to stabilize their work force, as in the agreement between the international executive board of the Brewery Workers and the United States Brewers association jointly to finance and administer a workmen's compensation plan and a pension fund.[30]

Unions could also be advantageous in highly competitive industries. As a leading CIO left-winger has recently written in his memoirs, from World War I through the 1930s the Amalgamated Clothing Workers of America "did much to regulate a disorderly industry. It offered the bosses production experts, bank loans [from the Amalgamated Bank], a disciplined work force. It reduced cutthroat competition by stabilizing costs. It helped the manufacturers themselves to organize."[31]

Of course most employers, particularly those in manufacturing industry, continued to oppose unionization until after the initial organizing drives of the CIO in the late 1930s. But even during the 1900s and 1910s many corporations that chose not to deal with unions except under great compulsion had developed a new understanding of the meaning of unionism. When forced to recognize a union as the result of a successful strike, most companies did so calmly.

The AFL was able to survive as a stable and increasingly bureaucratic organization by accommodating itself to this situation, which meant abandoning unskilled production workers in many industries. The IWW and other revolutionary industrial unionists tended to see the AFL's response to this situation as a betrayal of the working class. This was partly true. The AFL leaders preferred to consolidate their own unions and positions of power, rather than risk these in attempting to organize workers in the mass production industries. But, as IWW's and socialists of various kinds were to find out (if not understand), once the large corporations came to see the necessity for making concessions to the workers, the revolutionary potential in unionism dissolved. Some corporations recognized unions with relatively little struggle, others kept out the unions but made concessions to the workers, and—as we have seen—when the IWW was involved, the government itself could step in and impose the conditions sought by the union, while destroying the union itself.

But expecting that the fight for improvement of conditions on the job would bring into the open the underlying class antagonisms inherent in capitalism, left-wingers in the IWW, and later in the CIO, fought militantly on the job around immediate issues. In doing so they eschewed "politics"—which would have meant building a movement not centered around the place of work and the immediate issues that arose there. But the struggle around these issues, rather than leading workers to a revolutionary consciousness, could more easily teach them to avoid unions whose purpose went beyond that of winning immediate demands, particularly if these unions were more fiercely resisted by employers and government alike.

The history of the IWW shows that workers did draw just such conclusions. They relied on the IWW almost exclusively in times of crisis, when the conservative unions refused aid. The experience of the CIO reinforced this conclusion. The CIO used Communists and others as militant organizers, but only in the context of assurances given by the union's leadership to corporations and government leaders. And the leftists within the unions prided themselves on being "responsible"—on following orders from the conservative CIO leaders and not raising the question of socialism within their unions.

In fulfilling the promise of the IWW—organization of the unskilled in the mass production industries—the CIO followed the political philosophy of the AFL. Once the basic organizing was done, the CIO could merge with the AFL, from which it had originally split. The IWW was saved from this fate by maintaining a consistently anti-capitalist attitude and by refusing to seek recognition in the form of contracts, or even to bargain collectively. The price paid by revolutionaries within the CIO for choosing their path was absorption into a liberal corporation (or being discarded when their organizing abilities were no longer needed). The price the IWW paid for its path was failure to become a stable mass movement.


IV

When the IWW was organized in the early 1900s, the relationship of the large corporations to the federal and state governments was in the initial stages of the developments that led to the New Deal and to post–World War II liberalism. That process was uneven and difficult to comprehend, since it did not have the full support of the large corporations, much less that of the entire business community. At first, reforms were limited to attempts at regulation of various kinds of business practices. By the second decade of the century there were also attempts to limit child labor, to guarantee compensation for industrial accidents (workmen's compensation laws), and to regulate working conditions and hours of work. These included the La Follette Seaman's Act of 1915, the Adamson Act of 1916 establishing the eight-hour day on railroads, and various state laws regulating hours of work for women. The leaders of the Progressive movement were coming to see stabilizing society and rationalizing and expanding production as the function of the capitalist state, as well as of individual employers or corporations. Of course, the state apparatus had always been used to maintain order and defend capitalist property, just as the several state and federal governments had subsidized particular businesses when it was deemed desirable for the general community of business (as in the subsidization of canal construction in the early 1800s and railroads then and after the Civil War). But the role of the state as a mediator among various interest groups on behalf of the large corporations was becoming more important.

Neither the IWW nor any other organization on the left understood the implications in these changes, but the Socialists at least understood the central importance of the state and the need to combat capitalism in its class (political) sphere as well as in the particular spheres of individual capitalists or corporations (the workplace).

In contrast, the various syndicalist groups, both in and out of the IWW, were increasingly anti-political. The most strongly "anti-political" tendencies did not necessarily belong to the IWW. William Z. Foster, for example, quit the IWW in 1911 to form his own Syndicalist League of America and to work within the AFL. Foster insisted that labor unions alone could represent the interests of the working class. He "bitterly" opposed the "international Socialist Party," which, he said, was "an interloper and parasite."[32]

When he left the IWW to enter the "main stream" of the labor movement, Foster managed to become secretary of the AFL organizing committee that led a successful strike to gain recognition for a union among packinghouse workers in Chicago stockyards in 1917. On the basis of that success Foster was appointed to lead the 1919 AFL attempt to organize the steel industry—which culminated in the Great Steel Strike of that year. From Foster's perspective the AFL was "making straight for the abolition of capitalism," and was "going incomparably faster toward this goal than any of the much-advertised, so-called revolutionary unions, in spite of the latter's glittering preambles."[33]

Within the IWW, at least until 1913, Haywood represented the other side of this general tendency. From 1907 (when he was acquitted of the Steunenberg murder) to 1913 (when he was recalled from its national executive committee) Haywood devoted his major energies to the Socialist party. But even then, as Joseph Conlin points out, Haywood and other socialist IWW's reserved a secondary role for the party. As Haywood said, "the labor union will come to stand for socialism," and the Socialist party will "become a mere phase of the labor movement."[34]

Although Haywood's views, and those of the IWW as an organization, diverged steadily from those of the Socialist party after 1912, their perspectives shared an underlying theory. Socialist parliamentarism was based on an evolutionary vision of the development of the industrial working class into a majority, and on the belief that the experience of capitalist oppression, both in the workplace and elsewhere, would "naturally" create a socialist conscious-ness. In this sense, parliamentarism was the equivalent of IWW belief in the natural development of revolutionary consciousness among workers thrown into union struggles. Both relied on a "natural" process of the growth of a revolutionary movement among industrial workers. The difference was over the manner in which power could be won—with the IWW vision being a general uprising of workers on the job and a seizure of the factories, and the Socialist vision being the winning of an electoral majority, and then either a voluntary or a forced transfer of power.

Within this shared understanding of capitalist development, the Socialist party's path gave it an added advantage: seeking electoral majorities meant seeking the broadest possible base of support consistent with developing socialist principles. The Socialists included among their constituency skilled and unskilled workers, journalists, Christian socialists, small and tenant farmers, while the IWW's experience—being wanted only where the trade unions would not go—gave it a continually narrower field of operation, and of vision. Furthermore, by the 1900s, when both the Socialist party and the IWW were organized, the spontaneous anti-capitalism of industrial workers was on the wane, while opposition to the social policies of the large corporations and awareness of the responsibility of a steadily more integrated society for regulating business practices were on the rise. In this situation the appeal of the Socialist party went well beyond the ranks of the industrial working class, while that of the IWW was to narrower and narrower sections of it.

But essentially both the IWW and the Socialist party—and indeed, all other revolutionary organizations of the period—shared the belief that the industrial working class was to be the key agent of revolutionary change, and that the experience of unionism was the primary path to a socialist consciousness. That understanding was only natural in a period in which unions were still fiercely resisted by employers and had not yet won recognition from either the federal government or the corporations as a legitimate and responsible interest group within a liberal corporate state.

NOTES

1. Karl Marx, *The Poverty of Philosophy* (New York, 1963), pp. 172-73. In later years Marx became less sanguine about this perspective, but it remained the implicit basis of his politics. In *Capital,* Marx wrote: "The advance of capitalism develops a working class, which by education, tradition, habit, looks upon the conditions of that mode of production as self-evident laws of nature. The organization of the capitalist process of production, once fully developed, breaks down all resistance." Vol. 1, p. 809.

2. Leninism shares both of these traditions. The primacy of the party is combined with a conception of seizure of power resembling a political general strike directed at the state apparatus rather than the factories. The strength of Leninism was its rejection of the evolutionary determinism of both parliamentary and economist socialism. For this reason, many Socialists viewed it as a departure from orthodox Marxism.

3. See Carl E. Shorske, *German Social Democracy, 1905-1917* (New York, 1955), for an account of this process.

4. See James Weinstein, *The Decline of Socialism in America, 1912-1925* (New York, 1967 and 1969), pp. 29-53.

5. Among the recent books on the IWW are Melvyn Dubofsky, *We Shall Be All: A History of the IWW* (Chicago, 1969); Joseph R. Conlin, *Big Bill Haywood and the Radical Union Movement* (Syracuse, 1969); Conlin, *Bread and Roses Too: Studies of the Wobblies* (Westport, Connecticut, 1969); Robert F. Tyler, *Rebels of the Woods* (Eugene, Oregon, 1967);

Patrick Renshaw, *Wobblies* (London, 1967); and Philip S. Foner, *The Industrial Workers of the World* (New York, 1965).

6. *Proceedings, the Founding Convention of the IWW* (New York, 1969), pp. 142–43.

7. *Ibid.*, p. 1.

8. John Hutchinson, *The Imperfect Union* (New York, 1970), pp. 25–27.

9. *Proceedings*, pp. 1, 143, 586.

10. John Laslett, *Labor and the Left* (New York, 1970), pp. 21–25.

11. *Ibid.*, pp. 263–65.

12. Dubofsky, pp. 255–58; Donald B. Cole, *Immigrant City: Lawrence, Massachusetts, 1845–1921* (Chapel Hill, 1963), chapter 10.

13. For the Communist version, see Foner, chapter 17; for the liberal view, see Daniel Bell, "Marxian Socialism in the United States," in Donald Egbert and Stow Persons, eds., *Socialism and American Life* (Princeton, 1952), pp. 286ff.

14. See Weinstein, *Decline*, pp. 32–33.

15. Berger to Job Harriman, Milwaukee, July ? 1912, Socialist Party papers, Milwaukee County Historical Society.

16. The free speech fights were a series of struggles by the IWW to establish the right of its members to hold public meetings and to speak in the streets of various cities on the West Coast. The pattern in a free speech fight consisted of an IWW organizer attempting to speak on a street corner, being arrested, then being immediately replaced by another organizer, until the local jails were overflowing and the expense of jailing, feeding, and trying the "offenders" too much for the city to sustain. In the successful free speech fights, IWW's won the right to speak in public. The first major such fight was in Spokane, Washington, in 1909. The last, in which the IWW was clearly defeated, was in San Diego in 1912. See Dubofsky, pp. 173–97.

17. Weinstein, *Decline*, pp. 34–35.

18. Dubofsky, pp. 287–90.

19. *Ibid.*, p. 346.

20. Nevertheless, despite the IWW's neutral position on the war, the effect of wartime developments was to bring the party and the IWW closer together in spirit. This was in large part of result of the total support given the war by the AFL, and particularly of its militant anti-socialism in these years. Victor Berger expressed the feeling shared by many Socialists in a letter to the Secretary of the IWW in May 1918, which he sent along with a contribution to their defense fund. "Frankly speaking," Berger wrote, "I did not think much of the Industrial Workers of the World and their tactics in the past and I do not agree with syndicalism as such today—but I will gladly admit that the IWW have stood the test of being a class organization infinitely better than the trade unions. Gompers' cohorts have in the main proved to be the tail end of capitalism. That tail end is now being used as a weapon of the capitalist class very much like the crocodile uses his tail.

"I am beginning to believe that the IWW (or some labor organization that will succeed it but that will inherit its matchless spirit) is destined to take the place of the American Federation of Labor in our country and fulfill the mission in which the AFL has failed." Berger to A. Wouri, Milwaukee, May 6, 1918, Socialist Party papers, box 8, Milwaukee County Historical Society.

21. *Proceedings*, p. 575.

22. *Ibid*, p. 579.

23. See Robert V. Bruce, *1877, Year of Violence* (Chicago, 1970), pp. 180, 176, 136, 182.

24. See Irving Bernstein, *The Lean Years* (Baltimore, 1966), pp. 55–63. Another indication of the impact of rising productivity was the substantial decline in the number of children employed in industry. In 1910, one of four boys between the ages of ten and fifteen, and one in eight girls of the same ages, worked to support themselves or their families. By 1920 only one of sixteen boys and one of thirty-three girls in the same age levels worked. As children left the labor market, and as older workers suffered increasing unemployment, the shift in the need for labor from manufacturing and extractive industries to retailing, service and other non-manual occupations pulled a larger number of women into the work force—from 8.3 million in 1920 to 10.6 million in 1930. The employment of more women did not reflect a shortage of industrial workers, which had been the meaning

of the large-scale employment of children in industry in earlier decades, but a shift of investment into new areas.

25. Thorstein Veblen was one of a few who pondered these developments. Alongside the development of a large unskilled work force, Veblen saw a growing strata of technicians and engineers, who, as hired hands, had no inherent loyalty to capitalism. Technicians and engineers were a new sector of the working class, essential because of the highly integrated political economy to any revolutionary movement. "No movement for the disposition of the vested interests in America," he wrote, "can hope for even temporary success unless it is undertaken by an organization that is competent to take over the country's productive industry as a whole, and to administer it from the start on a more efficient plan than that now pursued." Technicians were an essential part of a revolutionary movement, he argued, because revolutionaries would take over a highly complex and technically developed system of production and distribution, but Veblen did not think that the technicians could effect a revolution by themselves. While he did not see breaking down divisions of labor as the goal of a revolutionary movement, he argued the need for "solidarity of sentiment between technicians and the working force engaged in transportation and in the greater underlying industries," and also for active support from "trained workmen in the great generality of the mechanical industries." This was "nearly indispensable from the outset." Rejecting the idea that skills were simply breaking down and that the unskilled could alone make the revolution, Veblen scoffed at the IWW as an organization, in his elitist phrase, of "irresponsible wayfaring men of industry." To those who viewed the IWW as a revolutionary threat he remarked: "If there is any assertion to be made without fear of stumbling it will be, that this flotsam of industry is not organized to take over the highly technical duties involved in the administration of the industrial system." See Veblen, *The Engineers and the Price System* (New York, 1947), pp. 95, 167–68, 90.

26. *Proceedings*, p. 579.

27. Weinstein, *Decline*, p. 15.

28. Robert Ozanne, *A Century of Labor-Management Relations at McCormick and International Harvester* (Madison, Wisconsin, 1967), pp. 105–6, 101.

29. Quoted in Weinstein, *The Corporate Ideal in the Liberal State, 1900–1918* (Boston, 1969), p. 13.

30. Laslett, p. 53.

31. Len De Caux, *Labor Radical* (Boston, 1970), p. 337. De Caux was editor of the *CIO News* from 1937 to 1947. The Amalgamated established uniform work standards in cooperation with the employers, thereby aiding them to organize among themselves.

32. Earl C. Ford and W. Z. Foster, *Syndicalism* (Chicago, 1912).

33. *Ibid.*

34. *The Auto Worker*, August 1920, p. 7.

# revolutionary nationalism and the Afro-American

## HAROLD W. CRUSE

Harold W. Cruse, the author of *The Crisis of the Negro Intellectual,* argues for revolutionary black nationalism and accepts black capitalism as a means toward that end. His central point that self-determination is the essence of all colonial struggles is crucial to an understanding of contemporary differences within the black community. C. L. R. James, for example, was greatly influenced by Marcus Garvey, but ultimately rejected Garveyism and concluded that even black capitalism would not lead to the acquisition of political and economic power. James Boggs believes that in an effort to protect its capitalist institutions, "the white power structure is seeking once again to reenslave black people by offering them black capitalism." President Nixon's support of such organizations as NEGRO would seem to bolster that contention. They agree with Cruse that the black community should control its own existence, but argue that an alternative to the continued exploitation of black workers by corporate ownership is needed.

REVOLUTIONARY NATIONALISM AND WESTERN MARXISM

Many of western Marxism's fundamental theoretical formulations concerning revolution and nationalism are seriously challenged by the Cuban Revolution. American Marxism, which, since World War II, has undergone a progressive loss of influence and prestige, is challenged most profoundly. For, while most American Marxists assert that the Cuban Revolution substantiates their theories of nationalism, national liberation and revolution, in fact, the Cuban success is more nearly a *succes de circonstance.* Orthodox Marxists were unable to foresee it, and, indeed, they opposed Castro until the last minute. One would hope that such a development might cause American radicals to reevaluate their habitual methods of perceiving social realities, but in the spate of written analyses of the Cuban Revolution one looks in vain for a new idea or a fleeting spark of creative theoretical inspiration apropos of the situation in the United States.

Harold W. Cruse, "Revolutionary Nationalism and the Afro-American," *Studies on the Left,* Vol. II, no. 3 (1962), 12–25.

The term "Negro" was always in disrepute among the Nationalists and only recently among certain other groups and individuals in the ranks of unaffiliated "revolutionaries." The accepted term among some is "Afro-American." The term "Negro" is used throughout this essay because it it convenient and more generally recognized. It was not many years ago that the term "Afro-American" was condemned by Negro intellectuals and derided for smacking of "black nationalism."

The failure of American Marxists to work out a meaningful approach to revolutionary nationalism has special significance to the American Negro. For the Negro has a relationship to the dominant culture of the United States similar to that of colonies and semi-dependents to their particular foreign overseers: the Negro is the American problem of underdevelopment. The failure of American Marxists to understand the bond between the Negro and the colonial peoples of the world has led to their failure to develop theories that would be of value to Negroes in the United States.

As far as American Marxists are concerned, it appears that thirty-odd years of failure on the North American mainland are now being offered compensatory vindication "90 miles from home." With all due respect to the Marxists, however, the hard facts remain. Revolutionary nationalism has not waited for western Marxist thought to catch up with the realities of the "underdeveloped" world. From underdevelopment itself have come the indigenous schools of theory and practice for achieving independence. The liberation of the colonies before the socialist revolution in the west is not orthodox Marxism (although it might be called Maoism or Castroism). As long as American Marxists cannot deal with the implications of revolutionary nationalism, both abroad and at home, they will continue to play the role of revolutionaries by proxy.

The revolutionary initiative has passed to the colonial world, and in the United States is passing to the Negro, while western Marxists theorize, temporize and debate. The success of the colonial and semi-colonial revolutions is not now, if it ever was, dependent upon the prior success of the western proletariat. Indeed, the reverse may now be true; namely, that the success of the latter is aided by the weakening of the imperial outposts of western capitalism. What is true of the colonial world is also true of the Negro in the United States. Here, the Negro is the leading revolutionary force, independent and ahead of the Marxists in the development of a movement towards social change.

## THE AMERICAN NEGRO: A SUBJECT OF DOMESTIC COLONIALISM

The American Negro shares with colonial peoples many of the socioeconomic factors which form the material basis for present day revolutionary nationalism. Like the peoples of the underdeveloped countries, the Negro suffers in varying degree from hunger, illiteracy, disease, ties to the land, urban and semi-urban slums, cultural starvation, and the psychological reactions to being ruled over by others not of his kind. He experiences the tyranny imposed upon the lives of those who inhabit underdeveloped countries. In the words of a Mexican writer, Enrique Gonsales Pedrero, underdevelopment creates a situation where that which exists "only half exists," where "countries are almost countries, only fifty percent nations, and a man who inhabits these countries is a dependent being, a sub-man." Such a man depends "not on himself but on other men and other outside worlds that order him around, counsel and guide him like a newly born infant."*

From the beginning, the American Negro has existed as a colonial being. His enslavement coincided with the colonial expansion of European powers and was nothing more or less than a condition of domestic colonialism. Instead of

*Enrique Gonsales Pedrero, "Subdesarollo y Revolucion," *Casa de las Americas,* (August–September, 1960).

the United States establishing a colonial empire in Africa, it brought the colonial system home and installed it in the Southern states. When the Civil War broke up the slave system and the Negro was emancipated, he gained only partial freedom. Emancipation elevated him only to the position of a semi-dependent man, not to that of an equal or independent being.

The immense wealth and democratic pretensions of the American way of life have often served to obscure the real conditions under which the 18 to 20 million Negroes in the United States live. As a wage laborer or tenant farmer, the Negro is discriminated against and exploited. Those in the educated, professional, and intellectual classes suffer a similar fate. Except for a very small percentage of the Negro intelligentsia, the Negro functions in a sub-cultural world made up, usually of necessity, only of his own racial kind. This is much more than a problem of racial discrimination. It is a problem of political, economic, cultural, and administrative underdevelopment.

American Marxists, however, have never been able to understand the implications of the Negro's position in the social structure of the United States. They have no more been able to see the Negro as having revolutionary potentialities in his own right, than European Marxists could see the revolutionary aspirations of their colonials as being independent of, and not subordinate to, their own. If western Marxism had no adequate revolutionary theory for the colonies, it is likewise true that American Marxists have no adequate theory for the Negro. The belief of some American Marxists in a political alliance of Negroes and whites is based on a superficial assessment of the Negro's social status: the notion that the Negro is an integral part of the American nation in the same way as is the white working class. Although this idea of Negro and white "unity" is convenient in describing the American multi-national and multi-racial makeup, it cannot withstand a deeper analysis of the components which make American society what it is.

Negroes have never been equal to whites of any class in economic, social, cultural, or political status, and very few whites of any class have ever regarded them as such. The Negro is not really an integral part of the American nation beyond the convenient formal recognition that he lives within the borders of the United States. From the white's point of view, the Negro is not related to the "we," the Negro is the "they." This attitude assumes its most extreme expression in the Southern states and spreads out over the nation in varying modes of racial mores. The only factor which differentiates the Negro's status from that of a pure *colonial status* is that his position is maintained in the "home" country in close proximity to the dominant racial group.

It is not at all remarkable then, that the semi-colonial status of the Negro has given rise to nationalist movements. It would be surprising if it had not. Although Negro Nationalism today is a reflection of the revolutionary nationalism that is changing the world, the present nationalist movement stems from a tradition dating back to the period of the first World War.

Negro Nationalism came into its own at that time with the appearance of Marcus Garvey and his "Back to Africa" movement. Garvey mobilized large sections of the discontented urban petit-bourgeois and working class elements from the West Indies and the South into the greatest mass movement yet achieved in Negro history. The Garvey movement was *revolutionary nationalism* being expressed in the very heart of western capitalism. Despite the obvious parallels to colonial revolutions, however, Marxists of all parties not only rejected Garvey, but have traditionally ostracized Negro Nationalism.

American Marxism has neither understood the nature of Negro Nationalism, nor dealt with its roots in American society. When the Communists first promulgated the Negro question as a "national question" in 1928, they wanted a national question without nationalism. They posed the question mechanically because they did not really understand it. They relegated the "national" aspects of the Negro question to the "black belt" of the South, despite the fact that Garvey's "national movement" had been organized in 1916 in a northern urban center where the Negro was, according to the Communists, a "national minority," but not a "nation," as he was in the Southern states. Of course, the national character of the Negro has little to do with what part of the country he lives in. Wherever he lives, he is restricted. His "national boundaries" are the color of his skin, his racial characteristics, and the social conditions within his sub-cultural world.

The ramifications of the national and colonial question are clear only if the initial bourgeois character of national movements is understood. However, according to American Marxism, Negro movements do not have "bourgeois nationalist" beginnings. American Marxists have fabricated the term "Negro Liberation Movement"—an "all-class" affair united around a program of civil and political equality, the beginnings of which they approximately date back to the founding of the National Association for the Advancement of Colored People in 1909. True, the NAACP was, from its inception, and is still, a bourgeois movement. However, it is a distortion to characterize this particular organization as the sole repository of the beginnings of the Negro bourgeois movement. For, such a narrow analysis cannot explain how or why there are two divergent trends in Negro life today: pro-integration and anti-integration. That is to say, it does not explain the origins of the Nationalist wing, composed of black Nationalists, Black Muslims, and other minor Negro Nationalist groupings, as an outgrowth of basic conflicts within the early bourgeois movements (circa 1900), from which also developed the present day NAACP–Martin Luther King–student coalition.

Furthermore, the Marxian version of the NAACP's origins does not explain why the Nationalist wing and the NAACP wing oppose each other, or why the overwhelming majority of Negroes are "uncommitted" to either one. There is widespread dissatisfaction among various classes of Negroes with the NAACP's approach to racial problems. On the other hand, in recent years, the Nationalists have been gaining support and prestige among "uncommitted" Negroes. This is especially true of the Muslims, the newest Negro Nationalist phenomenon.

The rise of free African nations and the Cuban Revolution have, without a doubt, stirred up the latent nationalism of many Negroes. The popular acclaim given Fidel Castro by the working class Negroes of Harlem during his visit in the fall of 1960 demonstrated that the effects of the colonial revolutions are reaching the American Negro and arousing his nationalist impulses. Many Negroes, who are neither Nationalists nor supporters of the NAACP, are becoming impatient with the NAACP–Martin Luther King–Student legalistic and "passive resistance" tactics. They suspect that the long drawn out battle of attrition with which the NAACP integration movement is faced may very well end in no more than pyrrhic victories. They feel that racial integration, as a goal, lacks the tangible objectives needed to bring about genuine equality. After all, "social" and "racial" equality remain intangible goals unless they are related to the seizure and retention of objectives which can be used as levers to exert political, social, economic, and administrative power in society. Power cannot be wielded from integrated lunch counters, waiting rooms, schools, housing, baseball teams, or love affairs, even though these are social advances.

There emerges from this dilemma a recognizable third trend, personified in the case of Robert F. Williams. Williams was forced to take an anti-NAACP position, but he was not a Nationalist and was critical of the 'Marxists." As a rebel, Williams' objectives were the same as those of the NAACP; he differed only in his *approach*. However, his seeming "revolutionary" stance is thwarted by the same lack of substance that makes a program of "racial integration" unsatisfactory to many Negroes. Williams resorted to arms for *defense* purposes—but arms are superfluous in terms of the objectives of racial integration. Arms symbolize a step beyond mere "racial integration," to the seizure of actual centers of social power. The adherents of this third trend—young social rebels who are followers of Williams' Monroe Movement—are faced with this predicament. They are neither avowed Nationalists nor NAACPers. They consider themselves "revolutionary," but are shy of having revolutionary objectives.

However, they are not a force as yet, and their future importance will rest, no doubt, upon how much influence the Nationalist wing will exert in the Negro community. In short, the main trends in Negro life are becoming more and more polarized around the issues of pro and anti-integration.

## INTEGRATION VS. SEPARATION: HISTORY AND INTERPRETATIONS

Negro historiography does not offer a very clear explanation of how the Negro has become what he is today. As written, Negro history appears as a parade of lesser and greater personalities against a clamor of many contending anonymous voices and a welter of spasmodic trends all negating each other. Through the pages of Negro history the Negro marches, always arriving but never getting anywhere. His "national goals" are always receding.

Integration vs. separation have become polarized around two main wings of racial ideology, with fateful implications for the Negro movement and the country at large. Yet we are faced with a problem in racial ideology without any means of properly understanding how to deal with it. The dilemma arises from a lack of comprehension of the historical origins of the conflict.

Furthermore, the problem is complicated by a lack of recognition even that it exists. The fundamental economic and cultural issues at stake in this conflict cannot be dealt with by American sociologists for the simple reason that sociologists never admit that such issues should exist at all in American society. They talk of "Americanizing" all the varied racial elements in the United States; however, when it is clear that certain racial elements are *not* being "Americanized," socially, economically, or culturally, the sociologists proffer nothing but total evasion, or more studies on the "nature of prejudice." Hence the problems remain with us in a neglected state of suspension until they break out in what are considered to be "negative," "anti-social," "anti-white," "anti-democratic" reactions.

One of the few attempts to bring a semblance of order to the dominant trends in the chaos of Negro history was made by Marxist historians in the 1930's and

1940's. However, it proved to be a one-sided analysis which failed to examine the class structure of the Negro people. Viewing Negro history as a parade from slavery to socialism, the Marxist historians favor certain Negro personalities uncritically while ignoring others who played vital roles. Major figures, such as Booker T. Washington and Marcus Garvey, who do not fit into the Communist stereotype of Negro heroes are ignored or downgraded. In the process, Marxist historians have further obscured the roots of the current conflict in racial ideology.

Under the aegis of other slogans, issues and rivalries, the pro-integration vs. anti-integration controversy first appeared at the turn of the century in the famous Booker T. Washington–W. E. B. DuBois debate. Washington's position was that the Negro had to achieve economic self-sufficiency before demanding his political rights. This position led Washington to take a less "militant" stand on civil rights than did other Negro leaders, such as DuBois, who accused Washington of compromising with the racists on the Negro's political position in the South.

It is not sufficient, however, to judge Washington purely on the political policies he advocated for the Negro in the South. For Washington gave voice to an important trend in Negro life, one that made him the most popular leader American Negroes have had. The Washington-DuBois controversy was not a debate between representatives of reaction and progress, as Communist historians have asserted, but over the correct tactics for the emerging Negro bourgeoisie.

From the Reconstruction era on, the would-be Negro bourgeoisie in the United States confronted unique difficulties quite unlike those experienced by the young bourgeoisie in colonial areas. As a class, the Negro bourgeoisie wanted liberty and equality, but *also* money, prestige, and political power. How to achieve all this within the American framework was a difficult problem, since the whites had a monopoly on these benefits of western civilization, and looked upon the new aspirants as interlopers and upstarts. The Negro bourgeoisie was trapped and stymied by the entrenched and expanding power of American capitalism. Unlike the situation in the colonial areas, the Negro could not seize the power he wanted or oust "foreigners." Hence, he turned inward toward organizations of fraternal, religious, nationalistic, educational and political natures. There was much frustrated bickering and internal conflict within this new class over strategy and tactics. Finally the issues boiled down to that of *politics vs. economics*, and emerged in the Washington-DuBois controversy.

In this context, it is clear that Washington's program for a "separate" Negro economy was not compatible with the idea of integration into the dominant white economy. In 1907 DuBois complained of Washington that:

He is striving nobly to make Negro artisans business men and property owners; but it is impossible, under modern competitive methods, for workingmen and property-owners to defend their rights and exist without the right of suffrage.

Yet, Washington could not logically seek participation in "white" politics in so far as such politics were a reflection of the mastery of whites in the surrounding economy. He reasoned that since Negroes had no chance to take part in the white world as producers and proprietors, what value was there is seeking political rights *immediately?* Herbert Aptheker, the leading Marxist authority on Negro history, quotes Washington as saying:

Brains, property, and character for the Negro will settle the question of civil rights. The best course to pursue in regard to a civil rights bill in the South is to let it alone; let it alone and it will settle itself. Good school teachers and plenty of money to pay them will be more potent in settling the race question than many civil rights bills and investigation committees.

This was the typical Washington attitude—a bourgeois attitude, practical and pragmatic, based on the expediencies of the situation. Washington sought to train and develop a new class. He had a longer range view than most of his contemporaries, and for his plans he wanted racial peace at any cost.

Few of the implications of this can be found in Marxist interpretations of Negro history. By taking a partisan position in favor of DuBois, Marxists dismiss the economic aspects of the question in favor of the purely political. However, this is the same as saying that the Negro bourgeoisie had no right to try to become capitalists—an idea that makes no historical sense whatsoever. If a small proprietor, native to an underdeveloped country, should want to oust foreign capitalists and take over his internal markets, why should not the Negro proprietor have the same desire? Of course, a substantial Negro bourgeoisie never developed in the United States. Although this fact obscured and complicated the problems of Negro Nationalism, it does not change the principles involved. Washington sought to develop a Negro bourgeoisie. He failed. But his failure was no greater than that of those who sought equality through politics.

Washington's role in developing an economic program to counteract the Negro's position is central to the emergence of Negro Nationalism, and accounts for much of his popularity among Negroes. Yet Aptheker makes the error of assessing Washington purely on political grounds. On this basis, of course, Aptheker finds him not "revolutionary" or "militant" in the fashion that befits a Negro leader, past or present. He rejects the historico-economic-class basis of Washington's philosophy, although these are essential in analyzing social movements, personalities, or historical situations. Aptheker has not seen Washington in the light of what he was: the leading spokesman and theoretician of the new Negro capitalists, whom he was trying to mold into existence. All that Aptheker has to say about Washington is summed up by him as follows:

Mr. Washington's policy amounted objectively to an acceptance by the Negro of second class citizenship. His appearance on the historical stage and the growth of his influence coincided with and reflected the propertied interests' resistance to the farmers and workers' great protest movements in the generations spanning the close of the nineteenth and the opening of the twentieth centuries. American imperialism conquers the South during these years and Mr. Washington's program of industrial education, ultra-gradualism and opposition to independent political activity and trade unionism assisted in this conquest.

Thus is the Marxian schema about the "Negro people" projected back into history—a people without classes or differing class interests. It is naive to believe that any aspiring member of the bourgeoisie would have been interested in trade-unionism and the political action of farmers. But American Marxists cannot "see" the Negro at all unless he is storming the barricades, either in the present or in history. Does it make any sense to look back into history and expect to find Negroes involved in trade-unionism and political action in the most lynch-ridden decade the South has ever known? Anyone reading about the South at the turn of the century must wonder how Negroes managed to survive at all, let alone become involved in political activity when such politics was dominated by the Ku Klux Klan. According to Aptheker, however, the Negroes who supported Washington were wrong. It was the handful of Negro militants from above the Mason-Dixon line who had never known slavery, who had never known Southern poverty and illiteracy, the whip of the lynch-mad KKK, or the peasant's agony of landlessness, who were correct in their high-sounding idealistic criticism of Washington. These were, Aptheker tells us, within a politically revolutionary tradition—a tradition which had not even emerged when Washington died!

After the Washington-DuBois debate, DuBois went on to help form the NAACP in 1909. Washington died in 1915. The controversy continued, however, in the conflict between the NAACP and the Garvey movement.

In 1916, Marcus Garvey, the West Indian-born Nationalist, organized his "Back to Africa" movement in the United States. Garvey had, from his earliest years, been deeply influenced by the racial and economic philosophies of Booker T. Washington. Adopting what he wanted from Washington's ideas, Garvey carried them further—advocating Negro self-sufficiency in the United States linked, this time, with the idea of regaining access to the African homeland, as a basis for constructing a viable black economy. Whereas Washington had earlier chosen an accommodationist position in the South to achieve his objectives, Garvey added the racial ingredient of Black Nationalism to Washington's ideas with potent effect. This development paralleled the bourgeois origins of the colonial revolutions then in their initial stages in Africa and Asia. Coming from a British colony, Garvey had the psychology of a colonial revolutionary and acted as such.

With the rise of Nationalism, DuBois and the NAACP took a strong stand against the Garvey Movement and against revolutionary nationalism. The issues were much deeper than mere rivalry between different factions for the leadership of Negro politics. The rise of Garvey Nationalism meant that the NAACP became the accommodationists and the Nationalists became the militants. From its very inception, the Negro bourgeois movement found itself deeply split over aims, ideology and tactics, growing out of its unique position of contending for its aims in the very heart of western capitalism.

Neither the nationalist side of the bourgeois movement nor the reformist NAACP wing, however, were able to vanquish the social barriers facing Negroes in the United States. The Garvey Movement found its answer in seeking a way out—"Back to Africa!" where the nationalist revolution had elbow room, where there was land, resources, sovereignty—all that the black man had been denied in the United States.

The Garvey era manifested the most self-conscious expression of nationality in the entire history of the Negro in the United States. To refrain from pointing this out, as Aptheker does in his essays on Negro history, is inexcusable. In his essay, "The Negro in World War I," Aptheker says: "What was the position of the Negro People during the years of Wilson's 'New Freedom'?" He then mentions the activities of the NAACP, the National Race Congress of 1915, and the formation in 1915 of the Association for the Study of Negro Life and History. But in discussing the racial unrest of the time, Aptheker fails to mention the Garvey movement, despite the fact that it had organized more

Negroes than any other organization in the three years following its establishment in 1916. The causes for these omissions are, of course, apparent: orthodox western Marxism cannot incorporate nationalism into its schema.

With the NAACP and the Garvey Movement growing apace, the "Negro People" had two "Negro Liberation Movements" to contend with. Never was an oppressed people so richly endowed with leadership; the only difficulty was that these two movements were at bitter odds with one another. Furthermore, within the Negro community, prejudice about lighter and darker skin coloring also served as a basis for class stratification. Thus, when retaliating against DuBois' criticisms of his movement, Garvey attacked him on the basis of his skin color, and assailed the assimilationist values of the upper class Negro leadership. In addition, the Garvey "blacks" and the NAACP "coloreds" disagreed as to which was the true "motherland"—black Africa or white America.

During the period when the Communists looked upon the Negro question as a national question, some Communist writers perceived the positive, as well as the negative, aspects of Garvey's appeal. Harry Haywood, for example, wrote that the Garvey movement "reflected the widening rift between the policies of the Negro bourgeois reformism and the life needs of the sorely pressed people." He sees in Garvey's "renunciation of the whole program of interracialism" a belief that the upper class Negro leadership was "motivated solely by their desire for cultural assimilation," and that they "banked their hopes for Negro equality on support from the white enemy." Haywood sympathized with this position, seeing in the "huge movement led by Garvey" a "deep feeling for the intrinsic national character of the Negro problem."

In 1959, the Communists withdrew the concept of "self-determination" in the black belt, and side-stepped the question of the Negro's "national character." Instead, they adopted a position essentially the same as the NAACP. Their present goal is to secure "with all speed" the "fullest realization of genuinely equal economic, political and social status with all other nationalities and individual citizens of the United States"—this to be accompanied by "genuinely representative government, with proportionate representation in the areas of Negro majority population in the South." This position is essentially no different from that supported by the NAACP.

Thus, it is not surprising that it is difficult to understand the present conflict within the Negro movement; the roots of the conflict have been obliterated. While most historians do not attempt at all to bring order to the chaos of Negro history, those that have—the Marxists—find it convenient from a theoretical standpoint to see Negroes in history as black proletarian "proto-types" and forerunners of the "black workers" who will participate in the proletarian revolution. This Aptheker–Communist Party mythology, created around a patronizing deification of Negro slave heroes (Denmark Vesey, Nat Turner, Sojourner Truth, Frederick Douglass, etc.), results in abstracting them from their proper historical context and making it appear that they are relevant to modern reality. Of course, there will be those Marxists who will argue that their inability to come to terms in theory with Negro Nationalism does not arise from an error in their interpretations of the role of the Negro bourgeoisie, of Washington, or of DuBois. They will defend all the historical romanticism and the sentimental slave hero worship of the Aptheker Cult. They will say that all this is "past history" and has no bearing on the "new situation." But if one takes this position, then of what value is history of any kind, and particularly, of what value is the Marxist historical method? The inability to view Negro history in a theoretical perspective leads to the inability to cope with the implications of Negro Nationalism.

## NEGRO NATIONALISM AND THE LEFT

To the extent that the myth of a uniform "Negro People" has endured, a clear understanding of the causes of Negro Nationalism has been prevented. In reality, no such uniformity exists. There *are* class divisions among Negroes, and it is misleading to maintain that the interests of the Negro working and middle classes are identical. To be sure, a middle class NAACP leader and an illiterate farmhand in Mississippi or a porter who lives in Harlem, all want civil rights. However, it would be far more enlightening to examine why the NAACP is not composed of Negro porters and farmhands, but only of Negroes of a certain "type."

What we must ask is why these classes are not all striving in the same directions and to the same degree of intensity. Why are some lagging behind the integration movement, and still others in conflict with it? Where is the integration movement going? Into what is the integration movement integrating? Is the Negro middle class integrating into the white middle class? Are integrated lunch counters and waiting stations commensurate with integration into the "mainstream of American life"? And what exactly *is* the "mainstream of American life"? Will the Negro ten percent of the population get ten percent representation in the local, state, and national legislatures?—or ten percent representation in the exclusive club of the "Power Elite"?

Why are some Negroes anti-integration, others pro-integration, and still others "uncommitted"? Why is there such a lack of real unity among different Negro classes toward one objective? Why are there only some 400,000 members in the NAACP out of a total Negro population of some 18 to 20 million? Why does this membership constantly fluctuate? Why is the NAACP called a "Negro" organization when it is an *interracial* organization? Why are the Negro Nationalist organizations "all Negro"? Why do Nationalist organizations have a far greater proportion of working class Negro membership than the NAACP? Finally, why is it that the Marxists, of all groups, are at this late date tail-ending organizations such as the NAACP (King, CORE, etc.), which do not have the broad support of Negro workers and farmers? We must consider why the interests of the Negro bourgeoisie have become separated from those of the Negro working classes.

Tracing the origins of the Negro bourgeoisie back to the Booker T. Washington period (circa 1900), E. Franklin Frazier, a Negro sociologist and non-Marxist scholar, came to the enlightening conclusion that "the black bourgeois lacks the economic basis that would give it roots in the world of reality." Frazier shows that *the failure of the Negro to establish an economic base in American society served to sever the Negro bourgeoisie, in its "slow and difficult occupational differentiation," from any economic, and therefore cultural and organizational ties with the Negro working class.* Since the Negro bourgeoisie does not, in the main, control the Negro "market" in the United States economy, and since it derives its income from whatever "integrated" occupational advantages it has achieved, it has neither developed a sense of association of its status with that of the Negro working class, nor a "community" of economic, political, or cultural interests conducive for cultivating "nationalistic sentiments." Today, except for the issue of "civil rights," no unity of interests exists between the Negro middle class and the Negro working class.

Furthermore, large segments of the modern Negro bourgeoisie have played a continually regressive "non-national" role in Negro affairs. Thriving off the crumbs of integration, these bourgeois elements have become de-racialized and de-cultured, leaving the Negro working class without voice or leadership, while serving the negative role of class buffer between the deprived working class and the white ruling elites. In this respect, such groups have become a social millstone around the necks of the Negro working class—a point which none of the militant phrases that accompany the racial integration movement down the road to "racial attrition" should be allowed to obscure.

The dilemma of the Negro intellectual in the United States results from the duality of his position. Detached from the Negro working class, he tries to "integrate" and to gain full membership in a stagnating and declining western society. At the same time, failing to gain entry to the status quo, he resorts to talking like a "revolutionary," championing revolutionary nationalism and its social dynamism in the underdeveloped world. But this gesture of flirting with the revolutionary nationalism of the non-west does not mask the fact that the American Negro intellectual is floating in ideological space. He is caught up in the world contradiction. Forced to face up to the colonial revolution and to make shallow propaganda out of it for himself, the American Negro intellectual is unable to cement his ties with the more racial-minded sections of the Negro working class. For, this would require him to take a nationalistic stand in American politics—which he is loath to do. Nevertheless, the impact of revolutionary nationalism in the non-western world is forcing certain Negro intellectuals to take a "nationalist" position in regard to their American situation.

Although Frazier does not delve into the nature of Nationalism or connect the rise of Nationalism with the failure of the Negro bourgeoisie to establish the "economic basis" of which he writes, it can be seen that the sense of a need for "economic self-sufficiency" is one of the causes for the persistence of nationalist groupings in Negro life. The attempt to organize and agitate for Negro ascendency in and control of the Negro market is expressed in such racial slogans as "Buy Black." The Negro nationalist ideology regards all the social ills from which Negroes suffer as being caused by the lack of economic control over the segregated Negro community. Since the Nationalists do not envision a time when whites will voluntarily end segregation, they feel that it is necessary to gain control of the economic welfare of the segregated Negro community. Moreover, many Negro Nationalists, such as the Black Muslims, actually believe that "racial separation" is in the best interests of both races. Others maintain this separatist position because of the fact of the persistence of segregation.

Thus, when Communists and other Marxists imply that "racial integration" represents an all class movement for liberation, it indicates that they have lost touch with the realities of Negro life. They fail to concern themselves with the mind of the working class Negro in the depths of the ghetto, or the nationalistic yearnings of those hundreds of thousands of ghetto Negroes whose every aspiration has been negated by white society. Instead, the Marxists gear their position to Negro middle class aspirations and ideology. Such Marxists support the position of the Negro bourgeoisie in denying, condemning, or ignoring the existence of Negro Nationalism in the United States—while regarding the reality of Nationalism in the colonial world as something peculiar to "exotic" peoples. The measure of the lack of appeal to the working classes of the Marxist movement is indicated by the fact that Negro Nationalist movements are basically working class in character while the new Negroes attracted to the Marxist movement are of bourgeois outlook and sympathies.

Ironically, even within Marxist organizations Negroes have had to function as a numerical minority, and were subordinated to the will of the white majority on all crucial matters of racial policy. What the Marxists called "Negro-white unity" within their organizations was, in reality, white domination. Thus, the Marxist movement took a position of favoring a "racial equality" that did not even exist within the organization of the movement itself.

Today, the Marxist organizations which advocate "racial integration" do not have a single objective for the Negro that is not advocated by the NAACP or some other reform organization. It is only by virtue of asserting the "necessity of socialism" that the Marxist movement is not altogether superfluous. It could not be otherwise. For Marxism has stripped the Negro question of every theoretical concern for the class, color, ethnic, economic, cultural, psychological, and "national" complexities. They have no program apart from uttering the visionary call for "integration plus socialism" or "socialism plus integration."

However, when Marxists speak of socialism to the Negro, they leave many young Negro social rebels unimpressed. Many concrete questions remain unanswered. What guarantee do Negroes have that socialism means racial equality any more than does "capitalist democracy"? Would socialism mean the assimilation of the Negro into the dominant racial group? Although this would be "racial democracy" of a kind, the Negro would wield no political power as a minority. If he desired to exert political power as a racial minority, he might, even under socialism, be accused of being "nationalistic." In other words, the failure of American capitalist abundance to help solve the crying problems of the Negro's existence cannot be fobbed off on some future socialist heaven.

We have learned that the *means* to the *end* are just as important as the end itself. In this regard, Marxists have always been very naive about the psychology of the Negro. It was always as easy matter for Marxists to find Negro careerists, social climbers, and parlor radicals to agree with the Marxist position on the Negro masses. However, it rarely occurred to Marxists that, to the average Negro, the *means* used by Marxists were as significant as the ends. Thus, except in times of national catastrophe (such as in the depression of the 30's), Marxist means, suitable only for bourgeois reform, seldom approximated the aspirations of the majority of Negroes. Lacking a working class character, Marxism in the United States cannot objectively analyze the role of the bourgeoisie or take a political position in Negro affairs that would be more in keeping with the aspirations of the masses.

The failure to deal adequately with the Negro question is the chief cause of American Marxism's ultimate alienation from the vital stream of American life. This political and theoretical deficiency poses a serious and vexing problem for the younger generation who today have become involved in political activity centered around the defense of Cuba. Some accept Marxism; others voice criticisms of Marxist parties as being "conservative," or otherwise limited in their grasp of present realities. All of these young people are more or less part of what is loosely called the "New Left" (a trend not limited to the United States).

It is now the responsibility of these new forces to find the new thinking and new approaches needed to cope with the old problems. Open-minded whites of the "New Left" must understand that Negro consciousness in the United States will be plagued with the conflict between the compulsions toward "integration" and the compulsions toward "separation." It is the inescapable result of semi-dependence.

The Negro in the United States can no more look to American Marxist schema than the colonials and semi-dependents could conform to the western Marxist time-table for revolutionary advances. Those on the American left who support revolutionary nationalism in Asia, Africa, and Latin America, must also accept the validity of Negro Nationalism in the United States. Is it not just as valid for Negro Nationalists to want to separate from American whites as it is for Cuban Nationalists to want to separate economically and politically from the United States? The answer cannot hinge merely on pragmatic practicalities. *It is a political question which involves the inherent right accruing to individuals, groups, nations and national minorities, i.e., the right of political separation from another political entity when joint existence is incompatible, coercive, unequal, or otherwise injurious to the rights of one or both. This is a principle that must be upheld, all expedient prejudices to the contrary.*

It is up to the Negro to take the organizational, political and economic steps necessary to raise and defend his status. The present situation in racial affairs will inevitably force nationalist movements to make demands which should be supported by people who are not Negro Nationalists. The Nationalists may be forced to demand the right of political separation. This too must be upheld because it is the surest means of achieving Federal action on all Negro demands of an economic or political nature. It will be the most direct means of publicizing the fact that the American government's policy on "underdeveloped" areas must be complemented by the same approach to Negro underdevelopment in the United States.

It is pointless to argue, as many do, that Negro Nationalism is an invalid ideology for Negroes to have in American life, or that the Nationalist ideas of "economic self-sufficiency" or the "separate Negro economy" are unrealistic or utopian. Perhaps they are, but it must be clearly understood that as long as racial segregation remains a built-in characteristic of American society, Nationalist ideology will continue to grow and spread. If allowed to spread unchecked and unameliorated, the end result can only be racial wars in the United States. This is no idle prophecy, for there are many convinced Negro Nationalists who maintain that the idea of the eventual acceptance of the Negro as a full-fledged American without regard to race, creed, or color is also utopian and will never be realized. These Nationalists are acting on their assumptions.

Can it be said, in all truth, that Nationalist groups such as the Black Muslims are being unrealistic when they reject white society as a lost cause in terms of fulfilling any humanistic promises for the Negro? For whites to react subjectively to this attitude solves nothing. It must be understood. It must be seen that this rejection of white society has valid reasons. White society, the Muslims feel, is sick, immoral, dishonest, and filled with hate for non-whites. Their rejection of white society is analogous to the colonial people's rejection of imperialist rule. The difference is only that people in colonies can succeed and

Negro Nationalists cannot. The peculiar position of Negro Nationalists in the United States requires them to set themselves against the dominance of whites and still manage to live in the same country.

It has to be admitted that it is impossible for American society as it is now constituted to integrate or assimilate the Negro. Jim Crow is a built-in component of the American social structure. There is no getting around it. Moreover, there is no organized force in the United States at present capable of altering the structural form of American society.

Due to his semi-dependent status in society, the American Negro is the only potentially revolutionary force in the United States today. From the Negro, himself, must come the revolutionary social theories of an economic, cultural and political nature that will be his guides for social action—the new philosophies of social change. If the white working class is ever to move in the direction of demanding structural changes in society, it will be the Negro who will furnish the initial force.

The more the system frustrates the integration efforts of the Negro, the more he will be forced to resolve in his own consciousness the contradiction and conflict inherent in the pro and anti-integration trends in his racial and historical background. Out of this process, new organizational forms will emerge in Negro life to cope with new demands and new situations. To be sure, much of this will be empirical, out of necessity, and no one can say how much time this process will take to work itself towards its own logical ends. But it will be revolutionary pioneering by that segment of our society most suitable to and most amenable to pioneering—the have nots, the victims of the American brand of social underdevelopment.

The coming coalition of Negro organizations will contain Nationalist elements in roles of conspicuous leadership. It cannot and will not be subordinate to any white groups with which it is "allied." There is no longer room for the "revolutionary paternalism" that has been the hallmark of organizations such as the Communist Party. This is what the "New Left" must clearly understand in its future relations with Negro movements that are indigenous to the Negro community.

# racial militancy and interracial violence in the Second World war

## HARVARD SITKOFF

Most black servicemen during World War II were limited to positions of floor moppers and cooks. They were excluded from prestige units such as the air and marine corps and segregated in theaters, USO centers, post exchanges, and even chapels, where signs pointed the way to worship for Catholics, Protestants, Jews, and Negroes. One can only conjecture about how many black servicemen died because the Red Cross could not find "black" blood plasma for the wounded.

Sometimes historians reveal such overpowering truths that we are reminded of E. H. Carr's admonition that good historians should have "the future in their bones." In the face of such compelling evidence of white society's violence toward and hate for black people as that presented by Harvard Sitkoff in the following article, the only question left is "Whither?"

---

World War II opened a quarter of a century of increasing hope and frustration for the black man. After a decade of depression, the ideological character of the war and the government's need for the loyalty and manpower of all Americans led blacks to expect a better deal from President Franklin D. Roosevelt. With a near-unanimity rare in the Negro community, civil rights groups joined with the Negro press and influential church, labor, and political leaders to demand "Democracy in Our Time!"[1] Individuals and organizations never before involved in a protest movement found it respectable, even expedient, to be part of the new militancy in the black community.[2] The war stimulated racial militancy, which in turn led to increased interracial violence that culminated in the bloody summer of 1943. Negro leaders then retreated, eschewing mass movements and direct action in favor of aid from white liberals for their congressional and court battles. While many of the goals of the early war years remained, the mood and tactics became increasingly conservative.[3] Paradoxically, the wartime violence which summoned forth the modern civil rights movement, enlisting in the struggle scores of liberal organizations and tens of thousands of whites previously blind or indifferent to American racism, also smothered the embryonic black movement for equality by tying it ever more closely to liberal interracialism, which all too easily accepted the appearance of racial peace for the reality of racial justice. By the end of the war two trends emerged which would shape the course of the next two decades. Jim Crow had stumbled badly enough to heighten the aspirations of many Negroes

Harvard Sitkoff, "Racial Militancy and Interracial Violence in the Second World War," *The Journal of American History* (December 1971), 661–681.

**285**

that they would soon share the American Dream; and leadership in the battle for civil rights had been taken over by various communist-front organizations, labor unions, religious groups fighting intolerance, and social scientists making a career of studying race relations.[4]

At the beginning of this war, unlike World War I, few Negro leaders asked blacks to close ranks and ignore their grievances until the war ended.[5] Rather, the very dependency of the government on the cooperation of the Negro intensified his demand for civil rights. "If we dont't fight for our rights during this war," said one Harlem leader, "while the government needs us, it will be too late after the war."[6] Memories of the false promises of World War I stirred a reader of the Amsterdam-Star News to write: "Remember, that which you fail to get now you won't get after the war."[7] Some Negro columnists openly advocated a prolonged war as the best hope for destroying the racial status quo. And the Negro press proclaimed the "time ripe for a new emancipation" and mobilized a "Double V" campaign to fight fascism and racism both abroad and at home.[8]

The Negro press headlined evidence of blacks excluded from defense jobs, blood plasma segregated by the Red Cross, abused Negro soldiers, and white hostility and violence. Circulation increased 40 percent as the Negro newspapers, functioning primarily to foster race solidarity and prod increasing militancy, campaigned to embarrass America's war for democracy by publicizing America's jim-crow policies and practices.[9] Membership in the National Association for the Advancement of Colored People multiplied nearly ten times during the war, and the number of its chapters tripled.[10] The Congress of Racial Equality, organized in 1942, experimented with non-violent action to end segregation in the North, and stimulated students at Howard University and interracial groups in various cities to begin sitting-in and experimenting with other forms of direct confrontation.[11] To "demand the right to work and fight for our country," A. Philip Randolph labored to build his March-on-Washington Committee into an all-black mass protest movement.[12] Even Negro fraternal, business, and professional societies collaborated in the battle against oppression on the homefront. Everywhere he turned, the urban black found new Negro organizations enlisting in the crusade and new leaders and journals exhorting him to demand equality. Each concession wrested from the government and every sign of the weakening of white supremacy added new converts, made fund raising easier and stimulated greater confidence and higher hopes.[13]

The establishment of the United Nations, the anti-imperialistic pronouncements of government officials, and a steady stream of articles, books, letters, and speeches—especially those of Pearl S. Buck, Eleanor Roosevelt, Wendell Willkie, and Henry Wallace—disputing the scientific basis of racism and urging America to practice what it preached, further augmented the militancy of black America.[14] The attempt to educate the public to stop discrimination and end prejudice reached its peak in 1944 with the publication of Gunnar Myrdal's An American Dilemma. Eschewing the socio-economic explanations popularized by American Marxists in the 1930s, Myrdal described the race problem as a moral problem for white America, brought about by the collision between the American Creed's promise of equality and liberty and the denial of them to the Negro. Woefully underestimating the extent and depth of American racism, Myrdal optimistically predicted that Americans would resolve their dilemma by ending discrimination and segregation.[15]

The growth of Negro political power also stimulated hope for change. The steady migration of blacks to the North and the return, after 1938, of many white Republicans to their traditional voting habits, prematurely led Negro leaders to believe that Franklin D. Roosevelt could be persuaded to support civil rights.[16] He refused to do so in 1940, but Willkie's strong bid for the Negro vote and the inclusion of a solid civil rights plank in the Republican platform forced the President to approve an anti-discrimination clause in the Selective Service Act, promote Colonel Benjamin O. Davis as the first Negro brigadier general, and appoint William Hastie as civilian aide to the secretary of war and Colonel Campbell Johnson as executive assistant to the director of Selective Service. Black political pressure also opened the way for new Reserve Officer Training Corps units in Negro colleges and an air force aviation school for blacks at Tuskegee.[17] These actions barely affected black life in America, but as possible first steps to be lengthened as the Negro vote grew in the North, they showed Negro leaders the power of the vote and the need for coordinated efforts. Moreover, the fact that President Roosevelt did respond, if only with gestures, increased black expectations. But the paucity of the response further clarified the disparity between Negro goals and gains—between democratic myths and realities.[18]

The experience of living in jim-crow America led the Negro to be acutely conscious of his deprivations and impatient with all impediments to first-class citizenship. Magazines and newspapers at the beginning of the war charted his plummeting morale and increased assertiveness.[19] Only a few blacks, mainly the followers of Leonard Robert Jordan's Ethiopia Pacific League and Elijah Muhammad's Temple of Islam, actually flirted with treason; many simply, but loudly, held their loyalty in check.[20] A Harlem doctor driving through Manhattan with a large sign on his car reading, "IS THERE A DIFFERENCE? JAPS BRUTALLY BEAT AMERICAN REPORTER GERMANS BRUTALLY BEAT SEVERAL JEWS AMERICAN CRACKERS BRUTALLY BEAT ROLAND HAYES & NEGRO SOLDIERS,"[21] expressed the bitterness of countless others, as did the black college student who asked: "The Army jim-crows us. The Navy lets us serve only as messmen. The Red Cross refuses our blood. Employers and labor unions shut us out. Lynchings continue. We are disfranchised, jim-crowed, spat upon. What more could Hitler do than that?"[22] NAACP responded to the new mood by repeatedly comparing Hitlerism with American racism and urging its followers: "Now Is the Time Not to Be Silent."[23]

The changing of signs on hiring gates from "No Help Wanted" to "Help Wanted, White," most stirred the militancy of lower-class blacks. After being first-fired during the Depression, they now found themselves last-hired, discriminated against in government training programs, excluded from many unions, and forced into the dirtiest and lowest paying jobs. To make matters worse, as the Depression in white America officially ended, the federal government drastically slashed welfare appropriations despite the fact that most blacks remained unemployed or underemployed.[24] Negro leaders established new committees and attended conferences requesting action, but their polite, formal protests and negotiations failed to budge President Roosevelt or the nation's leading industrialists and unions.[25]

As black discontent deepened, the established civil rights groups turned to mass protest meetings and picketing.[26] At the same time, Randolph issued a call for 10,000 blacks to march on Washington to demand federal action on job discrimination. Throughout the spring of 1941 the March on Washington

Committee mobilized lower-class blacks never previously recruited by any Negro organization. As his movement grew, NAACP, Urban League, and a score of staid, old-line Negro associations and leagues that had always shunned direct action hastily boarded Randolph's bandwagon.[27] Randolph kept countering presidential indifference by threatening to raise the number of angry marching blacks to 50,000 and then 100,000. A week before the scheduled march Franklin Roosevelt capitulated, agreeing to issue an executive order establishing the first President's Committee on Fair Employment Practices (FEPC) in exchange for cancellation of the embarrassing march on the nation's capital.[28] Although neither the original order nor the authority of FEPC ever fully met Negro expectations, President Roosevelt's action buoyed the most optimistic hopes of Negro organizations for further federal assistance. Similarly, the March-on-Washington Movement's apparent success in stirring thousands of blacks never before touched by the civil rights movement and in threatening the government with direct action graphically demonstrated the potential of mass black militancy.[29] The Chicago *Defender*, which in February labeled Randolph's proposal as "the miracle of the century," heralded the death of "Uncle-Tomism" and the new age of mass protest in July.[30]

To oppose discrimination in the armed services and the lack of black combat units, the two most bitterly resented aspects of American racism during the war, some young blacks publicly refused induction.[31] Various individuals and organizations such as the Chicago "Conscientious Objectors Against Jim Crow" tried to fight military segregation and racial quotas in the courts.[32] Countless other blacks just never showed up for examination or induction. Those who served often did so sullenly. "Here lies a black man killed fighting a yellow man for the glory of a white man," became a popular saying of black draftees.[33] In Harlem, a white draft board member noted: "When colored draftees came to the board for induction last year, I used to give them a little patriotic talk to make them feel good. But they didn't. They only laughed at me. Now I bow my head as they come in for their induction."[34]

The publicized denigration of blacks in the armed services caused both frustration and militant protest. Army policy at the beginning of the war strictly limited the quota of Negroes to be inducted and rigidly confined them to noncombatant units. Naval policy excluded them from the marines and coast guard and restricted blacks to being messboys in the navy.[35] While political pressure and war manpower needs slowly forced the armed services to move from exclusion to segregation to token integration, the great mass of blacks served throughout the war in service units commanded by white officers. They trained in segregated base camps, mostly in the South, and found themselves barred or jim-crowed by USO, service centers, theaters, and post exchanges.[36] Most bases even provided segregated chapels; the sign listing the schedule of religious services at one camp post read: "Catholic, Jews, Protestants, and Negroes."[37] Blacks who protested were harassed and intimidated; those who persisted in their opposition were transferred, placed in the stockade, or dishonorably discharged.[38]

The most chafing practice of the army, however, was its refusal to protect Negro servicemen off the post and its use of white military police to control blacks. Throughout the South a Negro in uniform symbolized "a nigger not knowing his place."[39] White bus drivers habitually refused to transport blacks to and from their bases. White military police enforced jim-crow seating restrictions, and off-base bars and restaurants used them to keep blacks out. To avoid friction with the local community, base commanders continuously enjoined blacks to obey the local customs of segregation and some even prohibited blacks from securing leave.[40] Little wonder that blacks equated army law with "white" law. Many blacks responded with cynicism and despair, and the war department regularly received reports on the low morale of the Negro soldier and accounts of black suicides, mental "crack-ups," desertions, and AWOL's due to discrimination and racist brutality.[41]

Other blacks responded by fighting back. Racial friction, sporadic conflict, and finally outright rioting became commonplace at nearly every army base in the South, many in the North, and even at a few in Australia, England, and the South Pacific.[42] As the experiences of war shattered the Negroes' illusions about white sincerity and destroyed their fear of white authority, "thousands of spontaneous and individual rebellions went unrecorded and unnoticed." Although the war department systematically suppressed most evidence of black revolt and labeled most of the deaths due to race battles as combat fatalities or "motor vehicle accidents," army statisticians, nevertheless, reported an unusually high number of casualties suffered by white officers of Negro troops and at least fifty black soldiers killed in race riots in the United States.[43]

In 1941, army authorities found a black private, arms and legs bound, lynched at Fort Benning. Brutality by the military police in Fayetteville, North Carolina, led to a pitched gun battle with black soldiers. Forty-three blacks went AWOL to escape the harassment and terrorization by whites in Prescott, Arizona. Black soldiers at Fort Bragg, Camps Davis, Gibbon, and Jackson Barracks fought white soldiers and police.[44] Although complaints and protests from Negro soldiers, chaplains, NAACP, and National Lawyers Guild poured into the war department and White House, neither would publicly respond.[45] The quantity and intensity of racial violence at military bases accelerated in 1942. The attempt by a military policeman to arrest a drunken black soldier in Alexandria, Louisiana, sparked a race riot that resulted in the shooting of twenty-eight Negroes and the arrest of nearly 3,000.[46] Other race riots broke out in New Orleans; Vallejo, California; Flagstaff, Phoenix, Arizona; Florence, South Carolina; Fort Dix, New Jersey; and the air force training school in Tuskegee.[47] The war department even refused to intervene when Beaumont, Texas, city policemen clubbed and shot a black soldier, and when a Negro army nurse was brutally beaten and jailed for defying the jim-crow seating arrangements on a Montgomery bus.[48]

Stories of race riots at Camps Stewart and Shelby, Forts Bliss and Benning, and March Field dominated the front pages of the Negro press along with accounts of southern peace officers killing black soldiers. Numerous bases reported Negroes wrecking post facilities and off-base restaurants that refused to serve them. Accounts of Negro soldiers going "over the hill" and battling with white military police increased dramatically. The growing fear of retaliatory violence by blacks led the governor of Mississippi to request the war department to move Negro regiments out of his state, and forced officers at some southern bases to order the removal of firing pins from the rifles of Negro servicemen.[49] Finally, after a bitter summer of violence, the war department officially acknowledged the existence of a serious morale problem among Negro troops and urged all white officers to treat blacks with the utmost care and diplomacy.[50]

The tensions and violence within the military mirrored the mushrooming conflict on the homefront. Both blacks and whites blamed the other for racial problems and both self-righteously sought advantage in the crisis of war. Many whites intensified their efforts to keep the Negro "in his place," regardless of the changes wrought by the war.[51] Each new protest against discrimination was seen as a sign of Negro disloyalty, and many feared that "the more they get the more they want." The more Negroes demanded their rights, the more white resistance stiffened, which led blacks to become even more impatient with second-class citizenship and determined to assert themselves.[52] The increasing competition between the races and the many petty irritations of war—the rationing, shortages, overcrowding, and high prices—engendered frustration, supersensitivity, and belligerency. The fatigue of long work weeks with little opportunity for recreation, the anxious scanning of casualty lists, the apprehension over a new job and a strange city, and the desire of noncombatants to prove their masculinity all fed the boiling racial cauldron.[53]

Government officials at all levels feared intervening in this explosive situation, contenting themselves with vague appeals to national unity. President Roosevelt, preoccupied with diplomacy and military strategy, and deeply dependent on southern support in Congress for his postwar foreign policy, let two southern aides, Mobilization Director James Byrnes and political secretary Marvin McIntyre, handle most racial matters.[54] Symptomatic of its approach to bury racial problems as deeply as possible—a mixture of blindness, patchwork compromise, and faith that good public relations could gloss over prior errors—the White House refused to do anything to prevent the riot by white Detroiters to keep Negroes from entering the Sojourner Truth public housing project. Warned well in advance of the trouble brewing, McIntyre sought only to avoid letting the conflict be publicized.[55] After the riot, the Office of Facts and Figures noted that unless strong and quick intervention by some high official, preferably the President, was not taken at once, disorders would follow.[56] The President did nothing. With little government action to relieve racial anxiety or enforce new norms, whites and blacks moved closer toward violence.[57]

The intensification of interracial rancor prompted various forms of violence, including lynchings.[58] Less dramatic, but more immediately affecting the racial climate, were the almost daily fights and incidents on public vehicles. Most involved Negro soldiers from the North refusing to honor southern racial etiquette and southern white migrants to the North refusing to mingle closely with blacks on the overcrowded busses, trolleys, and trains of industrial cities. Verbal abuse, shovings, slappings, and stabbings became everyday happenings, signifying the heightened racial animosity.[59]

The chaos, despair, and frustration arising from the Negro's resentment of the slow pace of racial progress and his accelerating hope for a better day, plus the bewilderment and anger of whites determined to maintain the racial status quo—expressed in and nurtured by three years of racial friction and conflict—exploded in an epidemic of interracial violence in 1943. The Social Science Institute at Fisk University reported 242 racial battles in forty-seven cities.[60] Throughout the North, juvenile delinquency increasingly turned into racial gang fights. Italo-American and Negro teenagers fought week-long battles in Newark and Philadelphia, while black and Polish gangs battled in Buffalo and Chicago.[61] Other racial gang fights were reported in Cambridge, Massachusetts, and Brooklyn.[62] The worst of these "zoot-suit" riots occurred in Los Angeles. A mob of over 1,000 whites, mainly sailors and soldiers, freely roamed the city attacking and stripping zoot-suited blacks and Mexican-Americans, while the city police, shore patrol, and military police looked the other way. Making no attempt to inquire into the causes of the riot, the Los Angeles City Council further stirred racial emotions by ordering the arrest for "vagrancy" of those who had been beaten and by declaring the wearing of a zoot-suit a misdemeanor.[63]

In mid-June, the Christian American Association of Texas spread a rumor that a Negro had raped a young white mother in Beaumont. A white mob of over 3,000, mainly workers from the Pennsylvania Shipyard fearing that FEPC would give their jobs to blacks, stomped through the Negro ghetto burning, pillaging, and terrorizing those in their path. War production stopped, businesses closed, thousands of dollars of property was damaged, one black and one white died, and more than seventy-five people were injured. Only a declaration of martial law and the swift, impartial action of the combined forces of local and state police, volunteers, and Texas Rangers quelled the riot.[64] In Mobile, the attempt to upgrade twelve Negro workers as welders in the yards of the Alabama Dry Dock and Shipbuilders Company caused 20,000 white workers to walk off their job and riot for four days. The League for White Supremacy, organized in 1942 to thwart the FEPC demand to end discrimination in the shipyards, had been agitating for a year unhindered by either company or union officials. It answered the company's decision to comply with FEPC policy by spreading a rumor that a black worker had just killed a white woman. While plant guards and local police looked on, gangs of whites attacked Negro workers with crowbars and wrenches and then rioted throughout the city. Only the belated entrance of federal troops finally stopped the riot, and FEPC backed down and agreed to the continuation of segregation in the shipyards.[65] Similar fears of Negro economic competition led to a series of hate strikes against the hiring of black workers in Maryland, Michigan, New York, and Ohio, and a violent battle between blacks and whites in the Sun Shipbuilding Yard at Chester, Pennsylvania.[66] A white walkout stopped Philadelphia's transportation system for a week when the city hired eight Negroes as trolley motormen, and a group of blacks in New Iberia, Louisiana, were driven out of town for setting up a welding school for Negroes—"the white people didn't want the colored folks to learn to be anything but sharecroppers and servants."[67]

Other cities beset by rumors of impending racial violence began taking extraordinary precautions to prevent riots. In Washington, the federal government worked behind the scenes with local Negro leaders and the municipal police force to keep a demonstration against the Capital Transit Company for refusing to hire black bus drivers from turning into an open race war.[68] A score of other cities hastily secured reinforcements for local police to avert rumored riots and instituted interracial committees, curfews, cancellation of leaves for local servicemen, and prohibitions on liquor.[69] While columnists publicly pondered the "threat of a domestic Pearl Harbor," racial rumors swept the nation.[70] Loose talk of Negro troops seizing the *Queen Mary* in a mutiny, of "Eleanor Clubs" (where Negro domestics organized a boycott and vowed to get "every white woman in her kitchen by Christmas"), of Disappointment Clubs (where blacks pledged to harass white women by promising to come to cook or clean on certain days and then not showing up), combined with tales of shovers, pushers, and bumpers clubs, whose members plotted to devote one day every week to walking in crowded areas and shoving whites, and rumors of blacks buying guns and a white counteroffensive against "uppity, out of line Negroes," kept many cities on edge.[71]

No city expected racial trouble more than Detroit, and none did less to prevent it. Forced to accommodate the more than 50,000 southern Negroes and

500,000 whites rushing into the city for employment in defense industries, with severe shortages of housing, recreation, and transportation, and an over-abundance of agitators and extremists of every color and persuasion, Detroit, the "Arsenal of Democracy," seethed with racism and hatred.[72] Racial clashes in schools, playgrounds, and factories, fights on busses and trolleys, and cross burnings throughout the city became accepted everyday occurrences.[73] The city was described as "a keg of powder with a short fuse."[74] When the riot finally exploded, Detroit's mayor told reporters: "I was taken by surprise only by the day it happened."[75]

The riot began when thousands of Detroiters, seeking relief from the hot, humid city streets, crowded into the amusement park on Belle Isle on Sunday, June 20. Small fights all through the day combined with rumors of a race war erupted into a riot on the bridge connecting the park with the city. News of the riot spread swiftly to every section of Detroit.[76] In the crowded ghetto blacks, tired of moving to find the Promised Land, tired of finding the North too much like the South, tired of being Jim-Crowed, struck out against "whitey" and his property and symbols of authority. Black mobs stoned passing motorists, hurled rocks and bottles at the police, stopped streetcars to beat up unsuspecting whites, and smashed and looted many of the white-owned stores in the ghetto.[77] White mobs, unhampered by the police, retaliated on all Negroes caught in white sections.[78] Throughout the melee, fresh rumors sustained the frenzy. Tales of babies killed and women raped served to justify the violent expression of old hatreds, while the excitement of a car burning in the night, the screeching wail of an ambulance siren, plenty of looted liquor, and a feeling of being free to do whatever one wished without fear of police reprisal fed the riotous appetite of the angry city.[79]

While city and state officials feared to act or ask for help and appeared unable to control the violence, and the White House and war department refused to intervene, the riot raged.[80] By Monday evening, nineteen police precincts, covering 75 percent of the Detroit area, reported riot activity. Most transportation lines had suspended operation and the fire department could no longer control the city's fires. Injured rioters and spectators were entering hospitals at the rate of one every other minute.[81] By the time federal troops finally arrived late Monday evening, Detroit's riot toll recorded thirty-four killed, more than 700 injured, over two million dollars in property losses, and a hundred million man-hours lost in war production.[82] Only the continued presence of soldiers patrolling the streets and armed military vehicles escorting busses and trolleys on their usual runs kept the continuing racial hysteria from erupting again. Throughout the summer anxiety increased, isolated racial fights continued, and rumors of blacks and whites collecting knives and guns for "the next one" heightened the tense atmosphere.[83]

Less than two months later, despite the extensive efforts of New York officials to maintain racial calm, a rumor of a Negro soldier killed by a white policeman triggered the same combination of deep grievances and war-bred tensions that had sparked the Detroit riot into an orgy of looting and destruction in Harlem.[84] The protest against discrimination and segregation, unemployment and restricted housing, police brutality, mistreatment of black soldiers, and the white-owned, rat-and-vermin-infested black ghetto led to the death of five Negroes, 500 injuries, and an estimated five million dollars of property damaged.[85] Once the rumor of another police killing swept through

Harlem, Walter White, executive secretary of NAACP, wrote, "blind, unreasoning fury swept the community with the speed of lightening." The young and the poor, goaded by the white-owned property they were powerless to possess, suddenly smashed the plate-glass windows of stores on all the main avenues in the ghetto, and "the Bigger Thomases of New York passed like a cloud of locusts over the stores of Harlem."[86]

Shocked by the extent of racial violence in the summer of 1943, and without a program to do anything about it, liberals and Negro leaders looked to the White House for leadership.[87] But President Roosevelt remained silent. Having been nurtured and elevated to power by the southern dominated and oriented Democratic party, he followed the century-old tradition of successful Democratic politicians by studiously avoiding interference with a state's right to control racial issues. Although Eleanor Roosevelt and some of the liberals in his administration cautiously urged him to support civil rights, the President continued to let his southern assistants—Byrnes, McIntyre, press secretary Stephen T. Early, and General Edwin "Pa" Watson, his military aide and secretary—handle all racial matters. They viewed civil rights issues as a danger to the fragile Democratic coalition as well as an unwarranted intrusion on the President's precious time, and the so-called Negro balance of power as far more expendable than southern votes in Congress. Consequently, they blocked all proposals for White House action and shuffled off complaints to David Niles, Jonathan Daniels, and FEPC—the Wailing Wall for minorities, virtually powerless to act but handy as a safety valve.[88] Secretary of War Henry L. Stimson and Secretary of the Navy Frank Knox took an even more standpat attitude on racial questions than Roosevelt's advisers. Both viewed the civil rights issue as an impediment to the war effort with which no compromise should be made. Both accepted notions of Negro inferiority and of black agitators, not even supported by their own people, unfairly taking advantage of a nation in the midst of war.[89] Even some of the President's liberal advisers, such as Harry Hopkins, failed to see civil rights as a major issue. Following Franklin Roosevelt's lead in replacing "Dr. New Deal with Dr. Win-the-War," they shelved their zeal for social reform for a new standard: "will it help to win the war? if not, the hell with it!"[90]

Moreover, the President would not respond affirmatively to the racial crisis because the congressional elections of 1942 increased his dependence on the southern Democrats and because the new pressures from the black community offended his sense of paternalism. With the Democrats receiving less than half the total major party vote for the first time since 1932, and the Republicans gaining forty-seven seats in the House, the southern bloc in Congress rode high, encouraging Roosevelt to weaken FEPC and pigeonhole all racial issues.[91] At the same time, the black demand for immediate change hampered his hope for a wartime consensus. To Roosevelt, the Negro always remained an unfortunate ward of the nation—to be treated kindly and with charity as a reward for good behavior. Nothing in his political past prepared him for the new black assertiveness. Throughout his administration he had worked with the conservative followers of Booker T. Washington in the South and the reliable Negro machine politicians of the North.[92] Despite the significant change in temper in the black community, Roosevelt continued to rely for advice on Negro matters on an elite coterie which included Lester Granger of the National Urban League; Dr. James Shepard, president of the North Carolina College for Negroes; Lester Walton, the minister to Liberia; and such prominent southern white liberals as

Daniels, Mark Ethridge, Frank Graham, and John Temple Graves. Steeped in the politics of gradualism, these men did little to help the President understand why blacks supported NAACP and the March-on-Washington Movement or why civil rights required new initiatives from the White House. They reinforced his inclination to avoid antagonizing southern politicians and to act only when he had a clear mandate from the people, and then only for the simplest, least fundamental solution.[93]

Maintaining an official silence throughout the summer of 1943, the administration hoped to defuse the racial issue by adhering to its standard policy of patronage, public gestures, and public relations. The President's aides first buried all pleas for a fireside chat on the riots and then killed plans to have Congress investigate the disorders.[94] Franklin Roosevelt's advisers then shelved all proposals for a governmental race relations commission in favor of the inoffensive appointment of Daniels to correlate personally all information on racial problems.[95] Even Marshall Field's innocuous plan to circulate pledges asking people not to spread rumors and to help to "win the war at home by combatting racial discrimination wherever I meet it," which the President liked, went unheeded.[96] Instead, new government films and press releases emphasized the recent gains of Negroes, and the government acted to handle future riots more efficiently by clarifying the procedure for calling in federal troops and approving Federal Bureau of Investigation Director J. Edgar Hoover's recommendation to grant draft deferments to members of urban police forces.[97] The following year Hoover announced his plan to round up the communist agitators causing racial unrest.[98]

The American left, however, did little to press a new racial policy on the White House. Most communist sympathizers continued to subordinate Negro rights to demands for a second front, and liberals, fearing continued violence, urged the Negro "to go slow," work with white allies, and avoid precipitating a white reaction.[99]

Social scientists who had earlier supported the more militant black leaders now began to work to divert aggression and control violence.[100] Scores of liberal organizations that had never before cared about the race problem suddenly awoke to the realization that they had to do something. Interracialism became an overnight fad: by the end of 1943 more than 100 local, state, and national commissions "to promote better race relations" had been established.[101] But since most of the liberals enlisting in the crusade for civil rights considered other issues more important, the committees floundered, doing nothing to attack the basic causes of racial unrest. Under the banners of ethnic democracy, interracial cooperation, and a more scientific understanding of group prejudice, most of the committees did little but broaden the channel of communication between Negro and white leaders, set up rumor-control bureaus and institute training sessions for police on human relations and effective handling of rioters.[102] Despite some worthy intentions, the committees functioned mainly as a buffer between blacks and their local government and widened the gap between bourgeois Negro leaders and the urban masses.[103] The more white liberals joined the movement, the more intent Negro leaders became in holding their support, by being accommodating, respectable, and a part of the larger progressive coalition. By the end of the war, interracialism had become the dominant tactic of the civil rights movement, while the committees which had spawned it, content to beget more committees, more surveys, and more reports, quietly faded away.[104]

The fear of continued violence by lower-class blacks and of an even greater period of violence after the war, like that following World War I, along with the emergence of interracialism, had a stunting effect on Negro militancy. Although the single greatest Negro victory since the Civil War, Executive Order 8802, had come because of an uncompromising, independent all-black effort, most of the old-line Negro leadership now retreated from their earlier militancy and began to entrust white liberals with the job of winning the Negro his rights.[105] Some did so because of their apprehension about controlling the aroused black masses or their jealousy of newly organized black groups, and some because they believed a minority without allies could never be successful once the war ended.[106] Moreover, the wartime prosperity of the Negro middle class demanded a movement that would conserve these gains, rather than one that might undo the progress made. Accordingly, by the end of 1943, almost all the Negro fraternal, labor, and professional groups once prominent in the militant battles against Jim Crow in the armed services and defense work, were supporting legislation for a permanent FEPC and "Hold Your Job" campaigns.[107] The once angry Negro press, regularly featuring full-page advertisements for war employment, directed much of their critical fire toward "irresponsible" blacks advocating sit-ins and civil disobedience.[108] And NAACP, the largest and richest of the Negro civil rights organizations, increasingly urged its chapters to get the movement out of the streets and into the courtroom and voting booth, and to back the national office in its support of an anti-poll tax bill, an aid to education bill, and an increase in social security coverage.[109]

In 1944 and 1945 the number of racial incidents declined, convincing many of the value of moderation. Negro and liberal leadership equated the decrease in interracial violence and the vocal support of whites with racial progress. Gradual reform, through legislation and court decisions, became the order of the day; capitalizing on the conscience of white America, the major tactic; and integration, the most sought objective.[110] Without any support from the established organizations and newspapers, the March-on-Washington Movement slowly faded away. With it went Randolph's hope for an all-black, mass direct-action movement—an organization of the masses, built on racial pride, that would force the white majority to heed the demands of black America. Following the lead of NAACP, Randolph turned his energies to building up the Negro vote and campaigning for a permanent FEPC.[111] Other Negro leaders exhorted blacks to mind their manners, be patient, and support liberal organizations.[112] Every week, it seemed, some new program of intercultural education, or interracial good-will, or another council on unity and amity appeared.[113] Not since the Civil War period had Negroes heard so many whites talking about freedom and racial justice; never before were so many journals and radio programs featuring items on race relations.[114] Civil rights had become respectable, and as whites flocked into the movement their views and needs predominated. The old Negro fighters for equality were quietly relegated to secondary and token positions. Meanwhile the talk of a new day coming grew louder and louder, convincing many that it was just around the corner while hiding from most Americans the fact that little or nothing was actually being done to eradicate the basic causes of racial inequality. But the mass of lower-class blacks did not have to be reminded of what the Boston *Globe* told its readers:

We have read about it. We have talked about it. We have held meetings and appointed committees and had more talk. We have passed the buck in all our talk. We blame the home, blame the schools, blame the police, blame the war. But what have we done—except talk?[115]

## NOTES

1. "Negro Organizations and the War Effort," Report from Special Service Division, April 28, 1942, Records of the Committee on Fair Employment Practice, RG 228 (National Archives); "Recent Factors Increasing Negro-White Tension," Special Service Division Memorandum, Nov. 2, 1942, Records of the Office of Government Reports, RG 44 (National Archives); Roy Wilkins to Walter White, March 24, 1942, Stephen J. Spingarn Papers (Harry S. Truman Library, Independence, Mo.); New York Times, Jan. 10, 1942.

2. Richard M. Dalfiume, Desegregation of the U.S. Armed Forces: Fighting on Two Fronts 1939-1953 (Columbia, Mo., 1969), 123n; Benjamin McLaurin, "Memoir," 36 (Oral History Collection, Columbia University); Charles S. Johnson, To Stem this Tide: A Survey of Racial Tension Areas in the United States (Boston, 1943), 131-39; Howard W. Odum, "Social Change in the South," Journal of Politics, 10 (May 1948), 247-48.

3. Herbert Garfinkel, When Negroes March: The March on Washington Movement in the Organizational Politics for FEPC (Glencoe, 1959), 144; Adam Clayton Powell, Jr., Marching Blacks: An Interpretive History of the Rise of the Black Common Man (New York, 1945), 172. See also Rayford W. Logan, ed., What the Negro Wants (Chapel Hill, 1944).

4. Lester B. Granger, "A Hopeful Sign in Race Relations," Survey Graphic, XXXIII (Nov. 1944), 455-56; "To Minimize Racial Conflict: Committees To Work on Human Relationships," American Century, LX (Jan. 1945), 80. See also Harold Cruse, The Crisis of the Negro Intellectual (New York, 1967), 163-64, 207-09, 299, 324, 534-35; "Education for Reality Understanding," Journal of Negro Education, XIII (Summer 1944).

5. Lester M. Jones, "The Editorial Policy of Negro Newspapers of 1917-18 as Compared with That of 1941-42," Journal of Negro History, XXIX (Jan. 1944), 24-31.

6. Charles Williams, "Harlem at War," Nation, 156 (Jan. 16, 1943), 88.

7. Quoted in Roi Ottley, 'New World A-Coming': Inside Black America (Boston, 1943), 314.

8. George S. Schuyler, "A Long War Will Aid the Negro," Crisis, 50 (Nov. 1943), 328-29, 344; Pittsburgh Courier, Oct. 5, 1940, Feb. 14, 1942; Chicago Defender, Dec. 13, 1941, March 14, 1942; Norfolk Journal and Guide, March 21, May 2, 1942; and "Government Blesses Separatism," Crisis, 50 (April 1943), 105.

9. Ralph N. Davis, "The Negro Newspapers and the War," Sociology and Social Research, XXVII (May-June 1943), 373-80; P. L. Prattis, "The Role of the Negro Press in Race Relations," Phylon, VII (Third Quarter 1946), 273-83; Thomas Sancton, "The Negro Press," New Republic, 108 (April 26, 1943), 557-60; Ernest E. Johnson, "The Washington News Beat," Phylon, VII (Second Quarter 1946), 127.

10. Charles R. Lawrence, "Negro Organizations in Crisis: Depression, New Deal, World War II" (doctoral dissertation, Columbia University, 1953), 103; Roy Wilkins, "Memoir," 83-88 (Oral History Collection, Columbia University); Report of the Department of Branches, April 14, 1941, NAACP Papers (Manuscript Division, Library of Congress).

11. Garfinkel, When Negroes March, 135-37; George M. Houser, "We Say No to Jim Crow," Fellowship, XI (April 1945), 61-63; CORE: A Brief History (New York, 1949).

12. A. Philip Randolph, "Why Should We March?" Survey Graphic, XXXI (Nov. 1942), 488-89; A. Philip Randolph, "Keynote Address to the Policy Conference of the March on Washington Movement," Francis L. Broderick and August Meier, eds., Negro Protest Thought in the Twentieth Century (Indianapolis, 1965), 201-10.

13. Raymond Hatcher to John Dancy, Feb. 1, 1943, Detroit Urban League Papers (University of Michigan Historical Collections, Ann Arbor); Roscoe E. Lewis, "The Role of Pressure Groups in Maintaining Morale among Negroes," Journal of Negro Education, XII (Summer 1943), 464-73; Thomas Sancton, "Something's Happened to the Negro," New Republic, 108 (Feb. 8, 1943), 175-79; Howard W. Odum, Race and Rumors of Race: Challenge to Crisis (Chapel Hill, 1943), 32-38.

14. Horace R. Cayton, "The Negro's Challenge," *Nation*, 157 (July 3, 1943), 10–12; Carey McWilliams, *Brothers under the Skin* (Boston, 1943), 17–20.

15. Gunnar Myrdal, with the assistance of Richard Sterner and Arnold Rose, *An American Dilemma: The Negro Problem and Modern Democracy* (2 vols., New York, 1944); Carl N. Degler, "The Negro in America—Where Myrdal Went Wrong," *New York Times Magazine* (Dec. 7, 1969), 152, 154, 160. Also see Charles S. Johnson, "The Present Status of Race Relations in the South," *Social Forces*, 23 (Oct. 1944), 27–32.

16. Pittsburgh *Courier*, June 29, 1940.

17. Will Alexander, "Memoir," 360 (Oral History Collection, Columbia University); Pittsburgh *Courier*, July 6, Aug. 24, 1940; Nancy and Dwight Macdonald, *The War's Greatest Scandal: The Story of Jim Crow in Uniform* (New York, 1943), 13–14; Henry L. Stimson Diary, Oct. 25, 1940, Henry L. Stimson Papers (Yale University Library).

18. Pittsburgh *Courier*, Nov. 2, 1940; White to Franklin D. Roosevelt, Nov. 4, 1940, PPF 1336, Franklin D. Roosevelt Papers (Franklin D. Roosevelt Library, Hyde Park).

19. Washington *Post*, March 26, 1944; Horace R. Cayton, "Negro Morale," *Opportunity: Journal of Negro Life*, XIX (Dec. 1941), 371–75; Kenneth B. Clark, "Morale of the Negro on the Home Front: World Wars I and II," *Journal of Negro Education*, XII (Summer 1943), 417–28; P. L. Prattis, "The Morale of the Negro in the Armed Services of the United States, *ibid.*, 355–63.

20. Roi Ottley, "A White Folks' War?" *Common Ground*, II (Spring 1942), 28–31; Alfred McClung Lee, "Subversive Individuals of Minority Status," *Annals of the American Academy of Political and Social Science*, 223 (Sept. 1942), 167–68; George Martin, "Why Ask 'Are Negro Americans Loyal?' " *Southern Frontier*, II (Feb. 1942), 2–3.

21. Ottley, *'New World A-Coming,'* 306–07.

22. Walter White, "What the Negro Thinks of the Army," *Annals of the American Academy of Political and Social Science*, 223 (Sept. 1942), 67.

23. "Nazi Plan for Negroes Copies Southern U.S.A.," *Crisis*, 48 (March 1941), 71; "Now Is the Time Not to Be Silent," *ibid.*, 49 (Jan. 1942), 7; Memorandum to NAACP State Branches, Dec. 12, 1941, NAACP Papers.

24. Garfinkel, *When Negroes March*, 17–21.

25. Robert L. Vann to Roosevelt, Jan. 19, 1939, June 13, 1940, OF 335; White to Roosevelt, March 13, 1941; and Edwin Watson to White, April 8, 1941, OF 93, Roosevelt Papers; McLaurin, "Memoir," 64–65, 295–96. Among the committees formed were the Pittsburgh *Courier's* Committee on Participation of Negroes in the National Defense Program; Adam Clayton Powell, Jr.'s Temporary National Protest Committee on Segregation; John A. Davis' Citizens Non-Partisan Committee for Equal Rights in National Defense; Committee on Negro Americans in War Industries, established by Phelps-Stokes Fund; and the Committee on Discrimination in Employment.

26. Pittsburgh *Courier*, Jan. 25, 1941; Walter White, *A Man Called White: The Autobiography of Walter White* (New York, 1948), 186–87; Florence Murray, ed., *The Negro Handbook* (New York, 1942), 72.

27. McLaurin, "Memoir," 36, 299; Lester B. Granger, "The President, the Negro, and Defense," *Opportunity: Journal of Negro Life*, XIX (July 1941), 204.

28. A. Philip Randolph to Roosevelt, May 29, 1941; Watson to Roosevelt, June 14, 1941, OF 93, Roosevelt Papers; McLaurin, "Memoir," 300–05.

29. Dalfiume, *Desegregation of the U.S. Armed Forces*, 118–22.

30. Chicago *Defender*, Feb. 8, June 28, 1941; Williams, "Harlem at War," 87.

31. McWilliams, *Brothers under the Skin*, 33–34; Dwight MacDonald, "The Novel Case of Winfred Lynn," *Nation*, 156 (Feb. 20, 1943), 268–70.

32. Minutes of the Board of Directors, Sept. 9, 1940, NAACP Papers; Chicago *Defender*, Jan. 11, 18, 1941; *PM*, July 18, 1942.

33. Edwin R. Embree, *Julius Rosenwald Fund: Review for the Two-Year Period 1942–1944* (Chicago, 1944), 2.

34. Earl Brown and George Leighton, *The Negro and the War* (New York, 1942), 8.

35. War Department Press Release, Sept. 16, 1940, OF 93; Confidential Memorandum from Steve Early to Watson, Sept. 19, 1940, PPF 2538, Roosevelt Papers; NAACP Press

Releases, May 8, July 31, 1942, NAACP Papers. Ulysses Lee, *United States Army in World War II: Special Studies: The Employment of Negro Troops* (Washington, 1966), 21–87.

36. Lucille B. Milner, "Jim Crow in the Army," *New Republic*, 110 (March 13, 1944), 339–42; "Jim Crow in the Camps," *Nation*, 156 (March 20, 1943), 429.

37. W. Y. Bell, Jr., "The Negro Warrior's Home Front," *Phylon*, V (Third Quarter 1944), 272.

38. Macdonald and Macdonald, *The War's Greatest Scandal*, 9–12; Dwight MacDonald to editors, "The Case of Alton Levy," *Nation*, 157 (Nov. 6, 1943), 538; "The Social Front," *Monthly Summary of Events and Trends in Race Relations*, 1 (Nov. 1943), 9.

39. "Negroes in the Armed Forces," *New Republic*, 109 (Oct. 18, 1943), 542–43.

40. Milner, "Jim Crow in the Army," 339–42; "Personalities on the Spot," *Monthly Summary of Events and Trends in Race Relations*, 1 (Sept. 1943), 26.

41. Bell, "The Negro Warrior's Home Front," 276–77. Also see Grant Reynolds, "What the Negro Soldier Thinks," *Crisis*, 51 (Nov. 1944), 352–54.

42. Lee, *United States Army . . . : The Employment of Negro Troops*, 348–79.

43. Charles E. Silberman, *Crisis in Black and White* (New York, 1964), 62–64.

44. Minutes of the Board of Directors, Sept. 8, 1941, NAACP Papers; Macdonald and Macdonald, *War's Greatest Scandal*, 2; Powell, *Marching Blacks*, 144; Pittsburgh *Courier*, Jan. 31, 1942.

45. White to Roosevelt, Aug. 13, 18, 20, 1941, OF 25; Ira Lewis to Roosevelt, Aug. 19, 1941; Gloster Current to Roosevelt, Sept. 26, 1941, OF 93, Roosevelt Papers; Chicago *Defender*, Aug. 30, 1941.

46. *Southern Frontier*, III (Feb. 1942), 1; Washington *Post*, March 26, 1944.

47. Macdonald and Macdonald, *War's Greatest Scandal*, 2–3; Powell, *Marching Blacks*, 144–45; New York *Times*, April 4, 1942.

48. McWilliams, *Brothers under the Skin*, 39; Randolph to Roosevelt, Aug. 1, 1942; Marvin McIntyre to Randolph, Aug. 6, 1942, OF 93, Roosevelt Papers.

49. Minutes of the Board of Directors, May 10, 1943, NAACP Papers; Chicago *Defender*, June 12, 19, 1943; Pittsburgh *Courier*, June 19, 1943; Florence Murray, ed., *The Negro Handbook 1944: A Manual of Current Facts, Statistics and General Information Concerning Negroes in the United States* (New York, 1944), 225; Powell, *Marching Blacks*, 145; "The Social Front," *Monthly Summary of Events and Trends in Race Relations*, 1 (Aug. 1943), 8–9.

50. "Negroes in the Armed Forces," 544.

51. "White Attitudes Toward Negroes," Report from OWI, Bureau of Intelligence, Aug. 5, 1942, Records of the Office of Government Reports, RG 44; "Race Tension and Farm Wages in the Rural South," Agriculture Department, Sept. 22, 1943, in OF 4245, Roosevelt Papers; Odum, *Race and Rumors of Race*, 7–8, 25, 42–43, 47–50; "Cities, North and South: A Reconnaissance Survey of Race Relations," *Monthly Summary of Events and Trends in Race Relations*, 1 (Oct. 1943), 11–12.

52. Pauli Murray to McIntyre, June 18, 1943, OF 93C, Roosevelt Papers; Sancton, "Something's Happened to the Negro," 175–79.

53. Arthur I. Waskow, *From Race Riot to Sit-In, 1919 and the 1960s: A Study in the Connections between Conflict and Violence* (Garden City, 1966), 220–23; Walter G. Muelder, "National Unity and National Ethics," *Annals of the American Academy of Political and Social Science*, 244 (March 1946), 10.

54. Roosevelt to Edwin Embree, March 16, 1942, OF 93, Roosevelt Papers; McIntyre to Roosevelt, March 2; James Byrnes to McIntyre, March 9, 1943, Records of the War Manpower Commission, RG 211 (National Archives); I. F. Stone, "Capital Notes," *Nation*, 156 (Jan. 23, 1943), 115.

55. McIntyre to C. F. Palmer, Jan. 19, 1942, OF 93, Roosevelt Papers; *NAACP Annual Report, 1942*, pp. 22–23, NAACP Papers. See also McIntyre to Roosevelt, Dec. 11, 1942, OF 4245-G, Roosevelt Papers, for McIntyre's attitudes toward racial protest.

56. Quoted in *PM*, June 28, 1943.

57. Bucklin Moon, *The High Cost of Prejudice* (New York, 1947), 60–61.

58. Jessie Parkhurst Guzman, ed., *Negro Year Book: A Review of Events Affecting Negro Life 1941-1946* (Tuskegee, 1947), 307–09; Murray, ed., *Negro Handbook 1944*, 169–72.

59. A. L. Foster to Dancy, June 10, 1943, Detroit Urban League Papers; Robert Lee Eichorn, "Patterns of Segregation, Discrimination and Interracial Conflict" (doctoral dissertation, Cornell University, 1954), 61–64; Allen Grimshaw, "Urban Racial Violence in the United States: Changing Ecological Considerations," *American Journal of Sociology*, LXVI (Sept. 1960), 117. See also "The Social Front," *Monthly Summary of Events and Trends in Race Relations*, 1 (Sept. 1943), 9; Odum, *Race and Rumors of Race*, 113–31.

60. *Monthly Summary of Events and Trends in Race Relations*, 1 (Jan. 1944), 2; Thomas Sancton, "The Race Riots," *New Republic*, 109 (July 5, 1943), 9–13; *Michigan Chronicle*, July 3, 1943.

61. White to Frank Murphy, June 30, 1943, Frank Murphy Papers (University of Michigan Historical Collections); *Monthly Summary of Events and Trends in Race Relations*, 1 (Aug. 1943), 1.

62. Embree, *Julius Rosenwald Fund . . . 1942–1944*, p. 6.

63. "Zoot-Suit War," *Time*, XLI (June 21, 1943), 18–19; Chester B. Himes, "Zoot Riots are Race Riots," *Crisis*, 50 (July 1943), 200–01; Carey McWilliams, "The Zoot-Suit Riots," *New Republic*, 108 (June 21, 1943), 818–20.

64. "The Social Front," *Monthly Summary of Events and Trends in Race Relations*, 1 (Aug. 1943), 6; Sancton, "The Race Riots," 10–11.

65. "Summary of a Report on the Race Riots in the Alabama Dry Dock and Shipbuilding Yards in Mobile," National Urban League, Detroit Urban League Papers; *Washington Post*, July 20, 1943.

66. "The Industrial Front," *Monthly Summary of Events and Trends in Race Relations*, 1 (Aug. 1943), 4–5; *ibid.* (Oct. 1943), 5; White, *A Man Called White*, 224–25; New York *Times*, Aug. 5, 1943.

67. "The Industrial Front," *Monthly Summary of Events and Trends in Race Relations*, 2 (Aug.-Sept. 1944), 6–7; Embree, *Julius Rosenwald Fund . . . 1942–1944*, p. 9.

68. Alexander, "Memoir," 167–68; Minutes of the Board of Directors, May 10, 1943, NAACP Papers.

69. Minutes of the Board of Directors, July 12, 1943, NAACP Papers; *Monthly Summary of Events and Trends in Race Relations*, 1 (Aug. 1943), 7–8.

70. Thomas Sancton, "Trouble in Dixie: I. The Returning Tragic Era," *New Republic*, 108 (Jan. 4, 1943), 11–14; Thomas Sancton, "Race Fear Sweeps the South," *ibid.* (Jan. 18, 1943), 81–83; Alexander, "Memoir," 696–99.

71. Odum, *Race and Rumors of Race*, 67–89, 96–103; Embree, *Julius Rosenwald Fund . . . 1942–1944*, p. 4; Johnson, "The Present Status of Race Relations in the South," 29.

72. Walter White, "What Caused the Detroit Riots"; "The National Urban League Report of the Detroit Riots," Detroit Urban League Papers.

73. Minutes of the Board of Directors, July 16, 1942, NAACP Papers; John Dancy Press Release, June 26, 1943, William Baldwin Memorandum, July 6, 1943, Detroit Urban League Papers.

74. Detroit *News*, Oct. 5–9, 1942; "Detroit Is Dynamite," *Life*, 13 (Aug. 17, 1942), 15–23.

75. *PM*, June 28, 1943.

76. Alfred McClung Lee and Norman D. Humphrey, *Race Riot* (New York, 1943); Robert Shogan and Tom Craig, *The Detroit Race Riot: A Study in Violence* (Philadelphia, 1964); Harvard Sitkoff, "The Detroit Race Riot of 1943," *Michigan History*, LIII (Fall 1969), 183–206.

77. Harold Kingsley, "Memorandum on Detroit Race Disturbance," June 23, 1943, Detroit Urban League Papers.

78. "Report of Thurgood Marshall, Special Counsel for the NAACP, Concerning Activities of the Detroit Police During the Riots, June 21 and 22, 1943," Mayor's Papers (Burton Historical Collection, Detroit Public Library).

79. Neil J. Smelser, *Theory of Collective Behavior* (New York, 1962), 71–73, 269.

80. Colonel R. G. Roamer, "Summary of Events in the Detroit Riot"; and Roamer-Lerch transcript, June 21, 1943, Records of the Office of the Provost Marshal General, RG 389 (National Archives).

81. William Guthner to F. W. Reese, Aug. 2, 1943, *ibid.*; Detroit *Free Press*, July 1, 1943.

82. Sitkoff, "The Detroit Race Riot of 1943," 192–96; White, *A Man Called White*, 226–27.

83. William Guthner, "Commander's Estimate of the Situation," Nos. I–IV, Records of the Office of the Provost Marshal General, RG 389; Fiorello La Guardia to Roosevelt, June 27, 1943, OF 93C, Roosevelt Papers.

84. White, *A Man Called White*, 233–41; Margaret Marshall, "Some Notes on Harlem," *Nation*, 157 (Aug. 21, 1943), 200–02.

85. Harold Orlansky, *The Harlem Riot: A Study in Mass Frustration* (New York, 1943), *passim*; Powell, *Marching Blacks*, 171–72.

86. Walter White, "Behind the Harlem Riot," *New Republic*, 109 (Aug. 16, 1943), 220–22.

87. Vito Marcantonio to Roosevelt, June 16, 1943; Philip Murray to Roosevelt, June 18, 1943; Douglas Horton to Roosevelt, June 27, 1943, OF 93C, Roosevelt Papers.

88. Malcolm MacLean to McIntyre, Feb. 24, 1942; Jonathan Daniels to Roosevelt, Sept. 28, 1944; and Frank Boykin to Watson, OF 93; David Niles to Daniels, Sept. 8, 1943; and A. V. Boren to Early, May 19, 1944, OF 4245-G, Roosevelt Papers. See also Helen Fuller, "The Ring Around the President," *New Republic*, 109 (Oct. 25, 1943), 563–65; "The Negro in Industry," *ibid*. (Oct. 18, 1943), 539; Joseph P. Lash, *Eleanor Roosevelt: A Friend's Memoir* (Garden City, 1964), 160, 217.

89. Stimson to Roosevelt, Feb. 16, 1942, OF 18, Roosevelt Papers; Stimson Diary, Sept. 27, Oct. 22, 23, 1940, June 18, 1941, May 12, 1942, June 23, 24, 1943, Stimson Papers.

90. Quoted in Arthur Krock, "Memoir," 86 (Oral History Collection, Columbia University).

91. Ed Pauley to Roosevelt, Dec. 14, 1942, PPF 1820, Roosevelt Papers; James A. Wechsler, "Pigeonhole for Negro Equality," *Nation*, 156 (Jan. 23, 1943), 122; "The Jim Crow Bloc," *New Republic*, 108 (Feb. 22, 1943), 240–41.

92. Roosevelt to George Foster Peabody, March 22, 1935, Dec. 12, 1935, PPF 660; Roosevelt to McIntyre, June 7, 1941, PPF 1248, Roosevelt Papers. See also Henry Stimson Memorandum on consultants on Negro Affairs, Feb. 18, 1943, Stimson Papers; Mary McLeod Bethune, "My Secret Talks with F. D. R.," *Ebony*, IV (April 1949), 42–51.

93. Mark Ethridge to Early, Aug. 20, 1941; Daniels to Samuel Rosenman, Sept. 9, 1943, OF 93; Daniels to Roosevelt, Sept. 24, 1943; and Daniels to Watson, Sept. 11, 1944, OF 4245-G, Roosevelt Papers. See also Thomas Sancton, "A Southern View of the Race Question," *Negro Quarterly: A Review of Negro Life and Culture*, 1 (Fall 1942), 197–200; John Temple Graves, "It's The Direction That Counts," *Southern Frontier*, III (April 1942), 2–3.

94. Many pleas for a presidential statement on the riots are in OF 93, Roosevelt Papers. Henry Wallace wanted the congressional plan to investigate the riots stopped because it "was bad from the standpoint of the 1944 election." Wallace to Roosevelt, July 7, 1943, PPF 1820, Roosevelt Papers. See also Roosevelt to Byrnes, Aug. 13, 1943, OF 88, *ibid*.

95. Harold L. Ickes to Roosevelt, July 15, 16, 26, 1943, OF 6; Francis Biddle to Roosevelt, July 15, Aug. 19, 1943, OF 93C; Biddle to Daniels, July 27, 1943; Daniels to Roosevelt, July 23, 1943; Daniels to Bishop Haas, July 28, 1943, OF 4245-G; Saul K. Padover, Memorandum, June 29, 1943, PPF 1820, *ibid*.

96. Marshall Field to Roosevelt, July 24, 1943, OF 93C, *ibid*.

97. Biddle to Roosevelt, July 15, 1943, OF 93C; and Daniels to Haas, Sept. 8, 1943, OF 4245-G, *ibid*.

98. J. Edgar Hoover to Daniels, Aug. 22, 1944, OF 4245-G, *ibid*.

99. See essays by Willard S. Townsend and Doxey A. Wilkerson in Logan, ed., *What the Negro Wants*, 163–92, 193–216; and James Boyd, "Strategy for Negroes," *Nation*, 156 (June 26, 1943), 884–87.

100. Gordon W. Allport, ed., "Controlling Group Prejudice," *Annals of the American Academy of Political and Social Science*, 244 (March 1946). See also Arnold M. Rose, *Studies in Reduction of Prejudice: A memorandum summarizing research on modification of attitudes* (Chicago, 1947); Goodwin Watson, *Action for Unity* (New York, 1947); Robert C. Weaver, "A Needed Program of Research in Race Relations and Associated Problems," *Journal of Negro Education*, XVI (Spring 1947), 130–35; Robin M. Williams, Jr., *The Reduction of Intergroup Tensions: A Survey of Research on Problems of Ethnic, Racial, and Religious Group Relations* (New York, 1947); Donald Young, "Techniques of Race Relations," *Proceedings of the American Philosophical Society*, 91 (April 1947), 150–61; and, in general, the work of Louis Wirth and his students at the Committee on Education, Training and Research in Race Relations at the University of Chicago.

101. *Monthly Summary of Events and Trends in Race Relations*, 1 (Jan. 1944), 2.

102. Embree, *Julius Rosenwald Fund . . . 1942–1944*, pp. 13–14; "Liberals and the Future," *New Republic*, 111 (Sept. 11, 1944), 310; *Monthly Summary of Events and Trends in Race Relations*, 1 (Sept. 1943), 1–2; *Monthly Summary of Events and Trends in Race Relations*, 1 (Dec. 1943), 2; Rebecca Chalmers Barton, *Our Human Rights: A Study in the Art of Persuasion* (Washington, 1955), 13.

103. A. A. Liveright, "The Community and Race Relations," *Annals of the American Academy of Political and Social Science*, 244 (March 1946), 106–07.

104. Langston Hughes, "Down Under in Harlem," *New Republic*, 110 (March 27, 1944), 404–05; Albert W. Hamilton, "Allies of the Negro," *Opportunity: Journal of Negro Life*, XXI (July 1943), 115–17; Lester B. Granger, "Victory Through Unity," *ibid.* (Oct. 1943), 148.

105. Sancton, "A Southern View of the Race Question," 199; Granger, "A Hopeful Sign in Race Relations," 455–56. Of the fourteen contributors to Logan's *What the Negro Wants*, only W. E. B. DuBois dissented from the general view that Negroes must avoid extralegal tactics and ally themselves with labor and liberals to secure first-class citizenship from the government.

106. Minutes of the Board of Directors, Sept. 14, 1942, NAACP Papers; *Monthly Summary of Events and Trends in Race Relations*, 1 (Oct. 1943), 2; McWilliams, *Brothers under the Skin*, 42–43.

107. "Programs of Action on the Democratic Front," *Monthly Summary of Events and Trends in Race Relations*, 2 (Nov. 1944), 105; "Negro Women Organize for Unity of Purpose and Action," *Southern Frontier*, IV (Dec. 1943), 2; Alvin E. Dodd, "Negro Employment Opportunities—During and After the War," *Opportunity: Journal of Negro Life*, XXIII (April-June 1945), 59–62; E. Franklin Frazier, *Black Bourgeoisie* (Glencoe, 1957), 49–50.

108. Garfinkel, *When Negroes March*, 144; Pauli Murray, "A Blueprint for First Class Citizenship," *Crisis*, 51 (Nov. 1944), 358–59.

109. Wilkins to Rev. F. S. Hardge, Dec. 10, 1944; Minutes of the Board of Directors, Dec. 14, 1943, NAACP Papers. See also "Negroes Fight on Four Major Fronts," *Southern Frontier*, V (Jan. 1944), 1–2.

110. "Racial Tensions Seem Easier," *Christian Century*, LXI (Aug. 30, 1944), 988; "To Minimize Racial Conflicts; Committees to Work on Human Relationships," *American Century*, LX (Jan. 1945), 80.

111. New York *Times*, July 4, 1943; Randolph to Wilkins, Jan. 31, 1944, NAACP Papers; Garfinkel, *When Negroes March*, 145–46; Cruse, *Crisis of the Negro Intellectual*, 208–09.

112. "The National Urban League Establishes Department of Public Education," *Opportunity: Journal of Negro Life*, XXII (Oct.-Dec. 1944), 184; "Negro Leader Supports White Liberals," *Southern Frontier*, VI (Nov. 1945), 2; Charles S. Johnson, "The Next Decade in Race Relations," *Journal of Negro Education*, XIII (Summer 1944), 442–44; Wilkins to White, Dec. 28, 1944, NAACP Papers. Significantly, White broke a thirty-five year old NAACP tradition of staying out of electoral politics by campaigning for Senator Robert Wagner. New York *Times*, Oct. 14, 1944.

113. Philip L. Seman, "Inter-faith—Inter-Race," *Monthly Summary of Events and Trends in Race Relations*, 2 (Aug.-Sept. 1944), 22; "Programs of Action on the Democratic Front," *ibid.* (Dec. 1944), 135; "Programs of Action on the Democratic Front," *ibid.* (Jan. 1945), 165–69.

114. "In the daily press and on the air," wrote Horace Cayton, "the Negro is getting more attention than he has enjoyed since the old Abolitionist days. And there is a growing awareness on the part of labor that the Negro problem requires action. In normal conditions all these things would be considered gains for the Negro. But they are *sporadic and unintegrated* and are insufficient to counteract the apparent inability of the government to set up a comprehensive plan." Quoted in McWilliams, *Brothers under the Skin*, 46–47. See also Liveright, "The Community and Race Relations," 106; "Institutes of Race Relations," *Monthly Summary of Events and Trends in Race Relations*, 2 (Aug.-Sept. 1944), 57–58; "The Negro: His Future in America: A Special Section," *New Republic*, 109 (Oct. 18, 1943), 535–50.

115. Boston *Globe*, Aug. 19, 1944. See also June Blythe, "Can Public Relations Help Reduce Prejudice?" *Public Opinion Quarterly*, 11 (Fall 1947), 342–60.

# women in twentieth century America

## NANCY E. SCHROM

The following article, originally printed in *Radical America,* co-authored by Ann D. Gordon and Mari Jo Buhle, and revised for this anthology is one of the rare contributions to women's history which considers women in terms of work and in relation to corporate America. Since gentility and helplessness were the ideal, for many years women were forbidden to step beyond their proper sphere: to work for pay was considered unfeminine. Immigrant and poor women, who needed to work, challenged the "cult of true womanhood," which claimed that women were biologically unsuited for labor. But not until the present, when middle-class women have become part of the work force, has the "cult" begun to topple.

While a full-length study of the roles women have played in society has yet to be done, this synthesis raises many of the issues to be further researched.

In preindustrial American society, men, women, and children shared productive economic functions in an organic family unit based on domestic production. Well before the turn of the twentieth century, massive and rapid industrialization broke down the traditional family structure and disrupted the web of social and economic relationships which characterized preindustrial society. As a result, women became American society's primary consumers in an economy in which the home no longer played a productive economic role.

Understanding the history of American women in the twentieth century depends in large part upon analyzing the importance of women's role as consumers in an economy which became based increasingly on mass consumption. In addition, two world wars and structural changes in the economy brought ever-increasing numbers of women into the labor force. Work for women, including married middle-class women, became respectable and desirable in the twentieth century. Much of women's recent history involves their experiences as workers.

Woman as consumer and woman as worker are the two most prominent images in twentieth century women's history. To analyze both involves not only looking at economic and social changes which have affected women, but also examining how these changes have affected women's relationships with each other: twentieth century women's history has been the story of women divided by class and economic role.

Despite dramatic social and economic changes, however, the ideological construct of woman and the role she should play in society—the nineteeth

Ann D. Gordon, Mari Jo Buhle, and Nancy E. Schrom, "Women in Twentieth Century America." This article has been revised for *Past Imperfect* by Nancy Schrom. It originally appeared as "Women in American Society: An Historical Contribution," *Radical America,* Vol. 5, no. 4 (July–August 1971), 39–53, 64–66.

century "Cult of True Womanhood"[1]—proved to be remarkably adaptable to twentieth century life. Ideas about woman's nature have changed in the last seventy years, but the traditional values associated with woman as guardian of the home and protector of morality which developed during the Industrial Revolution persisted in changed form well into the twentieth century. The persistence of the ideal despite its glaring incongruity with historical reality is the basic contradiction which emerges in the history of women in twentieth century America.

The fact that middle-class women became America's primary consumers in the first decades of the twentieth century is enormously important in understanding women's recent history. The same industrial developments which broke up the organic family unit in the late eighteenth and nineteeth centuries by sending men and working-class women into factory employment also affected women's traditional duties in the home. What women once produced in their own homes, they now could buy. The importance of woman's role as consumer was increased immeasurably by the emergence of the mass consumption economy early in the century. By 1920, American industry already was based primarily on the production of consumer goods. Canned goods, "store" bread, and clothing were on the market by the first decades of the twentieth century, and gas and electric appliances came into wide use in the 1920s. The proliferation of new products for the home has continued at an ever-increasing rate throughout the period.[2]

The economic changes which effected women's transition from co-producer in a domestic economy to consumer did not, in and of themselves, transform women's historical experience in a predetermined way. Rather, new economic conditions opened a number of potential alternatives for women which had not existed in previous centuries. Many feminists welcomed the technological improvements and new appliances: they could liberate women from the home. Charlotte Perkins Gilman, for example, urged that technological developments and labor-saving devices be employed to free women from the unspecialized and inefficient organization of housework. Community kitchens and technological innovations could revolutionize the organization of the modern home and leave women free for other pursuits.[3]

Early twentieth century feminists and social theorists combined an awareness of the liberating potential of the new economy with concern for the increasingly nonproductive nature of the middle-class homemaker's life. Psychotherapists and sociologists recognized the middle-class woman's "restlessness" and described the "nervous housewife" faced with an overabundance of spare time and feelings of inadequacy, boredom, and uselessness. As early as 1904, the economist Simon Patten wrote, "[historically] the household industries gave to the staying-home woman a fair share of the labor, but today they [household industries] are few and the 'homemaker' suffers under enforced idleness, ungratified longing, and non-productive time killing. . . ."[4] The image of middle-class women as social parasites, doomed to a symbiotic existence dependent on the more productive members of society, became a popular and compelling one.[5]

Despite the ceaseless increase of "labor-saving" products and appliances available to American women, and despite middle-class women's well-documented "restlessness" and discontent, the structure of the American home has been remarkably stable, and society at large has continued to see women primarily as homemakers. The persistence of the traditional ideology about women is linked integrally to women's economic role as consumers. The mature corporate economy has depended upon the consumption patterns of married middle-class women buying for their homes, and in order to carry out this role, women have had to be educated to accept their economic function. The "feminine mystique" was not a creation of advertisers, social scientists, and educators in the years after World War II, but rather has been in existence throughout the twentieth century as an updated version of the Cult of True Womanhood.

The decade of the 1920s has great historical significance for one trying to understand why Americans continued to think in traditional ways about women rather than adopting new alternatives which might have freed women from the home. It was in those years that the crucial importance of women's consumption patterns to the health of corporate capitalism became clear. In the twenties, social theorists, psychologists, educators, clergymen, and advertising executives told women in a variety of ways that their "natural" place was in the home and that their "real" job was motherhood. Homemaking and childrearing became specialized "professions" for the first time. Women could use the time they saved with new products and appliances to "put motherhood first,"[6] not embark on a career outside the home. Thus, at the same time that technological developments made it possible for women to spend less time at housework, cultural values demanded that they spend more time perfecting household arts.

The advertising industry and education were two of the most powerful institutions dedicated to inculcating the view that woman's psychological well-being and social responsibility lay in fulfilling her "natural" role in the home. The influence of these two institutions in the 1920s was especially significant and pervasive because advertising and education affected more women than in any previous period in American history.

Advertising became a major business in the twenties. The relatively small amount of advertising copy that existed before 1920 performed a limited and almost purely descriptive function. After World War I, however, advertising became important as a means of creating consumer demand and emotional needs. Hence, the amount of advertising copy not only vastly increased in the 1920s, but its style and approach were different as well: advertising became emotional and personal in an effort to link consumption with achievement and sexual success. In short, the twenties saw the advent of what Betty Friedan in the 1960s called "the sexual sell."[7]

Most of the advertising copy in the twenties was directed at women—a pattern familiar throughout the twentieth century. Because historical changes had taken away any productive economic and social reasons why women should stay in the home, advertising campaigns were particularly concerned with investing women with a contemporary sense of importance and productivity. Much of the advertising directed at women attempted semantically to turn consumption into production. The housewife managing her home was compared to the businessman running his firm. "Through her dealings as business manager of the home," an advertisement for Ford read, "the modern women brings sound commercial sense to bear on her judgment of a Ford closed car." "Retail buying is a productive act," wrote one enthusiastic commentator on the new economic order.[8]

Education for women in the early twentieth century also had a profound effect on the ways in which American society viewed women and on what women thought about themselves. The twenties marked a revolution in the scope of American higher education: more than five times as many students attended college in 1930 as had in 1900, and much of this increase occurred in the 1920s. Women were going to college in large numbers for the first time. In the twenties, however, educators concerned with women students began to emphasize that women's economic role was different from man's and that women should be educated accordingly. Many educators emphasized that it had been the mistake of women's education in the past to give the impression that homemaking required no special preparation. To remedy this problem, home economics and child-study courses were introduced into college curricula in the early twenties. Even Vassar, hitherto a staunch proponent of educating women in the same fashion as men, introduced a "euthenics" department in 1923 which was devoted to educating women for their future roles as wives and mothers. Preparation for homemaking as a profession was seen as giving the position dignity. In addition, it trained women to be effective and voluminous consumers. Vassar's president stressed that "a women does not need the same education as a man. . . . A women's college should train the woman for the part she is to play in life. Over 75 percent of college women marry. Are they trained for their career as homemakers?"[9] Some institutions continued to emphasize educating women to break away from their traditional role, but more common in the 1920s was the philosophy that women should be educated for their traditional status rather than encouraged to change it.[10]

Views expressed about the education of women in the twenties set the stage for the rest of the century. Although more and more women have attended college, higher education for women often still is seen as a prelude to domesticity and as an opportunity to meet a suitable husband. Women students have fewer academic expectations of themselves and fewer expectations are placed on them.[11]

Efforts on the part of advertising and educational institutions to revitalize woman's role in the home have not been able to change the basic fact that work inside the home has not been regarded as socially productive in twentieth century America. As Margaret Benston has stated, a capitalist society honors the production of exchange value, but regards the creation of use value as nonproductive because it does not receive financial remuneration. Because women have not been paid for housework, society has judged such work to be devoid of productive value. This fact has altered and fragmentized the relationships between men and women and between middle-class women and their working-class sisters, for in industrial society men and working-class women have worked outside the home in what society has deemed productive occupations.[12]

Largely because work in the home lost its social value, women in the twentieth century often have defined their personal liberation in terms of productive and meaningful work in the world of men. World War I marked the first large-scale movement of middle-class women into the labor force. The upward trend in employment has continued to the present: by the mid-1960s, more than a third of the female population was in the labor force and over a third of all married women were employed. This latter statistic is particularly striking because in the early years of the century, the great majority of women workers were single and very young. Cultural and ethnic values generally mitigated against a woman staying in the labor force after she had married unless severe economic hardship required the woman's income.[13]

This shift in employment patterns was due in part to the role of the world wars in forcing acceptance of married middle-class workers and making work outside the home respectable for women. However, the role of the wars in bringing middle-class women into the labor force can be overestimated. After both wars, the number of middle-class women workers declined for a temporary period, as many women returned to what they regarded as their permanent occupation: homemaker. In addition, although the wars brought about a striking increase in the number of middle-class women in the labor force, they did not help produce an alteration of consciousness in thinking about women's role. War work was almost always industrial in nature, with few intrinsically satisfying qualities. It gained its respectability by being temporary patriotic duty rather than a permanent career. In addition, no collective solutions were available for women who combined marriage with a war job. During World War II, for instance, a government propaganda tract urging women to work offered only vague individual solutions for the problems involved in combining working with housework and childcare. Women were instructed to "budget their time better," move to smaller, easier to care for homes, and buy prepared food.[14]

The economic transition in the 1920s from manufacturing to a predominance of service industries which employed large numbers of white collar workers was more important than the world wars in changing the nature of middle-class women's employment outside the home. The number of telephone operators, secretaries, typists, stenographers, and clerks rose dramatically in the 1920s setting the pattern for most middle-class women's employment. In the 1960s, three-fifths of the total number of working women had white collar jobs.[15]

The work experiences of middle-class women have differed strikingly from those of working-class women. No matter what type of work a middle-class woman has performed, work has been a consciously made choice and an effort to find self-fulfillment and independence, not an economic necessity. Exactly the reverse has been true of the twentieth century working-class woman who has entered the labor force because it was the only choice open to her.

In the late nineteenth and early twentieth centuries, an ever-increasing number of women, particularly immigrant women, entered industrial employment. Women made up a substantial proportion of the industrial work force in the nineteenth century, particularly in the years before the Civil War, but their numbers had always been much smaller than the number of women employed in domestic service or agricultural work. Industrial expansion and the introduction of new machinery which simplified and specialized the production process led to the employment of large numbers of unskilled women workers to perform jobs once performed by men. By 1900, 24.7 percent of women workers were engaged in industrial pursuits, second only to the 39.4 percent in domestic service.[16]

Working-class women performed a large variety of jobs outside the home. Early twentieth century garment shops, cigar factories, paper-box factories, and textile mills hired large numbers of women. In more recent years, women moved into the electrical, aviation, and automobile industries. Women in domestic service worked as waitresses, hotel workers, personal servants, and laundry workers.

Work in factories or in domestic service was hardly "liberating": the hours were long (well over sixty a week in factories in the years before strong union contracts and protective legislation) and working conditions were degrading and poor. Factories were dark and cramped and fire protection was unknown. Poor conditions frequently were exacerbated by requirements that workers pay fines for lateness and pay for their own materials. In the needle trades early in the century, for example, workers often had to buy their own needles and thread and paid for their own electrical power. As industry became increasingly routinized and specialized, and industrial production was subdivided into an ever-greater number of processes, speed-up and monotony added to its dehumanizing qualities. "In the shops we are not called by the name; we have numbers," one young woman garment worker said in 1909. "We work so steadily that in most cases we do not know the girl who works next to us."[17]

Sexist discrimination was widespread in industry. Not only were women paid about half of men's wages, on the average, in the early part of the century, but they had fewer opportunities open to them to learn a skilled trade.[18]

In short, women, particularly in the early decades of the twentieth century, had little control over the conditions of their employment and, like other marginal workers, were forced into a position of undermining wage standards and conditions in the workplace.

The labor movement early in the century did little to alleviate the industrial woman's plight. Organized labor vacillated and hedged on the issue of women workers. Although the American Federation of Labor occasionally hired a woman organizer and endorsed the necessity of organizing women workers, the Federation's pronouncements accomplished little. Part of the difficulty was due to the exclusionary policies of many locals which blindly refused to acknowledge that women had become a permanent part of the work force. As late as the 1920s there were still ten internationals which did not admit women.[19]

Underlying organized labor's lack of action were several assumptions about women workers. Union officials often expressed the traditional views that women were invariably temporary workers and that women were working for "pin money" or out of selfish disregard for their familial responsibilities. Women, like black and immigrant workers, were accused of strikebreaking and lowering hard won standards and benefits.[20]

Stereotypic assumptions about women workers and AF of L indifference, however, were not the greatest obstacles to the unionization of women. The unskilled nature of most working women's jobs set them apart from the early labor movement which was concerned with skilled tradesmen. Then too, a union organizer had to face obstacles in the consciousness of working women themselves: many working women did see themselves as temporary workers, working only until they got married. Understandably, many young women workers often looked forward to marriage as liberation from the harsh conditions of the factory.[21]

The first major breakthroughs in organizing women came in industries in which women made up a large proportion of the work force and from unions which were dedicated to organizing along industrial lines rather than on a trade basis. Not surprisingly, these first advances were made in the garment trades. With a series of organizational strikes in the early 1900s, the International Ladies' Garment Workers Union successfully organized tens of thousands of young immigrant women. In the 1930s, the CIO made similar advances by organizing women workers in electrical, textile, and automobile industries.[22] An increasing number of women have entered the labor movement throughout the twentieth century and woman's permanent place in industry has been acknowledged, but the relationship of women to the sources of union power parallels to some degree her general situation in industry. Union hierarchies, like business ones, have been men's preserves. Women make up a majority of the rank and file in the ILGWU, for instance, but the union is exclusively male in its leadership.

Although many women industrial workers have organized collectively, the historical record for women workers in nonindustrial pursuits has been bleak. The most oppressed of women workers—women who have worked in laundries or as waitresses or servants—have never fully realized the benefits of organiza-tion despite sporadic and usually unsuccessful attempts to organize them. The workplaces have been isolated, the labor supply unlimited, and workers' bargaining power weak or nonexistent.

On the other side of the economic spectrum, middle-class white collar employees have shown very little interest historically in organizing around common demands and in resistance to common forms of exploitation. This difference stems from the different nature of working-class and middle-class employment as well as different motivations for working. The oppression involved in factory work, especially in the early decades of the century, is a tangible reality. Then too, industrial employment is characterized by a sharp dichotomy between the position of the employer and the position of the worker. White collar employment, however, usually has not involved the physical oppression associated with industrial work: working conditions have been endurable and the jobs less strenuous. In addition, white collar employment generally has been accorded higher status than factory work, in part due to the fact that basic skills in the English language as well as some specialized skills, such as typing, are required. In white collar employment, lines between workers and management generally are more fluid and ambiguous than they are in industrial employment and are often characterized by more personal contact.[23] Finally, middle-class women in the labor force often see themselves primarily as consumers and as homemakers who work, rather than as workers first and foremost.[24]

The differences in economic roles and personal expectations between wor-king-class and middle-class women were also reflected in the feminist movement in the early part of the century. Working-class women were apathetic to the goals of organized feminism. They did not see the movement as furthering their collective aims of better working conditions and unionization. Their indifference to the movement was not unfounded. The National American Women's Suffrage Association, for example, was at best indifferent to the unionization of women workers, and some important suffragists were openly hostile to organized labor and immigration. Another important factor in its failure to attract working-class women was the movement's single-minded emphasis on suffrage. Most working women did not regard obtaining the vote as a real improvement in their condition, while middle-class suffragists often saw the vote as the only important goal of the movement. For them, suffrage was an end in itself.[25]

Women in the organized feminist movement accepted the economic transfor-mation of middle-class women from co-producer to consumer and incorporated it into their thinking about their own lives and about their place in society. In addition, early twentieth century feminists combined this acceptance of consumerism with an acceptance of the nineteenth century ideal of woman as imbued with fixed and unchanging moral and biological characteristics and responsibilities to care for children and the home. No longer advancing the individualistic political and legal arguments of nineteenth century feminism, early twentieth century feminists argued that women were different, morally and socially. For precisely these reasons women should be allowed to vote; the political system needed women's influence. Spokeswomen in the movement constantly stressed that the home and the community were interrelated and interdependent, and that to women as buyers fell the responsibility for insuring that the work they used to perform inside the home now was performed efficiently, safely, and equitably outside it. Accordingly, women spearheaded campaigns for pure food legislation and other consumer-oriented reforms.[26]

The arguments employed by the feminist movement early in the twentieth century ignored many of the contemporary trends involving women—particularly the increasing participation of working-class women in the industrial labor force. Although some organizations within the larger woman's movement attempted to bridge the gap between working-class women and their middle-class counterparts, and although there was a great deal of talk about "sisterhood" within the movement, early twentieth century feminism remained tied to its middle-class moorings. Generally, attempts at cross-class cooperation were based on urging middle-class women to use their buying power as a way to help their working-class sisters. The Consumer League movement, the union label organizations, and women's labor groups stressed that women controlled their communities' purchasing power, and for that reason should be knowledgeable about labor conditions. For example, during the 1909 shirtwaist strike, the Women's Trade Union League urged middle-class women to insist upon the waistmakers' union label when buying waists: "Now is the time for women of New York, Philadelphia, and in fact everywhere where American shirtwaists are worn, to rise in their might and demonstrate that with them bargain-hunting can be subordinated to principle and that they have said goodbye to the products of the sweatshop. . . . Friends, let us stop talking about sisterhood and MAKE SISTERHOOD A FACT."[27] But despite some earnest efforts, serious cross-class cooperation within the woman's movement failed.

The woman's movement's emphasis on the middle-class woman's consumer role, its acceptance of the nineteenth century ideal of women as morally superior to men, and its solitary emphasis on winning the vote help to explain not only the movement's failure to reach working-class women, but also its inability to move beyond its immediate goal of the franchise. For much of the nineteenth century, feminism was a bold movement, daring to challenge not only women's political inequality, but also the social institutions which defined woman's role: marriage and the family. By the early twentieth century, however, organized feminism fought only for the right to vote and attempted to avoid controversy. By the time the Nineteenth Amendment was enacted into law, the vote was no longer a way to help reach the goal of woman's social equality; it was an end in itself.[28]

In the years after 1920, feminism as a movement became increasingly isolated. Much has been written about woman's nature and about woman's fulfillment since the passage of the Nineteenth Amendment, but almost invariably it has been phrased in individualistic terms. Women generally have had little sense of their common difficulties and their collective power, and thus have attempted individual solutions to problems of identity, sexuality, work, and self-fulfillment.

The movement's limited vision in the early twentieth century helps explain the decline of feminism after 1920, but changing attitudes toward sexuality are perhaps even more important for an understanding of what happened to the feminist movement and feminist consciousness. Early twentieth century feminists usually accepted the nineteenth century stereotype of woman as devoid of sexual needs. Liberation included the right to abstain from sexual relations and marriage. By 1920, however, ideas about sex had changed, and feminine sexuality was openly discussed. Although it is possible to overestimate the impact of the "new woman" in the decade of the twenties, it is clear that those years witnessed a new openness about woman's sexuality. One index of such openness was the relatively rapid acceptance of the birth control movement. Although Margaret Sanger's early efforts in the years before World War I met with public indignation and legal reprisals, by the 1920s a large majority of young middle-class women approved of contraceptive use.[29] Intellectual currents were also important in shaping and reflecting new social trends. After World War I, popularized Freudian psychology contributed to changing notions about feminine sexuality, particularly because of Freud's emphasis on the centrality of sex in human motivation. Feminists such as Charlotte Perkins Gilman and Carrie Chapman Catt, however, who lived and wrote throughout the twenties, decried the "new morality" and the individualistic and hedonistic "new woman." It is not surprising, then, that young women who came of age after the suffrage amendment was passed and who had not been caught up in the struggle for the vote did not respond to traditional feminist ideology which stressed sexual repression and denial.[30]

The changes in ideas and norms concerning feminine sexuality which constituted the "new morality" are not only important for understanding the decline of feminism but also are crucial for understanding twentieth century women's relationships with one another. In this regard it is important to stress that the "new morality" has not been totally liberating. True, for most of the twentieth century women have not had to endure the sexual repression which characterized nineteenth century Victorian standards. On the other hand, the new definition of woman's sexuality has separated women from each other. With the reaffirmation of feminine sexuality, the traditional notion of sisterhood which characterized women's relationships with each other in the nineteenth century broke down. Many nineteenth century women internalized the societal view of themselves as more moral, pure, and pious than men and, as a result, often found emotional fulfillment in friendships with other women.[31] Women in the twentieth century, on the other hand, were expected to have emotional attachments only to men. Because women have competed on an individual basis for men's attention, the possibilities of women coming together to develop feminist consciousness and to realize their own power lessened.

Contemporary views on feminine sexuality which emerged in the 1920s have further divided middle-class women from working-class women. In the nineteenth century, women were divided from their sisters in similar fashion, but with some important variations. The working-class woman in the previous century was not affected by many of the repressive aspects of Victorian morality. In the twentieth century, however, working-class women generally have not shared the personally liberating aspects of the "new morality." They are not affected by the tenets of Freudian psychology and the open discussion of sexual matters that the popularization of psychoanalytic theories engendered. Often, because of religious prohibitions or lack of knowledge, they have not had access to effective methods of birth control. Working-class women's views on sexuality have often been influenced by fear of unwanted pregnancies, ignorance of contraceptive techniques, and unfulfilling sexual relations.[32]

The twentieth century affirmation of feminine sexuality also has been essential to the updated Cult of True Womanhood. The heightened emphasis on woman as a sexual being has formed the basis behind the arguments which advertisers, educators, and psychologists have advanced during the century to convince women that their emotional fulfillment depended upon accepting their "natural" role in the home. Whereas in the nineteenth century women were defined—and defined themselves—by careful avoidance of sexuality and the physical aspects of marriage and maternity, women in the present century often have been defined with reference to their sexuality alone. Because sexuality has been considered the only major factor necessary to explain women's motivations, behavior, and path to self-fulfillment, women have been further separated from male-oriented society. Women have been told in the twentieth century that they may find fulfillment only through marriage and motherhood. Deviation from these norms has indicated psychological and sexual maladjustment and personal unhappiness.[33] As one sociologist wrote in the late twenties, "Once the advocates of feminine independence may have believed that it would truly be the way to happiness. But the modern girl, who has seen the loneliness of older, unmarried friends, is beginning to discount the rewards from a material success that must be accomplished at the expense of love."[34]

Hence, throughout much of the present century, to be a feminist has meant to be "maladjusted" sexually. The view that women's fulfillment has depended upon fulfilling her roles as mother and wife, however, by no means has been limited to psychoanalytic theorists. The ways in which the advertising industry has made use of these assumptions about woman's nature have already been discussed. In addition, women themselves often have internalized the twentieth century stereotype. Margaret Sanger, for instance, urged women to liberate their "feminine spirit" and extolled the mystical virtues and rewards of motherhood. Actually, here views were not far removed from those of the Cult of True Womanhood.[35]

The history of women in twentieth century America, then, is a history of social division and fragmentation. Women have been separated across generations and across classes. The different economic roles of worker and consumer have divided women from each other. All twentieth century American women, however, have continued to be defined in terms of a limited stereotype. The definition of women in terms of marriage and motherhood, despite its increasing irrelevance to changing economic and social realities, has been an important factor in educating women to fulfill their economic role as American society's most important consumers. Finally, because there has not been a strong feminist tradition in America throughout most of the twentieth century, American women growing up in these years have had to accept and internalize this "feminine mystique" or react against it as individuals. Only in very recent years has feminist consciousness reemerged. To the current feminist movement belongs the task of attempting to understand and surmount the effects of class division and social fragmentation on American women. To the present movement also belongs the task of freeing women to understand themselves historically in light of the social and economic conditions which affect their lives, rather than in terms of their sexuality alone.

Nancy E. Schrom　　**311**

# REFERENCES

1. For a description of the nineteenth century ideal, see Barbara Welter, "The Cult of True Womanhood, 1820–1860," *American Quarterly*, XVIII (Summer 1966).

2. For a full discussion on the introduction of new appliances and "labor-saving" devices, the best source is the President's Committee on Recent Social Trends, *Recent Social Trends* (Washington, D.C., 1932). Other good, but short, discussions can be found in Ross M. Robertson, *History of the American Economy* (New York: Harcourt, Brace, and World, 1964) and in Carl N. Degler, "Revolution Without Ideology: The Changing Place of Women in America," in *The Woman in America*, Robert Jay Lifton, ed. (Boston: Houghton Mifflin, 1964).

3. Charlotte Perkins Gilman was an exceptionally prolific writer. Her best and most useful work is *Women and Economics* (New York: Harper & Row, 1966). Also see her novel, *What Diantha Did* (New York: Charleton, 1910).

4. Simon Patten quoted in Theresa Schmid McMahan, *Woman and Economic Evolution* (Madison: University of Wisconsin, 1908). Alice Beal Parsons, *Woman's Dilemma* (New York: Thomas Y. Crowell, 1924). The problem of the "nervous housewife" was discussed in a number of works in the early part of the century. See especially Abraham Meyerson, *The Nervous Housewife* (Boston: Little, Brown, 1920). Christopher Lasch in *The New Radicalism in America* (New York: Vintage, 1965) documents the "restlessness" of women in the first decades of the twentieth century. For early analyses of woman's role as consumer, see Bertha Lucas, *The Woman Who Spends: A Study of Her Economic Function* (Boston: Whitcomb and Barrows, 1904); Lorinne Pruette, *Women and Leisure* (New York: E. P. Dutton, 1924); Olive Schreiner, *Women and Labour* (New York: Frederick A. Stokes, 1911); Julia Jesse Taft, *The Woman Movement from the Point of View of Social Consciousness* (Chicago: University of Chicago, 1915); Thorstein Veblen, "The Economic Theory of Women's Dress," *Popular Science Monthly* (November 1894). The best recent study is Betty Friedan, *The Feminine Mystique* (New York: Norton, 1963).

5. See especially Charlotte Perkins Gilman, *Women and Economics*, previously cited; Lorinne Pruette, previously cited.

6. See *Ladies' Home Journal*, July 1922, p. 47.

7. Betty Friedan, *The Feminine Mystique*, previously cited. For a good discussion of the advertising industry in the twenties, including the image of women in advertising, see Otis Pease, *The Responsibilities of American Advertising: Private Control and Public Influence, 1920–1940* (New Haven: Yale University Press, 1958).

8. *Ladies' Home Journal* (August 1924), p. 49; Benjamin Andrews, "The Home Woman as Buyer and Controller of Consumption," *The Annals of the American Academy of Political and Social Science*, CXLIII (May 1929), p. 41.

9. Quoted in *The New York Times* (May 23, 1926), Section ix, p. 8.

10. For a discussion of women's education in the 1920s see Willystine Goodsell, *The Education of Women* (New York: Macmillan, 1923). Iva Peters, *Social and Vocational Orientation for College Women* (Richmond: Southern Women's Educational Alliance, 1926) is also useful.

11. The most useful analysis of the woman college student in recent years is in Nevitt Sanford, *The American College* (New York: Wiley, 1962). Betty Friedan, *The Feminine Mystique*, previously cited, has a very useful discussion on women's education. Sylvia Plath's novel, *The Bell Jar* (New York: Harper and Row, 1971), powerfully delineates the stresses and contradictions a woman faced in college in the 1950s.

12. Margaret Benston, "The Political Economy of Women's Liberation," *Monthly Review* (September 1969). See E. P. Thompson, "Time, Work Discipline, and Industrial Capitalism," *Past and Present* (1967) for a discussion of clock time and task orientation.

13. Esther Peterson, "Working Women," in Robert Jay Lifton, ed., *The Woman in America*, previously cited. For a discussion of married women who did work in industry in the early twentieth century, see Robert Smuts, *Women and Work in America* (New York: Columbia University Press, 1959).

14. See, for example, Laura Baker, *Wanted: Women in War Industry* (New York: E. P. Dutton, 1943) and Margaret Culkin Banning, *Women for Defense* (New York: Duell, Sloan, & Pearce, 1942). The amount of material on women's war work is considerable. For World War I see Mabel Daggett, *Women Wanted* (New York: George Doran, 1918). For World

War II see Katharine Anthony, *Out of the Kitchen, Into the War* (New York: Knopf, 1943) and Mabel Gerken, *Ladies in Pants: A Home Front Diary* (New York: Exposition, 1949).

15. Esther Peterson, previously cited, p. 154.

16. Helen Sumner, "History of Women in Industry in the United States, " *Report of the Condition of Woman and Child Wage Earners in the United States,* Vol. IX, United States Senate Document 645, 61st Congress (Washington, 1911). The *Bulletins* of the Women's Bureau are also invaluable. *Bulletin* Number 104, "The Occupational Progress of Women, 1910–1930" (Washington, 1933) is especially valuable.

17. *The New York Call,* December 16, 1909, p. 2.

18. Robert W. Smuts, previously cited, is a useful work. Working women's experiences in industry in the early decades of the twentieth century are very well documented by working women themselves, by social reformers, and by middle-class women who worked in industry for a short time and recorded their experiences. Some of the most notable works include Dorothy Richardson, *The Long Day: The Story of a New York Working Girl as Told by Herself,* in William O'Neill, ed., *Women at Work* (Chicago: Quadrangle, 1971); Sue Ainslie Clark and Edith Wyatt, *Making Both Ends Meet* (New York: Macmillan, 1911); Bessie Van Vorst, *The Woman Who Toils: Being the Experience of Two Ladies as Factory Girls* (New York: Doubleday, 1903). Elizabeth Baker, *Technology and Women's Work* (New York: Columbia University Press, 1964) is valuable. Alice Henry's works are the best single source for women's early experience in unions.

19. See *The Trade Union Woman* (New York: D. Appleton, 1915) and *Women and the Labor Movement* (New York: George Doran, 1923). Also see John B. Andrews and W. D. P. Bliss, "History of Women in Trade Unions," *Report of the Condition of Woman and Child Wage Earners in the United States,* Vol X, United States Senate Document 645, 61st Congress (Washington, 1911).

20. See Alice Henry, already cited.

21. See, for example, Louis Odencrantz, *Italian Women in Industry: A Study of Conditions in New York City* (New York: Russell Sage Foundation, 1919). See also Alice Henry's works, previously cited, for the best discussions of the difficulties facing the union organizer. Agnes Nestor's autobiography, *Woman's Labor Leader* (Rockford, Illinois: Bellevue Books, 1954), is a valuable source. (Agnes Nestor organized women glove workers and was an officer of the National Women's Trade Union League.)

22. One of the most valuable recent studies concerned with the garment workers, although not specifically concerned with the problems of women workers, is Peter Laslett, *Labor and the Left* (New York: Basic Books, 1970). A number of histories of the early years of the ILGWU exists. None of them are concerned with the special issues and problems of women workers. See, for example, Louis Levine, *The Women Garment Workers: A History of the International Ladies' Garment Workers* (New York: B. W. Huebsch, 1924). Rose Schneiderman's memoirs, *All for One* (New York: P. S. Eriksson, 1967), contains interesting material on her experiences as an organizer in ILGWU locals.

23. For a fascinating discussion of this point, see Elinor Langer, *Inside the New York Telephone Company,* in William O'Neill, ed., *Women at Work,* previously cited.

24. See Elinor Langer, previously cited.

25. The most important discussions of the feminist movement's relationship to working-class women are Aileen Kraditor, *The Ideas of the Woman Suffrage Movement* (New York: Columbia University Press, 1965) and Aileen Kraditor, ed., *Up From the Pedestal* (Chicago: Quadrangle, 1968). Also see William O'Neill, *Everyone Was Brave: A History of Feminism in America* (Chicago: Quadrangle, 1969).

26. Aileen Kraditor, *The Ideas of the Woman Suffrage Movement,* previously cited; William O'Neill, *Everyone Was Brave,* previously cited. Good source material for the consumer orientation of the feminist movement is in Rheta Childe Dorr, *What Eight Million Women Want* (Boston: Small, Maynard, 1910) and in the materials collected about the women's club movement. Jane Cunningham Croly, *The History of the Women's Club Movement in America* (New York: H. G. Allen and Co., 1898), is the most readily available source. Jane Addams was also concerned with this aspect of the feminist movement. See Christopher Lasch, ed., *Jane Addams: A Centennial Reader* (New York: Macmillan, 1960).

27. *The New York Call,* December 29, 1909, p. 4.

28. The most complete history of organized feminism is Eleanor Flexner, *Century of Struggle* (New York: Atheneum, 1968). Another useful work is Mildred Adams, *The Right*

to be People (Philadelphia: Lippincott, 1967). For a discussion of the decline of feminism, see William O'Neill, *Everyone Was Brave*, previously cited. Also see William O'Neill's article, "Feminism as a Radical Ideology," in Alfred Young, ed., *Dissent* (DeKalb, Illinois: Northern Illinois University, 1968). Organized feminism continued into the 1920s with the National Woman's Party, the successor to the Congressional Union. The National Woman's Party carried out an extensive campaign throughout the twentieth century for an equal rights amendment. The most valuable source of information on the NWP is its periodical, *Equal Rights*.

29. Excellent source material on young women's views on contraception in the 1920s is contained in Phyllis Blanchard, *New Girls for Old* (New York: Macauley, 1930). The best recent study of Margaret Sanger and the birth control movement is David Kennedy, *Birth Control in America* (New Haven: Yale University Press, 1970). An older but still useful study of birth control in America is Norman Himes, *Medical History of Contraception* (Baltimore: Johns Hopkins, 1936). Also see Margaret Sanger's own works, especially *My Fight for Birth Control* (New York: Farrar and Rinehart, 1931). An excellent new study of the impact of Freudian thought on America, although it does not cover the decade of the twenties, is Nathan Hale, *Freud and the Americans* (New York: Oxford University Press, 1971). Useful discussions of the changes in marriage and the family appear in William O'Neill, *Divorce in the Progressive Era* (New Haven: Yale University Press, 1967), and in Carl Degler, "Revolution Without Ideology," previously cited.

30. Secondary materials on the "New Woman" include James McGovern, "Woman's Pre-World War I Freedom in Manners and Morals," *Journal of American History*, LV (September 1968) and Christopher Lasch, *The New Radicalism in America*, previously cited. Source material is abundant. Magazines in the twenties, particularly *The Nation, Harper's*, and *The New Republic*, were very concerned with the woman issue, and contain a voluminous amount of contemporary debate on the "New Woman." Also see Phyllis Blanchard, *New Girls for Old* (New York: Macauley, 1930), which is particularly useful for information on contemporary sexual attitudes, and Freda Kirchwey, ed., *Our Changing Morality* (New York: A. and C. Boni, 1924). Fiction is also of value in seeing the emergence of the "new woman." See Kate Chopin, *The Awakening* (New York: Duffield, 1906); David Graham Phillips, *Susan Lenox* (New York: D. Appleton, 1931); and the novels of Floyd Dell and Robert Herrick. "New women's" autobiographies include Mabel Dodge Luhan, *Intimate Memories, Movers and Shakers* (New York: Harcourt, Brace, 1933) and Isadora Duncan, *My Life* (New York: Boni & Liveright, 1927). For the reactions of traditional feminists to the New Morality, see Charlotte Perkins Gilman, "Toward Monogamy," *The Nation*, 118 (June 11, 1924) and "Woman's Achievements Since the Franchise," *Current History*, 27 (October 1927). Also see Carrie Chapman Catt, "Suffrage: Only an Episode in an Age-Old Movement," *Current History*, 27 (October 1927). Dorothy Bromley's short article, "Feminist—New Style," *Harper's*, 155 (April 1925), is illustrative of young women's negative attitudes toward feminism.

31. For a discussion on this point, see William R. Taylor and Christopher Lasch, "Two Kindred Spirits: Sorority and Family in New England, 1839-1846," *New England Quarterly*, XXXVI (March 1963).

32. For a discussion of working-class sexual attitudes and relations, see Mirra Komarovsky, *Blue Collar Marriage* (New York: Vintage, 1962) and Lee Rainwater, *And the Poor Get Children* (Chicago: Quadrangle, 1960).

33. The psychoanalytic discussions of women have been the most influential in this regard. For classical psychoanalytic discussion about woman's nature, see Helene Deutsch, *The Psychology of Women, A Psychoanalytic Interpretation* (New York: Grune and Stratton, 1944). Also see Ferdinand Lundberg and Maryna Farnham, *Modern Woman: The Lost Sex* (New York: Harper, 1947), for the application of popular psychoanalytic thinking to women's lives in the early post-World War II period. Erik Erikson's neo-Freudian approach to woman's nature has been influential. See "Inner and Outer Space: Reflections on Womanhood," in Robert Jay Lifton, ed., *The Woman in America*, previously cited. The classical Freudian approach has not gone without refutation. See Clara Thompson's works for a psychoanalytic viewpoint which takes issue with Freud's views on women. One of her best articles is "Cultural Pressures in the Psychology of Women," *Psychiatry*, V (August 1942).

34. Phyllis Blanchard, *New Girls for Old*, previously cited, pp. 237-38.

35. For a good, although brief, discussion of this point, see David Kennedy, *Birth Control*

*in America,* previously cited, Chapter 2. Also see Margaret Sanger, *Women and the New Race* (New York: Brentano's, 1920). Beatrice Hinkle, a psychoanalyst in the twenties, also exemplifies this point in her work. See, for example, "Changing Marriage," *Survey Graphic,* 57 (December 1926); "New Morals for Old," *The Nation,* 119 (November 19, 1924); and "Why Feminism?" *The Nation,* 125 (July 6, 1927).

# bibliography

The civil rights movement resulted in a number of sophisticated analyses of white racism and nativism. See especially Thomas F. Gossett, *Race: The History of an Idea* (Schocken, 1965), and Joel Kovel, *White Racism: A Psychohistory* (Vintage Books, 1970). Arthur Waskow's *From Race Riot to Sit-In, 1919 and the 1960's* (Doubleday, Anchor, 1966) illuminates the connections between racial violence and international conflict. See also Elliott Rudwick, *Race Riot at East St. Louis* (World Publishing, 1966). Gustavus Myers' *History of Bigotry in the United States*, rev. ed. (Capricorn, 1960), which was originally published in 1943, has been brought up to date by Henry Christman and remains an indispensable guide to the persecution of racial and ethnic minorities. Three outstanding anthologies are Barry Schwartz and Robert Disch, eds., *White Racism: Its History, Pathology and Practice* (Dell, 1970); Lewis Carlson and George Colburn, *In Their Place: White America Defines Her Minorities, 1850–1950* (Wiley, 1972); and Paul Jacobs, Saul Landau, and Eve Pell, *To Serve the Devil*, 2 vols. (Vintage Books, 1971). See also William L. Patterson, ed., *We Charge Genocide* (International Publishers, 1970).

Radical black historians see racism as a primary element in America's development. See especially Sidney M. Willhelm, *Who Needs the Negro?* (Schenkman, 1970), which predicts that black people will be massacred when their labor is no longer needed; Rayford Logan, *The Betrayal of the Negro: From Rutherford B. Hayes to Woodrow Wilson* (Collier, 1965); Vincent Harding, "Beyond Chaos: Black History and the Search for a New Land," in John A. Williams and Charles F. Harris, eds., *Amistad I* (Vintage Books, 1970); and John Henrik Clarke, Esther Jackson, Ernest Kaiser, and J. H. O'Dell, eds., *Black Titan: W.E.B. DuBois: An Anthology By and About W.E.B. DuBois* (Beacon Press, 1970). Bernard Sternsher's anthology *The Negro in Depression and War: Prelude to Revolution, 1930–1945* (Quadrangle Books, 1970) includes articles by DuBois, Mary McLeod Bethune, and Richard Dalfiume, and Ernest Kaiser's important essay "The Federal Government and the Negro, 1865–1955," which was originally published in *Science and Society* (Winter 1956). See also Kaiser's "Recent Literature on Black Liberation Struggles," *Science and Society* (1969). "In Defense of the People's Black and White History and Culture," *Freedomways* (1970, parts I, II, III); and Mark Naison, "Marxism and Black Radicalism in America," *Radical America* (May–June 1971).

Important works on the black liberation movement include John Henrik Clarke, "The New Afro-American Nationalism," *Freedomways* (Fall 1961); Earl Ofari, *The Myth of Black Capitalism* (Monthly Review Press, 1970); James Boggs, *The American Revolution: Pages from a Negro Worker's Notebook* (Modern Reader Paperbacks, 1963); and Boggs, *Racism and the Class Struggle: Further Pages from a Black Worker's Notebook* (Modern Reader Paperbacks, 1970). For an analysis of the relationship between the Communist Party and the black community see Wilson Record, *Race and Radicalism: The NAACP and the Communist Party in Conflict* (Cornell University Press, 1964).

The summer 1969 issue of *Labor History* was devoted to "The Negro and the American Labor Movement." Reissued with additions and changes, and an introduction by Herbert Gutman, it is an invaluable source: Milton Cantor, ed., *Black Labor in America* (Greenwood Press, 1970). See also Julius Jackson, ed., *The Negro and the American Labor Movement* (Doubleday, Anchor, 1968).

Recent events have led to renewed interest in certain radical groups, especially the anarchist I.W.W. See especially Philip Foner, "The IWW and the Black Worker," *Journal of Negro History* (January 1970); Melvyn Dubofsky, *We Shall Be All: A History of the IWW* (Quadrangle Books, 1969); Michael Ebner, "The Passaic Strike of 1912 and the Two IWW's," *Labor History* (Fall 1970); and Vernon Jensen and Melvyn Dubofsky, "The IWW: An Exchange of Views," *Labor History* (Summer 1970). Harvey O'Connor's *Revolution in Seattle* (Monthly Review Press, 1964) is an important personal memoir supplemented by much research. For other radical movements see Lillian Symes and Travers Clement, *Rebel America: The Story of Social Revolt in the United States*, rev. ed. (Beacon Press, 1972), with an incisive introduction for the new edition by Richard Drinnon; Neil Betten, "The Great Depression and the Activities of the Catholic Worker Movement," *Labor History* (Spring 1971); and Joseph R. Starobin, *American Communism in Crisis, 1942–1957* (Harvard University Press, 1972). For an account of the activities of the left wing of the C.I.O., see Len De Caux's autobiographical *Labor Radical* (Beacon Press, 1970).

Because of the belief that radical movements are un-American, one response to radicalism has frequently been nativist hysteria. See Richard Hofstadter, *The Paranoid Style in American Politics* (Knopf, 1965); Harry N. Scheiber, *The Wilson Administration and Civil Liberties* (Cornell University Press, 1960); Louis F. Post, *The Deportation Delirium of 1920* (Ch. H. Kerr, 1923); Robert K. Murray, *Red Scare: A Study in National Hysteria* (University of Minnesota Press, 1955); and Roger Daniels, *The Politics of Prejudice* (Atheneum, 1968). Standard works on nativism and general histories of immigration range from the consensus melting-pot school of Oscar Handlin's *The Uprooted* (Little, Brown, 1951) to the mainstream-liberal examinations of nativist attitudes represented by John Higham, *Strangers in the Land, rev. ed. (Atheneum, 1970); William Preston, Jr. Aliens and Dissenters: Federal Suppression of Radicals, 1903–1933* (Torchbooks, Harper & Row, 1963); and Barbara Miller Solomon, *Ancestors and Immigrants* (Wiley, 1956).

For works on women, see the excellent bibliography in Ann D. Gordon, Mari Jo Buhle, and Nancy E. Schrom, "Women in American Society," *Radical America* (July–August, 1971); Gerda Lerner's brief but useful *The Woman in American History* (Addison-Wesley, 1971); Lerner's masterful *Black Woman in White America: A Documentary History* (Pantheon, 1972); Juliet Mitchell, *Woman's Estate* (Pantheon, 1972); and Aileen Kraditor, ed., *Up From the Pedestal* (Quadrangle Books, 1968). William O'Neill's *Everyone Was Brave: A History of Feminism in America* (Quadrangle Books, 1969) is well researched but suffers from his male bias. As yet there are almost no significant biographies of radical women. One exception is Richard Drinnon's work of rare distinction, *Rebel in Paradise: A Biography of Emma Goldman* (University of Chicago Press, 1961).

No listing of books about the discriminated is complete without some reference to those who discriminate. See especially, C. Wright Mills, *The Power Elite* (Oxford University Press, 1956); G. William Domhoff, *The Higher Circles: The Governing Class in America* (Vintage Books, 1970); Domhoff's more general *Who Rules America?* Prentice-Hall, 1967); E. Digby Baltzell, *The Protestant Establishment: Aristocracy and Caste in America* (Vintage Books, 1966); and Gabriel Kolko, *Wealth and Power in America: An Analysis of Social Class and Income Distribution* (Frederick A. Praeger, 1962).

in and out of the ivory tower:
the historian's dilemma

Those who, like Marc Bloch, regard the study of history as essential to an understanding of the problems of the living face a deep conflict today. The question of scientific objectivity as opposed to the political responsibility of scholars is an old one. Presently, the war in Indochina and increasing domestic violence challenge the scholar's ability to remain aloof from the political arena.

Historians must ask themselves if activism distorts scholarship: Are the two irreconcilable? There are those who believe that the revolutionary's job is to make the revolution and who consider scholarship and study anathema to that task. Others fear that this anti-intellectual assault will result in mindless conflict. They regard scholarship as crucial to an understanding of the sources of power in America and therefore essential for meaningful social change.

The disdain of young activists for intellectuals who continue to see the validity and relevance of intellectual work is reinforced by the unwillingness of many professional historians to join other citizens in condemnation of the war in Indochina. At a time when colleagues in other professions were using their associations' annual meetings to go on record in opposition to the war, historians refused to do so. The American Historical Association insisted that an antiwar statement was a violation of the hallowed ground of neutral scholarship.

The question remains: What action can a historian take, particularly if he believes that the solution to the crisis lies in the direction of social revolution at home? For the mainstream liberal historian the dilemma does not exist. No one really objects to Eric Goldman or Arthur M. Schlesinger, Jr., taking administration advisory positions or working actively on behalf of one or another liberal presidential candidate. Such behavior is accepted as not being antithetical to the role of scholar and historian.

But for the historian who believes in more fundamental and radical solutions, the problem takes on a new dimension. James Weinstein, a well-known radical historian and member of the editorial collective that publishes *Socialist Revolution,* argues that many avowed radicals themselves posit a false dichotomy between scholarship and action. For him, theory itself is part of revolutionary practice. Achieving a socialist understanding of history is seen as a prerequisite to forging a radical consciousness that will lead to structural transformation. Implicit in Weinstein's argument is the contention that the results hoped for so desperately by movement activists will be impossible to attain without the careful, reflective theoretical work that socialist intellectuals have the duty to engage in. He argues that many in the movement, such as historian Staughton Lynd, accept the dichotomy created by the mainstream historians. Like the liberals, they fail to understand that theory contributes to a self-conscious understanding of corporate capitalism. Certain radical activists and mainstream liberal historians play into each other's hands.

For Karl Marx, the hours he spent studying in the British Museum were basic for his critique of the mechanism of nineteenth century capitalism. For radical historians, the work they do in archival collections and at the typewriter is basic to their understanding of advanced capitalism and central to their commitment to social change. Perhaps we can begin to stop responding to events and developments imposed on us by others if we develop the resources and knowledge of how the mechanisms of control and domination in our society are maintained. Since the mainstream historian is not going to engage in this task, it is left to the radical scholar to apply himself—with the tools of scholarship, commitment, and integrity—to this task.

Three of the selections in this chapter represent accounts and documents pertaining to the developing conflict within the American Historical Association. James B. Gilbert and Ronald Radosh present accounts of the issues and events that played a part in the 1968 and 1969 American Historical Association conventions. The proper role to be taken by historians and by their professional association on the war is debated in an exchange of letters between John K. Fairbank and Howard Zinn, who were involved on opposite sides at the 1969 convention.

# what is radical history?

## HOWARD ZINN

Howard Zinn is a noted antiwar activist and the author of a number of works, including *The Southern Mystique, SNCC: The New Abolitionists,* and *Vietnam: The Logic of Withdrawal.*

In this essay, taken from his book *The Politics of History,* Zinn directly confronts the question of what role is to be played by the radical historian. He favors a history that is written from the viewpoint of the oppressed, that exposes the pretensions of government, and that shows the possibility of a better way of life.

---

Historical writing always has some effect on us. It may reinforce our passivity; it may activate us. In any case, the historian cannot choose to be neutral; he writes on a moving train.

Sometimes, what he tells may change a person's life. In May 1968 I heard a Catholic priest, on trial in Milwaukee for burning the records of a draft board, tell (I am paraphrasing) how he came to that act:

> I was trained in Rome. I was quite conservative, never broke a rule in seminary. Then I read a book by Gordon Zahn, called *German Catholics and Hitler's Wars.* It told how the Catholic Church carried on its normal activities while Hitler carried on his. It told how SS men went to mass, then went out to round up Jews. That book changed my life. I decided the church must never behave again as it did in the past; and that I must not.

This is unusually clear. In most cases, where people turn in new directions, the causes are so complex, so subtle, that they are impossible to trace. Nevertheless, we all are aware of how, in one degree or another, things we read or heard changed our view of the world, or how we must behave. We know there have been many people who themselves did not experience evil, but who became persuaded that it existed, and that they must oppose it. What makes us human is our capacity to reach with our mind beyond our immediate sensory capacities, to feel in some degree what others feel totally, and then perhaps to act on such feelings.

I start, therefore, from the idea of writing history in such a way as to extend human sensibilities, not out of this book into other books, but into the going conflict over how people shall live, and whether they shall live.

I am urging value-laden historiography. For those who still rebel at this— despite my argument that this does not determine answers, only questions; despite my plea that aesthetic work, done for pleasure, should always have its place; despite my insistence that our work is value-laden whether we choose or not—let me point to one area of American education where my idea has been accepted. I am speaking of "Black Studies," which, starting about 1969, began to be adopted with great speed in the nation's universities.

These multiplying Black Studies programs do not pretend to just introduce another subject for academic inquiry. They have the specific intention of so affecting the consciousness of black and white people in this country as to diminish for both groups the pervasive American belief in black inferiority.

This deliberate attempt to foster racial equality should be joined, I am suggesting, by similar efforts for national and class equality. This will probably come, as the Black Studies programs, not by a gradual acceptance of the appropriate arguments, but by a crisis so dangerous as to *demand* quick changes in attitude. Scholarly exhortation is, therefore, not likely to initiate a new emphasis in historical writing, but perhaps it can support and ease it.

What kind of awareness moves people in humanistic directions, and how can historical writing create such awareness, such movement? I can think of five ways in which history can be useful. That is only a rough beginning. I don't want to lay down formulas. There will be useful histories written that do not fit into preconceived categories. I want only to sharpen the focus for myself and others who would rather have their writing guided by human aspiration than by professional habit.

1. *We can intensify, expand, sharpen our perception of how bad things are, for the victims of the world.* This becomes less and less a philanthropic act as all of us, regardless of race, geography, or class, become potential victims of a burned, irradiated planet. But even our own victimization is separated from us by time and the fragility of our imagination, as that of others is separated from us because most of us are white, prosperous, and within the walls of a country so over-armed it is much more likely to be an aggressor than a victim.

History can try to overcome both kinds of separation. The fascinating progression of a past historical event can have greater effect on us than some cool, logical discourse on the dangerous possibilities of present trends—if only for one reason, because we learn the end of that story. True, there is a chill in the contemplation of nuclear war, but it is still a contemplation whose most horrible possibilities we cannot bring ourselves to accept. It is a portent that for full effect needs buttressing by another story whose conclusion is known. Surely, in this nuclear age our concern over the proliferation of H-bombs is powerfully magnified as we read Barbara Tuchman's account of the coming of the First World War:[1]

War pressed against every frontier. Suddenly dismayed, governments struggled and twisted to fend it off. It was no use. Agents at frontiers were reporting every cavalry patrol as a deployment to beat the mobilization gun. General staffs, goaded by their relentless timetables, were pounding the table for the signal to move lest their opponents gain an hour's head start. Appalled upon the brink, the chiefs of state who would be ultimately responsible for their country's fate attempted to back away but the pull of military schedules dragged them forward.

There it is, us. In another time, of course. But unmistakably us.

Other kinds of separation, from the deprived and harried people of the world—the black, the poor, the prisoners—are sometimes easier to overcome across time than across space: hence the value of historical recollection. Both the *Autobiography of Malcolm X* and the *Autobiography of Frederick Douglass* are history, one more recent than the other. Both assault our complacency. So do the photos on television of blacks burning buildings in the ghetto today, but the autobiographies do something special: they let us look closely, carefully, personally behind the impersonality of those blacks on the screen. They invade our homes, as the blacks in the ghetto have not yet done; and our minds, which we tend to harden against the demands of *now*. They tell us, in some small degree, what it is like to be black, in a way that all the liberal clichés about the downtrodden Negro could never match. And thus they insist that we act; they explain why blacks are acting. They prepare us, if not to initiate, to respond.

Slavery is over, but its degradation now takes other forms, at the bottom of which is the unspoken belief that the black person is not quite a human being. The recollection of what slavery is like, what slaves are like, helps to attack that belief. Take the letter Frederick Douglass wrote his former master in 1848, on the tenth anniversary of his flight to freedom:[2]

I have selected this day to address you because it is the anniversary of my eman-cipation . . . Just ten years ago this beautiful September morning yon bright sun beheld me a slave—a poor, degraded chattel—trembling at the sound of your voice, lamenting that I was a man . . .

When yet but a child about six years old I imbibed the determination to run away. The very first mental effort that I now remember on my part, was an attempt to solve the mystery, Why am I a slave . . . When I saw a slave driver whip a slave woman . . . and heard her piteous cries, I went away into the corner of the fence, wept and pondered over the mystery . . . I resolved that I would someday run away.

The morality of the act, I dispose as follows: I am myself; you are yourself; we are two distinct persons. What you are, I am. I am not by nature bound to you nor you to me. . . . In leaving you I took nothing but what belonged to me . . .

Why do we need to reach into the past, into the days of slavery? Isn't the experience of Malcolm X, in our own time enough? I see two values in going back. One is that dealing with the past, our guard is down, because we start off thinking it is over and we have nothing to fear by taking it all in. We turn out to be wrong, because its immediacy strikes us, affects us before we know it; when we have recognized this, it is too late—we have been moved. Another reason is that time adds depth and intensity to a problem which otherwise might seem a passing one, susceptible to being brushed away. To know that long continuity, across the centuries, of the degradation that stalked both Frederick Douglass and Malcolm X (between whose lives stretched that of W. E. B. DuBois, recorded in *The Souls of Black Folk* and *Dusk of Dawn*) is to reveal how infuriatingly long has been this black ordeal in white America. If nothing else, it would make us understand in that black mood of today what we might otherwise see as impatience, and what history tells us is overlong endurance.

Can history also sharpen our perception of that poverty hidden from sight by the foliage of the suburbs? The poor, like the black, become invisible in a society blinded by the glitter of its own luxury. True, we can be forcefully reminded that they exist, as we were in the United States in the 1960's when our sensibilities had been sharpened by the civil rights revolt, and our tolerance of government frayed by the Vietnamese war. At such a time, books like Michael Harrington's *The Other America* jabbed at us, without going back into the past, just supplying a periscope so that we could see around the corner, and demanding that we look.

Where history can help is by showing us how other people similarly situated, in other times, were blind to how their neighbors were living, in the same city. Suppose that, amidst the "prosperity" of the 1950's, we had read about the

1920's, another era of affluence. Looking hard, we might find the report of Senator Burton Wheeler of Montana, investigating conditions in Pennsylvania during the coal strike of 1928:[3]

All day long I have listened to heartrending stories of women evicted from their homes by the coal companies. I heard pitiful pleas of little children crying for bread. I stood aghast as I heard most amazing stories from men brutally beaten by private policemen. It has been a shocking and nerve-racking experience.

Would this not suggest to us that perhaps in our time too a veil is drawn over the lives of many Americans, that the sounds of prosperity drown out all else, and the voices of the well-off dominate history?

In our time, as in the past, we construct "history" on the basis of accounts left by the most articulate, the most privileged members of society. The result is a distorted picture of how people live, an underestimation of poverty, a failure to portray vividly the situations of those in distress. If, in the past, we can manage to find the voice of the underdog, this may lead us to look for the lost pleas of our own era. True, we could accomplish this directly for the present without going back. But sometimes the disclosure of what is hidden in the past prompts us, particularly when there is no immediate prod, to look more penetratingly into contemporary society. (In my own experience, reading in the papers of Fiorello La Guardia the letters from the East Harlem poor in the twenties, made me take a second look at the presumed good times of the fifties.)

Is the picture of society given by its victims a true one? There is no one true picture of any historical situation, no one objective description. This search for a nonexistent objectivity has led us, ironically, into a particularly retrogressive subjectivity, that of the bystander. Society has varying and conflicting interests; what is called objectivity is the disguise of one of these interests—that of neutrality. But neutrality is a fiction in an unneutral world. There are victims, there are executioners, and there are bystanders. In the dynamism of our time, when heads roll into the basket every hour, what is "true" varies according to what happens to your own head—and the "objectivity" of the bystander calls for inaction while other heads fall. In Camus' The Plague, Dr. Rieux says: "All I maintain is that on this earth there are pestilences, and there are victims, and it's up to us, so far as possible, not to join forces with the pestilences." Not to act is to join forces with the spreading plague.

What is the "truth" about the situation of the black man in the United States in 1968? Statistics can be put together which show that his position has improved. Statistics can be put together which show that his situation is as bad as it always was. Both sets of statistics are "true."[4] But the first leads to a satisfaction with the present rate of change; the second leads to a desire for quickening the rate of change. The closest we can come to that elusive "objectivity" is to report accurately all of the subjectivities in a situation. But we emphasize one or another of those subjective views in any case. I suggest we depart from our customary position as privileged observers. Unless we wrench free from being what we like to call "objective," we are closer psychologically, whether we like to admit it or not, to the executioner than to the victim.

There is no need to hide the data which show that some Negroes are climbing the traditional American ladder faster than before, that the ladder is more crowded than before. But there is a need—coming from the determination to represent those still wanting the necessities of existence (food, shelter, dignity, freedom)—to emphasize the lives of those who cannot even get near the ladder.

The latest report of the Census Bureau is as "true," in some abstract sense, as the reports of Malcolm X and Eldridge Cleaver on their lives. But the radical historian will, without hiding the former (there are already many interests at work to tell us that, anyway) emphasize those facts we are most likely to ignore—and these are the facts as seen by the victims.

Thus, a history of slavery drawn from the narratives of fugitive slaves is especially important. It cannot monopolize the historiography in any case, because the histories we already have are those from the standpoint of the slaveholder (Ulrich Phillip's account, based on plantation diaries, for instance), or from the standpoint of the cool observer (the liberal historian, chastising slavery but without the passion appropriate to a call for action). A slave-oriented history simply fills out the picture in such a way as to pull us out of lethargy.

The same is true in telling the story of the American Revolution from the standpoint of the sailor rather than the merchant,[5] and for telling the story of the Mexican War from the standpoint of the Mexicans. The point is not to omit the viewpoint of the privileged (that dominates the field anyway), but to remind us forcibly that there is always a tendency, now as then, to see history from the top. Perhaps a history of the Opium War seen through Chinese eyes would suggest to Americans that the Vietnamese war might also be seen through Vietnamese eyes.[6]

2. *We can expose the pretensions of governments to either neutrality or beneficence.* If the first requisite for activating people is to sharpen their awareness of what is wrong, the second is to disabuse them of the confidence that they can depend on governments to rectify what is wrong.

Again, I start from the premise that there are terrible wrongs all about us, too many for us to rest content even if not everyone is being wronged. Governments of the world have not been disposed to change things very much. Indeed, they have often been the perpetrators of these wrongs. To drive this point at us strongly pushes us to act ourselves.

Does this mean I am not being "objective" about the role of governments? Let us take a look at the historical role of the United States on the race question. For instance, what did the various American governments do for the black person in America right after the Civil War? Let's be "objective," in the sense of telling *all* the facts that answer this question. Therefore we should take proper note of the Thirteenth, Fourteenth, Fifteenth Amendments, the Freedman's Bureau, the stationing of armed forces in the South, the passage of civil rights laws in 1866, 1870, 1871, and 1875. But we should also record the court decisions emasculating the Fourteenth Amendment, the betrayal of the Negro in the 1877 Hayes-Tilden agreement, the nonenforcement of the civil rights acts. Ultimately, even if we told all, our emphasis in the end would be subjective—it would depend on who we are and what we want. A present concern, that citizens need to act themselves, suggests we emphasize the unreliability of government in securing equal rights for black people.

Another question: to what extent can we rely on our government to equitably distribute the wealth of the country? We could take proper account of the laws passed in this century which seemed directed at economic justice: the railroad regulation acts of the Progressive era, the creation of the graduated income tax in the Wilson administration, the suits against trusts initiated in the Theodore Roosevelt and Taft administrations. But a *present* recognition of the fact that the allocation of wealth to the upper and lower fifths of the population has not fundamentally changed in this century would suggest that all that legislation has only managed to maintain the status quo. To change this, we would need to emphasize what has not so far been emphasized, the persistent failure of government to alter the continuing inequities of the American economic system.

Historians' assessments of the New Deal illustrate this problem. We can all be objective by including in any description of the New Deal both its wealth of reform legislation and its inadequacies in eradicating poverty and unemploy - ment in America. But there is always an emphasis, subtle or gross, which we bring to bear on this picture. One kind of emphasis adds to a feeling of satisfaction in how America has been able to deal with economic crisis. Another stimulates us to do more ourselves, in the light of the past failure at dealing with the fundamental irrationality by which our nation's resources are distributed. The needs of the present suggest that the second kind of historical presentation is preferable.[7]

Thus, it is worth putting in their proper little place the vaunted liberal reforms of the Wilson administration. For instance, in a situation like the Ludlow Massacre of 1914, Wilson called out the federal troops not when the striking miners of Colorado were being machine-gunned by the Baldwin -Felts detectives or their homes burned by the National Guard, but when they began to arm and retaliate on a large scale. To take another case, it is useful to know that social security measures were proposed in 1935 beyond those supported by FDR, but that he pushed more moderate proposals. In the light of our belated recognition that social security payments are now and have always been pitifully inadequate, how we view FDR's social security program may or may not reinforce our determination to change things.

A radical history, then, would expose the limitations of governmental reform, the connections of government to wealth and privilege, the tendencies of governments toward war and xenophobia, the play of money and power behind the presumed neutrality of law. It would illustrate the role of government in maintaining things as they are, whether by force, or deception, or by a skillful combination of both—whether by deliberate plan or by the concatenation of thousands of individuals playing roles according to the expectations around them.

Such motivating facts are available in the wealth of data about present governments. What historical material can do is to add the depth that time imparts to an idea. What one sees in the present may be attributable to a passing phenomenon; if the same situation appears at various points in history, it becomes not a transitory event, but a long -range condition, not an aberration, but a structural deformity requiring serious attention.

For instance, we would see more clearly the limitations of government investigating committees set up to deal with deep-rooted social problems if we knew the history of such committees. Take Kenneth Clark's blunt testimony to the National Advisory Commission on Civil Disorders, which was set up after the urban outbreaks of 1967. Pointing to a similar investigation set up after the 1919 riot in Chicago, he said:[8]

I read that report . . . of the 1919 riot in Chicago, and it is as if I were reading of the investigating committee on the Harlem riot of '35, the report of the investigating committee on the Harlem riot of '43, the report of the McCone Commission on the Watts riot. I must again in candor say to you members of this Commission—it is a kind of Alice in Wonderland—with the same moving picture, reshown over and over again, the same analysis, the same recommendations, and the same inaction.

3. *We can expose the ideology that pervades our culture—using "ideology" in Mannheim's sense: rationale for the going order.* There is the open sanctification of racism, of war, of economic inequality. There is also the more subtle supportive tissue of half-truths ("We are not like the imperialist powers of the nineteenth century"); noble myths ("We were born free"); pretenses ("Educa - tion is the disinterested pursuit of knowledge"); the mystification of rhetoric ("freedom and justice for all"); the confusion of ideals and reality (The Declaration of Independence and its call for revolution, in our verbal tradition; the Smith Act and its prohibition of calls for revolution, on our lawbooks); the use of symbols to obscure reality ("Remember the *Maine*," vis-à-vis rotten beef for the troops); the innocence of the double standard (deploring the violence of John Brown; hailing the violence of Ulysses Grant); the concealment of ironies (using the Fourteenth Amendment to help corporations instead of Negroes).

The more widespread is education in a society, the more mystification is required to conceal what is wrong; church, school, and the written word work together for that concealment. This is not the work of a conspiracy; the privileged of society are as much victims of the going mythology as the teachers, priests, and journalists who spread it. All simply do what comes naturally, and what comes naturally is to say what has always been said, to believe what has always been believed.

History has a special ability to reveal the ludicrousness of those beliefs which glue us all to the social frame of our fathers. It also can reinforce that frame with great power, and has done so most of the time. Our problem is to turn the power of history—which can work both ways—to the job of demystification. I recall the words of the iconoclast sociologist E. Franklin Frazier to Negro college students one evening in Atlanta, Georgia: "All your life, white folks have bamboozled you, preachers have bamboozled you, teachers have bamboozled you; I am here to debamboozle you."

Recalling the rhetoric of the past, and measuring it against the actual past, may enable us to see through our current bamboozlement, where the reality is still unfolding, and the discrepancies still not apparent. To read Albert Beveridge's noble plea in the Senate January 9, 1900, urging acquisition of the Philippines with "thanksgiving to Almighty God that He has marked us as His chosen people, henceforth to lead in the regeneration of the world," and then to read of our butchery of the Filipino rebels who wanted independence, is to prepare us better for speeches about our "world responsibility" today. That recollection might make us properly suspicious of Arthur Schlesinger's attempt to set a "historical framework" for Vietnam comprised of "two traditional and entirely honorable strands in American thinking," one of which "is the concept that the United States has a saving mission in the world."[9] In the light of the history of idea and fact in American expansionism, that strand is not quite honorable. The Vietnam disaster was not, as Schlesinger says, "a final and tragic misapplication" of those strands, a wandering from a rather benign historical tradition, but another twining of the deadly strands around a protesting foreign people.

To take another example where the history of ideas is suggestive for today: we might clarify for ourselves the puzzling question of how to account for American expansion into the Pacific in the post–World War II period when the actual material interests there do not seem to warrant such concern. Marilyn B. Young, in her study of the Open Door period, indicates how the mystique of being "a world power" carried the United States into strong action despite "the lack of commercial and financial interest." Thus, "The Open Door passed into the small body of sacred American doctrine and an assumption of America's 'vital stake' in China was made and never relinquished."[10] Her book documents the buildup of this notion of the "vital stake," in a way that might make us more loath to accept unquestioningly the claims of American leaders defending incursions into Asian countries today.

For Americans caught up in the contemporary glorification of efficiency and success, without thought of ends, it might be liberating to read simultaneously *All Quiet on the Western Front* (for the fetid reality of World War I) and Randolph Bourne's comment on the American intellectuals of 1917:[11]

> They have, in short, no clear philosophy of life except that of intelligent service, the admirable adaptation of means to ends. They are vague as to what kind of a society they want or what kind of society America needs, but they are equipped with all the administrative attitudes and talents necessary to attain it. . . It is now becoming plain that unless you start with the vividest kind of poetic vision, your instrumentalism is likely to land you just where it has landed this younger intelligentsia which is so happily and busily engaged in the national enterprise of war.

4. *We can recapture those few moments in the past which show the possibility of a better way of life than that which has dominated the earth thus far.* To move men to act it is not enough to enhance their sense of what is wrong, to show that the men in power are untrustworthy, to reveal that our very way of thinking is limited, distorted, corrupted. One must also show that something else is possible, that changes can take place. Otherwise, people retreat into privacy, cynicism, despair, or even collaboration with the mighty.

History cannot provide confirmation that something better is inevitable; but it can uncover evidence that it is conceivable. It can point to moments when human beings cooperated with one another (the organization of the under-ground railroad by black and white, the French Resistance to Hitler, the anarchist achievements in Catalonia during the Spanish Civil War). It can find times when governments were capable of a bit of genuine concern (the creation of the Tennessee Valley Authority, the free medical care in socialist countries, the equal-wages principle of the Paris Commune). It can disclose men and women acting as heroes rather than culprits or fools (the story of Thoreau or Wendell Phillips or Eugene Debs, or Martin Luther King or Rosa Luxemburg). It can remind us that apparently powerless groups have won against overwhelming odds (the abolitionists and the Thirteenth Amendment, the CIO and the sit-down strikes, the Vietminh and the Algerians against the French).

Historical evidence has special functions. It lends weight and depth to evidence which, if culled only from contemporary life, might seem frail. And, by portraying the movements of men over time, it shows the possibility of change. Even if the actual change has been so small as to leave us still desperate today, we need, to spur us on, the faith that change is possible. Thus, while taking proper note of how much remains to be done, it is important to compare the consciousness of white Americans about black people in the 1930's and in the 1960's to see how a period of creative conflict can change people's minds and behavior. Also, while noting how much remains to be done in China, it is important to see with what incredible speed the Chinese Communists have been able to mobilize seven hundred million people against famine and disease. We need to know, in the face of terrifying power behind the accusing shouts against us who rebel, that we are not mad; that men in the past, whom we know, in the perspective of time, to have been great, felt as we do. At moments when we are tempted to go along with the general condemnation of revolution, we need to refresh ourselves with Thomas Jefferson and Tom Paine. At times when we are about to surrender to the glorification of law, Thoreau and Tolstoi can revive our conviction that justice supersedes law.

That is why, for instance, Staughton Lynd's book, *Intellectual Origins of American Radicalism*, is useful history. It recalls an eighteenth-century Anglo-American tradition declaring:[12]

> . . . that the proper foundation for government is a universal law of right and wrong self-evident to the intuitive common sense of every man; that freedom is a power of personal self-direction which no man can delegate to another; that the purpose of society is not the protection of property but fulfillment of the needs of living human beings; that good citizens have the right and duty, not only to overthrow incurable oppressive governments, but before that point is reached to break particular oppressive laws; and that we owe our ultimate allegiance, not to this or that nation, but to the whole family of man.

In a time when that tradition has been befogged by cries on all sides for "law and order" and "patriotism" (a word playing on the ambiguity between concern for one's government and concern for one's fellows) we need to remind ourselves of the *depth* of the humanistic, revolutionary impulse. The reach across the centuries conveys that depth.

By the criteria I have been discussing, a recollection of that tradition is radical history. It is therefore worth looking briefly at why Lynd's book has been criticized harshly by another radical, Eugene Genovese, who is a historian interested in American slavery.[13]

Genovese is troubled that *Intellectual Origins of American Radicalism* is "plainly meant to serve political ends." If he only were criticizing "the assumption that myth-making and falsifying in historical writing can be of political use" (for instance, the history written by so-called Marxists in the Stalinist mode) then he would be right. But Genovese seems to mean something else, for Lynd is certainly telling us the straight truth about the ideas of those early Anglo-American thinkers. He says a historical work should not deal with the past in terms of "moral standards abstracted from any time and place."

Specifically, Genovese does not like the way Lynd uses the ideas of the Declaration of Independence as a kind of "moral absolutism" transcending time, connecting radicals of the eighteenth century with those of the twentieth, while failing to discuss "the role of class or the historical setting of the debates among radicals." He is critical of the fact that "Lynd never discusses the relation of these ideas to the social groups that hold them" and claims Lynd "denies the importance of the social context in which ideas occur," rather seeing the great moral truths as "self-evident and absolute." This means to Genovese that Lynd "thereby denies the usefulness of history except for purposes of moral exhortation." He says Lynd leaves out "the working class, the socialist movements" and the "counter-tendencies and opposing views of the Left," thus making the book "a travesty of history."

It is a powerful and important criticism. But I believe Genovese is wrong—not in his description of what Lynd does, but in his estimate of its worth. His plea not to discuss the past by moral standards "abstracted from time and place" is inviting because we (especially we professional historians) are attached to the anchor of historical particularity, and do not want some ethereal, utopian standard of judgment. But to sbstract from time and place is not to remove completely from time and place; it is rather to remove enough of the historical detail so that common ground can be found between two or more historical periods—or more specifically, between another period and our own. (It is, indeed, only carrying further what we must of necessity do even when we are discussing *the* moral standard of any one time and place, or *the* view of any one social movement—because all are unique on the most concrete level.) To study the past in the light of what Genovese calls "moral absolutism" is really to study the past *relative* to ideals which move us in the present but which are broad enough to have moved other people in other times in history.

The lure of "time and place" is the lure of the professional historian interested in "my period" or "my topic." These particularities of time and place can be enormously useful, depending on the question that is asked. But if the question being asked is (as for Lynd): What support can we find in the past for values that seem worthwhile today?—a good deal of circumstantial evidence is not especially relevant. Only if *no* present question is asked, does all the particular detail, the rich, complex, endless detail of a period become important, without discrimination. And that, I would argue, is a much more abstract kind of history, because it is abstracted from a specific present concern. That, I would claim, is a surrender to the absolute of professional historiography: Tell as much as you can.

Similarly, the demand for "the role of class" in treating the natural-right ideas of Locke, Paine, and others, would be very important if the question being asked was: how do class backgrounds and ideas interact on one another (to better understand the weaknesses of both ideological and utopian thinking today). But for Staughton Lynd's special purpose, another emphasis was required. When one focuses on history with certain questions, much is left out. But this is true even when there is a lack of focus.

Similar to the professional dogma requiring "time and place" is a dogma among Marxist intellectuals requiring "the role of class" as if this were the touchstone for radical history. Even if one replaced (as Genovese is anxious to do) the economic determinism of a crude Marxism with "a sophisticated class analysis of historical change," discussing class "as a complex mixture of material interests, ideologies, and psychological attitudes," this may or may not move people forward toward change today. That—the total effect of history on the social setting today—is the criterion for a truly radical history, and not some abstract, absolute standard of methodology to which Marxists as well as others can get obsessively attached.

For instance, Genovese agrees that one of the great moral truths Lynd discusses—the use of conscience against authority as the ultimate test for political morality—was a revolutionary force in the past. But for Genovese this is a historical fact about a particular period, whereas: "Lynd seeks to graft them on to a socialist revolution, the content of which he never discusses. He merely asserts that they form the kernel of revolutionary socialist thought, although no socialist movement has ever won power with such an ideology. . . ." This is precisely the reason for asserting a moral value shared by certain eighteenth-century thinkers (and, on a certain level, by Marx and Engels): that socialist movements thus far have not paid sufficient attention to the right of conscience against *all* states. To be truly radical is to maintain a set of transcendental beliefs (yes, absolutes) by which to judge and thus to transform any particular social system.

In sum, while there is a value to specific analysis of particular historical situations, there is another kind of value to the unearthing of ideals which cross historical periods and give strength to beliefs needing reinforcement today. The trouble is, even Marxist historians have not paid sufficient attention to the Marxian admonition in his *Theses on Feuerbach:* "The dispute over the reality or nonreality of thinking which is isolated from practice is a purely scholastic question." Any dispute over a "true" history cannot be resolved in theory; the real question is, which of the several possible "true" histories (on that elementary level of factual truth) is *true,* not to some dogmatic notion about what a radical interpretation should contain, but to the practical needs for social change in our day? If the "political ends" Genovese warns against and Lynd espouses are not the narrow interests of a nation or party or ideology, but those humanistic values we have not yet attained, it is desirable that history should serve political ends.

5. *We can show how good social movements can go wrong, how leaders can betray their followers, how rebels can become bureaucrats, how ideals can become frozen and reified.* This is needed as a corrective to the blind faith that revolutionaries often develop in their movements, leaders, theories, so that future actors for social change can avoid the traps of the past. To use Karl Mannheim's distinction, while *ideology* is the tendency of those in power to falsify, *utopianism* is the tendency of those out of power to distort. History can show us the manifestations of the latter as well as the former.

History should put us on guard against the tendency of revolutionaries to devour their followers along with their professed principles. We need to remind ourselves of the failure of the American revolutionaries to eliminate slavery, despite the pretensions of the Declaration of Independence, and the failure of the new republic to deal justly with the Whiskey Rebels in Pennsylvania despite the fact a revolution had been fought against unjust taxes. Similarly, we need to recall the cry of protest against the French Revolution, in its moment of triumph, by Jacques Roux and the poor of Gravillers, protesting against profiteering, or by Jean Varlet, declaring: "Despotism has passed from the palace of the kings to the circle of a committee."[14] Revolutionaries, without dimming their enthusiasm for change, should read Khrushchev's speech to the Twentieth Party Congress in 1956, with its account of the paranoid cruelties of Stalin.

The point is not to turn us away from social movements but into *critical* participants in them, by showing us how easy it is for rebels to depart from their own claims. For instance, it might make us aware of our own tendencies—enlightened though we are—to be paternal to the aggrieved to read the speech of the black abolitionist Theodore S. Wright, at the 1837 Utica convention of the New York Anti-Slavery Society. Wright criticized "the spirit of the slaver" among white abolitionists. Or we might read the reply of Henry Highland Garnet in 1843 to the white abolitionist lady who rebuked him for his militancy:[15]

> You say I have received "bad counsel." You are not the only person who has told your humble servant that his humble productions have been produced by the "counsel" of some Anglo-Saxon. I have expected no more from ignorant slaveholders and their apologists, but I really looked for better things from Mrs. Maria W. Chapman, anti-slavery poetess and editor pro tem of the Boston *Liberator* . . .

The history of radical movements can make us watchful for narcissistic arrogance, the blind idolization of leaders, the substitution of dogma for a careful look at the environment, the lure of compromise when leaders of a

movement hobnob too frequently with those in power. For anyone joyful over
the election of socialists to office in a capitalist state, the recounting by Robert
Michels of the history of the German Social Democratic Party is enlightening.
Michels shows how parliamentary power can be corrupting, because radicals
elected to office become separated from the rank and file of their own
movement, and are invested with a prestige which makes it more difficult to
criticize their actions.[16]

> During the discussions in the Reichstag concerning the miners' strike in the basin of the
> Ruhr (1905), the deputy Hue spoke of the maximum program of the party as "utopian,"
> and in the socialist press there was manifested no single symptom of revolt. On the first
> occasion on which the party departed from its principle of unconditional opposition to all
> military expenditure, contenting itself with simple abstention when the first credit of
> 1,500,000 marks was voted for the war against the Hereros, this remarkable innovation,
> which in every other socialist party would have unquestionably evoked a storm from one
> section of the members . . . aroused among the German socialists no more than a few
> dispersed and timid protests.

Such searching histories of radical movements can deter the tendency to make
absolutes of those instruments—party, leaders, platforms—which should be
constantly subject to examination.

That revolutionaries themselves are burdened by tradition, and cannot
completely break from thinking in old ways, was seen by Marx in the
remarkable passage opening The Eighteenth Brumaire of Louis Bonaparte:

> Men make their own history, but they do not make it just as they please; they do not
> make it under circumstances chosen by themselves, but under circumstances directly
> found, given and transmitted from the past. The tradition of all the dead generations
> weighs like a nightmare on the brain of the living. And just when they seem engaged in
> revolutionizing themselves and things, in creating something entirely new, precisely in
> such epochs of revolutionary crisis they anxiously conjure up the spirits of the past to
> their service and borrow from them names, battle slogans and costumes in order to
> present the new scene of world history in this time-honored disguise and this borrowed
> language . . .

How to use the past to change the world, and yet not be encumbered by it—both
skills can be sharpened by a judicious culling of past experience. But the
delicate balance between them cannot come from historical data alone—only
from a clearly focused vision of the human ends which history should serve.

History is not inevitably useful. It can bind us or free us. It can destroy
compassion by showing us the world through the eyes of the comfortable ("the
slaves are happy, just listen to them"—leading to "the poor are content, just look
at them"). It can oppress any resolve to act by mountains of trivia, by diverting
us into intellectual games, by pretentious "interpretations" which spur
contemplation rather than action, by limiting our vision to an endless story of
disaster and thus promoting cynical withdrawal, by befogging us with the
encyclopedic eclecticism of the standard textbook.

But history can untie our minds, our bodies, our disposition to move—to
engage life rather than contemplating it as an outsider. It can do this by
widening our view to include the silent voices of the past, so that we look
behind the silence of the present. It can illustrate the foolishness of depending
on others to solve the problems of the world—whether the state, the church, or
other self-proclaimed benefactors. It can reveal how ideas are stuffed into us by

the powers of our time, and so lead us to stretch our minds beyond what is given. It can inspire us by recalling those few moments in the past when men did behave like human beings, to prove it is *possible*. And it can sharpen our critical faculties so that even while we act, we think about the dangers created by our own desperation.

These criteria I have discussed are not conclusive. They are a rough guide. I assume that history is not a well-ordered city (despite the neat stacks of the library) but a jungle. I would be foolish to claim my guidance is infallible. The only thing I am really sure of is that we who plunge into the jungle need to think about what we are doing, because there *is* somewhere we want to go.

## NOTES

1. Barbara Tuchman, *The Guns of August*, Macmillan, 1962, p. 72.

2. Herbert Aptheker, *A Documentary History of the Negro People*, Citadel, 1951, p. 2.

3. New York *Daily News*, February 6, 1928.

4. See Vivian Henderson, *The Economic Status of Negroes*, Southern Regional Council, 1963. One sentence in the *Report of the National Advisory Commission on Civil Disorders*, Bantam, 1968, p. 13, reveals the complexity: "Although there have been gains in Negro income nationally, and a decline in the number of Negroes below the 'poverty level,' the condition of Negroes in the central city remains in a state of crisis."

5. Jesse Lemisch, "The American Revolution from the Bottom Up," Barton Bernstein, ed., *Towards a New Past*, Pantheon, 1968.

6. See the letter of Commissioner Lin to Queen Victoria in Teng, Ssu-yü, and Fairbank, John K., *China's Response to the West*, Harvard University, 1954, p. 24.

7. This should not be confused with "the search for culpability," as Jerald S. Auerbach puts it, criticizing the New Left critics of the New Deal. The point is not to denounce the New Deal of FDR, nor to praise it; that kind of historical evaluation is useless. . . . Auerbach, in "New Deal, Old Deal, or Raw Deal: Some Thoughts on New Left Historiography," *Journal of Southern History*, February 1969, mistakes the intention of those who (like myself in *New Deal Thought*, Bobbs-Merrill, 1966, or like Paul Conkin, in *The New Deal*, Thomas Crowell, 1967) stress the inadequacies of the Roosevelt reforms. Our aim is not castigation of past politics, but stimulation of present citizens.

8. *Report of the National Advisory Commission on Civil Disorders*, Bantam, 1968, p. 483.

9. Richard Pfeffer, ed., *No More Vietnams*, Harper & Row, 1968, pp. 7, 8.

10. Marilyn Young, *The Rhetoric of Empire*, Harvard University, 1968, p. 231.

11. "Twilight of Idols," *The Seven Arts*, October 1917, reprinted in Randolph S. Bourne, *War and the Intellectuals*, Harper (Torchbook edition), 1964, p. 60.

12. Staughton Lynd, *Intellectual Origins of American Radicalism*, Pantheon, 1968, p. vi.

13. *New York Review of Books*, September 26, 1968.

14. For a marvelous historical document of this aspect of the French Revolution, see Scott, ed., *The Defense of Gracchus Babeuf Before the High Court of Vendome*, University of Massachusetts Press, 1967.

15. Herbert Aptheker, *A Documentary History of the Negro People*, Citadel, 1951.

16. Robert Michels, *Political Parties*, Free Press (Collier edition), 1962, p. 154.

# scholarship or commitment: a hassle of historians

## JAMES B. GILBERT

James B. Gilbert, Associate Professor of History at the University of Maryland, discusses the beginnings of the conflict between scholarship and activism as it affected the historical profession. In his assessment of the events which transpired at the 1968 annual meeting of the American Historical Association, Gilbert noted that the "political function of the historian . . . is up for grabs," and he itemizes the pressures upon the historian which come from students and the historian's own desire to be relevant to the need for social change.

Milling around in the corridors of New York's Statler-Hilton during the American Historical Association meeting, December 28-30, thousands of graduate students and professors must have felt that this was Mayor Daley's revenge. The meeting, originally scheduled for Chicago, was moved to New York after a strong demand by the membership not to convene in the city that had shown the world the grim guts of the Democratic Party. Enormous confusion resulted from overcrowded halls and elevators which seemed to run nonstop from the basement to the roof. Long lines of graduate students waited patiently to use house phones, that didn't always work, trying to establish get-it-yourself job interviews. Interesting positions were available, of course, but these were filled by a process resembling the National Football League player draft. And for those few superstar historians, always looking for a new job, there was the ritualistic greeting which has become almost like a fraternal handshake: "Are you happy at . . . ?" The skillful answer blends present dissatisfaction and a suggestion of wanderlust with a denial of disloyalty to the current alma mater—into one word.

Aside from an unusually heavy dose of frenzy, this convention was most notable for its politics and for the efforts to organize a caucus of radical historians. "We all know that something is wrong with the AHA," claimed Arthur Waskow, "but we don't know what it is." The American Historical Association is one of the largest liberal organizations in the country. But its political leanings are incidental to its function, and the result has been a liberalism of indifference. The Association publishes a journal, acts as a clearing house for jobs, and holds conventions which are both reunions and scholarly events. Behind these benign activities, however, there lies the power of numbers of men who command the attention of a great many students and who carry publishing houses into the black with the purchases they require for courses. As in other professions, the AHA reflects the activities of its members. Scholarly

James B. Gilbert, "Scholarship or Commitment: A Hassle of Historians," *The Nation*, Vol. 208, no. 3 (January 20, 1969), 77–78.

papers presented at such conventions sample the work being done in the field, whether radical or conservative. The search for originality insures attention to such ideas.

The current convention suggested, however, that the detachment of the historical profession may not be permanent. The political function of the historian, whether he likes it or not, is up for grabs. He is under pressure from students to make his work reveal something about the nature of social change. And often he is concerned to reconstruct the past because of his malaise about the present nature of.American society.

Such attitudes provided the gist of the panel discussion on Saturday night, December 28, of the relationship of the historical profession to politics. However irrelevant or disastrous it may seem to the younger generation of historians, the cold war showed itself alive and well in the mind of Arthur Schlesinger, Jr., who chaired the meeting. Countenancing the decision to quit Chicago, Schlesinger suggested that historians also might take a swipe at the Russians for their invasion of Czechoslovakia by refusing to attend, or if in attendance, by protesting, at the International Congress for Historical Sciences in Moscow two years hence. The more traditional position was expressed by AHA president, John K. Fairbank, who suggested that no political position ought to be implied in the organization's activities or in the selection of convention sites. Perhaps he understood, as Schlesinger did not, that if it were a policy to make symbolic protests against countries for the evils of their foreign policies, very few meetings could be convened anywhere. Both Schlesinger's and Fairbank's remarks were wide of the focus provided by the most important speech of the evening. Christopher Lasch's appeal to historians to involve themselves with new ideas and with unused concepts, his demand that they stop being ideologues for the *status quo,* brought the question of history and politics to the point where it belonged.

Lasch's suggestions were echoed in efforts to organize a radical caucus within the AHA. Perhaps, since historians are among the last of the large social sciences to produce a radical caucus, it was inevitable that there should be a twin birth. The reason for two competing caucuses stems primarily from the growing separation between scholarship and political activism within the university. The aim of radical historians can no longer be merely the confron-tation of conservative ideas and establishments. They must deal also with the problems which beset the whole Left today.

The first radical caucus was held on December 28, sponsored primarily by graduate students from the University of Wisconsin. Before an audience of about 700, several speakers chided the AHA for some of the statements of its past presidents, defended the usefulness of scholarship, and called for the creation of some sort of formal organization. After twenty minutes or so of groping around, avoiding arguments and issues, a newsletter was established— in lieu of further talk. As the audience melted away, some to publishers' cocktail parties, the meeting folded. It looked as if the scholarly Left might once more paste over its splits and factions with newsprint.

But the second caucus on Sunday, December 29, revealed that the first meeting has been merely a dress rehearsal. A smaller audience heard Eugene Genovese, Christopher Lasch and Helmut Gruber tackle the problem of radical scholarship. Lasch's remarks best caught the meaning of the present dilemma in personal terms. The breakdown of liberalism, he argued, had destroyed the rationale for the disjointed work which historians were doing. Isolated monographic studies could still be written in pursuit of truth; nothing diminished their value, but the historian himself had difficulty seeing the relevance of his work to social change. The meeting itself was testimony to the desire of historians to alter this situation. To overcome this isolation, Lasch proposed a larger, national organization whose aims would go beyond the academic world—an organization to which scholars could contribute their work and political activities.

This translation of the acknowledged split between scholarship and activism into political terminology stated what was unsaid on the previous afternoon. As Eugene Genovese put it, the issue was whether to defend the university and work within it to transform it according to the ideals it glibly asserts, or by a revolutionary act to confront it and expose its links to other institutions in society. The issue was between professionalism and 100 per cent radicalism, even though most positions were between these two extremes.

Behind Genovese's statement was the question of the meaning and uses of radical scholarship. The radical professor, because of his successes in working within the structure of the university, is obviously on the defensive. The internal structure and the exterior relationships of that institution have all been called into question by the left-wing students, who demand that the historian make his work relevant. The results of such demands have so far been inconclusive; much of the dialogue among scholars has broken on the definition of terms. Relevancy, radicalism, even professionalism, are words sufficiently ambiguous to serve as slogans for different programs of educational reforms.

# annual set-to:
# the bare-knuckled historians

## RONALD RADOSH

This discussion of the 1969 annual meeting of the American Historical Association by
Ronald Radosh reveals the passion with which historians were forced to confront their
role in society one year after the issue was first raised at their association's gathering.
Two new issues emerged at this meeting. One was the challenge to the social role of
historians raised by New Left activists; the other was the formal demand that the
association take a position against the war in Vietnam. As this article points out, once
again the scholars—including noted radical scholars—and the activists were often on
opposite sides on both issues.

There was evident last year at the annual meeting of the American Historical
Association a concern about the relevance of the historian's work to social
change, and the growing split between scholarship and political activism [see
James Gilbert, "A Hassle of Historians," *The Nation*, January 20, 1969]. The
1969 meeting disclosed an even more seriously divided association. A slim
majority of historians present showed preference for the older concept of
neutral scholarship, while a large and vocal minority of liberal, radical and
younger scholars asked the AHA members to demonstrate their concern about
the state of today's world.

This generalization, however, does not tell the whole story. For the type of
action suggested and analysis presented by leaders of the "radical caucus,"
particularly by Staughton Lynd and Arthur Waskow, almost frustrated the
development of a meaningful radical critique. Speaking on behalf of the caucus,
even though many of its adherents did not agree with their proposals, Lynd and
Waskow called for substantive changes in the AHA itself; a commitment by the
organization not only to "historical studies" but "to the intellectual liberation of
Americans," as well as to a demystification of "the holders of power." They
asked for granting of power within the AHA to students and "the historically
concerned public," both groups that Lynd and Waskow argued "the professional historian should be serving." Finally, they urged creation of a "special
fund for the Liberation of Historians," that would "encourage nonprofessional
members of the public to become historians."

Lynd stressed these proposals when making his bid for the presidency of the
association (he received some 400 votes), but they never came formally before
the convention floor. They were, however, subject to extensive debate at a pre-
convention caucus meeting held December 27. The debate revealed that the
Waskow-Lynd group had no conception of dealing with professional historians

Ronald Radosh, "Annual Set-to: The Bare-Knuckled Historians," *The Nation*, Vol. 210, no.
18 (February 2, 1970), 108–110.

as a constituency with its own problems and needs, one that might very well be won over by an intelligent radical critique of the role of the university, scholarship and the position of intellectuals in society.

Rather, they seemed to follow the analysis offered by Richie Rothstein, chairman of the radical and activist New University Conference. Rothstein called on historians to function alongside other radical professors in extra-disciplinary issues. The need, he wrote, was to build "people's identity as cadre of a radical movement (who happen to be engaged in the vocation of history) rather than as honest historians (who happen to be radicals)." The issue to Rothstein was "professionalism," and the professionalism of the radical or Socialist historian was as bad as any other kind. To Rothstein, the AHA meeting should be used merely to recruit "young historians who have been touched by the movement."

Instead of developing an appeal to historians on their own terrain, the caucus spent hours debating where and how to demonstrate against the war and repression. They finally chose the Justice Department. As for history itself Lynd favored development of "guerrilla history," in which participants in mass struggles would be asked to speak on their own behalf. Missing the essential difference between one who chronicles history and being a historian, Lynd seemed to mirror the worst anti-intellectualism within the New Left.

Despite criticism, Lynd came up with no viable statement of what it meant to write history that serves the public. The public, after all, is hardly composed of militant New Left activists. Moreover, Lynd could not explain why it should be thought reactionary to use professional skills to write history. No plumber would let an academic into a house to fix a sink (or at least into his union), but Lynd seemed to argue on behalf of the plumber (if he is a revolutionary plumber) writing history. Having given up on the profession before the convention even started, it was perhaps inevitable that Lynd and Waskow would favor actions of the type that movements traditionally engage in, but that have no particular relevance to questions facing historians and university professors.

The hostility to the profession was odd, since the AHA bent over backward to hear scores of papers by Socialist and radical historians, many of them papers of broad political and social concern. Panels were presented on "Laos and Vietnam," "The Age of Suspicion Revisited," "Radical Intellectuals and the Institutions of Power." Moreover, many non-professionals competent to comment were invited. Carey McWilliams spoke on the Alger Hiss case, I. F. Stone on muckraking, and Paul Goodman on anarchism.

The questions ignored by Lynd were formally taken up at a large panel that was part of the official program. At the meeting on "What is Radical History?" about 1,000 gathered to hear seven radicals define what they mean by the term. Ann Lane of Rutgers University started things off by asserting that radical history did not exist. There were radicals and Socialists who wrote history, some of it good and some bad, and those with a Socialist viewpoint had to write better history and convince their audience that their interpretation was valid. Lynd disagreed. Arguing for guerrilla history, he cited the example of Cuban revolutionaries who taped the experiences of youth reconstructing the Isle of Pines. The other panelists presented various approaches between Lane and Lynd, but the audience drifted away as the topic of discussion shifted to where and how AHA members should demonstrate against the war.

The climax of the convention was the annual business meeting. An event that usually attracts 150 of the few thousand present, was attended by 2,000 to 3,000 historians, and they met for two nights in a row until the late hours of the morning. The issue that pulled people in was sponsorship by the Lynd-Waskow group of a long and unwieldy resolution urging withdrawal from Vietnam and an end to repression of the Black Panther Party. A substitute resolution, introduced by historians William L. Neumann and Blanche W. Cook, "deplored and condemned" the war, urged withdrawal of all military involvement, and a reassessment of the fundamental assumptions behind U.S. foreign policy. In the interest of unity, Lynd agreed to support the substitute, and this resolution eventually lost by a vote of 647 to 611.

At the first night's business meeting the assembled delegates, particularly the anti-war group, received a severe shock. Leading the academic, essentially conservative and Vital Center historians was Eugene D. Genovese, perhaps the most noted Marxist scholar in the United States, and a historian whose own contribution to Socialist thought has been immense. Back in 1965, Genovese had been the victim of an onslaught against academic freedom because of the strong pro-National Liberation Front views he expressed at a local teach-in.

The argument presented by Genovese was that any motion against the war meant that those who favored the war would be forced to resign from the AHA. He stressed that he had always opposed the war, but pointed out that the majority of the American people support the war and that, while they were possibly misguided, they were as moral as the war's opponents. Ignoring the fact that either motion would have put only those present at the business meeting, and not the association, on record, Genovese and his supporters argued that to adopt such a motion would mean that historians would have to accept and teach the views it expressed.

If they rejected such coercion, Genovese claimed, they would have to resign from the AHA. Branding the large anti-war group as a bunch of "totalitarians" . . . Genovese ended his speech by screaming at the top of his lungs that the time had come to isolate the group, and to "put them down, put them down hard, once and for all." The most conservative members of the association thereupon stood and cheered. One could hear such libertarian and scholarly cries as "kill the Panthers," "kill the Vietcong" and "kill Lynd and Waskow." Indeed, one member launched a physical attack on Arthur Waskow. . . .

The most cogent and perceptive reply was delivered during the second night's debate by Fred Ciporen, a doctoral candidate from Wisconsin teaching history at Manhattan Community College and Brooklyn College. As a younger historian closer to student activists, Ciporen sought to tell his colleagues why they should go on record in opposition to the war. Universities and professors could not be neutral, Ciporen said, and their pretense to neutrality was hypocrisy while the killing and napalming went on. Pointing out that the nation was political, and that professors played a part in politics by their very abstention, Ciporen pleaded with the association to take a stand. How, he asked, could historians tell their children years later that they did nothing when others were trying to make history?

The arguments of the young activists did not persuade the majority. Genovese was backed by the noted intellectual historian and former peace candidate, H. Stuart Hughes. Repeating the totalitarian characterization of the anti-war group, Hughes asserted that any anti-war resolution would "politicize" the AHA—as if it had not been politicized. Stating that all present knew his own background and anti-war credentials, he recalled that the last time he had been in Washington was at a large anti-war rally, two and one half years ago! Where, many of the younger historians thought to themselves, had Mr. Hughes been in the interim?

The leadership of Genovese and Hughes had a more serious negative effect. That these two noted scholars, identified with the Marxist Left in one case and with the peace movement in the other, would use their talents to attack the anti-war group hindered the efforts of those who favored an intelligent blending of scholarly work and public concern. The actions of Genovese, particularly, seemed to vindicate the anti-intellectual attack on the irrelevance of Socialist scholars and their work.

Perhaps this defeat was averted by a paper delivered on the final convention day by Jesse Lemisch, a historian who had been dismissed from the University of Chicago because his "political concerns interfered with his scholarship." In what may have been the most telling and fundamental critique presented before the AHA, he proposed that the supposedly apolitical stars of the profession (Allan Nevins, Arthur M. Schlesinger, Jr., Samuel Eliot Morison, Oscar Handlin, Daniel Boorstin and others) were implicit cold warriors who sought to use history as a vehicle in the fight against communism. Lemisch's paper, "Present-Mindedness Revisited: Anti-Radicalism as a Goal of American Historical Writing since World War II," argued persuasively that what so many object to is not that a scholar should take a political position but that he should hold views contrary to Establishment shibboleths. His paper received a standing ovation from a good part of the large audience.

Lemisch may have helped to answer the question of what is radical history. For in his paper, he showed that when a historian challenges the ideological presuppositions of the most revered historians, and exposes their hidden and subtle present-mindedness, he was demolishing the argument of Genovese and Hughes that the academy is neutral and that historians are above politics. Lemisch presented a challenge to AHA members both politically and intellectually—but on their own terrain as working intellectuals involved in an association of colleagues and in an active professional life. Few who heard Lemisch's talk will be able to swallow the belief that they belong to an apolitical profession. His paper brought back vividly the meaning of the coda used by William Appleman Williams for *The Contours of American History* in 1961: "You commit yourself, and then—you see."

# exchange on the historian and the Vietnam war

## JOHN K. FAIRBANK AND HOWARD ZINN

The concern with which traditional historians viewed the "politicization" of their profession is shown in the letter addressed to Howard Zinn by the noted Asian historian, John K. Fairbank. Fairbank presents the arguments supported by the bulk of traditional historians, who felt that voting as an association against the war in Vietnam would have violated their professional sensibilities.

In his answer, Howard Zinn humorously but sharply chastises Fairbank for the latter's part in closing off debate at the 1969 meeting of the American Historical Association. Most important is Zinn's refusal to separate his role as historian from that of citizen. Zinn argues that an undue concern for the sanctity of one's profession allows historians to surrender their rights as citizens to speak out on the crucial matters of war and peace, life and death. "Silence," he argues, "is political decision."

---

AN OPEN LETTER TO HOWARD ZINN

Dear Howard,

Since I have so greatly admired your altruism and moral courage, I naturally would not have joined in our briefly-famous Struggle for the Mike on December 28 without having a point, in fact, two points:

1. Chairmen are entitled to recognize members of an assembly regardless of who has lined up at a mike. Speaking is a privilege more than a right. If a right, it would have to be pro-rated, and you had already spoken more than your pro-rated share.

2. Your resolution showed a lack of discrimination. The vast majority of the assembly would, I am sure, have voted anti-Vietnam War if given a chance in an *ad hoc* meeting separate from AHA official business. They voted you down because they did not believe the Vietnam War had affected their rights, opportunities, and procedures as historians, and because they opposed "politicization" of our professional association, that is, getting AHA officially to take a position on a public policy issue of concern to us all as citizens but not of concern primarily to us as historians. The AHA exists for professional purposes only.

This distinction lies at the heart of the pluralism that gives the AHA its legal freedom from interference, intimidation, or coercion by the government or other

Reprinted by permission of the American Historical Association, Washington, D. C. John K. Fairbank and Howard Zinn, Exchange on the Historian and the Vietnam War, *AHA Newsletter* (1970), 14–19.

political forces. "Politicization" is no joke. It can cut both ways. If we today could use AHA to support a worthy non-professional cause, others tomorrow could manipulate it for an evil cause. In other words, academic freedom has a distinct institutional basis that we should not act to destroy.

All this amounts to saying that the only freedom we can count on is freedom under law. This makes possible great demonstrations and many other forms of expressing dissent. It also requires that one recognize parliamentary rules and the agreed-upon limits to the usefulness of professional associations. Having got results in the public scene by using your legal rights, you of all people should recognize that our structure of legal distinctions is worth preserving.

*Harvard University*                                                              JOHN K. FAIRBANK


PROFESSOR ZINN REPLIES


Dear John:

I would not call it a "Struggle for the Mike." It was more like the Spanish-American War. Granted that the Mike was Cuba, helpless before both of us, and that I (Spain) might be said to have violated its privacy and independence by occupying its space first. We would have to add that you (Uncle Sam or Uncle John) came upon the scene with the air of affection for all (you wandered up the aisle, came up to me at the mike, put your hand on my shoulder, fondled the mike with love, whispered a few professional nothings in my ear) and then pulled the mike out of my hand with the genial ferocity of Teddy Roosevelt, thus violating both me and the Mike.

If I had done that to you, it would have been ascribed by some to typical radical hooliganism; the other way around, one could only call it Manifest Destiny.

Your unilateral decision that I had spoken more than my "pro-rated share" was not exactly the kind of obeisance to the rule of law which you profess; that rule of law says that the chairman decides whom to recognize; he can always ignore someone at the mike and recognize anyone standing up at his seat, or at some other mike, if he thinks there has been an inequitable distribution of speaking-time. For the Radical Opposition to try hard to get the floor by appearing as often as possible at one of several unoccupied mikes, when the chairman of the meeting—the man with the most parliamentary power—is of the Establishment, does not seem unreasonable.

But that's not really important. I bring it up only because I assume that a bit of historical retrospection may sharpen our present sensibilities. It is your second point that deserves serious discussion. Let's forget Spain now and discuss Vietnam.

You say that an anti-Vietnam War resolution would have passed easily if presented at an *ad hoc* meeting separate from A.H.A. official business. But neither you nor anyone else speaking for the Establishment position (Stuart Hughes, Eugene Genovese, or others) proposed such a meeting to convene then and there. Instead, you proposed to adjourn the meeting, period. (When the official meeting did end, you will note that the mikes were immediately cut off, so that even an announcement of an *ad hoc* meeting of radical historians could not be made to the departing assemblage.) In other words, none of you demonstrated any enthusiasm for taking any action on the Vietnam War, officially or *ad hoc.*

Personally, I don't much care what is the form of the meeting that passes such a resolution; I assume we are the same bodies, minds, spirits, whatever parliamentary rigamarole we go through to give our action another kind of official imprint. (I have the image of the sanitation worker at the beach, asked to save a drowning man, replying: "My business is garbage. But I'll be happy to go to the locker and put on my life-saver's uniform. Otherwise, it might spoil my professional reputation.") But you do care very much that we don't take action on Vietnam *as historians,* and that requires comment.

You say that the A.H.A. should not "officially" take a position on the war because the war affects us as citizens but not as historians. Let us assume the war does not affect us "as historians"; let us say that the taking of our students to war does not affect us as teachers of history; let us say that the momentous *historical* fact of the war will not affect the content of our historical studies. It only affects us "as citizens." Well, when *do* you assemble with other citizens to speak out on the crucial issues of our time? You spend almost all the days of the year in assemblies with other people as historians of the United States, as members of the Harvard faculty, as members of the History Department of the University, as members of the Association for Asian Studies, as teacher and students of History 291, etc.—and in none of these can you express your concerns as a citizen. Are we limited to prayers at night and other rare moments away from professional activities?

What can democracy possibly mean if not that people assembled whenever and wherever they can, for whatever reason, may express their preferences on the important issues of the day? If they may not, democracy is a fraud, because it means that the political leaders have effectively isolated the citizenry by taking up their time in various jobs, while the leaders make the policies, and the citizens, in 99 per cent of their life, remain silent, reserving moments of expression to biennial gestures in the voting booth, comments to friends over lunch, and mutterings to oneself from time to time. If all Americans, in all the thousands of assemblies that take place through the year, insist on keeping out of politics because neither war nor racial persecution nor poisonous vapors coming in through the library window, affect them as historians, chiropodists, clerks, or carpenters—then "pluralist" democracy is a facade for oligarchical rule.

It's no wonder that the war goes on, because all those concerned for the sanctity of their "profession" have surrendered their rights as citizens to speak out wherever they are, whatever they are doing, on matters of life and death. If you were at a meeting of historians in Germany in 1936 would you take the same position in the midst of the killing of Jews? If you were at a meeting of historians in Mississippi in the midst of the lynching of blacks, would you also insist you could not speak "as historians"? If you want to invoke prudence and profit, that is one thing. But there is no moral principle in a position that allocates a small portion of our spare time for moral indignation and the largest part of our lives for immoral silence.

You worry about "politicization" of the A.H.A. and argue that refraining from political stances will protect the A.H.A.'s freedom. We can also argue for universal virginity as a way of preventing venereal disease. But this is worse, because our political virginity is a fiction. Our silence in the face of war, racism, and other social evils is not freedom for us; it is freedom for the political leaders of the country to have their way and count on our inaction. Silence is a political decision. They have given us books, degrees, good jobs to play with, and the bargain is: don't interfere with what we're doing to the world. And not just to the world. To us, to our sons, to our students. We can separate ourselves in theory as historians and citizens. But that is a one-way separation which has no return: when the world blows up, we cannot claim exemption as historians, not even if it happens during an A.H.A. convention.

You say that avoiding "politicization" protects our "academic freedom," gives us "legal freedom from interference, intimidation, or coercion by the government or other political forces." But to stay out of politics "as historians" is to protect our freedom to stay apolitical in most of our working hours. If we give up our fight to take political stands on crucial matters, there is no need by the government to bother us, because we are then already interfered with, intimidated, coerced. But, you might say, we are not interfered with in the stacks or intimidated at our professional meetings, or coerced through our professional journals. Then, we have purchased our freedom to remain professionals at the cost of our freedom as citizens.

To have the A.H.A. support a good cause today means that "others tomorrow could manipulate it for an evil cause." But to refrain from supporting a good cause today does not at all prevent anyone tomorrow from manipulating the A.H.A. for an evil cause. Evil does not operate by legal precedent, but by power. And to refrain is already to be manipulated for an evil cause; while evils by political leaders usually involve action, those of citizens are usually the result of passivity.

To discuss your proposition that "the only freedom we can count on is freedom under law" requires much more space than we have here for adequate discussion. I would say only that such a proposition is destructive of freedom; when we assume that the law is the great protector of our freedom we have already surrendered moral principle to whatever power happens to be enthroned. The law may help freedom; it may hurt it. To give the law blanket endorsement is to be ahistorical. Under law, in modern times, caste systems have been maintained, wealth has been monopolized, wars have been fought. And when people begin to protest, outside those limited mechanisms of dissent carefully assigned by the law itself to protesters, the cry for "law and order" is always raised by those more afraid of the dissenters' threat to their own petty privileges than of the perniciousness protected by law.

John, I assume we are still friends, despite the Spanish-American War. It is the future that counts.

*Boston University*                                                    HOWARD ZINN

# can a historian be
# a socialist revolutionary?

## JAMES WEINSTEIN

James Weinstein is the author of *The Corporate Ideal in the Liberal State* and *The Decline of Socialism in America*. Presently a member of the executive committee of The New American Movement, Weinstein defends the role of professional historian as socialist revolutionary. Readers should note his critique of the approach toward history and politics taken by Staughton Lynd, a well-known activist historian whose work is defended in the selection by Howard Zinn.

Every part of the movement faces the same apparent dilemma: a mass revolutionary potential, mass discontent and searching, a deep-reaching rejection of the values of corporate America, and a narrow group of militants or "activists" with no perspective for realizing the potential, unable to relate to the mass except in occasional, sporadic outbursts. This split between a radical "activist" elite and the potentially revolutionary mass exists in society at large, but it also exists within the individual personalities of movement activists and of movement intellectuals.

In its personal form the split is between most radicals' conception of themselves as radicals and their understanding of themselves as individuals living in bourgeois society. Student radicals have difficulty accepting them-selves as students, and therefore find it difficult to relate to others as students. They see themselves as "legitimate" only when they deny their own existence as students in favor of an existence as "revolutionaries." The same used to be true of most women radicals, and remains true of those outside that wing of the Women's Liberation movement made up of women who understand that the basis of their radicalism, the thing that potentially unites them with the great majority of women, is their oppression as women: that the basis for a revolutionary movement among women is a politics that grows out of their particular situation. But with the exception of this section of the women's movement and of the revolutionary nationalist movements among blacks and various "third world" groups, there is a general inability to accept oneself as a concrete person, and a strong tendency to define one's radicalism in terms of a denial of one's actual existence. In so doing, however, most radicals also must reject those who are unwilling or unprepared to make this seemingly total transformation. The mass is rejected in favor of an elite.

For students who think of themselves as "middle class," this personal split, this denial of self, grows out of an understanding—an implicit theory—that there is some key social group or movement through which revolution will

James Weinstein, "Can a Historian Be a Socialist Revolutionary?" *Socialist Revolution*, Vol. I, no. 4 (July–August 1970), 97–106.

become a reality. Part of that theory is that "middle class" radicals must escape from their own experiences in order to organize in behalf of others. This belief reflects a lack of comprehension of the diversified nature of the proletariat and a denial both of the possibility of a diversified movement and of popular revolutionary consciousness. The common thread that runs through the various movement splinters is the idea that only a narrowly defined group can be truly revolutionary—whether that group is the industrial working class, the "third world," or the detached, full-time activists themselves.

This idea is not the result of a socialist analysis of the political economy of the modern United States, but is an acceptance of dominant bourgeois social thought, according to which people act only in their own narrow immediate group interest, and are defined in terms of their income levels or occupation, rather than by class. Just as most of the movement allows bourgeois social science to define the social structure of the United States, so is its radicalism molded by an acceptance of bourgeois social categories.

This was demonstrated by the actions and attitudes of the Radical Caucus at the recent (April 16-18) meeting of the Organization of American Historians in Los Angeles. The Radical Caucus that met at Los Angeles had been formed at the December 1969 meeting of the American Historical Association. At that meeting Staughton Lynd had run for the presidency of the AHA against the candidate of the official nominating committee. His candidacy was attacked not only by members of the profession's establishment, but also by Eugene D. Genovese, now at Rochester University. The experience of the December AHA meeting led to a broadening of interest in the Radical Caucus and to the beginnings of involvement of several historians who had sat out the Lynd-Genovese fight. Many of those who became active after December did so for two reasons: they did not want to be identified with Genovese; they did not want "radicalism" to be represented by Lynd.

Actually, these two reasons reduce themselves to one, for the principles involved are opposite sides of the same coin. As Lynd described the debate between himself and Genovese (*Liberation*, February 1970), the difference was between "activists" like himself and those who think it their job "to do the socialist scholarship and someone else's job to do the socialist action." There is some truth to this assertion as it applies to Genovese and a few others, but Lynd smeared all "historians associated with the Socialist Scholars Conference" with this description. Clearly there are some "radical" historians engaged in Marxist historical work who disdain any connection with existing movements.

But Lynd neglects to examine the nature of his "activism," preferring instead to let it stand as the only alternative to what he sees as the abstraction of theory from practice. In fact, both as an activist and as a historian, Lynd is an empiricist acting entirely within the framework of bourgeois categories. Thus, while the Marxist "scholars" are abstracted from existing social movements, the "activists" are permeated with the prevailing bourgeois notions of radicalism. The activists accept empiricism in place of developing revolutionary theory, while their activity is informed by the liberal definition of radicalism.

Both aspects of this became clear at the OAH convention, where the Radical Caucus engaged in political action within the business meeting and where Lynd gave an example of his idea of "What Is Radical History?" at a Radical Caucus counter-session. At the convention, there were some fifteen to twenty people who organized the Radical Caucus and perhaps as many as a hundred others who were sympathetic to it and interested initially in becoming a part of it. These people came to various meetings of the Caucus, but left in confusion or despair. Some returned a second or even a third time, but by the end of the three days, the Caucus was smaller than at the beginning and the dozens of historians who had identified in some way with it and with "radicalism" were more isolated and homeless than at the beginning.

The reasons for this became clear in the discussions of the resolutions to be introduced by the radicals at the business meeting and about running a candidate for vice president of the OAH (in opposition to the official candidate, Richard Hofstadter). The content of the resolutions was not seriously discussed, except as a function of the possibility of their acceptance by the majority of the convention. The anti-Vietnam war resolution, for example, was discussed almost entirely in terms of whether or not it might be adopted. The general feeling was that a straight anti-war resolution, calling for withdrawal, might be acceptable to the majority, and that such a resolution was, therefore, not radical. To guarantee that a resolution was radical it was necessary to frame it in such a way that it would be unacceptable to the majority, and so the resolution was written to include a statement on the suppression of the Panthers.

Such a statement might have been appropriate as a means of pointing to the dependence of American democracy on expansion, and to the historical connection between expansion and racism. It might have been a means of forcing the convention to confront the idea that racism has been inherent in American capitalism, which from the beginning defined success in terms of the ability to impose itself upon other, weaker peoples, and saw its religious and political institutions as superior to all others. But the framers of the resolution clearly did not intend to make these connections. The Johnson-Lynd resolution, on which the final resolution was partly based, had instead accepted the liberal myth of the American past. Its conclusion was that "Respect for America . . . can be achieved *once again* if we rededicate ourselves to the cause of human liberty and human welfare." (Emphasis added.)

In any case, the discussion within the Caucus made it apparent that anything that might be accepted by the convention, anything that made sense to those present at the meeting, could not be considered radical. Implicit in this view were two things: (1) an acceptance of the liberal image of radicalism as irrational, far out, and negative; (2) the idea that historians are an enemy class, at one with the establishment that dominates the profession. A conscious acceptance of the second idea, of course, would preclude the organization of a radical caucus within the OAH in the first place. How can there be a radical caucus of historians if historians are enemies? It would also lead to self-contempt and rejection. And, in fact, when the resolutions were defeated (as anticipated and hoped for), one of the leaders of the Caucus whispered that he *was* ashamed to be a historian.

The attitude of the women's caucus (a coalition of women historians of various political views) contrasted sharply with that of the Radical Caucus. Several members of the women's group also participated in the Radical Caucus, but the groups met separately and the women drew up their own resolutions. These they read to the Radicals, but only in order to get support for them. The women, unlike the Radicals, knew what they wanted, took themselves seriously as practicing historians, and framed resolutions that were militant, but intended for adoption. The main resolution included two instructions to the OAH, that it "undertake to receive, solicit and publicize information relating to specific instances" of discrimination against women in employment, admissions, grants, awarding of degrees, salary, working conditions, and consideration of promotion, and that it form a committee to deal with "the status of women in the historical profession" and "evaluate and make recommendations concerning the treatment of women in textbooks of American history used in secondary schools, colleges and universities." Professor John Caughey of UCLA moved to weaken the women's resolution by dropping these two instructions, but his amendment was defeated and the resolution was adopted as submitted. It was the only resolution adopted.

The decision to run a candidate against Hofstadter for vice president of the OAH was similarly unthought-out. No one knew why Hofstadter should be opposed, although we all knew his politics were no good. Finally, largely because several others (all of whom were faculty members) declined to run, a graduate student in history from San Francisco State College was nominated. He utilized his candidacy to discuss the content of the Caucus resolutions against the war and repression, for open enrollment, and for freedom of political action of faculty, students, and other university employees, and in opposition to discrimination against women.

The result of all this, the resolutions and the candidacy, was a strange mixture. On the floor the candidate handled himself well and the debate over the resolutions was serious. Although the resolutions lost, the meeting was almost evenly divided; often the margin of defeat was only ten to twenty votes in a total of some three hundred fifty or more. Several "established" faculty members spoke in behalf of various resolutions. On the other side, the establishment leadership performed badly. After the vote on the women's resolution, Kenneth Stampp of Berkeley moved that the meeting adjourn before consideration of the "political" resolutions on Vietnam and academic freedom. This was in direct violation of the pledge of the leadership of the OAH and created anger from many and embarrassment to the leadership. After a "debate" in the form of several points of order, adjournment was defeated. Then, on the academic freedom resolution, C. Vann Woodward moved a substitute resolution to have the executive secretary of the organization meet with the AAUP and tell that inert organization how concerned historians were about political firings. His substitute was criticized for excluding students and non-faculty employees, and as an evasion of responsibility on the part of those present. But it carried. In both instances the established leaders displayed a fear out of proportion to their positions, and revealed their own underlying contempt for democratic rights.

The true weakness of the Radical Caucus was not apparent in the business meeting, however, since the Radicals behaved with dignity and blended in with non-Caucus supporters of the resolutions, who were numerous, principled, and serious. On the immediate political issues, despite their attempts to be "radical" by making the resolutions unacceptable, the Caucus got widespread support. And yet the Caucus itself appeared to lose strength in the course of the meetings.

The reason for this was apparent in the Caucus meetings before the business meeting, on the resolutions, as already noted, but most important in the session on "What Is Radical History?" The session crystallized the weaknesses in the

Caucus in that it showed the conception of "radical" history to be the mirror image of "ruling class history," rather than something substantially different; and at the same time it showed the idea of "radical" politics, at least as Lynd presented it, to be entirely tactical, that is, entirely within the bourgeois mode of thought.

The session was a slice of life, with Lynd presenting to the meeting a woman, Genora (Johnson) Dollinger, who had led the Women's Emergency Brigade during the 1936–37 sit-down strike at General Motors in Flint, Michigan. Lynd introduced Mrs. Dollinger with some comments on "history from the bottom up," which, he said, was designed to show that the initiative and ideas for action often came from the rank and file, rather than from the leaders, as most liberal historians assert. He read a section of Sidney Fine's *Sit Down* that attributed the decision to occupy Chevrolet Building No. 4 to several leaders, and singled out Bob Travis and Roy Reuther of the International staff as the principal originators of the stratagem. But, Lynd argued, Kermit Johnson, a local leader, really thought up the plan. This was important, because it gave some insight into the origins of the tactics and the nature of effective political action. Building No. 4 was important because all Chevrolet engines were manufactured in that one location. Closing it down would close down Chevrolet production, and as a matter of fact, Lynd observed, General Motors learned something from this seizure and subsequently built several plants to make engines in different locations.

After this introduction, Lynd presented Dollinger to the audience as a woman who, as the wife of Kermit Johnson, had been instrumental in organizing the Women's Emergency Brigade that helped win the sit-down strike. Introducing her, Lynd said he was giving the audience of historians an example of how ordinary people make history. Dollinger then related her experiences in organizing the Brigade and in helping occupy and defend the Chevrolet buildings under siege. Her account was exciting and interesting in itself, but it did little or nothing to explain how history from the bottom up differs from history from the top down. In the course of her account and in answer to questions, Dollinger related that her father had been wealthy; that her uncle was a vice president of the Chevrolet division of General Motors; and that she had become a radical because her parents had conservative ideas about women, while "as a sort of premature women's liberationist," she thought girls should do things in the world just like boys. As a result of her revolt, she had married an auto worker and joined the Young People's Socialist League (YPSL) before the strike; she was already a socialist radical when it began. In organizing the Emergency Brigade, she said, she had followed military order, appointing herself captain and her assistants lieutenants.

As a Socialist Party member, Dollinger (then Mrs. Johnson) was involved in discussions about the tactics of the sit-down in the early stages of the strike. The local party leadership was conservative and feared the sit-down tactics would isolate the strikers, so Dollinger appealed to "the man I thought closest to God, Norman Thomas." When Thomas got her letter, he passed it on to a professor of economics in Chicago, who was then in charge of labor policy for the Party. This professor, who had never been in a strike before, came up to Flint to investigate the situation. Although he knew little or nothing about strike tactics, the professor was very sympathetic to the workers, examined the situation carefully, and then "rendered his decision." The decision was to go ahead with the tactics finally used. "If it weren't for him, his decision, the whole history of labor would have been different," Dollinger concluded.

As Dollinger understood the strike, it "shook the workers' way of living," and brought "this giant octopus [General Motors] to its knees." Yet in the question period she told us that she now refused to go back to strike reunions, because despite the success of the union, conditions were now just as bad in GM as before the strike, and, of course, General Motors was as strong as ever.

Lynd did not respond to this by asking what had gone wrong in the larger sense. He did not ask any questions about the nature of trade unionism, about the meaning of making recognition of the union, and therefore institutionaliza-tion of collective bargaining and contractual relations, the central thrust of working class activity. Instead, he asked simply: what happened to the militancy? Maybe, he suggested, it was the nature of the contracts (their particular content); or maybe the fault of Communist Party strategy; or maybe the development of bureaucracy. Something, some instrument, must be at fault, he implied, rather than the social relations in behalf of which the militants fought. The possibility that the workers were militant in behalf of a trade unionism that tied them closer to the system, that integrated their lives more tightly with that of the corporation, never occurred to Lynd. For him it was sufficient that the workers, those at the bottom, were engaged in militant activity.

Dollinger's story contradicted Lynd's presentation of it as history from the bottom up, but even if she had been born poor, had been radicalized in the course of the strike, had organized her brigade along democratic lines, and had referred her indecision to the members of the brigade, rather than to Norman Thomas, the results would undoubtedly have been the same. This illustrates the fault of Lynd's concept of history from the bottom up: it cannot explain or understand the *meaning* of actions taken by those at the bottom because it does not examine their relationship to the actions and consciousness of those at the top. For just as the meaning of ruling class thought and actions cannot be understood without knowing what was going on in the under classes, neither can the activity of the under classes be understood except in the context of the actions and consciousness of the upper classes.

This raises the question of the usefulness of the concept of radicalism, now that a socialist consciousness is widespread in the new left. Both in history and in the movement "radicalism" has no content. It is purely formal. It operates within bourgeois categories If the establishment likes decorum, disruption is radical. If straights wear their hair short, it is radical to wear it long. If the corporations oppose contractual relations with unions, it is radical to fight for these. If establishment historians write history by examining only ruling class sources—and increasingly the better liberal historians do not—then it is radical to use only lower class sources. The problem with this concept of radicalism is that it is purely responsive. Content is lost in a process of reaction to the initiatives of those in power. The ruling class is left in a position to steer militancy (and radicalism) in the direction advantageous to itself. The question in the case of the sit-down strike is complex, and fighting for the recognition of the union may well have been the correct tactic at that time. But certainly for revolutionaries, organizing the union could not have been the primary aim of working class activity. Whether or not the tactics pursued were appropriate, however, whether a different form of unionism was possible, or a different relationship of organized socialists to the union was desirable, cannot be answered in the framework in which they were presented by Lynd.

For socialists, as for blacks, other "third world" groups, and women, the question that historians should be asking, if they wish to contribute to the development of revolutionary politics, is "What went wrong?" Why are our respective movements so weak? Why have we met with nothing but frustration in seeking to achieve our historic goals? The version of "history from the bottom up" presented to the Radical Caucus at the OAH meeting cannot answer these questions; it doesn't even ask them. It is too busy celebrating successful tactics and militant actions, too busy attempting to give "radicals" "their own history"—which is to say, a false sense of accomplishment, and therefore a pious satisfaction with the past. That historians who understand the past in this manner prefer to be known as activists rather than as historians is understandable. The catch is that their activity is informed by the same mode of thought as their historical work, and ultimately faces the same problems: a one-dimensional glorification of motion; a dependence on fortuitous events or the actions of others; a lack of sustained or coherent direction.

## ABOUT THE AUTHORS

Blanche Wiesen Cook received her Ph.D. from Johns Hopkins University in 1968. She is currently Assistant Professor of History at John Jay College, City University of New York and has been a member of its faculty since 1968. Her areas of specialization are U.S. history, American and British peace movements, and violence and social change in the United States. Dr. Cook is the senior editor of Garland Library of War and Peace and has written articles for the *Journal of American Studies*.

Alice Kessler Harris, Ph.D., Rutgers University, 1900, is Assistant Professor of History at Hofstra University and has been a member of its faculty since 1968. She previously taught at Douglass College. Her areas of current academic interest are labor history and immigrant history. Dr. Harris also served in an advisory capacity on the Academic Freedom Committee of the American Civil Liberties Union.

Ronald Radosh received his Ph.D. from the University of Wisconsin in 1967. He is currently Associate Professor of History at Queensborough Community College and on the faculty of the Graduate Center, City University of New York. Dr. Radosh's areas of specialization include twentieth century United States, American labor and radical history, and U.S. foreign policy. He is the author of *America: From World War II Through 1970*, *Conservative Critics of the American Empire*, and *American Labor and United States Foreign Policy*.

A NOTE ON THE TYPE

The text is set in Melior, a typeface designed by Hermann Zapf and issued in 1952. Melior, like Times Roman, was created specifically for use in a newspaper. With this functional end in mind, Zapf nonetheless chose to base the proportions of its letterforms on those of the Golden Section. The result is a typeface of unusual strength and surpassing sublety.

This book was composed by Volt Information Sciences, Inc., N.Y. Printed and bound by Von Hoffmann Press, Inc., St. Louis, Missouri.